Studies in Luke,
Acts, and Paul

Studies in Luke, Acts, and Paul

C. Kavin Rowe

William B. Eerdmans Publishing Company
Grand Rapids, Michigan

Wm. B. Eerdmans Publishing Co.
4035 Park East Court SE, Grand Rapids, Michigan 49546
www.eerdmans.com

© 2024 C. Kavin Rowe
All rights reserved
Published 2024
Printed in the United States of America

30 29 28 27 26 25 24   1 2 3 4 5 6 7

ISBN 978-0-8028-8274-5

Library of Congress Cataloging-in-Publication Data

A catalog record for this book is available from the Library of Congress.

Contents

Preface   vii

List of Abbreviations   ix

PART 1: CHRISTOLOGY, GRECO-ROMAN CULTURE, AND CANONICAL RECEPTION   1

1. Luke-Acts and the Imperial Cult   3
   A Way through the Conundrum?

2. The God of Israel and Jesus Christ   24
   Luke, Marcion, and the Unity of the Canon

3. Luke and the Trinity   46
   An Essay in Ecclesial Biblical Theology

4. The Grammar of Life   73
   The Areopagus Speech and Pagan Tradition

5. Reading *World Upside Down*   95
   A Response to Matthew Sleeman and John Barclay

6. The Book of Acts and the Cultural Explication of the Identity of God   110

7. The Ecclesiology of Acts   133

8. History, Hermeneutics, and the Unity of Luke-Acts   146

9. Literary Unity and Reception History   171
   Reading Luke-Acts as Luke and Acts

Contents

10.	Acts 2:36 and the Continuity of Lukan Christology	179
11.	**Authority and Community**	201
	Lukan Dominium *in Acts*	

PART 2: BIBLICAL STUDIES AND THEOLOGY IN PRACTICE   215

12.	St. Paul and the Moral Law	217
13.	The Trinity in the Letters of St. Paul and Hebrews	233
14.	**New Testament Iconography?**	249
	Situating Paul in the Absence of Material Evidence	
15.	**Romans 10:13**	274
	What Is the Name of the Lord?	

Bibliography	309
Index of Authors	339
Index of Subjects	345
Index of Scripture	351
Index of Other Ancient Sources	359

Preface

These essays reflect an attempt to think holistically. At first glance, however, they may seem to have no more in common than multiple touch points in the largest textual areas of the New Testament: Luke, Acts, and Paul. The studies range rather widely, after all, and deal with topics that occupy specialists in different fields and subfields. And in one respect, of course, the essays do simply exhibit a history of interest in various topics or agreeing to requests to write on something that seemed important to me. But on closer inspection, when read together, the essays show what it could be like to think on the other side of an already-integrated inquiry.

Regardless of the topic under consideration, the interpretative effort in every case involves a refusal to separate thought into this kind or that kind— and then to correlate a particular kind with, say, a "historical method" or theology or politics or anything else. It is all too tempting on our side of modernity to abstract certain moments or habits in our thinking and turn them into methods. The problem with a method way of doing things is not that we cannot learn from studies that try to be "history" or "theology" alone and leave everything else to the side; the problem is that human beings do not really think like that, and for the simplest of reasons: we cannot. To the degree that we think at all, we think with the minds that we are, which is to say that the full human density of intellectual life is present all the time whether we want it to be or not. There are, of course, different styles or flavors of thinking, different sources and discourses, different foregrounds and backgrounds, and so forth. What there is not, however, is a method that itself thinks. The human being living its one life in the midst of time is the one who thinks.

Whether the subject is the Roman imperial cult or the absence of distinctively Christian material culture from the earliest period or an exegetical puzzle in a Pauline letter or the connection between Scripture and Christian doctrine or the reception of Luke and Acts, the effort has thus always been to pursue the question through asking other questions from a variety of areas of thought. Putting it this way makes it clear that I take question/answer to be the

Preface

fundamental movement of inquiry and that coming to a distinctive position on an area of research is at least as much a matter of asking integrated questions that emerge from a thinking life as it is consulting the right material from the right places. One does have to know some things about the imperial cult, for example, to write an essay on it, but thinking through the intersections of idolatry, community, linguistics, politics, and theology—and much more—is, I think, the only way to come to a worthwhile historical judgment about it vis-à-vis early Christian life. In short, what I hope readers of these essays will take away beyond additional knowledge is the sense that thinking well about early Christianity and its texts requires us to think well about a host of other important things, too.

Abbreviations

AB	Anchor Bible
ABD	*Anchor Bible Dictionary.* Edited by David Noel Freedman. 6 vols. New York: Doubleday, 1992
A. J.	Josephus, *Antiquitates judaicae*
Alex.	Lucian, *Alexander* (*Pseudomantis*)
ANF	Ante-Nicene Fathers
Ann.	Tacitus, *Annales*
ANRW	*Aufstieg und Niedergang der römischen Welt: Geschichte und Kultur Roms im Spiegel der neueren Forschung.* Part 2, *Principat.* Edited by Hildegard Temporini and Wolfgang Haase. Berlin: de Gruyter, 1972–
ANTC	Abingdon New Testament Commentaries
Apol.	Tertullian, *Apologeticus*
1 Apol.	Justin, *Apologia i*
2 Apol.	Justin, *Apologia ii*
BAGD	Bauer, Walter, William F. Arndt, F. Wilbur Gingrich, and Frederick W. Danker. *Greek-English Lexicon of the New Testament and Other Early Christian Literature.* 2nd ed. Chicago: University of Chicago Press, 1979
BBB	Bonner biblische Beiträge
BBR	*Bulletin for Biblical Research*
BDAG	Danker, Frederick W., Walter Bauer, William F. Arndt, and F. Wilbur Gingrich. *Greek-English Lexicon of the New Testament and Other Early Christian Literature.* 3rd ed. Chicago: University of Chicago Press, 1999
BDF	Blass, Friedrich, Albert Debrunner, and Robert W. Funk. *A Greek Grammar of the New Testament and Other Early Christian Literature.* Chicago: University of Chicago Press, 1961
B. J.	Josephus, *Bellum judaicum*

Abbreviations

BZNW	Beihefte zur Zeitschrift für die neutestamentliche Wissenschaft
C. Ap.	Josephus, *Contra Apionem*
C. Ar.	Athanasius, *Orationes contra Arianos*
Carm.	Horace, *Carmina*
CBQ	*Catholic Biblical Quarterly*
CCSG	Corpus Christianorum: Series Graeca. Turnhout: Brepols, 1977–
CCSL	Corpus Christianorum: Series Latina. Turnhout: Brepols, 1953–
Cels.	Origen, *Contra Celsum*
Conf.	Philo, *De confusione linguarum*
CQ	*The Classical Quarterly*
CSEL	Corpus Scriptorum Ecclesiasticorum Latinorum
Def. orac.	Plutarch, *De defectu oraculorum*
Descr.	Pausanias, *Graeciae descriptio*
Disc.	Dio Chrysostom, *Discourses*; Epictetus, *Discourses*
Div.	Cicero, *De divinatione*
DJD	Discoveries in the Judaean Desert
DOP	*Dumbarton Oaks Papers*
EKKNT	Evangelisch-katholischer Kommentar zum Neuen Testament
Ep.	Seneca, *Epistulae morales*
Eun.	Gregory of Nyssa, *Contra Eunomium*
EV	English versions
ExAud	*Ex Auditu*
Fid.	Ambrose, *De fide*
FRLANT	Forschungen zur Religion und Literatur des Alten und Neuen Testaments
Haer.	Irenaeus, *Adversus haereses*
HBT	*Horizons in Biblical Theology*
Hist. eccl.	Eusebius, *Historia ecclesiastica*
Hom. Heb.	John Chrysostom, *Homiliae in epistulam ad Hebraeos*
HThKNT	Herders Theologischer Kommentar zum Neuen Testament
ICC	International Critical Commentary
Int	*Interpretation*
JBL	*Journal of Biblical Literature*
JR	*Journal of Religion*

Abbreviations

JRS	*Journal of Roman Studies*
JSJ	*Journal for the Study of Judaism in the Persian, Hellenistic, and Roman Periods*
JSNT	*Journal for the Study of the New Testament*
JSNTSup	Journal for the Study of the New Testament Supplement Series
JTS	*Journal of Theological Studies*
KEK	Kritisch-exegetischer Kommentar über das Neue Testament
Legat.	Philo, *Legatio ad Gaium*
Let. Aris.	Letter of Aristeas
LIMC	*Lexicon Iconographicum Mythologiae Classicae*. Edited by H. Christoph Ackerman and Jean-Robert Gisler. 8 vols. Zurich: Artemis, 1981–1997
LSJ	Liddell, Henry George, Robert Scott, Henry Stuart Jones. *A Greek-English Lexicon*. 9th ed. with revised supplement. Oxford: Clarendon, 1996
LXX	Septuagint
m.	Mishnah
Metam.	Apuleius, *Metamorphoses*; Ovid, *Metamorphoses*
Mor.	Plutarch, *Moralia*
MS(S)	manuscript(s)
MT	Masoretic Text
NA[27]	*Novum Testamentum Graece*, Nestle-Aland, 27th ed.
Nat. d.	Cicero, *De natura deorum*
NICNT	New International Commentary on the New Testament
NPNF[2]	*Nicene and Post-Nicene Fathers*, Series 2
NT	New Testament
NTD	Das Neue Testament Deutsch
NTS	*New Testament Studies*
Od.	Homer, *Odyssey*
OED	Oxford English Dictionary
OT	Old Testament
Pan.	Epiphanius, *Panarion*
PBSR	*Papers of the British School at Rome*
PG	Patrologia Graeca [= *Patrologiae cursus completus: Series graeca*]. Edited by Jacques-Paul Migne. 162 vols. Paris, 1857–1886

xi

Abbreviations

PL	Patrologia Latina [= *Patrologiae cursus completus: Series latina*]. Edited by Jacques-Paul Migne. 217 vols. Paris, 1844–1864
Praep. ev.	Eusebius, *Praeparatio evangelica*
ProEccl	Pro Ecclesia
Resp.	Plato, *Respublica*
Sat.	Juvenal, *Satirae*
SBLDS	Society of Biblical Literature Dissertation Series
SBLSP	*SBL Seminar Papers*
SC	Sources chrétiennes
SEG	Supplementum epigraphicum graecum
SJT	*Scottish Journal of Theology*
SNTSMS	Society for New Testament Studies Monograph Series
SP	Sacra Pagina
Strom.	Clement of Alexandria, *Stromateis*
SVF	*Stoicorum Veterum Fragmenta*. Hans Friedrich von Arnim. 4 vols. Leipzig: Teubner, 1903–1924
TDNT	*Theological Dictionary of the New Testament*. Edited by Gerhard Kittel and Gerhard Friedrich. Translated by Geoffrey W. Bromiley. 10 vols. Grand Rapids: Eerdmans, 1964–1976
ThWNT	*Theologisches Wörterbuch zum Neuen Testament*. Edited by Gerhard Kittel and Gerhard Friedrich. 10 vols. Stuttgart: Kohlhammer, 1933–1979
TLL	*Thesaurus Linguae Latinae*
Ver. hist.	Lucian, *Vera historia*
WBC	Word Biblical Commentary
WUNT	Wissenschaftliche Untersuchungen zum Neuen Testament
ZNW	*Zeitschrift für die Neutestamentliche Wissenschaft und die Kunde der Älteren Kirche*

Part 1

CHRISTOLOGY, GRECO-ROMAN CULTURE, AND CANONICAL RECEPTION

READINGS IN LUKE AND ACTS

Luke-Acts and the Imperial Cult

♦ A WAY THROUGH THE CONUNDRUM?

DIFFICULTIES IN THE SUBJECT

The interpreter who wishes to study the theme of Luke-Acts and the imperial cult will be met immediately with several, rather large difficulties. In the first place, one has to reckon with the provincial nature of the Roman Empire. Fergus Millar put it memorably in the concluding admonition of a well-known essay:

> The moral is simple. The Republic, it may be, can be seen from Rome outwards. To take this standpoint for the Empire is to lose contact with reality. Not only the pattern of literary evidence, or the existence of an immense mass of local documents, but the very nature of the Empire itself, means that it can only be understood by starting from the provinces and looking inward.[1]

The implications for our study of the NT are rather obvious. To be able to discern concretely an NT document's relation to "Rome"—here a cipher for the web of complexes that made up what we call the Roman Empire—one would

---

1. Fergus Millar, "The Emperor, the Senate and the Provinces," in *Rome, the Greek World, and the East*, ed. Hannah M. Cotton and Guy M. Rogers, vol. 1, *The Roman Republic and the Augustan Revolution* (Chapel Hill: University of North Carolina Press, 2002), 291.

"Luke-Acts and the Imperial Cult: A Way through the Conundrum?" was originally published in *Journal for the Study of the New Testament* 27, no. 3 (2005): 279–300. Copyright 2005 SAGE Publications. DOI: 10.1177/0142064X05052507. (With response article three years later by Justin R. Howell, "The Imperial Authority and Benefaction of Centurions and Acts 10.34–43: A Response to C. Kavin Rowe," *JSNT* 31, no. 1 [2008]: 25–51.)

Part 1: Christology, Greco-Roman Culture, and Canonical Reception

need, at the very least, to know the province of the document's composition and/or destination. But despite generations of offered solutions, aside from some generally assured results (e.g., the Western provinces are excluded), this is precisely what we do not know for Luke or for Acts.[2] Indeed, whatever one's opinion of Richard Bauckham's proposals about the "Gospels for all Christians," it is noteworthy that, if his arguments work at all, they probably work best for Luke.[3]

A second and correlative difficulty lies in the nature of the imperial cult itself. One of the most commonly accepted results in the study of the cult is the fact that the cult was different in the Latin West than it was in the Greek East.[4] Though a notorious problem in itself,[5] there remains general agreement, for example, that the "divinity" of the emperor was construed one way in Rome and another in Ephesus, and probably still another in a city like Corinth, which, though in Greek Achaia, was in fact refounded as a Roman *colonia*.[6]

Moreover, the cult would have differed under particular emperors. It was not the same under Augustus or Tiberius as it was under Caligula—who, for example, moved in his short principate from forbidding sacrifice to his *genius* to receiving "direct worship in Rome"[7]—nor under Nero as it was

---

2. Cf. Joseph A. Fitzmyer, *The Gospel according to Luke*, 2 vols., AB 28/28A (Garden City, NY: Doubleday, 1981–1985), 1:57: "As for the place of the composition of the Lucan Gospel, it is really anyone's guess."

3. Richard Bauckham, ed., *The Gospels for All Christians: Rethinking the Gospel Audiences* (Grand Rapids: Eerdmans, 1998).

4. Duncan Fishwick, *The Imperial Cult in the Latin West: Studies in the Ruler Cult in the Western Provinces of the Roman Empire*, 2 vols. (Leiden: Brill, 1989–1992), I/1:92–93, is concise.

5. See, e.g., the discussion of Steven J. Friesen, *Twice Neokoros: Ephesus, Asia and the Cult of the Flavian Imperial Family* (Leiden: Brill, 1993), 146–52. Cf. the recent study of Manfred Clauss, *Kaiser und Gott: Herrscherkult im römischen Reich* (Stuttgart: Teubner, 1999), the first sentences of which are intentionally provocative: "Der römische Kaiser war Gottheit. Er war dies von Anfang an, seit Caesar und Augustus, er war es zu Lebzeiten, er war es auch im Westen des römischen Reiches, in Italien, in Rom" (17).

6. Cf. Elias Bickerman, "Consecratio," in *Le culte des souverains dans l'empire romain*, ed. Willem den Boer (Geneva: Fondation Hardt, 1973): "A universal cult of the ruler did not exist in the Roman Empire. Each city, each province, each group worshiped this or that sovereign according to its own discretion and ritual" (9; this remark was challenged in the ensuing discussion). Steven J. Friesen, *Imperial Cults and the Apocalypse of John: Reading Revelation in the Ruins* (Oxford: Oxford University Press, 2001), speaks of "imperial cults."

7. A. D. Nock, "Religious Developments from the Close of the Republic to the Reign of Nero," in *The Cambridge Ancient History* (Cambridge: University Press, 1934), 10:497.

Luke-Acts and the Imperial Cult

under Vespasian and others. Chronological reality here is phenomenological difference.

The third major difficulty for our topic derives from the conjunction of these differences due to locale and time with the various levels at which one can read Luke-Acts. Assuming our attempt to relate Luke-Acts to the cult, should we read the gospel in light of a particular reconstructed situation under Augustus and Tiberius, and Acts predominately under Nero? Or, assuming the typical dating of Luke-Acts to circa 85–95, should we read the entire narrative under the shadow of Domitian? Then again, these questions might falsely frame the hermeneutical choice. Perhaps we can read the text both as ancient "history" chronicling the events of circa 30–60 and contemporary commentary on the mid to late 80s or 90s. But even here where we can make use of textual depth, unless we correlate our reading with local data, we risk losing sight of the material reality of the cult itself and conjuring a generalized phantom.

And just at this juncture we face another gap in our knowledge, which is related to our ignorance about the place or destination of Luke-Acts. We do not know where exactly the author of Luke-Acts has been, or when he has been where he has been, or, excepting the Gospel of Mark, whence he draws his information,[8] or—perhaps most importantly—what he would or would not have known about the cult in particular towns, cities, or provinces.[9] Leaving aside the problem of precise dating, suppose Luke had been in Ephesus—a city in which the transformation of public space due to permeation with the material presence of the imperial cult is well documented—concurrently with the seven- or eight-meter colossus of Titus/Domitian:[10] Did he know of it? What would he have made of it?

What about the two colossi, mentioned by Josephus, in the temple at "the mouth of the harbor" in Caesarea Maritima?[11] Or again, suppose he had been on the Acropolis in Athens and seen the Roma-Augustus temple near the Parthenon. Did he read of Augustus as σωτήρ on the architrave?[12] Or the *Res gestae*

---

8. Luke's supposed "we-source," for example, remains notoriously problematic.

9. For a helpful introduction to the relation between municipal and provincial cults, see Friesen, *Imperial Cults*, 23–131.

10. Whether this particular statue is to be identified as Titus or Domitian is still debated. For Titus, see Friesen, *Twice Neokoros*, 60–63; for Domitian, see Simon R. F. Price, *Rituals and Power: The Roman Imperial Cult in Asia Minor* (Cambridge: Cambridge University Press, 1984), 187, 255.

11. Josephus, *B. J.* 1.21.7 §414.

12. For a concise discussion of this diminutive temple, see Michael C. Hoff, "The Poli-

Part 1: Christology, Greco-Roman Culture, and Canonical Reception

on the Augustan temple in Pisidian Antioch, a temple "which was visible from miles away to every traveller approaching the colony from the west"?[13]

The hole in our knowledge at this point is occasioned by the final major difficulty—namely, the fact that the imperial cult is not discussed or dealt with directly in Luke-Acts. In fact, it never comes up. This absence is particularly surprising since "travellers in the empire would not have been surprised to meet the cult wherever they went: they would have found the cult located both in local communities and in the associations formed of these communities in particular Roman provinces."[14]

It is quite impossible that Luke did not know of the imperial cult; one thus might expect him to have given some guidance to "Theophilus" with respect to this important aspect of daily life in the empire (e.g., do or do not continue to participate in temple activities associated with the emperor).[15] But trolling

---

tics and Architecture of the Athenian Imperial Cult," in *Subject and Ruler: The Cult of the Ruling Power in Classical Antiquity*, ed. Alastair Small (Dexter, MI: Thompson-Shore, 1996), 185–200, esp. 180–94.

13. See Stephen Mitchell, *Anatolia: Land, Men, and Gods in Asia Minor*, 2 vols. (Oxford: Clarendon, 1993), 1:104–5 (105).

14. Price, *Rituals and Power*, 2–3. Cf. Géza Alföldy, "Subject and Ruler, Subjects and Methods: An Attempt at a Conclusion," in Small, *Subject and Ruler*, 255: "This cult was in a certain sense the most important cult of the Roman Empire before the triumph of Christianity.... In the cult of the emperor ... practically everybody was involved. This is true in a double sense. Spatially, the ruler-cult was carried out at Rome as well as in all the towns of Italy and the provinces, and even in private houses. Socially, it was spread through all classes and groups."

15. Hans-Josef Klauck's question in a slightly different context is here on target: if Luke knew about the cult, "Warum konnte, warum wollte Lukas nicht deutlicher werden?" ("Des Kaisers schöne Stimme. Herrscherkritik in Apg 12,20–23," in *Religion und Gesellschaft im frühen Christentum: Neutestamentliche Studien*, WUNT 152 [Tübingen: Mohr Siebeck, 2003], 265). Klauck's essay is perceptive, but problems remain. Unless Luke wrote during Nero's reign, it seems unlikely that he would need to be implicit (the rhetorical device σχῆμα) in his criticism of Nero. That is, Klauck is correct that of the emperors Nero was the one with whom a "divine voice" was associated, but by Luke's time one could have probably criticized him openly (see below). Thus it seems unlikely that, if Acts 12:20–23 is an implicit critique of the imperial cult, the target would be Nero. However, if the target is not Nero, then the point about the "divine voice" is lost, and thus the connection between the implicit critique and the imperial cult. Moreover, that "Plutarch makes outspoken criticisms of the self-deification of Hellenistic kings without any feeling that what he says might be taken as reflecting on Roman practice" (Nock, "Religious Developments," 10:489n2), could be taken to illustrate the perceived difference between a *Herrscherkult* and the *Kaiserkult* even in antiquity.

in the deep waters of the narrative for this kind of direction is in vain. The catch just is not there.

Asking after the why of this absence summons a host of attendant complications. Perhaps it was too dangerous to speak critically of the emperor—an assured implication of *Kaiserkultkritik*. At times, if we believe Tacitus in the opening of the *Annals*, this was the case: "The histories of Tiberius and Caligula, of Claudius and Nero, were falsified through cowardice while they flourished."[16] Yet the danger of speaking openly against a Roman emperor did not always apply; for example, deceased emperors could be—and were—roundly disparaged.[17] Perhaps Luke's work was intended for Christians only and, given his emphasis on continuity with Israel, simply assumed incompatibility with the imperial cult, something akin to the worship of human beings rejected in Acts 14.[18] But at least until the outbreak of the Roman War, there was enough room even in Jerusalem to make a twice-daily sacrifice for the emperor.[19] Perhaps, however, Luke hoped that his work might also be read by non-Christians and wisely avoided a head-on confrontation with the normal and expected religio-political requirements of those he attempted to persuade.[20] Or perhaps Luke was so decidedly pro-Rome that he needed

---

16. Tacitus, *Ann.* 1.1. Cf., e.g., Tacitus, *Ann.* 14.52; Pliny, *Epistulae* 3.5; Cassius Dio, *Historiae Romanae* 62.29.4; 67.13.2–4. For Domitian in particular, see K. M. Coleman, "The Emperor Domitian and Literature," *ANRW* 2.32.5 (1986): 3087–115, who concludes: "Domitian however was not insensitive to the blandishments of literature; but where writings implied a political stance, they were not to be borne."

17. Indeed, Tacitus's statement cited just above continues to the effect that, after the emperors died, the histories were distorted in precisely the opposite manner—i.e., through "the influence of still rankling hatreds." Cf., e.g, Juvenal, *Sat.* 2.29-33; 4.38. Neither Pliny nor Tacitus nor Suetonius nor Dio refrains from criticism of Nero or Domitian. Cf. in a different genre the tragedy *Octavia*, falsely ascribed to Seneca but probably composed not too long after the death of Nero, which is an outright castigation of Nero's behavior. From the Jewish side, the excoriation of Caligula in Philo's *Legatio*, with its contrast between the joy at Caligula's ascendance and the despair at his madness, could hardly be more rhetorically effective.

18. One thinks immediately of Jervell's proposals over the last thirty years or so. Cf., e.g., Jacob Jervell, *Luke and the People of God: A New Look at Luke-Acts* (Minneapolis: Augsburg, 1972).

19. Josephus, *B. J.* 2.10.4 §197; 2.17.2 §409. Josephus says the sacrifice was at the expense of the Jewish people (*C. Ap.* 2.77), while Philo, if referring to the same thing, claims that the emperor paid for the daily sacrifices (*Legat.* 157, 317).

20. Cf., e.g., Johannes Weiss, *Über die Absicht und den literarischen Charakter der Apostelgeschichte* (Göttingen: Vandenhoeck & Ruprecht, 1897), who argued that Acts was an apologia addressed to pagans in an effort to refute Jewish accusations.

to suppress talk of the imperial cult in order to preserve the possibility of coeval existence between church and empire. Perhaps. As for knowledge, we have it not.

Such foregoing difficulties converge in a certain sense around the issue of particularity. On the one hand, recent work on the imperial cult has thrown into great relief the need for radical particularity in order to achieve accurate phenomenological description: the "where" and "when" determine "what" it is. On the other hand, particularity is exactly what we lack for Luke-Acts. The problem is severe enough with respect to a direct correlation between the imperial cult and Luke-Acts that it almost calls into question our ability to say something definite about the subject.

Approaching the Subject

Coming to terms with the above difficulties necessarily involves some methodological ground clearing. There are at least four different ways in which one could try to approach the problem, all of which have certain advantages but ultimately prove unsatisfactory. The first is to redate Luke-Acts to the reign of Nero, as, for example, did John Robinson somewhat notoriously.[21] The differences in the cult due to chronology would here be reduced. And, under Nero, the theory that it could have been dangerous for Luke to write openly against the emperor and his cult would have a certain plausibility. Yet this option can be moved aside rather quickly. The consensus on a post-70, post-Markan date rightly still holds sway.[22]

Second, in view of Luke's obvious concern to situate his narrative within the Roman world (Luke 2:1; 3:1, etc.), one might endeavor to read the text as a kind of conscious religious counterpoint to the imperial cult, an alternative way to participate in the *saeculum aureum*. Such a positioning of Luke-Acts would then be able to take account of the widespread sense of *pax* that accompanied the consolidation of power under the reign of Augustus while simultaneously avoiding the anachronistic distinction between religion and politics in relation to the cult. Thus, the well-known similarities in Lukan vocabulary to the pagan religio-political culture—εἰρήνη, σωτηρία, and so on—provide the touchstone for arguments about Luke's Christianized version of the *pax Romana*.

But the problems accompanying such a venture outweigh the benefits. The

---

21. J. A. T. Robinson, *Redating the New Testament* (Philadelphia: Westminster, 1976).
22. See Fitzmyer, *Luke*, 1:53–57.

threat of "parallelomania" lurks conspicuously nearby, waiting to expose the fact that similar wording—that is, "parallels"—may have nothing to do with similarity in content; common language may simply reflect mutual cultural-linguistic imbeddedness rather than "influence," "a reaction to," and so forth.[23] Further, serious liability emerges at the place where one's *Vorverständnis* of the imperial counterpoint threatens to skew significantly the Lukan text.[24] Regardless of the accuracy of one's picture of the imperial counterpoint, perception of the relation of Luke-Acts to the imperial cult is here lost, as the distinctiveness of Luke-Acts itself is swamped by the wave of Virgil, Horace, Velleius, and others. These aforementioned weaknesses bear also upon the final problem: the danger that the concrete relation between Luke-Acts and the imperial cult is sketched according to the background of political religion in the imperial period rather than the foreground of what the text itself actually says and the evidence of particular locations.

Third, one might go through the entire narrative, comb out the cities and towns that are mentioned, and then attempt to correlate them with what we know about the cult in these specific places. Such correlation would allow us to take account of the necessary particularity in the cult with respect to locale as well as the particularities of the Luke-Acts narrative. But the problem of precise dating would still remain:[25] At what time should we correlate Luke's Ephesus material, for example, with what we know of the ancient city, before or after the addition of the temple to Domitian (which after his death was

23. Samuel Sandmel's presidential address to the SBL, "Parallelomania," *JBL* 81 (1962): 1–13, is still relevant.

24. See, e.g., Allen Brent, *The Imperial Cult and the Development of Church Order: Concepts and Images of Authority in Paganism and Early Christianity before the Age of Cyprian* (Leiden: Brill, 1999), which, though commendable for its effort to take the cult seriously as religion, grinds Luke-Acts through the mill of (alleged) parallels to the point of serious distortion: "The fulfillment of the object of republican religion by Augustus was the real counterfoil to Luke's picture of Christianity as the fulfillment of the cult of the Temple of Judaism" (75); the "apostolic foundation of the Christian cultus is therefore to be seen reflecting contra-cultural images with reference to the college of the Fratres Arvales" (136), etc.

25. In this respect it is interesting that the list in Hans-Josef Klauck, *The Religious Context of Early Christianity* (Edinburgh: T&T Clark, 2000), 324, which correlates cities mentioned in the NT with a map or catalogue in Price's *Rituals and Power*, does not include "temporal duration." Klauck's choice to limit the list in precisely this way is understandable (the list would have been "too complicated"), but it points directly to the nature of the problem. At this point a considerable difference emerges between Luke-Acts and the Pauline letters, the latter of which can be correlated quite well with specific local data. I do not intend to deny, however, that Acts may at times furnish valuable pieces of information relative to particular locations that, e.g., might supplement the Pauline material.

rededicated to the Flavian founder Vespasian)?[26] Or Rome with Rome, before or after the great fire and Nero's scapegoating of the Christians?

Moreover, such an approach—taken in one direction—might assume far too much in the way of our knowledge about the Lukan author in relation to the Lukan texts. That is to say, an interpretation that is funded through a correlation of data from specific cities with particular locations mentioned in Luke-Acts is susceptible to the charge of eisegesis exactly at the point of our ignorance of Luke's mental processes. Leaving aside the already mentioned problem of precise date, did Luke, in fact, reflect upon the architectural shape of the Ephesian square or the size or "meaning" of the imperial statues and so on in order to allow such matters to exert influence, however subtly, in the composition of his narrative? That is, to put it generally and more simply, when writing about events of the early church in a certain place, if Luke knew about the imperial cult in that place, did he have it in mind? The short answer is, in the absence of explicit textual indication, we will never know. We thus run the risk of reading the text in light of our own constructions of Luke's knowledge of a particular place as they play into our interpretation of his narrative.

But what if such an approach is taken in another direction—namely, toward how inhabitants of certain locations might have heard the reading of Luke's text in light of their daily experience with the furniture and workings of the cult? That is, if we move away for the time being from what Luke might or might not have thought and toward the likely effect of the text in a given location, may we not divine something of the relationship between Luke-Acts as text and the imperial cult? Perhaps we might then be able to move backward and say something well founded about Luke's general intention.

But even here the methodological advance seems plagued with the problem that comes at the intersection of locale with date: the time at which the text would have been read matters for calculating its effect. Because of this intersection it becomes necessary to take a cross section or slice of time, but this very necessity brings with it a definite arbitrariness: there exists no logico-historical compulsion to pick a certain time for a specific place rather than another.

Yet there remains the possibility that elements in the text of Luke-Acts by virtue of their clarity and/or audacity would have been heard in connection to the imperial cult irrespective of chronological difference. If such elements exist, they would certainly operate at a general level, but for that reason they may be all the more telling.

---

26. See Price, *Rituals and Power*, esp. 135–36, 139 (fig. 3 = upper square in Ephesus), 140, 255; Friesen, *Twice Neokoros*, 59–62.

Luke-Acts and the Imperial Cult

Fourth, in light of the steady stream of studies that have taken up the question of Luke's attitude toward Rome,[27] one might note the abundance of seemingly "pro-Roman" passages in Luke-Acts and, on that basis, conclude, for example, either that Luke was unconcerned with the cult or that for apologetic reasons he decided not to press the matter. In both cases the correlation would be between Luke's positive evaluation of the *Imperium* and the absence of explicit engagement with the cult.

Conversely, one might be persuaded by the minority view of Cassidy and others that sees in the message of Luke-Acts a content or subject matter (*die Sache*) that is fundamentally disruptive to the existing order (e.g., the exalted shall be brought low and the humble raised up).[28] The view of the connection between Luke-Acts and the imperial cult would then receive its decisive push from the "anti-Rome" passages.

The inherent danger in the attempt to discern Luke's relation to the imperial cult via his larger (non-)apologetic concerns is what we might call the pendulum effect: a to and fro between purportedly positive and purportedly negative passages. If one, for example, (a) notices with T. D. Barnes that "no Roman official in ... Acts ... regards Christianity as a punishable offence"[29] and then (b) places the correlative weight on the positive passages,[30] the view of the connection between Luke-Acts and the imperial cult could be interpreted in one direction. However, if one (a) interprets the "reversals" in the Magnificat as a critique of the Roman status quo and then (b) places the correlative weight on other negative passages,[31] the view of the connection between Luke-Acts and the imperial cult could be interpreted in another direction. This swing from one side to the other on the basis of the same text suggests the need for caution in a construction of Luke's attitude toward Rome, as both sets of passages are in fact part of one narrative.

The stress, however, upon the larger issue of the portrayal of the Roman Empire in Luke-Acts can in fact help to orient us correctly in thinking about

---

27. For a brief survey, see Alexandru Neagoe, *The Trial of the Gospel: An Apologetic Reading of Luke's Trial Narratives*, SNTSMS 116 (Cambridge: Cambridge University Press, 2002), 3–24.

28. See, e.g., Richard A. Horsley, *The Liberation of Christmas: The Infancy Narratives in Social Context* (New York: Crossroad, 1989); Richard J. Cassidy and Philip J. Scharper, eds., *Political Issues in Luke-Acts* (Maryknoll, NY: Orbis Books, 1983).

29. T. D. Barnes, "Legislation against the Christians," *JRS* 58 (1968): 33.

30. E.g., Luke 7:1–10; 23:47; Acts 3:13; 13:7–8; 19:31, 37, etc.

31. E.g., Luke 4:5; 12:30; 18:32–33; 19:38 (addition of βασιλεύς); 21:12–13; 22:24; Acts 4:11, 25–26; 16:21, etc.

Part 1: Christology, Greco-Roman Culture, and Canonical Reception

our topic. If Simon Price's oft-noted statement that the imperial cult "constructed the reality of the Roman empire"[32] is anywhere near the mark, then this larger theme of Luke-Acts and Rome bears directly upon the question of Luke-Acts and the imperial cult. But an approach that seizes upon certain passages to the neglect of others—a scholarly ride on the pendulum to one side—and marks a relation to the imperial cult from only one set of passages probably distorts the unity of the narrative and is unlikely to have taken sufficient account of the complexity of Luke-Acts. Yet the possibility exists that there is something intrinsic to the text or story of Luke-Acts that provides enough governing conceptual and narrative-historical force to guide our reading of the "Rome" passages and at the same time to suggest a fairly tangible relation to the cult even in all its particularity.

Exegesis and the Imperial Cult

C. K. Barrett once remarked, "No Roman official would have ever filtered out so much of what to him would be theological and ecclesiastical rubbish in order to reach so tiny a grain of relevant apology."[33] Barrett's observation, though aimed only at the earlier *apologia pro ecclesia* hypothesis, helps nevertheless to draw the line between the many difficulties encountered in the previous two sections and the textual weight needed to correlate Luke-Acts with the imperial cult. For, as Barrett saw, discerning a relation between Luke-Acts and Rome is not a matter of finding tiny grains to place under a magnifying glass and amplify beyond their intrinsic narrative-historical importance. Much to the contrary, in light of the aforementioned problems, if an open passageway between Luke-Acts and the cult exists at all, the way through will need to be marked clearly. There is therefore a necessity for a point of exegetical entry that at once has manifest significance for the entirety of Luke-Acts and allows us to trace the path between the Lukan writings and imperial cult. There exists just such an entry point.

Chapter 10 occupies a place of central narrative and theological importance in Acts. Narratively, Saul has just transformed from persecutor to God's σκεῦος ἐκλογῆς to the Gentiles (9:15). The story then moves immediately to justify theologically Paul's mission through Peter's experience with Cornelius. This narrative-theological justification continues through Acts 11:18, at which time

---

32. Price, *Rituals and Power*, 248.
33. C. K. Barrett, *Luke the Historian in Recent Study* (Philadelphia: Fortress, 1970), 63.

the story returns to Saul to include his ministry (ἡ διακονία, 12:25) in Antioch (11:25–26, 30; 12:25). The events in chapter 10 are the pivot upon which the mission to the Gentiles turns.[34]

The climax of Acts 10 is Peter's speech wherein the (Lukan) gospel is proclaimed to the Gentiles for the first time. Whatever its pre-Lukan history,[35] the set for this speech in its present context is carefully constructed. After a vision ἐν Καισαρείᾳ, Cornelius, a pious ἑκατοντάρχης—and thus probably a Roman citizen[36]—of the Italian Cohort,[37] sends to Joppa two of his οἰκέται and one εὐσεβὴς στρατιώτης to ask for Peter. Upon their return to Caesarea, Cornelius falls prostrate and begins προσκυνεῖν Peter. Peter responds with proper Jewish theology—"Get up! I am only a human being!"[38]—and thereby rejects

34. The importance of the unit 10:1–11:18 is widely recognized. The compressed *Forschungsbericht* in Haenchen's commentary remains important (Ernst Haenchen, *The Acts of the Apostles: A Commentary*, trans. Bernard Noble and Gerald Shinn, rev. R. McL. Wilson [Philadelphia: Westminster, 1971], 355–63).

35. Jacob Jervell, *Die Apostelgeschichte: Übersetzt und erklärt*, KEK 3 (Göttingen: Vandenhoeck & Ruprecht, 1998), 317, summarizes well the breadth of opinion: "Der Abschnitt [10.1–11.18] ist als kunstvolle Komposition im ganzen auf vorlukanische Tradition zurückzuführen, oder fast alles ist Lukas selbst zuzuschreiben."

36. A. N. Sherwin-White, *Roman Law and Roman Society in the New Testament* (Grand Rapids: Baker, 1992), 160: "Cornelius and Julius . . . were not necessarily Roman citizens. The bulk of the auxiliary troopers were *peregrini*, and only became Roman citizens after twenty-five years of service. But about Cornelius there is less serious doubt. His troop, one of the *cohortes Italicae*, belonged to a special group recruited originally in Italy, though it is true that auxiliary units were kept up to strength after their formation by local recruitment, which Josephus specifically mentions in Judaea [*B. J.* 2.13.7]." Yet just a few pages earlier he wrote: "There can be no certainty that any of the centurions in the stories of Acts or Gospels [*sic*] was a Roman. Even Cornelius at Caesarea seems to be a provincial, living with his kinsmen" (156). Michael P. Speidel, "The Roman Army in Judaea under the Procurators," *Ancient Society* 13/14 (1982/1983): 233–40, argues that both Cornelius and Julius were Roman citizens. Whether Cornelius was Italian or Syrian, however, seems impossible to know.

37. For a concise discussion of this unit, see T. R. S. Broughton, "The Roman Army," in *The Beginnings of Christianity, Part 1: The Acts of the Apostles*, ed. F. J. Foakes Jackson and Kirsopp Lake (London: Macmillan, 1933), 5:427–45, esp. 441–43; or Speidel, "Roman Army." On centurions, see Yann Le Bohec, *The Imperial Roman Army* (London: Batsford, 1994), 43–45, 65, 74–76. The Imperial cult in the army is a difficult topic in its own right. See, e.g., Michael P. Speidel, "The Cult of the Genii in the Roman Army and a New Military Deity," *ANRW* 2.16.2 (1978): 1542–55, who notes that the army's "monuments to the Genius of the emperors are so numerous that they reflect a particular attachment of the army to their supreme commanders, even if one allows for the unusually rich documentation from the army camps" (1543).

38. The sentence could hardly be more emphatic: καὶ ἐγὼ αὐτὸς ἄνθρωπός εἰμι. Cf. the stress on ἄνθρωποι in Acts 14:15.

Part 1: Christology, Greco-Roman Culture, and Canonical Reception

improper obeisance to and/or worship of human beings. Heeding Peter's rebuke, Cornelius takes him inside where "many" (πολλοί) have gathered to hear Peter speak. The scene thus opens with Gentile characters, evolves in a Gentile's house that is full of Gentiles, and takes place in the most important Gentile city in the land—the city of the Gentile Καῖσαρ by the sea.[39] Moreover, Cornelius and those with him are prepared to hear Peter's words as from God: "Now then, we are all here before God to hear everything the Lord has commanded you to say" (10:33).

The Greek of Acts 10:36–37 is notoriously problematic. A decent translation is nevertheless possible:

> You know the word that he sent to the people of Israel preaching peace through Jesus Christ: this one is Lord of all. You know what has happened throughout the whole of Judaea, beginning in Galilee after the baptism that John preached, as God anointed in the Holy Spirit and power Jesus of Nazareth, who went about benefacting and healing all who were oppressed by the devil, for God was with him.[40]

Many commentators and contemporary translations take the sentence οὗτός ἐστιν πάντων κύριος to be parenthetical and translate "he is Lord of all."[41] But, in fact, Luke did not leave ἐστίν to imply the subject "he"; nor did he write the

---

39. By the time Luke wrote, Caesarea Maritima had become a Roman colony (under the principate of Vespasian). For recent work on the city, see, e.g., Avner Raban and Kenneth G. Holum, eds., *Caesarea Maritima: A Retrospective after Two Millennia* (Leiden: Brill, 1996), and Terence L. Donaldson, ed., *Religious Rivalries and the Struggle for Success in Caesarea Maritima*, Studies in Christianity and Judaism 8 (Waterloo, ON: Wilfrid Laurier University Press, 2000).

40. As in the NRSV, e.g., here the ὑμεῖς οἴδατε of 10:37 is taken to go also with the beginning of 10:36 because τὸν λόγον is in the accusative case. The other compelling option is that of Harald Riesenfeld, "The Text of Acts x.36," in *Text and Interpretation: Studies in the New Testament*, ed. Ernest Best and R. McL. Wilson (Cambridge: Cambridge University Press, 1979), 191–94, which treats τὸν λόγον as an apposition resuming the preceding clause: "(this is) the word which he sent . . ."

41. E.g., C. K. Barrett, *A Critical and Exegetical Commentary on the Acts of the Apostles*, 2 vols., ICC (Edinburgh: T&T Clark, 1994–1998), 1:522; Ulrich Wilckens, *Die Missionsreden der Apostelgeschichte: Form- und traditionsgeschichtliche Untersuchungen* (Neukirchen-Vluyn: Neukirchener Verlag, 1961), 48; RSV, etc. An exception is Robert C. Tannehill, *The Narrative Unity of Luke-Acts: A Literary Interpretation*, 2 vols. (Minneapolis: Fortress, 1986–1990), 2:139–40. Cf. also Beverly Roberts Gaventa, *The Acts of the Apostles*, ANTC (Nashville: Abingdon, 2003), 170.

relative ὅς.⁴² Instead, he wrote the demonstrative pronoun οὗτος. Interpretations that (if unwittingly) ignore the grammar here end by downplaying the directive force of οὗτος—*this one*.

Taken seriously, οὗτος excludes the idea that the sentence is parenthetical in importance and instead points to the dramatic nature of Peter's claim: Jesus Christ, this one, is the κύριος πάντων.⁴³ The underside of the stress that the demonstrative places on this claim is that there are others who are acknowledged as κύριος. Οὗτος thus serves as a countering device and raises the volume of the πάντων: *this one*—and not someone else—is the κύριος of all.⁴⁴

The context for this claim is remarkable. The narrative has turned a corner, explicitly rejected pagan reverence/worship, and now looks out upon an active mission to the Gentiles. Consider the scene: the leading Gentile character, a ranking member of the Roman military; the city, founded in honor of Augustus; the audience, a group of Gentiles;⁴⁵ the sermon, the inaugural for the mission. These elements taken in toto create an ethos in which the presence of the Roman Empire is keenly felt. And it is into this setting that Peter introduces the crucified Jesus—οὗτος—as the κύριος πάντων.

My argument is that, as this scene in Caesarea unfolded before them, auditors of the Lukan text throughout the empire would have heard the stress of this claim in connection with the Roman emperor and his cult.⁴⁶ The plenteous evidence for the application of κύριος to the emperor is both literary and archaeological. For this short chapter a few examples will have to suffice.

---

42. The suggestion of equivalence between οὗτος and ὅς is the problem in the otherwise perceptive remarks of T. E. Page, *The Acts of the Apostles* (London: Macmillan, 1911), 149.

43. Cf. the emphasis on the demonstrative οὗτος in Acts 2:36 (τοῦτον τὸν Ἰησοῦν).

44. Though highly significant, due to the restrictions of space I cannot deal with the impact of this claim in terms of its relation to the manifold use of κύριος for other deities (Zeus, Osiris, etc.; see W. H. Roscher, *Ausführliches Lexikon der griechischen und römischen Mythologie* [Leipzig: Teubner, 1884–1937], II/1:1755–69). My argument is not that Luke intended to refer only to the Roman emperor, but rather that the data makes it impossible to exclude the emperor in what would have been heard (i.e., there are no indications that the auditors would be expected to filter out the emperor as κύριος). The specific angle of vision for the chapter is of course determined by the assigned topic.

45. Gaventa, *Acts*, 171, also notes the importance of the location.

46. The scene here is thus used narratively for historical leverage. The argument is not, therefore, about what the "real" Cornelius in a particular house in Caesarea in the late 30s or early 40s would have heard (though of course the proximity to the Gaius incident is interesting) but about the historical situation around the time of Luke-Acts in light of the impact the narrative would have had upon its auditors.

Part 1: Christology, Greco-Roman Culture, and Canonical Reception

A striking instance occurs in the *Discourses* of Epictetus—once a slave of Nero's secretary Epaphroditus and later expelled from Rome by Domitian (only to become an acquaintance of Hadrian)—which refers to the emperor as ὁ πάντων κύριος καῖσαρ.[47] So, too, Suetonius famously indicates that Domitian wished to be called *dominus et deus noster*,[48] and Martial knows this as well: the god Janus promised length of days to Domitian, "the Lord and God of the whole world [*omni terrarium domino deoque*]."[49] An inscription from the city Acraephiae in Boeotia entitles Nero ὁ τοῦ παντὸς κόσμου κύριος Νέρων,[50] and we read of him as (ὁ) κύριος in hundreds of papyri and ostraka.[51] From Crete we hear of the last Flavian as [τῆς] τοῦ κυρίου αὐτοκράτορο[ς] Δομιτιανοῦ. And in Achaia, though his name was later erased, Domitian was styled by the proconsul τοῦ κυρίου ἡμῶ[ν].[52] Philo, too, refers to Caligula as κύριος, once as δεσπότης καὶ κύριος in the eloquent speech of Agrippa I and once in the Jewish assembly's address: κύριε Γάιε.[53] Moreover, when one moves past

---

47. Epictetus, *Disc.* 4.1.12.
48. Suetonius, *Domitianus* 13.2.
49. Martial, *Epigrams* 8.2.5–6 (cf. 5.8.1; 10.72.3). It is questionable whether Domitian himself demanded these titles (it is granted that those outside of the Imperial court would have used the expression; see the summary in Leonard L. Thompson, *The Book of Revelation: Apocalypse and Empire* [Oxford: Oxford University Press, 1990], 104–7). The problem, so the argument runs, is that if he did, we would expect to see this expression in Statius or Quintilian, both of whom wrote for Domitian. But it does not appear in their writings. Nor can one find *dominus et deus* on coins, inscriptions, etc. from Domitian's reign. Yet official policy in Rome was always a different matter than popular sentiment or even the emperor's own predilections (cf., e.g., M. P. Charlesworth, "The Refusal of Divine Honours: An Augustan Formula," *PBSR* 15 [1939]: 1–10). Thus Statius (*Silvae* 1.6.80), e.g., may have sought to portray Domitian in a good light when he mentioned that, upon being acclaimed *dominus* at one of his Saturnalia, the emperor forbade the people from using the title (one could easily compare Augustus's refusal of the title *dominus* at another public occasion [Suetonius, *Divus Augustus* 53.1–2]). Regardless of his intention, Statius certainly knew of Domitian as *dominus*. Moreover, one ought to beware the argument *e silentio*—where it might be possible to explain the absence on other grounds, the positive evidence should receive the weight.
50. Wilhelm Dittenberger, ed., *Sylloge Inscriptionum Graecarum*, 3rd ed. (Leipzig: Herzelium, 1917), II.814, lines 30–31, p. 507. Cf. Jdt 6:4: Nebuchadnezzar is κύριος of the whole earth (refers in historical time, like 2 Maccabees, to the Seleucid period).
51. See, e.g., index 1 in P. M. Meyer, ed., *Griechische Texte aus Ägypten* (Berlin: Weidmannsche Buchhandlung, 1916), or the indices in the SEG volumes.
52. Dittenberger, *Sylloge Inscriptionum Graecum*, II.821D, lines 1–2. Dittenberger notes: "Nomen Domitiani erasum est post damnatam memoriam senatusconsulto" (513 n. 7).
53. Philo, *Legat.* 286, 356. Josephus, *B. J.* 6.2.5. §134, refers to Titus as ὁ κύριος, but it is doubtful whether this use carries a titular sense.

Domitian (omitting Nerva) into the reigns of Trajan, Hadrian, and others, the examples seem only to increase.[54]

It is in fact undeniable that Luke, too, knew of the Roman emperor as κύριος. In Acts 25:13–27 the procurator Festus, having just arrived in Caesarea, asks King Agrippa II for advice, for Festus does not quite know what to do with Paul, whom the previous procurator (Felix) left as prisoner. The rub, as it were, is that Paul has appealed to Caesar, but Festus does not know what charges to put before the emperor. Indeed, says Festus to Agrippa, "I have nothing solid to write τῷ κυρίῳ about him" (25:26). This is the only time in the NT that the emperor is called κύριος, and here it has a double reference: to Nero within the time of the narrative and (most likely) to Domitian in historical time. The line between the external evidence and the Lukan text is thus clearly drawn via this single use of κύριος.

Taken by itself, it is of course possible that this corroborating reference ranks only as "an insignificant detail"[55] in the history of imperial appellation. But read within Luke-Acts, it bears an intrinsic narrative importance, specifically as it confirms the connection between the κύριος of Acts 10:36 and the Roman emperor. Following hard on the heels of the οὗτος, the use of πάντων in 10:36 precludes ultimate allegiance to the emperor on the part of the Gentile neophytes. When ecclesial practice begins to reflect this confession, it would probably not be too much to say that a seed of martyrdom has been sown.

Acts 10:36 thus opens the possibility of a concrete connection with the Roman emperor through the word κύριος not only because of the evidence external to Luke-Acts but also because of the Lukan narrative itself. Yet it still remains to justify internally—that is, narratively—the weight we have placed upon this verse. Is Acts 10:36 only a minor element within Luke-Acts, and have we, therefore, magnified a tiny grain beyond its intrinsic significance?

---

54. The Egyptian materials are obviously the largest in number (papyri from Oxyrhynchus, Memnoneia, etc.); yet even this fact has to be understood carefully. For example, though they originated in Alexandria (ca. 105), some lead seals bearing κύριος for Trajan were actually found in Fyon (SEG 66 [1996], 2115). Numismatic evidence constitutes an exception to this general picture, but official language from Rome was normally more reserved: "On coins, which can be trusted to reflect official language, we find *Kyrios* first at Alexandria of Trajan, then not till the time of Marcus Aurelius and Fucius Verus" (A. D. Nock, *Early Gentile Christianity and Its Hellenistic Background* [New York: Harper & Row, 1964], 35). Cf. Dio Chrysostom, *Disc.* 45.4, who tells of Smyrna's acclamation of Trajan as τῶν ὅλων κύριον.

55. Adolf Deissmann, *Light from the Ancient East* (New York: Doran, 1927), 354.

Part 1: Christology, Greco-Roman Culture, and Canonical Reception

Κύριος in Luke-Acts

In my view, it would be virtually impossible to overemphasize the importance κύριος has for Luke.[56] Though the subject is vast, here we must be content with a few observations supporting such an assertion. The first is simply statistical: Luke uses κύριος roughly two hundred times in Luke-Acts, about one hundred in each book. In addition, κύριος is used far more than any other christological title—over twice as many times as χριστός, for example, which several scholars (incorrectly) take as the most important title.[57]

The second observation is redactional/authorial: Luke is the only one of the (canonical) gospel authors to use the absolute ὁ κύριος consistently and expansively for Jesus in his earthly career (7:13, etc.). Moreover, he repeatedly unifies the vocative and non-vocative cases at the level of his narrative. We may think, for example, of Jesus's encounter with Zacchaeus—"Zacchaeus said to τὸν κύριον, 'Look, half of my possessions, κύριε, I give to the poor'" (Luke 19:8)—or the story of Ananias's vision in Acts 9:10-11: "ὁ κύριος said to him in a vision, 'Ananias . . .' And he said, 'Here I am, κύριε.' And ὁ κύριος [said] to him, 'Rise up . . .'"

Luke also provides christological reading directives for the parables via ὁ κύριος. We may take an example from the double tradition. Both Luke and Matthew place the material about the "hour of the thief" (Luke 12:39-40; Matt 24:43-44) side by side together with that of the "faithful manager/slave" (Luke 12:42b-48; Matt 24:45-51). But whereas Matthew simply juxtaposes the two sets of material, Luke connects them with a question from Peter and places the latter set as Jesus's answer and explication: "And Peter said, 'κύριε, are you telling this parable for us or for everyone?' And ὁ κύριος said . . ." The double tradition then picks up again, as Luke continues, "Who then is the faithful and prudent manager whom ὁ κύριος will put in charge of his household . . . ?" In Luke 12:41-42 we thus have an immediate κύριος sequence in which the first two uses refer to Jesus and the third refers to the κύριος of the parable. This sequence interrupts the flow of Jesus's parabolic teaching to introduce Jesus himself as κύριος and in this way effects a blending together of the κύριος in the world of the parable and that of the larger narrative.[58]

---

56. I attempted to give due emphasis to κύριος in Luke's Gospel in my *Early Narrative Christology: The Lord in the Gospel of Luke* (2006; repr., Grand Rapids: Baker Academic, 2009).

57. E.g., Fitzmyer, *Luke*, 1:197.

58. On parables and allegory, see Hans-Josef Klauck, *Allegorie und Allegorese in synoptischen Gleichnistexten*, Neutestamentliche Abhandlungen 13 (Münster: Aschendorff, 1978).

Furthermore, only once in Luke's appropriation of Mark does he change κύριος to something else, and this can be explained on other grounds.[59] By contrast, Luke adds or changes to a form of κύριος in passages from both the double (e.g., 7:19) and triple tradition (e.g., 18:41; 22:61), and Luke has at least twenty-five unique passages with κύριος to Matthew's seven.

Third, we may note a few examples of the christological importance of the narrative placement of κύριος. (1) In Luke 1:43 Elizabeth refers to Mary as ἡ μήτηρ τοῦ κυρίου μου. This is the first time that Jesus himself appears in the narrative, and his appearance is coincident with his identity as the Lord: ὁ κύριος in the womb. That Jesus's existence and naming as "the Lord" are coextensive indicates that κύριος is constitutive of christological identity in the Third Gospel. For Luke, there is no point at which Jesus is not κύριος. Such an introduction profoundly shapes Lukan Christology and our perception of Luke's use of κύριος in the rest of Luke-Acts, for it is in fact as κύριος that Luke first brings Jesus into the story.[60]

(2) Luke 2:11 is the first time that χριστός occurs in the gospel. The fact that in its very first occurrence χριστός appears not by itself but in juxtaposition with κύριος carries significance ipso facto. The Messiah is the Lord, and thus is Jesus's messianic status inextricably bound with his identity as κύριος.

(3) Luke first introduces the vocative κύριε—typically thought to be little more than "sir"—in a context in which its meaning is unquestionably exalted (5:1-11; cf. 6:46). Other arguments aside, Peter's switch in 5:1-11 from ἐπιστάτα to κύριε and accompanying confession of sin at the knees of the κύριος settle the question. The reader/auditor is thus prepared to hear in subsequent vocatives a Lukan christological conviction and a fuller import than an ordinary Greco-Roman address.

(4) Luke 24:34 states that ἠγέρθη ὁ κύριος. This is the last time that anyone speaks of Jesus in the gospel, and it stretches back through the narrative to the first, in 1:43 where Elizabeth speaks of Jesus in the womb as ὁ κύριος. This first and last use form an *inclusio* that brackets the gospel in terms of the identity of Jesus as ὁ κύριος: from beginning to end, Jesus is κύριος.

(5) Acts displays remarkable concern for continuity with the gospel precisely at the point of Jesus's identity as κύριος. Indeed Ἰησοῦς and κύριος are

---

59. Luke 9:33 has ἐπιστάτα, as does Matt 17:4, where Mark has κύριε in 9:5. In contrast to the interpretations in the secondary literature, in its Lukan contexts ἐπιστάτης consistently carries a negative connotation.

60. The importance of Jesus's introduction for Lukan Christology is supported by Luke's own preference for speaking of Jesus in the gospel narrative: ὁ κύριος.

Part 1: Christology, Greco-Roman Culture, and Canonical Reception

frequently yoked, as in Acts 1:21, which uses ὁ κύριος Ἰησοῦς to speak about the resurrected Lord Jesus in his earthly ministry: "So one of the men who have accompanied us during all the time that ὁ κύριος Ἰησοῦς went in and out among us, beginning from the baptism of John until the day when he was taken up from us—one of these men must become with us a witness to his resurrection" (1:21; cf. 4:33; 8:16, etc.). Of similar import is Acts 2:36. The exalted Lord at the right hand of God (2:34–35) is the same Lord (and Christ) as the Jesus who was crucified. Acts 2:36, therefore, harks back to Luke 2:11 and serves to establish a unity in the identity of the earthly and exalted κύριος (and χριστός) via narrative continuity.

(6) Finally, we may mention the often-noticed ambiguity that attends many of Luke's uses of κύριος. Rather than a reflection of accidental or imprecise language,[61] the ambiguity carries a profound point: the act of Jesus κύριος in heaven is that of God the Lord—that is, of the κύριος οὐρανοῦ καὶ γῆς (Acts 17:24: οὗτος οὐρανοῦ καὶ γῆς ὑπάρχων κύριος; cf. Luke 10:21). That the οὐρανὸς καὶ γῆ of 17:24 correspond formally to the πάντων of 10:36 need hardly be said.

In light of these (brief) observations, it should be apparent that, far from an isolated detail or parenthetical addition, Acts 10:36 provides a remarkable and dramatic abbreviation of Luke's christological use of κύριος. In this way it is a material link to the κύριος Christology of the entire Luke-Acts narrative, and its intrinsic narrative importance is therefore confirmed. "This one"—οὗτος—is in fact κύριος in Luke-Acts.

Implications

The correlation between Acts 10:36 and the imperial cult depends upon the conjunction of evidence external and internal to Luke's narrative, the artistry with which Luke creates the Cornelius-Peter meeting, the audacity of Peter's claim, and the manifest importance of κύριος in Luke-Acts. Taken together, these elements would shape the effect of the text in the Greco-Roman world so that in the word κύριος an ancient auditor could have perceived the rumbling of rival claims. The juxtaposition of the κύριοι, I have urged, is too obvious to be missed, and it is too potent to be accidental. May we then

---

61. E.g., James D. G. Dunn, "ΚΥΡΙΟΣ in Acts," in *The Christ and the Spirit*, vol. 1, *Christology* (Grand Rapids: Eerdmans, 1998), 241–53: "It would probably be fairer to see his usage as indicative of an unreflective stage in early christology" (253).

Luke-Acts and the Imperial Cult

draw the old conclusion that Luke presents a *Christuskult* in opposition to the *Kaiserkult*?[62] No. And, yes.

The narrative complexity and lack of direct discourse foreclose the possibility of pat answers to any facet of Luke's relation to Rome. Within the ambit of the Rome question, Luke's type of history is realistic, or at least wrought with considerable verisimilitude: there are some decent Romans (the centurion at the cross, Julius of the Augustan Cohort, et al.) and some deleterious ones (the Philippian στρατηγοί in Acts 16:19–40, Felix, et al.); Pilate did not initiate the charges against Jesus, but he did permit his crucifixion with two other criminals; there was a riot in Ephesus, but civilized debate in Athens, and so on. Thus it is clear that on the one hand Luke-Acts nowhere approaches the frontal attack on the machinery of Rome we find in Revelation. Even in Acts 10, as a member of the Roman army Cornelius is a character whose contour is paradigmatic, a "shining example of unprejudiced openness to the gospel."[63]

But on the other hand, the conceptual nature of the claim to universal lordship is not derivative but generative or controlling. It is not one piece of the conceptual puzzle of Christology but the structure itself into which the other pieces fit. It is at this level—that of the ordering principles of thought and their concomitant relation to praxis—that conflict could begin to break out. No matter how positive Luke's portrayal of the virtues of the Roman Empire and people, there is at bottom a rival claim to universal lordship. Thus in Acts 10, for example, the piety of Cornelius, the setting in Caesarea, and so forth actually highlight the contrast in the claim. The simple question "Who is the Lord of all?" is answered by Luke one way and by Rome another:

> The emperor's overwhelming and intrusive power had to be represented not in terms of a local hero but of a universal god. Standing at the apex of the hierarchy of the Roman empire the emperor offered the hope of order and stability and was assimilated to the traditional Olympian deities.[64]

The way in which this contrast plays out in Luke-Acts has primarily to do with the nature and shape of Jesus's lordship. That is to say, the rival claim not

62. E.g., Deissmann, *Light*, 349–92.
63. Ulrich Mauser, *The Gospel of Peace* (Louisville: Westminster John Knox, 1992), 94.
64. Price, *Rituals and Power*, 233. Nock, *Early Gentile Christianity*, 34, asserts that "it may be doubted whether there is in the use of *Kyrios* any conscious contrast of anything that would be felt as such between Jesus and the Emperor." Here Nock overlooks the internarrative significance of κύριος in Luke-Acts and the different content of κύριος signified by the words "Jesus" and "emperor."

Part 1: Christology, Greco-Roman Culture, and Canonical Reception

only involves ascription of universality to the same title but also extends to the content of "lordship." Rather than as wielding "overwhelming and intrusive power," or, as Seneca put it for the young Nero, arbitrating "life and death for the nations,"[65] κυριότης in Luke-Acts is construed in terms of the humility or service of the κύριος. One may immediately and rightly think of the second temptation, in which Jesus rejects authority over the οἰκουμένη. But another passage is perhaps most notable in keeping with our focus. During the disciples' second dispute over who was the greatest, Jesus admonishes them not to be like the "kings of the Gentiles, who κυριεύουσιν them." Rather, says Jesus, reversing the common understanding of power, let the greatest become the youngest and the leader, the servant, "for who is greater, the one who reclines at table or the servant? Is it not the one who reclines? But I am in your midst as the one who serves" (22:25-27). Indeed, in Luke 12:37 the κύριος who, upon his return, finds his δοῦλοι awake will serve them while they recline at table.[66]

As a whole, however, Luke is far more concerned with the story of Jesus and the church than with the narration of particular incidents that deal unambiguously with "Rome." This lack of direct attention to Rome is due partly to the intensity of this christological and ecclesiological focus and partly to the fact that Christian conflict with the emperor and his empire during Luke's time was not widespread.

There was, of course, no legal compulsion to participate in the imperial cult until the middle of the third century under Decius, and, insofar as the imperial cult figured into later persecutions, it should probably not be separated from other civic cults.[67] Moreover, even Pliny's much earlier letter to Trajan evidences genuine confusion over just what to make of the "Christians," and Trajan's response is certainly less than a coherent policy.[68] Yet a group whose praxis would accord with the confession of Acts 10:36 would eventually run up against the imperial κύριος.

---

65. Seneca, *De clementia* 1.2.
66. See above for the "allegorical" nature of κύριος in this parable.
67. See Fergus Millar, "The Imperial Cult and the Persecutions," in den Boer, *Le culte*, 145-65, esp. 164.
68. For Trajan's decision, Tertullian's quip is pertinent: "O sententiam necessitate confusam!" "What a decision, how inevitably entangled!" (*Apol.* 2.7). Cf., however, Bickerman's remarks in the discussion of Millar's essay mentioned in the previous note: "As Petronius says, the governor was imperator of his province; it was up to him to decide whether and how the Christians of his province were to be persecuted. There was not and could not have been a general rule on this subject. Yet, there could have been some pronouncement of some emperor touching the persecution of the Christians" (den Boer, *Le culte*, 171).

In fact, where conflict can be seen at an early point in ecclesiastical history, the identity of the κύριος πάντων often plays a role. The description of Jesus as κύριος κυρίων (and βασιλεὺς βασιλέων) twice in Revelation is immediately evident (17:14; 19:16 in reverse order).[69] And the account of Polycarp's martyrdom, wherein Polycarp refuses to say κύριος καῖσαρ and perform the sacrifices, is well known.[70] But we might also do well to recall, with Deissmann, the earliest Christian work in Latin (ca. 180), in which the proconsul Saturninus offers the possibility of "the pardon of our *dominus* the emperor," if only the Christians will swear by the *genius* "of our *dominus* the emperor."[71] In the subsequent justification of his conduct, the Christian Speratus responds, *Cognosco domnum meum, imperatorem regum et omnium gentium*.[72] So, too, though the textual lacuna obscures the context, the Epistle to Diognetus 7.7 preserves a likely reference to something similar: "they are cast to the wild beasts in order that they might deny τὸν κύριον." Perhaps, however, in the end it was Tertullian who in later (and more clearly worked out) terms best reflected the substance of the Lukan view of the emperor and his cult: "I will plainly call the emperor *dominus*, but only in the common manner when I am not forced to call him *dominus* in the sense of God."[73] Put in Lukan language, Christians may refer to the κύριος καῖσαρ as κύριος, as indeed Luke himself does (Acts 25:26), but Jesus κύριος is the κύριος πάντων (Acts 10:36).

---

69. Cf. 1 Tim 6:15, where Jesus is called μόνος δυνάστης ὁ βασιλεὺς τῶν βασιλευόντων καὶ κύριος τῶν κυριευόντων. In light of 1 Tim 6:13, where Jesus is commended for making τὴν καλὴν ὁμολογίαν before Pilate, 1 Tim 6:15 may indicate that the Imperial cult is somewhere in view. But because 1 Timothy as a whole does not evidence a direct relation to the Imperial cult, this is less sure than in Revelation.

70. Martyrdom of Polycarp 8.2. Cf. Josephus, *B. J.* 7.10.1 §§418–19, who relates that Sicarii (even their children) captured in Alexandria refused to call Caesar δεσπότης under torture designed solely (μόνος) for this purpose.

71. *Passio Sanctorum Scillitanorum* (*Pass. Sanct. Scill.*) 1, 5 (this phrase is used three times).

72. *Pass. Sanct. Scill.* 6. (The Greek version reads: ἐπιγινώσκω τὸν κύριον ἡμῶν.) The *dominus* here is certainly Jesus because of the allusion to Jesus's "render unto Caesar." Speratus asserts that he pays his taxes "because [*quid*] I acknowledge my Lord . . ." The Latin text set in parallel to a later Greek counterpart can be found in the appendix to J. A. Robinson, ed., *The Passion of S. Perpetua* (Cambridge: Cambridge University Press, 1891), 112–17. Cf. *Mart. Apoll.* 3. On *domnum* for *dominum*, see "dom(i)nus," in *TLL*, 5:1907–35, or A. Forcellini's *Lexicon Totius Latinitatis*, 2:193.

73. Tertullian, *Apol.* 34.1.

The God of Israel and Jesus Christ

♦ LUKE, MARCION, AND THE UNITY OF THE CANON

INTRODUCTORY REMARKS

In the study of history it is now almost a commonplace to note that the portrayal of certain persons or groups by their enemies or opponents is at best not accurate to the degree that we would wish and at worst totally distorted by the nature of the polemic. A well-known example from the world of NT scholarship of the apprehension of this methodological principle is the debate over Paul's portrayal of the Judaism of his period. In opposition to much of the accepted view of Judaism disseminated by Bultmann and others, E. P. Sanders's 1977 *Paul and Palestinian Judaism* sparked a widespread rethinking of the relationship of Paul's portrayal of Judaism to a Judaism that would be allowed to speak on its own terms—that is, from its own sources. Though Sanders's own picture has received critique,[1] his methodological point is accepted by scholars on all sides of the debate: in order to come to the best understanding possible of a person or group, we must first let them speak for themselves.

---

1. See, e.g., Charles H. Talbert's presidential address to the Catholic Biblical Association, "Paul, Judaism, and the Revisionists," *CBQ* 63 (2001): 1–22, and the literature cited therein.

"The God of Israel and Jesus Christ: Luke, Marcion, and the Unity of the Canon" was originally published in *Nova et Vetera*, English Edition 1/2 (2003): 359–80. It is reproduced with permission.

This paper was delivered as a lecture for a joint Heidelberg-Tübingen OT/NT conference (January 31–February 1, 2003) organized around the theme "In welchem Sinne ist die Schrift Verbindlich?" The text has only a few minor alterations and thus reflects in both orientation and style certain aspects pertinent to a set theme and to a particular location and audience. Further, due to the constraints of time and space, no attempt has been made within the footnotes to defend each subsidiary position taken herein with respect to complex and still-debated issues in Lukan scholarship.

The God of Israel and Jesus Christ

When we come to Marcion this methodological conviction, however, does not get us very far, except in the way of cautionary warning, since no writings of his are preserved except for partial appearances in the works of others. We must begin our study therefore with a caveat: The representation of Marcion or Marcionite theology in, for example, Tertullian's *Adversus Marcionem* is not necessarily the same as the way in which Marcion or his followers would have presented their own theology.[2] However, the position described by Tertullian does exist as a theological possibility, and it is to such a possible theological position that I take the word "Marcionite" to refer. But the precise relationship between the sources for Marcion's theology, their accuracy, and so on I will have to leave to the church historians.[3]

The God of Israel, Jesus, and the Gospel of Luke in Marcionite Theology

The purpose of this section is to remind us of the central issue that Marcionite theology raises and its implications for the relation of the Old and New Testaments (and, therefore, also for the possibility of the unity of the canon). The opening remarks of book 4 of Tertullian's *Adversus Marcionem* bring the crucial point of importance immediately to the fore.

For Tertullian, Marcion's *Antitheses* (ἀντιθέσεις, "Contradictions"), a work in which the latter set parts of (what we call) the Old and New Testaments against each other, made "such a division between the Law and the Gospel as thereby to make two separate gods [*duos deos dividens*], opposite to each other [*proinde diversos*], one belonging to one instrument (or, as it is more usual to say, testament [*testamenti*]), one to the other" (4.1). Tertullian had no problem agreeing to a difference in dispensation as reflected in the Old and New Testaments: "I do not deny a difference in records of things spoken, in precepts for good behaviour, and in rules of law . . ." (4.1). His irreconcilable disagreement with Marcion, however, was at the most basic of theological levels: that of the identity of God. In point of fact, Tertullian's admission of

---

2. There is nevertheless a general and significant agreement between the diverse sources. For a very succinct discussion of this agreement, see the introduction of Ernest Evans's translation of Tertullian, *Adversus Marcionem* (Oxford: Clarendon, 1972), ix–xi.

3. See, e.g., Gerhard May's brief piece "Marcion ohne Harnack" and the first section of papers from the Mainz 2001 conference, "Die Quelle zu Marcion," in *Marcion und seine Kirchengeschichtliche Wirkung / Marcion and His Impact on Church History*, ed. Gerhard May and Katharina Greschat together with Martin Meiser, TU 150 (Berlin: de Gruyter, 2002).

Part 1: Christology, Greco-Roman Culture, and Canonical Reception

dispensational difference hinges on the self-sameness of the God of the Old and New Testaments, for the sentence cited just above continues: "provided that all these differences [i.e., things spoken, behavioral precepts, rules of law] have reference to one and the same God [*unum et eundem deum*], that God by whom it is acknowledged that they were ordained and also foretold" (4.l).[4] Thus Tertullian does not reject the manifest difference between the Old and New Testaments but denies that this difference requires us to posit two different gods.

This then is the issue raised by Marcionite theology: the relation of the God of the OT to the God of the NT and to Jesus Christ himself. Marcionite theology holds that the God of the Old and the God of the New are not the same God; the creator and warrior god of the OT is an entirely different entity from the good God and Father of Jesus Christ: "Marcion of Pontus developed this doctrine, with shameless blasphemy of the God of whom the law and the prophets tell, saying that he is the creator of evil things . . . but that Jesus came from that father who is high above the God who made the world."[5] Thus, for the Marcionites, the god of Israel and Jesus Christ have nothing to do with one another except at the level of total discontinuity and contradiction, as the *Antitheses* were arranged to show.

It is of considerable interest for our purpose that in addition to certain "Pauline" epistles (the pastorals and Hebrews were omitted from the ἀποστολικόν), Marcion selected Luke for his two-part canon as the one gospel that would best fit with his teaching of a theology—in the strict sense—of separation.[6] Of the explanations of his choice that have been offered, I wish to note especially Harnack's suggestion that "der 'heidenchristliche' und asketische Charakter des 3. Evangeliums gegenüber dem 1. und 2., nachdem die drei ersten Kapitel des Werks getilgt waren, muß ihm sympathisch gewesen sein."[7] While Lukan asceticism has not seen great discussion lately,[8] the rest of Harnack's view fits well with the traditional emphasis of modern scholarship upon Luke's Hellenism and further raises the important

---

4. Tertullian, *Marc.* 4.1 (PL 2.362BC).

5. Irenaeus, *Haer.* 1.27.2 (PG 7.1.688A).

6. The text was entitled simply εὐαγγέλιον, the one gospel.

7. Adolf von Harnack, *Marcion: Das Evangelium vom fremden Gott: Eine Monographie zur Geschichte der Grundlegung der katholischen Kirche*, 2nd ed. (Darmstadt: Wissenschaftliche Buchgesellschaft, 1996), 250*.

8. Though see Susan R. Garrett, "Beloved Physician of the Soul? Luke as Advocate for Ascetic Practice," in *Asceticism and the New Testament*, ed. Leif E. Vaage and Vincent L. Wimbush (New York: Routledge, 1999), 71–95.

question of the theological significance of the opening scenes of the Lukan narrative for a reading of Luke's Gospel.

Though reconstructing Marcion's exact gospel text is not possible on the basis of the evidence we possess,[9] there is an important, well-established fact about this text in relation to the beginning of the canonical Luke. In contrast to his treatment of the larger body of the Lukan Gospel, where for the most part it would appear that Marcion carefully excised and/or inserted what was necessary for his theology, Marcion's version of the Gospel of Luke retained only a small part of one verse of the first three chapters (3:1) and the last third of chapter 4.[10] Rather than pointing to Marcion's knowledge of a Lukan text without chapters 1–2,[11] such a total omission points, I think, to a Marcionite insight of fundamental material significance: it is simply not possible to read the Gospel of Luke with its opening chapters along Marcionite lines.

Why not? The simple but accurate answer is that the feel of these beginning chapters is just too Jewish. All of it had to go. But we may ask further, Jewish in what sense? Custom, ethos, allusions, or references to the OT? Certainly that is the case. The Jewishness of the beginning of Luke's Gospel, however, runs much deeper than the general feel or atmosphere and emerges fully only at the intersection of what we might call theology proper and Christology—exactly that place where Marcionism carved out its distinctive teaching and held its appeal. This intersection and its implications underlie the necessity of the Marcionite rejection of the beginning portions of Luke's Gospel. The God of Israel and Jesus Christ must be kept separate, but the opening of the Lukan narrative will not allow such a separation. In fact it eliminates the possibility of conceiving of the God of Israel apart from Jesus Christ and vice versa.

---

9. David Salter Williams, "Reconsidering Marcion's Gospel," *JBL* 108 (1989): 477–96, draws out several of the difficulties and then attempts to reconstruct twenty-three different "explicit correlated readings" (i.e., passages that both Tertullian and Epiphanius cite explicitly). Williams's conclusion is that while there are certainly differences front the "modern, eclectically restored form" of Luke, Marcion's gospel nonetheless stood "closer to Luke than any other extant Gospel" (482).

10. At this point, I follow Harnack's reconstruction in *Marcion* (183–240).

11. In asserting that Marcion did in fact know of Luke with chapters 1–2, I follow such scholars as Harnack, Loisy, Metzger, Zahn, et al. for the opposite position; see, e.g., F. C. Conybeare, "Ein Zeugnis Ephräms über das Fehlen von c. 1 und 2 im Texte des Lucas," *ZNW* 3 (1902): 192–97; and John Knox, *Marcion and the New Testament: An Essay in the Early History of the Canon* (Chicago: University of Chicago Press, 1942). An important part of the question entails an opinion about the composition of Luke 1–2; for this matter, Joseph A. Fitzmyer, *The Gospel according to Luke*, 2 vols., AB 28/28A (Garden City, NY: Doubleday, 1981–1985), 1:309–12, is brief and judicious.

Part 1: Christology, Greco-Roman Culture, and Canonical Reception

Whether or not the actual Marcion grasped this matter in the way I have put it cannot be known, but the in toto rejection of 1:1–4:30 could be seen to point that way. Regardless, I began with Marcion because the theology of separation raises in acute form an important question in relation to the *Verbindlichkeit* of the canon in both its external and its internal dimensions—who is the God of the Bible?—and because Marcion's rejection of the OT and concomitant treatment of Luke's Gospel sets this issue before us in sharp relief.[12] We will now make a few remarks about reading strategy and Lukan OT hermeneutics, and then turn to the opening portions of the Gospel of Luke and focus on the introduction of Jesus into the narrative as κύριος as a way to open up the Lukan view of the relation of the God of Israel to Jesus Christ.

The God of Israel, Jesus, and the Gospel of Luke: Lukan Theology

Reading Strategy

At least since the time of Heidelberger Martin Dibelius, it has been assumed with confidence that the birth-infancy narrative is by and large later in origin than most of the material of the body of the gospel. One of Raymond Brown's monumental studies, *The Birth of the Messiah*, has in general confirmed this accepted hypothesis of an earlier generation.[13] At times in the history of modern scholarship, however, this historical point—the relative lateness of the birth-infancy narrative—has disproportionately, indeed incorrectly, influenced the interpretation of the gospel as a whole, as in, for example,

---

12. I have not attempted to translate "Verbindlich" or "Verbindlichkeit" into English due to the absence of a one-word equivalent. Part of the reason for the translation difficulty has to do with the fact that this one German word points in two directions. First, it can point to the inner relation of Scripture to itself, so to speak (a kind of internal Verbindlichkeit), and, second, it can point to our relation to the canon (a kind of external Verbindlichkeit). Thus the conference theme had two subheadings: (1) Vielstimmigkeit und Einheit der Schrift, and (2) Zum Problem der Normativität des Kanons. While the internal and external dimensions can be distinguished formally, they cannot be separated, hence the general idea of the lecture: to problematize the distinction between external and internal as one of separation while accepting the descriptive difference. In this light, the lecture is best understood if seen as beginning with a question of external Verbindlichkeit, moving toward internal Verbindlichkeit, and then on that basis back out toward external Verbindlichkeit.

13. This is not to deny that the birth-infancy narrative contains traditions that may themselves be quite early.

Conzelmann's relegation of Luke 1–2 to a position of unimportance in his famous book *Die Mitte der Zeit*.[14] Yet the basic fact remains that despite various attempts at reconstruction (proto-Luke, etc.), we have neither a single copy of Luke's Gospel without the birth-infancy narrative nor any really substantial evidence that the early followers of Jesus were acquainted with a Lukan Gospel minus the first two chapters.

The importance of this observation is at least twofold. First, if we want to understand *Lukan* theology, we must read the Lukan Gospel as Luke shaped it,[15] and this means taking seriously the placement of the first chapters at the beginning of the gospel. Of course, Luke himself makes just this point with the use of the expression ἀκριβῶς καθεξῆς in his προοίμιον. His narrative, he claims, is written "accurately in sequence,"[16] at least in the literary sense.

Second, the importance of Luke's term διήγησις is presupposed. It is, in fact, the word that tells us in what way Luke wants his gospel, or first book (πρῶτον λόγον; Acts 1:1), to be read: as a narrative. Despite the breaks or gaps in the narrative and the somewhat awkward but typical ἐγένετο δέ transitions, for example, the gospel as a whole is nonetheless characterized by Luke in his highly self-conscious preface as a διήγησις, and the gospel is therefore best understood if read this way. In terms of our particular study, this means that the way in which κύριος occurs in the narrative—its placement, its first and subsequent appearances, its relation to what comes before and after, and so forth—assumes first place in the order of interpretation. The uses of κύριος in the *Umwelt*, what we believe to have been likely, possible, or impossible in the Jewish and larger Mediterranean world of the first century, Luke's relation

---

14. Cf. also, e.g., Julius Wellhausen's slim commentary *Das Evangelium Lucae* (Berlin: Reimer, 1904), which begins outright with Luke 3:1.

15. In this sense it really does not matter whether Luke composed chs. 1–2 first or last, whether he had them as a tradition and, after minor editing, simply affixed them to the body of the gospel, etc. Whatever his compositional practice or treatment of his sources, it remains clear that he wanted chs. 1–2 to be a part of his total narrative.

16. "Accurately in sequence" seems to me to be the best literal translation of ἀκριβῶς καθεξῆς. Whether or not, and, if so, to what extent, Luke meant this in the strict sense of chronological agreement with actual events is impossible to know for sure. That Luke meant "accurately in sequence" in terms of the literary presentation itself seems to me to be confirmed by the nature of the preface (διήγησις, ἀσφάλεια, etc.), his use of καθεξῆς elsewhere (Luke 8:1 [in order or sequence; NRSV: "went on through"; Acts 3:24 [in order or sequence; NRSV: "those after him"]; Acts 11:4 [in order; NRSV: "step by step"]; Acts 18:23 [in sequence or in order; NRSV: "place to place"]), and both his respect for and rearrangement of Mark. See the brief discussion in Fitzmyer, *Luke*, 1:288–99, who himself thinks "literary order" is "the most evident sense of the adverb" (1:299).

Part 1: Christology, Greco-Roman Culture, and Canonical Reception

to his sources, and so on, are all important hermeneutical factors with which we would have to deal in a larger study. But, acknowledging the necessary and helpful reflexivity that exists between narrative interpretation and factors external to the narrative proper, such external factors set in relation to the meaning of κύριος in Luke's Gospel must not be allowed to override the meaning generated by the narrative. The narrative has the first move, as it were.

Lukan Old Testament Hermeneutics

It has become well-known in contemporary Lukan exegesis that Luke 1–2 displays a remarkable concern for continuity with the events, prophecies, and promises of the history of Israel. Such continuity is frequently, and rightly in my view, seen primarily in terms of Luke's use of the OT.[17] Luke Timothy Johnson may be correct that in its finer details Luke's method in using the OT is subtle and "eludes . . . detection."[18] But there are nonetheless a number of important observations for us to make about Lukan OT hermeneutics here in chapters 1–2 that have immediate bearing upon the interpretation of κύριος in the birth-infancy narrative.

Luke cites Scripture directly only twice (2:23, 24: both times prefaced with ἐν [τῷ] νόμῳ κυρίου), but the entire birth-infancy narrative is richly allusive,[19] to the point that Nils Dahl suggested that Luke's intention was to "write the continuation of the biblical history."[20] Against Raymond Brown's bridge metaphor,[21] which fails because for Luke there is no gulf between the old and the new, Dahl's choice of the word "continuation" is apt. This is, in fact, the very point of Luke's numerous OT allusions: there is continuity in the continuation

---

17. See, e.g., Joel B. Green's excellent essay "The Problem of a Beginning: Israel's Scriptures in Luke 1–2," *BBR* 4, no. 1 (1994): 61–85.

18. Luke Timothy Johnson, "Luke-Acts," *ABD* 4:409. For a comprehensive review of the treatment of Luke's use of the OT, see most recently Dietrich Rusam's Bonn habilitation, *Das Alte Testament bei Lukas*, BZNW 112 (Berlin: de Gruyter, 2003).

19. E.g., Gen 11–21 (Luke 1:5–2:52); 1 Sam 1:1–2:10 (Luke 1:5–2:52, esp. 1:46–55); Judg 13:2–25 (Luke 1:5–24); Dan 7–10 (Luke 1:5–2:52); Zeph 3:14–17 (Luke 1:26–33); Isa 2:9–12 (Luke 1:46–55); Isa 7:14 (Luke 1:27); Isa 9:6–7 (Luke 1:26–38); Isa 42:6 (Luke 1:79; 2:32); Isa 49:6 (Luke 1:32); Isa 52:10 (2:30–31); 2 Sam 7:12–16 (Luke 1:32–33); Mic 4:7–5:5 (Luke 2:1–14); Mal 3:1 (Luke 1:17, 76); Mal 4:5–6 (Luke 1:17).

20. Nils Dahl, "The Story of Abraham in Luke-Acts," in *Studies in Luke-Acts*, ed. Leander Keck and J. Louis Martyn (Philadelphia: Fortress, 1966), 139–58, esp. 153.

21. Raymond Brown, "Luke's Method in the Annunciation Narratives of Chapter One," in *Perspectives on Luke-Acts*, ed. Charles Talbert (Edinburgh: T&T Clark, 1978), 126–38, esp. 138.

The God of Israel and Jesus Christ

of the action of the God of Israel that stretches from the Jewish biblical history to Jesus Christ. However, this continuation is not wooden. The promises in the OT and their fulfillment in Luke's time are not perfectly balanced or correlated. Luke does not work from a rigid prophecy-fulfillment scheme;[22] nor are the prefigurations in the OT of character and event (e.g., Abraham, Sarah, Hannah) read in simple typological correspondence with the characters and events of Luke's time. Rather, Luke's reading of the LXX[23] enables him to shape his story to exert pressure upon the reader by means of atmospheric resonance. The characters and events of the OT are everywhere present and nowhere mentioned. The reader of the narrative in Luke 1–2 simply breathes the air of OT, thereby rendering direct citation of the LXX superfluous. For those who have ears to hear, the stories of Abraham and Sarah and Isaac, and Hannah and Samuel, and Samson, and King David, and the prophecies and promises of Isaiah, Daniel, Zephaniah, Micah, and Malachi echo throughout each line of the birth-infancy narrative. The hallowed past extends into the hallowed present even as this present reaches back into the past. The promises and their fulfillment form a single narrative grounded in the God of Israel's act in Jesus. As Paul Minear wrote nearly forty years ago, the "stories in Luke 1–2 unfold in such a way as to disclose a single skein of events, all of which stem from the marvelous fulfillment by God of his covenant promises to Israel."[24]

What Minear and others[25] have seen clearly as a result of Luke's use of the OT in chapters 1–2 is that the unity of the birth-infancy narrative itself and

---

22. Martin Rese, *Alttestamentliche Motive in der Christologie des Lukas*, Studien zum Neuen Testament 1 (Gütersloh: Gütersloher Verlagshaus Gerd Mohn, 1969), 37–41, 134–35, is correct when he argues in relation to Luke-Acts as a whole that a rigid prophecy-fulfillment scheme can obscure the distinctiveness and uniqueness of Luke's OT citations. Rese purposefully does not treat allusions to the OT, but his point holds here as well. This is not to deny the strong elements of prophecy and fulfillment that are obviously apparent (Schubert, Farris, et al.) but is instead to point to Luke's varied and multifaceted use of the OT.

23. In light of recent Septuagintal studies it is necessary to clarify in what way the term "Septuagint/LXX" is being used. At this point in this chapter, "the LXX" (the article is grammatically preferable in normal English usage) is used in the very general sense of the Greek-language OT (assuming here that Luke's OT texts were in Greek). Elsewhere in the chapter, when citing from the Greek OT, I will use "the LXX" to mean the critically reconstructed text of the Göttingen edition LXX.

24. Paul S. Minear, "Luke's Use of the Birth Stories," in Keck and Martyn, *Studies in Luke-Acts*, 111–30, esp. 116.

25. See, e.g., the interpretive aside "God's Purpose, the Scriptures, and the 'Beginning' of Luke-Acts," in Joel B. Green, *The Gospel of Luke*, NICNT (Grand Rapids: Eerdmans, 1997), 51–57.

Part 1: Christology, Greco-Roman Culture, and Canonical Reception

the continuity of the "new" events with the "old" depend upon the purpose and action of God. Thus are such unity and continuity theological in the strict sense of the word, as it is the same God who provides the continuation of that which had been promised in the Scriptures of Israel: there are fulfillment and unity of divine identity and purpose.

What has unfortunately not been as clearly seen is the depth or nature of this theological continuity. A primary reason is that Lukan theology and Christology have been kept too far apart. In this separation Luke's portrayal of God and of God's act in Jesus has been hidden from view. Conversely, Luke's view of Jesus and the animating power of his life have also remained insufficiently explored. In my judgment, both sides of this problematic could be helped by giving explicit and consistent attention to the question of the identity of God and of Jesus in relation to Luke's use of κύριος.

Luke 1:43

In the birth-infancy narrative, κύριος is used frequently in an unambiguous way to refer to the God of Israel (κύριος ὁ θεὸς τοῦ Ἰσραήλ; 1:68), and this usage normally displays septuagintal influence in both tone and diction. Luke writes, for example, in 1:6 of Zechariah and Elizabeth that they were righteous before God, πορευόμενοι ἐν πάσαις ταῖς ἐντολαῖς καὶ δικαιώμασιν τοῦ κυρίου ἄμεμπτοι, and in 1:9 that Zechariah entered τὸν ναὸν τοῦ κυρίου to perform his priestly service. The use of κύριος for God alone that began in 1:6 extends through 1:38 where we encounter Mary's famous response to the news that she will bear God's Son: ἰδοὺ ἡ δούλη κυρίου· γένοιτό μοι κατὰ τὸ ῥῆμά σου. Between 1:38 and 1:39, however, there is a narrative gap during which time the conception of Jesus occurs. We are not told directly that he is conceived, but we can infer it on the basis of the encounter between Elizabeth and Mary in which Elizabeth refers to the "fruit" (καρπός) of Mary's womb (1:42) and addresses Mary as ἡ μήτηρ τοῦ κυρίου μου. And it is with this address that Jesus himself appears in the narrative for the first time: ὁ κύριος in the womb.

As mentioned above, prior to 1:43 κύριος is used exclusively for God (ten times), but now Jesus himself enters the narrative for the first time and is given the name/title ὁ κύριος. Elizabeth's acclamation, furthermore, is rooted in the Holy Spirit and, rather than issuing in a greeting of mere oriental politeness,[26]

---

26. Werner Foerster in G. Quell and W. Foerster, "κύριος κτλ.," *ThWNT* 3:1038–98: "In orientalischer Hoflichkeit mag (rein auf den Sprachgebrauch gesehen) Elisabeth die Maria 'Mutter meines Herrn' nennen" (1085) = *TDNT* 3:1039–98: "It is probably with oriental

shows Jesus to be the κύριος to whom she gives her allegiance: she calls him "my" κύριος. Elizabeth then continues: "Blessed is she who believed that there would be a fulfillment of what was spoken to her παρὰ κυρίου." In this crucial moment of Jesus's introduction, Elizabeth's confession effects a double referent of the word κύριος between the as yet unborn and human κύριος of Mary's womb and the κύριος of heaven, who has taken away Elizabeth's shame (1:25, κύριος) and given the promise of the fruit of Mary's womb.

Perhaps the fact that an overlap now exists between κύριος and κύριος is an obvious linguistic observation. Yet it is a crucial one. If one were to hear the gospel read aloud (as would have been the case in the ancient world),[27] one would not be able to hear a difference between κύριος and κύριος but would instead experience a resonance, especially if the occasion was a Christian gathering for (charismatic) worship and edification in the 80s or 90s AD.[28]

1:6: τοῦ κυρίου
1:9: τοῦ κυρίου
1:11: κυρίου
1:15: τοῦ κυρίου
1:16: κύριον τὸν θεόν
1:17: κυρίῳ
1:25: κύριος
1:28: ὁ κύριος
1:32: κύριος ὁ θεός
1:38: κυρίου
1:43: τοῦ κυρίου
1:45: κυρίου
1:46: τὸν κύριον

In light of the OT context of Luke 1–2, Luke's frequent use of κύριος for the God of Israel, and the movement of the Lukan narrative, it becomes possible to draw the conclusion that the dramatic moment of 1:43 in the narrative

politeness, so far as linguistic usage is concerned, that Elisabeth can call Mary 'the mother of my Lord'" (1086).

27. For an excellent discussion of early Christian literacy, see Harry Y. Gamble, *Books and Readers in the Early Church: A History of Early Christian Texts* (New Haven: Yale University Press, 1995), esp. 2–10.

28. By the time Luke's Gospel would have been read, Jesus had already been acclaimed and worshiped as κύριος for at least three decades (cf. the pre-Pauline hymn in Phil 2:5–11).

Part 1: Christology, Greco-Roman Culture, and Canonical Reception

bespeaks a unity of identity[29] between YHWH and the human Jesus within Mary's womb by means of the word κύριος. Such a unity is not for Luke, as one might want to claim in the case of John, theologically propositional or based upon predication. Rather, the unity is narratively constituted: by means of the same word and the flow of the narrative, Luke creates a space wherein an overlap cannot help but take place, and which thus results in a doubleness in terms of the referent of κύριος.

Two further points are important in helping us continue to move forward. First, it is possible to speak this way because of the Holy Spirit. The reason that κύριος is now constitutive of Jesus's identity and that the one word κύριος has a twofold referent is because of the work of the Holy Spirit in the conception of Jesus. In the birth-infancy narrative of Luke, Jesus's life cannot be thought of apart from the Power of the Most High, as it is the Holy Spirit, God in his life-giving *Seinsweise*,[30] or τρόπος ὑπάρξεως,[31] who begins the new baby's life as ὁ κύριος. Thus it is that by the power of the Spirit, God's life is now bound up with Jesus's life to such a great extent and with such intensity that they share the name/title κύριος.

Second, unlike the Tetragrammaton, κύριος is not univocal. The word can refer to rulers, deities, slave masters, colt owners, and the like. Luke himself, for example, uses κύριος for Nero in Acts 25:26, and one can quite rightly assume that no overlap in identity between Jesus (or God) and Nero is intended (though there is a contrast). If, then, our interpretation of the overlap between the God of Israel and Jesus through the word κύριος is on target, we would need to see evidence in other parts of the narrative that would confirm the binding of the same word to these two different persons/characters in the narrative in particular, as distinct from other possible ref-

---

29. In this context I use "identity" to mean that which is essentially related to identifying the thing in question: As we will see, to speak of who Jesus is in Luke's Gospel is already and simultaneously to speak of the God of Israel, and to speak of who the God of Israel is, is already and simultaneously to speak of Jesus. One cannot identify Jesus as who he is apart from the God of Israel, and vice versa. There is a binding of the two persons (unity) with respect to who they are (identity). For Luke, there does not seem to be a "personal or individual existence" (*OED*, s.v. "identity") of Jesus in abstraction from God or of God in abstraction from Jesus. Yet there is a distinction between κύριος ὁ θεός and κύριος χριστός. On this point, see below.

30. Karl Barth, *Die Kirchliche Dogmatik* I/1 §9.2, pp. 379ff. *Church Dogmatics* I/1 §9.2, pp. 359ff.

31. Cappadocians: e.g., Basil of Caesarea, *De Spiritu Sancto* 46 (PG 32.152B); Gregory of Nyssa, *Eun.* 1 (PG 45.316C). For other uses, see the list in G. W. H. Lampe, ed., *A Patristic Greek Lexicon* (Oxford: Clarendon Press, 1961), 1434-35.

erents and/or overlaps. In other words, does our interpretation play out in the rest of the narrative?

Luke 2:11

Many scholars both past and present have taken χριστός to be the most important christological title for Jesus in Luke.[32] I think that this assessment is incorrect, or at best highly debatable, but the details of this matter can wait for another time. What is important to note now is something that is significant in itself: The first time χριστός occurs in the gospel narrative it occurs with κύριος. Luke does not write, as he is perfectly capable of writing elsewhere, χριστός or ὁ χριστός and leave it at that. Instead, he evidently wants the reader/auditor to read/hear χριστός together with κύριος right at the outset.

I agree with Fitzmyer and others that we should, with the best Greek manuscripts and in light of Acts 10:36, read two anarthrous nominatives (χριστὸς κύριος) at 2:11 rather than correct to χριστὸς κυρίου in light of the expression ὁ χριστὸς κυρίου just fifteen verses later in Luke 2:26.[33] But this decision does not determine the meaning automatically. "Christ, the Lord" is the most common English reading, but the "anointed Lord" (taking χριστός as an adjective) is also possible. One might also propose the "lordly Messiah" as the meaning, though this is somewhat awkward grammatically. The first rendering keeps the titles separate and distinct (so Fitzmyer); the latter two bring them together.

I submit that whatever their various etymological and cultural histories, Luke here uses both words together in a mutually determinative manner: χριστός conveys which and what kind of κύριος Jesus is, and κύριος discloses the depth of Jesus's messianic identity. This way of putting it would seem to require, in English at least, translating in a rather jarring way such that both titles are kept separate and intact as nominative nouns: "Christ Lord." This jarring translation, however, points immediately toward a larger narrative interpretation that would bring the words together (the messianic κύριος and the Lord who is the χριστός).

The importance of 2:11 for our focus is that it serves to maintain both a distinction and a unity. On the one hand, Jesus is not the same person in the narrative as the κύριος who remains κύριος πατήρ in heaven (cf. in this context 2:9, 15, 26; cf. 11:3); Jesus is the messianic κύριος, who is born on earth. On the

---

32. E.g., E. Earle Ellis, *The Gospel of Luke*, New Century Bible, 2nd ed. (Grand Rapids: Eerdmans, 1981), 9-12, 32-36; Fitzmyer, *Luke*, 1:197.

33. Contra, e.g., Paul Winter, "Lukanische Miszellen," *ZNW* 49 (1958): 65-75.

Part 1: Christology, Greco-Roman Culture, and Canonical Reception

other hand, there is a unity between them such that they are both κύριος with respect to their basic identity. Of interest in this connection is Dibelius's suggestion that Luke added ὅς ἐστιν χριστὸς κύριος with its titles to the pre-Lukan message ἐτέχθη ὑμῖν σήμερον σωτὴρ ἐν πόλει Δαυίδ and thus created some tension with the other nearby uses of κύριος, which refer to God (2:9, 15, 26).[34] Whether or not Dibelius's hypothesis is true we cannot know—I am increasingly skeptical about unverifiable source hypotheses for Luke 1–2[35]—but his recognition of the tension speaks again for a narrative overlap between Jesus and the God of Israel arising out of the word κύριος. In other portions of the Luke-Acts narrative, such a tension between the proper referents of κύριος is so pronounced as to be fully ambiguous, rendering an exegetically responsible choice between Jesus and God impossible, as we shall see in Luke 3:4–6.

Luke 3:4–6

In order to see the significance of 3:4–6 clearly, we should first make mention of 1:76. In Luke 1:76 Zechariah, filled with the Holy Spirit, prophesies that his son John will go "ἐνώπιον κυρίου ἑτοιμάσαι ὁδοὺς αὐτοῦ." Luke 1:76 is fully ambiguous in itself as regards the identity of the κύριος. That is, one cannot decide on exegetical grounds whether the κύριος is the God of Israel or Jesus. In fact, we can go further and assert that the the alternative of YHWH or Jesus forced upon the text by many exegetes turns out to be a false dichotomy. Alfred Plummer, for example, writes that "here κυρίου means Jehovah, not the Christ,"[36] while Bovon, Fitzmyer, and Jeremias, among others, think the

---

34. Martin Dibelius, "Jungfrauensohn und Krippenkind. Untersuchungen zur Geburtsgeschichte Jesu im Lukas-Evangelium," in *Botschaft und Geschichte: Gesammelte Aufsätze von Martin Dibelius*, ed. Gunther Bornkamm (Tübingen: Mohr Siebeck, 1953–1955), 1:62–63.

35. Henry J. Cadbury's judgment is prudent: Luke's "personal style is never so totally wanting as to prove alien origins for a passage, and is never so persuasive as to exclude the possibility that a written source existed, although the source be no longer capable of detection by any residual difference in style" (*The Making of Luke-Acts* [London: Macmillan, 1927], 67). Though with a slightly different emphasis, Raymond Brown, *The Birth of the Messiah* (Garden City, NY: Doubleday, 1977), 246, cites this passage from Cadbury in order to assess the current state of the question: "The linguistic opponents have fought one another to a draw at the present moment of our scientific research."

36. Alfred Plummer, *A Critical and Exegetical Commentary on the Gospel according to St. Luke*, ICC (New York: Charles Scribner's Sons, 1898), 42. So also Friedrich Bleek, *Synoptische Erklärung der drei ersten Evangelien* (Leipzig: Wilhelm Engelmann, 1862), 63; C. F. Evans, *Saint Luke* (London: SCM, 1990), 186; H. J. Holtzmann, *Hand-Commentar zum Neuen Testament. Erster Band: Die Synoptiker—Die Apostelgeschichte* (Freiburg im Breisgau:

κύριος is Jesus.³⁷ Johannes Weiss shrewdly attempts to have it both ways—that is, he sees the ambiguity—but leaves the matter uninterpreted: κυρίου "scheint nach V. 17 auf Gott bezogen werden zu mussen; vielleicht aber hat Lk es auf Christus bezogen, da er sonst κυρ. so braucht (im Gegensatz zu ὕψιστος)."³⁸ In any case, in the next edition of the commentary, the ninth, Father Bernhard flattened Johannes's judgment and, noting the change from the eighth edition, asserted that the κυρίου refers to YHWH.³⁹

Mohr Siebeck, 1889), 36; Erich Klostermann, *Das Lukasevangelium*, Handbuch zum Neuen Testament (Tübingen: Mohr Siebeck, 1919), 388; Gerhard Schneider, "Gott und Christus als Kyrios nach der Apostelgeschichte," in *Begegnung mit dem Wort*, ed. J. Zmijewski and E. Nellessen, BBB 53 (Bonn: Peter Hanstein Verlag, 1980), 161–74, esp. 167; and Schneider, *Das Evangelium nach Lukas: kapitel 1–10*, Ökumenischer Taschenbuchkommentar zum Neuen Testament (Gütersloh: Gütersloher Verlagshaus Mohn; Würzburg: Echter-Verlag, 1977), 62 (though here Schneider asserts that in light of the whole Gospel κύριος may be seen to refer to Jesus, but the immediate context requires "God" to be the referent).

37. François Bovon, *Das Evangelium nach Lukas*, vol. 1, EKKNT 3 (Zürich: Benziger; Neukirchener-Vluyn: Neukirchener Verlag, 1989), 108; Joachim Jeremias, *Die Sprache des Lukasevangeliums: Redaktion und Tradition im Nicht-Markusstoff des dritten Evangeliums* (Göttingen: Vandenhoeck & Ruprecht, 1980), 23; Fitzmyer, *Luke*, 1:385. So also A. R. C. Leaney, *A Commentary on the Gospel according to St. Luke*, Black's New Testament Commentaries (London: Black, 1958), 90, and William Manson, *The Gospel of Luke*, Moffatt New Testament Commentary (London: Hodder & Stoughton, 1930), 15.

38. Bernhard Weiss and Johannes Weiss, *Die Evangelien des Markus und Lukas*, Meyer Kritisch exegesticher Kommentar über das Neue Testament, 8th ed. (Göttingen: Vandenhoeck & Ruprecht, 1892), 318. The eighth edition of the Meyer series commentary was done by Johannes.

39. Bernhard Weiss, *Die Evangelien des Markus und Lukas*, Meyer Kritisch exegesticher Kommentar über das Neue Testament, 9th ed. (Göttingen: Vandenhoeck & Ruprecht, 1901), 294. Klostermann, *Das Lukasevangelium*, 388, mistakenly disagrees with "Bernhard" (it should be Johannes; Bernhard thinks otherwise, at least by 1901). Perhaps Klostermann realized his mistake, for in the second edition (1929) he drops the reference to Weiss. One also wonders if Klostermann did not in fact become more sympathetic with Johannes's statement in the eighth edition of the Meyer commentary. After declaring that in light of 1:16–17 the κυρίου of 1:76 certainly refers to God, Klostermann writes: "Lc selbst mußte dann die Beziehung auf den Messias Jesus hineingelegt haben" (28). Johannes Weiss himself, however, later seems to have agreed with his father (see *Die Schriften des Neuen Testament. Erster Band: Die drei alteren Evangelien. Die Apostelgeschichte* [Göttingen: Vandenhoeck & Ruprecht, 1906], 392, where Jesus/Messiah is not even mentioned). A serious problem with the approach of Weiss and Klostermann is that while they attempt to work on two different levels, that of the pre-Lukan context and the Lukan one, they frequently merge the two levels and lose consistency. Such a merger also creates methodological and hermeneutical confusion, as can be seen in the use of other Lukan narrative clues (1:16–17) to support the pre-Lukan hypothesis about referent (1:76).

Part 1: Christology, Greco-Roman Culture, and Canonical Reception

This either/or dichotomy is widespread, but in every case it begins with a false assumption about the relation of Lukan theology and Christology that, when carried over into exegesis, obscures the theological significance of the use of κύριος and smothers the actual dynamic of the text. The doubleness in the referent of κύριος retains the ambiguity present in the text and allows the ambiguity to be understood as both/and. To speak of the God of Israel as κύριος is to speak of Jesus as κύριος, and vice versa. This unity is confirmed in Luke 3:4-6.

Luke 3:1 begins formally the body of the gospel and opens with specific historical indications of the time at which the "fulfilled" (1:1) events took place. John the Baptist, now a grown man, appears from the wilderness as a prophet, fulfilling his vocation as a herald by trumpeting forth anew the words of the prophet Isaiah:[40]

> φωνὴ βοῶντος ἐν τῇ ἐρήμῳ
> ἑτοιμάσατε τὴν ὁδὸν κυρίου,
> εὐθείας ποιεῖτε τὰς τρίβους αὐτοῦ
> πᾶσα φάραγξ πληρωθήσεται
> καὶ πᾶν ὄρος καὶ βουνὸς ταπεινωθήσεται
> καὶ ἔσται τὰ σκολιὰ εἰς εὐθείαν
> καὶ αἱ τραχεῖαι εἰς ὁδοὺς λείας
> καὶ ὄψεται πᾶσα σὰρξ τὸ σωτήριον τοῦ θεοῦ

> The voice of one crying out in the wilderness:
> Prepare the way of the Lord!
> Make straight his paths!
> Every valley shall be filled,
> And every mountain and hill shall be made low!
> And the crooked places shall be made straight,
> And the rough places shall be made smooth!
> And all flesh shall see the salvation of God!

This citation of Isaiah 40:3-5 in Luke 3:4-6 is the fulfillment of Zechariah's prophecy in Luke 1:76 and forces again the question of the identity of the κύριος. In the Isaiah quotation itself the κυρίου of 40:3 (Luke 3:4) clearly refers to YHWH, as does the τοῦ θεοῦ of 40:5 (Luke 3:6). In Luke's narrative,

---

40. This passage is also discussed in "Luke and the Trinity: An Essay in Ecclesial Biblical Theology," pp. 46-72.

The God of Israel and Jesus Christ

however, the referent of the κυρίου is, as in the prophecy of 1:76, ambiguous. Because 3:4–6 is an OT quotation, the κύριος in 3:4 is unquestionably the μόνος κύριος of the OT; because John the Baptist in Luke's narrative literally does prepare the way for Jesus structurally, sequentially, and as his prophet, the κύριος indubitably refers to Jesus (the absolute ὁ κύριος is used at least thirteen times in Luke's Gospel). Exegesis that would see here only a reference to Jesus simply ignores the multiple uses of κύριος for God earlier in the narrative and the force of the point that this passage is an indisputable citation from the OT.[41] Conversely, exegesis that would see here only a reference to God simply ignores the structure and movement of the gospel.[42]

Furthermore, as in Mark 1:3, in Isaiah 40:3 (Luke 3:4) there is a small but significant difference between the septuagintal text and Luke's citation of this same text. Where the LXX reads εὐθείας ποιεῖτε τὰς τρίβους τοῦ θεοῦ ἡμῶν, "make straight the paths of *our God*" (Isa 40:3), Luke reads εὐθείας ποιεῖτε τὰς τρίβους αὐτοῦ, "make straight *his* paths" (Luke 3:4).[43] It is tempting to argue with Bovon, Green, Schneider, Schürmann, and others that the αὐτοῦ adds clarity and provides the interpretative key.[44] The exegetical move would then be to assert on this basis that Luke, with Mark,[45] intends that the κύριος of 3:4 refer to Jesus—hence the substitution of αὐτοῦ for τοῦ θεοῦ ἡμῶν. This argument, however, moves in the wrong direction. In reality, the αὐτοῦ produces precisely the reverse effect. It removes clarity and creates ambiguity, as it removes the noun and substitutes a pronoun, thus throwing all the weight back upon κύριος. As a result, the referent of the αὐτοῦ in itself is unclear and is dependent upon who one takes the κύριος to be—a decision that is fraught with ambiguity.

It is exegetically impossible to resolve the ambiguity of the κύριος with an either/or dichotomy. There is simply no way to settle the issue with certainty. A both/and exegesis avoids pressing the text into a preconceived either/

---

41. So, e.g., I. Howard Marshall, *The Gospel of Luke: A Commentary on the Greek Text* (Exeter: Paternoster, 1978), 136, who identifies the κύριος as Jesus, "not as God."

42. So, e.g., Bleek, *Synoptische Erklärung*, 159, who gives the complete weight to the OT quotation and speaks of a people prepared for YHWH.

43. On the reading of Codex Bezae, see below.

44. Bovon, *Das Evangelium nach Lukas*, 1:170; Green, *Luke*, 171; Schneider, "Gott und Christus," 167 n. 36; Heinz Schürmann, *Das Lukasevangelium*, 2 vols., Herders theologischer Kommentar zum Neuen Testament Bd. 3 (Freiburg: Herder, 1969–1982), 1:160 n. 98. So also, e.g., Evans, *Saint Luke*, 106, and Plummer, *Luke*, 87.

45. Mark is much more clear here than Luke. Mark begins outright with Jesus and John the Baptist, and there are no other previous occurrences of κύριος, as in the Lukan text, that cause one to wonder about the referent of κύριος.

Part 1: Christology, Greco-Roman Culture, and Canonical Reception

or mold and instead reflects the tension inherent within the text. As in the prophecy in 1:76, so here in its fulfillment the ambiguity of the κύριος overlap captures the fundamental correlation between the God of Israel and Jesus expressed in the doubleness of the single κύριος.

Wirkungsgeschichte: The impact of the overlap and ambiguity in Luke's use of κύριος can be seen already in the clarifying tendency of the scribes of Codex Bezae (D), though for D one cannot speak of a systematic clarification. A good example is the reading of Bezae here at Luke 3:4–6. The best way to see the significance is to compare the relevant parts of the text of the LXX, the best Lukan reading, and D.

φωνὴ βοῶντος ἐν τῇ ἐρήμῳ
ἑτοιμάσατε τὴν ὁδὸν *κυρίου*,
εὐθείας ποιεῖτε τὰς τρίβους τοῦ θεοῦ ἡμῶν
… καὶ ὄψεται πᾶσα σὰρξ τὸ σωτήριον τοῦ θεοῦ (LXX)

φωνὴ βοῶντος ἐν τῇ ἐρήμῳ
ἑτοιμάσατε τὴν ὁδὸν *κυρίου*
εὐθείας ποιεῖτε τὰς τρίβους *αὐτοῦ*
… καὶ ὄψεται πᾶσα σὰρξ τὸ σωτήριον *τοῦ θεοῦ* (Luke)

φωνὴ βοῶντος ἐν τῇ ἐρήμῳ
ἑτοιμάσατε τὴν ὁδὸν *κυρίου*
εὐθείας ποιεῖτε τὰς τρίβους *ὑμῶν*
… καὶ ὄψεται πᾶσα σὰρξ τὸ σωτήριον *κυρίου* (D)

The differences of D are striking. Whereas in the septuagintal text the κύριος ambiguity does not exist because of the clear continuity of θεός (τοῦ θεοῦ ἡμῶν to τοῦ θεοῦ; this is not to mention that the possibility of ambiguity did not yet exist), in the D text the ambiguity does not exist because of the change to direct address (the significance of the ὑμῶν)[46] and scribal adjustment toward κύριος. Thus, in the Bezae reading the removal of θεός and the second use of κύριος, coupled with John's direct address to the crowds, clearly point

---

46. So, rightly, George Edward Rice, "The Alterations of Luke's Tradition by the Textual Variants in Codex Bezae" (PhD diss., Case Western Reserve University, 1974), 44. Rice treats only Isa 40:3 and argues that the purpose of the Bezae scribes was to heighten the role of John the Baptist. That such a tendency exists in D may well be the case. But if one looks at the entire quotation from Isaiah (40:3–5), the more immediate explanation here is that of an alteration for christological purposes.

toward a scribe's christological interpretation of κύριος. The Lord of whom John speaks in D is Jesus. In the gospel alone, a similar christological tendency can also be seen, for example, at 7:13, 13:15, and 22:61, where D reads Ἰησοῦς in place of κύριος.[47]

Luke 20:41-44

There is no need here for a detailed investigation of our final passage from the gospel, but it is important nonetheless to mention. A significant question emerges from the fact that Jesus is clearly ὁ χριστὸς κυρίου (2:26) and simultaneously ὁ κύριος (1:43, etc.) and χριστὸς κύριος (2:11): How do the nominative and the genitive fit together? That is, how can Jesus be both *the Lord* (κύριος) and the Christ *of the Lord* (κυρίου)? Precisely this matter is at issue in Luke 20:41-44, where on the basis of Psalm 110:1 it is the Lord who raises the same question: "David therefore calls him κύριον; how then is he his son?" (20:44).

Two observations are pertinent to our purpose here. First, as with 2:11, Luke preserves a distinction between the messianic κύριος (David's son, ὁ χριστός) and the κύριος in heaven (ὁ κύριος)[48] at whose right hand the exalted Messiah will sit. Conzelmann's description, therefore, of Luke's use of κύριος for God and for Jesus as a *Vermischung* is inaccurate.[49] Even within the single word κύριος Luke is careful to preserve a distinction between, to use other language, the κύριος υἱός and the κύριος πατήρ. In light of this preserved distinction, the overlap in the referent of the word κύριος should not be understood in terms of a meshing or mixing together of two different persons/characters (as *Vermischung* implies), but rather in terms of the narrative continuity and unity of identity of Jesus and the God of Israel together as κύριος, as I have attempted to describe above.

Second, this distinction between the messianic and heavenly κύριος (or Father and Son) is grounded in an OT text, which is to say that there is scrip-

---

47. Cf. Luke 1:9 where D reads θεοῦ instead of κυρίου and 24:3 where D omits τοῦ κυρίου Ἰησοῦ altogether.

48. NA[27] does not print the article. The text-critical problem here is difficult to solve. However, when one takes account of the fact that the D scribes have a noticeable tendency to alter uses of κύριος throughout the gospel text, then B is the only strong MS left with an anarthrous reading. In this light, I would tend to go with the majority of the best Greek MSS and read the article. But an articular reading is not certain, and, in any case, Luke's point remains the same with both readings.

49. See Hans Conzelmann, *Die Mitte der Zeit* (Tübingen: Mohr Siebeck, 1954), 4.1.2 "Vater, Sohn, Geist," esp. 165, 172.

Part 1: Christology, Greco-Roman Culture, and Canonical Reception

tural justification for Luke's use of κύριος for both the God of Israel and Jesus. The connection to the OT highlights once again the importance of the Jewish Scripture for a major facet of Lukan Christology.

Acts 2:36 and 10:36

The last two passages we need to consider are in Acts. The first passage is Acts 2:36b, which, after citing Psalm 110:1 (109:1 LXX), reads: "God has made him [Jesus] both Lord [κύριος] and Christ [χριστός]." We cannot know for certain whether this confession is an early piece of kerygma adapted by Luke or an original part of the Lukan speech-composition.[50] Regardless, to read this verse in itself as an expression of Lukan theology is wrongheaded. It is clearly not the case that Luke believes Jesus to have become κύριος and/or χριστός only with his resurrection and exaltation—the entire Lukan narrative tells against such an interpretation. Instead, we should see this passage as strategically incorporated into the larger narrative and seek to discern its meaning and function in that connection. With the larger narrative context in mind, the contribution that Acts 2:36 makes to the understanding of κύριος has to do with the significance of the resurrection for Jesus's identity as ὁ κύριος.

Between the earthly and exalted Jesus are his crucifixion and death. Jesus's crucifixion as a criminal[51] and ultimately his death quite understandably threatened his identity as ὁ κύριος. But in raising Jesus from the dead, God the Father ensures the continuity of the messianic κύριος through suffering and death. From his conception by the power of the Holy Spirit Jesus is κύριος, but the resurrection nevertheless makes a profound difference for Lukan Christology, for it vindicates Jesus as the κύριος πάντων and establishes his rule over all (effected in the spread of the gospel). Thus the difference between Luke 1:43 and Acts 2:36 is not one of identity but one of place (earthly and heavenly Lord) and effect (universal mission). Through its development the narrative "appears as the path of character,"[52] meaning in this case that the identity of the

---

50. On speeches in the Mediterranean world, Charles H. Talbert, *Reading Acts: A Literary and Theological Commentary on the Acts of the Apostles* (New York: Crossroad, 1997), 45–47, manages to be lucid and brief without oversimplifying the matter.

51. In Luke's story, I take the centurion's judgment of Jesus as δίκαιος (23:47) as pointing toward existing accusations of Jesus's criminality. Cf. Jesus's question to the arresting party in 22:52 (λῃστής is used frequently in Josephus for the "bandits"), the description of Barabbas (λῃστής), and the crucifixion of the two criminals (κακοῦργοι) alongside Jesus.

52. Paul Ricoeur, *Oneself as Another*, trans. Kathleen Blarney (Chicago: University of Chi-

character is inseparable from the narrative in which he appears. Indeed, "the identity of the character is constructed in connection with that of the plot."[53] Jesus κύριος, then, is in Acts the same character in the still-unfolding same story that began in Luke 1–2: there is a narratively constituted continuity of identity through his crucifixion, death, and resurrection.

Acts 10:36 declares that Jesus is κύριος πάντων. Epictetus says the same thing of the Roman emperor,[54] and similar pronouncements exist in surviving inscriptions.[55] So also, from the domain of the mystery cults, in Plutarch's *Moralia* Osiris is ὁ πάντων κύριος. In relation to the Roman emperor, I would see here a rival claim to ultimate and definitive lordship, and in relation to the gods and goddesses of the mystery cults, a clash with the κύριοι πολλοί, to use Pauline language. But what about in relation to the Jewish God, who in OT theology is certainly the only κύριος πάντων? Nehemiah 9:6, for example, says simply: σὺ εἶ αὐτὸς κύριος μόνος (You yourself are the only κύριος!; 2 Esdras 19:6 LXX).[56] This universal lordship continues clearly even within the Gospel of Luke itself, where Jesus addresses the God of Israel as πάτερ κύριε τοῦ οὐρανοῦ καὶ τῆς γῆς, which is, of course, formally the same thing as κύριος πάντων (10:21; Marcion omits καὶ τῆς γῆς).[57]

The only way the κύριος πάντων predication of Jesus would not constitute a rival claim or a clash—indeed an outright Marcionite rejection of the God of Israel—would be if God and Jesus could both be κύριος πάντων in such

---

cago Press, 1992), 146. See esp. ch. 5, "Personal Identity and Narrative Identity," and ch. 6, "The Self and Narrative Identity."

53. Ricoeur, *Oneself as Another*, 141.

54. Epictetus, *Disc.* 4.1.12 (the Roman emperor is ὁ πάντων κύριος καῖσαρ).

55. E.g., ὁ τοῦ παντὸς κόσμου κύριος Νέρων (Ditt., Syll³ 11.814, Ins. 30–31).

56. Cf. e.g., Deut 6:4: ἄκουε, Ἰσραήλ· κύριος ὁ θεὸς ἡμῶν κύριος εἷς ἐστι (Hear, O Israel: The Lord our God, the Lord is one!); Isa 2:11 (cf. 2:17): καὶ ὑψωθήσεται κύριος μόνος ἐν τῇ ἡμέρᾳ ἐκείνῃ (And the only κύριος will be exalted in that day!); Isa 42:8: ἐγὼ κύριος ὁ θεός· τοῦτό μού ἐστιν τὸ ὄνομα· τὴν δόξαν μου ἑτέρῳ οὐ δώσω (I am the Lord God, this is my Name; my glory I will not give to another!); Ezek 39:7: καὶ τό ὄνομά μου τὸ ἅγιον γνωσθήσεται ἐν μέσῳ λαοῦ μου Ἰσραήλ καὶ οὐ βεβηλωθήσεται τὸ ὄνομά μου τὸ ἅγιον οὐκέτι καὶ γνώσονται τὰ ἔθνη ὅτι ἐγώ εἰμι κύριος ἅγιος ἐν Ἰσραήλ (And my holy name will be made known in the midst of my people Israel and my holy name will no longer be blasphemed. And the Gentiles will know that I am κύριος, the Holy One of Israel), etc. For similar expressions in the OT apocrypha and pseudepigrapha, see Henry J. Cadbury, "The Titles of Jesus in Acts," in *The Beginnings of Christianity, Part I: The Acts of the Apostles*, ed. Kirsopp Lake and Henry J. Cadbury (London: Macmillan, 1933), 5:361–62.

57. Luke also has Paul say this of God in the Areopagus speech (Acts 17:24). Interestingly, Fitzmyer, *Luke*, 1:117, classifies the phrase "Lord of heaven and earth" as an Aramaism in light of the parallel with 1QapGen 22:16.

Part 1: Christology, Greco-Roman Culture, and Canonical Reception

a way that there was no conflict between them. On OT theological grounds, there is simply not room for two κύριοι πάντων. Indeed, in an OT framework the idea of two κύριοι πάντων is a logical contradiction.

Ἰησοῦς κύριος πάντων is in the end only a possibility because in some way Jesus shares an identity with the Lord of Israel that is narratively constituted through the word κύριος. This shared identity as κύριος both derives from and interprets the κύριος overlap and ambiguity of the narrative (the latter of which is considerably more pronounced in Acts). The possibility and continuity lie with God himself in the power of his Holy Spirit, and thus is the continuity between the Old and the New, strictly speaking, theological.

Conclusions

We began with the Marcionite severing of the God of Israel from Jesus Christ and the attempt to read some of the Lukan Gospel in light of such a complete separation. We then turned to a few important texts in Luke's Gospel and in Acts and saw that contrary to the Marcionite reading, the unity between the God of Israel and Jesus Christ in the Lukan narrative is so strong that we could say with Hans Frei that Jesus κύριος is the "manifestation of the presence of God acting."[58] Or, to put it more precisely for our question here: Jesus is the presence of the God of Israel acting. In this connection clarity emerged with respect to a material agreement between the Lukan narrative and Marcionite theology—namely, that the person of Jesus Christ is a potential theological threat to the OT precisely at the point of his relation to the God of Israel: if the God of the Jewish Scripture and the God of Jesus Christ are not the same God, the unity of the old and the new collapses. But it is also exactly at this point that Marcionite and Lukan theology part ways, toward a strict separation and discarding of the OT on the one hand, and toward a unity of the old and the new at the most basic level of the identity of the God of Israel and Jesus Christ on the other.

When one looks at Luke, then, the *Verbindlichkeit* in relation to the OT inheres less in explicit textual clues than it does in the presentation of the divine reality, or, differently said, the continuity of the selfsame God. So, at both

---

58. Hans W. Frei, "Theological Reflections on the Accounts of Jesus' Death and Resurrection," in *Theology and Narrative: Selected Essays*, ed. George Hunsinger and William C. Placher (New York: Oxford University Press, 1993), 74.

a theological-confessional level and a literary-presentational one, the binding authority of the OT derives from God.

This raises for us the following interconnected questions: What exactly is the relation between internal and external *Verbindlichkeit*? Is it simply that as a community we have decided that a positive relationship to the OT is necessary, and that we could have just as easily decided on the Marcionite option, only we did not? Or, is there some logic or force—or something—within this sort of internal *Verbindlichkeit* that guides us of necessity in certain ways rather than in others in terms of our binding attachment (external *Verbindlichkeit*) to the OT?

Luke's answer—that is, the internal answer—is that it is the same God. Must not that also be our answer—the external one? And, if so, does not that raise the question of the divine authority of the text vis-à-vis the community's reception of this text? (Which points again, of course, toward the relation of internal and external *Verbindlichkeit*, as well as to the question of legitimate and illegitimate forms of *Sachkritik*.)

Luke and the Trinity

◆ AN ESSAY IN ECCLESIAL BIBLICAL THEOLOGY

The Problem of the Bible and the Creeds

In his programmatic essay "Über Aufgabe und Methode der sogenannten neutestamentlichen Theologie" in 1897,[1] William Wrede forcefully articulated the position that dogmatic theological categories of thought are "alien to the biblical writers"[2] and, thus, that the study of NT theology should have nothing whatsoever to do with dogmatic theology.[3] Wrede concluded his essay with an outright rejection of any connection between the Bible and theology and the meaningfulness of the terms "New Testament" and "theology" in relation to each other: "a theology which has biblical character, and is got from the Bible . . . can be set aside as irrelevant to us. . . . The name New Testament theology is wrong in both its terms. . . . The appropriate name for the subject-matter is: early Christian history of religion."[4] Only a few years later,

---

1. Translated into English by Robert Morgan as "The Task and Methods of 'New Testament Theology,'" in *The Nature of New Testament Theology*, ed. Robert Morgan (Naperville, IL: Allenson, 1973), 68–116.

2. Wrede, "Task and Methods," 69.

3. Wrede's program is the clearest logical outworking of the crisp distinction between dogmatic theology and historical investigation initiated by Johann Philipp Gabler in 1787 in his inaugural address *De justo discrimine theologiae biblicae et dogmaticae regundisque recte utriusque finibus*, translated by J. Sandys-Wunsch and L. Eldredge as "On the Proper Distinction between Biblical and Dogmatic Theology and the Specific Objectives of Each," *SJT* 33 (1980): 133–58.

4. Wrede, "Task and Methods," 115–16 (cf. 68–70). Though many of the philosophical assumptions of Wrede's day have been utterly demolished (e.g., complete objective neutrality

---

"Luke and the Trinity: An Essay in Ecclesial Biblical Theology" was originally published in *Scottish Journal of Theology* 56, no. 1 (2003): 1–26. It is reproduced with permission.

Luke and the Trinity

in 1899-1900, Adolf von Harnack, the jewel in the magnificent high-culture crown of liberal Protestant theology, delivered the lectures in Berlin that were to be published in book form under the title *Das Wesen des Christentums* and immediately translated into English as *What Is Christianity?* In these lectures Harnack elegantly expressed the widely accepted position of his time that the "philosophical" doctrinal formulations of the ecumenical creeds are abstract and "theoretical" distortions of the simple message of the gospels: "the living faith seems to be transformed into a creed to be believed; devotion to Christ, into Christology."[5]

Though it lost some of its sway through the Barthian revolution, this aspect of the theological program advanced in the nineteenth century—here at its peak in Wrede and Harnack—continued to exercise massive influence throughout the twentieth century. This influence, however, is by no means limited to "historians of religion" or theological liberals. The section on the Trinity in the first volume of Emil Brunner's *Dogmatics* is marvelous evidence of the vast power of this strain of thought. In writing about the "mystery" of the triunity of God, Brunner averred that "there is no trace of such an idea in the New Testament. This '*mysterium logicum*' . . . lies wholly outside the message of the Bible."[6] Tracing this influence still further, in an essay published in

---

on the part of the interpreter), this basic historicist orientation toward the NT is still exceedingly widespread today. See, e.g., Heikki Räisänen, *Beyond New Testament Theology* (London: SCM, 1990).

5. Adolf von Harnack, *What Is Christianity?* (Philadelphia: Fortress, 1986), 193. Especially instructive here is Harnack's polemic against the "Greek" church both past and present wherein he argues that the fact that the church "has not suppressed the Gospels" has saved the Greek church from some (though not all) of the "destructive" effects of its intellectualizing doctrines of the two natures of Christ and the Trinity (228-37). See also, e.g., Willibald Beyschlag, *New Testament Theology, Or, Historical Account of the Teaching of Jesus and of Primitive Christianity according to the New Testament Sources*, 2 vols. (Edinburgh: T&T Clark, 1899), esp. 1:73, 79; 2:88ff.; Wilhelm Bousset, *The Faith of a Modern Protestant* (New York: Charles Scribner's Sons, 1909), esp. 47f.; Wilhelm Hermann, *The Communion of the Christian with God* (Philadelphia: Fortress, 1971), esp. 34ff., 126ff., 134ff.; and Ernst Troeltsch, "Faith and History," in *Religion in History* (Minneapolis: Fortress, 1991), 134-45, esp. 145.

6. Emil Brunner, *Dogmatics*, vol. 1, *The Christian Doctrine of God* (Philadelphia: Westminster, 1950), 226; emphasis added. It is to Brunner's credit that he persistently keeps in view the fully developed doctrine of the Trinity. However, his assertion that this "mystery" is "the result of . . . transcendental speculation" (38) is quite in keeping with Wrede and Harnack. See also Rudolf Bultmann, "The Christology of the New Testament," in *Faith and Understanding* (Philadelphia: Fortress, 1969), 262-85; Bultmann, "The Christological Confession of the World Council of Churches," in *Essays: Philosophical and Theological* (New York: Macmillan, 1955), 273-90.

Part 1: Christology, Greco-Roman Culture, and Canonical Reception

2000 the evangelical scholar John Goldingay sang in praise of narrative but thought Trinitarian doctrine harmful to the reading of the Bible. The doctrine of the Trinity is "two stages removed from most of the NT narratives" and is "three stages removed from most biblical narrative," by which he means the OT. Further,

> if one starts from biblical narratives and asks after their theological freight, the vast bulk of their theological implications does not emerge within a trinitarian framework. . . . That is true (perhaps especially true) if we are interested in theological implications in the narrowest sense, in what biblical narrative tells us about God. For all its truth and fruitfulness, the doctrine of the Trinity seriously skews our theological reading of Scripture.[7]

THE EXEGETICAL NECESSITY OF TRINITARIAN DOGMA

Wrede, Harnack, Brunner, and Goldingay span more than a century of time and represent widely divergent theological perspectives as well as differing areas of expertise. They demonstrate, in their diversity, the enduring and far-reaching predominance of a mode of thought. Wrede was a NT critic and pioneering member of the *Religionsgeschichtliche Schule*; Harnack, a noted liberal historian of dogma; and Brunner, a "neo-orthodox" systematic theologian. Goldingay is a conservative evangelical OT scholar. Yet they all draw a clear line between the theological language and discourse of the Bible and the early creeds of the church. When pressed, this line of thought discloses the underlying assumption of a fundamental difference between the God about whom the Bible speaks and the God as known in church tradition and expressed in creedal formulations. It is my contention that this breach between the Bible and the early creeds of the church is the result of a fundamental misreading of the biblical text and of the early creeds, particularly at the point of the identity of God as Trinity. This is, of course, not to say that every single biblical writing

---

7. John Goldingay, "Biblical Narrative and Systematic Theology," 130–31, in *Between Two Horizons: Spanning New Testament Studies and Systematic Theology*, ed. Joel B. Green and Max Turner (Grand Rapids: Eerdmans, 2000), 123–42. Of a similar nature are all the now-popular attacks upon any kind of "dogma" as ideological imposition upon the Bible. See, e.g., Werner G. Jeanrond, "After Hermeneutics: The Relationship between Theology and Biblical Studies," in *The Open Text: New Directions for Biblical Studies*, ed. Francis Watson (London: SCM, 1993), 85–102, esp. 100; Jeanrond, "Criteria for New Biblical Theologies," *JR* 76, no. 2 (1996): 233–49.

contains the doctrine of the Trinity or even that the doctrine is fully expressed in any one writing.[8] In fact, the word "Trinity" is conspicuously absent.[9] Nor is it to say that it is possible or desirable to return to a precritical theological and hermeneutical situation or to read the Bible as if the Enlightenment had never occurred. However, it is to say that there is an organic continuity between the biblical testimony and the early creeds,[10] and that the creeds can serve as hermeneutical guidelines to reading the Bible because it is in fact the biblical text itself that necessitated the creedal formulations. There is an exegetical *necessity* to Trinitarian doctrine.

Typically, to the degree that this exegetical necessity is explored at all, it is explored under the rubric of propositional equality or expression such that the operative questions have only to do with predication:[11] Where is Jesus called God (θεός)? Where is the one God called Father, Son, and Spirit? and so forth. As a whole, this manner of investigation lends itself predominantly to Pauline, Deutero-Pauline, and Johannine texts,[12] while the Synoptic Gospels

---

8. No biblical writing taken alone is sufficient for the Nicene or Chalcedonian formulations. For the precise Trinitarian formulations of the later creeds reflection upon the full wealth of the OT and NT together is needed.

9. Karl Barth, *Church Dogmatics* I/1 (Edinburgh: T&T Clark, 1936), 308, wittily exposes the weaknesses of the point that the word "Trinity" (and "essence," "*homoousios*," etc.) does not occur anywhere in the biblical text: "Now this objection can be raised against every dogma and against theology in general and as such. It would also have to be raised against proclamation, which does not stop at the mere reading of scripture but goes on to explain it too."

10. On the distinction between judgments and the conceptual terms in which judgments are rendered and on the way in which this distinction pertains to the complicated problem of what it means "to say the same thing," see David S. Yeago, "The New Testament and Nicene Dogma: A Contribution to the Recovery of Theological Exegesis," *ProEccl* 3, no. 2 (1994): 152–64, esp. 159ff.

11. By way of thematic extension, all relevant studies of Pauline terms like μορφή, εἰκών, etc., the Johannine λόγος, etc., are brought under the same umbrella; thus, the literature is endless. In the way of general introduction to the issue, see appendix 3 in Raymond Brown's excellent little book, *An Introduction to New Testament Christology* (New York: Paulist, 1994), which is structured around θεός predication. Another recent example is Murray J. Harris, *Jesus as God: The New Testament Use of Theos in Reference to Jesus* (Grand Rapids: Baker, 1992). So, too, the classic title Christologies of the 1950–1960s move along the same lines: see Oscar Cullmann, *The Christology of the New Testament*, rev. ed. (Philadelphia: Westminster, 1963; German ed. 1957); Ferdinand Hahn, *The Titles of Jesus in Christology: Their History in Early Christianity* (New York: Word, 1969; German ed. 1963); and Vincent Taylor, *The Names of Jesus* (London: Macmillan, 1962); Taylor, *The Person of Christ in New Testament Teaching* (London: Macmillan, 1958).

12. Not surprisingly, not many texts emerge as possible contributors to Trinitarian the-

Part 1: Christology, Greco-Roman Culture, and Canonical Reception

are virtually ignored.[13] This oversight is due primarily to the way in which the Trinitarian question has been pursued and to the widespread assumption of a self-evident low Christology (and, hence, minimal connection with Trinitarian thinking) in the Synoptics in comparison with Paul and John.[14] However, the exegetical necessity of Trinitarian doctrine does not rest on only a handful of NT texts, but instead has to do with the fundamental logic of the biblical narrative taken as a whole, the OT together with the NT. The purpose of this chapter is to broaden the way in which the exegetical necessity of Trinitarian theology has frequently been understood in the post-Enlightenment period by

---

ology; John 1:1-18; 20:28; 1 John 5:20; 1 Cor 12:4-6; 2 Cor 13:13; Phil 2:5-11; Eph 4:4-6; Col 1:15-20; Heb 1:8-9; 2 Pet 2:1 (1 John 5:7, the *Comma Johanneum*, is a late addition), and even some of these texts were used to show that Jesus was not equal to God (see Brown, *New Testament Christology*, 174f.). An exception to the stress upon predication in the Pauline "Trinitarian" texts is Ulrich Mauser, "One God and Trinitarian Language in the Letters of Paul," *HBT* 20, no. 2 (1998): 99-108, who discerns an essential connection between the language of Paul's larger thought and the deeply embedded nature of the "triadic formulas" within this larger thought.

13. With the obvious exception of Matt 28:19.

14. When the question is the relation of the NT to Trinitarian theology, the concentration has been (perhaps unintentionally) almost exclusively upon the Pauline and Johannine texts (except for the obvious point, promulgated by Harnack as the essence of Christianity, that the Synoptics evidence Jesus's calling God "Father"). In addition to the sparsely scattered relevant comments in the works mentioned in n. 11, see, e.g., Barth, *Church Dogmatics* I/1, 313, 370, 400-402; Robert Jenson, *Systematic Theology*, 2 vols. (Oxford: Oxford University Press, 1997-1999), 1:92-93; Jürgen Moltmann, *The Trinity and the Kingdom* (Minneapolis: Fortress, 1993), 61-96, 122-24 (Moltmann does, however, recognize the narrative element of Trinitarian theology [64, 74, 76, 81] and gives brief attention to the Matthean version of Jesus's baptism [65-66]); Wolfhart Pannenberg, *Systematic Theology*, 3 vols. (Grand Rapids: Eerdmans, 1991-1998), 1:264-70, 301-5. Arthur W. Wainwright, *The Trinity in the New Testament* (London: SPCK, 1962), has a broader focus and includes aspects of function (Jesus as judge, etc.). Nonetheless, aside from the "Father" motif of the Synoptics, his actual treatment of NT texts is heavily weighted toward the Pauline and Johannine material. An exception to all of this is Nils Dahl's essay "Trinitarian Baptismal Creeds and New Testament Christology," in *Jesus the Christ: The Historical Origins of Christological Doctrine*, ed. Donald H. Juel (Minneapolis: Fortress, 1991), 163-86, which, though only a short and general overview, is a brilliant discussion of the relation of the early church's confessional formulas to the Trinitarian grammar of the NT confessions. In this essay Dahl also laments the fact that, excepting Wainwright's book and an article by K. L. Schmidt in 1938, "New Testament scholars have, by and large, left it to historians of Christian doctrine and theologians to discuss the relationship between the dogma and the New Testament data that were discussed in the later trinitarian and christological controversies" (166). So also in Athanasius, *Four Discourses against the Arians* (NPNF² 4:306-447), the governing NT interpretative texts are Pauline and Johannine, as they are in St. Basil, *On the Spirit* (NPNF² 8:2-50).

offering an exegetical-theological interpretation of the birth-infancy narrative in the Gospel of Luke (Luke 1-2) and exploring its implications for exegesis in the opening scene in the body of the gospel (Luke 3:1-6).

My thesis is that attention to the question of the identity of God in the narrative of Luke-Acts compels us to speak in Trinitarian terms. As mentioned above, the Trinitarian dogma of the later church in all its specificity is obviously not explicitly formulated in Luke-Acts.[15] However, the necessity of speaking of the one God in a threefold way is the response to the pressure exerted upon the reader by the biblical narrative itself. Correspondingly, the Trinitarian nature of the one Lord enables us to read the text and interpret its pressure with understanding. That is, the question of the identity of God enables us to see the exegetical necessity of Trinitarian doctrine, and Trinitarian doctrine, in turn, makes sense of and illumines its exegetical necessity.

My method will be to focus on two titles/names given to Jesus (κύριος and σωτήρ) with their respective OT echoes and background and on the way in which these titles/names function within the narrative.[16] This focus brings a

---

15. The question may thus be raised as to whether the use of the term "Trinity" is legitimate when applied to the Bible, in this case Luke-Acts. While I would not want to advance the claim that the narrative of Luke-Acts is latent Trinitarian theology in every single respect, I will retain the use of the word "Trinity" on the basis that the same general, but essential, judgment is made in Luke-Acts and the creedal formulations regarding the threefold distinction within the one God's identity and act.

16. Of logical and systematic necessity, this essay does not deal with the fairly widespread use of κύριος and σωτήρ in the Greco-Roman world for the Roman emperors (cf. Acts 25:26 where Festus says he has nothing to write to the Roman emperor [τι γράψαι τῷ κυρίῳ οὐκ ἔχω]) and the gods/goddesses of the mystery religions (e.g., Osiris ὁ πάντων κύριος in Plutarch, *De Iside et Osiride* 355). It should at least be noted, however, that Luke's use of κύριος and σωτήρ would have carried enormous theopolitical weight and could have functioned as a frontal challenge to the Roman Empire and the various pagan religions therein. See, among others, Allen Brent, *The Imperial Cult and the Development of Church Order: Concepts and Images of Authority in Paganism and Early Christianity before the Age of Cyprian* (Leiden: Brill, 1999), esp. 73-139; Manfred Clauss, *Kaiser und Gott: Herrscherkult im römischen Reich* (Stuttgart: Teubner, 1999); Dominique Cuss, *Imperial Cult and Honorary Terms in the New Testament* (Fribourg: University Press, 1974), 53-71; Adolf Deissmann, *Light from the Ancient East* (New York: Doran, 1927), esp. 344-45, 349-54, 363-64; Mark Edwards, Martin Goodman, Simon Price, and Christopher Rowland, eds., *Apologetics in the Roman Empire: Pagans, Jews, and Christians* (Oxford: Oxford University Press, 1999); W. Foerster and G. Fohrer, "σωτήρ," *TDNT* 7:1003-24; Ernst Lohmeyer, *Christuskult und Kaiserkult* (Tübingen: Mohr Siebeck, 1919); Simon R. F. Price, *Rituals and Power: The Roman Imperial Cult in Asia Minor* (Cambridge: Cambridge University Press, 1984); G. Quell and W. Foerster, "κύριος," *TDNT* 3:1039-98; and Lily Ross Taylor, *The Divinity of the Roman Emperor* (Middletown, CT: American Philological Association, 1931).

Part 1: Christology, Greco-Roman Culture, and Canonical Reception

force to bear upon the reader that pushes toward a Trinitarian understanding of God's identity. This narrative/titular approach[17] will assume the continuity of the God of the OT with the God of Luke-Acts and will press upon us the question of the relation of the Holy Spirit to Jesus and to the God of Israel.

The Identity of the Lord/Savior in OT Narrative

Brevard Childs was right when he wrote that the "church's struggle with the Trinity was not a battle against the Old Testament, but rather a battle for the Old Testament."[18] Historically and dogmatically, the emergence of Trinitarian thinking resulted from the conjunction of the exclusive devotion to the one God of Israel, the existence of Israel's Scripture,[19] and the "Christ event." This is also the case narratively in Luke-Acts, particularly as expressed in the birth narrative of Luke 1–2. In order to see the conjunction of these elements and their significance in shaping the Trinitarian theology in Luke's birth narrative, attention must be given to the use of κύριος and σωτήρ in the OT.

---

17. This approach accords with the articulate position of Leander Keck, "Toward the Renewal of New Testament Christology," *NTS* 32, no. 3 (1986): 362–77, esp. 368ff., who cautions against the "title-dominated" approach to christological analysis of the Gospels. However, the approach adopted in this essay also recognizes that the titles used within the narrative were chosen for a particular reason and carry weight from their past use (in this case from the OT). It is thus appropriate to focus on the way the titles are used in the story and at the same time to investigate the reason why the story uses these titles (which necessitates OT and cultural study). Both Luke Timothy Johnson, "The Christology of Luke-Acts," in *Who Do You Say That I Am? Essays on Christology*, ed. Mark Allan Powell and David R. Bauer (Louisville: Westminster John Knox, 1999), 49–65, and Jack Dean Kingsbury, "Jesus as the 'Prophetic Messiah' in Luke's Gospel," in *The Future of Christology: Essays in Honor of Leander E. Keck*, ed. Abraham J. Malherbe and Wayne A. Meeks (Minneapolis: Fortress, 1993), 29–42, though they differ in their conclusions, read Luke-Acts as a narrative whole and focus on the title/designation "prophet." One further point to make is that the focus here on two titles in particular should not be understood as a comprehensive christological claim over against the use of other titles, prophetic imagery, etc. Luke's Christology is a multifaceted presentation of a single person.

18. Brevard Childs, *Biblical Theology of the Old and New Testaments* (Minneapolis: Fortress, 1992), 376. Childs here draws upon Barth's exact point with respect to Paul and the OT (see *Church Dogmatics* I/1, 319).

19. On the issue of OT canon, see now Stephen B. Chapman, *The Law and the Prophets: A Study in Old Testament Canon Formation*, Forschungen zum Alten Testament 27 (Tübingen: Mohr Siebeck, 2000).

Κύριος and the OT

1. The fundamental connection between the Hebrew form יהוה (YHWH), God's name in the OT, and the Greek form κύριος as this same name, is unshakable. Though there has been considerable debate over the exact relationship between the Tetragrammaton (YHWH, יהוה) and its rendering in Greek OT MSS, it is exceedingly probable that κύριος was used to translate YHWH near the time of the NT,[20] and it is certain that κύριος was understood to be equivalent to the divine name. Κύριος was used by Josephus,[21] Philo,[22] the author of the Letter

---

20. The evidence for this point is debated. However, given the widespread use of κύριος and its Aramaic equivalent in and around the time of the NT (see nn. 21-27) and given the way in which the Tetragrammaton appears in, for example, the MT-oriented Deuteronomy sections of Papyrus Fouad 266 [848] (written in Hebrew square characters by a second scribe in a space very nearly equivalent, if not identical, to the full Greek KYPIOC), I think it highly likely that κύριος was used in at least some of the LXX MSS before the time of the NT. The theological point that I will advance below, however, does not rest on this position because Luke himself uses κύριος for YHWH. See esp. Zaki Aly and Ludwig Koenen, *Three Rolls of the Early Septuagint: Genesis and Deuteronomy* (Bonn: Rudolf Habelt, 1980); W. W. Graf Baudissin, *KYRIOS als Gottesname im Judentum und seine Stelle in der Religionsgeschichte: Erster Teil: Der Gebrauch des Gottesname Kyrios in Septuaginta* (Giessen: Töpelmann, 1929); Joseph A. Fitzmyer, *The Gospel according to Luke*, 2 vols. AB 28/28A (Garden City, NY: Doubleday, 1981-1985), 1:201-2; Fitzmyer, "The Semitic Background of the New Testament *Kyrios*-Title," in *A Wandering Aramean: Collected Aramaic Essays* (Chico, CA: Scholars Press, 1979), 115-42; George Howard, "The Tetragram and the New Testament," *JBL* 96 (1977): 63-83; Johan Lust, "Mic 5,1-3 in Qumran and in the New Testament and Messianism in the Septuagint," in *The Scriptures and the Gospels*, ed. C. M. Tuckett (Leuven: Leuven University Press, 1997), 65-88; Albert Pietersma, "Kyrios or Tetragram: A Renewed Quest for the Original Septuagint," in *De Septuaginta: Studies in Honour of John William Wevers on His Sixty-Fifth Birthday*, ed. Albert Pietersma and Claude Cox (Mississauga: Benben, 1984), 85-101; Patrick W. Skehan, "The Divine Name at Qumran, in the Masada Scroll, and in the Septuagint," *Bulletin of the International Organization for Septuagint and Cognate Studies* 13 (1980): 14-44, esp. 34-38; W. G. Waddell, "The Tetragrammaton in the LXX," *JTS* 45 (1944): 158-61, and bibliographies therein.

21. *A. J.* 13.68 cites Isa 19:19: "Ἡσαΐας ὁ προφήτης τοῦτο προεῖπεν· ἔσται θυσιαστήριον ἐν Αἰγύπτῳ κυρίῳ τῷ θεῷ." The only other time Josephus uses κύριος for the God of Israel is in *A. J.* 20.90 (Izates addresses YHWH as ὦ δέσποτα κύριε . . . τῶν πάντων δὲ δικαίως μόνον καὶ πρῶτον ἥγημαι κύριον). Fitzmyer, "Semitic Background," 121, is surely right that these two isolated instances argue against any kind of Christianizing of the MS of Josephus with respect to κύριος.

22. See esp. *De plantatione* 85-86 and *De mutatione nominum* 18-24. See also the discussion of Nils A. Dahl and Alan F. Segal, "Philo and the Rabbis on the Names of God," *JSJ* 9, no. 1 (1978): 1-28.

Part 1: Christology, Greco-Roman Culture, and Canonical Reception

of Aristeas,[23] Paul (Rom 10:13),[24] Mark (1:3), Luke (Acts 2:25), and other NT writers[25] to translate YHWH and to address the God of Israel. The Qumran community and the book of Daniel both use the Aramaic equivalent of κύριος for God.[26] Furthermore, κύριος would have functioned as the *qĕrê* (what is read) in the worship of the Greek-speaking synagogues, and the worshipers would have heard κύριος as the name of the God of the OT.[27]

23. See the conflated citation of Deut 7:18 (with Ps 110:4?) in Let. Aris. 155.

24. The Achilles' heel of Wilhelm Bousset's *Kyrios Christos: A History of the Belief in Christ from the Beginnings of Christianity to Irenaeus* (Nashville: Abingdon, 1970) has always been 1 Cor 16:22, μαραναθά, which preserves the Aramaic wording of the primitive church (as does Didache 10:6). It is difficult to know whether to translate μαραναθά as a perfect "our Lord has come" (מָרַן אֲתָא) or an imperative (מָרַן אֲתָא or מָרָנָא תָא) "our Lord, come." In light of Rev 22:20b (ἔρχου, κύριε Ἰησοῦ) I think it most likely to be an imperative, "Our Lord, come!"

25. We possess no NT MS with anything other than κύριος or θεός (infrequent) or abbreviations thereof as a translation of the Tetragrammaton. Howard, "Tetragram and the New Testament," makes an interesting case for a possible early transcription of the Tetragrammaton in the NT texts themselves, but his logic and attempt must in the end be judged as fanciful due to the complete lack of NT MS evidence.

26. Dan 2:47 (מָרֵא שְׁמַיָּא); 5:23 (מָרֵא מַלְכִיו); and esp. 1QapGen. See Joseph Fitzmyer, "New Testament *Kyrios* and *Maranatha* and Their Aramaic Background," in *To Advance the Gospel: New Testament Studies*, 2nd ed. (Grand Rapids: Eerdmans, 1998), 218–35; Fitzmyer, "Semitic Background," 116ff.; Lust, "Mic 5,1–3 in Qumran"; Martin Rösel, *Adonaq—warum Gott "Herr" genannt wird* (Tübingen: Mohr Siebeck, 2000), 217–21. In a still unidentified fragment from Qumran Cave 4, dated to the first century BC or early first century AD, there is possible evidence of the use of κύριος for YHWH. See 4Q126 (4Q *Unidentified gr*) in DJD IX, 219–21. See also the brief remarks, prior to the publication of 4Q126, of E. Ulrich, "The Biblical Scrolls from Qumran Cave 4: An Overview and a Progress Report on Their Publication," *Revue de Qumran* 14 (1989): 207–28, esp. 211: "One fragment, however, does have κυριο[, the first five letters of a possible equivalent for the Tetragrammaton, and the diction is plausibly Septuagintal or biblically-related."

27. On the importance of bilingualism for early Christianity, see Joseph Fitzmyer, "The Languages of Palestine in the First Century A. D.," in *A Wandering Aramean*, 29–56; and Martin Hengel, "Christological Titles in Early Christianity," in *The Messiah: Developments in Earliest Judaism and Christianity*, ed. James H. Charlesworth (Minneapolis: Fortress, 1992), 425–60, esp. 441–42 and n. 52. (Hengel emphasizes the importance of worship as a central locus of christological development. He also thinks κύριος would have certainly functioned as the *qĕrê* in the Greek-speaking synagogues.) Though Jerome (Ep. 25, *Ad Marcellam*; CSEL 54:219) knows of some who pronounced ΠΙΠΙ (a misunderstood transcription of the Tetragrammaton) "pipi" or "pee-pee," this utterance can hardly have been the norm, particularly in an early Jewish Christianity that knew well the intricacies of the divine name pronunciation prohibition. I find it near impossible to believe, in fact, that Greek-speaking Jewish Christians would have said out loud anything other than κύριος regardless of what they actually saw in the text. Fitzmyer's question, "What did a Greek-speaking Jew say

Luke and the Trinity

2. The relevant uses of κύριος for YHWH in the OT are enormous in number and therefore not necessary to list in detail. For this chapter it is especially important to keep in mind the monotheistic exclusivity of the divine name; the texts below are chosen accordingly:

Deuteronomy 6:4: ἄκουε Ἰσραήλ· κύριος ὁ θεὸς ἡμῶν κύριος εἷς ἐστιν
(Hear O Israel: The Lord our God, the Lord is one Lord! 2 Esdras 19:6 LXX)

Nehemiah 9:6: σὺ εἶ αὐτὸς κύριος μόνος
(You yourself are the only Lord!)

Zechariah 14:9: ἐν τῇ ἡμέρᾳ ἐκείνῃ ἔσται κύριος εἷς καὶ τὸ ὄνομα αὐτοῦ ἕν
(In that day the Lord will be one and his Name one!)

Isaiah 42:8: ἐγὼ κύριος ὁ θεός, τοῦτό μού ἐστιν τὸ ὄνομα· τὴν δόξαν μου ἑτέρῳ οὐ δώσω
(I am the Lord God, this is my Name; my glory I will not give to another!)

Σωτήρ and the OT

1. Σωτήρ was used in the LXX almost exclusively for the God of Israel.[28] YHWH as σωτήρ is a fundamental component of his identity and is used across genre and historical period throughout the OT. Further, as with κύριος, σωτήρ would have been used in the worship of the Greek-speaking synagogues in prayer and reading and would have been connected with YHWH's unique saving activity.

2. There are numerous illustrative OT texts. The following texts were chosen because of their verbal and thematic echoes within Luke-Acts and because the connection between the Lord God's identity and his activity as Savior is explicit.

Esther 5:2: καὶ γενηθεῖσα ἐπιφανὴς . . . ἐπικαλεσαμένη θεὸν καὶ σωτῆρα
(And she was glorious in appearance [and] called upon God even the Savior.)

---

when he read his Scriptures and found in it either the tetragrammaton or the letters ΠΙΠΙ?" ("Semitic Background," 123), gets at this point.

28. The only exception is in Judges where σωτήρ is used three times (3:9, 15; 12:3) to speak of the judges whom God has appointed.

Psalm 26:1: κύριος φωτισμός μου καὶ σωτήρ· τίνα φοβηθήσομαι;
(The Lord is my Light and my Savior! Whom shall I fear?)

Psalm 61:3: καὶ γὰρ αὐτὸς θεός μου καὶ σωτήρ μου
(He is my God and my Savior.)

Psalm 64:6: ἐπάκουσον ἡμῶν, ὁ θεὸς ὁ σωτὴρ ἡμῶν, ἡ ἐλπὶς πάντων τῶν περάτων τῆς γῆς
(Listen to us, O God our Savior, the hope of all the ends of the earth!)

Psalm 78:9: βοήθησον ἡμῖν, ὁ θεὸς ὁ σωτὴρ ἡμῶν, ἕνεκα τῆς δόξης τοῦ ὀνόματός σου
(Help us, O God our Savior, for the glory of your name!)

Isaiah 12:2–6: ἰδοὺ ὁ θεός μου σωτήρ μου κύριος, πεποιθὼς ἔσομαι ἐπ αὐτῷ καὶ σωθήσομαι ἐν αὐτῷ καὶ οὐ φοβηθήσομαι, διότι ἡ δόξα μου καὶ ἡ αἴνεσίς μου κύριος καὶ ἐγένετό μοι εἰς σωτηρίαν. . . . καὶ ἐρεῖς ἐν τῇ ἡμέρᾳ ἐκείνῃ, ὑμνεῖτε κύριον, βοᾶτε τὸ ὄνομα αὐτοῦ, ἀναγγείλατε ἐν τοῖς ἔθνεσιν τὰ ἔνδοξα αὐτοῦ, μιμνήσκεσθε ὅτι ὑψώθη τὸ ὄνομα αὐτοῦ. ὑμνήσατε τὸ ὄνομα κυρίου, ὅτι ὑψηλὰ ἐποίησεν· ἀναγγείλατε ταῦτα ἐν πάσῃ τῇ γῇ. ἀγαλλιᾶσθε καὶ εὐφραίνεσθε, οἱ κατοικοῦντες Σιων, ὅτι ὑψώθη ὁ ἅγιος τοῦ Ισραηλ ἐν μέσῳ αὐτῆς.
(Behold! The Lord is my God and my Savior! I have trusted in him. And I will not fear because the Lord is my glory and my praise and he has become my salvation! . . . In that day you will say, "Sing to the Lord! Shout out his name! Proclaim to the Gentiles his glorious deeds! Make it known that his name is exalted! Sing praise to the name of the Lord because he has done wonderful things! Proclaim these things to all the earth! Exult and rejoice, you who dwell in Zion, because the Holy One of Israel is exalted in your midst!")

Isaiah 62:11: ἰδοὺ γὰρ κύριος ἐποίησεν ἀκουστὸν ἕως ἐσχάτου τῆς γῆς· εἴπατε τῇ θυγατρὶ Σιών, ἰδού σοι ὁ σωτὴρ παραγίνεται
(For, behold! The Lord made it heard to the end of the earth. Say to the Daughter of Zion, "Behold! The Savior comes to you!")

Micah 7:7: ἐγὼ δὲ ἐπὶ τὸν κύριον ἐπιβλέψομαι· ὑπομενῶ ἐπὶ τῷ θεῷ τῷ σωτῆρί μου
(I will look to the Lord; I will wait upon God my Savior.)

Sirach 51:1: ἐξομολογήσομαί σοι, κύριε βασιλεῦ, καὶ αἰνέσω σε θεὸν τὸν σωτῆρά μου
(I will give thanks to you, O Lord and King, and will praise you as God my Savior.)

The Lord/Savior in Lukan Narrative

In the wake of the proposals of Hans Frei,[29] George Lindbeck,[30] and now Robert Jenson,[31] the point does not need laboring that narrative is an essential form of theology. The fundamental truth of such an insight is connected with the nature of many of the biblical documents themselves[32] and with the canon itself read as a whole. Simply put, the Bible is full of stories, and the Bible as a whole is a story. The metanarrative of God and his creation contains individual narratives within it. In this respect the use of the OT in the NT as historical and theological presupposition, citation, allusion, echo, and so on exhibits a narrative reflexivity and assumes tremendous theological importance. The grand old story of the God of the OT with his creation, and particularly with his elect people Israel, is woven into and is inextricably bound up with the many and various stories that attempt to capture this God's action in Jesus Christ. And these new stories, in turn, depend upon, relate to, and illumine the old. Luke 1–2 is an excellent example of such narrative and theological interplay. Though Luke cites Scripture directly only twice (2:23, 24), the entire birth-infancy narrative is richly allusive[33] and shows that Scripture is the matrix within which the person of Jesus and the events surrounding his life are to be interpreted. Conversely, the life and person of Jesus interpret the direction

---

29. Hans W. Frei, *The Eclipse of Biblical Narrative: A Study in Eighteenth and Nineteenth Century Hermeneutics* (New Haven: Yale University Press, 1974).

30. George A. Lindbeck, *The Nature of Doctrine: Religion and Theology in a Postliberal Age* (Philadelphia: Westminster, 1984).

31. Jenson, *Systematic Theology*.

32. This point is succinctly and powerfully explored by David Tracy, *The Analogical Imagination: Christian Theology and the Culture of Pluralism* (New York: Crossroad, 1981), 275-81.

33. E.g., Gen 11–21 (Luke 1:5–2:52); 1 Sam 1:1–2:10 (Luke 1:5–2:52, esp. 1:46–55); Judg 13:2–25 (Luke 1:5–24); Dan 7–10 (Luke 1:5–2:52); Zeph 3:14–17 (Luke 1:26–33); Isa 2:9–12 (Luke 1:46–55); Isa 7:14 (Luke 1:27); Isa 9:6–7 (Luke 1:26–38); Isa 42:6 (Luke 1:79; 2:32); Isa 49:6 (Luke 2:32); Isa 52:10 (Luke 2:30–31); 2 Sam 7:12–16 (Luke 1:32–33); Mic 4:7–5:5 (Luke 2:1–14); Mal 3:1 (Luke 1:17, 76); Mal 4:5–6 (Luke 1:17).

Part 1: Christology, Greco-Roman Culture, and Canonical Reception

and purpose of Scripture. The history of Israel blends with the coming of Jesus such that there is a continuity of story.

In recent years biblical scholars, too, have appropriated the implications of narrative as a means of theological discourse for the reading of the gospels.[34] In his slender volume on the theology of the Gospel of Luke, Joel Green correctly notes that the insight into "the imbeddedness of all thought in tradition and story has opened up the potential for reading the Gospel of Luke . . . in fresh ways."[35] The implication for this study regarding theological form and thrust is obvious, but significant nonetheless. Luke's theology, in both the strict and the general sense, is not expressed primarily through propositions but through the vehicle of narrative. Thus if the question of the identity of God is to be pursued exegetically, it must be done by paying close attention to the movement of the narrative. Further, special attention must be given to the influence and presence of the OT in Luke's narrative, for it is through the unitive intertwining of the movement of the narrative with the OT that the identity of God is apprehended.

The importance of Luke 1–2 in relation to the larger narrative was denied by Hans Conzelmann in his famous book of 1954,[36] but more recently Luke 1–2 has correctly received scholarly rehabilitation as the beginning of Luke's narrative and thus is recognized as an essential part of the whole.[37] In the following

---

34. Among many others, see Eugene Boring, "The Christology of Mark: Hermeneutical Issues for Systematic Theology," *Semeia* 30 (1985): 125–53; John R. Donahue, "The Literary Turn and New Testament Theology: Detour or New Direction?," *JR* (1996): 250–75; Jack Dean Kingsbury, *Conflict in Luke: Jesus, Authorities, Disciples* (Minneapolis: Fortress, 1991); Kingsbury, *Matthew as Story* (Minneapolis: Fortress, 1988); Gail R. O'Day, *Revelation in the Fourth Gospel: Narrative Mode and Theological Claim* (Philadelphia: Fortress, 1986); David Rhoads and Donald Michie, *Mark as Story: An Introduction to the Narrative of a Gospel* (Philadelphia: Fortress, 1982); Charles Talbert, *Reading Luke: A Literary and Theological Commentary on the Third Gospel* (New York: Crossroad, 1982); Robert C. Tannehill, *The Narrative Unity of Luke-Acts: A Literary Interpretation*, 2 vols. (Minneapolis: Fortress, 1986–1990).

35. Joel B. Green, *The Theology of the Gospel of Luke* (Cambridge: Cambridge University Press, 1995), 2. See also his recently published commentary that makes heavy and helpful use of such narratological insights: Joel B. Green, *The Gospel of Luke*, NICNT (Grand Rapids: Eerdmans, 1997).

36. Hans Conzelmann, *Die Mitte der Zeit* (Tübingen: Mohr Siebeck, 1954). Published in English translation as *The Theology of St. Luke* (London: Faber & Faber, 1960).

37. See, e.g., Raymond Brown, *The Birth of the Messiah* (Garden City, NY: Doubleday, 1977), 26f., 241–43; Paul S. Minear, "Luke's Use of the Birth Stories," in *Studies in Luke-Acts*, ed. Leander Keck and J. Louis Martyn (Philadelphia: Fortress, 1966), 111–30; and Robert C. Tannehill, *Luke*, ANTC (Nashville: Abingdon, 1996), 40–41.

exegesis I will assume the unity of Luke 1–2 with the body of the gospel both in terms of single authorship[38] and in terms of theological continuity and seek to offer a reading on the basis of this continuity in the opening of the body of the gospel in 3:1-6.

Luke obviously does not so clearly conceive of a preexistent Logos in the way that it is found in the prologue to John's Gospel or of the preexistence of Christ Jesus as it is expressed in the hymn in Philippians 2:5-11. Nevertheless, there is a strong incarnational theology in the movement of the narrative in Luke 1–2. It is at the point of this incarnation of YHWH that the Trinitarian grammar of Luke-Acts begins to emerge.

Throughout Luke 1:5-38 it is clear that κύριος refers only to YHWH, the God of the OT (though 1:17 presents an interesting case, on which see note 45 below). Several expressions, when taken in their narrative setting, make this referent abundantly evident:

1:6: ἐντολαῖς καὶ δικαιώμασιν τοῦ κυρίου (the commandments and ordinances of the Lord)
1:9: τὸν ναὸν τοῦ κυρίου (the temple of the Lord)
1:11 : ἄγγελος κυρίου (an angel of the Lord)
1:16: κύριον τὸν θεὸν αὐτῶν (the Lord their God)
1:32: κύριος ὁ θεός (the Lord God)
1:38: ἡ δούλη κυρίου (the servant of the Lord)

Between 1:38 and 1:39, however, there is a narrative gap during which time the conception of Jesus occurs. In light of 1:43 this narrative gap can be seen as the moment of the incarnation of YHWH, passed over in silence, but captured in the overlapping identity of the κύριος. For in 1:43 Elizabeth, filled with the Holy Spirit, addresses Mary as "ἡ μήτηρ τοῦ κυρίου μου" (the mother of my Lord!). This is the first time that Jesus himself appears in the narrative, and it is at this point that Jesus takes on the title/name κύριος. This dramatic moment

---

38. By this I mean only to say that chs. 1–2 are intentionally and essentially related to the rest of the gospel. What Luke's sources were and whether he wrote chs. 1–2 before or after completing the rest of the gospel are, as Talbert says, "well nigh impossible to answer" (Charles Talbert, "Prophecies of Future Greatness: The Contribution of Greco-Roman Biographies to an Understanding of Luke 1:5–4:15," in *The Divine Helmsman: Studies on God's Control of Human Events Presented to Lou H. Silberman*, ed. James L. Crenshaw and Samuel Sandmel [New York: Ktav 1980], 129). For brief discussions on these matters, see also Brown, *Birth of the Messiah*, 240-50, and Joseph Fitzmyer, *Luke the Theologian: Aspects of His Teaching* (New York: Paulist, 1989), 28-30.

Part 1: Christology, Greco-Roman Culture, and Canonical Reception

in the narrative identifies YHWH with the human Jesus within Mary's womb by means of the overlapping resonance of κύριος. There is a fundamental correspondence between the one God of the OT and the person of Jesus such that they share the same name. The doubleness that this overlap creates in the referent of the κύριος finds its theological interpretation in an incarnational unity between YHWH and Jesus.

But it is in fact impossible to speak about this incarnational unity of the κύριος apart from the Holy Spirit. In Luke's narrative Jesus's human existence is from his conception entirely dependent upon the Holy Spirit. In the annunciation scene Gabriel tells the virgin Mary (παρθένος twice in 1:27) that the very life of the baby within her will be by the overshadowing of the δύναμις ὑψίστου—that is, the πνεῦμα ἅγιον (1:35; cf. 24:49). The synonymity of the πνεῦμα ἅγιον with the δύναμις ὑψίστου is fully consonant with the OT (and the Second Temple period) as an expression of the dynamism of the εἷς κύριος of Israel.[39] In the movement of the Lukan narrative we see this dynamic divine inner life played out as the Holy Spirit is a distinct entity in itself, and

---

39. E.g., Gen 1:2; Ps 33:6; 51; 104:30; 139:7; Isa 11:2; 32:15; 42:1; 44:3-5; 63:10-14; Ezek 36:27; 37:1-14; Hag 2:5; Zech 4:6; Joel 3:1-5, etc. An older but still interesting study that deals with God's dynamism in the OT is G. A. F. Knight, *A Biblical Approach to the Doctrine of the Trinity*, SJT Occasional Papers 1 (Edinburgh: Oliver and Boyd, 1953). For the dynamism of the one God as understood in the Second Temple texts, see, among many others, Richard Bauckham, *God Crucified: Monotheism and Christology in the New Testament* (Grand Rapids: Eerdmans, 1998); Larry Hurtado, *One God, One Lord: Early Christian Devotion and Ancient Jewish Monotheism*, 2nd ed. (Edinburgh: T&T Clark, 1998); N. T. Wright, *The Climax of the Covenant* (Minneapolis: Fortress, 1991), 120-36; Wright, "Jesus and the Identity of God," *Ex Aud* 14 (1998): 42-56; Wright, "One God, One Lord, One People: Incarnational Christology for a Church in a Pagan Environment," *Ex Aud* 7 (1991): 45-58; Wright, *The New Testament and the People of God*, vol. 1 of *Christian Origins and the Question of God* (Minneapolis: Fortress, 1992). C. K. Barrett, *The Holy Spirit and the Gospel Tradition* (New York: Macmillan, 1947), is still helpful in drawing out the Hebraic thought of Luke 1-2, though, of course, his study needs much modification in terms of his Jewish/Hellenistic distinction. Hippolytus, writing on the creation of the world by God, rightly captures in philosophical language the essential judgments made in the OT about the plurality within the one God: "God, subsisting alone, and having nothing contemporaneous with himself, determined to create the world.... Beside him there was nothing; but, while existing alone, he existed in plurality [μόνος ὢν πολὺς ἦν], for he was not without his Word, his Wisdom, his Power, and his Counsel [ἄλογος, ἄσοφος, ἀδύνατος, ἀβούλευτος]" (*Against the Heresy of Noetus* 10 [*ANF* 5:227]). Cf. Tertullian, *Against Praxeas* 5 (*ANF* 3:600), "For before all things God was alone.... He was alone because there was nothing external to himself. Yet even not then was he alone; for he had with him that which he possessed in himself, that is to say, his own Reason."

yet is not other than God, but is indeed God's power.⁴⁰ God's Spirit is indeed God himself but in repetition or doubleness in the conception of Jesus. God remains God "above" the world and at the same time in the Holy Spirit "comes upon" and "overshadows" the earthly woman Mary.

Thus in the Lukan birth narrative there is a triplicity in the life of God that is made known through the conception of Jesus. The εἷς κύριος (Deut 6:4), the God of Israel, is fully transcendent as the Creator of the world and as the God behind the events that have come to be fulfilled in Luke's time (1:5–38). This God incarnates himself in the person of Jesus with an intensity that justifies the overlapping identification and doubleness in referentiality of the single divine name κύριος. And this kyriotic unity is effected precisely by the power of God, the Holy Spirit. In Luke the entire birth-infancy event is surrounded by and involves a Trinitarian understanding of God and of his relation to the world.

Attention to the title σωτήρ within Luke's narrative confirms the incarnational unity between YHWH and Jesus (again, by the power of the Holy Spirit) and explicitly extends it to the realm of soteriology. Here it is possible to be more brief because the essential line of thought has been laid out with respect to the κύριος overlap. The only difference is that whereas κύριος is both name and title, σωτήρ is strictly a title both in respect to YHWH, the God of the OT, and in respect to Jesus. Nonetheless, the title is situated within a narrative, and attention to the logic of the narrative leads to the recognition of the overlap of soteriological identity through the use of σωτήρ.

The Magnificat begins with Mary's adoration of God (τὸν κύριον) and her jubilation in "τῷ θεῷ τῷ σωτῆρί μου" (1:47). This twofold praise of God loudly echoes a multitude of OT texts (see above) and clearly links the κύριος of the OT with his saving activity as σωτήρ. The only other time σωτήρ is used in the gospel is in 2:11 where an ἄγγελος κυρίου announces to the shepherds that a human baby is their σωτήρ and that he is χριστὸς κύριος. Reading the

---

40. I take it as beyond the need for demonstration or argument that the Holy Spirit is a distinct entity (a "person" in later terminology) or character in the narrative of Luke-Acts. However, the relation of the Holy Spirit to God requires exceedingly careful formulation if it is to be interpreted. It is not that the Holy Spirit is God and yet distinct from *God*, but rather that the Holy Spirit is God and distinct *within* God, hence the formulation above to which this note is attached. Eduard Schweizer, *The Good News according to Luke* (Atlanta: John Knox, 1984), 66, helpfully calls the Holy Spirit the life of God. In addition, K. L. Schmidt, "Le problème du Christianisme primitif," *Revue d'histoire et de philosophie religieuses* 18 (1938): 126–73, rightly notes that ἅγιος in relation to πνεῦμα functions as personal identification: "l'Esprit est compris comme le Saint Esprit, comme une personne" (140). See also Geoffrey Wainwright, "The Holy Spirit," in *The Cambridge Companion to Christian Doctrine*, ed. Colin E. Gunton (Cambridge: Cambridge University Press, 1997), 273–96, esp. 278–80.

Part 1: Christology, Greco-Roman Culture, and Canonical Reception

two texts together in the narrative produces a unified soteriological identity between YHWH and Jesus (κύριος) in their role as Savior (σωτήρ).[41] And this unified soteriological identity is only possible by the power of the Holy Spirit (1:35).

This interpretation of the theological significance of κύριος and σωτήρ is dependent upon the logic of the narrative itself. As mentioned above, Luke does not write propositional statements such that each particular point can be analyzed in itself for consistency and coherence. Rather, the narrative stands or falls as a whole. The entire web of complexes in Luke 1–2 forms a single presentation,[42] so that the picture of God presented by the birth-infancy narrative is seen and taken as a whole. To isolate this or that aspect is to distort the total picture and misapprehend the subject matter with which Luke presents the reader. The Trinity of the one God emerges from the conception of Jesus as the incarnation of God by the power of the Holy Spirit and is rendered by the narrative read in its entirety such that to speak of God in the Lukan birth narrative is to speak simultaneously of the human person Jesus, the God of the OT, and the Holy Spirit.

The question naturally arises as to whether the interpretation heretofore advanced is borne out by the rest of the narrative in Luke-Acts. The answer is an emphatic yes. There are numerous texts that could be marshaled in support of a Trinitarian reading of Luke-Acts, and many of them are listed in the appendix. For the purpose of this chapter, as a kind of test case, we will examine the implications of the Trinitarian reading of the birth-infancy narrative for the reading of the opening scene in the body of the gospel. This test case will allow us to see how the overlap of identity and act through the OT and Luke's narrative blend to open wide interpretative vistas. First, however, brief mention needs to be made of 1:76.

In Luke 1:76 Zechariah, filled with the Holy Spirit, prophesies that his son John will go "ἐνώπιον κυρίου ἑτοιμάσαι ὁδοὺς αὐτοῦ!" Luke 1:76 is fully ambiguous in itself as regards the identity of the κύριος. And this, it may be said, is precisely the point of the kyriotic overlap. The alternative of YHWH *or* Jesus forced upon the text by many exegetes is a false dichotomy. Alfred Plummer, for example, wrote that "here κυρίου means Jehovah, not the Christ,"[43] while

---

41. Luke Timothy Johnson, *The Gospel of Luke*, SP (Collegeville, MN: Liturgical Press, 1991), 44, misses the narrative theological significance and inaccurately imposes a distinction upon the Greek between "Lord" and "Savior" (God) and "lord" and "savior" (Jesus) that it will not bear.

42. See Minear, "Luke's Use of the Birth Stories," 129.

43. Alfred Plummer, *A Critical and Exegetical Commentary on the Gospel according to*

Fitzmyer thought the κύριος was Jesus.[44] This either/or dichotomy is a historicist assumption carried over into exegesis that obscures the theological significance of the use of κύριος and prevents apprehension of the subject matter. The doubleness inherent in the incarnational unity of the κύριος necessitates that the ambiguity be understood as both/and. To speak of YHWH is to speak of Jesus and vice versa. This unity is confirmed in Luke 3:4-6.

St. Luke, ICC (New York: Charles Scribner's Sons, 1898), 42. Plummer is a perfect example of an exegete who completely missed the theological weight of κύριος in the movement of the Lukan birth-infancy narrative. In translating κύριος as Christ or Messiah, as he did for the key text of 1:43 (29), he obscured the narrative overlap of "Lord." Thus he read 1:76 only in light of 1:16-17 and was not able to take account of 1:43 (42).

44. Joseph A. Fitzmyer, *The Gospel according to Luke*, 2 vols., AB 28/28A (Garden City, NY: Doubleday, 1981-1985), 1:385. Fitzmyer raises the question of ambiguity more explicitly than does anyone else but in the end is nonetheless compelled to resolve this ambiguity. The pressure exegetes feel to remove and explain away the obvious ambiguity and their corresponding tendency to shy away from theological implications are quite remarkable. See, e.g., Green, *Luke*, 118, who sees the ambiguity in a way but fails to make anything of it, and Donald L. Jones, "The Title Kyrios in Luke-Acts," *SBLSP* 74, no. 2 (1974): 85-101, who sets the κύριος as Jesus over against the κύριος as God (88). Johnson, *Gospel of Luke*, avoids the issue altogether. John Philipose, "Kurios in Luke: A Diagnosis," *Bible Translator* 43, no. 3 (1992): 325-33, totally misunderstands the basic issue at stake when he suggests that in contexts where κύριος clearly refers to God it should be translated as "God . . . to avoid confusing the average reader" (326). One also witnesses these same tendencies with respect to the ambiguous uses of κύριος in Acts. E.g., Henry J. Cadbury, "The Titles of Jesus in Acts," in *The Beginnings of Christianity, Part I: The Acts of the Apostles*, ed. Kirsopp Lake and Henry J. Cadbury (London: Macmillan, 1933), 5:354-75, sees in the ambiguity only a dichotomy and prevents the ambiguous uses of κύριος from having any bearing on his discussion of κύριος as applied to Jesus in Acts: "Many cases of κύριος in Acts, perhaps the majority, are quite *ambiguous*, since they could mean *either* God *or* Jesus. Both these and the cases where it plainly means God may well be omitted from consideration" (359; emphasis added). An article by Gerhard Schneider, "Gott und Christus als Kyrios nach der Apostelgeschichte," in *Begegnung mit dem Wort*, ed. J. Zmijewski and E. Nellessen, BBB 53 (Bonn: Peter Hanstein Verlag, 1980), 161-74, provides an interesting counterpoint to Cadbury's neglect of ambiguity while sharing the same either/or view. Schneider systematically analyzes the ambiguous uses of κύριος in Acts and in every single case concludes that κύριος is either God or Jesus. That his analysis is untenable, however, is evident at the end of the article when he acknowledges that Luke's readers/auditors might not have been able to distinguish clearly between God and Christ as the referent of κύριος and speaks of God in his self-revelation as present in Christ, etc. (171-73). This concession, of course, is to reopen the very question of the theological meaning of the ambiguity. The only exception of which I am aware that is an explicitly exegetical study is J. C. O'Neill, "The Use of Kyrios in the Book of Acts," *SJT* 8, no. 2 (1955): 155-74. Barth, *Church Dogmatics* I/1, esp. 400-406, also sees the issue clearly.

Part 1: Christology, Greco-Roman Culture, and Canonical Reception

Luke 3:1 begins the body of the gospel and opens with specific historical indications of the time at which the "fulfilled" (1:1) events took place. John the Baptist, now fully grown, appears from the wilderness as a prophet, fulfilling his vocation as a herald by trumpeting forth anew the words of the prophet Isaiah:

> φωνὴ βοῶντος ἐν τῇ ἐρήμῳ
> ἑτοιμάσατε τὴν ὁδὸν κυρίου,
> εὐθείας ποιεῖτε τὰς τρίβους αὐτοῦ
> πᾶσα φάραγξ πληρωθήσεται
> καὶ πᾶν ὄρος καὶ βουνὸς ταπεινωθήσεται
> καὶ ἔσται τὰ σκολιὰ εἰς εὐθείαν
> καὶ αἱ τραχεῖαι εἰς ὁδοὺς λείας
> καὶ ὄψεται πᾶσα σὰρξ τὸ σωτήριον τοῦ θεοῦ

> The voice of one crying out in the wilderness:
> Prepare the way of the Lord!
> Make straight his paths!
> Every valley shall be filled,
> And every mountain and hill shall be made low!
> And the crooked places shall be made straight,
> And the rough places shall be made smooth!
> And all flesh shall see the salvation of God!

This citation of Isaiah 40:3–5 in Luke 3:4–6 is the fulfillment of Zechariah's prophecy in Luke 1:76 and forces again the question of the identity of the κύριος. In the Isaiah quotation itself the κυρίου of 40:3 (Luke 3:4) clearly refers to YHWH, as does the τοῦ θεοῦ of 40:5 (Luke 3:6). In Luke's narrative, however, the referent of the κυρίου is, as in the prophecy of 1:76, ambiguous. Because 3:4–6 is an OT quotation, the κύριος in 3:4 is unquestionably the εἷς κύριος of the OT; because the Baptist in Luke's narrative literally does prepare the way for Jesus structurally, sequentially, and as his prophet, the κύριος indubitably refers to Jesus (the absolute ὁ κύριος is used at least twelve times in Luke's Gospel).[45] Further, where the LXX reads εὐθείας ποιεῖτε τὰς τρίβους

---

45. Those who would see here only a reference to Jesus simply ignore that this is an indisputable citation from the OT. Conversely, those who would see here only a reference to God simply ignore the structure and movement of the gospel. I mentioned above that 1:16–17 is an interesting case regarding κύριος. We are now sufficiently into the exegesis for me to offer my reading. Briefly, 1:16–17 is to be read as an intimation of the coming incarnation;

τοῦ θεοῦ ἡμῶν, "make straight the paths of *our God*" (Isa 40:3), Luke reads εὐθείας ποιεῖτε τὰς τρίβους αὐτοῦ, "make straight *his* paths" (Luke 3:4).[46]

It is tempting to argue with Joel Green that the αὐτοῦ adds clarity and provides the interpretative key.[47] The exegetical move would then be to assert on this basis that Luke intends that the κύριος of 3:4 refer clearly to Jesus—hence the substitution. This argument, however, moves in the wrong direction. In reality, the αὐτοῦ produces precisely the reverse effect. It removes clarity and creates ambiguity. The simple reason is that the αὐτοῦ and the κυρίου in 3:4 are inseparably bound both grammatically and with respect to identity. Thus the referent of the αὐτοῦ in itself is unclear and is dependent upon whom one takes the κύριος to be[48]—a decision that is fraught with ambiguity.

The ambiguity of 3:4 is reinforced by and extends to the phrase τὸ σωτήριον τοῦ θεοῦ in Luke 3:6. How is this genitive to be read? Is this salvation something that God effects or is it in some way God himself? It is exegetically impossible to resolve the ambiguity of the κύριος or of the nature of the σωτήριον with an either/or dichotomy. There is simply no way to settle the issue with certainty. A both/and exegesis is more honest as it avoids pressing the text into a preconceived either/or mold and instead reflects the dialectic tension inherent within the text. As in the prophecy in 1:76, so here in its fulfillment the kyriotic overlap captures the fundamental correlation between YHWH and Jesus expressed in the duality of the single κύριος. The implications of this incarnational theology for the understanding of τὸ σωτήριον τοῦ θεοῦ fuse the oppositional ways of understanding the genitive into the same reality. The citation read as a whole within Luke's narrative, then, portrays the soteriological coming of YHWH in the human person Jesus in such a way that there is a unity of identity and of act.

---

however, there is not an overlap in 1:16–17 because the incarnation has not happened in the narrative yet—Jesus has not yet been conceived by the power of the Holy Spirit.

46. To my mind, text-critical issues allow a very strong comparison in this case. Codex Bezae reads ὑμῶν, which is not in any of the LXX MSS or any other NT MS. The only other variant listed in NA[27] is that of three Syriac MSS that have the equivalent of τῷ θεῷ ἡμῶν. This reading tradition, however, is essentially that of the dominant LXX MSS. The only LXX MSS that read αὐτοῦ are late (they range from the eighth to the thirteenth century).

47. Green, *Luke*, 171.

48. I have chosen not to pursue the argument of intentionality with respect to Luke's use of Isa 40:3–5. However, if Luke (a) had a manuscript that read τοῦ θεοῦ ἡμῶν or had memorized this passage of Isaiah with τοῦ θεοῦ ἡμῶν and (b) was consciously changing the wording of this manuscript or that of his memory to αὐτοῦ, then the substitution of αὐτοῦ would only press the point of ambiguity even more strongly. Further, it should be noted that if Luke is following Mark (1:3) here, Luke expands the quotation considerably.

Part 1: Christology, Greco-Roman Culture, and Canonical Reception

Excursus: The thrust of the interpretation of κύριος has been upon the incarnational unity of YHWH and Jesus by the power of the Holy Spirit. The purpose of this brief excursus is to respond to an important point raised by Joseph Fitzmyer that could have negative implications for an incarnational reading. Fitzmyer recognizes that the use of κύριος for Jesus "would have meant putting him on the same level as Yahweh," but asserts that this use was "without . . . identifying him" with YHWH since Jesus "is never referred to as *'abbā*."[49] The use of the "*kyrios*-title" for both Jesus and YHWH suggests only a "*Gleichsetzung* not an *Identifizierung*—because [Jesus] is not *'abbā*."[50] Fitzmyer's erudition is unquestionably impressive, but here his exegetical and theological misunderstanding of the kyriotic overlap and unity is striking. First, Fitzmyer assumes that what Jesus and YHWH share is only a title: "[Jesus] was somehow regarded as worthy of the same title otherwise employed for Yahweh."[51] The other side to this assumption is that the κύριος title denotes only function or status—equality, not identity.[52] The immediate problem here is that κύριος is not simply used as a title for YHWH; it is also his name. It does not merely describe YHWH or his action as do other titles (e.g., σωτήρ); other titles are appellations connected with who YHWH is, but κύριος is the unique identity of the God of Israel. Further, there is no cleft between YHWH and his name.[53] The divine subject is totally identified with

---

49. Fitzmyer, *Luke*, 1:202.

50. Fitzmyer, "*Kyrios* and *Maranatha*," 223. Cf. Fitzmyer, "Semitic Background," 130 and nn. 36, 90.

51. Fitzmyer, "Semitic Background," 130. At this particular point Fitzmyer mentions the hymn to Christ in Phil 2:6-11, but the essay as a whole is much broader and carries this assumption throughout (as does his other work listed above).

52. Cf. Reginald H. Fuller, *The Foundations of New Testament Christology* (New York: Scribner, 1965), 68, who argues that the application of LXX κύριος passages to Jesus "does not mean . . . that the distinction between Jesus and God is blurred, or that Jesus was by now regarded as a divine being in an ontological sense. All that the LXX usage opens up at this stage is a *functional* identity between the exalted Kyrios and the Yahweh-Kyrios of the Old Testament and the LXX" (emphasis added).

53. For theological reflection on the significance of the divine name, see esp. Brevard S. Childs, *The Book of Exodus: A Critical, Theological Commentary* (Philadelphia: Westminster, 1974), 411ff. Cf. Christopher Seitz, "Handing Over the Name: Christian Reflection on the Divine Name YHWH," in *Trinity, Time, and Church: A Response to the Theology of Robert W. Jenson*, ed. Colin E. Gunton (Grand Rapids: Eerdmans, 2000), 23-41; Seitz, "The Call of Moses and the 'Revelation' of the Divine Name," in *Theological Exegesis: Essays in Honor of Brevard S. Childs*, ed. Christopher Seitz and Kathryn Greene-McCreight (Grand Rapids: Eerdmans, 1999), 145-61; and Gerhard von Rad, *Old Testament Theology*, 2 vols. (New York: Harper & Row, 1962-1965), 1:186ff. Though there are a few passages that can give rise to the

Luke and the Trinity

and present in his name—κύριος is YHWH. The question, then, is seriously skewed from the outset when it is couched only in terms of what it might mean for Jesus to share the same title as YHWH. Instead, the question is what it means for Jesus to share the same name. And while no one would deny that κύριος functions as a title for Jesus, it is also to be understood as a name. This is especially true in Paul in such texts as Philippians 2:9–11 and Romans 10:13,[54] but it also applies to Luke in, for example, Acts 2:21, 25. Further, Luke 13:35 is narratively fulfilled in Luke 19:38, which is itself a literal fulfillment of Psalm 118:26—Jesus literally comes in the name of the κύριος, for he shares this same name. Second, the distinction between equality and identification is not true to the movement of the Lukan birth-infancy narrative and underestimates the importance of narrative itself as a means of theology. I do not think Luke 1:43 as read in the context of the narrative can be said to bear the weight of such a *Gleichsetzung/Identifizierung* distinction. On the contrary, it makes much more sense to read 1:43 as a dramatic moment in the narrative that unveils the incarnational identity of the one κύριος. Third, the objection to an overlap of identity that turns on the fact that Jesus was never called "Abba" is a misunderstanding of the use of the name κύριος and of the identity of YHWH. There is a common a priori assumption, which Fitzmyer seems to share, that the God of the OT, YHWH/κύριος, is the Father only. This, however, is the case neither in Luke's narrative nor in proper Trinitarian theology. In fact, it is the very use of κύριος itself that alerts us to the duality in the divine name. Of course Jesus is not Abba; he is the Son! Of course the Father is not Jesus; he is the Father! But *both* the Father *and* the Son bear the divine name κύριος. The Lukan narrative assumes the differentiation of the Father and the Son,[55] but nonetheless gives the divine name both to

---

question of whether God's name is distinct from God himself (the clearest is Isa 30:27–28), what is actually emphasized is YHWH's immanence or self-manifestation, not at all the name YHWH as a distinct entity apart from God (this is particularly clear in the LXX where τὸ ὄνομα κυρίου is most naturally understood as a circumlocution for YHWH).

54. See C. Kavin Rowe, "Romans 10:13: What Is the Name of the Lord?," *HBT* 22, no. 2 (2000): 135–73, reprinted in this volume at pp. 274–307.

55. A fascinating study in this respect is that of René Laurentin, *Structure et théologie de Luc I–II* (Paris: Gabalda, 1957). Laurentin argues that Luke has two theological plans in chs. 1–2, structural/historical and allusive (to OT). These two plans blend together to focus upon Jesus's entry into the temple as a fulfillment of Mal 3:1ff.—Jesus is YHWH who has come suddenly into his temple. If Laurentin is anywhere near the mark, it is interesting to note that Jesus as YHWH who has come into his temple is still the Son and the Father still the Father; in fact, Jesus' first words in the gospel are "τί ὅτι ἐζητεῖτέ με; οὐκ ᾔδειτε ὅτι ἐν τοῖς τοῦ πατρός μου δεῖ εἶναί με;"

Part 1: Christology, Greco-Roman Culture, and Canonical Reception

the Father and to Jesus. Hence, the use of κύριος expresses the unity of the εἷς κύριος (Deut. 6:4), which is differentiated within this identity into the Father and the Son. The duality of Father and Son in the Lukan narrative is no threat to the unitive identity of the one Lord. Correlatively, the unitive identity of the one Lord does not in any way preclude differentiation into Father and Son as it is found in the Lukan narrative. Further, in proper Trinitarian theology God is triune from eternity and is the subject matter of the entire Christian Bible, not just the NT.[56] Thus, Trinitarian theology allows for differentiation within the identity of the εἷς κύριος of the OT and at the same time maintains the unity of the εἷς κύριος as economically expressed in the NT.[57]

Conclusion: Luke's Trinitarian Kyriology

In opposition to the long-standing and influential idea that the Trinitarian understanding of God as developed and clarified in the ecumenical creeds and councils of the first centuries of the Christian church is an alien framework forced upon the biblical text and is a departure from biblical ways of thinking about God, this chapter has argued that there is an exegetical necessity to the triplicity within the one God. The particular point that requires Trinitarian interpretation is the kyriotic overlap made possible by the Holy Spirit as expressed in the movement of the Lukan narrative taken as a whole. To the fundamental question "Who is God in Luke-Acts?" a Trinitarian answer has been given through a probing of Luke's birth-infancy narrative as it plays out in the gospel. The triplicity within the one God "is in fact exegesis of this text. It is not . . . arbitrarily contrived speculation whose object lies elsewhere than in the Bible."[58] Thus the biblical text and the later doctrine that seeks to exegete the canon as a whole both speak about the one Lord of the OT as

---

56. See recently Bruce D. Marshall, *Trinity and Truth* (Cambridge: Cambridge University Press, 2000), 34ff.

57. I think Trinitarian theology appropriately helpful in this case even though the discussion in the excursus has of necessity been limited to Father/Son. As we have seen in the Lukan narrative, the Holy Spirit is constitutive of the relationship of the Son with the Father (for the systematic aspect, see esp. Pannenberg, *Systematic Theology*, 1:268ff.). It is interesting to note that in Paul the κύριος can also be called the Spirit (2 Cor 3:17, 18). Cf. also the third article of the Creed of Constantinople, which reads, in response to "we believe" (πιστεύομεν), "καὶ εἰς τὸ πνεῦμα τὸ ἅγιον τὸ κύριον τὸ ζωοποιόν." In this case τὸ κύριον is of necessity neuter in order to agree with τὸ πνεῦμα and corresponds grammatically and formally to the second article "ἕνα κύριον Ἰησοῦν Χριστόν."

58. Barth, *Church Dogmatics* I/1, 333.

incarnating himself in the person of Jesus by the Holy Spirit. There is a basic continuity of judgment regarding the identity of the God who made himself known in the life of the people of Israel and in the "Christ event." This continuity of judgment, however, is not finally about the intellectual agreement of a creative construal of the human mind but about the selfsame divine reality outside of the biblical text and about whom the early creeds seek to speak on the basis of the biblical text. Here, then, lies the deeper error in the line of thought espoused by Wrede, Harnack, Brunner, and Goldingay. It fails to read the Bible in light of its subject matter—that is, the actual living God outside of the text to whom the text points—and thus fails to discern the continuity of God himself as Trinity.

While it is true that the debates surrounding the creedal formulations leaned more heavily toward the "immanent" Trinity and that the biblical witness is oriented more heavily toward the "economic" Trinity,[59] these two must not be held apart but in fact are entirely complementary as seen in light of the foregoing exegesis. The economy of the one God who remains κύριος in heaven (Father) and by the Holy Spirit is κύριος as Jesus (Son) is expressive of the dynamism of God's immanent reality. Again, the point is not that the biblical writers were consciously thinking in later creedal terms. That is not the issue. Instead, the point is that of real and essential continuity between the biblical text and the later creeds with respect to the identity of God. To interpret the text in relation to the question of God's identity, not merely to repeat its storyline, is of necessity to speak of a triplicity within the one God. That is to say, the Trinitarian understanding of God is a response to the pressure exerted by the biblical text itself, as seen in the opening of Luke's Gospel, when read through the lens of the question of the identity of God.

Appendix: Selection of Significant Texts for Trinitarian Reading

While these texts are placed in a list, it is important to remember that it is not in reading the statements in themselves that their Trinitarian nature becomes apparent. Rather, to grasp the significance of these texts one must read them within the narrative as a whole.

---

59. Childs, *Biblical Theology*, 378.

Part 1: Christology, Greco-Roman Culture, and Canonical Reception

1. Gospel of Luke

Luke 1:68; 1:78–79; 19:44 read together (cf. 7:16):

1:68: κύριος ὁ θεὸς τοῦ Ἰσραήλ . . . ἐπεσκέψατο . . . τῷ λαῷ αὐτοῦ; "the Lord God of Israel . . . visited . . . his people."

1:78–79: ἐπισκέψεται ἡμᾶς ἀνατολὴ ἐξ ὕψους ἐπιφᾶναι τοῖς ἐν σκότει καὶ σκιᾷ θανάτου καθημένοις; "the dawn from on high will visit us, to appear to those sitting in darkness and in the shadow of death."

19:44: ἀνθ' ὧν οὐκ ἔγνως τὸν καιρὸν τῆς ἐπισκοπῆς σου; "because you did not know the time of your visitation" (reason for destruction).

Luke 3:16: Jesus will baptize ἐν πνεύματι ἁγίῳ.
Luke 3:21–22: baptism of Jesus (scene in its entirety).
Luke 4:1, 14: confirmation and continuation of conceptional and baptismal identity in relation to the Holy Spirit.
Luke 4:8; 24:52 read together:

4:8: κύριον τὸν θεόν σου προσκυνήσεις καὶ αὐτῷ μόνῳ λατρεύσεις (conflation of Deut 5:9 [Exod 20:5] and 6:13).

24:52: καὶ αὐτοὶ προσκυνήσαντες αὐτόν [Jesus].

Luke 4:2; 4:12 read together:

4:2: ἡμέρας τεσσεράκοντα πειραζόμενος ὑπὸ τοῦ διαβόλου.

4:12: οὐκ ἐκπειράσεις κύριον τὸν θεόν σου (Deut 6:16).

Luke 4:18: Isaiah 61:1f. citation: πνεῦμα κυρίου is upon Jesus.
Luke 5:8: Peter's reaction to Jesus: Σίμων Πέτρος προσέπεσεν τοῖς γόνασιν Ἰησοῦ λέγων, ἔξελθε ἀπ' ἐμοῦ, ὅτι ἀνὴρ ἁμαρτωλός εἰμι, κύριε!
Luke 5:17–26 (cf. 7:48f.): Jesus forgives sins; Pharisees oppose this "blasphemy" with Jewish confession μόνος ὁ θεός (the only/one God); Jesus insists on his (Son of Man's) authority to forgive sins on earth; paralytic and people glorify God.

Luke and the Trinity

Luke 7:50; 8:48, 50; 17:19: Jesus or God through Jesus as object of πίστις and worker of saving activity (σῴζω) reflects correlation of identity as σωτήρ.

Luke 8:39 (cf. 9:43; 11:20): unity of act between God and Jesus in exorcism of the Gerasene demoniac. Jesus instructs the healed demoniac to go home and tell ὅσα σοι ἐποίησεν ὁ θεός, and in response the healed demoniac preaches ὅσα ἐποίησεν αὐτῷ ὁ Ἰησοῦς.

Luke 10:21: Jesus rejoices ἐν τῷ πνεύματι τῷ ἁγίῳ and prays to Father as Lord: ἐξομολογοῦμαί σοι, πάτερ, κύριε τοῦ οὐρανοῦ καὶ τῆς γῆς.

Luke 11:13 read together with 24:49: unity of source, Father and Jesus, in the gift of the Holy Spirit: Father in heaven is the giver of the Holy Spirit (ὁ πατὴρ [ὁ] ἐξ οὐρανοῦ δώσει πνεῦμα ἅγιον τοῖς αἰτοῦσιν αὐτόν; 11:13); Jesus sends the Holy Spirit upon the disciples (ἐγὼ ἀποστέλλω τὴν ἐπαγγελίαν τοῦ πατρός μου ἐφ' ὑμᾶς . . . ὕψους δύναμιν; 24:49; cf. Acts 1:2 and 1:4 with 2:33).

Luke 13:35 and 19:38: Psalm 118:26 citation is ambiguous and precisely so as literally fulfilled in the coming of Jesus κύριος, the name of the God of the OT.

Luke 17:15–19 (13:12–13): unity of act between God and Jesus in healing. The healed Samaritan leper returns δοξάζων τὸν θεόν and prostrates himself at the feet of Jesus. Jesus asks him if none of the other healed lepers returned δοῦναι δόξαν τῷ θεῷ.

Luke 24:52–53: unity between worshiping risen and ascended Jesus and blessing/praising the God of Israel in his temple: καὶ αὐτοὶ προσκυνήσαντες αὐτὸν ὑπέστρεψαν εἰς Ἰερουσαλὴμ . . . καὶ ἦσαν διὰ παντὸς ἐν τῷ ἱερῷ εὐλογοῦντες τὸν θεόν.

Redactional observation: Luke is the only one of the gospel authors to use consistently and expansively ὁ κύριος for Jesus during his earthly ministry (Luke also unifies the alleged discrepancy between the vocative and absolute use of κύριος [e.g., 12:41–42; cf. Acts 1:21]). Cf., though, Mark 5:19!

Literary observation: Luke's narrative brackets Jesus's identity as ὁ κύριος (1:43 and 24:34). Luke 24:34 further establishes the continuity between the earthly, crucified, and risen κύριος Jesus.

2. Acts

The overlap of kyriotic identity and soteriological role is so apparent in Acts that it is not necessary to list all the important texts. I will simply make a few observations that could be followed throughout Acts.

Acts 1:24 and 4:29: prayer to Jesus and God as κύριος (cf. Acts 7:54–8:1).

Part 1: Christology, Greco-Roman Culture, and Canonical Reception

Acts 2:17–21 and Joel 3:1–5 (EV 2:28–32): the christological transformation in the overlap of κυρίου (2:20–21) necessitates a soteriological Trinitarian reading of this citation within its context in Acts. It is the God of the OT who will pour out his Spirit (God himself) such that all who call upon the name of Jesus (YHWH) will be saved. Cf. 4:12: about Jesus Christ of Nazareth (4:10–11) it is said that οὐκ ἔστιν ἐν ἄλλῳ οὐδενὶ ἡ σωτηρία οὐδὲ γὰρ ὄνομά ἐστιν ἕτερον ὑπὸ τὸν οὐρανὸν τὸ δεδομένον ἐν ἀνθρώποις ἐν ᾧ δεῖ σωθῆναι ἡμᾶς. Cf. Isaiah 52:6.

Acts 2:25–28: Christological transformation of κύριος of Psalm 16:8–11.

Acts 3:15: Jesus is the ἀρχηγὸς τῆς ζωῆς.

Acts 10:36: Jesus Christ is κύριος πάντων.

Acts 15:16–17 and Amos 9:11–12: kyriotic unity of YHWH and Jesus.

Overlap of object of πίστις: Jesus's name (3:16); the Lord (9:42; 11:17); Lord Jesus and God (16:31 with 16:34); repentance toward God and faith toward our Lord Jesus (20:21); Christ Jesus (24:24).

Overlap of content of proclamation: Word of God (4:31; 6:7; 11:1; 13:5; etc.); word of the Lord (8:25; 13:48–49; 15:36; etc.); name of Jesus (5:40; 8:12; 9:27, 11:20; etc.); kingdom of God (8:12; 19:8; 28:23, 31).

Spirit: of Lord: of God (5:3–9) and of Jesus (16:7)

Worship of humans and humanity of Jesus: Acts 10:25 and 14:8–20 in light of Luke 24:52 (cf. Luke 5:8; 17:15–19; etc.).

MS confusion: there is frequent confusion in the MS tradition over θεός and κύριος and where Jesus is meant and where God is meant (e.g., 13:44; 16:32).

The Grammar of Life

• THE AREOPAGUS SPEECH AND PAGAN TRADITION

> There are many who well understand how to view the particular, but who at the same time are unable to keep the totality *in mente*. Every such view, although otherwise meritorious, can only bring about confusion.
>
> —Søren Kierkegaard, *The Concept of Anxiety*

INTRODUCTION

The Areopagus speech in chapter 17 of the Acts of the Apostles is without a doubt one of the most striking scenes in the entire narrative.[1] It is not, as Philipp Vielhauer, Paul Schubert, and others have thought, the apogee of Acts, but the passage has played a particularly important role in the history of theology and biblical interpretation.[2]

---

1. Thus is the secondary literature on this passage almost endless. Of modern commentators on Acts, Gerhard Schneider, *Die Apostelgeschichte*, 2 vols., HThKNT (Freiburg: Herder, 1980–1982), 2:234, offers the most helpful delineation of the main lines of scholarship. Though of course more has been written since the publication of Schneider's second volume, his brief outline remains a trustworthy guide to the intellectual map of past interpretation. Émile Beurlier, "Saint Paul et L'Aréopage," *Revue d'histoire et de littérature religieuses* 1 (1896): 344–66, is concise for the patristic period.

2. That a scholar as observant as Jacob Jervell, *Die Apostelgeschichte: Übersetzt und erklärt*, KEK 3 (Göttingen: Vandenhoeck & Ruprecht, 1998), 453, can call the Areopagus speech an "Intermezzo" should immediately caution against any overstatement of the scene's narrative importance. See Philipp Vielhauer, "On the 'Paulinism' of Acts," in *Studies in Luke-*

"The Grammar of Life: The Areopagus Speech and Pagan Tradition" was originally published in *New Testament Studies* 57 (2011): 31–50. It is reproduced with permission.

Part 1: Christology, Greco-Roman Culture, and Canonical Reception

As early as the second century, Christian exegetes were keen to draw attention to the allusions to the texts, critical thought, and common practice of the Greco-Roman world in Paul's speech as a way to develop an account of the pagan knowledge of God.[3] In establishing the connections between Jesus and Socrates—and thus between Christian revelation and pagan theological knowledge—Justin Martyr, for example, drew attention to the fact that Socrates above all others had encouraged the Athenians to come to know "the unknown God."[4] And shortly thereafter, that connoisseur and critic of all intellectual finery, Clement of Alexandria, read Paul's use of the *Phaenomena* of Aratus as precedent for his own argument that pagan philosophy had indeed attained to truth in serious theological matters.[5] Further on, in the Latin West, Ambrose of Milan cited 17:27–28 as evidence of all humanity's participation in God and the capacity of reason that followed therefrom: grounded as it is in God's own supreme rationality, argued Ambrose, our corresponding rational nature predisposes and enables us all to seek God.[6] Thomas Aquinas would

---

Acts, ed. Leander E. Keck and J. Louis Martyn (Philadelphia: Fortress, 1966), 33–50, esp. 34; and Paul Schubert, "The Place of the Areopagus Speech in the Composition of Acts," in *Transitions in Biblical Scholarship*, ed. J. Coert Rylaarsdam (Chicago: University of Chicago Press, 1968), 235–61, esp. 261.

3. Examples of pagan tradition that were evident to early Christians are too numerous to name. We shall mention only one particularly striking example known to Acts commentators for a long time: for Origen the echoes of Socrates's trial reverberated so loud through the scene in Athens that he believed Socrates himself to have been tried before the Areopagus. Of course, Socrates was not tried before the Areopagus but before the People's Court in the agora. The fact that Origen thought the council was the Areopagus simply shows the power of Luke's story to evoke analogically shaped "historical" connections.

4. Justin Martyr, 2 *Apol.* 10.6 (πρὸς θεοῦ δὲ τοῦ ἀγνώστου αὐτοῖς διὰ λογοῦ ζητήσεως ἐπίγνωσιν προὐτρέπετο εἰπών . . .). I use here the critical edition of Miroslav Marcovich, *Iustini Martyris Apologiae Pro Christianis* (Berlin: de Gruyter, 1994). Marcovich also notes the possible allusion to Acts 17:23 (p. 28). There remains serious debate on the issue of Justin's knowledge of Acts (or lack thereof). For a judicious discussion, see Andrew Gregory, *The Reception of Luke and Acts in the Period before Irenaeus: Looking for Luke in the Second Century*, WUNT 2/169 (Tübingen: Mohr Siebeck, 2003), 317–21.

5. Clement of Alexandria, *Strom.* 1.19. The *Phaenomena* of Aratus was a wildly popular book by ancient standards. It was translated into Latin by no less a man than Cicero himself and also—in a very unusual move at that time—translated into Arabic.

6. Ambrose, *Epistola* 43 (to Horontianus). For the Greek East, see Jaroslav Pelikan's excellent treatment of the Cappadocians in *Christianity and Classical Culture: The Metamorphosis of Natural Theology in the Christian Encounter with Hellenism* (New Haven: Yale University Press, 1993). Though it is sometimes implicit, throughout the book Pelikan relates the Cappadocians' theological self-understanding and methods to Paul's speech (see esp., e.g., 167, where Acts 17:22-28 is cited as the overall framework for part 2 of Pelikan's book).

later agree. In the very first question of his *Summa*, Aquinas states that "holy teaching uses the authority of philosophers who have been able to perceive the truth by natural reasoning, for instance when St Paul quotes the saying of Aratus."[7] Later interpreters such as John Calvin perhaps focused more on Paul's "apologetic" strategy—his attempt to establish common ground with the Athenians as a way to convince them of the superior truth of the Christian gospel—but the underlying premise was basically the same as it was in the preceding exegesis: pagans may not yet have attained to fullness of Christian knowledge, but inasmuch as Aratus and others testified to the truth, they were doubtless on the way.[8]

With few exceptions,[9] modern NT scholars have for the most part simply reproduced the earlier readings, albeit with less overt philosophical analysis and a closer focus upon Luke's own role in shaping Paul's speech.[10] Indeed, it has long been a scholarly commonplace in the modern period to contrast Paul's rejection of natural theology in Romans 1 with Acts 17 as a way to differentiate Paul's own theology from Luke's supposedly rather un-Pauline formu-

---

7. Thomas Aquinas, *Summa Theologiae* Ia.1.8.2. I am aware of the debate over how best to construe Aquinas's understanding of "natural knowledge" (i.e., it is not an alternative to theological knowledge). But such matters cannot occupy us here.

8. See Calvin's *Commentary on Acts*, esp. his remarks on 17:22-34. That the Areopagus text was important to Calvin's thinking about the knowledge of God may be seen easily enough in the first chapter of book 1 of the *Institutes* (1.1.1; 1.5.3, etc.). Reflection on the "apologetic" dimension of Paul's speech occurred in the earlier period, too, of course. Indeed, for the view that Athenagoras's distinction between arguments "on behalf of the truth" and "concerning the truth" owes its intellectual foundations to Paul's Areopagus discourse, see T. F. Torrance, "Phusikos kai Theologikos Logos, St Paul and Athenagoras at Athens," *SJT* 41 (1988): 11-26. As far as I can discern, Athenagoras does not actually cite Acts 17, but Torrance may well be correct that the structure of his thought—at least as Torrance himself presents it—reflects a careful consideration of Paul's speech. For the connection between Paul's speech and the early Apologists, see the concise article of H. Gebhardt, "Die an die Heiden gerichtete Missionsrede der Apostel und das Johannesevangelium," *ZNW* 6 (1905): 236-49.

9. See, e.g., C. K. Barrett, *A Critical and Exegetical Commentary on the Acts of the Apostles*, 2 vols., ICC (Edinburgh: T&T Clark, 1994-1998), 2:850-51.

10. Analyzing the speeches in Acts has long been a kind of cottage industry in NT studies. Of course there has also been some debate over the question of cultural influence on Paul's speech, with Dibelius far on one side (pagan) and Gärtner on the other (Jewish). But most NT scholars would now view such Hellenistic/Jewish dichotomies as unnecessary, particularly when dealing with a culturally complex figure such as Luke. Furthermore, attention to the animating narrative moves of Acts as a whole precludes the ability to abstract "pagan" from "Jewish" elements when thinking about the Areopagus discourse: Acts is plainly concerned with both aspects of Mediterranean life and weaves them inseparably into the fabric of the text.

Part 1: Christology, Greco-Roman Culture, and Canonical Reception

lations.[11] Even where the contrast with Paul would not be drawn so sharply, the reading of Luke's material theological position has been, by and large, the same.[12] Major commentators—Conzelmann, Johnson, Fitzmyer, and so on—and other astute readers of Acts have all taken the Areopagus speech to argue for a deep theological *Anknüpfungspunkt* between pagan philosophical thinking and Paul's proclamation. Common vocabulary—the citation and allusions to pagan tradition—entails theological commensurability.[13]

What is remarkable about this long history of reading Acts 17 is that it constitutes a relatively stable and coherent hermeneutical tradition in spite of all the manifest differences in time, geographical location, historical analysis, argumentative focus, philosophical commitments, philological skill, felicity in expression, and so forth. When all is said and done, the Areopagus speech still emerges clearly as a kind of locus classicus for "natural theology."[14] To be sure, there remain substantive differences between, on the one hand, those who would make a distinction between analytical judgments that are cognitively correct *in se* (e.g., Acts 17:28) and the actual theological awareness of the speakers of those judgments (the "poets"),[15] and, on the other, those who would see no need to differentiate, for example, the epistemic status of Aratus's theological understanding of humanity's origins from a Jewish or Christian self-understanding (e.g., from the ancient world, Aristobulus; see below). Still, with more or less precision, the vast majority of Acts' interpreters take the presupposition of Luke's argument in chapter 17 to be that human beings as such—irrespective of the kind of knowledge marked by the names Israel and the church—know the one true God from the world he made and/or an

---

11. Vielhauer's article cited in n. 2 above is of course the classic statement of this position.

12. E.g., F. F. Bruce, *The Book of the Acts* (Grand Rapids: Eerdmans, 1954), 345–68; or Rudolf Pesch, *Die Apostelgeschichte*, 2 vols., EKKNT 5 (Neukirchener-Vluyn: Neukirchener Verlag, 1986), 2:141–42.

13. E.g., Paul Walaskay, *Acts* (Louisville: Westminster John Knox, 1998), 166: Paul is "far removed from the world of the Bible"; his "address was a reflection on Stoic theology." Stephen G. Wilson, *The Gentiles and the Gentile Mission in Luke-Acts*, SNTSMS 23 (Cambridge: Cambridge University Press, 1973), 214: Luke thinks the Gentiles' "basic response [is] correct but misguided."

14. See, e.g., the brief remarks of Daniel Marguerat, "Paul après Paul: une histoire de réception," *NTS* 54 (2008): 319. There were exceptions in the ancient world, too, of course. John Chrysostom, for example, took the logic of Paul's speech to be entirely critical rather than an attempt to establish common ground or engage in Christian apologetics (*Homiliae in Acta apostolorum*, Homily 38).

15. In more traditional language, this is the difference between the order of being and the order of knowledge.

introspectively generated awareness of his presence and/or philosophical anthropology.[16] It may be that such knowledge is in need of supplementation or even correction, but true knowledge of the true God it nevertheless remains.[17] Perhaps Clement said it best: "It is evident," wrote Clement, "that by employing poetic examples from the *Phaenomena* of Aratus, [Paul] approves of the well-spoken words of the Greeks and discloses that through the 'unknown God' the Creator God [τὸν δημιουργὸν θεόν] was in a roundabout way honored by the Greeks."[18]

Given the power and longevity of this way of thinking, it is really no less remarkable that this is not what Acts 17 actually argues. Indeed, whatever the merits of larger theories about a philosophically or experientially based natural theology, they cannot be earned on the basis of a close reading of Acts 17. Paul's Areopagus speech is not a paean of the Greek intellectual or spiritual achievement. It is instead the presentation of an alternative pattern of life.

---

16. See James Barr's chapter on the speech in *Biblical Faith and Natural Theology* (Oxford: Oxford University Press, 1994). In a sense Barr is right, of course, that the "importance of the Areopagus speech for traditional natural theology is too obvious to require exemplification" (21 n. 1). Yet it is helpful nevertheless to see something of the cumulative hermeneutical weight of a particular way of reading the speech. Paul's speech is not without its importance in other spheres of argumentation: we might remember, for example, Milton's *Areopagitica* (pub. 1644), whose allusive title recalled not only Isocrates's discourse but also Paul's. It was, says Milton, "especially Paul" who saw no contradiction in the attempt to insert the wisdom of the Greek poets into Holy Scripture. Milton's larger point was about censorship, and his actual political position was more dissimilar than similar to that of Isocrates (Milton obviously favored less censorship). This is simply to note that Paul's speech actually works somewhat better for Milton's purposes than Isocrates's: in Milton's way of seeing things, Paul had at least been able to read the Greeks.

17. Clement of Alexandria, *Strom.* 1.19. Subtle exegetes have attempted to distinguish between various degrees of "supplementation" or "correction"—the philosophers need less correction than the wider populace. See, e.g., the article of Gerhard Schneider, "Anknüpfung, Kontinuität und Widerspruch in der Areopagrede Apg 17,22-31," in *Kontinuität und Einheit*, ed. Paul-Gerhard Müller and Werner Stenger (Freiburg: Herder, 1981), 173-78, wherein the "Widerspruch" is explicated entirely in terms of the Christians and Stoics together over against the everyday pagan. Rudolf Bultmann, "Anknüpfung und Widerspruch: Zur Frage nach der Anknüpfung der neutestamentlichen Verkündigung an die natürliche Theologie der Stoa, die hellenistischen Mysterienreligionen und die Gnosis," *Theologische Zeitschrift* 2 (1946): 401-18, is typically thought-provoking: for Bultmann, the *Anknüpfung* just is the *Widerspruch*.

18. The critical text is that of Otto Stählin (updated by Ludwig Früchtel), *Clemens Alexandrinus* II, Die griechischen christlichen Schriftsteller 15 (Berlin: Academie, 1960), here 58-59. Perhaps the most interesting contemporary reading on this question is—unsurprisingly—the Gifford Lectures (e.g., Gilson, Barth, Pelikan, Barr, Hauerwas, et al.).

Part 1: Christology, Greco-Roman Culture, and Canonical Reception

The remainder of this chapter shall be devoted to a rereading of Acts 17 on the assumption that this long interpretive history has by and large worked within a restricted ambit of thought and, therefore, contributed fundamentally to the occlusion of the exegetical vision needed to grasp the pattern of Lukan reasoning in this passage. After establishing the necessary exegetical basis on which to reflect hermeneutically about the meaning of Paul's discourse, the chapter will conclude with a final statement about the direction of our thought if it is to follow (or not) the argument of Acts 17.

Exegesis

In order to see clearly the shape of Luke's theology as it is expressed in Acts 17, we must think several things simultaneously. Because, however, we obviously cannot write about them all simultaneously, we shall have to discuss these matters in order on the way to comprehending their significance with a single glance. There are five principal points.

(1) The Hermeneutical Narrative Context of the Speech: Analyses of the speeches in Acts have been crucially important in demonstrating beyond reasonable doubt that Luke wrote them himself (as did ancient historiographers more generally).[19] But this focus also courts a hermeneutical danger, namely, the substitution of a different interpretive context—that of the scholarly template provided for speech analysis—for the one Luke has created through the construction of his narrative.[20] As more recent scholarship has shown, ignoring the hermeneutical importance of narrative is hardly the way to develop a sophisticated reading of a passage whose meaning is inextricably tied to the overall development of a whole story.[21] In relation to the Areopagus speech,

---

19. As is well known, NT scholars have frequently looked for Luke's sources for his speeches. My formulation above is not intended to deny that Luke may well have had access to traditions/sources that helped him shape the speeches (or even exercised both formal and material restraints upon his literary creativity); its intent, rather, is simply to point to the significance of something recent scholarship has made unavoidable: any argument for a source/tradition behind the speeches must pass through the elegant and consistent manner by which Luke—throughout the speeches in Acts—has rendered literarily that which he has received. See also n. 43 below.

20. See C. Kavin Rowe, "Acts 2:36 and the Continuity of Lukan Christology," *NTS* 53 (2007): 37–56, reprinted in this volume at pp. 179–200.

21. See, e.g., Joel B. Green, "The Problem of a Beginning: Israel's Scriptures in Luke 1–2," *BBR* 4, no. 1 (1994): 61–85.

this point becomes particularly important due to the interpretively indispensable remarks that preface the entire speech:

> While Paul was waiting for them at Athens, his spirit was vexed within him as he saw that the city was full of idols. So he argued ... in the marketplace every day with those who chanced to be there. Some of the Epicurean and Stoic philosophers also met him; and some said, "What would this poser say?" Others said, "He seems to be a preacher of foreign divinities"—because Paul had preached Jesus [masc.] and the resurrection [fem.]. And they seized him and brought him to the Areopagus, saying, "We have the right to know what this new teaching is you present. For you bring some strange things to our ears. We want to know, therefore, what these things mean." (17:16–20; my translation)

The point of hermeneutically preparatory remarks, of course, is to position the reader in certain ways rather than others prior to the coming material. In this case, Luke positions his readers in at least three particularly significant ways. First, by narrating Paul's reaction to Athens as a whole—he is "vexed" at its rampant "idolatry"—Luke points explicitly to the overriding theological evaluation of the city's spiritual and intellectual traditions (17:16). Whatever the rich cultural heritage of Athens, Paul's focus lies elsewhere—that is, on the malformation of religious life.

Second, the term used by the Stoics and Epicureans to disparage Paul's philosophical sophistication draws on the larger cultural encyclopedia to alert the reader to watch for coming allusions to pagan works. Σπερμολόγος, as Demosthenes, Dio Chrysostom, and other public intellectuals knew, was a word used to brand opponents as posers, loafers in the agora who had, at best, picked up a few prooftexts from one of the florilegia floating around the cities.[22] Their "scraps" of knowledge, so the term suggests, hardly amounted to true philosophical understanding. Of course, by this point in the discourse of Acts, those who insult the main characters utter judgments that the readers of the narrative simply distrust. No Christian reader of Acts would think to agree with the slur of the Stoics and Epicureans. To the contrary, through Luke's careful frontloading of this spurious charge, Acts' readers are both inoculated against such a suspicion—it is gotten out of the way, as it were—and encouraged to discern in the coming allusions to pagan philosophical/religious traditions a deep argumentative significance.

22. E.g., Demosthenes, *De corona* 18.127 [269]; Dio Chrysostom, *Disc.* 32.9.

Third, it is noteworthy that Paul is actually on trial. This fact has often been overlooked by NT scholars who assume that the phrase ἐπὶ τὸν Ἄρειον πάγον refers simply to the hill of Ares where Paul made his speech. But in fact, "the Areopagus" refers more precisely to ἡ ἐξ Ἀρείου πάγου Βουλή, which, unsurprisingly, took its name from its meeting place: the hill of Ares. As T. D. Barnes convincingly showed, the frequent assertion that the council no longer met at this place is basically groundless.[23] Its sole piece of (alleged) hard ancient evidence is a single statement in Pseudo-Demosthenes, and even that has now been discredited by Barnes. The reason, therefore, that Luke does not distinguish between "Areopagus as hill upon which Paul spoke" and "Areopagus as city council before which Paul spoke" is that such a distinction would have been pointless.

Moreover, it is exceedingly difficult to make sense of Luke's use of ἐπιλαμβάνομαι and the phrase ἐν μέσῳ on the idea that Paul was simply and cordially escorted to the hill for a better audience (17:19, 22). The former word is most often used in the Lukan writings to refer to the "seizing" or "laying hold of" the Christians,[24] and the latter is almost always "amidst."[25] So, too, δύναμαι in δυνάμεθα γνῶναι τίς ἡ καινὴ αὕτη ἡ ὑπὸ σοῦ λαλουμένη διδαχή (17:19) is not the polite "may we" of the RSV, etc. but more like "we have the [legal] right to know," as in Acts 25:11 or P.Oxy. 899 (line 31; second/third centuries).[26] In short, Paul was seized and brought to the tribunal that had the legal right to try him for the specific charges brought against him (see below), and it is in the midst of this council that he speaks and from which he departs (17:33; ἐξῆλθεν ἐκ μέσου αὐτῶν). As Barnes rightly observed, "The obvious meaning of the words in Acts should be accepted: Paul was taken before the Areopagus, i.e. before the council sitting on the hill."[27]

A trial setting is also presupposed by the deep resonance with Socrates's famous trial, in which the crime of "introducing new/strange divinities" figured

---

23. Timothy D. Barnes, "An Apostle on Trial," *JTS* 20 (1969): 407–19.

24. Cf. esp. Acts 16:19 where Luke, as he does here in 17:19, employs ἐπιλαμβάνομαι with the preposition ἐπί in order to speak about Paul and Silas's appearance before certain authorities: "Having seized [ἐπιλαβόμενοι] Paul and Silas, they dragged them into the agora ἐπὶ τοὺς ἄρχοντας" (cf. ἐπὶ τοὺς πολιτάρχας in 17:6). See also Luke 23:26; Acts 16:19; 17:6; 18:17; 21:30, 33. Cf. Jerome's translation of ἐπιλαμβάνομαι in 17:19 as *apprehendere* (*et apprehensum eum ad Areopagum duxerunt*).

25. Cf. esp. Acts 27:21: σταθεὶς ὁ Παῦλος ἐν μέσῳ αὐτῶν εἶπεν· ἔδει μέν, ὦ ἄνδρες; see also Luke 2:46; 8:7; 10:3; 22:27; 24:36; Acts 1:15; 2:22.

26. LSJ 452.

27. Barnes, "Apostle on Trial," 410.

prominently.[28] From Xenophon and Plato to Josephus and Justin Martyr, the ancients spoke of the charges against Socrates in terms of his attempt to bring into Athens new or strange deities, and of the corresponding rejection of the gods of the polis.[29] Diogenes Laertius, for example, who evidently believed that he was citing from the original affidavit, wrote that "Socrates is guilty of refusing to recognize the gods recognized by the polis, and of introducing other, new divinities."[30] Obviously Luke could not have read Diogenes Laertius; nor do we have any firm evidence that he knew Xenophon or Plato. But the similarity between Luke's careful phrasing and the grammatical fundament upon which ancient testimony is constructed would be obvious to anyone acquainted with the philosophic or even popular traditions surrounding the death of Socrates: ξένων δαιμονίων (v. 18), ἡ καινὴ αὕτη ἡ διδαχή, ξενίζοντα, εἰσφέρεις (vv. 19–20), ξένοι, καινότερον (v. 21).

Indeed, Athens itself was reputed to be a place of considerable risk for all who would deal in foreign religious matters, as figures from Euripides to Josephus were well aware. Citing the case of Ninus the priestess, for example, Josephus informs his readers that in Athens the "penalty decreed for any who introduced a foreign god was death."[31] And despite being the home of antiquity's greatest thinkers and scholars, wrote Apuleius, the city's treatment of Socrates had nevertheless resulted in its "perpetual ignominy":[32] Athens was the place where everyone knew that to bring in foreign or new deities was to invite trial and court death.

Luke's culturally careful and philologically precise narration creates the analogical space in which the trial of Socrates informs that of Paul. Readers of Acts are thereby enabled to see in the seizure of Paul the potential for death. Like Socrates, Paul appears before the governing Athenian council under the

---

28. It is important to note that the interpretive move runs the other way as well: the Socratic echoes also rightfully reinforce the reading of the scene as a trial. That Socrates was tried in the People's Court does not substantively alter the impact of the resonance: it merely helps to describe more precisely the actual shape of the analogy.

29. The other charge frequently reported was that of "corrupting the youth"—which was in essence yet another political charge. On this point, see Peter Garnsey, "Religious Toleration in Classical Antiquity," in *Persecution and Toleration*, ed. W. J. Shells (London: Blackwell, 1984), 1-27.

30. Diogenes Laertius, *Lives* 2.40. Cf., e.g., Xenophon, *Memorabilia* 1.1.1, 3, et passim; Plato, *Apologia* 24BC, 28E–30E et passim; Josephus, *C. Ap.* 2.262-264; Justin Martyr, *1 Apol.* 5.4.

31. Josephus, *C. Ap.* 2.267-68. Cf. Euripides, *Bacchae*, lines 255-59.

32. Apuleius, *Metam.* 10.33.

suspicion of introducing strange, new deities (Jesus and Resurrection), and, like Socrates, Paul may well meet his end.

(2) Δεισιδαίμων: NT exegetes have frequently observed that Paul's opening line can be read in standard terms as a *captatio benevolentiae*: "And Paul, standing in the middle of the Areopagus, said, 'Men of Athens, I perceive that you are exceptionally religious [δεισιδαιμονέστερος] in every way'" (17:22).[33] As all ancient rhetors and important councils knew—and as Luke clearly did himself (see esp. Acts 24:2–3, for example)—such a move was a conventional way to win goodwill at the outset of a case. To read Paul's sally in this way presupposes, of course, that δεισιδαιμονέστερος is best rendered "exceptionally religious" rather than "superstitious" (another entirely valid meaning of the word).[34] Opening one's *apologia* with a highly charged and well-known insult—"I perceive that you are all *superstitious*"—would hardly qualify as a rhetorically suave *captatio benevolentiae*: as a way to angle for one's life in political waters, it would seem rather inexpedient, to say the least.

Yet, as other scholars have seen, the reader is well aware that Paul is already vexed at the city's rampant idolatry.[35] It would therefore make more sense, so this line of thinking goes, to read δεισιδαιμονέστερος in accordance with 17:16. As Luke tells it, Paul does not think the Athenians are particularly pious but exceptionally superstitious—or in Jewish theological language, idolatrous.

But in fact, as Hans-Josef Klauck has rightly observed, to believe one is forced to choose between these two readings is already to have missed the Lukan literary technique and ruined its point. For δεισιδαιμονέστερος is at

---

33. E.g., Ernst Haenchen, *The Acts of the Apostles: A Commentary*, trans. Bernard Noble and Gerald Shinn, rev. R. McL. Wilson (Philadelphia: Westminster, 1971), 520. See, however, Apuleius, *Metam.* 10.7, and Lucian, *Anacharsis*, or *Athletics* 19, both of whom speak of the dangers of trying to influence the Areopagus through rhetorical maneuvering.

34. Haenchen, *Acts of the Apostles*, 520, thinks that "superstition" is an entirely modern concept. If by this Haenchen means to say that we as moderns know that the tricks involved in palm-reading, crystals, etc. are nothing but tricks—and therefore unreal and untrue in some sort of metaphysical sense—then of course he is right. The conception of the cosmos that buttressed the seriousness with which the ancients took their soothsayers is no longer ours. However, if we simply understand "superstitious" to mean a kind of gross exaggeration and distortion of otherwise common features of religious life in the ancient world (as does Plutarch in his *De superstitione*, for example), then our translation is on solid ground. On this matter and the word itself, see P. J. Koets, Δεισιδαιμονία: *A Contribution to the Knowledge of the Religious Terminology in Greek* (Purmerend: Muusses, 1929), and, more recently, Dale B. Martin, *Inventing Superstition: From the Hippocratics to the Christians* (Cambridge, MA: Harvard University Press, 2004).

35. See the concise discussion in Barrett, *Acts*, 2:836.

one and the same time "exceptionally religious" and "quite superstitious."[36] That is to say, in the story world, the Areopagus hears the former—the Paul of Acts does not blunder verbally so badly or so quickly—while the reader, who is positioned hermeneutically by vv. 16–21, also hears the latter. To be sure, translation into English obscures the simultaneity of meaning in the one Greek word. But this should hardly be the cause of interpretive error. Luke's point is rather clear. Through a deft use of dramatic irony, Luke unifies historical verisimilitude—and rhetorical skill—with theological judgment and, precisely in so doing, alerts the readers of Paul's speech to its multilevel discourse.[37] Grasping the import of the speech, therefore, will involve considerably more than a flat or simplistic reading at a single level of meaning. At the very least, it will involve the ability to comprehend the rhetorical simultaneity of different levels of meaning.

(3) "An unknown god": In the pyramid of well-known phrases from the Areopagus speech, "to an unknown god" would surely vie with "in him we live and move and have our being" for the top. Though we have yet to discover an inscription with θεὸς ἄγνωστος in the singular, this fact is of little to no interpretive consequence.[38] More significant is Paul's attempt to tie this inscription together with a theology of creation. Given the charge of "newness," it is unsurprising that Luke depicts Paul's first argumentative move as an effort to rebuff this charge. "What you worship unknowingly,"[39] this I proclaim to you." I do not, implies Paul, bring in anything new at all. Rather, the one to whom I testify has preceded me here in Athens.

It is perhaps this remark more than any other that has led interpreters of the NT to think that Paul here extols the Athenians' theological knowledge—that

---

36. E.g., Hans-Josef Klauck, *Magic and Paganism in Early Christianity: The World of the Acts of the Apostles* (Edinburgh: T&T Clark, 1999), 81–82. See also Daniel Marguerat, "Luc-Actes entre Jérusalem et Rome: Un procédé lucanien de double signification," *NTS* 45 (1999): 70–87, esp. 75. Marguerat's article provides multiple instances of Luke's semantic skill in constructing purposefully ambiguous statements.

37. On dramatic irony as a major Lukan literary technique, see C. Kavin Rowe, *Early Narrative Christology: The Lord in the Gospel of Luke* (2006; repr., Grand Rapids: Baker Academic, 2009).

38. See, e.g., P. W. van der Horst, "The Unknown God," in *Knowledge of God in the Graeco-Roman World*, ed. R. van den Broek, T. Baarda, and J. Mansfeld (Leiden: Brill, 1988), 19–42.

39. It is possible to read the participle ἀγνοοῦντες as yet another instance of dramatic irony: if one translates "unknowingly" for the ears of the Areopagus, Paul's statement is much less offensive—because theologically critical—than if one translates "ignorantly." Again: the connotative difference exists in Greek in the same word; it is only in English that the choice must be made.

Part 1: Christology, Greco-Roman Culture, and Canonical Reception

is, that Luke portrays Paul as the consummate natural theologian. Long has the Unknown God been known in Athens!

Such a reading would hardly be unreasonable were it not for the fact that what Luke actually speaks of is not knowledge but *ignorance* of God. Such is the point of the alpha-privative—the God about whom Paul testifies remains unknown in Athens. The inscription "to the unknown God," when taken literally, is thus to be read not as commendation of the Athenians' theological penetration but instead as Athenian self-testimony to their need for the kind of knowledge that comes with Paul's preaching. In short, the Athenians worship in ignorance and, as a precise epistemological correlate of this fact, do not know it.

(4) Aratus and the Rest: Understanding that Paul must avoid the charge of "newness" should remove any surprise at Paul's transition from the (now) famous inscription to theological criticism of a kind that could be found among many pagan philosophers. Modern theologians who naturally agree with the declaration οὐκ ἐν χειροποιήτοις ναοῖς κατοικεῖ οὐδὲ ὑπὸ χειρῶν ἀνθρωπίνων θεραπεύεται προσδεόμενός τινος (17:24–25) need do no more to remember its seriousness in the ancient world than reread Pausanias, who reports virtually countless instances of caring for divine images. The ivory statue of Athena on the Acropolis in Athens, to take a geographically relevant example from Pausanias's ramblings, was treated with water to counteract the destructive effects of an overly arid location. And, even restricting ourselves to the same passage in Pausanias, we learn also that the image of Zeus in Olympus was regularly saturated with olive oil, and that of Asclepius in Epidarus built over a cistern.[40]

But of course this is unsurprising. Images of the gods were wiped down, scraped clean, brought food, proffered mirrors—if they happened to be vain enough—chained, put on trial, exiled, and so on. In short, both in their shrines and without, they were the objects of a whole range of practices that could be seen, under the gaze of the philosopher's eye, as crude statements about divinity itself. Divinity, such practices might imply, was tied essentially to its images and, therefore, could be said to require all manner of shelter and ministrations. Socrates, Plato, Varro, Seneca, Epictetus, Plutarch, the much-maligned and little-understood "atheists," the Epicureans—the list could go on and on—all inveighed against such superstition and endeavored to sever the connection between crass conceptions of materially determined divinity and, as they saw it, divinity properly conceived. As Seneca once put it: "To beings who are

---

40. Pausanias, *Descr.* 5.11.10–11.

sacred, immortal and inviolable, [people] consecrate images of the cheapest inert material. [These images] are called divinities, but if they were suddenly brought to life and encountered, they would be regarded as monsters."[41]

Paul's statement in vv. 24–25 resonates well with such sentiments and, in so doing, connects pieces of philosophical grammar to his theological discourse. Indeed, this is but the initial move in a continuing effort to speak with easily recognizable words of pagan tradition. When in 17:27, for example, Paul proclaims that "God is not far from each one of us," he could be paraphrasing his contemporary Seneca: "We do not need . . . to beg the keeper of a temple to let us approach his image's ear, as if in this way our prayers were more likely to be heard. God is near you, he is with you, he is in you."[42] "In him we live and move and have our being" (17:28a) evokes a wide enough range of familiar philosophical thinking to have scholars scurrying from Plato to Posidonius and Epimenides to Epictetus in the effort to ferret out Luke's "source."[43] And, as all Acts scholars know, when Luke writes, "As even some of your poets have said . . ." (17:28), he then immediately cites one of the opening lines of Aratus's *Phaenomena*, a book whose ancient fame would be hard to overestimate: τοῦ γὰρ καὶ γένος εἰμέν (*Phaenomena* 5; Acts 17:28b, ἐσμέν). Of course, Aratus himself may well echo the commencement of Cleanthes's *Hymn to Zeus*.[44] If so, Luke's citation draws easily upon two layers of well-known tradition and seamlessly orchestrates their incorporation into the movement of the discourse. In short, Luke constructs Paul's *apologia* as an argument against the charge of bringing in new/strange divinities by means of an apparently appeasing recognition and reception of pagan philosophical traditions vis-à-vis "divinity" or "the Deity" (esp. 17:29).

---

41. Seneca, *De superstitione* (*apud* Augustine, *De civitate Dei* 6.10); cf., among many possible examples, Plutarch's *Numa* 8.7–8 or his *De superstitione*, esp. 167.

42. Seneca, *Ep.* 41.1; cf., inter alios, Dio Chrysostom, *Disc.* 12.28.

43. This is yet another place where a better sense of Luke's literary style would serve us well. Just to the degree that we comprehend that Luke is not a rigid copyist or a wooden interpreter of the texts and traditions he knows, we will find unnecessary the need to search for a "source" from which Luke derived his philosophical-sounding sentences. Indeed, the whole search for a source can be interpreted as the effect of the power of allusion—as Luke here puts it to work—upon modern scholars of his text. That is, we do not search for a source to understand Luke's text but, to the contrary, precisely because we already move within the sphere created by the allusion. In Gadamer's terms, the search for a source is not to go behind the text as we have it but rather is itself a part of the text's effective history and, in a sense, counts as a certain kind of evidence that we have already understood at least part of what Luke means to say.

44. *SVF* 1.537 (pp. 121–22).

Part 1: Christology, Greco-Roman Culture, and Canonical Reception

It is tempting to read this as a theology of rapprochement, a rhetorically suave defense against "newness" and "foreignness" that works precisely because it establishes an equivalence between what Paul preaches and what the wisest pagans have always known. On this reading, Paul's proclamation and certain constitutive aspects of pagan philosophical thinking point to the same truth. Luke thus presents Paul in the hermeneutically charged act of "translation."[45]

Of course, to translate something is simply to say the same thing in another language. As any who have thought about translation could testify, however, even the easiest cases, when scrutinized, can turn out to be mortifyingly difficult.[46] In this case, to speak of "same-saying" posits a basic synonymy between two fundamentally different grammars for the whole of life—pagan and Christian—on the basis of a vocabulary common to Luke's argument and classic pagan texts and traditions of thought.[47] To be sure, various and sundry attempts at same-saying or translation were common in the ancient world. The second-century Jewish thinker Aristobulus, to take only one salient example, also cited the opening praise of Zeus in Aratus's *Phaenomena* and simply substituted "God" for "Zeus." As Aristobulus put it, the "inherent meaning" of the latter was finally the same as the former.[48] But reading Paul's speech

---

45. See, e.g., the classic statement by Martin Dibelius, "Paul in Athens," in *Studies in the Acts of the Apostles* (London: SCM, 1956), 78-83: the Areopagus speech is a "manner of constructing a Christian theology not on biblical, but on philosophical, especially Stoic, ideas" (82). The fundamental translational assumption here of course is that a Christian theology actually could be erected on a Stoic basis. For a more recent example, see, among many possible options, Ben Witherington III, *The Acts of the Apostles: A Socio-rhetorical Commentary* (Grand Rapids: Eerdmans, 1998), who asserts that Paul "is making a proclamation of monotheism in its Christian form" (518). Unwittingly perhaps, such a formulation treats Christianity as a subset of a more general theological reality ("monotheism"). In this way of thinking, monotheism is the ultimate truth toward which both pagan philosophy and Christianity point, and is therefore the theological ground that makes possible a genuine translation: pagan philosophy and Christianity are ultimately about the same thing, as it were, even though they use different languages to speak of it. Whether Witherington intends this or not is unclear, for later in the commentary he seems both to retreat from this statement and to reaffirm it (534-35). That many scholars take "monotheism" to be the theological essence of Christianity, the "highest" form of religion in general, and so forth needs no elaboration. See, e.g., the introduction by Polymnia Athanassiadi and Michael Frede, eds., *Pagan Monotheism in Late Antiquity* (Oxford: Clarendon, 1999), 1-20.

46. Think, for example, of the multifaceted questions that one must engage to explain Luther's translation of ἐκκλησία not by *Kirche* but by *Gemeinde*.

47. See below on ancient philosophy as a way of life.

48. Eusebius, *Praep. ev.* 13.12. For the text and translation of Aristobulus, see Carl R.

86

through the conceptual grid of "translation" entirely overlooks the crucial fact that in Luke's text the pagan philosophical vocabulary has been incorporated into a radically different overall interpretive framework: the biblical story that stretches from Adam to the return of Jesus Christ.

(5) Creation to Consummation: Whether or not Luke knew Paul's thinking in Romans 5:12-21 is debatable, but it is nonetheless significant that the "story" Luke tells in Paul's Areopagus speech narrates the human drama in relation to Adam on the one hand and Jesus Christ on the other. Of course, Luke's Paul is attentive to his immediate context and so employs his rhetorical skill accordingly: neither figure is overtly named. And this makes good political sense: the denizens of the Athenian court know of neither man. But it is beyond doubt that the Christian readers of Acts know the identity of the man whom God raised from the dead and appointed to judge the world in righteousness (17:31).[49] No less clear is the identity of the "one" from whom God made "every nation of humanity to dwell on the whole face of the earth" (17:26).[50] For Luke no less than for Jews or other early Christians, it is in Adam that humanity has its origins (cf. Luke 3:38).

By situating human existence within God's creative purpose in Adam and eschatological end in Jesus Christ, Luke enframes the totality of human life. He is thus able to narrate the whole of human history in terms of a drama of divine hope and human ignorance. "And he made from one every nation of humanity . . . that they should seek God in the hope that they might feel after him and find him. But he is not far from each one of us. . . . The times of ignorance God overlooked, but now he commands all people everywhere to repent" (vv. 26-30).[51] That is to say, the history of humanity unfolds in just such a way as to require repentance—the necessary correlate of acknowledging the man whom God has raised from the dead (vv. 30-31).

Holladay, *Fragments from Hellenistic Jewish Authors*, vol. 3, *Aristobulus* (Atlanta: Scholars Press, 1995), 171-73.

49. So, rightly, Barrett, *Acts*, 2:852, among others.

50. This is yet another instance of Luke's use of dramatic irony: the members of the Areopagus can well hear a connection to Stoic "oneness" doctrine, but the readers of Acts know of course that the "one" is Adam. Cf. Marguerat, "Luc-Actes entre Jérusalem et Rome," 75.

51. Many English translations of Acts 17:27 suggest that the Gentiles have found God. This is a mistake. The optative mood of ψηλαφήσειαν and εὕροιεν expresses the wish or hope of God's creative purpose but not the fact that the Gentiles have "touched and found." Indeed, Luke's point is just the opposite: *despite* such a hope the Gentiles have remained ignorant of God; that is, they have *not* touched or found God. The καί γε that begins the next sentence makes this point explicit.

Part 1: Christology, Greco-Roman Culture, and Canonical Reception

It is within this totalizing framework—what things human could transpire before Adam or after the end of the world?—that the appropriation of pagan tradition occurs. Aratus, Cleanthes, the deep similarity with Stoic theological vocabulary, and so on all appear within the perspective created by the order of thought that begins with Adam and ends with Jesus Christ. To grasp the importance of this hermeneutical context for "reading" pagan tradition is at once to see that Luke's appropriation is not translation. It is, rather, a transformation of preexisting tradition at the most fundamental level of the unity between thought and life. In truth, the pagan philosophical grammar is sufficiently reorganized to the point that it speaks a different language.

Hermeneutics as a Way of Life

If we take in the five exegetical points above with a single glance, three crucially important and interrelated insights immediately become apparent. First, by placing the vocabulary of pagan philosophy inside the hermeneutical context of creation (vv. 24, 26) and eschaton (vv. 30–31), Luke renders obsolete the original structures of meaning in which the pagan phrases occur and, therefore, radically alters their sense. Precisely because words cannot themselves be Stoic or Platonist or anything else—they are "Stoic" only because of the larger interpretive scheme in which they are located, namely Stoicism—their occurrence in Paul's Areopagus speech bespeaks their transformation.

To know that God is "not far" from us is not to cultivate an inner awareness of the possibilities of self-transcendence or our materially deep ties to ultimate reality—*Deus sive Natura*, as Spinoza later put it—but is to become aware of the creative telos of the Lord of heaven and earth (vv. 24–27). To be "God's offspring" is no longer, as the *Phaenomena* of Aratus would construe it, to be children of Zeus who can read the meaning in the stars but is instead, on Luke's counter-reading, to be children of the living God who reject the confusion between Creator and creature. In the overall logic of the speech, that is to say, Aratus's line is situated within the theological direction of Genesis 1—from God toward humanity—and is thus reversed: humanity's divine origin actually testifies to the break between God (Creator) and world (creature) and, hence, excludes our ability to image God. Inasmuch as humans are the living offspring of the living God, we cannot image him (esp. vv. 28–29). To live and move and have our being in God, therefore, is to know as "ignorance" the way of life that constructs "God" from the materials of the human imaginative arts and sciences.[52] In short, to read the allusions to pagan traditions in Acts 17 is to encounter the truth of the words not on their own terms but on Luke's.

Second, seeing the truth of pagan tradition on Luke's terms is not only an apperceptive adjustment, cognitive correction, or internal realignment of the intellect. Rather, as the end of Paul's speech makes so clear, to shift from the "unknown God" to knowledge of him is to move into and inhabit the way of life constituted by repentance and the recognition of the identity of the man who was raised from the dead.[53] "The times of ignorance God overlooked— but now (!) he commands everyone everywhere to repent" (v. 30). The kind of knowledge at which Luke's discourse aims is a theological perspective that is nothing short of a way of being in the world, an overall pattern that takes account not only of intellection but of a whole life. Thus, in the Lukan sense, to overcome "ignorance" (ἄγνοια, v. 30) is finally to live a different life.

To put this point in relation to the rest of Acts: the Areopagus discourse should not be read as an aberration within Luke's narrative of an otherwise deeply disruptive Christian mission in the wider Greco-Roman world. In Lystra, Iconium, Philippi, Corinth, Ephesus, and so on, the Christian mission as it is depicted in Acts not only encounters but even engenders considerable cultural chaos. In accordance with such a narrative pattern, the speech in Acts 17 is yet another powerful example in Luke's larger literary program of the collision between the Christian habitus and (locally) antecedent pagan traditions, a moment in which the wisdom of those who do not know God is transfigured by the bearer of the message of Jesus's resurrection.[54] Athens is not little Lystra, of course, and so the collision is more subtle or layered—in a word, philosophical. But it is, at bottom, a collision nonetheless. What is at stake in the appropriation and transformation of pagan tradition is not a simple difference in theoretical viewpoint but the difference in the total configuration of life that emerges out of conflicting claims to truth about the ultimate origin and destiny of humanity. Human beings, created by the God of Israel, now find their telos—in every significant sense of the word—on a particular day and in relation to a particular man. God "has fixed a day on which he will

---

52. With characteristic clarity, Barrett, *Acts*, 2:850–51, remarks, "From nature the Greeks have evolved not natural theology but natural idolatry."

53. Cf. Alfons Weiser, *Die Apostelgeschichte*, 2 vols. (Gütersloh: Gerd Mohn, 1981–1985), 2:479–80. Weiser's concise and well-formulated excursus constitutes another exception to the dominant interpretive trend.

54. See esp. ch. 2 of C. Kavin Rowe, *World Upside Down: Reading Acts in the Graeco-Roman Age* (Oxford: Oxford University Press, 2009).

Part 1: Christology, Greco-Roman Culture, and Canonical Reception

judge the world in righteousness by a man whom he has appointed" (v. 31).[55] Human life is therefore to be lived in light of the intersection and existentially thick correlation between the whole world and the resurrection of Jesus. To put it differently, in the Lukan way of seeing things, the revelation of the unknown God results in a way of patterning human life that is oriented toward the last day. It is this life, so Paul's speech would claim, to which the Athenians must turn to know God and to live rightly in the world.

Third, taken together, points one and two sharpen the case against reading Acts 17 as "translation" by exposing the fact that for the translation to work it would have to presuppose a synonymous take on a total context for life. But of course, as the work of Pierre Hadot and others has shown, it was no less the case for ancient philosophy than it was for early Christianity that to "think" philosophically was to "live" in a pattern of life.[56]

Because thinking and living were sundered on the way to modernity—"philosophy" now seems to refer only to the former—as a matter of course we moderns inhabit an intellectually problematical way of reading ancient philosophy. We tend to think, that is, that philosophy in the Greco-Roman world was thinking about thinking (epistemology/logic), or thinking about living (ethics), or thinking about the world (physics/cosmology).[57] But, more properly described, ancient philosophy was a certain kind of *thinking life* in which thinking and living were not simply close correlates but were intimately, even inseparably, intertwined. "O Philosophia—Guide of life," began Cicero's well-

---

55. This determination of the entire cosmos by a specific human being reveals the deep unity between the vastness and the particularity of Luke's theological vision: the totality of what is, is immediately and irrevocably related to the one whom God raised from the dead. And this relation, moreover, is one that determines the lives of all who now live. Such is the underlying logic of repentance for "everyone, everywhere."

56. See the collection of essays in Pierre Hadot, *Philosophy as a Way of Life: Spiritual Exercises from Socrates to Foucault* (Oxford: Blackwell, 1995). For a brief entrée into Hadot's thought, see his *The Present Alone Is Our Happiness: Conversations with Jeannie Carlier and Arnold I. Davidson* (Stanford, CA: Stanford University Press, 2009). Arthur Darby Nock's famous description of philosophy as that which provides the best analogy to early Christianity because it offered a "scheme of life" is in fundamental agreement with basic aspects of Hadot's position.

57. The well-known Stoic division of philosophy into logic, physics, and ethics—which can be traced at least to Xenocrates, the onetime head of the Platonic Academy—is of course in view here. The point is to draw attention to how readily we assimilate such a division into our own terms without realizing that it was a division that corresponded not to three different kinds of abstract philosophical discussion but instead to sets of "spiritual exercises" intended to lead the practitioner more deeply into the philosophical life.

known hymn to philosophy.[58] Epistemology, ethics, physics, and so on were readings of the world that emerged out of and were directed toward an overall existential posture and lived intellectual pattern. As Plutarch put it when comparing statecraft to philosophy: the hoi polloi "think that philosophers [are those] who sit in a chair and converse and prepare their lectures over books. But the continuous practice of statecraft and philosophy, which is daily seen in acts and deeds, they fail to perceive." "Socrates philosophized," continues Plutarch, "but he did not set out benches or seat himself in an armchair or observe a fixed hour for conversing or promenading with his students. Instead, he joked with them . . . drank with them . . . served in the army or lounged in the agora with some of them and finally was imprisoned and drank the poison. He was the first to show that human life at all times and in all its parts, in all its pathos and its deeds, admits of philosophy."[59] In antiquity, philosophy was nothing less than "a mode of existing-in-the-world, which had to be practiced at each instant, and the goal of which was to transform the whole of the individual's life."[60]

Of course, to put things this way is to risk turning the philosophers into ancient existentialists.[61] This they were not. After all, with few exceptions,[62] in practice neither Stoicism nor Platonism nor much anything else was fundamentally incompatible with the everyday tasks or sense of community that came with immersion in civic life.[63] Nevertheless, philosophers from Plato to

58. Cicero, *Tusculanae disputationes* 5.5: "O vitae Philosophia dux . . ." Book 5 contrasts Philosophia with Fortuna as ultimate determinative factors in one's happiness. Cicero's position, of course, is that—despite the manifest agonies inflicted by Fortuna (esp. 5.1)—Philosophia provides the pattern of life by which virtue, and thus happiness, can be obtained.

59. Plutarch, *Whether an Old Man Should Engage in Public Affairs* (*An seni respublica gerenda sit*) 26. Cf., among many other examples, the opening lines of *On Stoic Self-Contradictions* (*De Stoicorum repugnatiis*), which emphasize the unity of philosophic thought and life.

60. Hadot, *Philosophy as a Way of Life*, 265.

61. A risk Hadot constructively exploits in his essay on the figure of Socrates (*Philosophy as a Way of Life*, 147–78).

62. Certain kinds of Cynics would constitute the primary exception (e.g., Diogenes of Sinope). The criticism of Epicurean hypocrisy we find, for example, in Cicero's *Nat. d.* 1.115 presupposes their participation in normal religious/civic life.

63. The general lack of reflection on this aspect of ancient philosophy is a weakness in Hadot's work. He does address this matter in relation to the Skeptics, who directly affirmed the importance of daily life, but as a whole it is disregarded vis-à-vis other philosophical traditions. When Hadot says, for example, that there is a "rupture between the philosopher and the conduct of everyday life" or that a philosopher's daily life is "utterly foreign to the everyday world" (*Philosophy as a Way of Life*, 57–58), he obscures the fact that traditional

Part 1: Christology, Greco-Roman Culture, and Canonical Reception

Marcus Aurelius to Plotinus were engaged in the attempt to live out a total life as both a striving for and a reflection of the deepest wisdom on ultimate matters.[64] In Plato's classic formulation, philosophy was not just thinking; it was training for death.[65]

Thus in the fullest sense, for Luke to have translated the Christian way of being into a Stoic one,[66] he would have had to say that the pattern of life that is called Stoicism is the same as the total pattern of life that is called Christianity. This he plainly does not do.[67] Indeed, what Luke says is that there is a very different way to understand the cosmos and humanity's place therein. The end of human life is now (cf. τὰ νῦν in v. 30) to be seen in terms of the rhythm of existence that is repentance and in light of the eschatological reality of the coming Judge. The implications for the interpretation of this speech should thus be clear. In the deepest sense, readers of Acts who advocate for translation as the interpretive lens through which to see Paul's speech either fail to take ancient philosophy seriously as philosophy or unwittingly mistake

---

philosophical schemes of life could quite easily incorporate large segments of the political and economic status quo. That Aristotle was a tutor to Alexander, or that Seneca (with Burrus) helped to run the empire while Nero was young, or that Marcus Aurelius drew from Epictetus (or that Marcus Aurelius was himself an emperor!), and so on, should considerably complicate the thesis that the "spiritual exercises" of the philosophers were intended to remove them entirely from normal daily life. Elsewhere it seems that Hadot does recognize this point, but he does not reflect on its significance (e.g., *What Is Ancient Philosophy?* [Cambridge, MA: Harvard University Press, 2002], 108). It may well be that Hadot is focused more on the ideal philosophical life than what actually took place, but the critical point about the weight of everyday life—even for philosophers—remains.

64. Even the Skeptics had a view (!)—namely, that these matters could not be definitely decided.

65. See, e.g., his *Phaedo*.

66. Despite the fact that in the ancient world the Christians were occasionally lumped together with the Epicureans—on the idea that both groups denied the gods and were therefore "atheists" (see, e.g., Lucian, *Alex.* 25, 38)—commentators on Acts have rightly seen that Epicureanism is prima facie incompatible with Christianity in a way that constitutes a marked difference from Stoicism. The latter philosophy is really the only one of the two whose echoes rumble loudly enough in Paul's speech to raise serious questions for our consideration.

67. Moreover, this "same-saying" would have to hold for the entirety of the Acts narrative in that the whole of the way Luke tells the story would need to be translatable into a Stoic way of life. That is, were Luke to have written the Areopagus discourse in such a way as to make the argument for translation, we would expect to be able to map Stoicism and Acts onto one another without any major difficulties (or else accuse Luke of gross conceptual ineptitude).

bits and pieces of verbal or conceptual overlap for a pattern of life—or, alas, do both at once.

Conclusion

Against the long tradition of reading Paul's Areopagus speech as a "translation" of Christian theological convictions into pagan philosophical terms, this chapter has argued that the traditional way of understanding this portion of Acts overlooks hermeneutically indispensable exegetical details and the larger conceptual issues involved in speaking about the translation of one kind of thinking life into another. The idea that merely using the same words—from Aratus, Cleanthes, Seneca, or whomever—would issue in agreement on a total pattern of life is simply an illusion. Common vocabulary is in itself never more than common vocabulary. The crucial question is rather about the larger grammar in which particular words or phrases occur.

In the case of the Areopagus speech, meticulous attention to the narrative logic of the scene reveals a fundamentally Christian grammar—one in which words gain their meaning from their embeddedness in a linguistic pattern whose ordering syntactical principles derive from the coordination of a specific human being's life history with an eschatological conception of the world.[68] To the extent that recognizing the truth of this coordination requires the form of knowledge given through repentance and the forgiveness of sins, Acts 17 speaks of a regulative schema for human life no less than for our thought. Attending to the vocabulary common to Acts and pagan tradition thus opens out not upon similarity but upon an existentially rich difference.

To put this point another way, Luke's method of telling the story of Paul's speech does not lead him to articulate narratively a manner of thinking that would—were it to exist—encompass both Stoicism and Christianity as total ways of life, a kind of general or more comprehensive grammar that would transcend intellectually the particularities of Christian language about the world (or Stoic language—or whatever). To the contrary, Luke recognizes the conflict and confrontation that occurs when irreducibly particular patterns of life offer irreducibly different ways of being. Of course, he also knows that were Paul to make this overly explicit in Athens, he could lose his life. Luke thus crafts a careful speech that employs vocabulary common to Christian and pagan tradition alike (indeed, enough to save Paul's life) but whose mean-

---

68. Cf. Schneider, *Apostelgeschichte*, 2:234.

Part 1: Christology, Greco-Roman Culture, and Canonical Reception

ing is fundamentally evangelistic (enough to cause the full range of mockery, continued interest, and conversion[69]). That modern scholars have had trouble avoiding the temptation to reduce this theological move to a more general hermeneutics is not surprising given our typical neglect of rigorous philosophical thinking, but it is not for that reason any less obfuscating when it comes to Paul's speech. In Lukan logic, neither Stoicism nor Christianity is subsumed under anything else. They are—and remain—different and competing languages about the truth of the world.

---

69. Of particular interest is the group (οἱ δέ) that says, "We will hear you again about this." I do not take this to signify the philosophical possibility of translation but rather to gesture toward the complex realities of kerygmatic communication. This group hears words they have heard before while simultaneously realizing that something has changed—that their philosophical traditions have been (re)interpreted in ways they do not (yet?) understand. Their interest is thus aroused. They are not resistant to the point of sneering, but neither are they brought to conversion.

Reading World Upside Down

◆ A RESPONSE TO MATTHEW SLEEMAN AND JOHN BARCLAY

Introduction

John Barclay and Matthew Sleeman have given me a great gift in taking time to read carefully *World Upside Down* and to engage its argument publicly. I am grateful to both of them for helping me to clarify my reasoning about the political contour of Acts and early Christianity and for extending the conversation about these important matters. I use the term "conversation" deliberately to signal something important about my understanding of the work *World Upside Down* was intended to do. In brief, that work was to open a certain kind of dialogue—not only about Acts but also about a whole range of other significant questions that find deep engagement within the pages of the NT and in antiquity more generally. What follows should not be understood in the first instance, therefore, as a simple defense of my argument. Of course, I cannot help but think I am correct about some of the issues that have been raised, and there will thus be a decent amount of defense-like argument. But, truth be told, this is more in the letter of the thing. The spirit of my response should be understood as an attempt to reason together in search of common wisdom. We all have much to learn.

"Reading World Upside Down: A Response to Matthew Sleeman and John Barclay" was originally published in *Journal for the Study of the New Testament* 33, no. 3 (2011): 335–46. Copyright 2011 The Author(s). DOI: 10.1177/0142064X10396141. This journal issue included a discussion of *World Upside Down* by Steve Walton, Matthew Sleeman, and John Barclay. I have retained the somewhat informal nature of the original discussion.

Part 1: Christology, Greco-Roman Culture, and Canonical Reception

The response will have four parts, each of which will deal with criticisms of the book:[1] (1) a brief statement about the purpose and argument of *World Upside Down*; (2) a specification of three areas in which Dr. Sleeman presses me for some elaboration and where I think he is right (one of these areas overlaps with one of Professor Barclay's concerns as well); (3) a response to Professor Barclay's two main criticisms; and (4), finally, a concluding reflection about the "tension" I tried to describe.

The Aim of *World Upside Down*

In general the aim of *World Upside Down* was, first, to dislodge a firmly entrenched way of reading Acts that fundamentally occluded the theological/political edge of the text and, second, to replace it with something better. This something better, I thought, needed to take account of at least four main things: (1) the whole narrative, rather than just certain pieces of it (e.g., the trial scenes); (2) the interconnections of ancient life (theology, politics, economics, etc.); (3) the way in which language is lived or practiced; and (4) the kerygmatic or truth claim of Acts.

In order to take account of all four things, I presented what I took to be the overarching theological vision of Acts as it was situated both within and over against certain constitutive features of Greco-Roman culture. To do this well, I thought, meant developing a rich enough set of conceptual resources within which the distinctive edge of Acts' Christian reasoning could be seen. But it also meant making some crucial choices about the way in which such conceptual resources were put to use. The central choice involved the attempt to depict Acts' political vision as a whole. All of the detailed exegetical work was in service of this larger depiction. That is to say, despite the ample amount of close reading and the nearly one hundred pages of endnotes, the book is a sketch. If its argument about the comprehensiveness of a pattern of being is right, the term "comprehensive" should nevertheless not be taken to suggest that all the details have been filled in. Indeed, they have not. Moreover, as Barclay notes in his response, Luke himself does not offer as much concrete description of early Christian communities as we might wish. What he offers instead is a vision, a pattern of lived thought that displays something of the main interconnections that make up Christian existence

---

1. For obvious reasons, I judge this to be more useful (and interesting) for the scholarly community than simply elucidating points of agreement.

Reading World Upside Down

in the Mediterranean world. In this sense, at least, perhaps Lukan politics in Acts is "underdressed."[2]

But it is hard to see how it could be otherwise. To offer a narrative vision for a new life is not to map all its specifics, but is instead to create the imaginatively productive conditions under which a community can rightly read and thus make its way in the world. *World Upside Down* was an attempt to sketch these productive conditions and inhabit as best as I could the generative force of the movement whose story is told in Acts.

Christian Communities, Heaven, and the Resurrection

There are three places in Dr. Sleeman's paper where he challenges me to think further about the way in which my thesis could be extended or deepened. First, in his section "Locating the 'New Cultural Reality'" Dr. Sleeman asks, "Where is this new cultural reality?"[3] One could, I suppose, say in Jerusalem, Antioch, Ephesus, Corinth, Athens, Thessalonica, and so on—in short, anywhere Christian communities are being formed. And, indeed, this is close to what Dr. Sleeman goes on to say. He speaks of the "third space" that is created by the coming together of Christians, for example. Of course, the earliest Christians did not actually build alternative spaces in the way pagans built temples (or Jews synagogues), and Dr. Sleeman may well mean to point more toward the distinctively Christian imaginative world created by Acts.[4] But the question itself nevertheless presses for an account of what characterizes the kind of space Christians "took up in public."[5] Professor Barclay asks for something similar, I think, when he says, "How did these churches organize their households, their children's upbringing, their slaves, their marriages (or

---

2. Oliver O'Donovan, *The Desire of the Nations: Rediscovering the Roots of Political Theology* (Cambridge: Cambridge University Press, 1996). O'Donovan himself notes that "the architecture of a Christian doctrine of society has yet to be established, though, of course, many components have been discussed often and well" (286). He is, however, quite concerned about discovering the political hermeneutics of Scripture in a sophisticated manner (see esp. 22, for example). I take it that, in principle at least, I am trying to do something close to what O'Donovan describes.

3. Matthew Sleeman, "The Vision of Acts: World Right Way Up," *JSNT* 33, no. 3 (2011): 330.

4. Cf. the use of Soja in Matthew Sleeman, *Geography and the Ascension Narrative in Acts*, SNTSMS 146 (Cambridge: Cambridge University Press, 2009).

5. Sleeman, "Vision of Acts," citing C. Kavin Rowe, *World Upside Down: Reading Acts in the Graeco-Roman Age* (Oxford: Oxford University Press, 2009).

renunciation of marriage)? How did they conduct their economic affairs . . . ? What was their involvement in sport, in the arts, in civic affairs?"[6]

Here are welcome words of admonition from both Dr. Sleeman and Professor Barclay. Because of my focus on larger narrative patterns, I did not give sufficient attention to the specific characterization of the communities in Acts. In part, as Barclay notes, this is because Acts itself is not rife with detail of this kind. But, in another sense, it is something my book lacks and which would strengthen the argument as a whole (and on which others could work). Still, it is not clear to me how much this absence really affects my main thesis. On the one hand, the claim for a new culture would obviously benefit from local illustrations thereof. On the other hand, Acts itself does not seem so concerned to provide us with the information on which to speculate. At this point at least, my reading may simply reflect the narrative foreground more so than the modern concern to illumine the sociological gaps in the story's detail. But the point is nevertheless an important one.

Second, Dr. Sleeman's suggestion that I should think more about the ascension and heaven as constitutive features of the "life stance" of the early Christians is also helpful. Sleeman is right that this is both an important feature of Acts and something to which I paid relatively little attention. In particular, Sleeman's claim that attention to these matters would deepen our understanding of the "extra-local" identity of the Christian communities across the Mediterranean[7] is intriguing and deserves further reflection.

Finally, Dr. Sleeman argues that I could have given more attention to the narrative development of the resurrection.[8] In one sense, the resurrection is implicit in much of what I say (e.g., speaking of ecclesiology as public Christology implies a sociopolitical outworking of the life history of Jesus, including his resurrection; that is to say, the Christian pattern of being after Jesus assumes resurrection as the outcome of violent death). But in another sense it is a striking omission precisely because it is *the* hope that underlies specifically Christian politics. So Jesus, so the Christians. Without the hope of the resurrection I doubt we could even speak coherently of Christian politics in the first and early second century. Oliver O'Donovan's *Desire of the Nations* is apropos once again. "The resurrection of the dead," says O'Donovan, "is the condition of true politics." "The church," he continues, "will frame its political witness with authenticity . . . [when] it confesses that it looks for the resurrection of the dead and the life of the world to come."[9]

---

6. John Barclay, "Pushing Back: Some Questions for Discussion," *JSNT* 33, no. 3 (2011): 323.
7. Sleeman, "Vision of Acts," 328.
8. Sleeman, "Vision of Acts," 329.
9. O'Donovan, *Desire of the Nations*, 288.

CULTURE: PAGANISM AND POLITICS

John Barclay's response criticizes *World Upside Down* along two interrelated lines: the threat of cultural demise (the unity of paganism or pagan religiousness) and the political shape of Acts/ancient life. The first criticism turns on the issue of pagan culture; the second on the way political language works. I shall take these in turn.

Culture and Paganism

In one sense, I am not saying much more than that we ought to take the silversmith Demetrius, for example, quite seriously in his articulation of the interconnection between theology and economic life and the way such a connection unfolds politically. So doing requires us to eschew basic, dichotomizing habits of thought in the modern world that would refer theology/religion to one sphere and economics or politics to another—and allows us, instead, to focus upon the structuring importance of the pagan gods within the larger interconnections that sustained ancient pagan life. When Barclay asks, "If [Luke] attacks the polytheistic beliefs which undergird all pagan religious practice, does this threaten to unravel 'pagan culture' as a whole?"[10] he reproduces—linguistically if not intentionally—two dichotomies I am explicitly working against: belief and practice, and religion and culture. Polytheism is not simply a belief system; nor is it reducible to something called "religion." It was a lived pattern that also undergirded much economic and political practice, as even a thinker as critical as Cicero knew well enough. There are three additional points that I want to emphasize.

First, I want to resist the idea that polytheism and the Christian view of God are simply substitutable, as if swapping the latter for the former left the rest of human life intact and unchanged. Of course Barclay is right that the Christian mission did not "entail the deconstruction of that [pagan] 'culture' as a whole"[11]—especially if by culture he means something close to everything in human life. But this was not my point. The point, rather, was that certain crucial interconnections that were necessary to the larger pattern of pagan life were dismantled and replaced by something else: new interconnections—and thus a new pattern, one that, for example, prohibits the sacrifice to the gods and instead requires the formation of "brothers and sisters" in communities

10. Barclay, "Pushing Back," 323.
11. Barclay, "Pushing Back," 323.

Part 1: Christology, Greco-Roman Culture, and Canonical Reception

of Jews and Gentiles that proclaim Jesus of Nazareth as Lord (and are centered upon common devotion to him, and so forth). Even with all the vast diversity and disagreement that existed in pagan culture, it is inconceivable that a decent description of pagan culture could make the organizing force of the gods peripheral or unimportant. But if the gods are taken as important, then the pattern of life that emerges in Acts on the basis of a break between God and the world is quite different—and, hence, so are the larger connections that make what a "culture" is or comes to be.

Second, I want to emphasize the difference between Christian criticism and the criticism, conflict, and contestation internal to pagan life. I agree with Barclay (and Mary Beard et al.) that pagan culture was extremely diverse and was constituted as much "by conflict and competition, as by harmonious integration."[12] But I do not think paganism was so diverse as to be able to encompass the extinction of polytheism. The difference between internal contestation and Christian criticism, that is, is not quantitative (as if they are really the same thing, and there is just more of it or a more intense form in the case of the Christians) but qualitative (it is a different kind of thing). James Rives, for example, confuses quantitative and qualitative difference when he presupposes a common continuum on which Christianity and other "nonconformist" groups can be located: Christianity, says Rives, was the "extreme" of nonconformity.[13] But there is no "religious" continuum *within* paganism that would allow for the destruction of polytheism. Christianity is, quite simply, something else. Where within the pagan diversity do we see anything like the Christian practical criticism? (By "practical criticism" I mean the formation of actual missionizing communities of Jews and Gentiles on the basis of a theological reading of the world that requires the community members to cease sacrificing to the gods and refuse ultimate allegiance to the emperor.) In short, the postmodern tendencies to see fragmentation and conflict are on target in many respects, but they meet their limit in the fact that paganism could not—as a whole—conceive of the end of the practice of polytheism. No

---

12. Barclay, "Pushing Back," 323. It should be said, however, that there are erudite classicists who, in full cognizance of the more recent postmodern-flavored treatments of diversity, argue for a unity in pagan religious practice: masterfully, for example, Robin Lane Fox, *Pagans and Christians* (New York: Knopf, 1986) and, from a religio-political angle vis-à-vis the Roman emperor, Clifford Ando, *Imperial Ideology and Provincial Loyalty in the Roman Empire* (Berkeley: University of California Press, 2000).

13. James B. Rives, *Religion and Authority in Roman Carthage* (New York: Oxford University Press, 1995), 251. In the epilogue to *Religion in the Roman Empire* (London: Blackwell, 2007), he is more nuanced.

matter what disagreements occur otherwise, in this basic but extraordinarily far-reaching and significant aspect, paganism shares a common horizon.

Third, I want to underline the difference between Christian and Jewish critical practice. The difference can be stated in two words: mission and permission. It is probably true, as Barclay writes, that "diaspora Jews and their proselytes were quite as critical of pagan belief and cultic practice as was Luke, but were also often so well integrated into the educational, social, economic and even political dimensions of civic life (see the Aphrodisias inscription) that it would be absurd to suggest that they threatened total cultural destabilization."[14] From the invectives in Second Isaiah through denunciations in the Second Temple period and beyond, Jews were just as critical of pagan idolatry as were the early Christians. But the practice of the criticism was different. Prior to the birth of Christianity, Jews did not—to my knowledge—engage in a worldwide, strategic, and conscious effort to draw any and all pagans away from their cultic practice and bring them into the Jewish way of life. At least according to Acts, the Christians did just this.[15] Moreover, the early Christians were not exempt—as Jews generally were until at least the early third century—from the imperial cult or pagan cultic practice more generally. (There were of course no official laws compelling individuals to participate in this or that Roman cult. This has a simple reason: prior to Christianity there would not need to be. Apart from the Jews, no one systematically refused or had any reason to refuse participation in all pagan cults.) These two differences (mission and permission) amount to a different overall way of being in the world vis-à-vis pagan culture. To sideline the importance of Christian mission for a reading of Acts or a construal of the politics of early Christianity is historically no less than narratively problematical. The difference between the sociopolitical practice of the early Christians and the diaspora (non-Christian) Jews at this point should not be forgotten.

Politics and Paganism

In relation to politics and paganism, I will make three principal points. There are obviously other matters to address—for example, the relevance of a "defi-

14. Barclay, "Pushing Back," 323.
15. Thus I wrote: "Jews and gentiles could coexist so long as the former did not actively missionize the latter—which the Christians did—and the latter did not seek to impose itself on the former. But such coexistence with Jews was fraught with problems whenever polytheism meant in practice anything other than a policy of leaving the Jews to their own ways" (Rowe, *World Upside Down*, 261 n. 69).

Part 1: Christology, Greco-Roman Culture, and Canonical Reception

nition" of politics—but the following points should be sufficient to extend the discussion.

First, Professor Barclay says, "It is striking that in practice, for most of early Christian history and for the vast majority of Christians, this collision [between Jesus and Caesar as "Lord"] did not arise, and many found ways of honouring Caesar as 'Lord' within (and, of course, beneath) their honour of Jesus as Lord: even Paul in Luke's narrative appeals to Caesar, without anxiety about a clash of allegiances."[16] In principle, there is nothing linguistically that would prevent a way of honoring two lords.[17] How "many" actually tried to do this we do not of course know, but Tertullian, for example, speaks for Barclay's suggestion when he cleverly says that he will call the emperor *dominus* as long as he is not required to call him *dominus*![18] The opposition that I see, however, is not in the simple use of the word "Lord," as if linguistic juxtaposition was problematical in and of itself. The issue has rather to do with the way in which the critical thrust of the Christian language—Caesar is no longer the Lord of all—was practiced or lived (as all language actually is in one way or another). The way this aspect of the language was practiced turned out to be politically confrontational: the Christians would not worship the emperor or sacrifice to the gods, both of which Rome itself required (cf. Pliny). The conflict comes, therefore, because Christian and Roman theopolitical proposals are incapable of simultaneous embodiment. When Barclay says that "a clash between Roman authority and Christian confession of Christ (as Lord of all, Acts 4.24) was *always* a possibility"[19] (emphasis added), he actually upholds the theoretical point I was making in that part of the book: the Christians have to deny what the Roman emperor has to be, the Lord of all. The clash is *always* potential—not because the Christians cannot in principle "honor" an emperor (1 Pet. 2:17) but precisely because this is politically/theologically insufficient for Rome itself.[20] The Christians were likely not a group that

16. Barclay, "Pushing Back," 326.
17. Barclay's language about Paul's appeal is more difficult, however, in light of the fact that the readers of Acts know Paul was put to death. We are not told whether Paul is "anxious" about his appeal, but we do know his appeal brought his demise. See Rowe, *World Upside Down*, esp. 231 n. 241.
18. Tertullian, *Apol.* 34.1.
19. Barclay, "Pushing Back," 325–26.
20. Indeed, in 1 Peter it is clear that despite the recommendation of 2:17 the Christians still suffer as Christians—*hos Christianos* (4:16)—and are encouraged in their suffering to "sanctify [*hagiasate*] Christ as Lord in your hearts, and be ready to offer an *apologia* to anyone who asks" (3:15). Again, unlike the Jews, the Christians were not exempt from Roman cultic practice and could not simply say to the Romans, as did the Jews in Jerusalem prior

was consciously subverting the empire in any kind of "hard" sense—in this I agree with Barclay—but their theological reasoning nevertheless positioned their social life over against the claims that were necessary to sustain Roman politics (in this Barclay appears to agree with me). The Christians do not set up "another king" (Acts 17:7) as a direct rival to the imperial throne; and yet when confronted by the political demands of the imperial king, the Christians obey him not. In my view, the vision of Acts makes Pliny's letter and many developments thereafter theologically and politically intelligible exactly because it articulates the irreducible conflict between the claims to ultimate sovereignty for God/Jesus on the one hand and the emperor and the Roman gods on the other.[21]

Second, there is the issue of Christian crimes (*flagitia*—an old chestnut!). Barclay suggests that the early Christians were "legally vulnerable only if they could be convicted of crimes" and that Luke is not so much concerned with whether the "Christians pose the threat of 'coup,' but whether they are criminals (of various sorts)."[22] It is true that in Acts causing *stasis* is not the only charge with which Luke is concerned (Barclay is right here to note Gallio's terminology in 18:14, *adikēma* or *rhadiourgēma ponēron*). Yet, in light of Christian practice

---

to the revolt in 66, we are loyal in that we make a sacrifice in the temple "on behalf of" the emperor (with the implicit/insider point: but not "to" him). Cf. Philo, *Legat.* 357.

21. Another way to put this point would be to say that Acts prepares the way not for Eusebius on Constantine but for the trials of the martyrs. While we agree on the ad hoc nature of persecution and the absence of any legal compulsion to participate in the imperial cult prior to Decius, Barclay and I differ, it seems, on how much weight to place on persecution/martyrdom in the early period (he wants less, I more). In my view, Barclay's historical judgments are perhaps more influenced by the overall outcome (Christianity ultimately "wins") than they are by the prevalence of positive examples. In the early period, it strikes me that martyrdom was an indispensable category within which Christian self-understanding took shape (Polycarp, Justin, etc.).

22. Barclay, "Pushing Back," 325. The idea that Christians were vulnerable only if they could be convicted of actual crimes is difficult to square with the Pliny/Trajan correspondence (it is more, in other words, than a "partial exception" to Barclay's point). The Christians are set free unpunished for anything whatsoever if they curse Christ and make offerings to the emperor and the gods. Had they been charged with murder, say, it is hard to see how cursing Christ would count as acquittal for the crime of murder. Apparently, no matter what the charges, all that is required is to renounce Christ and rejoin the normal rhythms of pagan life. Moreover, as Trajan makes clear in his reply, the Christians are not to be sought out (implying that they are not guilty of any wrong worth bringing to justice in itself). This is a very odd policy, but it is intelligible on the assumption that the Romans had not seen anything like the Christians before and therefore did not know what to do with them. In short, the issue really is the name itself.

Part 1: Christology, Greco-Roman Culture, and Canonical Reception

as it is narrated in the story, it is difficult to understand what the "crimes" would be if they were not associated with the gods and/or the emperor. In Philippi, for example, when the accusers say that the Christian missionaries ("Jews") advocate practices (*ethē*) that are illegal for *Romans* to practice (16:21), it is hard to know what to think of other than the gods/emperor (or what to make of the emphasis, particularly in a scene that takes place in a Roman colony). Or, again, along with several other scholars, I think the charges in Thessalonica make best sense in light of some version of a loyalty oath to the emperor (hence the stress on "another" in "another king": *basilea heteron*). What precisely are the Christians accused of doing (*prassousin*, 17:7) if not in some way rejecting the practical implications of loyalty to the emperor (e.g., participation in his cult, refusal of the loyalty oath, etc.; cf. *anastatosantes*, 17:6)? What should we call a group—other than "treasonous" or some approximate term—that violated the loyalty oath to the emperor by proclaiming another king?[23] Among the "many heavy charges" (*polla kai barea aitiomata*) brought to Festus by Paul's Jerusalem opponents there is something that moves Paul to declare that, in addition to the Jewish law and the temple, he has done "nothing against Caesar" (25:7–8). Why does he need to deflect a charge against Caesar? What would this charge be? The narrative force of these and like passages (e.g., Lysias's mistaking Paul for the Egyptian), in addition to the explicit charge of *stasis*—which comes up not only in the Ephesian riot (and would be implicitly present for any riot) but is in fact the legal charge that launches Paul's official trial—is simply hard to ignore. Again, I do not think Luke is arguing against a notion of "coup" in the sense of raising a large army to march on Rome, but more in the sense that would accompany Rome's worries about the political practice of a strange society (interestingly, of course, *hetaeria* is one of the two words—*superstitio* is the other—Pliny uses to characterize the Christian assembly; cf., e.g., from a later period Celsus's criticism in Origen, *Cels*. 1.1). In Acts, the Christians are obviously not interested in direct rebellion or insurrection, and yet their missionizing, common life positions them in such a way as to elicit the charge. To such a reading of their life, they must say "no."

Third, there is the related issue of Roman law.[24] "If," Barclay argues, Luke

23. Rowe, *World Upside Down*, 234 n. 29. Moreover, it is hard to understand why Barclay seems to oppose "crimes" with "coup," treason, and the like. Treason was a "crime": it had a particular, legally defined punishment, for example (in the case of Roman citizens, beheading).

24. Of course it is true that Roman provincial administration was an ad hoc affair. No one even remotely familiar with the workings of Roman administration could think otherwise. This fact is something that *World Upside Down* both makes quite explicit and—at other times—simply assumes as common scholarly knowledge.

can "keep open the gap between [the Christians'] practices/beliefs and the law, they can penetrate Roman society without legal trouble—of course to reshape that society, but neither cultural subversion nor political revolution are really in the frame."[25] Barclay is right that the Christians were not interested in political revolution, but how the narrative of Acts would fit a classically Niebuhrian argument about reshaping Roman society is hard to understand.[26] The aim of the early Christians in Acts is not to transform society but, to put it bluntly, to convert all pagans to Christianity. In this they did not succeed of course, but that the mission is supposed to be universal is, I think, beyond question.

Still, Barclay's suggestion that Luke attempts "to keep open a gap" between the Christians and Roman law is worth serious thought.[27] Moreover, when Barclay later says that Luke thought "law, even Roman law, was on the Christians' side, *whatever their detractors might think*,"[28] he not only agrees with me on the substance of the matter but also nicely encapsulates the tension he claims does not exist. Luke's reading of Roman law is a Christian reading of that law. As Gadamer, Carl Schmitt, and others have insisted, hermeneutics is as crucial for law as it is for history or theology (or life, for that matter). Gadamer showed that to know the law's interpretation just is to know its application, and yet law cannot interpret or apply itself. It requires interpreters and judges—in short, human beings—and, as such, cannot stand by itself either for or against the Christians. As a legal hermeneut, Luke does, therefore, occupy a space between Roman law and Christian life and interpretively shapes the former to fit the latter. The tension is that when it comes to the gods and/or the emperor, Rome cannot—and over time does not—agree (cf. from a later period Tertullian, *Apol.* 10.1–2: "we are accused of sacrilege and treason at once"). There is thus an irreducible legal, hermeneutical difference between the Christian reading of the Christian reality and the Roman reading of the Christian reality. Let us not forget: the voice that speaks in Luke's story is not that of the *lex Romana* itself; in Acts, the Roman law speaks with a distinctively Christian inflection. As all our rel-

---

25. Barclay, "Pushing Back," 325.

26. The third item here, "cultural subversion," is slightly more difficult. In agreement with Barclay, I doubt the early Christians had a conscious, worked-out program of cultural subversion. Nevertheless, how would one characterize the effects of the practical criticism of the gods (stop going to sacrifice to the gods because they are idols) if not as culturally subversive? Moreover, from the first until the last chapter of Acts, scarcely a scene goes by without some disruption or another that could in principle be tied to Christian presence.

27. Indeed, it coheres exactly with what I suggested in *World Upside Down*, esp. 148–50.

28. Barclay, "Pushing Back," 327; emphasis added.

evant pagan sources tell us, the Roman use of the Roman law vis-à-vis the Christians was rather different. Finally, then, we come to the question of the tension in Luke's work.

THE QUESTION OF THE TENSION

Professor Barclay thinks that I have exaggerated or created it; I think he has perhaps failed to see what it is about at its heart—though he comes very close to restating a central part of it when he says that "opponents of Christianity will attack it legally on the grounds that Christians practice 'crimes' (*flagitia*), while defenders (like Luke and the author of 1 Peter) insist that Christians, though untraditional and unpopular, are by no means criminal."[29] Indeed, here Barclay stands at the door and knocks. Once he adds to that statement the admission that cultural destabilization would attend pagan conversion to Christianity, he has entered the room.

The tension is really about the irreducibly particular ways to read the world and the fact that it is impossible to live them both at once. The question is not whether Luke and his hearers felt such a tension, but whether such a tension exists and—if it does—how it orders productively the intellectual grammar that informs the narrative patterns in Acts.

As best as I can make out, the pattern of Lukan thinking on this question is something like this: (1) Luke realizes what the Christian mission is going to do—its cultural/political potential; (2) Luke realizes—because of his knowledge of the Roman law—what Rome qua Rome will make of the Christians once the question is raised in any kind of serious way;[30] but (3) he does not accept this reading of the Christian mission because he knows what a politically seditious group is in Roman terms (out to challenge Rome directly in one way or another) and thinks that this is not the right way to describe what Christianity is: in Luke's view the Christian mission is the peaceful bringing of God's salvific light; so (4) he refuses the problematic understanding of the *Christianoi* by means of a rereading of Roman law in light of what he knows Christianity actually is and issues declarations of innocence from the mouths of the Roman officials in his

---

29. Barclay, "Pushing Back," 324.

30. Incidentally, there is no hint in Acts or for a long time thereafter that the impetus for criminal/political accusation comes from "the top" (Roman governors and the like). It comes instead from trouble with the local populace in one way or another.

story (in order to shape correctly the political imagination of his readers for what he sees on the horizon).³¹

Rome qua Rome will not understand Luke's claim that the early Christian mission is not actually seditious precisely because it cannot: it does not have the requisite categories of knowledge in which this kind of claim can make sense. For Luke, cultural destabilization is the outworking of God's salvific action in Jesus Christ; it is not criminal action or sedition. To understand the necessary connection between Jesus and a new reality (pattern of communal life in his name—the Way, ecclesia, etc.) is already to know that Christian political life truly is God's light, however destabilizing it may be for the present order. That is, for Rome to make the connection Luke makes between Christian political life and light, their particularized perspective would need to undergo a dramatic change (from pagan to Christian). Otherwise, what counts as sedition and what does not remains intractably in dispute. In sum: the issue of truth that is involved in the particularized reading of the Christian reality is what is ultimately at stake in the question of whether the Christians are problematic or not. If Luke is right, then they are not seditious: they are participating in the peaceful creation of a new way of life; if Rome is right, they are seditious. As far as I can see, there is no way around this conflict of interpretation.³²

"Stop sacrificing to the gods/participating in the cult of the emperor and instead worship Jesus and live as brothers and sisters in a community of fellowship" *could* be a peaceful transition to another set of arrangements that make a new culture, *if* the Romans were to admit that the Christians are right.³³ But absent such an admission (i.e., if the Christians are wrong), once the question about the Christians is raised, the Roman political and legal machinery is right—on its own terms—to detect in the *nomen ipsum* something strange and threatening.

A brief paraphrase—and slight caricature—of Luke's position may be helpful:

---

31. To take only one example, think of the significance of the fact that it is Luke alone in the synoptic tradition who has Pilate declare Jesus's legal innocence (cf. Luke 23:47, *dikaios*).

32. There is no third place to which one can be removed and from which one can evaluate political life. We are quite simply caught in the concrete situation of having to make evaluative judgments that derive from, correspond to, and even inform the particularized perspective from which we read the world.

33. For example, one could peacefully take down the Temple of Artemis, or convert it into a full-time bank, or melt down Athenian statues to make water basins or any number of other things. In short, there is no metaphysical necessity to violent confrontation.

Part 1: Christology, Greco-Roman Culture, and Canonical Reception

Come over to Jesus in repentance and you'll see that we're not only innocent but in fact creating peaceful communities. Your temples, idols, house gods, and so on will all have to go, and you will not be able to participate in the cult of the emperor or take loyalty oaths to him if they involve acclaiming him Lord of all or sacrifices or anything like that. But despite the fact that all these things are also connected to your livelihood (economics), your civic and military arrangements, your families, the deep history of your lives, and so forth—that is, we know the cultural web will undergo some serious unravelling—this is all for the good. Think what you get instead: *sotēria* in Jesus Christ! There will be some Gentiles/Romans who will not understand this and who will think our form of life problematic. But don't worry too much about this because we're not violent insurrectionists; the law, therefore, is actually on *our* side. We're innocent (*dikaios*) just like Jesus. And even if we're taken to the high levels of government (and the proconsul doesn't convert—which he may—remember Sergius Paulus!) and suffer and wind up getting killed like Jesus, that's not the end. The God who raised the innocent Jesus from the dead will raise us up too.

The tension Luke narrates is thus about the fact that cultural destabilization is at one and the same time the bringing of God's salvific light (Christian reading) and sedition (Rome). Luke understands this tension and writes the Acts narrative in such a way that it requires us to think through the juxtaposition between Christian claims and the pagan denial of those claims. Of course Luke does not actually think the Christians could take over the empire: he could not imagine such a thing.[34] And of course Romans such as Pliny do not actually think the Christians are a threat in any deep sense to their empire. The issue, rather, is about the potential of a catechized political imagination to bring about a fundamental restructuring of human life, the inevitable misinterpretation of the character of the restructuring, and the tenacity with which such restructuring can be resisted. In order to catechize Christians well in the political shape of their imagination (cf. Luke 1:1–4), Luke makes use of the tension that exists between Christian and Roman political claims to say what the Christian life is with all its social risks (it is culturally destabilizing), how it will be misinterpreted (it is not a sedition), and how it will be resisted (Jesus and Paul will be put to death despite their innocence).

Because it captures so well the connection between a politics of truth and the effects that follow in its wake, I conclude with a citation from Vaclav Havel's

---

34. Barclay, "Pushing Back," 325.

Reading World Upside Down

famous essay "The Power of the Powerless." "Why was Solzhenitsyn driven out of his own country?" Havel asks. His answer is striking:

> Certainly not because he represented a unit of real power, that is, not because any of the regime's representatives felt he might unseat them and take their place in government. Solzhenitsyn's expulsion was something else: a desperate attempt to plug up the dreadful wellspring of truth, a truth which might cause incalculable transformations in social consciousness, which in turn might one day produce political debacles unpredictable in their consequences.[35]

Havel is of course writing about the Communist regime of the Eastern Bloc—a time and place obviously very different and far removed from the events depicted in Acts. Still, as a way to help us think about the interpretation of early Christianity and its tension with the Roman Empire, Havel's remarks are richly suggestive: Christian politics does not occur at the level of "real power" but rather in its claim to drink from the wellspring of truth and its active, passionate invitation to all who are thirsty to come and drink too.

---

35. Vaclav Havel, "The Power of the Powerless," in *Living in the Truth* (London: Faber & Faber, 1986), 59. The entirety of Havel's essay—from his continuous imaginative depiction of the greengrocer who "lives in the truth" to the story of the far-reaching political effects caused by the suppression of "two obscure" Czech rock bands (63–65) to his distinction between different kinds of "opposition" (72–74)—is relevant to the issues under discussion here.

The Book of Acts and the Cultural Explication of the Identity of God

Introduction

New Testament scholars are not accustomed to reading Karl Barth for help with their historical and exegetical work. Yet, at one point at least, it is Barth above all others in our time who has seen clearly a central theological point without which many of the historical dynamics involved in "Christian origins" are virtually unintelligible: God is the measure of all things.[1] To speak properly of God in Barth's sense is to speak not of the grandest object within our horizon but of the reality that constitutes the total horizon of all human life and thought. God is not derivative of human culture (à la Feuerbach, Freud, et al.) but generative.

The hermeneutical corollary of Barth's insight is of momentous consequence and can be stated simply: what we think about God will determine what we think about everything else.[2] To speak of "God" is to invoke the context for all understanding, that to which all life and thought are related; to the extent that we live and think at all, therefore, we do so in light of our understanding—whether explicit or implicit—of God. Theology, that is, is never merely ideation. It is always and inherently a total way of life.

---

1. This theme is central to Barth's theology; it is difficult, therefore, to know where to point the reader. But see, e.g., Karl Barth, *Church Dogmatics* (Edinburgh: T&T Clark, 1957–1958), II/1 §26, esp. pp. 76, 117; §28, esp. pp. 312–13; §31, p. 562; III/1 §§40–41, esp. pp. 5–7, 11–13.

2. Cf., e.g., Barth's statement in *Dogmatics in Outline*, trans. G. T. Thomson (New York: Harper & Row, 1959), 50: "Everything that is said about creation depends absolutely upon this Subject."

"The Book of Acts and the Cultural Explication of the Identity of God" was originally published in *The Word Leaps the Gap: Essays on Scripture and Theology in Honor of Richard B. Hays*, ed. J. Ross Wagner, C. Kavin Rowe, and A. Katherine Grieb (Grand Rapids: Eerdmans, 2008), 244–66. It is reproduced with permission.

The Book of Acts and the Cultural Explication of the Identity of God

The early Christians were not Barthians. Yet to see that the contour of their life derived from their understanding of God is to penetrate to the core of the conflict that surrounded their birth and growth. From 1 Thessalonians (1:9) through Pliny's famous epistle (10.96) to the persecution under Decius and beyond, the clash of the gods was that which ultimately determined the shape of the collision between (emerging) Christianity and paganism.[3] There were of course confusion, diversity, difference, and complex interaction between paganism and Christianity. But the conflict as a whole and the instantiation of a new culture—for that is what it was[4]—are utterly inconceivable apart from the clash between the exclusivity of the Christian God and the wider mode of pagan religiousness.[5] To put it slightly differently: once one grasps the primary—sensu stricto—importance of God for a total way of life, the conflict becomes intelligible. Converting to the God of the Christians was not merely an adjustment of this or that aspect of an otherwise unaltered basic cultural pattern; rather, worshiping the God of the Christians simultaneously involved an extraction or removal from constitutive aspects of pagan culture (e.g., sacrifice to the gods) and a concomitant cultural profile that rendered Christians identifiable as a "group" by outsiders.[6] Yet the practices that created this cul-

---

3. There has long been phenomenological difficulty in identifying "paganism" as a single, unitary thing. Yet linguistic alternatives prove to create more problems than they solve; traditional usage is thus best retained so long as it is not understood to describe a monolithic religion, culture, power structure, etc. For a brief and lucid statement of the problem, see Robin Lane Fox, *Pagans and Christians* (New York: Knopf, 1987), 33.

4. See, e.g., Ramsay MacMullen, *Paganism in the Roman Empire* (New Haven: Yale University Press, 1981), 88; Frances M. Young, *Biblical Exegesis and the Formation of Christian Culture* (Cambridge: Cambridge University Press, 1997), 50, 70, 286-91.

5. Lane Fox is again concise on the problem of speaking of paganism as a single "religion"—it is, he argues, more like a pattern of religiousness. Still, this pattern displays enough of a common core and broad similarity that we can speak of it in something of a holistic way; see Lane Fox, *Pagans and Christians*, 31-38, 90, etc. In addition, I take it now for granted that "religion" in pagan antiquity was a public and political affair, that the attempt to privatize beliefs or piety perpetuates a modern mistake in the study of antiquity, and that these matters have been amply demonstrated in recent study; see, e.g., Simon R. F. Price, *Rituals and Power: The Roman Imperial Cult in Asia Minor* (Cambridge: Cambridge University Press, 1984), 15-16, 234-48; Robert Louis Wilken, *The Christians as the Romans Saw Them*, 2nd ed. (New Haven: Yale University Press, 2003), x. Cf. n. 95 below.

6. This is not necessarily to say, however, that in the early periods "Christian" is the word that would have been used. In many cases the Jewish Christian missionaries (Paul, etc.) would simply have been "Jews" to the outsiders (as in Acts 16:20, for example). It is also noteworthy that Tertullus presents Paul to Felix as a ringleader of a Jewish sect (αἵρεσις), the Nazarenes (Acts 24:5). Yet once Gentiles are in the picture, the word Χριστιανοί is doubtless

Part 1: Christology, Greco-Roman Culture, and Canonical Reception

tural profile were themselves dependent upon the identity of God. Christian ecclesial life, in other words, was the cultural explication of God's identity.

Taken as a whole, the narrative of the Acts of the Apostles is a rich exposition of this cultural explication of divine identity. In the book of Acts, the expansion of God's εὐαγγέλιον is coterminous with the creation of a people whom, in Luke's terms, God has taken out of the Gentiles for his name's sake (Acts 15:14: ὁ θεὸς ἐπεσκέψατο λαβεῖν ἐξ ἐθνῶν λαὸν τῷ ὀνόματι αὐτοῦ).[7] The revelation of God in Christ, that is, necessarily entails the formation of a people who bear witness to God's name.[8] In this way, volume two of Luke's overall literary project displays the narrative outworking of the claim of volume one that the salvation of God comes through Jesus Christ as an apocalypse to the Gentiles (Luke 2:30–32; Acts 13:47; cf. Isa 42:6; 49:9).

Space does not permit an elucidation of these matters from the entirety of Acts; that task belongs to a much larger project.[9] We shall therefore focus upon two instances in which the reconfiguration of divine identity necessitated by the witness of the early missionaries results in a clash between the

---

there soon, too: there is a community of Jews and Gentiles that behaves socially like Jews in some very important ways (one God, no sacrifice to pagan gods, etc.) but differs visibly from other Jews in some very important ways (the absence, for the most part, of dietary restrictions, no circumcision, no rigorous Sabbath keeping, the claim to follow Jesus as the Messiah, etc.). Acts 11:26; 26:28; 1 Pet 4:16 all suggest that Χριστιανός was first coined by outsiders. On this important issue, see David G. Horrell, "The Label Χριστιανός: 1 Peter 4:16 and the Formation of Christian Identity," *JBL* 126 (2007): 361–81.

7. For the OT echoes in this phrasing, see Nils A. Dahl, "A People for His Name (Acts xv. 14)," *NTS* 4 (1957–1958): 319–27. Though Dahl settles on Zech 2:15 LXX (2:11 Eng.) as the "most interesting parallel" to Acts 15:14, he also notes that "the number of similar [LXX] texts indicates that Acts xv. 14 is modelled upon the general pattern rather than upon any individual passage" (323). In my judgment, Dahl is correct to say that Luke's formulation in Acts 15:14 depends upon a larger reading of the OT (including Zech 2:14–17) in which "the conversion of Gentiles is seen as a fulfilment of God's promises to Israel: Luke ii. 29–32; Acts ii. 39; iii. 25; xiii. 47, etc." (327). As these remarks indicate, my way of putting the issue of the formation of a people (main text, above) hardly intends to say that Acts is unconcerned with Judaism and Jewish traditions; Luke is very much concerned with Judaism. Recent and extensive studies confirm this fact (see, e.g., the work of Joseph Tyson). By comparison, only scant attention has been given to Luke's concern with Gentiles/paganism. In fact, I know of only two recent attempts, the first of which is quite brief. See Hans-Josef Klauck, *Magic and Paganism in Early Christianity: The World of the Acts of the Apostles* (Edinburgh: T&T Clark, 1999); Christoph W. Stenschke, *Luke's Portrait of Gentiles Prior to Their Coming to Faith*, WUNT 2/108 (Tübingen: Mohr Siebeck, 1999).

8. In theological terms: theology proper is distinct but never separate from ecclesiology. God's revelation and the formation of a people are in fact one theological movement.

9. This project eventually became *World Upside Down*.

expansion of the gospel and essential assumptions of religio-cultural life in the ancient Mediterranean world: the accounts of Christian mission in Lystra (Acts 14:8–19) and in Philippi (16:16–24). These two scenes are exegetically advantageous because they exhibit *in nuce* the potential volatility inherent in much early Christian interaction with pagan culture. In so doing, they allow us to draw out something of the necessary interconnection between theology and politics.

Before moving to the exegesis, however, a brief word about interpretive method is in order.[10] The exegesis below proceeds on two simple assumptions: first, that word meaning is contextually dependent, and, second, that a text is most fruitfully interpreted with at least some understanding of the "cultural encyclopedia" relevant to the text's genesis.[11] Thus, on the one hand, my treatment of these two passages should not be read as two separate diachronic studies of Luke's historical accuracy, skill in creating *Lokalkolorit*, and so on.[12] To the contrary, in each case the entire narrative of Acts is assumed as the wider interpretive context in which exegetical understanding is to be had. On the other hand, this literary reading is resolutely historical, in the sense that the narrative of Acts is situated within the Mediterranean culture of its early auditors. With these clarifications in mind, we may turn now to the exegesis.

ACTS 14: PAUL AND BARNABAS AS HERMES AND ZEUS

> To all but a few of the highly educated, the gods were indeed a potential presence whom a miracle might reveal.[13]

---

10. For a thorough account of the present state of method in the study of Acts, see Todd Penner, "Madness in the Method? The Acts of the Apostles in Current Study," *Currents in Biblical Research* 2, no. 2 (2004): 223–93.

11. The language of "cultural encyclopedia" derives from Umberto Eco and refers to the wider cultural knowledge (tacit and explicit) assumed by the author and embedded in a text by virtue of its origin within a particular time in history. So, for example, in contrast to the cultural encyclopedia that is now relevant to modern democracies, Luke has no idea of that which many people now claim is necessary—namely, the separation of religion and politics; this crisp distinction is simply not part of his knowledge base. To access Luke's cultural encyclopedia is immediately to become aware of the inextricable unity of religion and politics in one form of life.

12. For an excellent study of Luke's accuracy in local description, see Peter Lampe, "Acta 19 im Spiegel der ephesischen Inschriften," *Biblische Zeitschrift* 36 (1992): 59–76.

13. Lane Fox, *Pagans and Christians*, 140.

Part 1: Christology, Greco-Roman Culture, and Canonical Reception

After escaping a second straight round of persecution (first in Pisidian Antioch, then in Iconium), Paul and Barnabas make their way through Derbe, Lystra, and the surrounding countryside preaching the gospel (εὐαγγελιζόμενοι ἦσαν, 14:7). In the Roman colony of Lystra, Paul dramatically heals a cripple who has been listening to him preach (14:9a), whom Paul recognizes as having the πίστις to be healed (τοῦ σωθῆναι, 14:9bc).[14] The effect upon the crowds is immediate and overwhelming: they respond with religious acclamation and prepare to make a sacrificial offering to Paul and Barnabas as Hermes and Zeus (14:11–13). The apostles,[15] delayed by their inability to understand Lycaonian,[16] finally rush forth to protest this pagan worship and to call for its abandonment on the basis of a reconfiguration of divine identity (14:14–18). As a result, after the arrival of some Jews from Antioch and Iconium, the crowds are persuaded to stone Paul (14:19).[17]

Though it is perhaps startling to moderns, it is hardly surprising that in the ancient world a display of power would occasion the acclamation οἱ θεοὶ ὁμοιωθέντες ἀνθρώποις κατέβησαν πρὸς ἡμᾶς (14:11). Not only was great theological importance attached to miracles,[18] but Greco-Roman religious sensibilities had long been under the "spell of Homer,"[19] in which the appearance of the gods in human form was to be expected: "gods in the guise

---

14. The parallels with Peter's act of healing in Acts 3:1–10 and Jesus's in Luke 5:17–26 have long been observed, as has the connection to Jesus's programmatic reading of Isa 61 in the synagogue in Nazareth (Luke 4:18–19). Cf. Luke 7:22.

15. Acts 14:4, 14, the only time Paul and Barnabas are called ἀπόστολοι in Acts.

16. Many scholars note that this detail helps explain why the sacrificial act progressed as far as it did without the apostles' interference. See, e.g., Henry J. Cadbury, *The Book of Acts in History* (Eugene, OR: Wipf & Stock, 2004), 22.

17. There is a marked emphasis upon the ὄχλοι. The word occurs five times in ten verses (14:11, 13, 14, 18, 19).

18. Ramsay MacMullen, *Christianizing the Roman Empire: A. D. 100–400* (New Haven: Yale University Press, 1984), 25–42, for example, has argued strongly for the importance of Christian "wonder-working" as a major factor in the story of how Christianity won the battle of religions in the empire (cf. his *Paganism in the Roman Empire*, 96–97).

19. The phrase "spell of Homer" is taken from Walter Burkert's treatment of that theme in his classic study *Greek Religion* (Cambridge, MA: Harvard University Press, 1985), 119–25. Burkert speaks of a "common Homeric literary culture" from the eighth century onward (8). The judgment about the importance of Homer's influence is ubiquitous among classicists. See, e.g., Lane Fox, *Pagans and Christians*, 110; A. D. Nock, "Religious Attitudes of the Ancient Greeks," in *Essays on Religion and the Ancient World*, ed. Zeph Stewart (Oxford: Clarendon, 1972), 2:534–50 (esp. 543, 550); Simon R. F. Price, *Religions of the Ancient Greeks* (Cambridge: Cambridge University Press, 1999), 6.

of strangers from afar put on all manner of shapes, and visit the cities."[20] This was no less true in various hamlets or in the interior of Asia Minor than it was in Greece itself: "Even in wretched Olbia, on the Black Sea, the wandering orator Dio (c. 100 A. D.) flattered his audience on their passion for Homer and his poems."[21]

Philosophers, of course, from Xenophanes and Plato to the time of the NT and beyond were critical of Homer's anthropomorphism of the gods, crudely interpreted.[22] Only through sophisticated demythologization of the inherited mythology could Aristotle, for example, make the views of the "forefathers and of the earliest thinkers . . . intelligible."[23] Among intellectuals, this criticism naturally gained considerable currency. Luke's contemporary Josephus, for example, praises "the severe censure" of the Homeric tales by the "leading thinkers" among the "admired sages of Greece."[24]

Yet if we take our measure from material remains and from the views presupposed by the critics' criticism—as well as from the kind of data we see in Pausanias's vivid descriptions of local piety, for example—we find that "far into the second and third centuries A. D., this piety of the majority survived the wit of poets and philosophers."[25] Alexander of Abonuteichos, to take but one outstanding case from the mid-second century AD, began his career by

---

20. Homer, *Od.* 17.485-86 (trans. Murray, LCL). Cf. Lane Fox, *Pagans and Christians*, 119: "Greek votive reliefs of all periods owe a large debt to sightings of their gods." For this theme in the apocryphal Acts, see Rosa Söder, *Die apokryphen Apostelgeschichten und die romanhafte Literatur der Antike* (1932; Stuttgart: Kohlhammer, 1969), 95-98.

21. Lane Fox, *Pagans and Christians*, 110. For a concise treatment of the excerpts from Homer (and other ancient material) that circulated in the ancient world, see Henry Chadwick, "Florilegium," in *Reallexikon für Antike und Christentum*, ed. Theodor Klauser et al. (Stuttgart: Hiersemann, 1950-), 7:1131-60.

22. For a helpful starting point, see Price's chapter "Greek Thinkers" in *Religions of the Ancient Greeks*. Harold W. Attridge, "The Philosophical Critique of Religion under the Early Empire," *ANRW* 2.16.1 (1978): 45-78, provides a significant overview of the discussion during the time of the NT. See also Daniel Babut, *La religion des philosophes grecs: de Thalès aux Stoïciens* (Paris: Presses Universitaires de France, 1974), who discerns a broad unity in the locus of the critique despite considerable historical development and points of material disagreement within such a focus (esp. 204-5).

23. Aristotle, *Metaphysica* 12.8.18 (1074B; trans. Tredennick, LCL). Aristotle here holds that the mythology of gods "human in shape or . . . like certain other animals" was developed "to influence the vulgar and as a constitutional and utilitarian expedient."

24. Josephus, *C. Ap.* 2.239-42 §§33-34 (trans. Thackeray, LCL alt.).

25. Lane Fox, *Pagans and Christians*, 115. One of the outstanding merits of Lane Fox's study is that, in terms of historical perception, he refuses simply to adopt the more sophisticated philosophical perspectives that are frequently the viewpoint of the literary sources

Part 1: Christology, Greco-Roman Culture, and Canonical Reception

addressing the people from a high altar, ... [congratulating] the city because it was at once to receive the god [Asclepius] in visible presence. The assembly—for almost the whole city, including women, old men, and youths, had come running—marveled, prayed and worshiped. Uttering a few meaningless words like Hebrew or Phoenician, he dazed the people, who did not know what he was saying save only that he everywhere brought in Apollo and Asclepius.[26]

After Alexander displayed his divine powers by producing a small snake he had secretly prepared for the occasion, the people "at once raised a shout [and] welcomed the god."[27]

Lucian is no doubt having a bit of fun here, but in point of fact the cult in Abonuteichos—geographically considered, a sure misfire for economic gain—was enormously successful and did center on Alexander and his pet snake. From around 150 to the mid-170s, "people flocked to this distant point where Providence seemed to have broken afresh into the world. Its god gave personal advice to Romans of the highest rank and sent an oracle to the Emperor himself."[28] If behind Lucian's satire, therefore, we glimpse a philosophically trained (Pythagorean) and religiously nimble Alexander, we must also see that his skillful charlatanry was well calculated to fit a vast believing public.

Nor is it any surprise that in Lystra the local priest of Zeus and the crowds instantly prepared to sacrifice to Paul and Barnabas (θύειν, Acts 14:13, 18), inasmuch as to worship the gods in antiquity was to sacrifice. Ovid's *Metamorphoses*, to cite a work obviously germane to Acts 14, opens its treatment of transformation with Jupiter's (Zeus's) account of his descent from Olympus "as a god disguised in human form [*deus humana ... imagine*]." After appearing at his destination, Jupiter reports, "I gave a sign that a god had come, and the common folk began to worship me."[29] Ovid's tale is significant, not

---

and instead attempts to correlate more closely the views presupposed by those sources with other types of evidence (inscriptions, statues, etc.). Cf. the insightful remarks of MacMullen, *Paganism in the Roman Empire*, esp. 77–79. On Socratic criticism as the cause of an Athenian "religious crisis," see the judicious discussion by Robert Parker, *Athenian Religion: A History* (Oxford: Clarendon, 1996), esp. 199–217, who notes that Socrates's criticism of the gods was taken to be socially dangerous only because of its (perceived) necessary link to a moral relativism (esp. 212).

26. Lucian, *Alex.* 13 (trans. Harmon, LCL alt.).
27. Lucian, *Alex.* 14 (trans. Harmon, LCL).
28. Lane Fox, *Pagans and Christians*, 242. Lane Fox's concise discussion situates the cult within the overall "normal" cultic practice of the empire (241–50).
29. Ovid, *Metam.* 1.200–220 (trans. Miller, LCL).

The Book of Acts and the Cultural Explication of the Identity of God

simply because he was still the most influential poet of Rome when it was composed (ca. 8 AD), but because it reflects, with Acts 14:8-18, a common *topos*, a standard way of thinking about the appearance of the gods and the human response to them (cf. Acts 10:25-26 and 28:1-10). Indeed, if we read on in the *Metamorphoses* to book 8, we find the delightful account of the visit of Jupiter and Mercury (Hermes)—*specie mortali*—to the Phrygian countryside, where they are (finally[30]) received hospitably by the old couple Baucis and Philemon, who eventually ask to serve as priests for the gods (i.e., to guard their temple, to preside over the sacrifices, etc., 8.707-8). The similarity to Luke's account of Paul and Barnabas in Lystra is striking, and it is not without good reason that Acts scholars have frequently drawn attention to this passage in the *Metamorphoses* as a possible basis for Luke's story.[31] Prima facie, one might easily think the Lystrans' eagerness to honor Paul and Barnabas makes excellent sense in light of their religious prehistory: Hermes and Zeus had been sighted in the interior of Asia Minor before.

Whether or not Luke knew the story in Ovid's *Metamorphoses* or a local tradition is largely indeterminable.[32] The syncretistic Jew Artapanus (second century BC), for example, tells of Egyptians who accorded Moses divine honors and designated him "Hermes" in response to his hermeneutical skill.[33] And Horace, too, suggests that Augustus was Mercury in human shape.[34] But that Luke shares with

---

30. They are first unrecognized in their human form and rejected: "To a thousand homes they came, seeking a place for rest; a thousand homes were barred against them" (Ovid, *Metam.* 8.628-629, trans. Miller, LCL).

31. Luke Timothy Johnson, for example, remarks that "Luke may well be playing off a literary motif concerning the hospitality shown to the gods Zeus and Hermes by residents of Phrygia.... These folk do not want to miss the chance to be the next Baucis and Philemon!" Johnson, *The Acts of the Apostles*, SP 5 (Collegeville, MN: Liturgical Press, 1992), 251; see also his earlier remark: "It is difficult to avoid the suspicion that Luke's account plays off such a tradition" (248). Cf., e.g., C. K. Barrett, *A Critical and Exegetical Commentary on the Acts of the Apostles*, 2 vols., ICC (Edinburgh: T&T Clark, 1994-1998), 1:677; Klauck, *Magic and Paganism*, 59.

32. Cf. Cilliers Breytenbach, "Zeus und der lebendige Gott: Anmerkungen zu Apostelgeschichte 14.11-17," *NTS* 39 (1993): 396-413, who argues that both Ovid and Luke draw upon local traditions (403).

33. See the text in Carl R. Holladay, *Fragments from Hellenistic Jewish Authors*, vol. 1, *Historians* (Chico, CA: Scholars Press, 1983), 210-11, frg. 3, lines 10-13 (*apud* Eusebius, *Praep. ev.* 9.27.6; Eusebius quotes at this point from Alexander Polyhistor). Because of his theological "synchronism," whether Artapanus was Jewish or pagan has been a point of contention, but the consensus now is that he was a Jew (see Holladay, *Fragments*, 1:189-90).

34. Horace, *Carm.* 1.2, lines 40-45 ("sive mutate iuvenem figura ales in terris imitaris

Part 1: Christology, Greco-Roman Culture, and Canonical Reception

Ovid and other Greco-Romans a basic understanding of the religious patterns that surround the appearance of the gods can hardly be denied. In this, as in other areas of his portrayal of paganism (see below), Luke is simply a man of his time. As Robin Lane Fox puts it, "Acts' author believed this response was natural."[35]

Where Luke's historical situatedness is forgotten, the critical theological edge of this carefully sketched scene is badly blunted. Ernst Haenchen, for example, asks with respect to the pagan response to Barnabas and Paul, "But is it really conceivable?" His answer is clearly that it is not:

> That the priest of Zeus would immediately believe that the two wonder-workers were Zeus and Hermes, and hasten up with oxen and garlands, is highly improbable.... It is not only the priest's credulity, moreover, but that of the people which is unconvincing. The healing of the cripple was admittedly a great miracle. But surely not so great as to persuade the Lycaonians that their very gods stood in their midst.[36]

But this reading is, at best, to replace ancient religious practice with its philosophical critique, or already to adopt unawares the perspective of Paul and Barnabas. At worst, it is no less than a radical modernizing of the text, in the sense that it dismisses fundamental aspects of pagan religion as mere silliness.[37]

By contrast, to become aware of the normalcy—indeed, the religious propriety—of the pagan reaction is to become aware of the requisite background against which Luke's scene derives its critical force. For Luke's call through the mouths of Paul and Barnabas is not simply an admonition to tweak a rite or halt a ceremony. It contains, rather, a summons that simultaneously involves the destruction of an entire mode of being "religious."

It is true, of course, that in a certain respect Paul and Barnabas appear "as genuine philosophers who reject such attempts at deification"[38] and in this way

---

almae filius Maiae patiens vocari Caesaris ultor"). Noted also in A. D. Nock, *Conversion* (Oxford: Clarendon, 1933), 237.

35. Lane Fox, *Pagans and Christians*, 100.

36. Ernst Haenchen, *The Acts of the Apostles: A Commentary*, trans. Bernard Noble and Gerald Shinn, rev. R. McL. Wilson (Philadelphia: Westminster, 1971), 432.

37. Klauck, *Magic and Paganism*, 57, remarks: "Apparitions of gods on earth in human form are a stable element of hellenistic piety—assertions to the contrary in some commentaries are nothing more than a sign that their authors have never read the 'Bible of the Greeks,' Homer's epics." Klauck does not mention whom he has in mind, and it is difficult to believe that Haenchen never read Homer, but Klauck's general point is sound.

38. Johnson, *Acts*, 251. Cf. Nock, "Religious Attitudes," 2:549.

The Book of Acts and the Cultural Explication of the Identity of God

evince a joining of hands with pagan philosophical criticism.[39] Yet simply to note this connection is to reduce the import of the passage to a single point of contact with a small minority in the wider culture.

With few exceptions, principal philosophical critique was directed more against superstition (see, e.g., Plutarch's περὶ δεισιδαιμονίας[40]) and overly literal interpretation of myth than it was against cultic practice.[41] In spite of the manifest theological problems exposed by his lucid dialogue on the nature of the gods, for example, Cicero believed firmly in the necessity of traditional cultic practice (*Nat. d.* 1.2.4) and was himself—despite *De divinatione*—a member of the College of Augurs (*Nat. d.* 1.6.14).[42] So too the same Plutarch who in his earlier years could rant against the impiety of the superstitious could later become a priest at Delphi with no sense of discontinuity. And the Stoics, despite Zeno's criticism of building temples to gods, "attend the mysteries in temples, go up to the Acropolis, do reverence to statues [προσκυνοῦσι . . . τὰ ἕδη], and place wreaths upon the

---

39. By the first century AD, this "refusal of divine honors" had become a highly complex, grand-scale political maneuver—specifically in relation to the Roman emperor—and varied as to its interpretation within the different parts of the empire. See, e.g., M. P. Charlesworth, "The Refusal of Divine Honours: An Augustan Formula," *PBSR* 15 (1939): 1–10; or Price, *Rituals and Power*, 72–77. Pseudo-Callisthenes's *Alexander Romance* (*The Life of Alexander of Macedon*) is frequently cited in relation to Acts (so Johnson, *Acts*, 249); see, e.g., 2.22: "I beg off from honors equal to the gods. For I am a mortal man and I fear such ceremonies. For they bring danger to the soul" (trans. Haight). But it should be acknowledged that even in this work Alexander does not always refuse the honors (e.g., 2.14) and that the third-century date and the weak historical core of the work make it difficult to relate to Acts.

40. On the complex associations surrounding this term and its cognates, which also occur in Acts 17:22 and 25:19, see P. J. Koets, Δεισιδαιμονία: *A Contribution to the Knowledge of the Religious Terminology in Greek* (Purmerend: Muusses, 1929).

41. Certain types of Cynics are the primary exceptions (e.g., Diogenes of Sinope and, if Eusebius is accurate, Oenomaus of Gadara). There were of course accusations leveled at Epicurus along these lines (recall, e.g., the linkage of Epicureans with Christians and atheists in Lucian, *Alex.* 38), but we must remember that Philodemus's *On Piety* defended Epicurus with respect to traditional religious practice, claiming even that he was initiated into the Eleusinian Mysteries. On this point in general, see Attridge, "Philosophical Critique"; Price, *Religions of the Ancient Greeks*, 135–37.

42. See too, of course, his *On the Laws*—modeled on Plato's similarly titled work—in which he argues for the necessity of religious practice for the good of Roman society; indeed, the "rites shall ever be preserved and continuously handed down in families, and . . . they must be continued forever" (*De legibus* 2.19.47, trans. Keyes, LCL). On Plato as the "first political thinker to argue that matters of belief can be criminal offences," see Price, *Religions of the Ancient Greeks*, 133–34.

shrines."[43] Even Epicureans, though considered by some to be atheists,[44] sacrificed to the gods.[45]

Luke's criticism, however, goes much deeper and aims at the very foundations that support the edifice of pagan religiousness in the effort to break the entire structure with a single biblical word—μάταια.[46] Accompanied by prophetic action—the rending of their clothes[47]—Paul and Barnabas characterize the whole scene as worthless, futile, or vain.[48] Though εἰκόνες/ἀγάλματα/ξόανα would hardly be excluded, the passage gives no indication that they are directly in view. At this point, images are not in themselves the problem. Rather, the critique reaches further, toward the entire religious complex of pagan deities and cultic sacrifice. Luke is not interested in philosophical reform or in demythologizing but in ἐπιστροφή, a conversion to a way of life incompatible with traditional pagan cults (cf. Acts 15:3, τὴν ἐπιστροφὴν τῶν ἐθνῶν; 26:20, καὶ τοῖς ἔθνεσιν ἀπήγγελλον μετανοεῖν καὶ ἐπιστρέφειν ἐπὶ τὸν θεόν).[49] Turn, say Paul and Barnabas, from these backward acclamations (the honor of mere humans as θεοί) and lifeless practices (sacrifice) to the living God.[50]

---

43. Plutarch, *Mor.* 1034B (trans. Cherniss, LCL).

44. See, e.g., Cicero, *Nat. d.* 2.30.76; Lucian, *Alex.* 38.

45. Plutarch, *Mor.* 1034C; cf. Cicero, *Nat. d.* 1.30.85, 123; 3.1.3.

46. The relevant occurrences are plentiful. See, e.g., (LXX) Lev 17:7; Amos 2:4; Isa 32:6; Jer 10:3, 15; Ezek 8:10. See also BDAG 621.

47. Though it may well be that "Halb nackt mit zerrissenen Kleidern (vgl. *Appian* Bell Civ I, 66,300) man kaum noch für einen Gott gehalten werden [kann]" (Rudolf Pesch, *Die Apostelgeschichte*, 2 vols., EKKNT 5 [Neukirchen-Vluyn: Neukirchener Verlag, 1986], 2:58), the more likely point for the narrative audience is similar to what one sees in the OT or, better, in Matt 26:65//Mark 14:63 when the high priest tears his clothes at the perceived blasphemy. Cf., from a later period, m. Sanhedrin 7.5.

48. Reading diachronically, the crowd in Lystra would hardly have heard μάταια with its larger biblical resonance (false god). Yet at the level of the narrative audience, Luke shapes the auditor's perception by the use of this theologically freighted word from the LXX.

49. Of course, pagans too could speak of ἐπιστροφή (Plato, *Resp.* 7.517Cff., of the task of educating the soul) or *conversio* (Cicero, *Nat. d.* 1.37.77, of the philosophers' attempt with the masses), but the point here is that such "turning" was compatible with traditional cultic practice, whereas for Luke it clearly is not, and the ultimate object toward which one is to turn is clearly different.

50. Barrett, *Acts*, 1:680, is right to note of ἐπιστρέφειν that "the verb has so fully taken on the sense of proclamation that it means almost to command: telling you to turn." The relationship to 1 Thess 1:9 has often been discussed; see, e.g., Ulrich Wilckens, *Die Missionsreden der Apostelgeschichte: Form- und traditionsgeschichtliche Untersuchungen* (Neukirchen-Vluyn: Neukirchener Verlag, 1961), esp. 86–87.

The criticism thus has both a deconstructive and a constructive dimension. On the one hand, where the pagan action would bring the human and divine almost entirely together, there is in the cry (κράζοντες) of Paul and Barnabas the explicit emphasis upon ἄνθρωποι in their sheer humanness, as it were, as an attempt to open a space between human beings and God. Καὶ ἡμεῖς ... ἐσμεν ἄνθρωποι is emphatic and, indeed, reminds the reader/audience of Peter's similar exclamation when confronted by a prostrate Cornelius: καὶ ἐγὼ αὐτὸς ἄνθρωπός εἰμι! (10:26).[51] In both cases, the speakers move to establish a common humanity with their audience and hence to drive an ontological wedge between themselves and the divine. In Acts 14:15 this attempt is further strengthened with the use of ὁμοιοπαθεῖς ... ὑμῖν, particularly as it counterbalances ἡμεῖς ... ἐσμεν. Ἡμεῖς ὁμοιοπαθεῖς ἐσμεν ὑμῖν ἄνθρωποι: "we" are just like "you"—human beings through and through. Ὁμοιοπαθεῖς would of course, to the ear of the philosophically trained auditor, seal the deconstructive case: a true θεός is one without πάθος.[52] Paul and Barnabas are human.

On the other hand, the message is not simply cease and desist. Rather, as Luke Johnson notes, the religious impulse of the crowds is received even as the official machinery is shut off. In this way, the reception of the pagan impulse involves an essential reinterpretation as to its telos—the living God. Barrett is correct that θεὸς ζῶν is "almost a proper name";[53] the potency of the name comes through in the utter contrast between death and life, the turning away from τούτων τῶν ματαίων toward θεὸν ζῶντα, the source of life itself: ἐποίησεν τὸν οὐρανὸν καὶ τὴν γῆν καὶ τὴν θάλασσαν καὶ πάντα τὰ ἐν αὐτοῖς (14:15).[54] To be the "living" God is to be Creator, to possess the life-giving power to do good and to bring rain and sustenance (14:17).

The pagan religious impulse is thus redirected toward the living God by a sweeping criticism and the unveiling of the true divine reality behind the gifts that sustain life in the natural world. Zeus was of course seen as the giver of good things—ἐπιδιδόναι γὰρ δὴ ἀγαθὰ αὐτὸν ἀνθρώποις[55]—and, in particular, as the rain god (Ζεὺς Ὑέτιος/Ὄμβριος, etc.). In fact, these two functions

---

51. On this point, see C. Kavin Rowe, "Luke-Acts and the Imperial Cult: A Way through the Conundrum?," *JSNT* 27 (2005): 279–300, esp. 290, reprinted in this volume at pp. 3–23. Cf. Barrett, *Acts*, 1:665, who notes that the "denial that apostles and evangelists are anything other than human" is a Lukan theme.

52. Cf. Josephus's criticism in *C. Ap.* 2.251 §35.

53. Barrett, *Acts*, 1:680.

54. Cf. Breytenbach, "Zeus und der lebendige Gott," 397, who notes the OT and early Jewish link between ὁ θεὸς ζῶν and his status as Creator.

55. Pausanias, *Descr.* 8.9.2, here of Zeus in Mantineia.

Part 1: Christology, Greco-Roman Culture, and Canonical Reception

could easily be linked, as Pausanias reports: "There is on Parnes another altar, and on it they make sacrifice, calling Zeus sometimes Rain-god [ὄμβριον], sometimes Averter of Ills [ἀπήμιον]."[56] In light of these well-known functions of Zeus,[57] the radical nature of the apostles' reinterpretation emerges in that it does not, in the manner of Aristobulus, for example, consist of a simple substitution of numinous realities—"that which you call Zeus is really the God of Israel."[58] It thus has no affinity with ancient pluralism (in which, e.g., divine names can be only incidental to divine realities[59]). Instead, it involves both a demolition of the pagan model in toto (worshiping Zeus is futile) and a call for a new construction of divine identity. Cilliers Breytenbach puts well the implicit theological ground: the God whom they preach is not only "der lebendige Gott" but "auch der *einzige* lebendige Gott."[60] At least as Luke would have it, the telos of the pagan religious impulse is not in need of a different

---

56. Pausanias, *Descr.* 1.32.2 (trans. Jones, LCL). "Averter of ills" can be read as the obverse of one who brings good. See ἀπήμιος and its cognates in LSJ (188; cf. ἀπήμων as "kindly" or "propitious" in Homer, *Od.* 7.266). For the ancient altar on Parnes, see Parker, *Athenian Religion*, 30–31. Breytenbach, "Zeus und der lebendige Gott," 399–403, provides an excellent summary of the relevant material for Zeus and Hermes in relation to Lystra in particular.

57. See the relevant material in Arthur Bernard Cook's monumental study *Zeus: A Study in Ancient Religion*, 3 vols. (Cambridge: Cambridge University Press, 1914–1940).

58. In citing the opening lines of Aratus's *Phaenomena*, Aristobulus simply substitutes θεός for Ζεύς/Δίς: "we have signified [that the power of θεός permeates all things] by removing the divine names Δίς and Ζεύς used throughout the verses; for their inherent meaning relates to θεός" (*apud* Eusebius, *Praep. ev.* 13.12). For the text and translation of Aristobulus, see Carl R. Holladay, *Fragments from Hellenistic Jewish Authors*, vol. 3, *Aristobulus* (Atlanta: Scholars Press, 1995), 171–73. Such theological moves were of course routine in the ancient Mediterranean world. To take only two of many possible examples, we may think of the closing hymn to Apollo in the first book of Statius, *Thebaid*, in which Apollo is asked for his blessings "whether 'tis right to call thee rosy Titan . . . or Osiris . . . or Mithras" (1.696–720, trans. Mozley, LCL); or, in a more philosophical vein, of Pseudo-Aristotle: "God being one has many names" (*De mundo* 401A). See also the discussion below on Acts 16 (pp. 124–29).

59. "Dis pater Veiovis Manes, sive vos quo alio nomine fas est nominare," ran an ancient Roman prayer; preserved in Macrobius, *Saturnalia* 3.9.10; cited in P. W. van der Horst, "The Unknown God," in *Knowledge of God in the Graeco-Roman World*, ed. R. van den Broek, T. Baarda, and J. Mansfeld (Leiden: Brill, 1988), 39. Modern religious relativism (in which, e.g., divine names reflect only the social location of the religious person) is of course also nowhere in sight.

60. Breytenbach, "Zeus und der lebendige Gott," 397. For a list of the allusions to the OT in 14:15–18, see esp. Gustav Stählin, *Die Apostelgeschichte*, NTD 5 (Göttingen: Vandenhoeck & Ruprecht, 1962), 193–94, who lists nine principal areas—with about twenty texts—that demonstrate the OT theological roots of Paul's exclamation.

The Book of Acts and the Cultural Explication of the Identity of God

or additional name; rather, the impulse itself requires a fundamentally new direction, from dead worship to the living God.

With such a message, it is no great wonder that the crowds, having barely (μόλις) been put off, are subsequently persuaded to attack (14:18–19).[61] This end to the episode in Lystra articulates narratively something of the offense caused by a collision of divine identity and the practices it entails. Contrary to much received scholarly wisdom, in Acts the gospel does not routinely meet with exuberant acceptance among the Gentiles (cf., e.g., 14:2 and the careful ὅσοι formulation of 13:48).[62] It may well be that God ἐν ταῖς παρῳχημέναις γενεαῖς εἴασεν πάντα τὰ ἔθνη πορεύεσθαι ταῖς ὁδοῖς αὐτῶν (14:16), but simply by its mention, the phrase intimates that the time has now come for Gentiles to turn away from their foolish ὁδοί toward the living God.[63] If idolatry is at least as much "an error about the management of society (a political error)"

---

61. Taking the pl. λιθάσαντες in v. 19 to include the crowds (in light of πείσαντες—what else would be its purpose?). So, rightly, Jacob Jervell, *Die Apostelgeschichte: Übersetzt und erklärt*, KEK 3 (Göttingen: Vandenhoeck & Ruprecht, 1998), 379 n. 607; Gerhard Schneider, *Die Apostelgeschichte*, 2 vols., HThKNT (Freiburg: Herder, 1980–1982), 2:162. Contra Klauck, *Magic and Paganism*, 60–61, who thinks (a) that Luke includes only the Jews from Iconium, and (b) that Luke needs correction—Paul would not have survived a Jewish stoning—so that a Gentile mob is in view. If one takes λιθάσαντες to include the crowds, Klauck's problem simply disappears.

62. So, rightly, Pesch, *Apostelgeschichte*, 2:59–60. Johnson, *Acts*, 251, forces the passage in a positive direction when he writes that this scene shows how God "is opening a door of faith for the Gentiles." Johnson is correct that the Gentiles are not simply condemned for their idolatry. In an important sense, they are open to divine visitation. However, to read the passage as something of a commendation of the Gentile impulse toward idolatry ("Luke portrays these rustics as having precisely the conditions for genuine faith," 251) goes too far and makes unintelligible the concluding evangelistic disaster. If God is opening a door for the Gentiles in Lystra (see μαθηταί in 14:22), it would seem to be on the basis of Paul's preaching (14:7) rather than this healing in particular (indeed, as Haenchen, *Acts of the Apostles*, 431, noted, the mention of πίστιν τοῦ σωθῆναι in 14:9 presupposes Paul's preaching). Moreover, the exhortation in 14:22 to the disciples in Lystra, Iconium, and Antioch seems to point to some level of persecution in these locations (παρακαλοῦντες ἐμμένειν τῇ πίστει καὶ ὅτι διὰ πολλῶν θλίψεων δεῖ ἡμᾶς εἰσελθεῖν εἰς τὴν βασιλείαν τοῦ θεοῦ). That "much suffering/many tribulations" could be the life of the disciples in Lystra is of course narratively compelling in light of the proximity of 14:22 to the Lystra story, though it could easily pertain also to the missionaries' prior experience in Pisidian Antioch and Iconium (13:50–14:6).

63. Jacob Jervell, *The Theology of the Acts of the Apostles* (Cambridge: Cambridge University Press, 1996), 19, takes v. 16 as a statement about God's absence from the history of Gentiles. Perhaps this is to go too far, but the narrative contrast with the description of God's continuous activity in Israel is certainly striking.

Part 1: Christology, Greco-Roman Culture, and Canonical Reception

as it is an error of the mind,[64] it should occasion no surprise that those who would be affected by the destabilizing power of its theological critique should attempt to drive the bearer of the message out of their community.

Acts 16: Paul and the Pythian Spirit

> Street prophets were strongly in evidence. We hear much about prophetic women, "pythonesses," as they were popularly known.[65]

After Paul's escape from Lystra, Luke narrates swiftly the passage through Derbe and Paul's eventual journey to the apostolic council (Acts 14:19–15:5). Upon approval from James and the council, Paul resumes his Mediterranean mission, and soon thereafter, in response to a vision, travels to the Roman colony of Philippi with his fellow missionaries (note the change to "we" in 16:10). In Philippi, after the conversion of Lydia (16:14–15), the missionaries are "opposed" (ὑπαντῆσαι) by a certain παιδίσκη with a πνεῦμα πύθωνα, whose oracles bring her masters (κύριοι) much economic benefit. Subsequent to their initial meeting, the mantic girl follows the missionaries around, crying (ἔκρα-ζεν), "These men are slaves τοῦ θεοῦ τοῦ ὑψίστου, who proclaim to you ὁδὸν σωτηρίας" (16:17).[66] Paul, who is greatly annoyed, exorcises the spirit in the name of Jesus Christ (16:18), and in turn, the girl's masters—with the ὄχλος and στρατηγοί (16:22–23)—see that Paul is removed from their midst. For our purposes, we may focus upon four aspects of the scene in Philippi.

First, recalling that ὕψιστος was "a term . . . vague enough to suit any god treated as the supreme being"[67] helps disclose the narrative force of v. 17's initial ambiguity. Within the world of the story there exists the linguistic and chronological space—Paul was followed for "many days" (πολλὰς ἡμέρας)—for the

---

64. Moshe Halbertal and Avishai Margalit, *Idolatry*, trans. Naomi Goldblum (Cambridge, MA: Harvard University Press, 1992), 163.

65. Lane Fox, *Pagans and Christians*, 208.

66. Cf. Luke 8:28, where the Gerasene demoniac cries out in a great voice (ἀνακράξας . . . φωνῇ μεγάλῃ), "What have you to do with me, Jesus, Son τοῦ θεοῦ τοῦ ὑψίστου?" In this pericope Luke speaks both of demons (pl., δαιμόνια) and of an unclean spirit (sg., τὸ πνεῦμα τὸ ἀκάθαρτον). These two different ways of speaking are presumably unified in the single name "Legion," which stands for the man's possession by many demons.

67. A. D. Nock, "The Guild of Zeus Hypsistos," in *Essays*, 1:425. See Arthur Bernard Cook, *Zeus: A Study in Ancient Religion*, 3 vols. (Cambridge: Cambridge University Press, 1914–1940), for Zeus; Barrett, *Acts*, 2:786, for other literature.

pagan misidentification of the God of Israel with the highest god in the (local) pantheon.[68] Indeed, if Stephen Mitchell is right, there are "good grounds for thinking that the place where this confrontation occurred was a sanctuary of Theos Hypsistos. . . . The cult of Theos Hypsistos is well attested epigraphically in cities of Aegean and Propontic Thrace around the middle of the first century AD."[69] In any case, such fusion and interchangeability of the divine were of course commonplaces in Greco-Roman antiquity, at both the popular and the philosophical levels. As Celsus would later put it, "I think . . . that it makes no difference whether we call Zeus the Most High (ὕψιστον), or Zen, or Adonai, or Sabaoth, or Ammon like the Egyptians, or Papaeus like the Scythians."[70]

This is hardly to say, of course, that the proclamation (καταγγέλλω[71]) presupposed by the narrative was itself polytheistic, as if Christian auditors/readers of Acts would be unaware of the specific identity of the Most High God. Rather, it is to point out that the reader can realistically imagine that the Gentile audience of Paul and his companions (ἡμεῖς, v. 17) would have heard the mantic's cry as a polytheistic interpretation of Christian proclamation—that is, these are the prophets of the Most High (ὁ ὕψιστος Ζεύς) who

---

68. So, rightly, e.g., Barrett, *Acts*, 2:786.

69. See Stephen Mitchell, "The Cult of Theos Hypsistos between Pagans, Jews, and Christians," in *Pagan Monotheism in Late Antiquity*, ed. Polymnia Athanassiadi and Michael Frede (Oxford: Clarendon, 1999), 110; cf. 115-21. A cultic site has yet to be found in Philippi in particular. Mitchell's suggestion depends upon (a) a coordination of Luke's use of προσευχή (Acts 16:13, 16) with the terminology of other known Theos Hypsistos "shrines," (b) the possibility that Lydia—as a god-fearer—would have already been involved in the worship of Theos Hypsistos, and (c) the widespread finds mentioned in the main text of this essay. Mitchell notes that the cult of Theos Hypsistos "from the Hellenistic period until the fifth century was found in town and country across the entire eastern Mediterranean and the Near East" (125-26). See too the concise treatment by Paul R. Trebilco, *Jewish Communities in Asia Minor*, SNTSMS 69 (Cambridge: Cambridge University Press, 1991), 127-44 (esp. 143 for this context).

70. *Apud* Origen, *Cels.* 5.41 (trans. Chadwick). The identification of Jupiter/Zeus ὕψιστος with the God of the Jews was of course present already in Varro (see the collection of texts in Menahem Stern, *Greek and Latin Authors on Jews and Judaism*, 3 vols. [Jerusalem: Israel Academy of Sciences and Humanities, 1974-1984], 1:210-11) and continued through late antiquity. See, e.g., Damascius, *Isidorus* 141 (*apud* Photius, *Bibliotheca*): "[Isidorus wrote] that on this mountain there is a most holy sanctuary of Zeus the Highest [ὕψιστος] to whom Abraham the father of the old Hebrews consecrated himself" (trans. Stern, 2:674). One does not have to argue that the populace was consciously aware of the Platonic or Stoic philosophical pressure toward one supreme being—refracted differently through different (local) gods—to note the intermingling of divine names (Zeus Sarapis/Attis/Dionysius, etc.).

71. For Luke's use of καταγγέλλω, see esp. Acts 4:2; 13:38; 16:21(!); 17:3, 18, 23; 26:23.

Part 1: Christology, Greco-Roman Culture, and Canonical Reception

provide healing (σωτηρία).⁷² Indeed, as Klauck suggests, this conscription of God's identity by local religious tradition may well be the (implied) reason for Paul's annoyance (v. 18).⁷³

The ambiguity in the phrase τοῦ θεοῦ τοῦ ὑψίστου, however, lasts only until the exorcism, at which time the identity of the Most High receives christological specification: ὁ θεὸς ὁ ὕψιστος is not Ζεὺς ὕψιστος (or any other "supreme being") but the God who works σωτηρία through the name of Jesus Christ (cf. Acts 4:12!). Moreover, prior to this specification, it is not clear within the world of the story that Paul's proclamation necessarily entails an attack upon pagan religiousness. But the explicit appearance of the name Jesus Christ involves a simultaneous confrontation with a pagan πνεῦμα and the economic practices that depend upon pneumatic presence. That the citizens of Philippi find the implications of this confrontation threatening is made clear by the ensuing events, in which the power of Jesus Christ is interpreted narratively as a force of subversion for the religio-economic habits of the polis (16:19–24).

Second, though some scholars note the possible meaning of πύθων as "ventriloquist,"⁷⁴ such a reading makes little sense here.⁷⁵ However much the double accusative may surprise us,⁷⁶ it seems clear that the meaning is something like "a pythian/pythonic spirit."⁷⁷ The description is not of linguistic trickery

---

72. On the non-eschatological meaning of σωτηρία for pagans, Nock, *Conversion*, 9, is concise.

73. Klauck, *Magic and Paganism*, 69.

74. Werner Foerster, "πύθων," *TDNT* 6:917–20.

75. See too the still-relevant critique of ventriloquism in general as a way to explain the phenomena of divination, prophecy, etc. in E. R. Dodds, *The Greeks and the Irrational* (Berkeley: University of California Press, 1951), 71–72, with notes.

76. Barrett, *Acts*, 2:785.

77. The girl, that is, has "a spirit, a pythian/pythonic one," taking the accusatives in apposition. Though a larger resonance with the official priestess (πυθία or πυθιάς) in Delphi or its mythological prehistory could well be intended (see Beverly Roberts Gaventa, *The Acts of the Apostles*, ANTC [Nashville: Abingdon, 2003], 238), "official" cultic religion is not primarily in view here. In the first instance, πύθων is used at this point, rather, in a more general sense of one of the many and various fortune tellers of the ancient world (see, e.g., the tale of the nameless but influential wanderer in Plutarch, *Def. orac.* 421A–E, or Lucian, *Alex.* 9, which mentions traveling mantics [μαντεύεσθαι] as if they were a commonplace; and Dio Chrysostom, *Disc.* 1.56, who contrasts a true mantic with the οἱ πολλοὶ τῶν λεγομένων ἐνθέων ἀνδρῶν καὶ γυναικῶν—the many men and women who are only said to be inspired). Cf. too the plural "pythons" in Pseudo-Clement, *Homiliae*, 9.16.3: ὅτι καὶ πύθωνες μαντεύονται ἀλλ' ὑφ' ἡμῶν ὡς δαίμονες ὁρκιζόμενοι φυγαδεύονται ("for even pythons prophesy, but they are cast out by us as demons, and put to flight"). Klauck, *Magic and Paganism*, 65–66, takes πύθων as a proper name, "a spirit, Python." This is an attractive

The Book of Acts and the Cultural Explication of the Identity of God

but of the animating spirit that is the source of the oracles (μαντευομένη, v. 16).[78] It is this spirit of divination—in Plutarch's language, the δαίμων[79]— that is the immediate target of Paul's exorcism. This emerges clearly in v. 18, where Luke is careful to differentiate the spirit (σοι) from the girl (ἀπ' αὐτῆς) through Paul's direct address to the πνεῦμα: "I charge you in the name of Jesus Christ to come out from *her*."

Thus it is, third, that the intense anger of the masters is narratively intelligible. It is not that Paul has announced the nature of a ventriloquist's linguistic trick to the wider public in order to enlighten their minds, but rather that he has destroyed the means by which the oracles were produced. The display of power through the evocation of the name Jesus Christ has removed *dynamically*—rather than simply epistemologically—the economic benefit derived from the possession of the girl. The masters own the παιδίσκη, not the πνεῦμα. The πνεῦμα has gone out (ἐξῆλθεν).[80] Indeed, the text may even suggest that this display of Jesus Christ's superior power is visible to the masters: they see (ἰδόντες) that the hope of their gain has gone out (ἐξῆλθεν).[81]

Finally, it is this dynamic character of the exorcism that is at bottom what is so fundamentally disruptive in Philippi. If Cicero is right, there had long been philosophical criticism of μαντική (*Div.* 1.4ff.; *Nat. d.* 2.3.9), at least in its more official forms.[82] Yet Paul's action is hardly the type of intellectual stroke that can be parried by the piety of the masses. To the contrary, the vanquishing of the pythonic spirit is a tear in the basic fabric of pagan popular religion in that it demonstrates publicly the weakness of the pagan πνεῦμα in the face of the

---

translation in view of the emphasis upon the πνεῦμα in v. 18; yet in light of Lukan style, it is probably better to retain the adjectival sense (see BDF §242).

78. On μαντεία, κτλ. as oracle, etc., see LSJ 1079–80. We may also note that μαντεύεσθαι is used only here in the NT and thus never of Christian prophets. Luke's usage follows that of the LXX, where μαντεύεσθαι, κτλ. are uniformly employed in a critical sense and not of Israel's prophets.

79. See *Def. orac.* 417 et passim.

80. Cf. Plutarch, *De Pythiae oraculis* 402B-C, who notes the worry about the πυθία that "the spirit [πνεῦμα] has been completely quenched and her powers have forsaken her" (trans. Babbitt, LCL), or *Def. orac.* 418D, where Cleombrotus speaks, for the moment, for those who believe that the defection of the oracles should be attributed to the departure of the δαίμονες (cf. also, e.g., *Def. orac.* 438C-D).

81. Of course, it is entirely possible that 16:19 simply means that the masters become aware that the oracles will stop. But in light of the "form" of exorcism stories in general, it would not be out of character for there to be a demonstration of the spirit's departure.

82. Cicero mentions Xenophanes. See also Dodds, *Greeks and the Irrational*, 190, who makes reference to Cicero's note, along with other evidence.

Part 1: Christology, Greco-Roman Culture, and Canonical Reception

missionaries and their message. Inasmuch as such religious life was woven together with material gain,[83] such a tear means the unraveling of mantic-based economics as well (v. 19). If it is anywhere near true that "prophetic persons were to be found everywhere, in the cities, the countryside, in every cultural zone of the Empire,"[84] the economic effect could well be considerable. In this sense, the masters of the παιδίσκη perceive rightly that the power of the name Jesus Christ extends beyond one mantic; Paul and Silas are in fact "disturbing the city" (v. 20).

Verse 21 thus encapsulates the juxtaposition of perspectives present in the conflict: καὶ καταγγέλλουσιν ἔθη ἃ οὐκ ἔξεστιν ἡμῖν παραδέχεσθαι οὐδὲ ποιεῖν Ῥωμαίοις οὖσιν. Of course, if we read from Luke's perspective and take οὐκ ἔξεστιν in v. 21 in a strictly legal sense, the charges are untrue and incapable of substantiation, as we know from the magistrates' decision to release Paul and Silas in peace (16:36, *prior* to their knowledge that Paul and Silas are Roman citizens). The missionaries are not calling for riotous insurrection (στάσις). Yet read from within the perspective of the characters who utter the charges, it must be admitted that, despite their motivation (v. 19), they have witnessed in Paul's exorcism the inherently destabilizing power of Jesus Christ for the pagan way of life. The recognition of the superior power of Jesus Christ is simultaneously the invalidation of the power claims of other πνεύματα. As Ramsay MacMullen has rightly noted, "The unique force of Christian wonder-working . . . lies in the fact that *it destroyed belief as well as creating it*—that is, if you credited it, you had then to credit the view that went with it, denying the character of god to all other divine powers whatsoever."[85] To adopt the ἔθη

---

83. In addition to this passage itself, see, e.g., Cicero, *Div.* 2.132–33, who mentions diviners who "prophesy for money" and "beg a coin": "I [Ennius] do not recognize fortunetellers, or those who prophesy for money, or necromancers, or mediums, whom your friend Appius makes it a practice to consult . . . for they are not diviners either by knowledge or skill. . . . From those to whom they promise wealth they beg a coin . . ." (trans. Falconer, LCL); and Plato, *Resp.* 2.364B–C, who knows of nonprofessional diviners that are the equivalent of door-to-door religious salesmen.

84. Lane Fox, *Pagans and Christians*, 207. Cf. Ramsay MacMullen, *Enemies of the Roman Order: Treason, Unrest, and Alienation in the Empire* (Cambridge, MA: Harvard University Press, 1966), 128: "In the Roman empire, a universal confidence that the future could be known either through rites of official priests on public occasions, or privately, produced an infinitely combustible audience for predictions." At the level of more official oracles, scholars have long noted that Plutarch's *De defectu oraculorum* is not the final word on the subject. Business in Delphi may have slowed, but it was booming in Abonuteichos. See, e.g., MacMullen, *Paganism in the Roman Empire*, 61–62 and 175–76 n. 55.

85. MacMullen, *Christianizing the Roman Empire*, 108–9.

advocated by these missionaries, as in fact happens in the Philippian pericope both preceding and following (Lydia and the jailer), would thus be to accept (παραδέχεσθαι) and to embody (ποιεῖν) a set of convictions that run counter to (οὐκ ἔξεστιν) the religious life of the polis. In this way, too, the ὄχλος and στρατηγοί—doubtless encouraged by the Ἰουδαῖοι/Ῥωμαῖοι contrast[86]—are given credible motive in the logic of the narrative to join in the attack (vv. 22–23). Harbingers of economic and/or religious disaster rarely elicit affection. Given such a confrontational display of power, it is hardly surprising that after their beating and imprisonment the missionaries are finally asked to leave the city (vv. 22–24, 39).

Conclusion

In an article that attempted to explore Luke's "common ground with paganism," F. G. Downing concluded that in Acts "only the persistent literalists are under attack."[87] At a glance, one can see how Luke's criticism of "literalist" views of statues and images (Acts 17:24–25, 29)—if taken in isolation—could generate such a conclusion. Upon a closer reading of the evidence, however, Downing's proposal can be seen to fall far short of the mark.

As the scenes in the Roman colonies of Lystra and Philippi illustrate, the apocalypse of God to the Gentiles does not merely offer a professor's remonstrance to the simpleminded but, much more radically, exposes the profound incommensurability between different theological frameworks and the resultant overall construal of human existence. This is no less true in Iconium, Thessalonica, Athens, Ephesus, and elsewhere. The particular narrative segments vary in intensity, of course,[88] but seen as a whole, the picture is one of collision between Christian mission and constitutive aspects of pagan culture. Gods and goddesses are challenged, important rulers and authorities inter-

---

86. For a compendium of ancient attitudes toward Jews, see Stern, *Greek and Latin Authors*. Roman citizenship is obviously an important aspect of this passage (cf. 16:37–38), particularly because of Philippi's status as a *colonia*, but the issues involved, regrettably, cannot be treated here.

87. F. G. Downing, "Common Ground with Paganism in Luke and Josephus," *NTS* 28 (1982): 557.

88. Many scholars, for example, would see Paul's speech in Athens as a placid, philosophical discussion. This view, however, overlooks the significance of the Socratic echoes and the role of the Areopagus as the Athenian tribunal. On this latter point in particular, see the excellent article of Timothy D. Barnes, "An Apostle on Trial," *JTS* 20 (1969): 407–19.

Part 1: Christology, Greco-Roman Culture, and Canonical Reception

vene, magicians and spirits are vanquished, money and jobs are lost, books are burned, riots break out, missionaries are persecuted and/or flee, and the world is turned upside down. Acts is thus not a book of minor cultural remodeling but rather a narrative exposition of another way of life. In Martha Nussbaum's terms, Luke attempts to "unwrite" the culture-forming stories of paganism by offering a different narrative that construes the entirety of reality in light of the God of Israel's act in Jesus.[89]

To unwrite culture-forming stories is not so much to criticize the various cultural details that exist in the foreground of life—particular forms of speech, patterns of behavior, and so on—as it is to redo the *background* of life against and because of which all of these particular details are intelligible. Such unwriting in its theological sense, that is, pertains to the entirety of life inasmuch as it attempts to rearticulate the comprehensive context in which the various aspects of life make sense.[90] To rearticulate the background of life is to re-create the world in which one lives; it requires, therefore, nothing less than a new way of being. Precisely in this way, the shift involved in coming to inhabit another comprehensive or background story is the move toward an alternative culture.[91]

---

89. Martha Nussbaum, "Narrative Emotions: Beckett's Genealogy of Love," *Ethics* 98 (1988): 225–54. Cf. διήγησις in Luke 1:1. Nussbaum's essay is focused upon (culturally constructed) "emotions" rather than theology per se. Yet her way of articulating the profound impact of alternative narratives provides a helpful language for thinking about the interface between the early Christians and pagans.

90. On the importance of the distinction between the "background" and "foreground" of life, see Charles Taylor, *Philosophical Arguments* (Cambridge, MA: Harvard University Press, 1995), esp. 132–33.

91. After two millennia of Christian influence upon the Western imagination, it can be difficult to grasp again what it would be like to have an entire theological horizon fundamentally undone, and yet this is precisely what we must attempt to do if we are to understand the cultural dynamics of the early Christian encounters with pagan culture. Paradoxically perhaps, in recent history it was Nietzsche who famously put clearly the issue of a totally and radically different pattern of life on the basis of a theological vision undone: "'Whither is God' [cried the madman]. 'I shall tell you. We have killed him—you and I. All of us are his murderers. But how have we done this? How were we able to drink up the sea? *Who gave us the sponge to wipe away the entire horizon? What did we do when we unchained this earth from its sun?* Whither is it moving now? Whither are we moving now? Away from all suns? Are we not plunging continually? Backward, sideward, forward, in all directions? Is there any up or down left? Are we not straying as through an infinite nothing? Do we not feel the breath of empty space? Has it not become colder? Is not night and more night coming on all the while? Must not lanterns be lit in the morning?'" Friedrich Nietzsche, *The Gay Science* §125, trans. Walter Kaufmann, in *The Portable Nietzsche*, ed. Kaufmann (New York: Viking, 1954), 95; emphasis added.

The Book of Acts and the Cultural Explication of the Identity of God

Such unwriting does not mean that Luke's theological vision is developed in an effort to engineer directly a political coup, as the depiction of Paul—echoing that of Jesus himself—makes plain.[92] Yet because of the structuring role of "God" for all of human life, the concrete explication of God's identity positions followers of the Way resolutely against the grain of pagan culture. Indeed, for Gentiles there is a "taking out" (λαβεῖν ἐξ, Acts 15:14). To embrace the theological vision of Acts is in principle at once to abandon traditional cultic practice; it is not to add yet another name to the high god atop the pyramid of powers but is to reject all other claims to ultimate divine power.[93] The early Christians thus differed substantially from pagan philosophy—the closest pagan analogue to early Christianity, as Nock saw long ago—and from pagan polytheism. Where the former could offer "a life with a scheme,"[94] it did not require a rejection of traditional cultic practices, even in the face of sophisticated theological criticism of those practices. Where the latter could absorb virtually countless divine beings, it was not structurally open to one that demanded the denial of the rest.

These differences point to a crucial aspect in the attempt to trace the cultural profile of God's identity—namely, the myth of pagan tolerance. It is true, of course, that philosophy had the intellectual space for criticism of a "superstitious" understanding of religious practice and that polytheism had substantial theological space for other gods. It is superficial and anachronistic, however, to assume that such space was roomy enough to accommodate a challenge that would potentially abolish entire sets of practices that held together the fabric of pagan life.[95] The ideals of modern Western liberalism

---

92. Paul is falsely accused of στάσις by the rhetorician Tertullus (Acts 24:5; cf. 23:10). Jesus, too, in contrast to Barabbas (Luke 23:18, 25), is not guilty of στάσις or perverting the people (23:14–15, 20, 22); he is, rather, δίκαιος, as the centurion at the cross confirms (23:47; cf. esp. 22:52). See further Rowe, "Luke-Acts and the Imperial Cult," 287–88, with notes.

93. On the pyramid of divine powers, see MacMullen, *Paganism in the Roman Empire*, 73–94.

94. Nock, *Conversion*, 167.

95. Cf. Seneca, *Ep.* 90, who wrote of philosophy: "From her side religion never departs, nor duty, nor justice, nor any of the whole company of virtues which cling together in close-united fellowship" (trans. Gummere, LCL). "Religion" as a separate or private sphere of life—distinct from politics, for example—is of course a modern construct: see, e.g., Lane Fox, *Pagans and Christians*, 82: "Civic cults . . . were only some of the many times for regulated worship in a pagan city. If we look beyond them, we can appreciate the gods' role on every level of social life and their pervasive presence . . . in early Christians' existence"; Nock, *Conversion*, 272: "Religion in Greece and Rome was not a distinct and separate aspect

have all too often been read back into antiquity.[96] As a leading ancient historian has recently put it:

> "Polytheism" ... is often seen as a tolerant and open religious system. It is associated with amateur priests, who lacked authority, and with an absence of dogma, orthodoxy and heresy. Already having many gods, it is attributed the capacity to accommodate even more at any time. This romantic view of Greek religious liberalism has little to commend it. The absence of dogmas did not entail that anything was permitted, nor was the pluralism of gods open-ended.[97]

Luke would agree. To follow the Way of God is to be confronted by the cultural limits of ancient pluralism. That such limits are, in the narrative of Acts, frequently enforced with violence only serves to indicate the depth of the conflict. God is the measure of all things: theology is a total way of life. This both historic paganism and the book of Acts seemed to sense, the one as threat and the other as promise.

---

of life, but something which ran through all its phases"; and Young, *Biblical Exegesis*, 50: "Ancient religion was indistinguishable from culture."

96. For the philosophical issue here, see Taylor's chapter entitled "The Politics of Recognition," in *Philosophical Arguments*, 225–56.

97. Price, *Religions of the Ancient Greeks*, 67. Cf. Parker, *Athenian Religion*, who writes that "no Greek surely would have supposed that an impious opinion should be permitted to circulate out of respect for freedom of speech" (209) and that, with respect to Athenian polytheism in particular, "we are dealing not with principled tolerance but with a failure to live up to intolerant principles" (210).

The Ecclesiology of Acts

Introduction

In a certain sense, dealing with the ecclesiology of Acts ought to be as easy as any topic in NT theology. The entire book of Acts, after all, is most fundamentally a story about the church. It seems we should be able to read Acts carefully and discern its teaching about the church. But, of course, this is not so easy.

There are several reasons why it is difficult to speak well about the ecclesiology of Acts. For one thing, Acts presents multiple Christian communities throughout its narrative, and it hardly takes much thought to see that in important ways the church in Corinth, for example, differs from that in Ephesus, which in turn differs from that in Lystra and Antioch and Jerusalem, and so on. For another, studying Luke's twenty-two uses of the word *ekklēsia* in Acts sheds surprisingly little interpretive light on the dynamic theological moves of the narrative as a whole. As NT scholars have often observed, it is difficult—perhaps frustratingly so—to find a particular pattern of usage. But absent such a pattern, our study of the word produces little more in the way of results than restatements of the context in which the word receives its meaning. Still more difficult is the fact that, almost reflexively, we tend to think of ecclesiology in relation to particular structures of various Christian denominations. Does the Acts of the Apostles lead to or support the Lutherans? the Presbyterians? the Methodists? the Baptists? the pope? Or none of the above? Such a focus does not necessarily produce the wrong questions—we should ask Scripture questions about church governance—but neither does it get to the heart of Acts' vision. The simple reason is that ecclesiology in Acts is less about the particulars of church order (though there is some of that) than it is about how

---

"The Ecclesiology of Acts" was originally published in *Interpretation* 66 (2012): 259–69. Copyright 2012 The Author(s). DOI: 10.1177/0020964312443192. (Reprinted in *Toward a Theology of Church Growth*, ed. David Goodhew [Burlington, VT: Ashgate, 2015], 77–89.) An earlier version of this essay was given as the 2011 Harrison Lecture at Mount Olive College.

Part 1: Christology, Greco-Roman Culture, and Canonical Reception

to be Christian in a world that did not know what being Christian was. That is the ecclesiology of Acts: a way of reasoning and habit of being that make Christianity a visible human witness to the Lord Jesus Christ in a world that did not know him.

Precisely because of this lack of knowledge, the best way to see the ecclesiology of Acts is to situate its political vision within the wider Roman world. This allows us to see clearly the particular tension that constituted the heart of Christianity's public witness and made it such a potent force. I will proceed in three steps. First, I will discuss one of the most memorable scenes from the second half of the book, the riot in Ephesus (Acts 19). Second, I will examine the series of scenes from Acts 25–26 that depict the trial of the apostle Paul. Third, by looking closely at a short scene in Thessalonica (Acts 17), I will explore the picture that emerges when the scene in Ephesus is held together with Paul's trial. The scene in Thessalonica provides the interpretive lens through which to look at the ecclesiology of Acts as a whole—because it captures in abbreviated form the animating theological moves that fund the Acts narrative.[1]

Christianity and the Destabilization of Greco-Roman Culture (Ephesus: Acts 19)

The first scene to consider is a riot in Ephesus, one of the most important cities in the ancient Mediterranean world. The story occurs in Acts 19:1–11. The central narrative line of this lengthy passage is as follows: The Christians arrive with their typical missionary program, and many people convert. Because conversion to the Christian movement involved the simultaneous rejection of the practices of magic, soothsaying, and the like, the new converts hold a public book burning in which they destroy their magic books. Shortly thereafter, an Ephesian silversmith named Demetrius accuses Paul and the other Christians of destroying his business in Ephesus and threatening the city's major temple. (This temple was the temple of Artemis, and Demetrius and his coworkers made shrines of the goddess and sold them in conjunction with the temple. Their business was directly dependent upon the flourishing of the temple.) Deme-

---

1. What follows is an abbreviation of the argument I made in *World Upside Down: Reading Acts in the Graeco-Roman Age* (Oxford: Oxford University Press, 2009). For a discussion of the proposals of that book, along with my response, see the March issue of *JSNT* (2011): 317–46.

trius's accusation is not a formal legal one—a particular kind of crime such as treason or improper use of magic—but is rather more of an attempt to incite a crowd against the Christian missionaries. It works: the people cry out, "Great is Artemis of the Ephesians," and drag some of Paul's companions into the city theater, and there they riot. This riot lasts for some time before the chief official of Ephesus arrives and quiets the crowd by reminding them that, because of their disorderly tumult, they are all in danger of being charged by the Romans with riotous sedition. The Christians then slip away more or less unharmed.

Out of all the interesting details in this story, I focus on only three. First is the importance of the Ephesian silversmith's charge. To his colleagues in business, Demetrius says:

> Men, you know that from this business we have our wealth. And you know that this Paul has persuaded and turned away a considerable crowd of people by saying that "gods made with hands are not gods." And you [therefore] know that there is danger not only that our business may come into disrepute but also that the temple of the great Artemis may count for nothing, and that she may even be deposed from her magnificence, she whom all Asia and the world worship. (19:25–27)[2]

Two millennia later, Demetrius's charge may appear somewhat overdone. But as abundant evidence demonstrates, it would be difficult to overestimate the importance of Artemis to Ephesian life. As a first-century inscription put it, the temple of Artemis was known as "the jewel of the whole province [of Asia] on account of the grandeur of the edifice, the age of its veneration of the goddess, and the abundance of its revenue."[3] It functioned not only as a "house of worship" but also as the arbiter for regional disputes, a bank, a holding facility for important civic archives, and an asylum for debtors, runaway slaves, and other persons in dire trouble. The temple sent its own representatives to the Olympic Games, was the beneficiary of private estates, had abundant sacred herds, owned considerable real estate from which it drew its famous revenue, and so on. In short, as one scholar wrote, Artemis of the Ephesians was "an indispensable pillar in the cultural structures and life of Asia, and was therefore a crucial factor in the lives of all . . . whom Christianity hoped to convert."[4]

---

2. All translations are my own unless otherwise noted.

3. See Rowe, *World Upside Down*, 45, 204 n. 209.

4. Richard Oster, "The Ephesian Artemis as an Opponent of Early Christianity," *Jahrbuch für Antike und Christentum* 19 (1976): 24–44, esp. 34.

Part 1: Christology, Greco-Roman Culture, and Canonical Reception

Taking seriously the cultural role of the Ephesian Artemis cult prevents the possibility of reading Demetrius's charge simplistically, as if Luke were simply exhibiting the cunning with which the silversmith enlisted others to rescue his business. On the contrary, the words of Demetrius articulate a more radical possibility: the potential for cultural collapse. As readers of Acts would know from earlier portions of the narrative (especially chs. 7, 14, 16, and 17), theological criticism of the kind Paul advocates does in fact depose Artemis and, hence, would dismantle this "indispensable pillar in the cultural structures and life of Asia." Through the mouth of Demetrius, Acts thus juxtaposes starkly the competing perspectives that form the clash of the gods: to understand the Christian mission is to perceive the theological danger posed to Artemis of the Ephesians. Consequently, it is to witness, says Demetrius, to the prospective disintegration of religiously dependent economics.[5]

It is no wonder, therefore, that after the compatriots of Demetrius hear his argument, they become "full of rage and cry out, 'Great is Artemis of the Ephesians!'" (19:28). Acts continues, "The city was filled with confusion and they rushed into the theater, dragging . . . Paul's travel companions" (19:29). That those whose livelihood depends upon the Ephesian goddess should vigorously defend her greatness is only natural. Demetrius speaks of a Christian politics that collides with fundamental features of Greco-Roman life on the basis of competing theologies.

For my limited purpose, the second important feature of this scene is the chief official's persuasion of the crowd. His basic point, with which many an ancient civic official could sympathize, is that rioting will not bring the desired outcome, but might well instead lead to profoundly undesirable consequences for them all. In order to get the crowd to agree with him—and therefore quit the theater and go home—the Ephesian official makes essentially two interconnected arguments. First, he skillfully negates Demetrius's charge against the Christian missionaries by drawing attention to the fact that the central cultic object of the Ephesian Artemis, a sacred stone, was not, strictly speaking, "made by hands." The sacred stone, so says the official, had been given by heaven/Zeus; that is, it had fallen from the sky.[6] For the ancient Ephesians, this meteorite was a religiously charged cultic image. The official's point is

---

5. That this problem would come to be associated with the Christians very soon after the composition of Acts can be seen in Pliny the Younger's famous correspondence with the emperor Trajan about the Christians (ca. 110/112).

6. Meteorites were not infrequently the objects of cultic veneration in the ancient world.

thus clear: Paul's central criticism—"gods made by hands are not gods"—does not apply to Artemis, because, in actuality, the cultic object was *not* made by hands. Moreover, the official points to the fact that business is booming as usual. "Is there anyone," he says, "who does not know that the city of the Ephesians is the temple warden of Artemis?" In short, the official argues that the missionaries are neither blasphemers nor temple robbers; there is no reason to worry about economic disaster on their account.

The chief official's second argument against the tumult is quite simple, and it makes an immediate impact. After reminding Demetrius and his group that there are legal means by which to deal with any official accusations (the Roman governor and the open courts), the Ephesian official informs the people that they are in danger of being accused of *stasis*. In this context, *stasis* means "riot-interpreted-by-the-Romans-as-sedition"—that is, a breach of the civic order required to sustain the *pax Romana*. That Rome was particularly nervous about crowd violence—and therefore particularly heavy-handed in their discipline thereof—is well known. One could think, for example, of Gaius's merciless slaughter of rowdy tax protesters in the circus, or of the decade-long revocation of Pompeii's ability to hold gladiatorial games, or Claudius's reduction of the revolting Lycians to slaves.[7] Whatever the specifics of the imagined response, the official's threat is clear enough to achieve its aim: he dismisses the people from the theater, and they go away. The Ephesian official's argument works: "the Christians are no worry to us"; therefore, the people should "go on home before we get into real trouble."

The third crucial feature of this scene is that focusing on the charge of Demetrius and its counterargument by the Ephesian official brings us to an interpretive choice vis-à-vis Christian politics according to Acts: Should we follow Demetrius (the Christians are culturally destabilizing and are therefore politically problematic) or the Ephesian official (the Christians are no worry to us)? To which voice in the narrative should we listen? With few exceptions, modern scholars have sided with the Ephesian official: the Christians do not fundamentally threaten larger cultural patterns and can even make rather good citizens. Indeed, to many readers of Acts, the Ephesian official's argument seems to cohere with Luke's overall vision of early ecclesial politics: because the Christians regularly appear before Roman officials (or those who represent their overall political interests) and because these officials speak of the innocuousness of the missionaries' efforts, Christianity according to Acts—so

---

7. See Rowe, *World Upside Down*, 48.

Part 1: Christology, Greco-Roman Culture, and Canonical Reception

this reading goes—is compatible, perhaps even cozy, with the wider political nexus named the Roman Empire.[8]

The problem with this reading is that Demetrius is actually right. Yes, the city official's words are clever and slick, but they also miss the point: As readers of Acts and any other early Christians would know, Jesus and Artemis are not compatible. If there are numerous conversions to the Christian movement, Demetrius will likely go out of business. The Christians are thus fundamentally disruptive to the practices necessary to sustain the worship of Artemis. That such disruption unfolds economically and politically is the necessary consequence of the inseparability of ancient religion from the rest of life.

If we take this kind of politics seriously, we could infer that the political shape of early Christianity is worrisome to the Roman world precisely because its theology strikes at the religio-economic heart of Roman order. The Christians are rebellious in a very basic sense and therefore, in the view of the Romans, need to be punished. Before concluding that the Christians are politically problematic for Roman order, however, we must consider carefully another scene where the issue of the Christian mission and its potential to engender *stasis* is on prominent display.

Christianity Is Not *Stasis* (Paul on Trial: Acts 25–26)

In contrast to Acts 19 where there is no formal trial, Acts 24:1–26:32 narrates Paul's actual trial for the crime of *stasis* (i.e., "sedition," again in the sense of riot-causing revolt). This is the last of several times in Acts in which the early Christians have been brought before Roman officials and yet one more in a series of confrontations where the accusation of disruption has been raised in relation to Christian life. In this particular case, Paul's judge is first Felix and then Festus, the successive Roman governors of Judea. The main narrative line of this complex scene is as follows: Because of Paul's apparent role in causing a riot in Jerusalem, a military tribune named Claudius Lysias apprehends him. When Lysias learns, however, that Paul is a Roman citizen, he sends him on from Jerusalem to the Roman governor Felix in the seaside city of Caesarea (the location of the governor's residence for the majority of his tenure). After hearing the case against Paul—wherein Paul is charged formally with inciting a seditious riot—Felix decides to put Paul in custody rather than to release him

---

8. Acts would thus on this reading be the first great piece of Constantinian Christian literature. Indeed, it has often been read that way (e.g., Haenchen, Conzelmann, et al.).

or have him executed (in Roman law, sedition was a capital crime). Two years pass with Paul in custody, and Felix is replaced by Festus, who also hears Paul's case. To make sure he understands the particularities of the Jewish argument, Festus invites the Jewish King Agrippa II along with some other important political officials to hear Paul's defense. Paul then makes his case, which he does by telling the story of his awakening to belief in Jesus of Nazareth's resurrection from the dead. Festus cannot make any sense of Paul's account as a legal defense speech (an *apologia*) and so turns to Agrippa for help. Agrippa then offers his judgment, which confirms Festus's rather vague intuition: Paul has committed no political crime worthy of death. The charge of leading a revolt (*stasis*) cannot be sustained.

I am again limited to only three central observations. First, quite in the face of the accusations brought against him, Paul resolutely maintains his innocence: "I have done nothing against the law of the Jews, against the temple, or against Caesar," he says to Festus and the rest (25:8). By this point in the narrative, readers of Acts know of course that Paul speaks as a reliable character in that story—after all, next to Jesus, Paul is Luke's hero—and we are therefore to read his declaration as the political truth (indeed, he has already made this declaration earlier in the story). As Paul represents it, the early Christian movement is not a direct attack on the Roman political system, a kind of religiously based bid for insurrection or imperial power. As far as Acts is concerned, Paul's declaration speaks rightly of the political shape of the Christian mission. The Christians are not out to stage a coup.

Second, it becomes all the more puzzling to take note of Festus's statement to King Agrippa about Paul. Because he cannot understand Paul's talk about the resurrection of Jesus, Festus does not know what to write to the emperor in his letter of transfer that would accompany Paul on his way to appeal his case in Rome. Festus thus says to Agrippa, "I have nothing to write to my Lord about [Paul]" (Acts 25:26). This is the only time in the NT that the Roman emperor is actually called "Lord" (*kyrios*). It was the correct thing for the emperor's officials to call him, as numerous texts, papyri, and inscriptions show. In fact, the emperor was not only styled as "Lord" *simpliciter* but, more comprehensively, as "Lord of all the world," as an inscription from Greece has it, or as we can read in Lucan, Martial, or Epictetus, for example.[9]

In Acts, however, the emperor is not called "Lord of all"; among human beings, that title is reserved for Jesus alone. Indeed, in Acts 10, the apostle Peter tells a centurion named Cornelius that Jesus is the one who is "the Lord of all":

9. See Rowe, *World Upside Down*, 106.

Part 1: Christology, Greco-Roman Culture, and Canonical Reception

> You know the word that he sent to the people of Israel preaching peace through Jesus Christ: this one is Lord of all. You know what has happened throughout the whole of Judea, beginning in Galilee after the baptism that John preached, as God anointed in the Holy Spirit and power Jesus of Nazareth, who went about benefacting and healing all who were oppressed by the devil, for God was with him. (vv. 36–38)

When readers of Acts later encounter the statement of Festus, we are thus required to think through a startling juxtaposition. In Acts, both Jesus and the Roman caesar are called *kyrios*; yet it is Jesus Christ—not the Roman emperor—who is the Lord of all. The obvious implication is that, according to Acts, the Christians' most basic and final allegiance is not to the Roman emperor but to the Lord of all, Jesus of Nazareth.

Third, the reason that Jesus is Lord of all—in the view of Acts—has to do with his resurrection from the dead. And that is Paul's point in his speech before Festus. Jesus, says Paul, must suffer, rise from the dead, and proclaim light both to the people (Israel) and to the nations (Gentiles) (cf. 26:23). That is, in maintaining his innocence of sedition, Paul does not articulate a normative general political scheme—monarchy, democracy, communitarianism, and so forth—but instead says that he is innocent of leading a revolt because Jesus has been raised from the dead: a confirmation of his life of peace and the beginning of the formation of peaceful communities of Jew and Gentile throughout the Mediterranean world. In effect, Paul says, "I'm not leading a revolt because obedience to the resurrected Jesus commits us to peace of just the kind he himself exemplified in his willingness to go innocently to his death and be raised by God."

On the face of it, to say the least, this is a rather odd defense in a Roman court setting. It is therefore unsurprising that a Roman official such as Festus—who has no Jewish theological sensibilities about resurrection from the dead and knows virtually nothing of Jesus of Nazareth—is genuinely perplexed. Indeed, Festus interrupts Paul and cries out, "Paul, you're crazy!" (26:24). Festus literally cannot understand Paul's defense as a proper legal defense. He thus turns to consult the Jewish King Agrippa, who has actually heard of the Christians. After discussion with Agrippa, Festus and his council decide that Paul is innocent. Quite crazy he may be, but he is not the ringleader of a politically seditious faction.

What is critical is the interpretive conundrum that arises when this passage is read together with the scene in Ephesus. In that scene, as we saw, Acts portrays the Christians as fundamentally disruptive to the patterns that sustain a culture—and therefore as threatening in a decisive sense to the wider world in which the rule of Rome is unfolding. But in the trial before Festus, Paul is flatly declared "unworthy of death"—that is, innocent of the capital crime of treasonous sedition. On the one hand, Luke narrates the movement of the Christian mission into the Gentile world as a collision with culture-constructing aspects of that world. From the perspective created by this angle of vision, the Christian mission and basic features of Greco-Roman culture are competing realities. On the other hand, Luke narrates the threat of the Christian mission in such a way as to deny that it is in direct competition with the Roman government. Of treason and sedition, says Luke, Christianity is innocent. The Christians are a basic threat, but they are not out to establish Christendom, as it were. New, threatening way of life? Yes. Coup? No. The question thus becomes: How do we account for this tension?

The history of NT scholarship—as well as Christian politics—demonstrates that it is all too easy to neglect one side of the tension and focus entirely on the other. The culturally destabilizing reality of the Christian mission is overlooked, and Christianity becomes a politically innocuous or even irrelevant "spiritual" movement; or the declaration of innocence of sedition is overlooked and Christianity is read as a liberating, overt frontal challenge to the Roman Empire. But, in fact, we should not be forced to choose one side or the other. Indeed, precisely because they are both parts of the same narrative, we should read them together. The task is to inhabit the narrative's tension and refuse to dissolve it. To that end, we turn to our final scene in the Acts of the Apostles.

Jesus the King: The Tension of Christian Politics (Thessalonica: Acts 17)

The scene in Acts 17:1–9 takes place in the city of Thessalonica. The central relevant matter is rather clear. As a consequence of their missionizing and the conversions that take place therewith, the Christians are hauled before the local authorities and accused in this way: "These people who have turned the world upside down have come here also, and Jason has received them; and they are all acting against the decrees of Caesar, saying that there is another king—Jesus" (17:6–7).

Much scholarly ink has been spilled in the effort to determine the precise nature of the imperial "decrees" against which the Christians are acting. But for the most part, such labor has been unnecessary for the simple reason that the

Part 1: Christology, Greco-Roman Culture, and Canonical Reception

text says directly what the accusation is: the Christians are accused of saying that there is "another king." The word "another" makes clear that the question is one of rivalry: "another," as in "not the one you now have." If we ask who the king is that Thessalonica now has, the answer is not hard to find. Indeed, the only historically plausible answer to this question in the mid to late first century is the Roman emperor. In Thessalonica the Christians are thus accused of challenging the throne of Caesar. It is precisely in setting Jesus up as king that the Christians run afoul of the "decrees of Caesar."

It is with good reason that many interpreters of the NT have thought that these charges were false. As we have seen with Paul's trial before Festus, Acts does speak of the Christians' innocence of sedition. Moreover, at the end of the scene here in Thessalonica, the Christians are forced to give collateral for their good behavior but are then set free, thus once again illustrating narratively their innocence of treasonous sedition.

But in exegesis, as in life, things are seldom as easy as they appear. In point of fact, it was no secret that the early Christians acclaimed Jesus as king. No reader of early Christian literature could think otherwise. The Gospel of Luke and the Acts of the Apostles are no exception. Throughout Luke's Gospel, Jesus is cast in a royal role. Indeed, he both enters Jerusalem and is crucified there explicitly as king. And in Acts, the missionaries repeatedly preach about the reality brought by Jesus's advent and resurrection as "the kingdom of God." The final sentence of Acts has Paul preaching in Rome itself about "the kingdom of God and the Lord (of all) Jesus Christ" (28:31). In short, the accusers in Thessalonica actually have a rather good case. Jesus is king. The interpretive question is thus what we should make of the fact that Jesus is actually another king—that in some way his kingship is juxtaposed to that of the Roman emperor—and that, at least as Acts tells it, such a kingship does not lead to a seditious revolt.

It has long been tempting for Christians to resolve this tension by insisting on a dualistic nature of the two kings or kingdoms. God's kingdom—in which Jesus is king—does not overlap in any kind of earthly or strictly political way with Caesar's (or, later, the rule of the state). It is possible to have both kings, because their sovereignty can be referred to different spheres (heaven and earth), modes of communal life (church and state), and so forth. In this reading, it would be true that Jesus is "another king" as the accusers in Thessalonica say, but inasmuch as his kingship is politically innocuous it is compatible with Caesar's. "Another" here would thus mean in its positive Christian construal a second, non-rival, different-kind-of-king.

But we have already seen that Acts would teach us to think with more nuance about this tension. In Acts, the kingdom is obviously not a "human kingdom" in the straightforward simplistic sense—and in this way, the Christian mission does not threaten Rome as did, for example, the Parthian kingdom on the eastern frontier. Yet, against all Gnostic or pietistic tendencies, the vision in Acts is of a kingdom that is every bit as much a human presence as it is a divine work. The kingdom of which Jesus is king is not simply spiritual, but also material and social, which is to say that it takes up space in public. It competes with Artemis in Ephesus, for example. And because public space is not neutral but contested space—the arena in which various readings of the world make their bid for adoption—the Christian mission's challenge to basic aspects and patterns of Greco-Roman culture is simultaneously a challenge to the order of Caesar, and thus in a crucial or fundamental sense to his claim to be the lord of all.[10]

To think with Acts, we must thus say both yes and no. Yes, the resurrection of Jesus threatens the stability of Roman life; no, the Christians are not guilty of *stasis*; yes, the Christians are bad for religiously based economics; no, they are not trying to take over the public market; yes, Artemis will be deposed; no, the Christians will not tear down the temple; yes, Jesus and not Caesar is Lord of all; but, no, the Christians are not violent revolutionaries. And so on.

If we take both the yes and the no seriously—if we take the tension described earlier and refuse to dissolve it—then it becomes apparent that the charges in Thessalonica are at once both true and false. They are false in that they attempt to place Jesus in an outright competitive relation to the Roman emperor. Such a positioning can lead only to a politics of revolt. But in Acts, the Christians have no dreams to expel the Romans from Jerusalem, or rise up and march on Rome, or take over the empire. Jesus is not, strictly speaking, that kind of a rival to Caesar, as if they were in the same contest competing for the same prize.[11]

And yet the charges are true in that Caesar is not the highest political authority (he is demoted, to say the least). The Christians owe their allegiance to the true Lord of all, and the politics of the Christian mission entails a call

---

10. Thinking analogically about Caesar's claim to be Lord of all: For Christians to kill other Christians because they are separated by different citizenships is to say in a very painful and practical way that Christian identity is subordinate to national identity—which in turn is to say that Caesar trumps Jesus, or, as my colleague Paul Griffiths puts it, "citizenship trumps baptism" (see his "'Allah Is My Lord and Yours': Talking with Ahmadinejad," *Christian Century* [October 17, 2006], 8-9). Caesar, that is, is the one who can command final, ultimate allegiance to the point of death.

11. Acts presupposes no deeper ontological basis upon which Jesus and Caesar play out their respective roles as claimants for the title "Lord of all." In Acts, Jesus simply is the Lord of all as the self-revelation of the God of Israel; and that is, as it were, the cosmic ontology—the arena in which everything else takes place.

Part 1: Christology, Greco-Roman Culture, and Canonical Reception

to a way of being that threatens to undo basic habits and practices of Greco-Roman life. As we saw in Ephesus, and as could be seen in many other places in the Acts narrative,[12] the Christian missionaries really do, in the words of their accusers in Thessalonica, turn the world upside down.

Focusing on the scene in Thessalonica highlights the irreducible conflict over the interpretation of the Christians—what their public space is about, as it were—precisely because we can answer both yes and no to the question of whether they turn the world upside down by proclaiming another king (or Lord). With respect to the examples above, when we focus upon the conflict with Artemis of the Ephesians, we must answer yes. But when we focus upon Paul's trial before the Roman governor Festus, we must answer no. The narrative program in Acts—of which these scenes are, to repeat, paradigmatic instances—thus resists interpretive reduction and requires for its interpretation complexity and constant movement in our political thought.

The program as a whole can be summarized in this way: Jesus is Lord of all, the king of the way of life called the kingdom of God. The early Christian mission is a new, worldwide, and publicly identifiable instantiation of this reality and, as such, calls into question religious/economic/political norms that help to both produce and sustain Greco-Roman culture. In this sense, the Christians are profoundly destabilizing and will continue to be so insofar as the wider Roman world remains unmoved by their call to a new pattern of life. Yet the political objectives of such destabilization are not in any way directly revolutionary (particularly not in the sense of an attempt to depose Caesar and place a new, Christian emperor on the throne). "Sedition" and "treason," therefore, are not the right vocabulary to describe the shape of Christian politics. In the Acts of the Apostles, the stark either/or of Roman politics is refused (either for Rome or against her, either innocent or guilty, either Caesar is Lord of all or there is revolt). In its place, Acts proclaims the possibility of another way of life. The lordship of Jesus in Acts leads neither to an *apologia* to/for Rome nor to an anti-Rome polemic. It is simply, but really, a new and different way. In short, theology here is politics.

Conclusion

Inasmuch as the deeper currents of Western (or North Atlantic) culture continue to flow against the normative commitments of Christian life,[13] we may

---

12. See ch. 2 of Rowe, *World Upside Down*.
13. See Charles Taylor, *A Secular Age* (Cambridge, MA: Harvard University Press, 2007).

be entering a time of reading Scripture that both requires and enables a richer analogical relation to the ancient world than has been possible or necessary in a very long time. Our world will doubtless not forget what Christianity is any time soon. Many of the commitments needed to sustain care of the sick and dying, for example, depend upon a specifically Christian view of the human being. Yet the fact is that it grows increasingly difficult to develop and maintain a Christian imagination that correlates with an all-encompassing pattern of life. Moreover, it is possible to imagine a future in which the Christian way of being is a minority whose life pattern is at odds with much of what the wider Western world will consider normal.[14] We return to Acts, therefore, at a propitious time in the life of the church to learn or relearn things that will allow our children in the faith to continue the form of life in the world that earned the name "Christian"—or to live out the life that proclaims Jesus is Lord of all in a world that will not recognize his lordship.

Of the things we should learn from Acts' ecclesiological vision, none is quite as important as the very basic sense that thinking theologically about the church requires us to discern the interconnections that make up a total way of life. That is, the church in Acts has really nothing to do with a discrete sphere of life or thought, as if ecclesiology could name a particular, limited set of ideas or practices in distinction from Christology, eschatology, anthropology, and so on. Rather, if we wish to talk about ecclesiology according to Acts, we must talk primarily about a theologically explicated habit of being that is noticeably different from the larger practices and assumptions that shape daily life in the Greco-Roman world. According to Acts, ecclesiology is simply the communal form of life that is living in obedience to the Lord of all; it is a form of life that is at once political and theological, or public and private, or, to say it only slightly differently, all-encompassing. This refusal to locate particular parts of the church in different spheres of life is the necessary presupposition to the existence of a people with the mode of being that is publicly identifiable in Acts' sense—the "Christians." If we, too, wish to live so that our children and grandchildren in the faith—and their children and grandchildren—can be known as "Christians," then, according to Acts, our ecclesiology will have to keep alive the distinction between church and world not merely on this or that contested point (e.g., euthanasia, abortion) but also in the concrete practice of a whole way of life that marks publicly its practitioners as those who live under the lordship of the Lord of all.

14. See David Bentley Hart, *Atheist Delusions: The Christian Revolution and Its Fashionable Enemies* (New Haven: Yale University Press, 2009).

History, Hermeneutics, and the Unity of Luke-Acts

This chapter does not dispute the notion that Luke-Acts can be read as a literary unity.[1] Nor does it take up the much-debated question of genre.[2] Instead, the chapter centers upon a historical difficulty that impinges upon our guild's (almost) unquestioned assumption that to read Luke-Acts together is to interpret this literary unity historically.[3] The argument receives its shape from

---

1. Johnson puts it well: "In addition to the prologues, the volumes are joined by an intricate skein of stylistic, structural, and thematic elements which demonstrate convincingly that the same literary imagination was at work in both." Luke Timothy Johnson, *The Gospel of Luke*, SP 3 (Collegeville, MN: Liturgical Press, 1991), 1.

2. Whether Luke and Acts belong in the same genre is still hotly contested. See, e.g., the recent and extensive essay of Charles H. Talbert with Perry Stepp, "Succession in Luke-Acts and in the Lukan Milieu," in *Reading Luke-Acts in Its Mediterranean Milieu* (Leiden: Brill, 2003), 19–55, which is used (in part) to buttress his widely known arguments in favor of a unified biographical genre.

3. For an exception to this assumption, see Mikeal C. Parsons and Richard I. Pervo, *Rethinking the Unity of Luke and Acts* (Minneapolis: Fortress, 1993). Parsons and Pervo mention five different kinds of unity, the last three of which they discuss in detail and dispute in at least some way: (1) authorial, (2) canonical, (3) generic, (4) narrative, and (5) theological. Unlike Parsons and Pervo, I do not think the narrative or theological unity of Luke-Acts can be called into question (and authorial unity is now a given). As they recognize, the question of genre remains debated, but even if Luke and Acts turn out not to belong in the same genre, this would not preclude their literary unity. The five and a half pages on canonical unity (a rather unclear designation) contain several interesting observations, particularly with respect to the differing textual traditions, but such observations are not developed any further. As will become clear, it is precisely these more tangible, historical matters that raise the greatest questions about the unity of Luke-Acts. On the various facets to the "almost complete consensus" regarding the unity of Luke-Acts, see the *Forschungsbericht* of J. Verheyden, "The Unity of Luke-Acts: What Are We Up To?," in *The Unity of Luke-Acts*, ed. J. Verheyden (Leuven: Leuven University Press, 1999), 3–56. On the different meanings of "unity" used in the scholarly literature, see I. Howard Marshall, "Acts and the 'Former

---

"History, Hermeneutics, and the Unity of Luke-Acts" was originally published in *Journal for the Study of the New Testament* 28, no. 2 (2005): 131–57, as a discussion article with responses by Luke Timothy Johnson and Markus N. A. Bockmuehl. Copyright 2005 SAGE Publications. DOI: 10.1177/0142064X05060098.

the thesis that the history of reception presents us with a problem to which we ought to give serious thought. In order to get at this problem, the chapter will sketch briefly the reception history relevant to our question, draw out the hermeneutical consequences thereof, and, finally, suggest further lines to follow in our reflection upon a first-rate difficulty in NT interpretation.

Reception History

Even for prophets the future can be rather hazy. Hananiah, after all, was presumably at least somewhat sincere. Yet—with no claim to the prophetic gift—I will hazard a prediction: reception history of the texts of the NT will come to constitute a greater and greater portion of the scholarly work in the field, partly because of the seeming eternal return of the same in the exegetical debates and partly because of the ability of the text's forward history to shed substantial light on substantive issues of interpretation.[4] A case in point is Andrew Gregory's recent study, a comprehensive and meticulous treatment of the *Reception of Luke and Acts in the Period before Irenaeus*.[5] It is Gregory's study, in fact, that provides the departure point for the problem with which we have to deal.

Treatise,'" in *The Book of Acts in Its Ancient Literary Setting*, ed. Bruce W. Winter and Andrew D. Clarke (Grand Rapids: Eerdmans, 1993), 163–82, esp. 164–72.

4. See, e.g., for Matthew's Gospel, W.-D. Köhler, *Die Rezeption des Matthäusevangeliums in der Zeit vor Irenäus*, WUNT 2/24 (Tübingen: Mohr Siebeck, 1987), and for John's, Titus Nagel, *Die Rezeption des Johannesevangeliums im 2. Jahrhundert: Studien zur vorirenäischen Aneignung und Auslegung des vierten Evangeliums in christlicher und christlich-gnostischer Literatur* (Leipzig: Evangelische Verlagsanstalt, 2000). For the Johannine corpus, see Charles E. Hill, *The Johannine Corpus in the Early Church* (Oxford: Oxford University Press, 2004). In terms of NT commentaries that display a concern with reception history, Ulrich Luz's goliath on Matthew stands above the rest.

5. Andrew Gregory, *The Reception of Luke and Acts in the Period before Irenaeus: Looking for Luke in the Second Century*, WUNT 2/169 (Tübingen: Mohr Siebeck, 2003). This work is a revised version of the author's Oxford PhD dissertation and, to date, is the only extensive investigation of Lukan reception history. Cf. the brief piece of Arthur J. Bellinzoni, "The Gospel of Luke in the Second Century CE," in *Literary Studies in Luke-Acts: Essays in Honor of Joseph B. Tyson*, ed. Richard P. Thompson and Thomas E. Phillips (Macon, GA: Mercer University Press, 1998), 59–76. Bellinzoni notes that his essay is a condensed version of a larger paper that he hopes to publish. At present, as far as I am aware, the longer paper has not been published. Interestingly, matters of reception history receive only a (rather vague) footnote in Verheyden's thorough survey of virtually every other significant area that pertains to the question of "unity" ("Unity of Luke-Acts," 6 n. 13).

Part 1: Christology, Greco-Roman Culture, and Canonical Reception

In a sense, Gregory's title gives the game away, even as it also acts as a provocateur to the typical NT scholar. Why not *The Reception of Luke-Acts in the Period before Irenaeus*? Why the bothersome little "and," *Luke and Acts*? Far from a careless or reckless run into academic obstacles, this "and" is purposively employed, for it points us implicitly to the results of the investigation.[6]

After a virtually exhaustive (not to say exhausting) tour through the many candidates for testimony to the reception of Luke and/or Acts prior to and including Irenaeus, Gregory concludes that, with only two exceptions, there is "no evidence . . . to demonstrate that Luke and Acts were read as two volumes of one work."[7] The first exception is Irenaeus himself, who, so contends Gregory, "explicitly treats Luke-Acts as a two volume work, and he reads each volume in light of the other."[8] Gregory's evidence for this interpretation of Irenaeus is essentially twofold: Irenaeus's knowledge of the common authorship of Luke and Acts, and the particular use of Luke and Acts in Irenaeus's argument in the opening section of *Adversus haereses* 3.

Taking the latter first, we may note that *Adversus haereses* 3.1.1 indubitably reflects Irenaeus's knowledge of the end of Luke and the beginning of Acts:[9]

> For it is not permitted to assert that [the apostles] preached before they possessed "perfect knowledge," as some have the audacity to affirm, glorying in themselves as correctors [*emendatores*] of the apostles. After our Lord rose from the dead, [the apostles] were invested with Power from on high [cf. Luke 24:49; Acts 1:8a] when the Holy Spirit came down [cf. Acts 1:8a], were filled with all gifts, and had perfect knowledge. They departed to the ends of the earth [cf. Acts 1:8b], preaching the glad tidings of the good things sent from God to us, and proclaiming the peace of heaven to those who have—all equally and each one in particular—the Gospel of God. *Matthew* produced a written gospel . . . *Mark* handed down to us in writing what

---

6. Cf. the suggestion of Parsons and Pervo regarding the appropriateness of the conjunction "and" (*Rethinking*, 127).

7. Gregory, *Reception of Luke and Acts*, 352.

8. Gregory, *Reception of Luke and Acts*, 39. This statement stands in some tension with his later remark that in the work of Irenaeus "Acts is not used separately from either the Gospels or from Paul but in close association with both" (301).

9. For our purposes it is sufficient to note the allusions to Luke 24:49 and Acts 1:8, but it should be said that for Irenaeus the entire beginning of Acts seems to be in mind. Whether or not Irenaeus actually needs Luke 24:49 for his argument to work is a fascinating question (see n. 11), but the point that he used this text remains (suggesting that Irenaeus, at least, thought Luke 24:49 necessary).

had been preached by Peter. So, too, *Luke* recorded in a book the Gospel preached by [Paul]. Then *John* . . . published a gospel during his residence in Ephesus.[10]

With respect to this passage, Gregory notes that "the unity of Luke-Acts plays an important part in Irenaeus's anti-Gnostic polemic, for it allows him to argue that there was no time when the apostles were without perfect knowledge, for they had such perfect knowledge from the moment they received power from on high after Jesus had risen from the dead."[11]

Gregory is to be commended for his sophistication in attempting to uncover the hermeneutical presupposition that underlies Irenaeus's argumentation. Yet to construe *Adversus haereses* 3.1.1 as evidence for the claim that Irenaeus "explicitly treats Luke-Acts as a two volume work, and he reads each volume in light of the other" is, at best, to exaggerate its significance.

It is certainly true that in making his argument Irenaeus coordinates the end of Luke with the beginning of Acts and, hence, uses what we would call the literary unity of Luke and Acts. Thus Irenaeus perceives—probably reflecting an awareness of the "chain-link interlock" described by Lucian[12]—

---

10. Irenaeus, *Haer.* 3.1.1. I use here the text printed in F. Sagnard, *Irénée de Lyon: Contre les hérésies, Livre III*, SC 34 (Paris: Cerf, 1952).

11. Gregory, *Reception of Luke and Acts*, 39-40. Gregory's reading of Irenaeus here is nuanced and remarkably perceptive. In light of contemporary Lukan scholarship, as well as the text of Luke-Acts itself, our initial, reasonable assumption may be that Irenaeus is speaking about the gift of the Holy Spirit at Pentecost in Acts 2. As odd as it may seem to us, however, Irenaeus's actual argument is rather different. His point here at the opening of book 3 (whose purpose, Irenaeus tells us, is to deal with the heretics' treatment of the Scriptures) is that the apostles had received the Holy Spirit—and hence had "perfect knowledge"—*before* they departed to the ends of the earth to preach the gospel (Acts 1:8b). Irenaeus thus reads Luke 24:49 together with Acts 1:8a in order to say that the apostles had received the Power from on high before they departed to preach, and he reads Acts 1:8b to announce their departure. The preaching of the apostles is thus from a point of perfect knowledge, and their testimony—i.e., the Scriptures—therefore need no correction. Exactly what text of Luke and Acts Irenaeus is reading or quoting from memory is a complex question and cannot be addressed here. On Irenaeus's biblical text, see William Sanday and C. H. Turner, *Novum Testamentum Sancti Irenaei Episcopi Lugdunensis* (Oxford: Clarendon, 1923). J. Lawson (*The Biblical Theology of Saint Irenaeus* [London: Epworth, 1948], 88 n. 1) suggests that the notion that the apostles had "perfect knowledge" is based upon John 14:26 and 16:13. As a background influence for the idea of "perfect knowledge" in this passage, Lawson's suggestion is plausible, and it illustrates well the complexity in attempting to identify biblical influence upon Irenaeus. But the Johannine texts are not in the foreground here in *Haer.* 3.1.1 as are the Lukan.

12. See Lucian, *Ver. hist.* 55. For a discussion of this narrative device in relation to the

that Luke and Acts go together narratively, that is, that the beginning of Acts overlaps with the end of Luke in order to pick up the gospel story and carry it forward.

However, Irenaeus's sequential coordination and perception of the "chain-link" bear little similarity to a literary-critical reading practice that self-consciously separates Luke from the other gospels to read with Acts as one work. Indeed, precisely what we do not see in Irenaeus is any kind of sustained reading of one "volume in light of the other"—that is, a reading of *Luke-Acts*. In point of fact, in the worthiest candidate for consideration, the passage cited just above, Irenaeus observes the connection between the story of Luke and Acts not in order to claim legitimacy for a unified reading of Luke-Acts but in the service of a "historical" argument for the authority of the *Tetraevangelium*: the fact that the apostles had perfect knowledge proves, contra the "correctors," that Matthew, Mark, Luke, and John need no correction—they are the gospel of God (cf. esp. the coordination of the four *Evangelia* with the single *Evangelium* in *Haer.* 3.11.9).[13] Irenaeus does not, then, ask how the ending of Luke and beginning of Acts go together, what Luke's larger point was in unifying the stories, what in the gospel prefigures the mission to the end of the earth, or any other questions that would presuppose a unified literary reading. Instead he simply takes the joint material in Luke 24 and Acts 1 as historical *facta* and argues on that basis.

Yet there is an important way in which Irenaeus does actually exhibit considerable reflection upon the fact that Luke and Acts must be taken together, that of their common authorship. As Hans von Campenhausen put it, "Luke, the author of Acts, is above all else the author of the Gospel of Luke . . . the authority of Acts . . . depends on the authority of the Gospel."[14] Gregory is

---

NT, see Bruce W. Longenecker, "Lukan Aversion to Humps and Hollows: The Case of Acts 11.27–12.25," *NTS* 50 (2004): 185–204.

13. Given the character of this "historical" argument, it is probably not too much to suggest that the fact that Luke in particular is the gospel that contains the information necessary to the argument is really of no importance to Irenaeus. Especially given the absence of a sustained reading of Luke-Acts, one can easily imagine that, if Matthew had been the gospel with the relevant information, Irenaeus would have used it. This is obviously an exercise in imagination, but it helps to illustrate that what *Haer.* 3.1.1 reflects in terms of Irenaeus's treatment of Luke's two volumes is Irenaeus's knowledge of the contents of each. It is not Irenaeus but modern critics who formulate such knowledge in the categories of literary unity and hermeneutical consequence. It is imperative that we do not conflate modern formulations with ancient reading practice.

14. Hans von Campenhausen, *The Formation of the Christian Bible*, trans. J. A. Baker (Philadelphia: Fortress, 1972), 201–2. Gregory (*Reception of Luke and Acts*, 39 n. 58) makes

History, Hermeneutics, and the Unity of Luke-Acts

thus correct to note that "Irenaeus ... argues those (unnamed) opponents who receive Luke's (Pauline) Gospel must accept also what Luke says concerning Paul in Acts: those who accept what Luke wrote in his former volume must accept also what he wrote in his second."[15]

But recognizing Irenaeus's acknowledgment of the common authorship of Luke and Acts is still not the same thing as evidence of a particular reading practice that separates Luke from the fourfold gospel to read alone with Acts.[16] Indeed, the use to which Irenaeus puts his knowledge is that Acts should be read not along with Luke in particular but along with the fourfold gospel. In this respect, Acts is, as Campenhausen rightly saw, Irenaeus's "second text"— the *Tetraevangelium* as a whole being his first.[17]

Irenaeus may well accept the Lukan authorship of both Luke and Acts[18] and make use of Luke's literary coordination of the beginning of Acts with the end of the gospel, but Irenaeus does not evidence a sustained reading of the two volumes together as a single work in a way formally similar to our literary-critical focus on one unified story. In terms of his actual reading practice and strategy, Acts is read in connection to four gospels, not one.

---

reference to Campenhausen as illustrating "Irenaeus' use of the unity of Luke-Acts to link Acts both with the fourfold Gospel and Paul," but fails to mention that the emphasis of Campenhausen's own account falls on the issue of authorship.

15. Gregory, *Reception of Luke and Acts*, 39.

16. One may also wonder about Irenaeus's argumentative tactics: if he were to separate Luke from the other gospels to read alone with Acts, would he not thereby undermine his basic argument regarding the theological necessity of the *Tetraevangelium* and play directly into the hands of his opponents who denied the necessity of the "four" (specifically, the variously striped Marcionites known for their reading of "Luke" without the other gospels; cf. *Haer.* 3.14.3-4)? On this point, see esp. his polemic in *Haer.* 3.11.9.

17. Campenhausen, *Formation of the Christian Bible*, 201. Note, too, that Irenaeus not only grants primary unity to Luke as part of the "fourfold" gospel but also grounds its fourfold character in the created order (four zones of the world, four winds, etc.) and in the activity of God, who has bound the four together "by one Spirit" (*Haer.* 3.11.8). Thus is the fourfold gospel theologically necessary in the strict sense (cf. Graham N. Stanton, "The Fourfold Gospel," *NTS* 43 [1997]: 319-21, 342-43). The theological necessity of the "four" does not preclude, of course, Irenaeus's freedom to relate particular material from within the individual gospels to Acts, but it does mean that, in terms of his overall hermeneutical practice, Acts is not isolated to read in relation to Luke alone but is instead taken with the fourfold gospel as a whole.

18. Though in fact his focus is more on the authority of Acts than upon authorship per se. Authorship is a derivative issue in the sense that it serves the purpose of establishing the authority and trustworthiness of Acts (in contrast to the position of his opponents).

Part 1: Christology, Greco-Roman Culture, and Canonical Reception

Gregory's second exception is the Muratorian Fragment. Even if we retain a traditional dating (which seems the best option),[19] it is again far from clear that the Muratorian Fragment supports the supposition that the two volumes of Luke and Acts were read as a single literary whole. Gregory's evidence for this claim is tied not to an indication of a literarily unified interpretation but rather, once more, to the issue of common authorship: "the association of the name of Luke with the third Gospel may be explained solely on the conjecture that he wrote Acts, and the observation that similarities between these two volumes, not least their respective dedications to Theophilus, require that they be read as a literary whole."[20]

In fact, however, the only "similarity" that the Fragment mentions is that of authorship.[21] That the writer of this fragmentary piece recognizes the common authorship of Luke and Acts is beyond dispute: "The acts of all [*omnium*] the apostles are written in one book. For the 'most excellent Theophilus' Luke summarizes the several things that in his own presence have come to pass."[22] But acknowledgment of common authorship, as we noted above, is still well removed from an explicit requirement to read the work Luke-Acts as a single,

---

19. Cf., convincingly, Stanton, "Fourfold Gospel," 322–25, and Bruce M. Metzger, *The Canon of the New Testament: Its Origin, Development, and Significance* (Oxford: Clarendon, 1997), 193–94, against A. Sundberg et al.

20. Gregory, *Reception of Luke and Acts*, 41. Gregory's prose both here in the sentence quoted above (missing a word?) and in this larger section is somewhat opaque and his actual argument difficult to discern. "The reference to Luke as a physician is additional to any information that we are given by Irenaeus, but it could come from Colossians 4, so that Luke's name, his profession and his status as companion of Paul may each rest on existing tradition, and these may then provide the grounds for the conjecture that Luke was the companion of Paul whose presence is to be detected in the we-passages of Acts. Here therefore is clear evidence that the association of the name of Luke with the third Gospel may be explained solely on the conjecture that he wrote Acts, and the observation that similarities between these two volumes, not least their respective dedications to Theophilus, require that they be read as a literary whole."

21. E.g., contrary to what Gregory seems to suggest with "their respective dedications" (in the sentence quoted above), the Muratorian Fragment does not actually mention the dedication to Theophilus in relation to the preface to Luke's Gospel but only in relation to the preface to Acts; yet Gregory himself knows this well, as he indicates explicitly (*Reception of Luke and Acts*, 42): "silence on the preface to Luke."

22. Lines 34–36. "Apostolic" authorship is of course part of what appears to be at issue. Cf. line 80: The Shepherd of Hermas is not to be read publicly with the "apostles," for, among other things, "it is after their time." Of course the lacuna at the beginning of the fragment and the "wretched state of the [existing] Latin text" (Metzger, *Canon of the New Testament*, 305) are well known and make perilous any guess as to the document's specific purpose.

literary whole, and the two should neither be confused nor be conflated. One should infer, moreover, from the phrase "third book of the Gospel" that the author of the Fragment reads Luke not with Acts as *Luke-Acts* but, as did Irenaeus, with the other three gospels.[23] Indeed, John is called the author of the *quartum evangeliorum*, the *fourth* of the gospels.[24] In any case, that the author of the Muratorian Fragment reads Luke and Acts together as a single, literary work similar to the way (post)modern NT exegetes do is highly doubtful, if not wholly wrong.

While the second-century evidence is not in itself valid for the end of the first century—we must always be wary of anachronism and arguments from silence—it is still worth our consideration.[25] Indeed, where it is not contradicted by earlier material, later evidence may help to shape our perception of the phenomenon in question, perhaps especially when the weight of the evidence is so entirely one-sided.

In this light, we may return to the preface in Acts. Though Acts 1:1-2 provides a clear and purposive link to Luke's Gospel,[26] it can nonetheless be read simultaneously as presupposing a separation between the two volumes that fits well with the situation noted by Gregory, in two interconnected respects in particular.

First, the address to Theophilus in Acts 1:1 can easily be interpreted to imply that he (they) has (have)[27] already read, and presumably understood, the

---

23. Line 2. Since, however, the beginning of the text is missing, there is no way to know for sure. But see Stanton, "Fourfold Gospel," 322-25.

24. Line 14. Noted also by Stanton, "Fourfold Gospel," 333. Significantly, Stanton remarks that the Muratorian Fragment explicitly mentions, as did Irenaeus, the Spirit as that which holds the Gospels together (324).

25. The relationship of the second-century evidence to Luke-Acts is not necessarily dependent upon the date of their composition, but neither is it unaffected by the date. In fact, the later one dates Luke and Acts, the more direct the relationship of our other second-century sources to them could be.

26. Cf. Stanton, "Fourfold Gospel," 334, who notes that "the short preface to Acts with its rededication to Theophilus was a conventional way of introducing the second roll of a single work" (cf. Longenecker, "Lukan Aversion," 188, with reference to "the seam between the two Lukan volumes"). The emphasis on literary unity is well placed, but specificity such as the "second scroll of a single work" may be problematical (see, e.g., Alexander's remarks cited below on p. 156).

27. Loveday Alexander is right to note that the address to Theophilus in no way means that Luke and/or Acts were written for private readership (*The Preface to Luke's Gospel: Literary Convention and Social Context in Luke 1.1-4 and Acts 1.1*, SNTSMS 78 [Cambridge: Cambridge University Press, 1993], esp., e.g., 188). If one grants that Theophilus is not a fictive addressee (and this can be contested), it seems impossible to decide for sure whether or not he was Luke's *patronus*.

Part 1: Christology, Greco-Roman Culture, and Canonical Reception

gospel. Brief reference is made to its contents, and Luke speaks of the first book he has "made" (ἐποιησάμην). Even for the author, then, reading the story of the gospel would not depend definitively upon Acts. Literarily, Luke's Gospel is more than "somewhat self-sufficient";[28] it is intelligible on its own.

Second, Acts 1:1–2 also seems to presuppose at least some chronological space between the two volumes,[29] space that might allow the gospel at least some time to become associated with other narratives focused explicitly on the life of Jesus (e.g., Mark) and which would thus make good sense as a sort of *Ausgangspunkt* for the different treatment of Luke and Acts in the second century.[30] The gospel, in other words, could well have been treated as a gospel (though of course the

---

28. Henry J. Cadbury, *The Book of Acts in History* (New York: Harper & Brothers, 1955), 139. Cadbury's remark here is significant because it is part of his explanation of how Luke was separated from Acts. It is interesting to note that even Cadbury mentions that the volumes were at least self-sufficient enough "to have prevented some modern readers from recognizing their unity" (139). Cadbury also implies that Luke almost foresaw the possibility or even likelihood of separation: "Fortunately our author had the judgment or foresight to make each of his two volumes somewhat self-sufficient" (139).

29. How much time elapsed between the writing of Luke and Acts is of course impossible to know. It has been common at least since Kenyon's suggestion to assume that the reason Luke and Acts were separated is precisely because of the limitation of scroll length (e.g., Cadbury, *Book of Acts in History*, 138): Luke would fit on one scroll and Acts on a second. The preface to Acts would then be seen as the short introduction to the second scroll. Yet, even if this were the case, we do not necessarily have to assume that he sent both scrolls together at once (see Gregory, *Reception of Luke and Acts*, 300–301). In any case, at the very least they were physically separate volumes. There also seems now to be the possibility that Luke used a codex or codices for his work (see Gregory, *Reception of Luke and Acts*, 300–301 n. 9), which would raise the question of the absence of a unified reading even more acutely given that Luke could have written Luke-Acts together on one codex. The likelihood of the possibility of a codex would, it seems, increase in proportion to a late dating of the Lukan material (yet see Harry Y. Gamble, *Books and Readers in the Early Church: A History of Early Christian Texts* [New Haven: Yale University Press, 1995], 63, who, despite the rapid and expansive adoption of the codex in early Christianity, argues that it is unlikely that a gospel would have first been written on a codex due to the former's narrative character). Again, it is important at this point to emphasize that we are dealing with probability and hypotheses, not firm knowledge. As Gregory (*Reception of Luke and Acts*, 301) notes, "We cannot say with certainty that Acts circulated independently before Irenaeus as we do not know how (or if) it circulated at all."

30. There are of course some who date Acts quite late (Knox, O'Neill, Koester, etc.). We should also note Gregory's finding—though remembering, too, his use of Koester's rigorous redaction criterion—that there exists no evidence of external attestation for Luke until the mid-second century and Acts slightly later (Gregory, *Reception of Luke and Acts*, 5 n. 11). Yet, as Gregory later notes regarding the absence of attestation, the "lack of evidence for the reception of Luke-Acts [sic] before the middle of the second century does not mean that these texts were not used, let alone not written" (353).

word would probably not have been used)³¹ prior to the "publication," or at least distribution, of Acts. In such an early association or grouping, Acts would not really even have had the chance to become inseparably attached to Luke.

In addition, even if we accept an early date for Acts (late first rather than second century),³² the widespread assumption in modern scholarship of an early *division* of Luke from Acts is actually without an indisputably solid foundation.³³ The only existing evidence that can be adduced in favor of this assumption is the preface in Acts, if this preface is taken to establish an original historical, chronological unity. Yet, as we have discussed above, the preface might as easily be interpreted as implying that "Theophilus" has already read Luke's first λόγος and that Acts came later. And if Loveday Alexander is correct, such a preface would not be anomalous in the ancient world:

---

31. For a recent study of εὐαγγέλιον, see James A. Kelhoffer, "'How Soon a Book' Revisited: ΕΥΑΓΓΕΛΙΟΝ as a Reference to 'Gospel' Materials in the First Half of the Second Century," *ZNW* 95 (2004): 1-34, who argues that εὐαγγέλιον as a literary designation predates Marcion, 2 Clement, and even the Didache. Kelhoffer places the *terminus a quo* after the writing of the synoptics, arguing that their authors did not use the word to designate a writing, and thus sees the time frame in which the designation emerged as chronologically rather narrow (between the composition of Matthew and the Didache).

32. Thus opening the space between the composition and attestation of Acts as wide as possible.

33. See Helmut Koester, *Ancient Christian Gospels: Their History and Development* (Harrisburg, PA: Trinity Press International, 1990), 332, for example, whose statement is remarkably confident: Luke and Acts "were originally two volumes of *one* work. . . . Luke's work has not been preserved in the form in which it was published by its author." François Bovon (*Luke*, vol. 1, *A Commentary on the Gospel of Luke 1:1–9:50*, Hermeneia [Minneapolis: Fortress, 2002], 1) is no less confident: the acceptance of Luke and Acts into the canon "led to the division of the two volumes . . . presumably against Luke's intentions. From that point on, the Gospel of Luke and the book of Acts ceased to be two volumes of a single work circulating at the book markets." Cf. also, e.g., Cadbury, *Book of Acts in History*, 139; Brevard S. Childs, *The New Testament as Canon: An Introduction* (Philadelphia: Fortress, 1984), 239; Stanton, "Fourfold Gospel," 334-35. See, however, W. A. Strange, *The Problem of the Text of Acts*, SNTSMS 71 (Cambridge: Cambridge University Press, 1992), 181: "There is no strong evidence to suppose that the two works were issued or ever circulated together" (cf. also Parsons and Pervo, *Rethinking*, 117-18 n. 6). Gregory is careful to say that we do not know that Luke and Acts circulated independently (*Reception of Luke and Acts*, 301-2). He is correct that absence of evidence is not the same as negative evidence (not knowing if something is the case is quite different from knowing it to be or not to be the case). Yet the somewhat strange reluctance to acknowledge separation on the basis of the prologue in Acts is unnecessary. It is also possible to understand the Muratorian Fragment to distinguish between the time at which Luke wrote the gospel (while with Paul, lines 4-6) and Acts (later when recollecting the things that transpired in his presence, lines 34-39).

Part 1: Christology, Greco-Roman Culture, and Canonical Reception

Our study of recapitulations in scientific treatises makes it less clear that the two [Luke and Acts] are necessarily so closely linked. Things seem to have been looser in practice than logic might demand. Not all multi-volumed works have recapitulations; and conversely, not all recapitulations signal a close literary unity of the type presupposed in current study of Luke-Acts. The critic who finds a unitary conception in the texts themselves may indeed find confirmation for this unity in the two prefaces. But . . . the critic who finds that the two works . . . are none the less very different in conception, need not find the prefaces a stumbling-block. The connection between two successive works of a corpus linked by recapitulations is not always as tight as we might expect.[34]

Moreover, as far as we know, though Luke was on occasion in the fourth position among the four gospels—thus giving the opportunity for Acts to follow—Luke and Acts were never placed beside each other in any ancient manuscript.[35] Of course, the composition of Luke and Acts, even if we accept a relatively late date,[36] came well before our existing manuscripts, but it is surely more than an unlikely coincidence that the (alleged) separation left no trace of an original unity at any point in the pre-Irenaean evidence or in subsequent, highly varied manuscripts.[37] In fact, the mention of common authorship of the two volumes in Irenaeus and in the Muratorian Fragment might point, if indirectly, to the fact that Acts was not universally known or acknowledged to have been written by Luke, despite the historically correct orthodox assumption.[38]

---

34. Alexander, *Preface to Luke's Gospel*, 145–46. "Scientific" for Alexander is of course not used "in the limited sense operating in the British educational system, where 'Science' is distinguished from 'Arts' or 'Humanities', but in a sense closer to that of the French, or of the German *wissenschaftlich*" (21).

35. Speculation about P[53] (P. Mich. Inv. 6652, third century) as an exception cannot be more than speculation due to the incompleteness of the MS (two leaves: Matt 26:29–40; Acts 9:33–10:1) and the debate over whether or not the fragments are part of the same codex (see Stanton, "Fourfold Gospel," 326 n. 32, and 334 n. 60). For Luke as the fourth gospel, see Metzger, *Canon of the New Testament*, 230–31 (and 231 n. 5), 296–97, 310. (Gregory's study may increase the likelihood that Luke and Acts were not together in the case of P[53], since if he is correct, there would be no precedent in the second century for this joining.)

36. Thus closing the space as much as possible between the composition and MS evidence of Acts.

37. See Gregory, *Reception of Luke and Acts*, 27–32, for a concise and careful discussion of P[75], P[4], and the reliability of MS evidence for a pre-Irenaean text of Luke.

38. See Cadbury, *Book of Acts in History*, 146.

Stanton's proposal, that "the acceptance of Luke into the fourfold Gospel led to its early separation from Acts,"[39] may thus make more sense the other way around: Luke and Acts were not divided because they were not really read together in the first place. By itself, Luke was rather naturally grouped with other gospels and found its way unhindered into the fourfold gospel rather early on.[40] Interestingly, with this view the unsettled history of Acts then becomes somewhat easier to understand. Its various placements in the canonical lists,[41] rejection by Marcion (if he knew it)[42] and other heretical groups who accepted Luke,[43] the discussion regarding its authority in Irenaeus and others vis-à-vis such rejection, and so on are difficult to account for in light of an original historical unity.[44] Yet if the two volumes were not read as one, much

39. Stanton, "Fourfold Gospel," 335.

40. This reversal of Stanton's suggestion might actually contribute to his overall argument of an early fourfold Gospel (though it is strictly speaking a separate issue): in terms of historical order the fourfold Gospel did not separate Luke from Acts, but the fact that Luke and Acts were separate made it easier to get the fourfold Gospel together. Though he opts for an original historical unity, Cadbury (*Book of Acts in History*, 139) also notes that "it was natural that the Gospel of Luke should be associated with other Gospels."

41. See, e.g., the lists in Alexander Souter, *The Text and Canon of the New Testament* (New York: Charles Scribner's Sons, 1920), 211-12, or appendixes II and IV in Metzger, *Canon of the New Testament*.

42. If Marcion did not know Acts, as, for example, Cadbury inter alia maintained (*Book of Acts in History*, 145), this would only strengthen the idea that Luke and Acts circulated independently. C. K. Barrett ("Acts and Christian Consensus," in *Context: Essays in Honour of Peder Johan Borgen*, ed. P. W. Bøckman and R. E. Kristiansen [Trondheim: Tapir, 1987], 19-33; and "The Third Gospel as a Preface to Acts? Some Reflections," in *The Four Gospels, 1992*, ed. F. Van Segbroeck et al. [Leuven: Leuven University Press, 1992], 2:1451-66), following the suggestion of Harnack that Luke was the first gospel to arrive in Pontus (explaining, at least in part, its high esteem), conjectured that Luke-Acts was in fact seen as a sort of first "New Testament" by Marcion. Marcion "based his own New Testament upon it, editing the gospel, and substituting for Acts . . . the Antitheses and the Pauline letters" ("Third Gospel as a Preface to Acts?," 1466).

43. See Adolf von Harnack, *The Origin of the New Testament and the Most Important Consequences of the New Creation* (London: Williams & Northgate, 1925), 66.

44. Harnack's statement may be overdone but is nevertheless worth recalling: "The placing of this book in the growing Canon shows evidence of reflection, of conscious purpose, of a strong hand acting with authority" (*Origin of the New Testament*, 67). In replying to Strange's thesis (*The Problem of the Text of Acts*) that Luke died with Acts in draft form (hence its late publication, by a western and non-western editor, in textually different forms), Stanton remarks that "neither Irenaeus nor the Muratorian Fragment presses a case for accepting Acts" ("Fourfold Gospel," 335). Perhaps it depends upon what Stanton means by "presses," as in fact just a few lines earlier he wrote—correctly reading Irenaeus in my view—that Irenaeus "insists that if his opponents accepted Luke's Gospel, they should also

Part 1: Christology, Greco-Roman Culture, and Canonical Reception

of the difficulty disappears: Luke came within the gravitational pull of the other gospels, and Acts was left to float about, as indeed it seemed to do.

Had Luke first written the gospel amidst, or sent it to, a particular community and then quickly followed it with Acts, and had this community existed without Mark, Matthew, John, or Q or any other sources, or at least been willing to set them aside (perhaps in accordance with Luke's intention in the gospel προοίμιον) so that they would not read such sources in harmony with Luke's Gospel, then there might have been a chance that Luke and Acts would have been read together as a literary whole. But over the distribution and circulation process—in short, the ins and outs of a community's reading practices—Luke himself would have had little to no control (particularly if Theophilus was his patron),[45] and an identifiable Lukan community has been notoriously hard, if not outright impossible, to find.[46]

---

accept Acts" (335). Irenaeus certainly takes it that Acts is ancient, but he nonetheless notes the need for its acceptance.

45. Cf. Gregory, *Reception of Luke and Acts*, 2, who notes in passing, "Once Luke released each volume he would have had no control over its circulation and copying."

46. Popular guesses both modern and ancient have included locations as diverse as Rome, Caesarea, the whole of Achaia, etc. (for a brief list, see, e.g., Joseph A. Fitzmyer, *The Gospel according to Luke*, 2 vols., AB 28/28A (Garden City, NY: Doubleday, 1981–1985), 1:57). Even if one is still inclined to argue, as would Philip F. Esler and David Sim, for example, that the gospels reflect specific communities to which they were addressed, the ability to pin precisely Luke or Acts on a map of the Mediterranean world is seriously lacking (Philip F. Esler, "Community and Gospel in Early Christianity: A Response to Richard Bauckham's *Gospels for All Christians*," *SJT* 51 [1998]: 235–48; David Sim, "The Gospels for All Christians? A Response to Richard Bauckham," *JSNT* 84 [2001]: 3–27). For the issue of gospel communities in general, see, e.g., the concise remarks of S. C. Barton, "Can We Identify the Gospel Audiences?," in *The Gospels for All Christians: Rethinking Gospel Audiences*, ed. Richard Bauckham (Grand Rapids: Eerdmans, 1998), 173–94, esp. 186–88. It is important at this point to note with Stanton ("Fourfold Gospel," 336) that "the older view that the individual gospels circulated only in limited geographical areas is no longer tenable: the papyri . . . indicate clearly that there was a great deal of contact between different regions around the Mediterranean." See, e.g., the essay of M. B. Thompson, "The Holy Internet: Communication between Churches in the First Christian Generation," in Bauckham, *Gospels for All Christians*, 49–70. We may also think in particular of the now-classic studies of Abraham Malherbe (*Social Aspects of Early Christianity* [Philadelphia: Fortress, 1983]) and Wayne Meeks (*The First Urban Christians* [New Haven: Yale University Press, 1983]), as well as that of Peter Lampe (*From Paul to Valentinus: Christians at Rome in the First Two Centuries* [Minneapolis: Fortress, 2003]), which have shown the importance of the travel between and interconnectedness among the early (usually Pauline) Christian communities. With respect to the circulation of texts in the ancient world, Loveday Alexander is willing to speak of "interweaving networks" ("Ancient Book Production and the Circulation of the

We may thus not only draw attention to the importance of Gregory's study in general[47] but even strengthen the overall impression it gives. If the two sole exceptions to Gregory's findings (Irenaeus and the Muratorian Fragment) are not really exceptions at all but, indeed, also count against the idea that Luke and Acts were read as Luke-Acts, and if my additional remarks point in the right direction, then our current interpretive practice certainly appears in a rather different light.

Consequences for Interpretation

> From the first generations Acts is little mentioned. We infer what happened largely by still later evidence rather than by contemporary knowledge. . . . The book itself tells much of its own history up to the time it was written. After that we are in the dark, as in a tunnel, and emerge only late and partially.[48]

The implication of the history of reception of Luke and Acts for our interpretation comes at the juncture between the course of history as we can detect it and our decision to work hermeneutically on a particular level in relation to this history. In reading Luke-Acts as a unity we have often proceeded on the assumption that this hermeneutical choice is more historical than, for example, the canonical choice that was eventually made to place John between Luke and Acts.[49] In one way, this hermeneutical claim to historical accuracy

---

Gospels," in Bauckham, *Gospels for All Christians*, 104). In a general sense, while they by no means prove its impossibility, such studies decrease the likelihood of a specifically Lukan community that would have read Luke's writings in isolation.

47. Gregory's study will surely also spark debate, perhaps especially over his application of Koester's redaction criterion to determine the reception of the texts. It may be, as Gregory recognizes, that Koester's criterion affords the best (only?) way we can know for sure that, say, Lukan rather than Lukan-like texts were directly received, but it may also filter out more than is necessary.

48. Cadbury, *Book of Acts in History*, 137.

49. Cf., among many possible examples, Gilmour's statement over fifty years ago: "While Mark and Matthew are complete in themselves, Luke is the first volume of a two-volume work. The fundamental unity of Luke-Acts has . . . been obscured in part by an accident of manuscript transmission whereby Luke has been included in the 'Gospel' section of the canon and Acts in the 'Apostle' section. The canonical separation by the Gospel of John is an unfortunate divorce." Samuel MacLean Gilmour, "The Gospel according to St Luke," in *The Interpreter's Bible*, ed. George A. Buttrick et al. (New York: Abingdon, 1952), 8:15–16.

is indisputably true. Even if he thought he was composing Scripture,[50] Luke almost certainly did not write the *Doppelwerk* with the idea of an NT canon in mind, least of all one in which John would be situated between his own two volumes (even if he knew a form of John's Gospel[51]).

Yet, in a different way, the hermeneutical choice to read Luke-Acts together may in an important sense be less historical than we have thought, especially if we mean here by "history" something like the course of the actual reading of Luke and Acts. If Gregory's study and our supplementations are near the mark, then we are virtually forced to ask whether Luke-Acts was *ever* routinely read as Luke-Acts in the earliest period. If the answer is, as Gregory's work suggests, a fairly clear no, then we will have to face the possibility that our interpretations of Luke-Acts as a unity may be (at best) as it was intended but not as it was: that is, our interpretations of Luke-Acts may not reflect the practice of the earliest readers after all.

We may thus ask: When speaking of what the ancient Christians may have made of *Luke-Acts*, are we, to state it candidly, simply engaging in an interpretive trick, a hermeneutical fudge that results in an easy welding of the ancient world together with our own? More precisely, do we not confuse literary unity with historical unity, at least insofar as how the text(s) would have been heard? A perfectly satisfying answer is hard to come by, but an important part of any attempt involves the relation between the course of history and our hermeneutical decisions.

At this point it may help to clarify the situation if we take a concrete example from the scholarly literature as a way toward a discussion of our problem. The explicit, sophisticated commitment to a unified interpretation of Luke-Acts makes Luke Johnson's commentaries in the Sacra Pagina series an ideal place from which to gain some illustrative clarity.

In the introduction to his commentary on the gospel, Johnson articulates clearly the hermeneutical commitment to literary unity that informs his work in both commentaries:

> The decision to read these separate texts as a single literary work means deliberately to adopt a literary-critical approach to the New Testament, and to

50. See Nils A. Dahl, "The Story of Abraham in Luke-Acts," in *Studies in Luke-Acts*, ed. Leander E. Keck and J. Louis Martyn (Philadelphia: Fortress, 1966), 139–58, esp. 153; and Smith's presidential address to the SBL (D. Moody Smith, "When Did the Gospels Become Scripture?," *JBL* 119 [2000]: 3–20).

51. Gregory (*Reception of Luke and Acts*, 56–69) has a judicious discussion of the most important recent work on this problem and concludes that at present the *status quaestionis* is that of "a continuing debate."

History, Hermeneutics, and the Unity of Luke-Acts

rely upon a contemporary literary designation in preference to a traditional perception of the texts or even their canonical placement. Although formal acknowledgement of Luke-Acts' literary unity is today almost universally given, few commentaries (if any) have yet taken that decision seriously in their treatment of the respective volumes. The present commentary intends systematically to exploit the implications of the designation "Luke-Acts."[52]

This commitment is consistently carried forward into his commentary on Acts. In the introduction to the second commentary he simply refers the reader—in good Lukan fashion—back to the previous volume where "the framework for reading both volumes as a single story was established."[53]

The literary-critical enterprise that reads Luke-Acts together is one that I fully support. It is in fact, as Johnson writes elsewhere, "magnificently rewarded by the results."[54] Yet precisely here, where we may be wooed by "results," the historical evidence for the reception of Luke and Acts points up hermeneutical slippage, or maybe even confusion, insofar as we endeavor on literary-critical grounds to tie our interpretation to the ancient world.

That study of the ancient world provides substantial insight into Luke's literary style, technique, sophistication, and the like is hardly debatable, and it is not here that our problem is located. The problem, rather, arises when from literary-critical assumptions about the unity of Luke-Acts we draw conclusions about the meaning of Luke-Acts for the early Christians who would

---

52. Johnson, *Gospel of Luke*, 1.

53. Luke Timothy Johnson, *The Acts of the Apostles*, SP 5 (Collegeville, MN: Liturgical Press, 1992), 2. Johnson continues: "Everything said there about the identity of the author, the circumstances of composition, the genre and purpose of the work, and the literary methods used by the author, need not be repeated in detail" (2). We may—perhaps a bit mischievously—wonder here about a fuller analogy with Luke-Acts: Johnson's commentaries are meant to be read together as a single whole with two parts. Yet there was never a historical, chronological unity to the commentaries since they were written and published apart. Moreover, at least in the Divinity School library of Duke University, Johnson's commentaries do not sit next to each other on the shelf. Luke is with the other Luke volumes and Acts with its companions (this is also true within the Sacra Pagina series itself). The library grouping obviously reflects the later "canonical" arrangements, but such an order is intelligible on reception-historical grounds.

54. Luke Timothy Johnson, "The Christology of Luke-Acts," in *Who Do You Say That I Am? Essays on Christology*, ed. Mark Allan Powell and David R. Bauer (Louisville: Westminster John Knox, 1999), 51. This is actually Johnson's response to his own observation (cued by Parsons and Pervo) that "the early separation of the Gospel and Acts in the process of canonization would argue for their separate treatment" (51).

Part 1: Christology, Greco-Roman Culture, and Canonical Reception

have heard the texts. Johnson's remarks at the end of his Acts commentary illustrate the predicament:

> For the final time, therefore, Paul announces a turn to the Gentiles with a ringing affirmation: the salvation from God has been sent to them, and they will listen! Luke's readers recognize this as the prophecy that has indeed taken place "among us" (Luke 1.1), and which has generated the question that made the writing of this narrative necessary in the first place: how did the good news reach the Gentiles, and did the rejection of it by the Jews mean that God failed in his fidelity to them? Luke's answer is contained in the entire narrative up to this point.[55]

Leaving aside the actual exegetical proposals, Johnson here moves from a unified literary-critical reading to what "Luke's readers" may have recognized (cf. "us"). Moreover, he implies that to answer the question "How did the good news . . . ?" the readers will have had to read Luke-Acts together: "Luke's answer is contained in the entire narrative up to this point." But to make this move is to confuse literary results with historical evidence.

Here then is the hermeneutical problem: the interpretation that Johnson claims the ancient Christian readers would have understood is predicated upon reading Luke and Acts together as a unified narrative, but the evidence from reception history makes it doubtful that early Christian readers would have read the two volumes together in this way. Johnson's interpretation, while literarily ingenious, thus appears to be historically implausible inasmuch as it depends on readers' perception of Luke-Acts. By extension, we may rightfully wonder about the historical viability of interpretations that claim a connection to an ancient Christian audience but depend in principle for their intelligibility upon the entirety of Luke-Acts as a single work. Thus, for example, when Gary Gilbert concludes his essay, "By echoing and repackaging various forms of Roman propaganda, Luke-Acts provides Christians with their source of legitimization and bolsters the nascent self-identification of the Christian community in the first and second centuries,"[56] we may point out that his interpretation presupposes the existence of Christian communities in the first and second centuries who

---

55. Johnson, *Acts of the Apostle*, 476; emphasis removed.
56. Gary Gilbert, "Roman Propaganda and Christian Identity in the Worldview of Luke-Acts," in *Contextualizing Acts: Lukan Narrative and Greco-Roman Discourse*, ed. Todd Penner and Caroline Vander Stichele, Society of Biblical Literature Symposium Series 20 (Atlanta: Society of Biblical Literature, 2003), 256.

would have read Luke-Acts together and, moreover, in such a way that this one work would have contributed substantially to the construction of their identity as Christians. Or when John Carroll states that his article "will develop a picture [of God] that would result from repeated reading, or hearing, of the narrative over a period of time—the sort of engagement that might have occurred in an early Christian community that treasured Luke's two books 'to Theophilus,'"[57] we may ask, But where are such Christians?[58] And, indeed, where is Luke-Acts?

---

57. John T. Carroll, "The God of Israel and the Salvation of the Nations," in *The Forgotten God: Perspectives in Biblical Theology: Essays in Honor of Paul J. Achtemeier on the Occasion of His Seventy-Fifth Birthday*, ed. A. Andrew Das and Frank J. Matera (Louisville: Westminster John Knox, 2002), 91. Cf., e.g., F. Gerald Downing, *Doing Things with Words in the First Christian Century*, JSNTSup 200 (Sheffield: Sheffield Academic, 2000), 198–217, who presupposes a single, first reading of Luke-Acts in his chapter on Theophilus's "first hearing of Luke-Acts." See, in this connection, P. J. J. Botha, "Community and Conviction in Luke-Acts," *Neotestamentica* 29, no. 2 (1995): 145–65, whose article assumes a unified reading of Luke and Acts in the attempt to specify "the occasion for the presentation of Luke-Acts" in analogy to the readings and performances that "were a common feature of the symposia and dinner parties" in the Greco-Roman world (150–51).

58. Cf. the widely recognized work of Philip F. Esler, which concludes that "Luke's two volumes may be described as an exercise in the legitimation of a sectarian movement, as a sophisticated attempt to explain and justify Christianity to the members of his community at a time when they were exposed to social and political pressure" (*Community and Gospel in Luke-Acts: The Social and Political Motivations of Lucan Theology*, SNTSMS 57 [Cambridge: Cambridge University Press, 1987], 222). Esler's general point, that Luke himself "theologized" in relation to a concrete community, may be correct (though it is debatable, as the controversy surrounding Bauckham's proposals regarding gospel audience have illustrated), but it does not ipso facto follow that this community would have read Luke-Acts together in a way analogous to modern critical practice, or even that Luke wrote Luke and Acts close together (e.g., his gospel could have gotten out and around, as it were, before he wrote Acts). In other words, monographs such as Esler's that read community out of Luke-Acts are arguably much more about Luke's overall socio-theological concerns, at least methodologically speaking, than they are about an actual community that reads Luke and Acts together as Luke-Acts. Barrett's hypothesis ("Acts and Christian Consensus" and "Third Gospel as a Preface to Acts?"; noted in n. 42) that Marcion knew of Luke-Acts does actually attempt to provide a distinct group within a particular locale (Pontus) that would have known of an original unity of Luke's two volumes (though obviously Marcion did not read them together). Yet Barrett's primary piece of evidence—a statement from the Mesopotamian bishop Marutha of Maipherkat (ca. 400 AD; "Acts and Christian Consensus," 31)—is hardly a suitable basis for such a conjecture, and we may also note that Barrett's hypothesis probably rests on the prior assumption of just the type of unity that is in question. Moreover, as intimated earlier, it seems prima facie to make better sense out of the situation to assume either that Marcion did not really know Acts (though this runs against the testimony—albeit polemical—of the early church fathers) or that he came to know Acts only after he knew Luke (thus making sense of the totality of the rejection of Acts).

Part 1: Christology, Greco-Roman Culture, and Canonical Reception

In other words, it is doubtlessly true on a literary level that Luke-Acts *can* "be read as a *single* story."[59] The problem is that historically it hardly ever—if ever—was.

An Open Question

To raise bedeviling hermeneutical and historical questions without offering clear, constructive answers is somewhat like dumping a puzzle onto the table without attempting to put the pieces together—one can easily see that there are various pieces to the puzzle but not necessarily how they should be arranged to form a coherent picture. We must do more than simply dump the puzzle out, but to say that we can at this point put all the pieces together may be to move too fast.

The dilemma we face is how to relate interpretations based on literary unity to the course of history that evidences separation—or, perhaps, to borrow from Raymond Brown in another context, how to relate "what most likely was meant by the first-century author" to what was "most likely understood by the first- [and second-] century audience."[60] It would seem that when we read Luke-Acts together as a single work, we have made the hermeneutical choice to focus upon Luke's intention (for traditional, "old-fashioned" hermeneuts), or the effect generated from reading two volumes together (for those of a more modish outlook), and given up claim to an understanding of the perception of the text by its early auditors. The necessary basis for literary-critical interpretation to claim historical insight into the early Christian reading of the Lukan writings has (so far) not been provided: an actual person or community that reads Luke and Acts together as the single story Luke-Acts, and, furthermore, to the exclusion of a sort of canonical current that allows Acts to be heard with Luke but not Luke with other gospels. Yet literary-critical interpretation of Luke-Acts divines something of Luke's overall purpose, plan, and theology, and is in this way historically closer to the genesis of the work and the person who wrote it (or at least the implied author) than a so-called historical interpretation that would attempt to trace more closely the actual reading of the work in two separate parts.

Conversely, it would seem that when we seek to read Luke and Acts as they were read and understood early on, we have made the hermeneutical choice

---

59. Johnson, *Gospel of Luke*, 4: Luke-Acts "must be read as a *single* story."
60. Brown, *An Introduction to the Gospel of John*, ed. Francis J. Moloney (New York: Doubleday, 2003), 111. Brown is speaking here about the purpose of a commentary.

to focus upon the course of history and of historical plausibility in relation to ancient Christian readers/auditors' perceptions and given up our right to draw historical conclusions on the basis of interpretations that presume literary unity. Yet in this respect we become somewhat further removed from Luke's intention and estranged from the literary dynamics of the two volumes. Alexandru Neagoe's new study of the "trial narratives" in Luke-Acts can serve as a final example to illustrate the problem.[61]

Neagoe argues persuasively that not only are the various trial scenes in Acts (Peter, Stephen, Paul, etc.) related to each other, but also that they are related literarily to the trial of Jesus in the gospel (which itself has "narrative precedents" in the gospel narrative). When the two volumes are read as Luke-Acts, the trial of Jesus thus helps by virtue of its reappearance in "retrospective references" to fund the interpretation of the trial scenes in Acts. When the scenes in Acts and in the Gospel of Luke are related to one another, it becomes clear—so Neagoe—that Luke's intention therewith was to display the defense of "the gospel" (*apologia pro evangelio*). The trial scenes, that is, are part of an overall literary project within Luke-Acts and in their connectedness reveal something basic to the Lukan project: the intention to defend the gospel via a two-volume literary work.

Even if one is disinclined to accept the claim that Luke's overall purpose in writing was to defend the gospel (*apologia pro evangelio* in the broadest sense), it can hardly be doubted that in relating the trials to one another Neagoe has drawn our attention to a salient literary feature of Luke-Acts. In so doing, he has, in my judgment, also opened a window onto something of Luke's intention. That is to say, through the elucidation of a particular literary dynamic of Luke-Acts, we have moved closer to Luke's intention in linking the scenes together, and perhaps even to his larger compositional purpose. Neagoe's study is thus a literary one and, to its credit, does not really push to say that the early Christians would have made the connections between Jesus's trial in the Gospel of Luke and the trials of Paul and so on in Acts. Perhaps the early Christians would have heard in Paul's trials echoes of Jesus's own trial, but to restrict such echoes to the Gospel of Luke is to make a literary decision about Luke's intentional narrative stitching, not—insofar as we now know—a historical one about the reading of the texts.

To make a historical determination about how the trials in Acts would have been heard in early Christian communities is to admit the serious likelihood

---

61. Alexandru Neagoe, *The Trial of the Gospel: An Apologetic Reading of Luke's Trial Narratives*, SNTSMS 116 (Cambridge: Cambridge University Press, 2002).

Part 1: Christology, Greco-Roman Culture, and Canonical Reception

that Acts was not heard as part of a work Luke-Acts but with several other writings. But to allow this separation of Luke from Acts is to lose contact with the literary dynamic of Luke-Acts in which the trials of Acts reach back to and are meaningfully informed by the trial of Jesus in Luke. Neagoe's study, that is, would lose its ability to be specific—and thus its tie to the Gospel of Luke in particular—as it would need to forfeit the possibility of reading a specifically Lukan trial of Jesus into the trials of Acts. The study could then hardly be said to be a study of Luke-Acts. Is there a way to relate these choices to one another in a coherent manner, or are our readings of Luke-Acts by necessity bifurcated into literary (Luke-Acts) and historical (Luke and Acts) interpretation?

Fully satisfying answers remain in the distance. Yet some differentiation may nonetheless help to move forward the discussion about the interpretation of Luke's work in light of its early reception, at least with respect to the issues involved. To suggest that historical interpretation may require us to read the volumes separately is not to say that a return to the present canonical shape of the material is the most accurate way of pursuing a connection to a *pre-canonical* audience's perception of the texts. Strictly speaking, a *canonical* interpretation is one that attempts to read Luke after Matthew and Mark but before John, and Acts after the four gospels and before the *corpus Paulinum*.[62] Acts' well-known, checkered canonization history—it was quite differently placed[63]—is alone sufficient reason to doubt the canonical route as a sufficiently historical one for the attempt to get at the earliest Christians' perception of the texts under discussion. Canonical interpretation is thus to be distinguished hermeneutically from questions of reception history and literary-critical interpretation of Luke-Acts. Yet how we might inquire historically after the potential impact of the gospel and Acts upon their earliest Christian readers/auditors is not sufficiently clear.

---

62. Of modern scholars, Robert Wall's commentary in the *New Interpreter's Bible* series is an excellent example of a canonical interpretation of Acts, of what it might mean to read Acts after the four gospels and before Paul's letters. Cf., however, the intriguing discussion of Childs (*New Testament as Canon*, esp. 239-40), in which he argues that "the canonical function of Acts was not determined by the order of its placement within the New Testament collection. . . . The canonical significance of Acts lies elsewhere, regardless of its order within the New Testament collection" (239). Yet Childs's canonical understanding does in fact take Acts as the framework for the interpretation of Paul, but perhaps in a way that is (somewhat?) independent of their actual order. In light of Childs's nuanced discussion, perhaps we should be even more specific within canonical criticism itself and term Wall's type of interpretation literary-canonical (in the sense of reading the present canonical material literarily in order).

63. E.g., after John, after Mark, after the Pauline epistles, etc.

It is probably both logical and, in light of what we know, academically sound to assume that we could know something of the impact of Luke's Gospel upon its early Mediterranean audience(s) (even if this something is rather general in nature);[64] yet when speaking about Christian communities we must bear in mind that the gospel's preface might well—though it is not strictly necessary—assume "Theophilus's" knowledge of other gospel-like writings. Whether Luke was then read by itself against or with these other accounts would depend on the community's reading practices, a point that I touched on above and about which we know practically nothing. But in theory, at least, Luke's Gospel could have been read by itself, and it seems a legitimate undertaking to wonder about how it might have been heard.

The case is not necessarily the same with Acts, which, insofar as we can discern, was neither meant to be read alone nor actually read alone, but always in conjunction with another early Christian writing or writings. But to assume that this other Christian writing was Luke's Gospel by itself is precisely what the reception history of the texts calls into question. It is of course possible to think of certain scenes or vignettes in Acts as having a particular impact on this or that audience. It is conceivable, for example, that various auditors in the ancient world could glean in a rather general sense from Paul's trials that the gospel is being defended (*apologia pro evangelio*), even if they were unable to perceive the literary and material connections of such trials to Jesus's trial in Luke's Gospel.[65] But this possibility of the impact of particular scenes hardly settles the larger question about Acts as a whole. Would not the perception of Acts by the early Christians vary considerably depending upon the other writings with which Acts was (or was not) read? To return to Johnson's proposal regarding the ending of Acts, can we really say, with reference to concrete

---

64. See, e.g., the still-important essay of Charles H. Talbert, "Prophecies of Future Greatness: The Contributions of Greco-Roman Biographies to an Understanding of Luke 1.5–4.1," in *Reading Luke-Acts in Its Mediterranean Milieu* (Leiden: Brill, 2003), 65–77. Cf. Talbert's careful remarks on "authorial audience" as "larger cultural milieu" in the lead essay of the same collection ("On Reading Luke and Acts," esp. 17–18). As I read him, Talbert does not presuppose an actual early Christian community for his interpretations, but rather in a technically sophisticated way construes the meaning of Luke's text primarily through the lens of larger Greco-Roman culture (specifically, relevant aspects of its "presupposition pool").

65. If Acts came after the Pauline letters, for example, the auditor's ability to connect the trial scenes in Acts to the Gospel of Luke would probably be greatly diminished. So, too, to take another example, in a canonical ordering where John precedes Acts, it is worth noting the serious differences in the narration of Jesus's trial before the Sanhedrin between John and Luke. Would hearing John's version not have an impact on the way in which one would hear the trials in Acts?

Part 1: Christology, Greco-Roman Culture, and Canonical Reception

Christian communities, how this ending would have been heard apart from the other texts with which it would have (and have not) been read? Would it not make a substantial difference, to take only the most obvious example, to hear the ending of Acts *before* rather than *after* the Pauline corpus if the issue at stake is anything like the theological question involved in Paul's mission to the Gentiles?

One hesitates to end a chapter without making some "new" proposal that will solve all difficulties and send us off to hermeneutically confident and exegetically fruitful work. But the topic is, as the puzzling reader has now realized, seriously perplexing and invites further reflection from and conversation with others. It seems then that the problem of history and hermeneutics in relation to Luke-Acts leaves us—at this point—with an open question. We are left, that is, with the need to think more clearly about the relation of literary-critical interpretation to the actual course of history and, conversely, about the relation of historical interpretation to Luke's intention and literary design. Perhaps, in short, what we are forced to do is to consider anew the actual course of history of reading *Luke and Acts* (reception history) in relation to Luke's intention and plan in *Luke-Acts* (literary interpretation). For Luke, it would seem, set out to write a two-volume work, even if he knew volume one would be read first, but the church as a whole did not take his point. Theologically, this turned out for the best,[66] but historically and for literary-critical interpretation it presents an open question.

To conclude, I shall simply summarize the main arguments of the chapter in the form of some theses and questions:

1. Insofar as Luke intended Acts to go with Luke as two volumes of a connected work, and insofar as they exhibit literary connectedness, it is clearly legitimate and valuable to study the two works as the literary unity Luke-Acts. Since, however, we have virtually no evidence that the early Christians actually treated the two volumes as a literary unity, such studies cannot claim to be recovering or reproducing the ways in which the early Christians read/heard Luke and Acts.
2. Since the two works were not read as a unity by the early Christians, there is certainly no reason why modern studies *must* treat the two as a connected unity in every dimension of the interpretive enterprise;[67] indeed, the claim

---

66. So, rightly, Stanton, "Fourfold Gospel," 341–46.
67. The claim that scholars *must* treat Luke and Acts together is of course widespread in modern research. See, e.g., W. Ward Gasque, *A History of the Criticism of the Acts*

that a unified reading is historically rooted—in the sense of grounded in actual reading practices—is, as far as we can ascertain, at best seriously disputable and perhaps even false. In the case of Luke's Gospel, this means that readings and studies of the gospel itself, as with Matthew, Mark, or John, are entirely appropriate.[68] Further, the evidence of early Christian readings would press us more toward studies of Luke in the context of other gospel traditions than toward studies of Luke-Acts.

3. There is probably a wide variety of ways in which Acts can legitimately and valuably be read, depending on whether the legitimacy of a reading strategy is connected with the author's intention and/or the literary character of the work—both of which would validate reading Acts with Luke—or with the evidence for Acts' early reception and its textual and canonical history, which would validate reading Acts in a variety of relationships (and canonical connections): as a sequel to the fourfold gospel tradition, as a prelude or sequel to the Pauline letters, and so on.

4. In relation to the preceding theses, we might, however, pose the question: Do we not forfeit an understanding of the literary dynamics of Luke and Acts if we separate them and/or join them together with other writings?[69]

---

of the Apostles, Beiträge zur Geschichte der biblischen Exegese 17 (Tübingen: Mohr Siebeck, 1975), 309, who concludes his learned monograph thus: "The primary gain of the recent criticism of Luke-Acts has been the recognition that the Gospel according to Luke and the Book of Acts are really two volumes of one work which must be considered together."

68. Contra, e.g., the critical remarks of Martin Rese, "Das Lukas-Evangelium. Ein Forschungsbericht," *ANRW* 2.25.3 (1985): 2298 n. 162: "Es war . . . sicher keine gute Entscheidung, in der Reihe 'Wege der Forschung' einen Band allein für das LkEv zu bestimmen." Rese's note comes at the conclusion of his report on the research of the first half of the twentieth century. The point at which the scholarly discussion advanced, argues Rese, was the apprehension of the unity of Luke-Acts. To return to a separate treatment of Luke and/or Acts is to forfeit understanding: "LkEv und Apg sind als ein einheitliches Werk anzusehen, und man wird keinem der beiden Einzelteile dieses Werks gerecht, wenn man es je für sich allein betrachtet. . . . Ohne diese Einsicht ist der jetzt noch zu behandelnde Abschnitt der Arbeit am LkEv nicht zu verstehen, und hinter diese Einsicht sollte keine Auslegung des LkEv mehr zurückfallen" (2298).

69. Cf. Loveday Alexander's comments in "Formal Elements and Genre: Which Greco-Roman Prologues Most Closely Parallel the Lukan Prologues?," in D. P. Moessner (ed.), *Jesus and the Heritage of Israel: Luke's Narrative Claim upon Israel's Legacy* (Harrisburg, PA: Trinity Press International, 1999), 11, on the preface of Acts: "Acts is 'Volume II': readers who begin here have missed a lot of essential information, very little of which will be directly explained for their benefit. . . . For the reader of Acts, in other words, the opening sentence makes it evident that the two volumes have to be read in sequence."

Part 1: Christology, Greco-Roman Culture, and Canonical Reception

Is it possible to retain the depth of understanding of both Luke and Acts gained by reading them together if we read them apart?[70]

5. Finally, to put the larger issue as simply as possible: What are the current interpretive options if we take seriously the possibility that Acts was intended to go with Luke but that they were not actually read together?

---

70. Cf. Barrett, "Third Gospel as a Preface to Acts?," 1453: "It is clear that the gospel . . . can be, and very often has been, read independently, and taken on its own makes the same good sense as Matthew, Mark, and John. But this does not in itself mean that it was not intended to serve the additional purpose of introducing a second volume which from the beginning was part of the author's plan."

Literary Unity and Reception History

◆ READING LUKE-ACTS AS LUKE AND ACTS

Every NT scholar knows that to speak correctly of Luke and Acts, we should talk of Luke-Acts. Or such is the conventional wisdom. Yet a consideration of the issues raised by the reception history of these texts problematizes our linguistic habits by forcing us to rethink some fundamental assumptions that shape our interpretation of the Lukan writings. In this respect Andrew Gregory's remarkably thorough spadework[1] uncovered central historical and hermeneutical problems with which NT scholars must deal—problems which I subsequently sought to press upon the field in my chapter "History, Hermeneutics and the Unity of Luke-Acts."[2] The present chapter continues this conversation.

The Present Situation, *in Nuce*

If we look first at the evidence "external" to Luke-Acts—ancient readers, copyists, and so on—we find no evidence of any interpretive practice that depends for its intelligibility upon the hermeneutical strategy of taking Luke-Acts as a single, unified literary whole. Furthermore, though the common authorship of Luke and Acts was discussed in antiquity, there exist no arguments to the effect that Luke and Acts should actually be read together as Luke-Acts. This is obviously not to say that Luke and Acts were unknown prior to Irenaeus.

---

1. Andrew Gregory, *The Reception of Luke and Acts in the Period before Irenaeus: Looking for Luke in the Second Century*, WUNT 2/169 (Tübingen: Mohr Siebeck, 2003).

2. C. Kavin Rowe, "History, Hermeneutics and the Unity of Luke-Acts," *JSNT* 28, no. 2 (2005): 131–57, reprinted in this volume at pp. 146–70.

"Literary Unity and Reception History: Reading Luke-Acts as Luke and Acts" was originally published in *Journal for the Study of the New Testament* 29, no. 4 (2007): 449–457. Copyright 2007 SAGE Publications. DOI: 0142064X07078995.

Part 1: Christology, Greco-Roman Culture, and Canonical Reception

It is, rather, to say that, insofar as it can be discerned, there is no indisputable indication that Luke and Acts were read as the literary unity we call Luke-Acts. Since Andrew Gregory's dissertation there have been a few minor articles that touch upon this topic,[3] but not one of them presents evidence that could qualify substantially this conclusion. With respect to the available data, we may thus say that Luke-Acts was not received as Luke-Acts.

There are of course debatable passages—chiefly, in my view, Justin Martyr's *First Apology* 50.12 and the opening of book 3 of Irenaeus's *Against Heresies*. But I would submit that, at best, what these passages demonstrate is, on the one hand, knowledge of the contents of Luke and Acts taken primarily as historical facts (Justin and Irenaeus) and, on the other, knowledge of the Lukan *authorship* of Acts (Irenaeus alone). What such passages almost certainly do *not* demonstrate is any kind of larger or sustained reading of Luke and Acts together as Luke-Acts, a hermeneutical approach, in other words, that depends for its coherence upon an actual reading practice that treats literarily Luke's two volumes as one unified work.[4]

From the perspective of reception history, we may thus summarize the situation as follows: no ancient author exhibits a hermeneutical practice that is founded upon the reading of Luke-Acts as one work in two volumes; no ancient author argues that Luke and Acts should be read together as one work in two volumes; and there is not a single NT manuscript that contains the unity Luke-Acts or even hints at this unity by placing Acts directly next to the Gospel of Luke.[5]

---

3. See, e.g., Arthur J. Bellinzoni, "The Gospel of Luke in the Apostolic Fathers," in *Trajectories through the New Testament and the Apostolic Fathers*, ed. Andrew F. Gregory and Christopher M. Tuckett (Oxford: Oxford University Press, 2005), 45-68, and François Bovon, "The Reception and Use of the Gospel of Luke in the Second Century," in *Reading Luke: Interpretation, Reflection, Formation*, ed. Craig Bartholomew et al. (Grand Rapids: Zondervan, 2005), 379-400 (with a response from Gregory).

4. My point here with respect to *Haer.* 3.1 is that, while Irenaeus may well perceive an essential connection between the end of Luke and beginning of Acts (so Gregory), this says more about Luke's literary ability than it does about Irenaeus's reading practice. When asking about the latter—i.e., does Irenaeus actually read a two-volume work as one (Luke-Acts)?—the answer is that he manifestly does not. In terms of hermeneutical strategy and practice, Irenaeus reads the *Tetraevangelium* together with Acts. With respect to Justin the situation is even more complex: it is arguable that *1 Apol.* 50.12 reflects the plotline of Luke-Acts, but it is also possible (as Gregory pointed out in private conversation) that 50.12 derives from Justin's knowledge of the end of Luke and Matthew (esp. 28:19-20). Of course, it has also been argued that Justin did not know Acts at all.

5. This despite the fact that Luke could assume the fourth position in the *Tetraevange-*

If we look, second, at the evidence internal to Luke-Acts, we find an absence of any concrete indication that Luke and Acts were issued together as one work. There is every reason to think that the two volumes are unified structurally, thematically, and theologically—which is to say literarily in a rather full sense—but it does not follow that the volumes had to be, or were intended to be, issued together as one work. To those who would invoke the preface of Acts as evidence to the contrary, it should be pointed out that (a) the (admittedly ambiguous) preface can easily be read to presuppose a chronological gap between the composition of Acts and the πρῶτος λόγος; (b) within Luke's literary milieu "recapitulatory" prefaces did not necessarily imply chronologically close composition;[6] and (c) Luke's Gospel is narratively intelligible on its own, apart from Acts (even Cadbury was quick to recognize this point; indeed, he offered it as a reason for their subsequent separation[7]). To be sure, for those who have ears to hear, there are various items in the gospel that receive their completion, as it were, in Acts (e.g., Simeon's prophecy in Luke 2:32 that Jesus will be a φῶς εἰς ἀποκάλυψιν ἐθνῶν points through Luke 7:1–10 toward the second volume). But such connections only show Luke's literary deftness as a writer. They do not say anything one way or another about the reception of the works; they do not render the gospel unintelligible by itself; and they do not show that Acts must have been bound together with Luke from the start.

Literary Unity and Reception History

In light of the foregoing sketch, we may make two important distinctions. (1) In contrast to Parsons and Pervo, I do not question the literary, theological, or "architectonic" unity of Luke-Acts. Indeed, I think it demonstrable that the author of the gospel did write Acts as a sequel to Luke.

However, what unity in this sense tells us has to do with Luke's literary achievement, his talent as an author; it does not—and this point bears repeating—tell us how the texts were actually read. Luke's narrative artistry,

---

lium (e.g., Codex Claromontanus, the Cheltenham canon, the Curetonian Syriac Gospels, Theophilus of Antioch, and NT MS 888).

6. Contra Luke Timothy Johnson, "Literary Criticism of Luke-Acts: Is Reception History Pertinent?," *JSNT* 28, no. 2 (2005): 161; see Loveday Alexander, *The Preface to Luke's Gospel: Literary Convention and Social Context in Luke 1.1–4 and Acts 1.1*, SNTSMS 78 (Cambridge: Cambridge University Press, 1993).

7. Henry J. Cadbury, *The Book of Acts in History* (New York: Harper & Brothers, 1955), 139.

his ability to write a richly textured, two-volume work, is emphatically not the same thing as what other people did with his writings: the intention and success of Luke the author should not be confused or conflated with the reception of Luke and Acts.

This simple distinction is actually far-reaching, in two senses: (a) Further demonstration of the literary unity of Luke-Acts as a response to my earlier article, to Gregory, or to Bockmuehl misses the point of the argument from reception history.[8] To take but one example, questions of whether the preface to Luke's Gospel refers to both volumes or to the gospel alone[9] really do nothing whatever to alter the force of the reception-historical argument, which is that we have no evidence that the two volumes were read together as Luke-Acts. Irenaean nuance aside, this is a historical fact that cannot be altered by additional attention to Luke's literary skill. To defeat Parsons and Pervo on "literary unity" is not yet even to grapple seriously with reception history. (b) To affirm the literary unity of Luke-Acts while questioning its actual reception as Luke-Acts suggests that we should speak both of Luke-Acts (when thinking in terms of Lukan theology, Christology, politics, etc.) and of Luke and Acts (when inquiring after what the texts' early auditors would have heard). Thus I agree with Luke Johnson that "a literary-critical reading . . . of Luke's entire narrative is best . . . for understanding his literary and theological voice"[10] but disagree that we can move assuredly from Luke's "voice" as displayed through both volumes to what ancient readers would have heard. In the case of the Lukan writings, reconstructing the latter on the basis of the former is exactly what is made difficult by the evidence from reception history. Despite the confidence of modern NT scholarship, the hermeneutical difference between the two modes of reading cannot so easily be collapsed into one interpretive process.

(2) Hence we come to the division among scholars of reception history that results from the absence of first-century evidence. On one side, there are those who think that the literary unity of Luke-Acts supplies sufficient ground for us to suppose that the writings were read together as Luke-Acts prior to their separation: ideal readers must be translated into a group of real readers.[11] On the

---

8. Gregory, *Reception of Luke and Acts*; Markus Bockmuehl, "Why Not Let Acts Be Acts? In Conversation with C. Kavin Rowe," *JSNT* 28, no. 2 (2005): 163–66.

9. See Michael F. Bird, "The Unity of Luke-Acts in Recent Discussion," *JSNT* 29, no. 4 (2007): 425–48.

10. Johnson, "Literary Criticism of Luke-Acts," 162.

11. See Andrew Gregory, "The Reception of Luke and Acts and the Unity of Luke-Acts," *JSNT* 29, no. 4 (2007): 459–72; Johnson, "Literary Criticism of Luke-Acts."

other, there are those who think that we have no evidence for such a smooth translation and that what later evidence we do possess points uniformly in the opposite direction:[12] ideal readers may not so easily be translated into real readers (literary unity does not offer us the concrete, requisite community or interpreters). With respect to the late first or early second century (assuming the more or less traditional dating of Luke and Acts), perhaps we are simply at a stalemate. Yet each view de facto presupposes an earlier state of affairs that allegedly renders intelligible the later evidence: the former view, that "somehow" Luke and Acts became separated in the history of transmission; the latter, that Luke and Acts may well have been read separately from the start. We thus arrive at the question of a historically plausible *Ausgangspunkt* for the subsequent history of the texts.

The Search for an *Ausgangspunkt*

To search behind our extant evidence for a plausible *Ausgangspunkt* is of course to deal with probabilities rather than with knowledge. Yet it is hardly unreasonable to ask whether there might be a situation that could explain well the subsequent developments. If we examine, then, the common hypothesis that Luke and Acts were *separated* at some point after their initial, joint publication, we find that it has less to commend it than we may have thought (cf. Bockmuehl: "There is no evidence that Acts *ever* became 'separated' from the Gospel, as is often assumed"[13]). To the absence of literary indications that a joint publication was necessary, we may add that if Luke and Acts were originally designed to fit almost exactly on one scroll each, as has long been suggested (Kenyon et al.), then it becomes much harder—rather than easier—to think of their mutual publication and interpretation. If on two separate scrolls, Luke and Acts were in a physically important sense primed or ready for different treatment, particularly if whoever received these scrolls already knew a gospel-like writing that would bear substantial similarity to Luke (say, the Gospel of Mark). Interestingly, of course, in the preface to his gospel, Luke mentions other such writings (πολλοί!) and for all practical purposes invites Theophilus to contrast Luke's account with the others. Whether the recipients of Luke's Gospel actually did compare or contrast different writings we cannot know. But we may surely observe that

---

12. Rowe, "History, Hermeneutics"; Bockmuehl, "Why Not Let Acts Be Acts?"
13. Bockmuehl, "Why Not Let Acts Be Acts?," 164.

Part 1: Christology, Greco-Roman Culture, and Canonical Reception

it would be natural for Luke's readers to associate the gospel with these other gospels or gospel-like writings.[14]

Moreover, there are the issues of the two different forms of the text of Acts (the "Western" text is almost 10 percent longer) and the varying placement of Acts in the canonical "lists" and NT manuscripts. With respect to the text of Acts, we may take notice of the important fact that it is more difficult to account for the messiness of Acts' textual situation with the supposition of a neat, joint publication with Luke—*Luke-Acts*—than it is to suppose that Acts' textual situation is at least in some way intrinsically related to the manner in which it actually began to circulate. Though hardly an attempt at a text-critical solution, to tie Acts' textual anomalies to its originating circumstances is to account better for (a) the fact that it is cited as authoritative in various forms without discrimination (e.g., Tertullian and Cyprian read the Western text; Clement of Alexandria, Origen, and Athanasius cite the Alexandrian; and Eusebius of Caesarea evinces a mixture of Western and non-Western readings) and (b) the dramatic difference between the textual problems in Acts and those of the other NT writings—especially the Gospel of Luke.

With respect to the placement of Acts in "lists" and NT manuscripts, it is well-known that Acts often introduces the Catholic Epistles (e.g., Athanasius's Easter letter of 367 and P[74]). To stay at this level of generality, however, is to obscure the considerable diversity of Acts' particular placement. It also seems to conclude the Catholic Epistles (e.g., "Pope Innocent to Exsuperius of Toulouse," ca. 400), as well as the *evangelium* (e.g., Eusebius, *Hist. eccl.* 3.25.1 and P[45]), which of course varied as to its order. It both introduces and follows the *corpus Paulinum* (e.g., the canon of Gregory of Nazianzus and the Cheltenham canon, respectively). And, at least in one fragmentary papyrus from the third century, a small portion of Acts is found with Matthew alone (P[53]). More strikingly, in Codex Claromontanus (ca. sixth century)—where Luke is the fourth of the four gospels—Acts occurs near the end of the list, between Revelation (which itself follows the Epistle of Barnabas) and the Shepherd of Hermas. How frequent or rare was such an odd positioning of Acts may be impossible to know, but it is probably not without significance that the final canon in the Apostolic Constitutions (Can. 85, ca. late fourth century) positions Acts thus: "Our sacred books are . . . the four Gospels . . . fourteen Epistles of Paul;

---

14. The mention of πολλοί in the preface also renders difficult the possibility of reconstructing a community that would know of only Luke's Gospel. Moreover, for all its differences from the Synoptics, even John—simply because of the intensity of focus on Jesus—is prima facie more like these gospels than Acts is like the gospels.

two Epistles of Peter; three of John; one of James; one of Jude; two Epistles of Clement; and the Constitutions dedicated to you, the bishops, by me, Clement, in eight books . . . ; and the Acts of us, the Apostles."[15]

Such variation prohibits our ability to trace a clear line of reception. If, however, we take the picture in somewhat of a holistic manner, Acts' unsettled canonical history is more readily comprehensible with the hypothesis that it circulated *ab initio* independently from the Gospel of Luke than with the idea that in the face of an ecclesial tradition of reading Luke-Acts, the two volumes were nonetheless later separated—but left *no trace whatever* of their original unity. At the very least, it is beyond doubt that in strong contrast to the Gospel of Luke, the role of Acts in the scriptural parameters of the church was far from clear. Indeed, perhaps this is the historical reality that underlies the surprising remarks of John Chrysostom in 401: "To many persons [Acts] is so little known, both it and its author, that they are not even aware there is such a book in existence."[16]

Given the physical (scrolls), textual (Western/non-Western), and canonical (various placement) picture—as well as the knowledge of the preexistence of other gospel-like writings with which Luke (but not Acts) could have easily and perhaps immediately been associated—does not a separate publication of Luke and Acts serve as a better point of departure for the separate treatment of these works we find in the second century and beyond? If the standard view requires a theory to explain Luke's separation from Acts (typically, the fogging "somehow"), the alternative view that would allow for separate publication and circulation, by contrast, has considerable explanatory power. Its solution is elegant and simple: Luke and Acts were not treated as Luke-Acts because they were not issued as one work in the first place; separate publication and circulation amounted to separate treatment. Of course, in terms of our actual data, this puts the matter in reverse. The lack of joint publication and circulation is what might make the best sense in light of the absence of evidence that the two works were read as a unified literary whole.[17]

---

15. Trans. Bruce M. Metzger, *The Canon of the New Testament: Its Origin, Development, and Significance* (Oxford: Clarendon, 1997), 313. Metzger's work is of course indispensable to this entire paragraph, as are the "selected documents" in Alexander Souter, *The Text and Canon of the New Testament* (New York: Charles Scribner's Sons, 1920), 205–37.

16. Cited also in Mikeal C. Parsons and Richard I. Pervo, *Rethinking the Unity of Luke and Acts* (Minneapolis: Fortress, 1993), 1.

17. The language of "publication and circulation" in this section derives primarily from Harry Gamble's chapter of that title in his seminal study *Books and Readers in the Early Church: A History of Early Christian Texts* (New Haven: Yale University Press, 1995). I use

Part 1: Christology, Greco-Roman Culture, and Canonical Reception

Concluding Reflections

I conclude with two observations that should merit further discussion and elaboration. First, in the study of the reception history of the NT documents, the differences between the various NT writings should not be overlooked or minimized. Indeed, they should be given careful attention.[18] Thus, for example, when Luke Johnson questions the usefulness of the reception history of Luke and Acts for the historical-critical imagination by drawing on Paul's Epistle to the Romans, he (inadvertently) obscures the central problem.[19] The point of my earlier article, that is, was not to object to the historical-critical method as such but rather to note the way in which the reception history of Luke and Acts *in particular* creates hermeneutical problems for the assumptions that undergird standard scholarly practice.

Johnson's conflation between Paul's writings and Luke's leads nicely to the second observation, which pertains to the importance of reception history for traditional NT studies. Because there are no "laws" or "principles" that govern the history of textual reception, the usefulness of a text's forward history to traditional historical-critical exegesis cannot be determined in general but, instead, only through specific investigation. To stay with Romans and Luke-Acts: the reception history of Romans does not render problematic the historically imaginative attempt of contemporary scholars to read this letter "within the frame of first-century social realities and rhetoric,"[20] for such history—as much as it illuminates important aspects of Romans—clearly does not undermine hermeneutically the presuppositions that support the modern reading strategy. The case is simply otherwise with Luke-Acts, where—at the very least—the study of reception history presents a complex and significant challenge to the dominant historical-critical practice.

---

it here as a way of raising an issue for further research (cf. Gregory, *Reception of Luke and Acts*, 300ff.). Gamble has taught us much about the publication and dissemination of ancient Christian and non-Christian texts, but he does not address comprehensively the question of publication and circulation as it relates to two- or multivolume works. Were the evidence to permit it, our ability to be more precise about questions of "publication" in relation to Luke-Acts would be greatly aided by a thorough study of the publication and distribution of two- and multivolume works. One might, for example, comb carefully through the data presented in Raymond J. Starr, "The Circulation of Literary Texts in the Roman World," *CQ* 37, no. 1 (1987): 213–23.

18. One instance of this, e.g., is that the Johannine Epistles do not have a uniform reception history.

19. Johnson, "Literary Criticism of Luke-Acts," 162.

20. Johnson, "Literary Criticism of Luke-Acts," 162.

Acts 2:36 and the Continuity of Lukan Christology

If, as Luke probably intended, one reads Luke's Gospel before moving on to Acts, then Peter's statement in Acts 2:36 may come as something of a surprise. At the end of a rather lengthy speech to the "men of Judea and all who live in Jerusalem" (2:14), Peter says, ἀσφαλῶς οὖν γινωσκέτω πᾶς οἶκος Ἰσραὴλ ὅτι καὶ κύριον αὐτὸν καὶ χριστὸν ἐποίησεν ὁ θεὸς τοῦτον τὸν Ἰησοῦν ὃν ὑμεῖς ἐσταυρώσατε. The rather startling part of the sentence, of course, is the statement that "God has made him both Lord and Christ, this Jesus whom you crucified."

The initial surprise at Peter's statement comes with good reason, for it certainly seems clear enough from the very beginning of the story in the gospel that Jesus is *already* Lord and Christ. Indeed, even while still in Mary's womb, Jesus is referred to as ὁ κύριος in Elizabeth's address to Mary: καὶ πόθεν μοι τοῦτο ἵνα ἔλθῃ ἡ μήτηρ τοῦ κυρίου μου πρὸς ἐμέ (Luke 1:43).[1] Moreover, the angels announce to the shepherds that Jesus—still only an infant in the storyline—is already κύριος and χριστός: "Today is born to you in the city of David a Savior, who is χριστὸς κύριος" (2:11). Prima facie, then, Peter's statement in Acts 2:36 seems to exist in serious tension with the christological claims of Luke's Gospel.

The purpose of the present chapter is to address this apparent tension in Lukan christological expression and, on the basis of our discussion, to offer an interpretation of the verse that situates it within the context of Luke-Acts,

---

1. For a recent challenge to the notion that Mary becomes pregnant immediately or soon after Gabriel's visit—held by the vast majority of modern exegetes (e.g., Dibelius, Fitzmyer, Johnson, Nolland, Schürmann, Schneider, et al.)—see the thought-provoking article of Michael Wolter, "'Wann wurde Maria schwanger?' Eine vernachlässigte Frage und ihre Bedeutung für das Verständnis der lukanischen Vorgeschichte (Lk 1–2)," *Von Jesus zum Christus: Christologische Studien*, ed. Rudolf Hoppe and Ulrich Busse, BZNW 93 (Berlin: de Gruyter, 1998), 405–22.

"Acts 2:36 and the Continuity of Lukan Christology" was originally published in *New Testament Studies* 53 (2007): 37–56. It is reproduced with permission.

Part 1: Christology, Greco-Roman Culture, and Canonical Reception

its proper framework for meaning. Taking account of the larger narrative and hermeneutical context of the verse allows both its particular force and Lukan christological coherence to remain. In order to make our way to the interpretive proposal, it is necessary, first, to chart the salient points in the history of interpretation and, second, to discuss the hermeneutical matters involved in coming to a correct understanding of the verse in its overall Lukan context. Thus, this chapter will proceed in three sections: (1) History of Interpretation; (2) Interpretive Context: The Framework for Meaning; and (3) A Reading.

History of Interpretation

Modern scholars were not the first to notice the christological potential of Acts 2:36. Tertullian, for example, drew upon Acts 2:36 in his polemic against Praxeas to argue that Christ was not the same person as the Father: "Jesus will be the same as the Christ . . . who was anointed by the Father. . . . Thus Peter says: 'Let all the house of Israel know that God has made him both Lord and Christ,' that is, *anointed*."[2] Later in the patristic period, moreover, the verse became a point of serious contention in the interpretive controversies between heterodox and orthodox theologians. Perhaps it was Paul of Samosata in the mid-third century who first seized upon the verse to bolster his position, though that is not certain.[3] What is certain is that by the time of the Arian controversy heterodox hermeneuts had appropriated Acts 2:36, along with

---

2. Tertullian, *Adversus Praxean* 28.3–4 (CCSL 2.1201; all translations are my own unless otherwise specified). Irenaeus also cites almost in full Peter's speech in Acts 2, but the citation occurs within a context of several other extended citations and evidences no awareness of an interpretive battle over 2:36 in particular (*Haer.* 3.12.2 [SC 3.209]).

3. In an argument over the interpretation of this passage, Athanasius writes: "If therefore they suppose that the Savior was not Lord and King before he became human and endured the cross, but only then began to be Lord, let them know that they bring the statements of Paul of Samosata out into the open again" (*C. Ar.* 2.15.13 [PG 26.173A]; here the ἀλλὰ τότε is to be taken with reference to the entire life of Christ rather than restricted to his execution upon the cross; it pertains, that is, to γένηται ἄνθρωπος καὶ σταυρὸν ὑπομείνῃ and not just to σταυρὸν ὑπομείνῃ: εἰ μὲν οὖν νομίζουσιν ὅτι καὶ πρὶν γένηται ἄνθρωπος καὶ σταυρὸν ὑπομείνῃ οὐκ ἦν κύριος καὶ βασιλεὺς ὁ σωτὴρ ἀλλὰ τότε ἀρχὴν ἔσχε τοῦ εἶναι κύριος γνώτωσαν ὅτι τὰ τοῦ Σαμοσατέως ἐκ φανεροῦ πάλιν φθέγγοντα ῥήματα). This passage need not do more than indicate Athanasius's view of the general position of Paul of Samosata (and here we must compare, e.g., Eusebius, *Hist. eccl.* 7.30, and Epiphanius, *Pan.* 65), but because Athanasius's remarks occur in the context of his discussion of Acts 2:36, they may at least suggest that Paul used this passage.

Acts 2:36 and the Continuity of Lukan Christology

Proverbs 8:22 and other similar texts (e.g., Col 1:15),[4] as evidence for their belief that Christ/the Son was a creature created by the Father. No obviously direct line can be drawn from Athanasius's *Orationes contra Arianos IV* through Epiphanius's *Panarion* and Ambrose's *De fide* to Gregory of Nyssa's *Contra Eunomium*, but the general similarity in the debate we find in these orthodox authors is unmistakable.[5]

The center of the exegetical argument over Acts 2:36 was the word "made" (ἐποίησεν). Insofar as we can reconstruct their interpretation, it seems that heterodox theologians from Arius to Eunomius took ἐποίησεν to refer to God the Father's creation of the Son. In one of the few surviving heretical works, for example, Eunomius put it clearly:

> We assert that the God of all things . . . begot and created before all things [ποιήσαντα πρὸ πάντων] as Only-begotten God our Lord Jesus Christ, through whom all things were made. . . . This Only-begotten God is not to be compared either with the one who begot him or with the Holy Spirit who was made through him, for he is less than the one in being a "thing made" [ὡς ποίημα], and greater than the other in being a maker. And indeed, a trustworthy witness of the fact that he was made [πεποιῆσθαι] is Peter . . . for Peter said, "Let all the house of Israel know . . . that God has made [ἐποίησε] him both Lord and Christ."[6]

The testimony of the church fathers supports this understanding as the general heterodox construal of the passage. Gregory of Nyssa, for example, writes that "those who force the word the opposite way say that by ἐποίησεν the Apostle makes known the pre-temporal generation of the Son."[7] So, too, Ambrose speaks of this construal as the Arians' "customary citation of [Acts 2:36]." If one reads more carefully, argues Ambrose, "it does not follow that the Son was made by God."[8]

---

4. For a list of "theologically significant passages of Scripture used by non-Nicenes," see the appendix with the same title in Richard Paul Vaggione, *Eunomius of Cyzicus and the Nicene Revolution*, Oxford Early Christian Studies (Oxford: Oxford University Press, 2000), 383–95.

5. Cf., e.g., John Chrysostom, *Hom. Heb.* 3.1 (PG 63.28), who also links Acts 2:36 together with Prov 8:22 in his argument against the Arians.

6. *Liber apologeticus* 26. I cite here the critical text and translation of Richard Paul Vaggione, *Eunomius: The Extant Works*, Oxford Early Christian Texts (Oxford: Clarendon, 1987), 68–71.

7. Gregory of Nyssa, *Eun.* 5.2 (PG 45.684D).

8. Ambrose, *Fid.* 1.15.95 (PL 16.573C). See also Athanasius, *C. Ar.* 2.15.11 (PG 26.168C–170C); cf. Epiphanius, *Pan.* 69.42.1–6 (PG 42.266–69).

In contrast to modern interpretation (see below), then, the primary divide in heterodox readings was not between Jesus's status in his earthly ministry and that of his resurrection/exaltation glory, but rather between his status as created versus uncreated being. Thus ἐποίησεν was related not to the actual life, death, and resurrection of Jesus but to God's action before the foundation of the world. God *made*—that is, created—the Lord and Christ; he did not exist coeternally with the Father.

The orthodox response in general was of course to deny the heretical reading of ἐποίησεν: "We say that it is impious to take ἐποιήσεν to refer to the divinity of the only-begotten."[9] This denial was accomplished, first, by drawing attention to the rest of Peter's remark: τοῦτον τὸν Ἰησοῦν ὃν ὑμεῖς ἐσταυρώσατε. When the Arians said, "Here we find 'made' in scripture," they did not see that "by 'this Jesus' the wording—for the wording is self-explanatory—means the Lord's human nature [τὴν ἐνανθρώπησιν κυρίου]. The meaning is clear from 'this Jesus *whom you crucified.*' This is plainly the flesh which they crucified, for they crucified flesh [σάρκα γὰρ ἐσταύρωσαν]."[10] On the basis of the conclusion of Acts 2:36, Athanasius, Epiphanius, Ambrose, and Gregory of Nyssa all argued that because it was absurd to speak of divinity being crucified, Peter was obviously not speaking here about the divinity of Christ but about his "flesh" or "humanity."

Within this larger focus upon the humanity of Christ, the verb "made" was related to the two poles of the life of Jesus, the incarnation and the res-

---

9. Gregory of Nyssa, *Eun.* 5.2 (PG 45.684D).

10. Epiphanius, *Pan.* 69.42.2 (I cite the recent translation of Frank Williams, *The Panarion of Epiphanius of Salamis*, 2 vols., Nag Hammadi Studies 35 [Leiden: Brill, 1987–1994]; cf. PG 42.268A). Cf. Athanasius, *C. Ar.* 2.15.12 (PG 26.171A): "For even Peter, after saying, 'He has made him Lord and Christ,' immediately added, 'this Jesus whom you crucified.' It is manifest to everyone—so let it be even to these [Arians], if they keep to the context [ἀκολουθία]—that he has been made according to his humanity and not according to the essence of the Logos. For what was crucified other than the body?" Cf. also, e.g., Ambrose, *Fid.* 1.15.95: "Let the ignorant [heretics] read the entirety [of the sentence], and let them understand it. For thus it is clearly written, 'God made this Jesus, whom you crucified, both Lord and Christ.' It was not the divinity that was crucified, but the flesh. This was possible in any event because the flesh is that which is able to be crucified" (PL 16.573C); Amphilochius of Iconium, *Fragmenta* 1.4–5: "It was not the divinity [ἡ θεότης] that died, but the humanity [ἄνθρωπος]" (CCSG 3.227); John Chrysostom, *Hom. Heb.* 3.1: Acts 2:36 does not refer to "the divine Word, but to that which is according to the flesh" (PG 63.28: εἴρηται . . . περὶ τοῦ θεοῦ λόγου ἀλλὰ τοῦ κατὰ σάρκα); Eustathius of Antioch, *Fragmenta* 72.6-10: "He made the suffering Jesus Lord, and not the Wisdom or Word . . . but rather the one who was raised up on the cross with outstretched hands [τὰς χεῖρας]" (CCSG 51.144).

urrection/exaltation. Gregory of Nyssa, for example, espoused both points of view simultaneously. He notes, on the one hand, that "the blessed Peter was indicating briefly and in passing the mystery according to the flesh [the incarnation],"[11] and, on the other, that "the apostle says that the humanity was exalted; it was exalted because it became Lord and Christ. And this happened after the passion. It is not, therefore, the pre-temporal existence of the Lord which the apostle proves by ἐποίησεν but the transformation of the humble to the exalted that was effected by 'the right hand of God.'"[12] If in this latter passage Gregory somewhat prefigured modern discussion of Luke's exaltation Christology,[13] it was far from his intention.[14] His larger point, rather, was that since the Son was Lord and Christ from all eternity according to his divine nature, Acts 2:36 can apply only to the human nature.

Second, Athanasius in particular offered a different reading of ἐποίησεν in which he coordinated Peter's earlier statement in Acts 2:22—"Men of Israel, listen to these words: Jesus of Nazareth, a man attested [ἀποδεδειγμένον] to you by God"—with the conclusion of the speech in 2:36. On this basis, Athanasius took the word ἐποίησεν as a virtual equivalent for ἀποδείκνυμι and, hence, read ἐποίησεν in context to mean that God "made him Lord not in general but 'toward' us, and 'in our midst,' which is the same as saying, '[God] manifested him.'" In this way, argued Athanasius, "the expression that [Peter] uses at the end, 'made' [ἐποίησε], is explained by what he said in the beginning with the word 'manifested' [ἀπέδειξεν]."[15]

Where the heretical exegetes read Acts 2:36 in relation to the doctrinal issue of the Son's eternal or non-eternal generation from the Father, they were rebuffed by the orthodox interpreters' attention to the primary context of the statement—Peter did seem to speak here of the crucifixion of the human Jesus. Yet, by directing the force of ἐποίησεν toward the human nature of Christ and by including the incarnation within the purview of ἐποίησεν, the ortho-

---

11. Gregory of Nyssa, *Eun.* 5.5 (PG 45.708D).

12. Gregory of Nyssa, *Eun.* 5.3 (PG 45.697A–B).

13. See the frequent repetition of ὑψόω and its cognates in *Eun.* 5.3 (PG 45.697A–D). Cf., of course, Acts 2:33 (τῇ δεξιᾷ οὖν τοῦ θεοῦ ὑψωθείς ...).

14. Gregory's statement should not be pressed too much into the service of modern interpretation: Gregory would clearly deny that the Son was made Lord in his divine nature "after his passion"—that is, at the resurrection (indeed, his polemic throughout the relevant sections of *Eun.* 5 functions in just this way).

15. Athanasius, *C. Ar.* 2.15.12 (PG 26.172B). Athanasius's citation of Acts 2:22 varies only slightly from the text in NA²⁷ (omitting Codex Bezae here): whereas in NA²⁷ ἀπὸ τοῦ θεοῦ follows ἀποδεδειγμένον, in the Athanasian text ἀπὸ τοῦ θεοῦ precedes ἀποδεδειγμένον.

Part 1: Christology, Greco-Roman Culture, and Canonical Reception

dox, too, indicated their willingness to situate and interpret the verse within a larger doctrinal framework. Given the fact that the orthodox framework was eventually to win out in the history of theology, it is not very surprising that Acts 2:36 does not appear to be a major point of interpretive debate until the modern period.[16]

The interpretation of Acts 2:36 in modern exegesis differed substantially from that of the ancient argument. The latter concentrated primarily on the implications of the statement for Christian doctrine, whereas the former has tended to focus upon the status of Acts 2:36 as evidence for pre-Lukan kerygma, and this usually in connection with the apparent inconsistency the verse produces within Luke's own Christology. Yet, to a striking degree, modern debate has resembled the ancient one in its concern with the word ἐποίησεν.[17]

William Wrede was not the first to return to the potential significance of ἐποίησεν in Acts 2:36, but his remarks were characteristically perceptive and helped to shape more than one generation of scholarly opinion. Wrede drew upon Acts 2:36 in an effort to support his thesis that Mark's "Messianic Secret" was a literary motif that reflected the historical fact that Jesus was not considered to be Messiah during his lifetime: "In his sermon at Pentecost in Acts 2.36 Peter says that God has *made* the Jesus whom the Jews crucified *both Lord and Christ*. In this it is implied that this has been done through his being raised from the dead. This saying quite by itself would prove that there was in primitive Christianity a view in accordance with which Jesus was not the messiah in his earthly life."[18] Wrede himself did not explicate the problems

---

16. It is of course interesting, however, that Luther makes reference to Acts 2:36 in relation to Rom 1:3-4 (in *Luther's Works*, vol. 25, *Lectures on Romans* [*Scholia*] [St. Louis: Concordia, 1972], 147). In this way he prefigures modern reconstructions of early Christology. Yet Luther does not evidence an awareness of the potential theological problems raised by these verses, though christologically speaking he does seem to read them in terms of a resurrection/exaltation schema (Jesus was not recognized as the Son of God until the coming of the Spirit after his resurrection/exaltation).

17. See, e.g., the emphasis on "made" in Oscar Cullmann, *The Christology of the New Testament*, trans. Shirley C. Guthrie and Charles A. M. Hall, rev. ed. (Philadelphia: Westminster, 1963), 181, 207; or the commentaries of Rudolf Pesch, *Die Apostelgeschichte*, 2 vols., EKKNT 5 (Zürich: Benziger; Neukirchen-Vluyn: Neukirchen, 1986), 1:124, 128, and Gerhard Schneider, *Die Apostelgeschichte*, 2 vols., HThKNT (Freiburg: Herder, 1980-1982), 1:276-77.

18. William Wrede, *The Messianic Secret*, trans. J. C. G. Grieg (Cambridge: Clarke, 1971), 216. For a concise consideration of Wrede's thesis in light of recent research, see Joel Marcus, *Mark 1-8: A New Translation with Introduction and Commentary*, AB 27 (New York: Doubleday, 2000), 525-27.

Acts 2:36 and the Continuity of Lukan Christology

that unfold naturally for Lukan Christology if one interprets Acts 2:36 in this way. Yet his reading of ἐποίησεν was clear enough—Jesus became Lord and Christ only at or after his resurrection.

Rudolf Bultmann read Acts 2:36 in like manner. Coordinating the verse with Romans 1:4, Bultmann followed Wrede's lead and asserted that "Jesus' messiahship was dated from the resurrection."[19] And though his larger concerns were quite different, Oscar Cullmann also interpreted Acts 2:36 in light of Romans 1:4 and the Christ-hymn in Philippians 2:5-11, thus arguing for a reconstruction of the early Christian recognition that "God not only resurrected [Jesus] but gave him lordship, 'made' him to be the *Kyrios* (Rom 1.4; Acts 2.36)."[20] In the reading of Wrede, Bultmann, and others, Jesus was made or "adopted" as χριστός (and κύριος) not during his lifetime but on account of his resurrection. Thus could Ulrich Wilckens speak of this passage in 1961 as a locus classicus "für eine alte, primitive, 'adoptianische' Christologie."[21]

In addition to offering a different reading, to which we shall return at the end of the chapter,[22] Wilckens himself criticized the predominant interpre-

---

19. Rudolf Bultmann, *Theology of the New Testament*, 2 vols. (New York: Charles Scribner's Sons, 1951–1955), 1:27.

20. Cullmann, *Christology*, 207. The German edition of Cullmann's *Christologie* (1957) was known to Wilckens.

21. Ulrich Wilckens, *Die Missionsreden der Apostelgeschichte: Form- und traditionsgeschichtliche Untersuchungen* (Neukirchen-Vluyn: Neukirchener Verlag, 1961), 170. The use of the term "adoptionist" to describe early christological positions has long been problematic. In contrast, e.g., to μοναρχία, μόναρχος κτλ., the term "adoptionist" in its christological sense does not occur in the ancient sources. With reference to early Christology (cf. the ecclesial disputes at the turn of the eighth and ninth centuries CE), this description was introduced into modern discussion by Adolf von Harnack in his *Lehrbuch der Dogmengeschichte* (in the fourth edition of this work, Harnack himself acknowledged that the term "'adoptianische' irreführend sein kann" but went on to say "ich weiss indess keine bessere"; *Dogmengeschichte*, 3 vols. [Tübingen: Mohr Siebeck, 1909], 3:214 n. 3). Harnack argued that the only surviving document to express clearly an adoptionist Christology was the Shepherd of Hermas (*Dogmengeschichte*, 1:212 n. 2), but this interpretation of the Shepherd is not without serious problems. Generally, the positions that would fall under Harnack's category were what Eusebius and others described simply as the belief that Christ was a ψιλὸς ἄνθρωπος and was therefore not divine in and of himself (see, e.g., *Hist. eccl.* 5.28 with reference to Artemon and Paul of Samosata). Given the role of Acts 2:36 in the Arian disputes over the nature of Christ's divinity, it is not improbable that this verse would have been used in earlier debates, but there is an absence of evidence and, hence, no ground upon which to base a firm decision.

22. We may note now that Wilckens rejected "adoptionist" as a correct description of the Christology expressed in Acts 2:36, preferring, as did Conzelmann, "subordination." In his commentary on Acts, Conzelmann largely followed Wilckens, though of course Con-

Part 1: Christology, Greco-Roman Culture, and Canonical Reception

tation on a significant point that helped to shape subsequent scholarly discussion. Rather than as a pre-Lukan piece of kerygma, Wilckens argued that Acts 2:36 derived from Luke himself ("dieser Satz als ganzer [stammt] von Lukas"[23]). For the period of scholarly activity after Wilckens, the title of Martin Rese's *New Testament Studies* article captured well the general perception of the principal interpretive alternatives: "Die Aussagen über Jesu Tod und Auferstehung in der Apostelgeschichte—ältestes Kerygma oder lukanische Theologumena?"[24]

On one side, scholars continued to hold that Acts 2:36 evidences Luke's dependence upon earlier tradition. C. K. Barrett put starkly this position in the mid-1990s: Acts 2:36 is "clear proof that Luke is at this point using a source; he would not have chosen to express himself in this way."[25] Not every scholar in this line of interpretation would want to claim certainty for the detection of a "source,"[26] but there would nevertheless be general agreement on the presence of identifiable pre-Lukan tradition in Acts 2:36.[27]

---

zelmann's own articulation of "subordination" was clear already in *Die Mitte der Zeit* (see Hans Conzelmann, *Acts of the Apostles*, Hermeneia [Philadelphia: Fortress, 1987], 21). For criticism of the employment of these terms in relation to Acts, see Jacques Dupont, "Les discours missionaires des Actes des Apôtres d'après un ouvrage recent," *Revue biblique* 69, no. 1 (1962): 37-60, esp. 53, 55-56.

23. Wilckens, *Missionsreden*, 174.

24. Martin Rese, "Die Aussagen über Jesu Tod und Auferstehung in der Apostelgeschichte—ältestes Kerygma oder lukanische Theologumena?," *NTS* 30, no. 3 (1984): 335-53. Rese notes: "In den fünfziger Jahren gab es im Blick auf die Aussagen über Jesu Tod und Auferstehung in der Apostelgeschichte einen erstaunlich weit verbreiteten Konsens: Diese Aussagen galten als Bestandteil des alten urchristlichen Kerygmas" (335). Rese also has a concise discussion of the "forschungsgeschichtliche Hintergrund" to the consensus of the 1950s.

25. C. K. Barrett, *A Critical and Exegetical Commentary on the Acts of the Apostles*, 2 vols., ICC (Edinburgh: T&T Clark, 1994-1998), 1:151. Cf., e.g., Eduard Schweizer, "Jesus Christus I," in *Theologische Realenzyklopädie*, ed. Gerhard Müller (Berlin: de Gruyter, 1987), 16:671-726: "Nach Lukas ist, anders als in den Vorlagen, schon der Irdische 'Herr', wird aber nach Act 2,36 erst durch die Auferstehung dazu" (702).

26. For an older example, see F. J. Foakes Jackson and Kirsopp Lake, "Christology," in *The Beginnings of Christianity, Part I: The Acts of the Apostles*, ed. F. J. Foakes Jackson and Kirsopp Lake (London: Macmillan, 1920), 1:345-418, who consider it "far more probable" that Acts 2:36 was drawn from a source than that the verse reflects the thought of the "editor" of Acts (367, esp. n. 2).

27. Cf., e.g., James D. G. Dunn's statement in *The Acts of the Apostles*, Epworth Commentaries (Peterborough: Epworth, 1996), 28: "The christology itself seems primitive at a number of points: . . . the resurrection/ascension as evidence that 'God has made him both Lord and Messiah' (2.36). Given the more developed christology at the period of Luke's

Acts 2:36 and the Continuity of Lukan Christology

On the other side, scholars have determined that the author of Acts himself wrote 2:36.[28] Such a position does not necessarily entail the denial of any influence upon Luke by earlier tradition, but it does cast the interpretive issue in terms of Lukan formulation.[29] Particularly important in this line of argument has been the attention given to the nature of speech composition in the ancient world.[30] On the basis of the well-known statements about speech composition in Thucydides and Lucian,[31] Christopher Tuckett, for example, suggested recently that "the speech in Acts 2 placed on Peter's lips may not tell us so much about Luke's own views, but more about what Luke thought were the kinds of things Peter said, or should have said, in the context in which the speech is now placed within the story."[32]

---

writing, it is unlikely that he was wishing to promote these emphases. It is more likely that he drew them from traditions or memories which his inquiry (or common knowledge) had brought to light." See, too, Ferdinand Hahn, *The Titles of Jesus in Christology: Their History in Early Christianity* (New York: Word, 1969), 106–7, and Ernst Haenchen, *The Acts of the Apostles: A Commentary*, trans. Bernard Noble and Gerald Shinn, rev. R. McL. Wilson (Philadelphia: Westminster, 1971), 187.

28. See, e.g., Richard F. Zehnle, *Peter's Pentecost Discourse: Tradition and Lukan Reinterpretation in Peter's Speeches of Acts 2 and 3*, Society of Biblical Literature Monograph Series 15 (Nashville: Abingdon, 1971), 67–68.

29. See, e.g., Rese, "Jesu Tod und Auferstehung," 347: "Das Ergebnis der Untersuchung der Aussagen zu Jesu Tod und Auferstehung in der Apostelgeschichte läßt sich in einem Satz formulieren: Diese Aussagen sind nicht Zeugnisse für das älteste Kerygma, sondern lukanische Theologumena, auch wenn Lukas sie unter Verwendung von Traditionen verschiedenster Art gebildet und nicht einfach aus der Luft gegriffen hat."

30. It is worth recalling at this juncture Cadbury's remarks of nearly seventy-five years ago: "Critics of the secular school would scrutinize [Luke's] speeches particularly. They were the most prized parts of the classical historians and the most carefully composed parts in contemporary historiography.... Like Thucydides and the other best composers of speeches he attempted to present what the speakers were likely to have said" (Henry Joel Cadbury, "The Speeches in Acts," in *The Beginnings of Christianity, Part I: The Acts of the Apostles*, ed. Kirsopp Lake and Henry J. Cadbury [London: Macmillan, 1933], 5:425 and 426–27 respectively). Cf. Arnaldo Momigliano, "Pagan and Christian Historiography in the Fourth Century AD," in *The Conflict between Paganism and Christianity in the Fourth Century*, ed. A. Momigliano (Oxford: Clarendon, 1963), 79–99, who famously (and hyperbolically) argued that prior to the historiographical method of Eusebius most ancient histories were "rhetorical work[s] with a maximum of invented speeches and a minimum of authentic documents" (89).

31. Thucydides, *Historia belli Peloponnesiaci* 1.22; Lucian, *Ver. hist.* 58.

32. Christopher M. Tuckett, "The Christology of Luke-Acts," in *The Unity of Luke-Acts*, ed. J. Verheyden (Leuven: Leuven University Press, 1999), 141. Strictly speaking, of course, Tuckett's view is not new. Recall, for example, Eckhard Plümacher, *Lukas als hellenisticher Schriftsteller: Studien zur Apostelgeschichte*, Studien zur Umwelt des Neuen Testaments 9

Part 1: Christology, Greco-Roman Culture, and Canonical Reception

Despite the differences between these two opinions regarding pre-Lukan tradition, there is a remarkable convergence at the point of the actual interpretation of Acts 2:36 itself. That is to say, Barrett and Tuckett may represent different answers to the *traditionsgeschichtliche* question, but they seem to be united in their opinion that Acts 2:36 promulgates a Christology that is recognizably different from Luke's own view. This convergence, we may suspect, is due to a similar reading of ἐποίησεν, in which the word is taken to say that Jesus is "now Lord and Messiah" and has been made so "by virtue of his resurrection."[33]

It is fascinating that, for all their differences in reasoning, in theological assumptions, and in *Sitze im Leben*, both the ancient and modern discussions share the hermeneutical practice of removing Acts 2:36 from its larger Lukan context in order to read it within the purview of some other interpretive framework. This is not to say that the church fathers were wrong to look to this verse for help with doctrinal controversy or that modern scholars should stay away from historical "reconstruction." It is, rather, simply to point to the possibility that Acts 2:36 might have a meaning within the overall context to which it is indigenous—namely, that of Luke-Acts—that fits well with the christological logic of the wider Lukan narrative.

To draw attention to such a "contextual possibility" is not to claim methodological innovation. Indeed, with considerable success, contemporary advocates of more literary approaches to Luke-Acts have urged scholars to recognize the inseparability of individual theological statements from their textual surroundings. As Beverly Gaventa put it in her brief treatment of the theology of Acts, "Lukan theology is intricately and irreversibly bound up with the story he tells and cannot be separated from it."[34]

(Göttingen: Vandenhoeck & Ruprecht, 1972), 72–79, who argued that, in a way similar to the mimetic method found in Greco-Roman historiography, Luke engages in "Archaisierung"—the stylistic device whereby archaic terms or expressions are employed to create the semblance of antiquity (Plümacher refers to Acts 2:36 on 72 n. 8). For a review and criticism of Plümacher's overall thesis, see Marion L. Soards, *The Speeches in Acts: Their Content, Context, and Concerns* (Louisville: Westminster John Knox, 1994), 135–43.

33. Joseph A. Fitzmyer, *The Acts of the Apostles: A New Translation with Introduction and Commentary*, AB 31 (New York: Doubleday, 1998), 260–61.

34. Beverly Roberts Gaventa, "Toward a Theology of Acts: Reading and Rereading," *Int* 42 (1988): 150. See also, e.g., Gaventa's recent commentary, *The Acts of the Apostles*, ANTC (Nashville: Abingdon, 2003), esp. 59; and the remarks of Luke Timothy Johnson, *The Gospel of Luke*, SP 3 (Collegeville, MN: Liturgical Press, 1991), 4: "To regard Luke-Acts as a story means, at the least, that we do not read it as a systematic treatise. Rather, we must seek Luke's meaning through the movement of the story" (emphasis removed).

Acts 2:36 and the Continuity of Lukan Christology

Despite this methodological pressure toward the narrative context in general,[35] when it comes to the interpretation of Acts 2:36 in particular, literary analyses of Luke-Acts have differed little from the prevalent trends in modern research. For all its profound theoretical differences from traditional historical scholarship, that is, in practice literary work on Acts 2:36 has remained within the ambit of the predominant modern interpretative construct. Robert Tannehill, for example, whose work helped to pioneer the literary study of Luke-Acts, assumes that Jesus is κύριος "*because* he is seated at God's right hand"[36]—that is, Jesus becomes κύριος by virtue of the resurrection. Thus Tannehill's understanding of Acts 2:36 itself is formally similar to that of Wrede, Bultmann, and others.

Yet the literary interpreter's concern to read contextually presses for the integration of Acts 2:36 with the larger christological perspective developed through the narrative. In so doing, the methodology and underlying philosophical insight of recent literary efforts provide a distinctive hermeneutical advantage for the interpretive problem posed by Acts 2:36 for Lukan Christology. To see the precise conceptual structure of such an advantage, however, we need first to explicate clearly the dominant interpretive contexts in which the verse has been read.

INTERPRETIVE CONTEXT: THE FRAMEWORK FOR MEANING

For the patristic period, it best befits analysis to think of the interpretive context in terms of the reading of ἐποίησεν in conjunction with "time." In het-

---

35. See, e.g., the insightful commentary of F. Scott Spencer, *Acts* (Sheffield: Sheffield Academic, 1997), or the treatment of William S. Kurz, *Reading Luke-Acts: Dynamics of Biblical Narrative* (Louisville: Westminster John Knox, 1993). Cf. Luke Timothy Johnson, *The Acts of the Apostles*, SP 5 (Collegeville, MN: Liturgical Press, 1992), 1: "What is most impressive . . . is not the story's historical verisimilitude, but the way Luke used it to give literary shape to a theological vision"; and, from a slightly different perspective, Charles H. Talbert, *Reading Acts: A Literary and Theological Commentary*, rev. ed. (Macon, GA: Smyth & Helwys, 2005), xxv–xxvi.

36. Robert C. Tannehill, *The Narrative Unity of Luke-Acts: A Literary Interpretation*, 2 vols. (Minneapolis: Fortress, 1986–1990), 2:352; emphasis added. Cf. the otherwise perceptive article of David P. Moessner, "Two Lords 'at the Right Hand'? The Psalms and an Intertextual Reading of Peter's Pentecost Speech (Acts 2.14–36)," in *Literary Studies in Luke-Acts: Essays in Honor of Joseph B. Tyson*, ed. Richard P. Thompson and Thomas E. Phillips (Macon, GA: Mercer University Press, 1998), 215–32, in which Acts 2:36 is read as the "establishing" of Jesus as Lord (esp. 218, 231); and Johnson, *Acts*, 52, 55.

Part 1: Christology, Greco-Roman Culture, and Canonical Reception

erodox interpretation, ἐποίησεν was read not in relation to the historical life of Jesus but in relation to pretemporal reality. Acts 2:36 was taken, therefore, to apply to the creation of the Son by the Father. In this line of interpretation, the Lukan context was rendered virtually irrelevant for the understanding of Acts 2:36. In orthodox interpretation, ἐποίησεν was read primarily in relation to the incarnation, though, as we saw above with Gregory of Nyssa, it could also be seen in relation to the resurrection. Acts 2:36 was taken, therefore, to apply only to the human nature of Christ—either at the point of its coming into being ("made") or its resurrection/exaltation after death—and the "making" of the divine nature of Christ by the Father was denied. Ἐποίησεν was, in the orthodox line of interpretation, at least returned to its context within the larger sentence in which it occurs, for it was related explicitly to the end of Jesus's life upon the cross. Yet, to the extent that the final clause of Acts 2:36 was used as a fillip for reflection not upon the resurrection but upon the incarnation, the interpretation of Acts 2:36 was only indirectly related to the Lukan context.

It goes too far to say that Acts 2:36 in the patristic period was simply a "prooftext" for predetermined theological positions. Many of the more interesting recent studies on patristic exegesis show the fundamental inadequacy of such a methodological caricature.[37] Acts 2:36 undoubtedly contributed to the formulation of dogmatic positions, even as it was used to support them. Yet we may nevertheless rather safely characterize the interpretive context of patristic reading as that of a "dogmatic debate" rather than of the Lukan writings (i.e., Luke-Acts). In this context an interpretation of Acts 2:36 within the overall Lukan narrative was unable to be given by either party, for the ingredients necessary to an interpretation determined by the Lukan context were left out and others—those of the dispute over the creation of the Son—were added in instead.[38]

In marked contrast to ancient interpretation, in the modern period it has seemed self-evident to NT exegetes that Acts 2:36 does not pertain to pretemporal theological matters. Instead, ἐποίησεν has been read explicitly in relation to the demise of the earthly life of Jesus and his subsequent resurrection by God. In this way, modern interpreters—here in similarity to the orthodox

---

37. The work of Frances M. Young is representative here, perhaps especially *Biblical Exegesis and the Formation of Christian Culture* (Cambridge: Cambridge University Press, 1997). For a sampling of her work, see the recent article "The 'Mind' of Scripture: Theological Readings of the Bible in the Fathers," *International Journal of Systematic Theology* 7, no. 2 (2005): 126–41.

38. An exception to this generalization is the interpretation of Athanasius cited in note 15 above, to which I return at the end of the chapter.

Acts 2:36 and the Continuity of Lukan Christology

church fathers—have adhered closely to the final clause of Acts 2:36 in an effort to secure their reading of ἐποίησεν. Moreover, many modern interpreters attempt to work with Acts or Luke-Acts as a particular textual unit and are therefore able to use the Lukan context in certain ways for interpretation. Yet, to the extent that ἐποίησεν is read as effecting a change in Jesus's status, the actual meaning of "made" in modern interpretation is determined not by the larger Lukan context but by an interpretive context provided by historical reconstruction.[39] This situation bears further comment.

It is certainly the case that interpreters who posit contradiction between Acts 2:36 and Lukan Christology presuppose a larger Lukan Christology—garnered of course from Luke's Gospel and other portions of Acts—against which Acts 2:36 is read. When Ernst Haenchen, to take an important example, argues that "the expressions [κύριος and χριστός], taken from older tradition, with which the speech is brought to a provisional end, use formulae that are at odds with Lucan Christology,"[40] he must have in mind a greater Lukan Christology against which Acts 2:36 stands.[41] In this sense, the larger Lukan context plays a role in the interpretive process of modern scholarship in the effort to sort out the perplexing nature of Acts 2:36.

But when the question is asked as to the context in which the interpretation of Acts 2:36 itself is given, the answer is not Luke-Acts but rather a historical reconstruction in which Acts 2:36 is seen to express a primitive Christology—whether the primitiveness be Luke's accurate preservation of an early kerygmatic formula or his own attempt at verisimilitude in the words of his character Peter. In this line of interpretation, as far as the meaning of Acts 2:36 is concerned, it matters little whether one favors a source theory (Barrett; cf. Dunn) or a speech-compositional one (Tuckett; cf. Rese). Both theories assume that what the verse means is that Jesus became Lord and Messiah by virtue of his resurrection, and both theories see this particular meaning as in

---

39. Of many possible examples, one may here think of the particularly clear section "The Earliest Christian Writings" in James D. G. Dunn, *Christology in the Making: A New Testament Inquiry into the Origins of the Doctrine of the Incarnation*, 2nd ed. (Grand Rapids: Eerdmans, 1989), esp. 36 (cf. 181).

40. Ernst Haenchen, *The Acts of the Apostles*, trans. Bernard Noble and Gerald Shinn, rev. R. McL. Wilson (Philadelphia: Westminster, 1971), 187.

41. See also, e.g., Jürgen Roloff, *Die Apostelgeschichte*, NTD 5 (Göttingen: Vandenhoeck & Ruprecht, 1981), 60: "Die Aussage, daß Gott Jesus 'zum Herrn und Gesalbten (= Christus) gemacht hat,' dürfte alter hellenistisch-judenchristlicher Tradition entstammen. Lukas hat sie schwerlich selbst geschaffen, da sie seinen eigenen christologischen Vorstellungen widerspricht."

Part 1: Christology, Greco-Roman Culture, and Canonical Reception

conflict with Luke's overall Christology. Thus, in this manner of reading, the meaning of Acts 2:36 turns out to be entirely consonant with the meaning it supposedly had in pre-Lukan Christology (source and/or "Peter").[42] One does not have to look far to find the reason for this agreement in meaning: Acts 2:36 is read within the interpretive context of a pre-Lukan reconstruction.

It goes too far to say that Acts 2:36 in the modern period is simply a "prooftext" for historical hypotheses (cf. esp. Wrede above). The verse also helped to create them. Yet we may safely characterize the interpretive context for Acts 2:36 in the vast majority of modern scholarship as a historically reconstructed pre-Lukan Christology rather than the Lukan writings. This mode of interpretation involves a subtle substitution in which the Lukan interpretive context for reading Acts 2:36 is replaced by an interpretive context created by historical reconstruction. In general, the Gospel of Luke and other parts of Acts may well be read contextually, but when it comes to Acts 2:36 in particular, another context is put in place, and this verse is read in relation to the newly substituted framework of meaning.[43] The possibility thus arises that the tension that modern interpreters perceive between Acts 2:36 and Lukan Christology is due less to the necessary force of the words in Acts 2:36 than it is to the collision of different interpretive contexts.

A Reading

The foregoing sections have undertaken to illustrate the inseparable hermeneutical connection between the actual interpretations of Acts 2:36 and the interpretive contexts in which this verse has been read. The critical import pertains to the profoundly important, if now obvious, observation that the sense of the words in Acts 2:36 varies with its operative interpretive context. There is nothing inherent to the grammatical structure or individual words of Acts 2:36 (esp. ἐποίησεν) that of necessity determines specifically the meaning of the verse across the historical, exegetical spectrum. Examining the dominant trends in both ancient and modern interpretation, therefore, helps us to gain substantial hermeneutical purchase in that the juxtaposition of the

---

42. Cf. esp. Hahn, *Titles*, 107, who rejects alternative interpretations of Acts 2:36 "because the text fits in excellently with that phase in the development of tradition which we have been discussing" (i.e., early Christology).

43. One suspects that this subtle substitution is precisely what has (unwittingly) happened when the interpretation of literarily oriented scholars (Tannehill, Moessner, Johnson, et al.) matches that of the pre-Lukan reconstruction.

Acts 2:36 and the Continuity of Lukan Christology

vastly different interpretive contexts brings clearly into focus the importance of a framework for interpretation. The necessity of identifying the framework best suited to the interpretation of Acts 2:36 for Lukan Christology is thereby made evident.

In relation to the topic under discussion, we may put the point formulaically: if we are interested in the meaning of Acts 2:36 for Lukan Christology, the wider Luke-Acts narrative is the best framework for interpretation, the requisite interpretive context. Of course, stated this way—especially in light of recent literary studies—the matter seems almost banal. And yet the history of interpretation outlined here suggests that such a bald statement is badly needed. Until we permanently register the philosophical point that linguistic intelligibility is context dependent—context is meaning's *conditio sine qua non*—we shall never get around to reading Acts 2:36 in connection to the wider narrative of which it is an integral part. Mutatis mutandis, the perennial relevance of James Barr's incisive critique of Kittel's *Wörterbuch* should not be forgotten when it comes to Acts 2:36: context matters for what we think the words mean.[44]

Acts 2:36 may indeed contribute to dogmatic debate, and reconstructing historically an earlier context in which to understand the verse is certainly a legitimate undertaking.[45] (Whether or not such hypotheses are successful in this case is a separate question.)[46] The point, however—to focus only upon modern interpretation—is that such a reconstruction provides another, *dif-*

---

44. "We may sum up these criticisms of TWNT by saying that the great weakness is a failure to get to grips with the semantic value of words in their contexts" (James Barr, *The Semantics of Biblical Language* [London: Oxford University Press, 1961], 231).

45. Cf. the remarks of Martin Rese, "Formeln und Lieder im Neuen Testament. Einige notwendige Anmerkungen," *Verkündigung und Forschung* 15, no. 2 (1970): 75–95: "Niemand wird bestreiten wollen, daß es im NT Formeln und Lieder gibt, die alter sind als ihr jetziger Kontext" (75). However, in the closing critical questions, Rese notes that skepticism regarding the original wording and context of earlier pieces of tradition arises, at least in part, from the reality "daß neutestamentliche Formeln und Lieder immer nur in sekundären Quellen überliefert sind" (94).

46. Cf., with a different focus, the comments of E. P. Sanders: "The topic 'Jesus' Galilee' indicates an effort to describe Jesus' environment or context—what New Testament scholars often call his 'background.' Since context is essential to understanding, this is part of the 'quest for the historical Jesus.' If we have a saying or an event and do not know the context, our fertile minds will make one up. The context that our brain supplies may be quite inaccurate, and the result may be misleading, but we automatically try to fit new information into what we already know" ("Jesus' Galilee," in *Fair Play: Diversity and Conflicts in Early Christianity; Essays in Honour of Heikki Räisänen*, ed. Ismo Dunderberg, Christopher Tuckett, and Kari Syreeni [Leiden: Brill, 2002], 3).

Part 1: Christology, Greco-Roman Culture, and Canonical Reception

ferent interpretive context from the *Lukan* one. To read Acts 2:36, therefore, as a pre-Lukan piece of kerygma (whether taken over by Luke or placed with historical verisimilitude in the mouth of Peter) and apply the reconstructed earlier meaning to Lukan Christology is to confuse different levels of meaning-determining discourse—what we have called the interpretive context—such that a non-Lukan context is substituted for the Lukan one. Loosing Acts 2:36 from its narrative mooring in the attempt to determine specifically the meaning of the verse in relation to Lukan Christology thus immediately involves a methodological confusion. This confusion prevents ipso facto an interpretation of the verse's meaning within Luke-Acts: in the act of disengaging any statement (or passage) from the narrative, the possibility of discovering that statement's meaning within the Lukan writings is actually forfeited, for the Lukan context itself is rendered inoperative as meaning-determining discourse. Even to begin an analysis of the meaning of Acts 2:36 for Luke's Christology, therefore, we will have to be methodologically committed to the literary effort to work with the Lukan context—that is, Luke-Acts. Due to the constraints of this chapter, in what follows I shall focus upon Luke's use of κύριος and simply note now that what can be said for κύριος can also, with different nuance of course, be said for χριστός.[47]

For our purposes it is unnecessary to list each noteworthy aspect of Luke's complex and richly varied use of κύριος. Instead, it shall suffice to attend to one central point, along with a few of its textual particulars, that bears directly upon the significance of Acts 2:36. This central point is that, for Luke, there was no moment at which Jesus was not κύριος.

As noted in the opening of the chapter, Jesus is already named κύριος while still in the womb (Luke 1:43). Indeed, it is at this exact moment—and thus as κύριος—that Jesus himself officially enters the narrative. The implication for Jesus's identity as developed through the narrative is that it simply cannot be thought apart from his identity as ὁ κύριος; in the Lukan story, Ἰησοῦς cannot be abstracted from κύριος. That is to say, if we take the sequence of the narrative seriously (cf. καθεξῆς in the προοίμιον), there was no Jesus who was not already and simultaneously κύριος. By speaking of one who was still in the womb as κύριος, Luke presses the christologically indispensable point that Jesus's very life and his identity as Lord are the same thing.

---

47. For a full elaboration of Luke's use of κύριος, see C. Kavin Rowe, *Early Narrative Christology: The Lord in the Gospel of Luke* (2006; repr., Grand Rapids: Baker Academic, 2009). The other statement that could be considered here is of course Acts 5:31, in which we read that God exalted Jesus as ἀρχηγός and σωτήρ (τοῦτον ὁ θεὸς ἀρχηγὸν καὶ σωτῆρα ὕψωσεν). Σωτήρ appears in the gospel for Jesus (2:11), and ἀρχηγός in Acts 3:15.

Acts 2:36 and the Continuity of Lukan Christology

It is this unity in identity that is, narratively speaking, confirmed from heaven in the angels' declaration that the newly born baby is χριστὸς κύριος (2:11). And it is this unity of identity that underlies the authorial preference, unique among the canonical gospels, expressed in Luke's repeated reference to Jesus as ὁ κύριος in the gospel narrative: "And seeing her, ὁ κύριος had compassion upon her" (7:13).[48]

In fact, Luke is at pains throughout the entire gospel to narrate Jesus's identity as ὁ κύριος upon the earth. Thus, for example, do numerous characters address Jesus as κύριε (5:8, 12; 7:6, etc.). Many scholars dismiss the vocative's relevance for Christology,[49] but in so doing they overlook Luke's use of a literary technique, dramatic irony, in which characters can say more than they know. Luke not only writes with historical verisimilitude—a Gentile may well instruct his messengers to address someone as κύριε (7:6)—but also skillfully encourages the auditor/reader to draw the christologically continuous line between the vocative and non-vocative uses of κύριος (cf., e.g., 12:41–42). Rather than either historical (low) or christological (high) in meaning, therefore, the Lukan vocative displays a both/and character. It is both christologically significant and historically credible. The κύριος is correctly addressed as κύριε, for that is indeed who he is, and yet those who address him as such say more, christologically speaking, than they could understand.[50] In brief, by introducing Jesus as ὁ κύριος, by writing repeatedly of him as ὁ κύριος, by juxtaposing vocative and non-vocative uses of κύριος (e.g., 10:38–42; 12:41–42; 14:21–23; 19:8; cf. Acts 9:10–11; 22:10; 26:15), by adjusting Mark's text (e.g., 6:5) or rewriting it to include further references to Jesus as κύριος (e.g., Luke 18:41 in 18:35–43 // Mark 10:46–52), and by composing unique material in which the word κύριος figures prominently (e.g., 10:1, 17, etc.), Luke creates a narrative Christology in which Jesus's identity as κύριος stands at the center.[51]

---

48. Cf. 7:19, 31 (dubious); 10:1, 39, 41; 11:39; 12:42; 13:15; 17:5, 6; 18:6; 19:8; 22:61; 24:3.

49. This tendency is widespread enough that one can take an example almost at random. See, e.g., C. F. D. Moule, *The Origin of Christology* (Cambridge: Cambridge University Press, 1977), 35: "First, the vocative . . . must be cleared out of the way. Many writers . . . make the mistake of counting instances of the vocative when they are preparing statistics for the application of *kurios* as a title to Jesus. But *kurie* is so common as a respectful address . . . that it would be truthful, statistically, to reckon a schoolboy's 'O Sir' as evidence that the schoolmaster had been knighted."

50. The Lukan use of the vocative presents a problem for English translators, who must choose between "Lord" and "sir" (or suitable variations thereof), thereby obscuring the both/and dynamic of the Lukan narrative. The problem, however, obviously does not exist in Greek (or in German for that matter).

51. For a full discussion of these points and others related to them, see Rowe, *Early Narrative Christology*.

Yet this identity was not without threat. In point of fact, in what is surely one of the more creative literary moves in the gospels, Luke withholds the word κύριος from the mocking, trial, execution, and burial of Jesus. Prior to this point, κύριος has occurred at virtually every twist and turn in the narrative, but with Peter's final denial in 22:61–62, Luke writes, "And ὁ κύριος turned and looked at Peter. And Peter remembered the word τοῦ κυρίου, how he had said to him, 'Before the cock crows today, you will deny me three times.' And he went out and wept bitterly." And with Peter's exit goes κύριος.

Thus it is just here, at the moment that Jesus is rejected by his last disciple[52] and begins to be mocked and beaten, that the word disappears from the story. This silence is striking; it is in fact the silence of death, that which the human verdict upon the identity of Jesus brings upon the Lord.

Not until the other side of the resurrection does κύριος reappear (24:3, 34). Its reappearance in the narrative on the other side of Jesus's death evidences, as Charles Talbert put it, "God's reversal of the human *no* to Jesus"[53] and thus proclaims the ongoing life of the Lord: "ὁ κύριος is truly risen" (24:34).

The opening of Acts continues the emphasis upon Jesus's identity as κύριος, picking up—at least in this respect—exactly where the gospel ended. Indeed, as the last words from any characters in the gospel name Jesus as κύριος (24:34; the eleven), so the very first word addressed to the resurrected Jesus in Acts is κύριε (1:6; the apostles). Moreover, Acts 1:21 refers back to the Jesus of the gospel as ὁ κύριος Ἰησοῦς and thereby establishes a well-crafted "chain-link" with the first mention of the resurrected one in Luke (24:3).[54] And, moving closer to the immediate context of the verse in question, twice in his Pentecost speech Peter "proves" that Jesus is the κύριος of whom Scripture has spoken (2:25 [Ps 15:8 LXX]; 2:34 [Ps 109:1 LXX]). Following Peter's speech, Luke continues to write frequently of Jesus as κύριος both in the story itself (ὁ κύριος Ἰησοῦς, e.g., in 8:16) and as a way in which Jesus is addressed (κύριε Ἰησοῦ, e.g., in 7:59 in Stephen's prayer).[55] In Acts Jesus is κύριος in his heavenly life

---

52. Peter is also the first one to address Jesus as κύριε in the gospel narrative (5:8).

53. Charles H. Talbert, "The Place of the Resurrection in the Theology of Luke," *Int* 46 (1992): 21.

54. On "chain-link" technique and the NT, esp. Luke-Acts, see Bruce W. Longenecker, "Lukan Aversion to Humps and Hollows: The Case of Acts 11.27–12.25," *NTS* 50 (2004): 185–204. On the text-critical problem here, see Rowe, *Early Narrative Christology*, 182–83 n. 86.

55. The precise number of times that Luke refers to Jesus as κύριος is difficult to determine because of the (well-known) ambiguity that attends many occurrences of κύριος in Acts. In round numbers, depending on text-critical decisions, ambiguity, and so on, it would be between forty-five and seventy times.

even as he was κύριος in his earthly life in the gospel. To be sure, there is a difference in location (earth/heaven), but there is unity in identity. For Luke, the one who was in Mary's womb, lived, died, and was raised is at every point along this continuum ὁ κύριος.

Luke thus comprehensively and deftly develops his κύριος Christology across both volumes of his literary project. The two volumes together tell the one story of the Lord of all (κύριος πάντων, Acts 10:36). It is in light of this larger literary and christological context of Luke-Acts that we may now return to Acts 2:36.

It is true that Peter does not have to speak the author's own Christology. Especially if we consider the manner of speech composition in the ancient world, Peter could theoretically say something that differed from Luke's point of view (cf., e.g., Tuckett above).[56] Given the immense care with which Luke has developed narratively the position that Jesus was Lord from his life's inception, it seems unlikely, however, that he would introduce a basic christological contradiction in the mouth of a main character—in fact, initially the most important spokesman for the nascent Christian movement[57]—at the climax of the first speech in the second volume.[58] In this reading, at a moment of great dramatic weight, Peter would proclaim a Christology that Luke considered to be false—indeed, to the extent that he felt the need to undermine it systematically with his own christological project. The entirety of the gospel would thus prepare the auditor/reader to hear Peter's bold words in Acts as christologically inaccurate.[59] If ἐποίησεν in Acts 2:36 has to mean what it allegedly means in the interpretive context of a pre-Lukan reconstruction, then perhaps we would be driven to just such a conclusion. But its meaning need not be that which entails a christological contradiction. It could mean something else altogether, as patristic interpretation illustrates. In fact, if we place the verse within its proper interpretive context, Acts 2:36 does mean something else.

56. The point would hold for a source theory such as Barrett's as well.

57. Indeed, Peter is the main character for the first half of Acts. Furthermore, as mentioned just above in n. 52, Peter is actually the first one to address Jesus as κύριε in the gospel (5:8).

58. Cf. Peter Balia, "Does Acts 2.36 Represent an Adoptionist Christology?," *European Journal of Theology* 5, no. 2 (1996): 137-42, esp. 140; and, Hahn's remark: "2.36 is regarded as a summarizing formula concluding the whole speech" (*Titles*, 106). Balia's short article was unknown to me until this article was completed, but I am delighted to note the correspondence between our interpretations—even to the point of acknowledging the insight of Athanasius—all the more so because of our independence.

59. According to Luke, Jesus was κύριος from his conception, but according to Peter in Acts 2:36, Jesus was not κύριος until after his resurrection.

Part 1: Christology, Greco-Roman Culture, and Canonical Reception

When thus situated, it becomes apparent that Acts 2:36 does not mean "it was only at his resurrection and ascension that God made Jesus Lord and Christ,"[60] that there was a change in Jesus's status, that he became something he was not before. On the contrary, Acts 2:36 *confirms* the already-established identity of Jesus as κύριος in the face of his rejection and death.[61] The verse is, in other words, a vivid abbreviation of the movement of the entire gospel story in which the identity of Jesus who was κύριος from the womb was threatened by his rejection and crucifixion but reaffirmed by his resurrection. Such a reading does not diminish the force of ποιεῖν but rather takes seriously ὁ θεός as its subject. In this way the emphasis is placed upon God's continuous action in the life of Jesus despite human violence, rejection, and death.[62] God's salvific will is not broken either by human resistance or by Jesus's death.[63] The Lord who was crucified has been raised. Acts 2:36 is thus consistent with the narrative Christology of the gospel.

The "making" of which Acts 2:36 speaks does not refer, therefore, to an ontological transformation in the identity of Jesus or his status (from not κύριος to κύριος) but to an epistemological shift in the perception of the human community. Indeed, such is the point of the imperative γινωσκέτω. Furthermore, ἀσφαλῶς (cf. Luke 1:4) occurs in the initial position, thus indicating its emphatic nature.[64] The resurrection and exaltation of Jesus should alter assuredly the knowledge of the "house of Israel" regarding Jesus's identity: "let the whole house of Israel *know assuredly* . . ." But God's action does not alter Jesus's identity itself. The resurrection, as Athanasius seemed to see, "manifested" God's reversal of the human rejection of Jesus precisely through the identity of the messianic Lord. It is to this reversal—expressed here in terms of the continuity of Jesus's identity—that the ἐποίησεν of Acts 2:36 points.[65]

---

60. C. K. Barrett, "Submerged Christology in Acts," in *Anfänge der Christologie*, ed. Cilliers Breytenbach and Henning Paulsen (Göttingen: Vandenhoeck & Ruprecht, 1991), 238.

61. Cf. Petr Pokorný, *Theologie der lukanischen Schriften* (Göttingen: Vandenhoeck & Ruprecht, 1998), 93: "Nach lukanischer Auffassung ist die Auferstehung ein anschauliches Zeugnis Gottes für Jesus als den Herrn und Messias (Act 2,36), welches sein ganzes Leben rehabilitiert"; and 152: "Der gekreuzigte Jesus ist durch die Auferstehung als der Herr im Sinne von Ps 110,1 (Act 2,34) und als Messias bestätigt (Act 2,36 vgl. 10,36)."

62. Cf. Gaventa, *Acts*, 79, who writes of the "sharp juxtaposition of God's action with that of humanity."

63. Cf. the emphasis on the firmness of "God's purpose" in Spencer, *Acts*, 39.

64. Thanks are due to Scott Spencer for drawing my attention to this point.

65. Despite Barr's earlier warning, one may still desire evidence that ποιέω can mean something other than "make/do." In fact, a consultation of the standard lexica reveals a remarkable range of meanings; moreover, ποιέω is one of the most commonly used verbs

Acts 2:36 and the Continuity of Lukan Christology

Wilckens of course made his way toward an interpretation that ran contrary to the prevailing consensus of the 1950s and asserted that Acts 2:36 applied to the entirety of the christological event. Jesus was Lord *"von Anfang an."*[66] A minority of exegetes have followed Wilckens's claim and appropriated his insight.[67] Quite recently, for example, Frank Matera saw that Acts 2:36 "should be read in light of the angel's announcement to the shepherds that a savior has been born who is Messiah and Lord (Luke 2.11). Since the resurrection is the moment when God enthrones his Son, Israel should now know who Jesus *always* was."[68] In the Lukan narrative, there was not a time when Jesus was not κύριος.

While such interpretations are undoubtedly on the right track, in my judgment they have in time amounted to little more than astute counter-assertions.[69] There has been need, in other words, to analyze the greater interpretive problematic and to offer argument for a reasoned rejection of the majority view in the modern period. Further, there has been the concomitant literary and

---

in Greek. Simple collection of linguistic data is thus rendered argumentatively irrelevant, as one is thrust back by this semantic breadth upon the particular context in question (here, to demonstrate that ἐποίησεν is consonant with the proposed interpretation; elsewhere, in Acts 1:1, e.g., to show that "wrote" renders ἐποιησάμην accurately, or that "chose" comes closest to ἐποίησεν in Mark 3:14, etc.). However, we may note with profit a similar use of ἐποίησεν within the Lukan corpus itself (see Luke 1:51, where, in the context of God's fulfillment of his promises, the word means something like "shown"—so, rightly, the NRSV, KJV, et al.) and also that Athanasius's argument mentioned above on p. 198 depends hermeneutically upon the linguistic judgment that ποιέω is virtually equivalent to ἀποδείκνυμι.

66. Wilckens, *Missionsreden*, 174: "Von Anfang an hat einerseits Gott in Erfüllung der Schrift diesen Jesus zum Herrn und Christus gemacht und ihn so in die zentrale Funktion der Heilsgeschichte eingesetzt, während andererseits dieser so von Gott ausgezeichnete Jesus von den Juden angefeindet und getötet worden ist."

67. See, e.g., Conzelmann, *Acts*, 21; Schneider, *Apostelgeschichte*, 1:276-77. Cf. Donald L. Jones, "The Title Kyrios in Luke-Acts," *SBLSP* 74, no. 2 (1974): 93, 94-95, 96; and Eric Franklin, *Christ the Lord: A Study in the Purpose and Theology of Luke-Acts* (Philadelphia: Westminster, 1975), 52-54.

68. Frank J. Matera, *New Testament Christology* (Louisville: Westminster John Knox, 1999), 268 n. 44. Cf. his earlier remark, "Jesus did not become the Messiah and Lord in function of his resurrection; he was already Messiah and Lord at his birth" (63). Cf. the concise discussion of H. Douglas Buckwalter, *The Character and Purpose of Luke's Christology*, SNTSMS 89 (Cambridge: Cambridge University Press, 1996), 184-91, esp. 189: "Acts presents a messianic unveiling of what was announced of Jesus in Luke's Gospel right from the start."

69. For example, the ground for Wilckens's opinion was essentially that of the Lukan authorship of the verse. However, given the nature of speech composition in the ancient world, one could hold simultaneously that Luke wrote Acts 2:36 and that it expresses a Christology contrary to Luke's (cf. Tuckett).

Part 1: Christology, Greco-Roman Culture, and Canonical Reception

theological need to situate Acts 2:36 within Luke's narrative Christology and thus to say how exactly this particular verse fits well within the larger Lukan project. In this light, the foregoing chapter has endeavored (a) to draw out, through an analysis of the operative interpretive contexts in both ancient and modern interpretation, the hermeneutical necessity of the κύριος Christology of Luke-Acts as the proper interpretive context for Acts 2:36, and (b) to interpret the meaning of this verse within this context. If this be done well, then it can be said that Acts 2:36 encapsulates the story of the κύριος χριστός told in the gospel and continued in Acts. Acts 2:36, that is, does not contradict Lukan Christology but expresses it.

Authority and Community

◆ LUKAN *DOMINIUM* IN ACTS

> The question of authority in its religious form is the first and last issue of life.
>
> —P. T. Forsyth, cited in R. R. Williams, *Authority in the Apostolic Age*

In contrast to community, authority is not exactly a popular topic. This situation probably derives in large part from the present intellectual and cultural context in which many of us, as heirs to a liberal democratic tradition, are predisposed to dislike the very mention of authority. But, as people living in the anti-authority fallout of the 1960s and '70s, perhaps also we do not know quite what to make of authority or how to talk about it constructively. In fact, when originally preparing this chapter, a remark from Gaius Cotta, the "academic" in Cicero's *De natura deorum*, kept coming back to me: "In almost all subjects," says Cotta to his opponents during their debate, "I am more ready to say what is not true than what is" (1.21.60).[1]

With respect to the theme of this chapter, Cotta's remark is as sobering as it is revealing. As John Schütz put it in his classic book on Paul: "For the student of the earliest Christian history and literature the problem of authority is very real even if its discussion must often be more oblique than direct."[2] Schütz has here put his finger on what we might call the dilemma of indirection: to get at

---

1. Cf. John Howard Schütz, *Paul and the Anatomy of Apostolic Authority* (Cambridge: Cambridge University Press, 1975), ix: "There is no reason to assume that we intuitively know what authority is and how it functioned in a radically new venture like early Christianity."
2. Schütz, *Paul*, 1.

"Authority and Community: Lukan *Dominium* in Acts" was originally published in *Acts and Ethics* (ed. Thomas E. Phillips; Sheffield: Sheffield Phoenix, 2005), 96–108. It is reproduced with permission.

the meaning of authority, one has to get at it by way of something else—that is, indirectly.

Despite the many inherent difficulties in such a discussion, I will attempt to bring some clarity to the topic and so to stimulate our thinking about Acts and ethics. This task will require five successive steps. First, en route to a serviceable methodology for the chapter, we will do a bit of concise but crucially important conceptual housecleaning in the effort to sweep out any underlying modern dust that might obscure our understanding of both authority and community in Acts. Second, we will need to mention briefly the working method that allows us a point of entry into the ethical underpinnings of the emergent Christian community. In this light, we will, third, come to an issue critical in any discussion of ethics, that of human equality. Fourth, we shall then focus upon the apparent antithesis of equality, the elevation of certain persons of the community. Finally, on the basis of the juxtaposition of these issues, we shall consider the nature of authority and community in Acts.

Prolegomena

First in the order of potential conceptual obstruction is a particular philosophical or theological anthropology. If, for our purposes here, we paint with broad strokes, we may say that in the wake of the Enlightenment the picture of the human being that emerges focuses upon the individual. This individual is, in turn, best characterized as autonomous, a subject whose freedom consists in the essence of having no rule or law—or authority—other than oneself (αὐτὸς νόμος).

Whether or not this anthropology is "completely mythical"[3] or "a conceit with which moderns delude themselves,"[4] what is certain is the effect that such an understanding has upon the construal of both authority and community. Where the human being is conceived of as an autonomous individual, authority—that which by definition involves "another"—can ultimately only

---

3. Herbert McCabe, "Obedience," in *God Matters* (London: Chapman, 1987), 227: "Now I hope to persuade you . . . that this idea of the individual, which forms the very basis of our society . . . is completely mythical; there are no such animals." McCabe's reflections in this brief essay are of basic importance for any treatment of authority.

4. Leander E. Keck, *Who Is Jesus? History in Perfect Tense* (Columbia: University of South Carolina Press, 2000), 164: "The notion of an autonomous self is a conceit with which moderns delude themselves."

be construed negatively—that is, as something that is fundamentally limiting to human freedom and potential or both. "Dominative authority," so said a modern scholar in line with such a view, "never pays dividends in the long run; in the end it will always strangle and kill, in the effort to secure outward conformity in the place of free assent."[5]

The effect of this anthropology upon one's view of community is much the same. To live with others is to be confronted by the need to dominate or the reality of being dominated. In both of these cases, the "other" is a menace to the autonomy of the self. In the former situation, the threat of a reversal (master to slave, for example) is ever nigh and the effort aimed at maintaining the order of the authoritarian status quo is ever required. In the latter, the self is obviously at the mercy of another.

The conception of the human being as a free, autonomous individual and its concomitant understanding of authority and community finally only exist together in outright and unhappy tension or, perhaps better, violent contradiction. It is true, of course, that even on this modern view authority might be "necessary"; but—and here is the crux—authority would be, as in the cliché, a necessary evil. It is no small wonder, then, that authority, as Yves Simon put it, has a bad name.[6]

The point with this prolegomena may be readily discernable, but it is not for that reason any less important: if the conceptual apparatus we employ to read Luke-Acts is outfitted with the modern anthropology of the autonomous individual and the corresponding negative views of authority and community, we will, at best, distort beyond recognition the understanding of authority as construed by the narrative of Acts. Luke's view of community is not one in which individuals are jockeying and elbowing for position. He does not envisage, that is, the infamous crab bucket, in which community is defined by pinching and clawing for place and authority by the luck and ability to claw to the top.

---

5. Henry St John, preface to *Authority in a Changing Church*, ed. John Dalrymple et al. (London: Sheed and Ward, 1968), ix. One suspects the influence of such anti-authority anthropology as described above in, for example, statements that move easily between the modern "good" of democracy and the movement of the early church as "democratic": "That everyone experienced the fit of the spirit implied that the spirit functioned as a principle of democratization" (Helmut Koester, "Writings and the Spirit: Authority and Politics in Ancient Christianity," *Harvard Theological Review* 84 [1991]: 354).

6. See Yves R. Simon, *A General Theory of Authority* (Notre Dame: University of Notre Dame Press, 1962).

Part 1: Christology, Greco-Roman Culture, and Canonical Reception

Method

We may begin by noting at the outset that an ultimately insufficient way in which to approach the question of authority in Acts is to do a word study of ἐξουσία. Even leaving aside worries about semantic fallacies, the term occurs too infrequently to allow us to draw substantive conclusions on this basis about the nature and shape of authority in Acts.[7]

I suggest, instead, that for heuristic purposes a more adequate starting point for exegetical reflection is to combine an insight from an ethicist into the interconnection between authority and community with an analysis of the picture of community life generated by Acts in toto. Building on the work of Simon and others, Stanley Hauerwas has noted that the meaning of authority is "dependent upon an understanding of the nature of human community and the moral good."[8] The methodological implication of this statement is that if we can in some way accurately describe the nature of a human community and the moral good that is its practice and belief, we will have seen what is meant by authority (even if such seeing is through a glass darkly).

The following reflections will thus derive from what we might call, for lack of better terminology, Lukan narrative community.[9] Reading community in

---

7. A possible exception is the occurrence of ἐξουσία in Acts 1:7, in which eschatological authority is placed in the hands of the Father. After the disciples ask the resurrected Jesus, "Lord, is this the time when you will restore the kingdom to Israel?" Luke writes, "And [Jesus] said to them, 'It is not for you to know the times [χρόνους] or periods [καιρούς] that the Father has set by his own authority [τῇ ἰδίᾳ ἐξουσίᾳ].'" In this way, ultimate authority actually rests with God, and this in fact does reflect the nature and shape of authority in Acts.

8. See his essay "Authority and the Profession of Medicine," in *Suffering Presence: Theological Reflections on Medicine, the Mentally Handicapped, and the Church* (Notre Dame: University of Notre Dame Press, 1986), 39. For a discussion of the definitional and conceptual differences between "power," "strength," "force," "violence," and "authority," see Hannah Arendt, *On Violence* (New York: Harcourt, Brace & World, 1969), 44–46. Arendt notes that of all of these phenomena, authority is "the most elusive" and, as a term, "the most abused" (45). Though her analysis is certainly profound, to the extent that she views the "hallmark" of authority as entailing "unquestioning recognition by those who are asked to obey," a problem remains. It does not need to be the case at all that recognition of authority is primarily unquestioning; indeed, one way to view authority is to see it as an argument about the order or structure of reality (this is especially clear in various arguments vis-à-vis authority in a religious or theological framework). Even once accepted, such an argument may continue to receive questioning while remaining authoritatively compelling overall.

9. I speak here purposefully of community rather than communities in order to indicate that the analysis will not focus upon the portrayal of particular, individual communities in Acts (e.g., Antioch or Jerusalem) but rather upon the total picture of early Christian life

Acts as a whole—that is, looking at the nature of this community—allows us to thematize authority for ethical analysis. Under the pressure of thematization, the text yields two issues of constitutive significance for the Lukan construal of authority—significance, that is, that extends throughout and gives shape to the total picture of authority as developed in the narrative community in Acts. The first issue is that of human equality.

THE EQUALITY OF ALL

The notion of equality (*égalité*) or egalitarian (*égalitaire*) ethics has of course achieved a great deal of popularity in recent years both through historical and avowedly ideological criticism of the biblical sources.[10] Despite the many trenchant critiques of the egalitarian enterprise,[11] the question of human equality

---

gained from reading Acts as a whole. Thus, in terms of the view of authority, I am not so much searching for pieces of historical information within the narrative as I am asking after the shape the narrative gives to authority through the overall depiction of Christian community.

10. One could think here especially of Elisabeth Schüssler Fiorenza's program of "discipleship of equals." See, e.g., the collection of several of her shorter essays entitled *Discipleship of Equals: Critical Feminist Ekklesia-logy of Liberation* (New York: Crossroad, 1993). In the first chapter of *Jesus: Miriam's Child, Sophia's Prophet* (New York: Continuum, 1994), Schüssler Fiorenza gives a particularly useful account of her own approach over the years. Cf. also, e.g., John Dominic Crossan, *The Historical Jesus: The Life of a Mediterranean Jewish Peasant* (San Francisco: HarperSanFrancisco, 1991) and *Jesus: A Revolutionary Biography* (San Francisco: HarperSanFrancisco, 1994).

11. See the devastating criticisms of such work by, for example, John H. Elliott, "Jesus Was Not an Egalitarian: A Critique of an Anachronistic and Idealist Theory," *Biblical Theology Bulletin* 32, no. 2 (2002): 75–91, and "The Jesus Movement Was Not Egalitarian but Family-Oriented," *Biblical Interpretation* 11 (2003): 173–210. Elliott concludes his critique: "The concept of equality/egalitarianism, as utilized by egalitarian theorists, is of recent modern vintage and historically incompatible with the conditions and perspectives of first century persons.... However much we moderns and heirs of the American and French revolutions cherish the hard won prize of political and legal (and in some domains economic and social) equality, we must as honest historians acknowledge that this is a development of the modern era and not to be found in the societies and even mentalities of antiquity" ("Jesus Movement," 203–5). Elliott does maintain, however, that in relation to "direct access to God" and "the media of salvation," the cultural, legal, and social disparities were relativized to the extent that they no longer had any bearing upon these, admittedly more religious and theological, matters ("Jesus Movement," 204–5). But he neglects the fact that this manner of relativizing is, of course, to speak of a type of equality in a crucially important sense (see the note below), even if it is to speak of equality in an explicitly theological, and therefore non-modern, sense.

Part 1: Christology, Greco-Roman Culture, and Canonical Reception

is not anachronistic when put to Luke-Acts. Indeed, when properly understood, the matter of human equality can be seen to be woven into the fabric of the narrative itself in such a way that to remove the concern for human equality would be to unravel the total story that Acts seeks to tell.[12]

The Cornelius material in Acts 10 is an appropriate place for our attention both because of its role as the major turning point in the narrative for the mission to the Gentiles and because the logic of the passage undergirds the Lukan view of the unity between Jew and Gentile as a whole, Luke's vision for "Christian" community.[13] The passage is therefore both foundational and representative in nature. As such it will serve not only to focus our vision but also to point us toward the nature of authority as displayed in the wider narrative.

Whether Peter's initial words to Cornelius and his houseguests in 10:28 accurately depict Jewish law is not our concern here;[14] rather, our focus is the theological declaration that opens the scene: "God has revealed [ἔδειξεν] to me

---

12. Lest it be missed: I am not simply advocating that we should ask whether or not Luke supports equality in a contemporary sense of the word (cf. Elliott's remarks in the note above). Indeed, I would argue that whatever we mean by "equality" will be dependent upon the particular context (historical, cultural, textual, etc.) in which the word is used. Thus the conceptual move here is to ask in what way the narrative of Acts construes equality, and the semantic-philosophical direction is from the text to the word: the term, that is, receives its meaning from the shape of the story. In this light, as we will see, it emerges that equality for Luke is something like the ultimate status of all humanity before God and the concomitant notion of salvation. In its basic structure, equality is, in other words, both anthropological and soteriological. In this way, the Lukan view of equality is derivative, depending upon the character of God and the significance of Jesus for all humanity. It is, hence, in a far-reaching sense, profoundly unmodern. The critical push in this section of the essay is thus to be seen as an attempt to carve out some space in which we can give a more nuanced account of what we mean by "equality" in relation to the biblical sources. So, e.g., Schüssler Fiorenza's conclusions are untenable in light of Elliott's critique, but Elliott himself, for the most part, simply adopts the same working definition of "equality" (no doubt in order to assess accurately egalitarian theory) and therefore downplays the importance of a soteriological construal of equality, such as we see in Acts.

13. Ch. 10 occupies a place of central narrative and theological importance in Acts, as the events narrated here are the pivot upon which the mission to the Gentiles turns. Narratively, Saul has just transformed from persecutor to God's σκεῦος ἐκλογῆς to the Gentiles (9:15). The story then moves immediately to justify theologically Paul's mission through Peter's experience with Cornelius. This narrative-theological justification continues through Acts 11:18, at which time the story returns to Saul to include his ministry (ἡ διακονία, 12:25) in Antioch (11:25–26, 30; 12:25).

14. The NRSV's rendering of ἀθέμιτος as "unlawful" is problematic (as is "ungesetzlich" in, e.g., Rudolf Pesch, *Die Apostelgeschichte*, 2 vols., EKKNT 5 [Neukirchen-Vluyn: Neukirchener Verlag, 1986], 1:341). For the issue involved here, see Beverly Roberts Gaventa, *The Acts of the Apostles*, ANTC (Nashville: Abingdon, 2003), 168.

that no one [μηδένα] is to call a human being common [κοινόν] or unclean [ἀκάθαρτον]" (10:28; cf. 10:14, κοινὸν καὶ ἀκάθαρτον).[15] Simply put, this is an astonishing claim: it levels anthropologically the worth of humanity; no human being (ἄνθρωπος) is to be called profane or unclean.

Such leveling fundamentally dismantles the easiest way of dividing humanity, the denigration of those who are different—that is, the denigration of the "other." Μηδείς, *no one*, can make the determination of κοινός or ἀκάθαρτος. On this view, we neither sit on nor stand before the judge's bench in a human court.

The statement further raises instantly the question of its ground. How can Peter the Jew say such a thing?

Cornelius and his guests do not have to wait long, for the ground of this anthropological leveling is given just a few verses later in the first words of Peter's speech: οὐκ ἔστιν προσωπολήμπτης ὁ θεός (10:34). It is somewhat difficult to translate this sentence precisely without unwanted semantic baggage. Not "to receive the face" is not really to be "impartial" (cf. NRSV et al.), a term that usually connotes the natural scientist's detached posture over an experiment (Dewey);[16] neither is it any better to say that God is "no respecter of persons" (KJV), a phrase that communicates divine aloofness in weighing human worth. Perhaps the best among the current options renders the sentence "God isn't one to play favorites." Yet this lack of favoritism is not due to God's indifference toward, or distance from, humans but rather to God's generosity to Jew and Gentile alike. The ground of the equality of humanity is thus conceptualized in strictly theological terms.[17] Because God is generous to all, there is no favoritism or judgment prima facie.

---

15. The personalizing "that I should call" of the RSV is a poor translation. The accusative μηδένα is the subject of the infinitive λέγειν.

16. An interesting case in point is Jerome H. Neyrey, "The Symbolic Universe of Luke-Acts: 'They Turn the World Upside Down,'" in *The Social World of Luke-Acts: Models for Interpretation* (Peabody: Hendrickson, 1991), 271-304, who writes of God's "impartiality," but then moves on to undermine the basic sense of the term by describing this aspect of God's character in terms of God's "mercy," which itself takes shape through "hospitality and inclusiveness." Cf. also Jouette M. Bassler, *Divine Impartiality: Paul and a Theological Axiom*, SBLDS 59 (Chico, CA: Scholars Press, 1982), who speaks of Paul's and Luke's use of divine impartiality as "acceptance" (e.g., 176).

17. For a more or less contemporary consideration of "authority" in relation to our concept of God, see Nicholas Lash, *Voices of Authority* (Shepherdstown: Patmos, 1976), esp. 10-12: "As Christians we should continually be asking ourselves the question: What concept of God, and of God's relationship to man, is implied by that notion of authority (whatever it may be) which we regard as relevant to, or appropriate for, our discussion of the Christian quest for truth—for right belief and right action?" (10). From the side of NT studies, cf. Neyrey, "Symbolic Universe of Luke-Acts," 296: "The essential apologetic for the new maps [people, holy places, body] which characterize the Jesus movement group ultimately resided in Luke's doctrine of God."

Part 1: Christology, Greco-Roman Culture, and Canonical Reception

The counterpart to this conviction or, better yet, its expression is Peter's claim in 10:36 that Jesus is κύριος πάντων.[18] The theology of God's generosity, that is, takes shape through the dominion of Jesus over all, both Jew and Gentile. Indeed, this is the thrust of Peter's speech and the conclusion to which it leads: Jesus is the one who has been appointed by God as "the Judge of the living and the dead" (10:42, κριτὴς ζώντων καὶ νεκρῶν), an expression that is obviously meant to signify all humanity. Thus it is that everyone (πᾶς) who believes in his name is forgiven (10:43).

Precisely in this christological conditioning of God's generosity is the seriousness of human equality that of an ultimate seriousness. Salvation—at least in its Lukan variation—is not based in any way on any type of "identity marker" but is instead open to all irrespective of the particularities of race, nationality, class, and gender. As the κύριος πάντων, Jesus stands in the role of both Judge and Savior of all people (cf. Acts 4:12). Seen from this point of view, humanity in its totality is one. That is to say, because of the God of Israel's generosity, human beings stand before the Lord Jesus together as equals. The polarity of "us" and "them" is thus dissolved. Or so at least it is taken this way in the narrative of Acts, as Peter's remarkable statement at the Jerusalem Council indicates: God does not distinguish between "us" and "them" (15:8–9, ὁ καρδιογνώστος θεὸς ... οὐθὲν διέκρινεν μεταξὺ ἡμῶν τε καὶ αὐτῶν).[19]

Exploring the ground of Peter's astonishing claim that no human (ἄνθρωπος) is to be called common (κοινός) or unclean (ἀκάθαρτος) has involved a particular narrative in which the equality of human beings depends not upon a universal democratic truth available to all rational creatures but

---

18. Many commentators and contemporary translations take the sentence οὗτός ἐστιν πάντων κύριος to be parenthetical and translate "he is Lord of all." In my judgment, this way of reading is to ignore the grammar here by downplaying the directive force of οὗτος—*this one*. "You know the word which he sent to the people of Israel preaching peace through Jesus Christ: this one is Lord of all. You know what has happened throughout the whole of Judaea, beginning in Galilee after the baptism which John preached, as God anointed in the Holy Spirit and power Jesus of Nazareth, who went about benefacting and healing all who were oppressed by the devil, for God was with him" (10:36–37). Cf. the similar use of οὗτος in Acts 2:36 (τοῦτον τὸν Ἰησοῦν); 17:3 (οὗτός ἐστιν ὁ Χριστὸς ὁ Ἰησοῦς); 17:24 (οὗτος οὐρανοῦ καὶ γῆς ὑπάρχων κύριος). On this point, see C. Kavin Rowe, "Luke-Acts and the Imperial Cult: A Way through the Conundrum?," *JSNT* 27 (2005): 279–300, reprinted in this volume at pp. 3–23.

19. To see clearly the soteriological dimension of equality, it is important to note at this point that Luke's coordination of the universal (God/humanity) and the particular (Jesus Christ) involves a construal of God's relation to humanity such that it is refracted through—and cannot be abstracted from—the particular human being Jesus Christ.

Authority and Community

upon the character of God and God's action in Jesus Christ. Indeed, though cognates intriguingly turn up in Paul on the one hand and in James on the other,[20] the specific word προσωπολήμπτης is used only here in the ancient world. Authority, from this angle, rests finally in the character of God and is expressed humanly in terms of an anthropological leveling. This is the significance of an assembly whose self-identity is not that of a voluntary association of autonomous individuals held together with contractual glue but a community in which the dominion of Jesus is reflected in the equality of all humans, Jew and Gentile.[21]

Yet, embedded within the very speech that presses for human equality is a statement that seems to elevate dramatically the role of certain members of this community. In 10:41 Peter says explicitly that the appearance of the resurrected Jesus was not to all the people but ἡμῖν (to us), the ones who were chosen by God ahead of time or in advance (προχειροτονέω). The second basic matter, then, with which we have to deal is the understanding of authority that issues from the structure of the community in which some members are in some way elevated above others.

THE ELEVATION OF SOME

A vast amount of attention has understandably been given to "the twelve" in the Lukan writings, as well as to the related issue of the Lukan understand-

---

20. See BDAG, s.v. προσωπολήμπτης and προσωπολημψία. As noted in Eduard Lohse, "προσωπολημψία κτλ.," *TDNT* 6:779, these cognates are presumably based upon the Septuagintal expressions πρόσωπον λαμβάνειν or θαυμάζειν πρόσωπον. In the NT, see Jas 2:1 (προσωπολημψίας); 2:9 (προσωπολημπτεῖτε); Rom 2:11 (προσωπολημψία); Eph 6:9 (προσωπολημψία); Col 3:25 (προσωπολημψία). See Bassler, *Divine Impartiality*, for a discussion of "impartiality" in the OT and later rabbinic materials (cf. appendix A, "The Linguistic Development of the Jewish and Jewish-Christian Idioms for Impartiality," 189–91).

21. The Cornelius story is representative for other portions of Acts in which the unity of Jew and Gentile is both explicitly and implicitly at issue. Following Peter's report to Jerusalem of his experience with Cornelius, for example, the assembly of Jew and Gentile (11:20; reading Ἑλληνιστάς with B, D², et al.) in Syrian Antioch is for the first time called Χριστιανοί. The clear implication is that to be a Χριστιανός is to be, as it were, in mixed company. Cf., e.g., the description of the community in Iconium and the opponents (Acts 14:1, 5). So, too, the Jews in Jerusalem in Acts 22 seem to like Paul's speech until he mentions his commission to the Gentiles, at which point Paul's audience decides that he ought not to live (22:22).

ing of apostleship.[22] With Bovon, Schmithals, and others,[23] I do not think that Luke invented the concept of the twelve. It is indubitable, however, that he places considerable emphasis on their importance—and on Peter much more than the others, though John receives some special attention as well. But we must also remember that Paul, who is called an ἀπόστολος only twice (Acts 14:4, 14),[24] is the prominent figure for a vast stretch of the narrative. Moreover, James the brother of Jesus and the so-called πρεσβύτεροι ("elders"; Acts 15:6, 23) are also clearly cast in leadership roles.

Though perhaps desirable for the analytic task involved here, it is highly doubtful that such manifest variety in leadership can be arranged neatly into separate tiers that reflect accurately the various levels of importance that were attached to the twelve or to Peter or to Paul.[25] The historical picture is irreducibly complex and the accompanying problems intractable. Nevertheless, it should hardly be controversial to say that, even when allowing for this historical complexity, the narrative of Acts is weighted heavily toward exactly this configuration: the twelve apostles, most especially Peter, and Paul.

The opening scenes of Acts could scarcely be more obvious in their concern with the apostles and the apostolic task. The very first sentence of Luke's second volume seeks immediately to root apostolic identity in the election of the apostles during Jesus's life: Luke speaks explicitly of the apostles "whom

22. The expression οἱ δώδεκα is used only once in Acts (6:2; cf. Luke 8:1; 9:1, 12; 22:3, 47). The classic study is Hans von Campenhausen, *Ecclesiastical Authority and Spiritual Power in the Church of the First Three Centuries*, trans. J. A. Baker (Peabody, MA: Hendrickson, 1997). See also Walter Schmithals, *The Office of Apostle in the Early Church*, trans. John E. Steely (Nashville: Abingdon, 1969).

23. Contra Günther Klein in his influential monograph *Die Zwölf Apostel: Ursprung und Gehalt einer Idee*, FRLANT 59 (Göttingen: Vandenhoeck & Ruprecht, 1961). François Bovon, "The Apostolic Memories in Ancient Christianity," in *Studies in Early Christianity*, WUNT 161 (Tübingen: Mohr Siebeck, 2003), 7–8, and Schmithals, *Office of Apostle*, 265–72.

24. Ann Graham Brock, *Mary Magdalene, the First Apostle: The Struggle for Authority*, Harvard Theological Studies 51 (Cambridge, MA: Harvard University Press, 2003), 149–51, notes the possibility that these occurrences do not reflect Luke's careful negotiation of the term but rather his source. It is of course striking that Luke does not use ἀπόστολος elsewhere for Paul, but Brock's proposal so clearly works to help her larger thesis that one cannot help but wonder about special pleading. For a balanced review of Brock, see that of Edith M. Humphrey, review of *Mary Magdalene, the First Apostle: The Struggle for Authority*, by Ann Graham Brock, *Review of Biblical Literature* 6 (2004): 366–70.

25. Cf. Campenhausen, *Ecclesiastical Authority*, 28: "The most impressive evidence against a simple organizational interpretation . . . is the fact that it is quite impossible to arrange the leading figures of primitive Christianity in any definite patterns, vertical or horizontal, which would allow us to delimit their mutual official rights and duties."

[Jesus] elected [ἐξελέξατο]" (1:2). And the brief recapitulation of the disciples' encounter with the resurrected Jesus includes in Jesus's last words to them the description of the apostolic task that will find its echo many times over later in the narrative, particularly in the self-understanding of Peter and Paul: "you shall be my witnesses [μάρτυρες]" (1:8; cf. Luke 24:48). This is, in fact, in the account of the primitive community in Acts 4:32–35, exactly what the apostles do: "And with great power," writes Luke, "the apostles gave testimony [τὸ μαρτύριον] to the resurrection of Jesus" (4:33). Moreover, as is well known, the same emphases appear in the reconstitution of the twelve with the enrolling of Matthias: the one who is to replace Judas must be firmly connected to the earthly life of Jesus and, therefore, be able to bear witness to Jesus's earthly demise and subsequent resurrection (1:21–22). Luke then carefully develops the theme of witness to Jesus's resurrection, as Peter repeats over and again with subtle variation what he first says in the climactic section of his Pentecost speech: "This Jesus God raised up and of that we are all witnesses" (2:32; cf. 3:15; 5:32; 10:39, 41).

Paul's vocation, no less than the original apostles, is characterized by his commission to be a witness to Jesus's resurrection. Indeed, as Austin Farrer observed long ago, Luke is in the broad sense of the term an "emphatic typologist."[26] With respect to his "apostolic" role as a commissioned witness (μάρτυς) to the resurrection of Jesus, Paul's vocation is in a crucially important way a type of the apostles'—especially that of Peter's.[27]

As the resurrected Jesus commissioned the apostles as witnesses (μάρτυρες) in the opening of Acts, so the resurrected Jesus commissions Paul as a μάρτυς to what the latter has seen and heard (Acts 22:15), which is—to risk the obvious—the resurrected Jesus: "You will be a witness to [Jesus] for all people," says Ananias in Paul's retelling of their meeting (22:15). Furthermore, the next time Paul narrates his conversion, Jesus himself says to Paul, "I have appeared to you for this purpose, to appoint you [προχειρίσασθαι, a close cognate of the word Peter uses of himself in 10:41] as a servant and witness" (26:16; cf. 22:17; 23:11; 26:22).

The typology here answers the problem of Paul's status and role in Acts vis-à-vis his absence from Jesus's earthly career. If the point of the criterion of

---

26. Austin M. Farrer, "The Ministry in the New Testament," in *The Apostolic Ministry: Essays on the History and the Doctrine of the Episcopacy*, ed. Kenneth E. Kirk (New York: Morehouse-Gorham, 1946), 134.

27. On the "typology" of Peter and Paul, cf., e.g., Acts 3:1–10 // 14:8–10; Acts 5:16 // 16:18; Acts 5:16 // 28:9; Acts 8:14–17 // 19:1–7; Acts 9:36–41 // 20:9–12; Acts 10:26 // 14:15; and Acts 12:6–11 // 16:24–34.

Part 1: Christology, Greco-Roman Culture, and Canonical Reception

historical continuity with the earthly Jesus is to guarantee testimony to this dead man's resurrection, then a direct vision of this same dead man as alive accomplishes the same thing. Luke's Paul of course had no doubt that Jesus was dead. In point of fact, he persecuted those who believed differently. The resurrection appearance was to establish that this Jesus was alive. Even Festus, who later accuses Paul of madness (μανία, Acts 26:24), seems to understand this much: the issue at stake between Paul and his accusers is about "a certain one named Jesus who died, but whom Paul asserted to be alive" (25:19).

At the outset and throughout his sequel, then, Luke constructs the nature of the principal leadership in his account of the early Christian movement—the twelve apostles, Peter, and Paul—in such a way as to build into this structure the necessity of a historical connection to the life of Jesus precisely because this history impacts the task of testimony. That is to say, the Jesus who was killed has been resurrected and is now alive. The leaders are leaders because they know this story from the inside, as it were, and they therefore bear witness to it in a way that others do not. Such is the significance of a community that believes itself to be founded and funded by a particular, irreplaceable story in which the definitive act of the God who is "the Lord of heaven and earth" (Luke 10:21; Acts 17:24) is fastened to the life history of Jesus from Nazareth.

Equality and Elevation: Concluding Reflections on Authority, Ethics, and Acts

In light of the foregoing discussion, we may put simply the questions that guide our concluding reflections: How does the deep concern for anthropological equality relate to the elevation of certain persons of the larger Christian community in the narrative, and what might our attempt to answer this question tell us about the construal of authority in the narrative of Acts?

The first of three steps is to note that commitments to anthropological equality and to the appointment of certain persons to positions of leadership stand in conflict with each other only if we accept the (modern) premise, noted at the beginning of the chapter, that authority is of necessity fundamentally detrimental to human beings. Acts, however, cannot be read profitably in these terms and this premise must be rejected. In marked contrast to much modern anthropology, for Luke the elevation of Paul and the apostles serves to underwrite human equality.[28]

---

28. Campenhausen, *Ecclesiastical Authority*, 13, is thus wrong to set equality and au-

Yet such underwriting occurs not because Luke perceives and articulates a natural truth about humanity or social life—it is self-evident, for example, that all human beings are by nature created equal, but nonetheless for decent civil life need the order that results from structures of authority: "We hold these truths to be self-evident, that all men are created equal, that they are endowed by their Creator with certain unalienable rights ... That to secure these rights, governments are instituted."[29] Instead, Luke's underwriting of human equality occurs for the sake of the witness to the God of Israel's act in the resurrection of Jesus. Luke does not first reflect upon the "good" that no human may be called κοινός or ἀκάθαρτος—the unity of Jew and Gentile—and from this good then draw the conclusion that the story of the death and resurrection of Jesus is helpful ethically and, hence, important. Much to the contrary, the particular narrative of which the "authoritative voices," to borrow from Alasdair MacIntyre,[30] are the principal bearers is the same narrative that roots the equality of humanity in the identity of the resurrected and exalted Jesus as Lord of all (κύριος πάντων) and, indeed, in the very nature of God as the one who is generous to all (προσωπολήμπτης). The latter section on the "elevation of some" is the narrative and conceptual presupposition of the former section on human equality: the story that Peter and Paul know from the inside is that which fully includes Gentiles under the dominion of the same Lord.

Thus we may say in a second step that in Lukan perspective authority is constitutive of community. It is significant that those who devote themselves to the teaching (διδαχή) of the apostles are concurrently involved in communal fellowship (κοινωνία), the breaking of bread and praying together that is the life of the early church (Acts 2:42). As in the account of Cornelius, so in Antioch, Iconium, and elsewhere, to live in the story of the dominion of the κύριος πάντων is to be in fellowship with "the other," Jew and Gentile. In this sense, authority is not really "top-down" as we usually think of it, with a

---

thority in opposition: "In the primitive community freedom reigns, but not equality. At no time is there a lack of outstanding personalities with their own particular vocation and authority." Cf., in a different context, Michel Foucault, *Discipline and Punish: The Birth of the Prison* (New York: Vintage Books, 1977), esp. 222, on the relation of discipline and equality.

29. The Declaration of Independence of the United States of America. The text of the Declaration of Independence can be found in many places, including the back of many good American dictionaries. For a convenient link to the text, as well as other information relevant to its history, go to www.ushistory.org/declaration.

30. Alasdair MacIntyre, "Patients as Agents," in *Philosophical Medical Ethics: Its Nature and Significance*, ed. Stuart F. Spicker and H. Tristram Engelhardt Jr. (Boston: Reidel, 1977), 200.

Part 1: Christology, Greco-Roman Culture, and Canonical Reception

few skilled elite controlling the masses, but instead "bottom-up" or supportive. For the dissolution of "us" and "them," the community depends upon, or stands upon, the authority of the message that itself provides the ground of this dissolution.

Finally, then, to think about authority in Lukan perspective is to refuse essentially negative accounts of authority in which authority is basically injurious to human flourishing or, at best, a necessary evil. Neither would it be right, however, to think of authority as a "good," something worth pursuing in itself; rather, perhaps it can be thought of as a possibility or condition in human community under which the common good is pursued and indeed furthered. Or, to put it more directly into Lukan terms: The resurrection and exaltation of Jesus the Lord (κύριος), to which the apostles, Peter, and Paul bear decisive witness, discloses the character of God toward all humanity. This divine character is itself explicated socially in a community in which need is addressed, possessions are shared, meals are eaten together, and defining boundaries of separation are broken.

Part 2

BIBLICAL STUDIES AND THEOLOGY IN PRACTICE

READINGS IN PAUL

St. Paul and the Moral Law

INTRODUCTION

Although St. Paul's thought has often been examined in discussions of natural law, on first glance it is not obvious that he would actually have had much to say about a universal moral law.[1] When Paul speaks of "law," he most frequently means the Torah, the Law given to the Jews by the God of Israel. The Jews were God's elect people, and Law was the pattern of life that expressed and maintained their covenant with God and publicly distinguished them from all non-Jews.[2] In Paul's thought, Torah is not equivalent to a universal moral

---

1. Paul nevertheless figures frequently in religious discussions of natural law. See, e.g., Jane Adolphe, Robert L. Fastiggi, and Michael Vacca, eds., *St. Paul, the Natural Law, and Contemporary Legal Theory* (Lanham, MD: Lexington Books, 2012). It is important to note that the meaning of the expression "natural law" has also undergone profound change in the modern world. See, inter alia, Russell Hittinger, "Natural Law and Catholic Moral Theology," in *A Preserving Grace: Protestants, Catholics, and Natural Law*, ed. Michael Cromartie (Grand Rapids: Eerdmans, 1997), 1–30. For the purposes of this chapter, I use the terms "universal moral law," "moral law," and "natural law" in as rudimentary a sense as possible: they mean the basic, normative way we are supposed to be in the world that can be discerned simply by thinking/observing/arguing with others, etc. Legitimate debate could be had about whether natural law and universal moral law mean or refer to the same thing. In my view, if one speaks of a/the moral law, one invokes norms that trade on metaphysical affirmations and commitments; if one speaks of natural law, one also invokes norms that trade on metaphysical affirmations and commitments. Whether the two sets of metaphysical affirmations and commitments are identical or not would vary depending on what exactly was intended by "moral" and "natural." In short, the words will mean what we use them to mean.

2. On the complicated question of the "Noachide" commandments and whether Jews thought Gentiles were expected to keep certain pre-Mosaic laws, see, inter alia, Markus

---

"St. Paul and the Moral Law" was originally published in *Christianity and Global Law*, ed. Rafael Domingo and John Witte Jr. (New York: Routledge, 2020), 17–30. Republished with permission of Taylor & Francis Informa UK Ltd – Books; permission conveyed through Copyright Clearance Center, Inc.

Part 2: Biblical Studies and Theology in Practice

law. In fact, the most likely ancient progenitors of much current natural law discussion were the Stoics.[3]

On further reflection, however, we can see in Paul several critical points about the way that human beings are, and are supposed to be, in the world that constructively intersect today's questions about a universal moral law. In this chapter, I discuss the principal Pauline passages that should figure in any treatment of Paul and natural law, and then reflect briefly on the theological consequences of the exegesis for the shape of Christian thought about global law.

Texts

Because Paul wrote so much of what is in the NT, it can be difficult to know where to focus. Yet there clearly are places in his letters and in NT traditions about him that are most relevant to our question. Those places are in his letter to the Romans and in the Acts of the Apostles. We must say clearly, however, that the following passages are treated in relation to Paul's overall theology and its reception in Acts rather than simply lifted out of context and made to speak on a contemporary question. All too often in the history of exegesis, readers of Scripture have practiced hermeneutical "snatch-a-verse" and reflected on a wider question in light of passages that are distorted by leaving their original grammatical home behind. Insofar as we seek Paul's wisdom on the question of natural law, we will have to read him—and his reception—in the context that gives his words their specifically Pauline meaning.[4]

Bockmuehl, *Jewish Law in Gentile Churches: Halakhah and the Beginning of Christian Public Ethics* (Edinburgh: T&T Clark, 2000), 145–73.

3. The Stoics are actually more complex and would not mean by "nature" what it is frequently taken to mean today. I have written about the meaning of Stoic words elsewhere; see in relation to the topic of this chapter, for example, the section on the words "God and World" in Rowe, *One True Life: The Stoics and Early Christians as Rival Traditions* (New Haven: Yale University Press, 2016), 226–28. Some scholars, of course, trace natural law back to Plato, but one would need to demonstrate that Plato's use of "nature" or of "law" or of "reason," and so on, means what is meant in any given modern natural law discussion to know that the continuity between the posited point of origin and current debate was real. See the discussion in Michael Bertram Crowe, *The Changing Profile of the Natural Law* (The Hague: Martinus Nijhoff, 1977), 1–27.

4. There are other passages one could read, of course, but sooner or later these must figure prominently. One could also think automatically of 1 Cor 6:1–11 in relation to Gentile courts of law, or Rom 13:1–7 in relation to various forms of government, but there are

Romans

On any account, Romans is Paul's most theologically elaborate missive. It is also the letter in which he deals most explicitly with the question of the Gentile knowledge of God. Precisely because Romans is an account of God's dealings with the Jews in past history and now in Christ Jesus, Paul finds that he must also write about the Gentiles' relation to God. To think about Israel's election in light of Christ is, for Paul, simultaneously to think about how the Gentiles fit into that history.

Romans 1:1–3:31

As most NT scholars now recognize, Romans 1:1–3:31 is the first major section of the letter. On the way to his main point, Paul deals extensively with Gentile knowledge of and obedience to the God of Israel. For the purposes of this chapter, four key points emerge from Paul's opening argument. First, Paul clearly affirms that God's creative power is written into creation in an obvious enough way that it makes sense to say God "has revealed" to everyone aspects of what it is to be God—namely, his eternal "God-ness" and "power" (1:19–20). This revelation is quite specific at this point: there is no mention of a divine law, moral or otherwise; Paul speaks of what later came to be called God's attributes.

Second, Paul characterizes the Gentile response to God's self-revelation in creation as rejection. Though they can "know God" in the sense of some divine attributes, the Gentiles have refused this knowledge: "Claiming to be wise, they became fools" (1:22). Their "reasonings" are not knowledge in any significant sense; they are, rather, senselessness, darkness, confusion, a covering over of the heart.[5]

---

many others. Richard Cassidy, e.g., focuses on 2 Timothy in "St. Paul: Between the Law of Caesar and the Justice of Christ in Second Timothy," and Mary Healy on Eph 5 in "St. Paul, Ephesians 5, and Same-Sex Marriage"; both essays are in Adolphe, Fastiggi, and Vacca, *St. Paul, the Natural Law, and Contemporary Legal Theory*, 1–20, 147–59, respectively. For the commitment to reception history as a hermeneutically illuminating way to understand an earlier writer's positions or the range of a text's plausible field of meaning, see Markus Bockmuehl, *Seeing the Word: Refocusing New Testament Study*, Studies in Theological Interpretation (Grand Rapids: Baker Academic, 2006).

5. Reading this passage to affirm that the Gentiles do in fact "have some knowledge of what is right and good through the law of creation and through conscience" is such a common mistake that one can pick an example almost at random. I cite Carl Braaten because of his indisputably excellent contributions to theology. It is therefore all the more striking

Part 2: Biblical Studies and Theology in Practice

Third, Paul's adduced evidence for this description of Gentile reasoning is not that Gentiles make poor analytic arguments, have no intellectual sophistication, or draw the wrong conclusions from what would otherwise be laudable insights. The evidence is practice. The Gentiles live in ways that disclose the worship of creation rather than God. The "truth" is that only God should be worshiped, but precisely by the way they live, the Gentiles show that their knowledge of God is a lie—idolatry (1:25).

Fourth, in 2:14–16 Paul states that

> whenever Gentiles who do not have the Law by nature do the things of the Law, even though they do not have the Law, they are a Law to themselves. These [Gentiles] manifest the work of the Law, written on their hearts, while at the same time their conscience also witnesses and among them their thoughts accuse or perhaps excuse them on that day when God will judge the secrets of men according to my Gospel through Christ Jesus.[6]

Throughout the history of discussion of non-Christian knowledge of God's law, these verses have been used repeatedly to argue that Paul believes in natural law. But in the context of the epistle, they actually say something quite different.

Paul's point is not that some Gentiles happen to know the universal moral law and behave accordingly while others do not. Nor is it that God has decided to write the moral precepts of the created order on some hearts and not others. Paul's point in the context of Romans is rather that God's promises in Jeremiah are now fulfilled in the life of Gentile Christians. The "new covenant" declaration from Jeremiah 31:31–34 (38:31–34 LXX) is brought to life in the ability of Gentile Christians to walk in the way of Torah. Torah, of course, is not a universal moral law but the covenant of the God of Israel with his people. Speaking of the Gentile Christians who do not have the Torah by birth but who, because of their reception of God's Spirit, exhibit the purpose of Torah in their lives makes an excellent transition to an argument against negligent Jewish Christians who do have the Torah by birth but whose lives testify against it (Rom 2:17–29). The counterpoint is rhetorically striking and effective.[7] The

---

that such a common mistake finds its way into his arguments about natural law. See Carl E. Braaten, "Response to Russell Hittinger," in Cromartie, *A Preserving Grace*, 36.

6. By nature (*physei*) is meant here "by birth"—i.e., they are not Jewish and thus are not born into the way of life that is Torah. *Physei*, that is, should not be read with *poiein* to require the translation "do by nature."

7. Moreover, it would make little sense to point to the observance of a/the natural law as the move to set up the discussion of Jewish Christian behavior that follows.

question at this point in Romans is about the place of the Gentiles vis-à-vis the election of Israel, not what morally praiseworthy behavior the Gentiles might have been up to in the world at large.[8] On that matter Paul has already decisively spoken only a few verses before (1:18–32).

Romans 1:1–3:31 contain the loci classici of Paul's alleged endorsement of a natural law. Paul's actual argument, however, complicates the attempt to find a universal moral law in his thought. In this section of Romans, Paul does not extol the "natural" knowledge of God or talk about a universal moral law. What he says instead is that the way that Gentile reason interacts with what God has revealed of himself in creation is idolatrously to distort that revelation. Quite in the face of the way God made the world, reason goes its own way, and that own way leads not to a discovery of God's attributes or to a law that reflects God's will for human behavior but to the absolutizing of creation. Reason here, for Paul, is not an abstract capacity native to all human beings but reason at work; and reason at work moves not toward God's revelation in creation but toward cloudiness, darkness, and brokenness. Gentile patterns of life are constitutive of the knowledge they possess, and such knowledge is, for Paul, tantamount to ignorance. The Gentiles have forsaken the truth and live a lie.

Romans 6–8

After treating the figures of Abraham and Adam (chs. 4 and 5), Paul turns toward the character of Christian existence within a creation that still longs for eschatological redemption (chs. 6–8). Two major points from this section of the letter bear on our current question. First is Paul's theological anthropology. In stark contrast to certain modern notions of human freedom, in which we will to choose what we choose and cannot be forced to choose anything that we do not will for ourselves, Paul's view of humanity is that we exist in slavery. Baptism into the reality of Christ's death and resurrection marks the transition from one slavery to another. Paradoxically, perhaps, this second slavery is for Paul what true freedom is (6:15–23). We do not move freely from one kind of unfettered self to another. Prior to baptism we are dominated by powers that are in principle beyond the power of our will: sin and death. We are slaves to sin and move in patterns of death. Upon transition to the true Lord, we

---

8. On the current interpretation and history of discussion of this passage, see especially Simon Gathercole, "A Law unto Themselves: The Gentiles in Romans 2.14–15 Revisited," *JSNT* 24, no. 3 (2002): 27–49.

become slaves to him—which is to say, we are freed from sin and death—and discover the patterns that lead to life eternal (6:23; ch. 7).

Second is Paul's understanding of creation. Like his fellow Jews, Paul believed both that the God of Israel created the world and declared it good and that the present world was in need of healing due to Adam's fall and paled in comparison to the world to come. In Romans 8, however, Paul teaches the Roman church that their understanding of the world cannot be separated from their understanding of Jesus Christ and the active work of the Holy Spirit. The healing has already begun (8:22–30). It is here *now*. But precisely because this healing is also and inextricably linked to hope, Paul describes the creation as still existing "in bondage to decay" (8:21). The healing of creation is *not yet* complete. The creation still waits "with eager longing" for the consummation of God's work in Christ.

What Paul's argument in Romans 6–8 means for an attempt to find a universal moral law is of course varied and complex. But two points stand out. The first relates to anthropology: an account of a universal moral law that presupposes a human knower whose mind can work unfettered by sin and darkness runs directly counter to Paul's view of human possibilities. At the very least, the quality of human knowledge, according to Paul, would always be bound up with the question of the will; there is no mind that can serve the Lord's truth apart from the will that is enslaved to one master or another. A thinking mind whose thoughts are free from the will's *dominus* is as un-Pauline an abstraction as is conceivable.[9]

The second point relates to the context in which one could (or not) discern a/the natural law—namely, creation. For Paul, creation is not an inert data set about which a debate could be had over whether a moral law can be discerned. The idea that one could read "universal law" off the face of creation is severely problematized by Paul's insistence that creation itself is in need of healing—that is, that it "presents" as broken. It may well be that those who are "in Christ" can see the healing that has begun, but apart from that discernment, the testimony of creation to the God who made it remains one not of natural law but of groaning.

Taken together, Paul's theological anthropology and understanding of creation mean that human beings emerge in a world in which we are already

---

9. Moreover, the coordination of sin and will means that even if there were a law to be discovered, we could not unproblematically obey it, as Paul forcefully argues in Rom 7:14–25, for example. The point of discovering a universal law we cannot obey makes sense in certain tendencies of Luther's law/gospel theology, but it is hard to account for otherwise.

caught. We long for freedom, redemption, and therapy, but we lack the fundamental power to bring them about. Without fail, we hinder ourselves time and again, and we are further ruined by active powers that seek to harm us. However Paul's theology might bear on the question of law, it will always impart a sobering sense that, in relation to the moral life, laws do not run deep enough to create the flourishing that human beings long for, the justice we strive for, and the healing we hope for.

ACTS OF THE APOSTLES

The Acts of the Apostles presents the bulk of the "canonical Paul," the Paul as he was interpretatively received and remembered. Acts narrates the earliest extended interpretation of Pauline missionary theology and, as such, offers ample opportunity for reflection on what this Paul makes of the wider Roman world. From all the rich material in Acts, two passages and their themes are most relevant for this chapter.[10]

Paul and Athens

When it comes to the question of the NT and pagan philosophy, no text is quite so beloved as Paul's Areopagus speech in Acts 17. There, it is often assumed, we see the quintessential endorsement of the wisdom of the Greeks and a translation of Christian truth into insights the Greeks share. This standard interpretation, however, fares poorly with a closer reading of the speech in the context of Acts itself. Removed from that context, Paul's speech could mean anything we make of it, but within its narrative home, the speech works to transform the meaning of pagan words rather than to endorse them on their own.

Ancient readers were given their first clues to the hermeneutical direction of Paul's speech by the introductory remarks. Athens is described as a place not of exalted university knowledge but of idolatry: "While Paul was waiting for them in Athens, he became vexed because he saw that the city was full of idols" (17:16). Paul's preaching is received not as the truth of all things but

10. It is customary in the modern period for NT scholars to argue that the Paul of Acts and the Paul of the Epistles should be kept apart. For certain tasks this makes some sense. But I take Bockmuehl's larger methodological point in *Seeing the Word* about "reception" to be correct, and apply it here in this way: in an attempt to assess the range of the NT's Paul for the question of a universal moral law, we would do well to examine his immediate reception within the NT text that most directly and elaborately speaks to this question.

as advocacy for the polytheistic worship of Jesus and another deity named "Resurrection" (17:18). Paul's vocabulary is heard not as evidence of real philosophical refinement but as the pretentious pretending of a poser (*spermologos*, v. 18). And Paul is not welcomed by the leading authorities but seized, arrested, and put on trial before the Areopagus Court. In short, Athens is a place where, immediately on its arrival, Christianity is misinterpreted, maligned, and manhandled. Readers of Paul's speech take this knowledge with them as they listen to Paul's defense before the Areopagus.

Typical defense speeches by the rhetorically trained opened with a *captatio benevolentiae*—an attempt to win the goodwill of the judge/audience—and prima facie Paul's is no different. "Men of Athens! I perceive that in every way you are *deisidaimonesteros*!" (17:22). The word *deisidaimonesteros*, however, is ambiguous. It can mean either "very religious" (a compliment) or "highly superstitious" (an insult). This skillfully placed ambiguity directs the reader to look for multilevel meaning in Paul's words as the speech unfolds.

Three brief examples will suffice to show the importance of the ambiguity for interpreting the speech.[11] First, in 17:23 Paul mentions an inscription he saw on his way through Athens that read "to an unknown god" and comments: "What, therefore, you worship unknowingly (ignorantly), I announce to you." Paul's immediate purpose is to ward off the charges of "bringing in strange and new teaching" by situating his preaching within Athenian history and culture. Paul knew that a conviction on these charges—the charges Socrates himself faced—was lethal. I'm not bringing in anything new, Paul suggests, because what I proclaim to you is the God who made heaven and earth (v. 24)—that God precedes even Athens! On the surface, it looks as though Paul says that the Athenians have been worshiping the true God all along, only they did not know it. As Paul moves on, however, the surface interpretation becomes more complicated, and the sense emerges that the theological stress of the phrase lies on their *ignorance*: what you worship ignorantly—that is, *without* theological knowledge.

Second, in 17:27, after extolling the creative power of "the God who made the world and everything in it," Paul speaks of this God's creative purpose for human beings: God made them so that "they should seek God in the hope that they might grope after him and find him. *And yet*, God is not far from each one of us." The language echoes what many philosophers would have eagerly affirmed. Paul's contemporary Seneca, for example, knew that "God

---

11. For fuller discussion, see C. Kavin Rowe, *World Upside Down: Reading Acts in the Graeco-Roman Age* (Oxford: Oxford University Press, 2009), 27–41.

was near you, with you, in you" (*Ep.* 41.1), which of course is to say that God was not far from each of us. There was no real need, Seneca knew, to go to the temples, offer sacrifices, and so on. But again Paul's words reveal another layer. "You shall seek the Lord your God and you will find him, if you search after him with all your heart and with all your soul" (Deut 4:29; Isa 55:6). The biblical text is in fact Paul's theological reservoir, the deep well from which his statement to the Areopagus is drawn. The ambiguity of the words discloses Paul's point: the God of Israel is the God whom humans are to seek. *And yet*, they have not found God. That is, Paul does not say here that the Gentiles have groped and found the God of Israel but that—*even though God is close to each one of us*—they have *not* found him. "These times of ignorance God has overlooked," Paul later continues, characterizing Gentile theological knowledge as "unknowing." On closer inspection, Paul's nearness language thus turns out to say something quite different from the pagan philosophers: even though God is so close, he has *not* been found; he is *unknown*. The image is of people groping around in the dark after something they cannot find but which stands ever so near to them.

Third, in 17:28 Paul finishes his statements about the relation between God and humanity by quoting from the opening lines of the hymn to Zeus in the Stoic Aratus's *Phaenomena*, an astrological book that was exceptionally popular in the ancient world: "we are his offspring." Read in its linguistic home, "we are his offspring" means quite simply that by nature human beings participate with their reason in the reason that is the structure of the eternally cycling cosmos. This structuring reason is often called "God" or "gods" or "Providence" and the like. Aratus's line expresses the coordination of same nature—human mind and the reason of the cosmic cycle. Paul, however, means something quite different. His reference is to Israel's Scriptures, specifically to Genesis 1 and 2, the God of Israel, and that God's image of himself in the creature he made and named *Adam* (Hebrew; Greek *anthrōpos*, "human being"). Unlike his near Jewish contemporary Aristobulus, Paul does not posit a metaphysical identity between the god mentioned in the *Phaenomena* and the God of Israel, or between the reason of humanity and that of Zeus; his point is, instead, that human beings find their lives enclosed within the scriptural story of the Jews. When Paul then mentions that we all come from one human being (*anthrōpos*), he invokes typical Stoic doctrine only to subvert it by means of the allusion to Adam. And by the end of the speech, the man whom God has appointed to bring justice to the world is, as all readers of Acts know, Jesus of Nazareth. "We are his offspring" is transformed to mean that the totality of human life is determined by our existence between Adam and Jesus.

Part 2: Biblical Studies and Theology in Practice

While many readers of Paul's defense speech before the Areopagus have seen him to be making an attempt to validate Greek philosophical insights and religious impulses, paying close attention to the way the language works in context reveals a different purpose. By the end of the speech, the terms of philosophical/religious discourse have been reset inside the biblical tradition and transfigured in light of the gospel. Their meaning is different from what they would mean in their host systems and texts, and they now testify on Paul's terms to the claim that Gentile knowledge of the God of Israel is best named as ignorance. As NT scholar C. K. Barrett once put it: "From nature the Greeks have evolved not natural theology but natural idolatry."[12]

Paul's Roman Citizenship and Trial in Acts

From at least Theodor Mommsen on, scholars of Roman jurisprudence have regularly noted the remarkable historical value in Acts' record of Paul's Roman citizenship and trial. The trial also raises fundamental questions about early Christianity's views of Roman law and what these views mean for a consideration of a universal moral law. Several points are in order.

First, as Acts presents it, Paul quite obviously knows and makes use of Roman legal traditions as he moves through his initial arrest, trial, and defense (*apologia*) in Acts. In the face of the lawyer Tertullus's accusation that Paul is the ringleader of the sect of the Nazarenes, for example, Paul cleverly redescribes his movement as taking one side of a much larger and inner-Jewish debate. He thereby makes use of the typical Roman legal posture toward such debates—that is, they have nothing to do with Roman law and should be settled by the Jews themselves (see the comment by Gallio, the governor of Achaea, in Acts 18:14–15). Contra the charge that he is guilty of riot-inducing sedition (*stasis*), Paul says instead that he came simply and piously to bring his people alms and offerings (24:16–17). And in defense of the accusation that he corrupted the Jerusalem temple, Paul flatly denies it and draws attention to the significant fact that his accusers are absent. Roman law technically required that a defendant's accusers be present; their absence constituted *destitutio* and could lead to the dismissal of the charges or even counter-charges.[13] And, finally, when the chips are down and it appears that Paul should and will be released—a verdict that accords with the evidence but that will also get him

---

12. C. K. Barrett, *A Critical and Exegetical Commentary on the Acts of the Apostles*, 2 vols., ICC (London: T&T Clark, 1998), 2:850–51.

13. Rowe, *World Upside Down*, 77.

ambushed and killed—Paul sets in motion an appeals process that will take him all the way to the imperial court in Rome. "I appeal to Caesar" (25:11) is a legal maneuver par excellence. Even the Roman governor Festus is now bound, as King Agrippa II makes clear to him: "This man could have been freed if he had not appealed to Caesar" (26:32). Someone who was unaware of Roman jurisprudence could never have pulled this trick out at just the right time and in front of just the right people, as Paul so skillfully did.

Paul also knew how to use his Roman citizenship for the advantage of Christians and to maneuver his way through tight spots for the sake of the gospel. In the Roman colony of Philippi, for example, Paul waits until the day after the magistrates have imprisoned him to let them know that he is a Roman citizen. When the magistrates send their soldiers secretly to let Paul out, he says to them, "[The magistrates] have beaten us publicly, uncondemned, men who are Roman citizens, and have thrown us into prison; and do they now cast us out secretly? No! Let them come themselves and take us out." This ace up the sleeve achieves the desired effect: Paul receives a public apology, the guard's life is saved, and the Christian community in Philippi gains a measure of protection. Paul of course could have simply informed the colony's officials on the previous day that he was a citizen and as such had legal privileges that should be respected. But he does not. He waits until the opportune time and then presses his advantage.

So, too, he knows that it is "illegal" to scourge a Roman citizen before trial (though of course in reality it was done). But Paul allows himself to be chained and stretched out for the flogging before he says, "Is it lawful for you to scourge a man who is a Roman citizen and uncondemned?" (22:25). He thereby gains a significant measure of tactical control vis-à-vis the Roman tribune Claudius Lysias. According to the logic of the narrative, Paul's motive here is not to save his hide. He is quite willing to suffer for the gospel, as he has made clear and put into practice time and again. His intent, rather, is to create the political wiggle room necessary for him to work between a rock and a hard place (the Jewish leadership who wish him dead and the Roman tribune who will punish capitally the one responsible for riotous commotion). Absent this room, Paul's life is forfeit and the chance to get to Rome eliminated. By taking advantage of the law of the saeculum, however, Paul secures time and space to move forward in his mission.

In Acts as a whole, then, Paul is nowhere depicted as knowing about or endorsing a universal moral law, but he is shown to be legally savvy in a manner that makes sense only with the supposition that some important aspects of Roman law have been well learned and that the Roman legal matrix is a me-

Part 2: Biblical Studies and Theology in Practice

dium within which Christians can maneuver for their benefit. The canonical Paul clearly puts Roman law to use in ways that, practically speaking, claim it as a relative or occasional good. Theologically put, Roman law can be said to serve God's purposes. Yet such service is clearly only ad hoc, and even in Acts it does not rise to the level of a universal good or norm. Roman law, for example, cannot save Jesus; nor can it save Paul. They are both declared innocent, and yet they are both arrested, tried, and eventually executed.[14]

The Pauline Contribution to the Question of a/the Universal Moral Law

There are other NT texts one could consider, but reading the main lines of Paul's thought in Romans and the reception of Paul in Acts brings us quickly to several central judgments about the Pauline contribution to the question of a universal moral law. First, and perhaps most surprisingly for Christian advocates of natural law, Pauline theology cannot be used to testify to the epistemic availability of a universal moral law. The most that can be said is that creation testifies to some of God's attributes, but human beings as such cannot see them; the attributes are hidden by the patterns of life that make the creation into the object of worship. The people named Israel/Church can receive knowledge about God and the law he wills, but this knowledge is the Torah and the life given by God's Spirit written on the hearts of those who believe. Absent the knowledge of God given from his side of things, God remains unknown, even though we are all his offspring.

Second, laws of the saeculum are not universal moral laws, even if they can on this or that occasion deliver justice (*dikē*). But they can be learned and productively used by Pauline Christians. Roman law, for example, can serve the Christian community's larger purpose by enabling Paul to escape Jerusalem and reach Rome. And a knowledge of Athenian legal history and traditions can enable Paul deftly to avoid what is in his view an untimely execution. Yet such laws are only ad hoc instances of good and cannot be relied upon to produce behavior that is consistently in accordance with the norms of the

---

14. Of course Acts does not portray Paul's death as the gospel does that of Jesus. But the reader of Acts knows about Paul's death and can see the foreshadowing again and again in the way Acts tells about Paul's mission (in his speech to the Ephesian elders, for example, in Acts 20:17–38). On this point, see especially Charles H. Talbert, *Reading Acts: A Literary and Theological Commentary on the Acts of the Apostles*, Reading the New Testament (Macon, GA: Smyth & Helwys, 2005), 231.

gospel or even with a relative justice. The Corinthian Christians lamentably use secular law to take each other to court, and pagan governors order imprisonment or execution or both.[15] As philosopher Hans-Georg Gadamer saw, in a deeply significant sense there is no real understanding of law without its human application: the application of the law is law. Theologically considered, the discernment needed to make good use of a secular law is bound up with the will of the discerner, which is to say that being enslaved to the masters of sin and death matters for one's perception of the good in law.

Third, Pauline anthropology leads directly to a question raised pointedly in the title of Luther's classic *The Bondage of the Will*. Put succinctly: the *is*, the *ought*, and the *can* or *cannot* all go together in a complex cluster of intertwined judgments. Taking a position on the existence of a universal moral law entails concomitant positions not only on human knowledge but also on our practical capacity and what we should expect to see in the exceedingly vast scope of human behavior. The matter of a universal moral law, that is, is not just noetic; it is a matter of possibilities of and actual being in the world. If human beings can know God's moral law but cannot do it, then we should not expect to track God's law in the life patterns of unregenerate humanity.[16] What we should expect instead, at least on Pauline terms, is something like evidence of its contradiction—the world testifies to God's law precisely through its inability to do it.[17] Between the view that our wills exist in bondage and cannot get to the good no matter how diligently we try and the view that they need only some divinely enlightened educational direction to do the good—pedagogically provided, say, by teachers who know the good toward which we should aim—there exists a substantive distance not only with respect to the problem of the will but also and simultaneously with respect to what we make

---

15. Interestingly, Tertullian, ever the lawyer he was trained to be, argues that the Roman practice here contradicts Roman law (i.e., there is no identifiable crime that goes with the name Christian—as stealing goes with thief, for example—and yet the Christians are treated as criminals and punished as such). This argument is an instance of ad hoc reasoning with the law to criticize its unjust application. See Tertullian's *Apology*.

16. On this point, see Susan E. Schreiner, "Calvin's Use of Natural Law," and Daniel Westberg, "The Reformed Tradition and Natural Law," both in Cromartie, *A Preserving Grace*, 51–76, 103–17, respectively.

17. Such evidence could, of course, be quite complicated in any of its particular instantiations. For example, we might observe that some peoples have the explicitly articulated prohibition against killing and think that this reflects knowledge of God's law. Paul's reply would likely move from this theoretical or noetic judgment (epistemology) to the practice (practical reason): but they kill anyway. The critical Pauline test for God's law is what we could call the *regula vitae*, that is, whether it shows up in life as the law that is lived.

Part 2: Biblical Studies and Theology in Practice

of the natural law's impact, or promise for human community, and how we see it showing up in the world. For the apostle Paul, the inability to do what God requires is the heart of the matter. The moral grain of humanity is no grain at all; it is, quite simply, the consequence of the broken will's wayward ways. Insofar as God's self-revelation can be seen "naturally" in the world, it shows up as rejection. Of course, to read human behavior of whatever kind as a rejection of the way God intends us to be rather than as just one more variation on the way humans go about being human, or to see signs of a created order rather than just a collection of variously and momentarily arranged phenomena, is already to reason Christianly about the whole ball of wax—which, after all, is what Paul is trying to do.

Fourth, taking Paul seriously for reflection on a universal moral law illustrates the truth of the crucial point made by Russell Hittinger and others that the difference between Christian and modern secular discourse about a "natural law" is grammatically—and thus substantively—vast. It may, on first glance, look as if all current discussants of a moral or natural law are talking about more or less the same thing. They use the same term, after all. But as we have learned from Wittgenstein, the "language game" in which a word is played, as it were, provides the context for word meaning. And the use of the word in that game provides the concept, or a related cluster of them, that one has. Use a word differently or in a different game and the concepts are different. Different language games, different use, different meaning, different concepts. When, therefore, the term "natural law" is used on the one hand to talk about the way the God of Jesus Christ intends human beings to be in the world and, on the other, is used to talk about the way human beings construct and live out their sense of self and its obligations in a world in which the Christian God does not exist, "natural law" means radically different things, and the conceptual arrangements that go with the respective uses are thus also seriously different. No amount of overlapping speech about "rights" or "dignity" or anything of that sort makes the understanding of "nature" or "law" or "natural law" turn out to exhibit the same, shared sense of what the world is or requires of its human citizens.

There are, indisputably, momentary convergences of judgment on this or that question of action or behavior. But these should be seen as historically contingent—some of them of course already influenced by the long history and deep penetration of Christianity in jurisprudential theorizing about the human being in virtually all forms in the North Atlantic West. Such ad hoc historically contingent convergences should be wisely celebrated, wisely taken advantage of, wisely made much of in legal practice, and so on, but they should not be mistaken for agreements based in a shared understanding of a universal moral law.[18] As time rolls on and cultural mores shift, these contingent agreements always can, and in many instances will, gradually disappear and become evident in retrospect not as the truths of natural law but as consequences or coincidences of history.[19] It is the way things have gone, not the way things must and always will go. Christians should not, therefore, be tempted into thinking that God can be sidelined for what we make of human behavior. Any Christian speech about a "universal moral law" that is informed by St. Paul means the way the God of Jesus Christ intends us to be in the world. If others speak of a moral or natural law but reject the Christian account of reality, then they use the same term but speak of something else.

Concluding Reflections

Whether or not Christians should make or endorse particular claims about a universal moral law depends, of course, on vastly more than a few NT texts. Whatever could be said about such a law, however, could not be said in direct contradiction to these texts without forfeiting—on this point at least—the practice that is Christian reasoning. On the basis of the foregoing exegesis, then, there are two final points worth making about the intersection of the biblical texts with the question of natural law.

The first point concerns Christian freedom. The lack of a universal moral law highlights the great freedom Christians have to work with or against—or ignore—any given law or set of laws. Our vision for the habits of our being is given in our theological understanding of reality, and that includes what we make of law(s). We do not, that is, start off discerning the precepts of a universal moral law and note how these precepts fit with Christian convictions about norms for various human behaviors or are supplemented by them. Instead, we begin reasoning Christianly and discern the fit between what we know to be

---

18. For an example of how "convergences" or ad hoc agreements can be put constructively to work without large-scale moral theories or background notions of universally binding norms, see H. Tristram Engelhardt Jr., *The Foundations of Bioethics*, 2nd ed. (Oxford: Oxford University Press, 1996).

19. Even as others might appear. The point is not that everything common will disappear but that things in common are ad hoc and will shift. Christians should be wisely alert to things in common and make of them practically what we are able to make of them. But we should not be fooled into thinking—to put it in Wittgensteinian terms—that secular grammar and Christian grammar are the rules of the same language.

Part 2: Biblical Studies and Theology in Practice

true and what shows up in the world at any given moment as law—whether that law is of the "state" sort, or transnational, or simply the currently prevailing claims of particular cultures and societies about the way human beings are or ought to be in the world ("rights" for example). This means that Christian life is essentially ad hoc when it comes to law; ad hoc is the visionary posture, that is, of the freedom to be in the world as Christians. Christians are not bound by an allegedly universal moral code that turns out, on closer inspection or simply by the revelatory power of the march of time, to be yet one more instance of a particular culture's convictions, habits, or ideals about human behavior. We are free to reason about law in all its forms.[20]

The second point concerns the need for wisdom. If under scrutiny many of our dilemmas in the modern world disclose competing accounts of freedom(s), and if Christians claim that we are free vis-à-vis laws that are supposedly related to various understandings of freedom(s), it cannot be overemphasized that what we need to develop is wisdom. To be free without wisdom is to be waywardly and recklessly foolish, in which case freedom is tragically reversed and ad hoc judgments amount to wreckage. If we learn from St. Paul and his reception in the NT how to think constructively about law, what we will learn is that to reason well about Christianity and law requires immersion in practices that produce and ingrain the wisdom that is the stuff of Christian prudential judgment and maturity. We should not expect to find a universal moral law that could compel universal acknowledgment or create behavioral norms that could establish the just society for which humans long, somehow overriding the propensity of the human condition to go our own way and worship that which is not God. In the absence of a moral law that could command global assent and obedience, that is, what human societies need most is genuine wisdom. When it comes to law, it is through wise judgments that Christians can contribute to the hopes we share with others for the broadest possible human flourishing.

---

20. A slightly different way to put the point about freedom is to speak of critical distance. Freedom vis-à-vis human laws always implies a critical distance from any given law. It is this critical distance that is presupposed in the Romans' early worries about Christian "obstinacy." The Romans did not of course speak of "critical distance" as the Christian political posture. But it is the fact of that distance—the willingness to insert Christian theological understanding between Roman law and Christian obedience to it—that renders intelligible the Roman mystification at the Christian refusal to worship/sacrifice to the gods/emperor.

The Trinity in the Letters of St. Paul and Hebrews

> About this we have much to say that is hard to explain.
>
> —Hebrews 5:11

Prolegomena

As we know from ancient biblical manuscript evidence, Hebrews frequently circulated with the rest of the *corpus Paulinum* and was considered the fourteenth of Paul's letters. Indeed, even our earliest attested form of the Pauline letters includes Hebrews (P[46]). This did not, however, prevent ancient scholars from expressing serious reservations or outright doubts about the Pauline authorship of Hebrews. Tertullian, to mention a prominent example, believed the author was Barnabas. Origen was less sanguine: about the author of Hebrews, he said, "only God knows."

Today it is safe to say that most scholars would agree with the ancient skeptics against the view of authorship implied by the manuscript tradition and accepted by Jerome and Augustine (among many others). Though there is hardly a consensus about the identity of Hebrews' author—the suggestions are many and varied (Barnabas, Apollos, Silas, Priscilla, etc.)—it would be exceedingly difficult to find a modern NT scholar who would argue for the Pauline authorship of Hebrews. Indeed, it would be only slightly less difficult to find academics in the mainstream of NT scholarship who would argue for the Pauline authorship of all thirteen of the Pauline epistles. From a typical NT scholar's perspective, therefore, grouping these fourteen texts together is likely to seem artificial.

"The Trinity in the Letters of St. Paul and Hebrews" was originally published in *The Oxford Handbook of the Trinity*, ed. Gilles Emery and Matthew Levering (New York: Oxford University Press, 2011), 39–54. Reproduced with permission of the Licensor through PLSclear.

Part 2: Biblical Studies and Theology in Practice

Hermeneutically considered, however, a modern judgment of this kind is in fact no more than the concrete evidence of privileging a certain kind of interpretive commitment over others, the kind that believes that the NT texts should be arranged according to authorship (as it is critically reconstructed). But, as everyone knows, plenteous other schemata are on offer. We could, for example, organize the texts according to the drift of their reception history, their canonical order, their genre, their similarity in patterns of thought, and so on. In each case, the ordering of the texts would result from a particular hermeneutical posture vis-à-vis the canonical witness and would require—no less than presuppose—theological justification for its adoption. In the case of this chapter, the justification is rather simple: grouping Hebrews together with Paul allows us to inhabit a particular stream of Christian reflection on the biblical texts as a way to direct our attention to certain theologically productive modes of reading that have by and large been forgotten in the modern period.

Yet we would be mistaken were we to think that a Pauline/Hebrews organization in particular would facilitate a more Trinitarian reading than any other, or help us to draw more clearly the lines between Scripture and its dogmatic explication. The reason, of course, is that the doctrine of the Trinity is not based upon a particular ordering of only a few biblical texts. It is instead the antecedent theological logic of the Christian canon as a whole. Offering an ultimate justification for grouping all the letters attributed to Paul together with Hebrews is therefore not only unnecessary but, strictly speaking, impossible in a chapter focused on the connection between these texts and the doctrine of the Trinity. The working procedure herein is instead no more complicated than seeing how the Trinitarian framework helps us to read well the language about God in these texts. Methodologically considered, however, such a statement could point in any number of different directions, and we must therefore elucidate its intent for this particular chapter.

Approach

Taking Trinitarian doctrine as the hermeneutical lens through which we consider Paul's letters and Hebrews entails the following points as basic corollaries to the more fundamental shape of the inquiry.

1. The texts considered below are not to be read as evidence of "prooftexting" in the manner of the old *dicta probantia/classica*. Despite the disdain of modern critics, it is true that we can still learn much from this older way of reading Scripture. For example, we always have particular schemata that

The Trinity in the Letters of St. Paul and Hebrews

help to structure our reading of Scripture; we cannot think, that is, without ordering thought. The schemata of the *dicta classica* are clear—above board, so to speak—whereas those of contemporary NT scholars are frequently hidden behind false and illusory notions of an exegesis that prescinds from larger doctrinal commitments. Paying attention to an overt schema should help us to become more aware of the way in which the order of our thought already directs our exegetical attention in certain ways rather than others.

Still, it is hard to deny that the manner by which these compendia remove particular words or phrases from their more immediate scriptural contexts ignores hermeneutically what is prima facie one of the most striking aspects of holy Scripture itself—namely, that it has discrete literary units ("books"). Put more directly: the methodological moves of the older prooftexting approach occlude the theological significance of the surface shape of Scripture. If modern biblical studies has anything crucial to teach us in this respect, it is that engagement with the literary texture of Scripture's surface forms a critical part of fruitful interpretation in our own time.

2. The texts considered below are also not focused interpretively by "predication." To put it bluntly, for many interpreters of Scripture, modern biblical criticism destroyed the possibility of taking the *dicta probantia* seriously as a way to conceive constructively the relation between Scripture and the church's doctrinal teaching. They therefore sought other methods by which to connect the Bible with doctrinal explication. Prominent among these was a mode of reading whereby the NT was explored for passages in which, for example, the word *theos* (God) was predicated of Jesus (e.g., John 1:1, 18; Rom 9:5, etc.). Because of their immediate relevance to what it would mean to think of Jesus as divine, these texts were thought to help fund materially the doctrine of the Trinity.

There is doubtless much to learn from the collection of such passages, but the problem remains that the exegetical procedure is still vulnerable to the critique of more skeptical scholars who see this approach as the residue of an older method of reading Scripture that extracted small amounts of texts for a predetermined outcome. Attending more carefully to the immediate context of these statements, so it was argued, disclosed not so much the prefiguration of later doctrinal truths as it did a complex set of exegetical ambiguities (e.g., the significance of the anarthrous use of *theos* in John 1:1 for the *Logos*). In short, though the predication approach helped to direct our attention to striking features of the scriptural texts, it remained within the ambit of a kind of exegesis that was unable to deal with the vast amounts of biblical material that would obviously not fit inside the range of texts generated by

Part 2: Biblical Studies and Theology in Practice

the methodology. It therefore furthered rather than countered the impression created by the older prooftexting model of reading—namely, that the Bible and Christian doctrine could only be related artificially through some version of an externally imposed schema.

3. The texts considered below are not examined through a lens ground by a (re)construction of a particular historical trajectory: a kind of reading structured by the question of "how we got here from there," or focused on the way in which Scripture raised theological issues that could only be settled after decades of rigorous doctrinal reflection. In more recent history—after the rise of the so-called historical consciousness—this approach has been rather common. All treatments of the development of doctrine, whether of a more liberal (e.g., Adolf Harnack) or more traditional (e.g., Alister McGrath) leaning, presuppose the theological importance of attending to the linear dimension of history and move from the biblical texts to the later creedal formulations.

Accounts of the relation between Scripture and the dogmatic tradition that are shaped by a conception of a historical trajectory that begins in Scripture and moves toward the creeds are particularly important. Their importance is not only because such accounts take seriously the historical shape of our noetic boundaries but also because they can be read—whether their author intends it or not—as attempts to foreground the economy of God's self-revelation. By attending carefully to the linear dimension of doctrine, studies premised on the significance of historical trajectory correspond to the epistemic priority of the economic Trinity and help us to (re)trace the path of theological knowledge from the economic to the immanent reality of God.

4. Instead of the three reading strategies just described, the approach in this chapter takes shape from the three primary considerations:

First, the theological grammar in the NT presupposes certain basic judgments about the identity of God. The particular grammatical moves of the texts could not be made, that is, unless larger theological judgments have been made that allow these linguistic possibilities. Put thetically: the NT speech could not have taken shape in precisely this way unless X or Y is true about God. This "unless" then requires explication in a theological idiom.

Second, the development of the doctrine of the Trinity was the explication of this "unless," the unpacking of the internal theological logic behind the particular form of Scripture's grammar. In part, of course, this is what it means to say that the immanent Trinity is ontologically prior to the economic (whereas the economic is epistemically prior to the immanent). But it is also what it means to say that Trinitarian doctrine is the lens through which we can rightly perceive the particular form of Scripture's speaking about the identity of the

God who has revealed himself there. To employ a Trinitarian framework to read Scripture, therefore, is hardly to impose an artificial schema upon the NT. It is instead to reason inside the theological patterns required to understand the language used to speak about God in the texts.

Third, precisely because the doctrine of the Trinity is the true reception of Scripture's particular way of speaking about the identity of the Christian God, it also constitutes an otherwise unavailable form of exegetical perception. Thinking in Trinitarian patterns does not obfuscate the specificity of argument in, for example, Romans or 1 Corinthians—turning it into, say, an actual argument about the Trinity—but rather interprets the particular language about God within the horizon of that language's subject matter (*res*). In this way, Trinitarian reasoning enables us better to understand the deep and theologically essential connection between the specific language of Scripture and the God who—always and antecedently—speaks it forth.

Hebrews and the Pauline Letters

Given the amount of material involved in treating Hebrews and Paul, we obviously cannot aspire to comprehensiveness. What we can do, however, is to select strategically important passages that have substantial bearing not only on our reading of the larger text under discussion (e.g., Heb 1 is important rhetorically for the whole of the letter) but also on our more central question. In so doing, we shall by and large omit discussion of the protracted exegetical debates that surround virtually every verse of these texts and shall instead simply display our readings of the selected passages on the way to a more synthetic judgment.

Hebrews

Hebrews is a complex text whose basic theological grammar exhibits many and various substantive connections to the doctrine of the Trinity. Because it would be impossible to canvas the entire letter, we must restrict our inquiry to particularly striking features of these connections. The opening two chapters of the letter relate directly to our central concern, and we shall therefore focus our attention there (though let it be noted that what can be said here about Hebrews applies elsewhere in the letter).

If Hebrews' theology has been thought to be "supersessionist"—a judgment that is in need of serious rethinking—it cannot be on account of its doctrine of

God. Indeed, the first verse of chapter 1 immediately and clearly identifies the God about whom Hebrews speaks as the God of Israel, the one who "spoke of old to our fathers by the prophets" (Heb 1:1). This is not a new God, a divine figure other than the Jewish God, the one who brooks no rivals, whose identity is bound together with his uniqueness, and whose demand for worship is therefore total and exclusive. Indeed, the opening of the letter both states and assumes that the *theos* of Hebrews is in no way anything other than the OT God.

This point is important to grasp clearly because immediately the letter begins to render more complex the identity of just that God by extending the range of language by which we could rightly speak of him: "But in these last days he has spoken to us by a Son, whom he appointed as the heir of all things, and through whom he also made the ages" (Heb 1:2). Over against the notion that the Son is a divine figure to be contrasted with God, Hebrews immediately speaks of their interrelation. The Son is the "radiance of God's glory and the exact representation of his nature" (Heb 1:3). To put it in contemporary language, the Son is not other than God but is in fact God expressed or externalized—embodied, as we will shortly see—in relation to the world. That the Son is not fundamentally other than God is immediately made explicit by the citation of Psalm 44 in which the address to God (*ho theos*) is extended to include the Son: "But of the Son he [God] says, 'Your throne, O God, is for ever and ever'" (Ps 44:7 LXX). The theological judgment underlying this hermeneutical move is rather clear: the Son is none other than the God of whom the psalm speaks.

It is generally well known that in the OT the creative and ordering power of the God of Israel was frequently rendered with metaphorical dexterity—spoken of as Word or Wisdom as, for example, in Proverbs 8:22—and that this way of speaking of God's relation to the world became quite common around the time of the NT. Hebrews may well owe much to this way of thinking about God, but the letter also moves in a profoundly new direction—namely, that "the Son" is not at all to be understood in a purely noetic sense. The Son of Hebrews, that is, is not a metaphorical way of speaking about God's mediated relation to the world, a kind of grammatical holding place that gestures toward the fact that the true, high God could never come directly into contact with the material realm. Indeed, Hebrews is resolute in affirming the Son's human life. The Son we hear of as *theos* in Hebrews 1:8 is none other than the Jesus we hear of in Hebrews 2:9: "But we see Jesus, who for a little while was made lower than the angels, crowned with glory and honor because of the suffering of death, so that by the grace of God he might taste death for everyone." That the suffering and death was that of a real human, moreover, is made clear on page after page of the letter. Jesus the Son partook of the "same nature" that other human beings have—that is, flesh and blood (Heb 2:14)—and he was tempted in precisely the same way that other humans are (which is why he is able to aid them in their temptations; Heb 2:18; cf. 4:15). He was the "pioneer and perfecter of our faith, who for the joy that was set before him endured the cross, despising the shame, and is seated at the right hand of the throne of God" (Heb 12:2).

It is this human life of the Son to which the statements in Hebrews 1:5–6 make reference: "For to which one of the angels did God ever say, 'You are my Son, today I have begotten you'? Or again, 'I will be a Father to him and he will be a Son to me'? And when he brought the Firstborn into the life of the world [*oikoumenē*], he says, 'Let all the angels of God worship him.'" Hebrews 1:5–6 does not deny, that is, that the Son is eternally *theos* but instead speaks from the perspective of post-resurrection knowledge about the entrance of the Son into the life of the world in the person of Jesus. The "begetting" of the Son, that is, does not point to the *creation* of the Son but to the beginning of his human life in the human realm, or *oikoumenē* (or perhaps, if the author of Hebrews indeed knows the traditions surrounding Jesus's baptism, it speaks of the beginning of Jesus's ministry). Even in his earthly life the "Firstborn"—a reference to Jesus's resurrection from the dead, not his creation (cf. Rom 8:29; Col 1:15, 18; Rev 1:5)—can be worshiped by the angels. In short, the figure of Jesus is the Son who God is—both in himself and in his creating and redeeming relation to the world.

That the Son is internal to the identity of God is at bottom what differentiates him from the angels. Modern readers might be perplexed by the amount of energy the author of Hebrews expends to distinguish the Son from the angels. But in fact, as Athanasius saw so clearly in his own way in the fourth century, the question that lies behind such a focus goes to the heart of God's identity. If God is the God of Israel, and if God's Son is Jesus the human being, why then—a good Jewish theologian should ask—can the Son be worshiped? How is this worship of the Son not idolatry? Is this not an affront to the one and only true God? Hebrews' way of navigating this basic question is through a grammar of contrast: Jesus should not be conceived as, or in analogy to, an angel.

Hebrews develops this contrast already in the opening of the letter: the Son has become "as much superior to the angels as the name he has obtained is more excellent than theirs" (Heb 1:4). The contrast is then deepened by citing a variety of OT texts, all of which are intended to emphasize the difference

Part 2: Biblical Studies and Theology in Practice

between the Son and the angels: "Of the angels [God] says, 'Who makes his angels winds and his servants flames of fire.' But of the Son he says, 'Your throne, O God, is for ever and ever'"; and, later, "But to which one of the angels has he said, 'Sit at my right hand until I make your enemies a footstool for your feet'? Are not all [the angels] ministering spirits who are sent forth to serve those who will inherit salvation?" (Heb 1:13–14; cf. 1:5–6). Thus it is no less than God himself who declares through Scripture the Son's superiority to the angels. And yet—in view of the use of Psalm 44:7 in Hebrews 1:8—it would be more precise to say that God declares his own superiority to the angels in the person of the Son. God does not, that is, declare the superiority of something other than God but speaks of himself as *theos* in the figure of Jesus the Son. As the text of Hebrews would have it, "Son" is thus internal to the meaning of "God."

Still, in the theology of Hebrews "God" is not collapsed into "Son" or "Jesus" any more than it excludes them. That is to say, "God" is sufficiently relational in its meaning to require of the reader nimbleness in thought, a movement between selfsameness and difference. To put it in the terms of Hebrews, the Son can both be called *theos* and "have" a *theos*. In the very same citation of Psalm 44 where the Son is clearly called "God," to take only the most striking example, we learn that "God" is not reducible to the Son. Addressing the Son, Hebrews 1:8–9 continues, "You have loved righteousness and hated lawlessness; for this reason God, *your God*, has anointed you" (cf. the expressions in Heb 1:3; 2:17; 10:12; 12:2; 13:20, etc.). Even within one citation, therefore, "God" (*theos*) is both the Son and yet not reducible to the Son.

Or again, if we ask who the *kyrios* is in Hebrews, "the Lord" is both Jesus the human being and the God of the OT. Not only does Hebrews 7:14 speak of Jesus clearly as "the Lord" who was descended from Judah (cf. Heb 13:20), in Hebrews 1:10–12 it is no less than God himself who addresses the Son as "Lord" through an OT text in which *kyrios* originally referred to the God of Israel: "You, O Lord [*kyrie*], did found the earth in the beginning, and the heavens are the work of your hands" (Ps 101:26. LXX). Yet in the citation of Psalm 110:4 in Hebrews 7:21 and elsewhere "the Lord" is clearly the God of Israel. In Hebrews 8:8, for example, Jeremiah 31 is cited with the characteristic "says the Lord," which plainly refers to God. Were we to attempt to assign one meaning of *kyrios* to Jesus and another to God, we would have already dismantled the language through which Hebrews presents God/the Lord and, therefore, moved away from the theological pattern created by Hebrews' continuous attempt to speak of the OT God and of Jesus together.

Hebrews mentions the Holy Spirit only seven times (Heb 2:4; 3:7; 6:4; 9:8, 14; 10:15, 29). Yet it does so in a way that makes clear the relational determination of the Spirit's identity. Speaking of the nature of salvation, the author of Hebrews says, "It was declared at first by the Lord, and it was attested to us by those who heard him, while God also bore witness by signs and wonders and various miracles and by gifts of the Holy Spirit distributed according to his own will" (Heb 2:3–4). Here the Spirit is explicitly described as God's Spirit—the Spirit's gifts are distributed according to God's will—and tied to the salvific life of Jesus (the Lord). To speak of the Holy Spirit, therefore, is also to speak of God and of the Lord Jesus (cf. the context in Heb 6:4 and 10:29).

Moreover, the Holy Spirit cannot be reduced to a simple metaphorical way to speak about God's presence, as if using Spirit language were but another way to speak of God's immanence. The Spirit in Hebrews is rather the one through whom Christ offered himself to God. As the author argues *a minore ad maius*: "For if the sprinkling of defiled persons with the blood of goats and bulls and with ashes of a heifer sanctifies for the purification of the flesh, how much more shall the blood of Christ—who through the eternal Spirit offered himself without blemish to God—purify your conscience from dead works to serve the living God!" (Heb 9:13–14). Or again, Hebrews clearly portrays God as the one who provides the voice of Scripture, but no less do we find the Spirit performing the same task—indeed, with the same basic scriptural text: "And the Holy Spirit also bears witness to us; for after saying, 'This is the covenant that I will make with them after those days, says the Lord, I will put my laws on their hearts and write them on their minds,' he then adds, 'I will remember their sins and misdeeds no more'" (Heb 10:15–17, citing Jer 31:33–34; cf. the speech of the Holy Spirit in Heb 3:7).

As will be obvious to any reader, the letter to the Hebrews employs a highly complex theological grammar primarily because Hebrews speaks of God in ways that simultaneously maintain and extend the discourse of the OT. "God" is none other than the God of the OT, and yet this God is described also in relation to a human Son that is internal to his eternal identity—Jesus the Christ—and in relation to the Holy Spirit. Moreover, in its defense of the propriety of Jesus worship (esp. chs. 1–2), Hebrews reveals a sense of the profound questions that surround its extension of the OT's theological discourse to a "flesh and blood" human being. To speak of the OT *theos* and Jesus *anthrōpos* together (Ps 44:7; Heb 1:8) is already to effect a dramatic revaluation of both terms. And to tie inextricably the Spirit of God to the self-offering of Jesus is yet again to revalue the meaning of Holy Spirit.

Hebrews does not itself so much articulate this revaluation as presuppose it. Later doctrinal language—Trinitarian reasoning, to be precise—developed the interconnection between the relation of the terms that Hebrews presupposes

Part 2: Biblical Studies and Theology in Practice

for its particular theological grammar. Hebrews' grammar, that is, becomes intelligible in light of a larger linguistic range that allows one to say God and Jesus and Spirit together. In this way, Trinitarian doctrine explicates the intelligibility of the particular theological language of Hebrews no less than it creates an exegetical perception of "God" in the text itself.

Pauline Epistles

As NT scholars have long emphasized, the letters by or attributed to the apostle Paul are occasional documents. They are not systematic treatises aimed at the elucidation of the whole of the Christian faith. They are—with only one real possible exception (Romans)—written as "words on target," pastoral responses to the particular problems and questions of early Christian congregations. Because of their character, it is an entirely unexceptional fact that the Pauline texts do not contain long discourses on the nature of God, person of Christ, and so forth. This is exactly what one would expect in occasional, pastorally targeted letters. However, it does not follow from the absence of such direct discourse that one can understand Paul quite apart from thinking through the theological judgments that form the possibility of several of his particular formulations. Indeed, to attend carefully to the grammar of the occasion is immediately to perceive the larger syntax in which the theological logic of such particular formulations is made possible. With respect to the view of God found in the Pauline epistles, Trinitarian reflection is the larger theological syntax that illumines and—ultimately—renders intelligible Paul's particular grammatical moves.

Obviously the Pauline corpus is too vast to survey in this chapter. We shall therefore select only four instances from across the corpus that will serve to establish paradigmatically the theological point of view from which the identity of God should be seen when thinking through the witness of the Pauline letters. These four instances are not chosen, however, because they are unusual (and therefore particularly interesting to academics) but precisely because they are typical of the theological grammar of the Pauline corpus as a whole (and therefore all the more important).

1 Corinthians 12

In chapter 12 of 1 Corinthians Paul begins to admonish the Corinthians for their misunderstanding of the importance of spiritual gifts. The church in

Corinth, it is well known, had an abundance of those who spoke in tongues, prophesied, and so forth. The question thus arose as to how the manifestation of the true (Holy) Spirit should be differentiated from its counterfeits ("spirits"). Paul instructs the Corinthians: "I want you to understand that no one speaking by the Spirit of God ever says, 'Jesus be damned!'; and, no one can say 'Jesus is Lord!' except by the Holy Spirit" (12:3).

What is initially intriguing about Paul's argument is that it does not argue for discerning the true Spirit by giving the Corinthians an extensive checklist of things that the Holy Spirit would or would not do through the Corinthians (scream profanity incoherently, foam at the mouth, attack people, and so on). He names only one thing, though of course it has both a negative and positive side: the Spirit never testifies to the permanent death of Jesus but, entirely to the contrary, leads one to confess that Jesus is Lord.

At its deepest level, the argument is that to know the manifestation of the true Spirit is to know the relational determination of the Spirit's identity. Such determination is by God on the one hand and Jesus on the other: God's Spirit is the one who enables the confession that the Lord is Jesus. Paul does not, of course, specify the proper method by which to construe this relational identity in any overtly metaphysical way. But he does say rather clearly that the way to differentiate the true from the false is to see the connection of the Holy Spirit to God the Father and Jesus the Lord. The Spirit of God, that is, cannot be abstracted from Jesus Christ. As Paul will later say, the Corinthians are baptized by the Spirit into one body (which of course is Christ; 1 Cor 12:12–13). In 1 Corinthians 12:4–6 this relational determination of God's identity is expressed in a neat parallelism:

> There are varieties of gifts—but the same Spirit (*to auto pneuma*)
> There are varieties of service—but the same Lord (*ho autos kyrios*)
> There are varieties of working—but the same God (*ho autos theos*)

Again, Paul's argument is not actually *about* God's relational identity. It is about how to know the true Spirit and the proper place and worth of spiritual gifts in Christian community. Yet God's relational identity is the ground upon which this argument is constructed, which is to say that the Trinitarian pattern of speech is the linguistic fundament of Paul's particular appeals. One can, of course, conceive of other ways in which he could make the same argument. But that is to miss the point (as hypotheticals often do). The point is rather that when attempting to shape the communal life of the Corinthians vis-à-vis the manifestation of the Holy Spirit, Paul draws upon a theological language that positions the Holy Spirit in relation to the "same Lord" and "same God."

Part 2: Biblical Studies and Theology in Practice

Of course, when "Lord" refers to Jesus, to say "same Lord" and "same God" almost in the same breath is to speak idolatrous nonsense—unless the referents of the words "Lord" and "God" are to be understood in a noncompetitive manner. And, indeed, Paul's argument gives us no reason to suspect that Lord competes with God. It is rather the case that Paul's seamless theological grammar requires us to think in terms of a reciprocally determining identity between the Lord and God. Differently said, while in the OT the question of competition between God and the Lord could never arise—the Lord was simply God, and vice versa—Paul's language extends the referent of "the Lord" to include Jesus in such a way as to condition what we mean when we now say "God." In brief, Paul's argument presupposes a linguistic interconnection between God, Jesus the Lord, and the Holy Spirit such that to speak of one is necessarily to invoke or imply the others. As Paul himself puts it: no one can confess that Jesus is Lord except by the power of God's Holy Spirit.

To receive such speech—to understand the theological possibility of the grammar—is already to reason in a Trinitarian pattern of thought. In this way, Trinitarian reasoning articulates theologically the ground of the text's grammatical moves and really is, therefore, the deeper presupposition of the particular Pauline argument in 1 Corinthians 12. That this is not an isolated instance but constitutive of Pauline argumentation as a whole could be easily shown from a variety of texts (e.g., 1 Cor 2:2–5; 2 Cor 13:13; Gal 3:1–5; Phil 3:3, etc.). Due to the necessary brevity of our reflection, however, we shall illustrate the material continuity with 1 Corinthians 12 by three further examples, each one of which is selected from a major textual area in the Pauline corpus (the *Hauptbriefe*, the deutero-Pauline letters, and the Pastoral Epistles).

Romans 5

Turning first to Romans, we can see several different places where a Trinitarian pattern of speech is employed (e.g., chs. 3, 9–11, etc.). A rather striking instance occurs in Romans 5:1–11, where Paul describes God's reconciling work. Commentators have long noticed that chapter 5 begins another major section in Paul's argument. Having established that justification occurs through the faithfulness of Jesus Christ (chs. 1–4), Paul now begins to describe such justification as "peace with God through our Lord Jesus Christ" (5:1). Of course, for Paul, peace in its Christian sense is not opposed to suffering; indeed, suffering provides the occasion for Christian hope (5:2–3). And hope "does not disappoint us because God's love has been poured into our hearts through the Holy Spirit which has been given to us" (5:5). God's love is not a fickle declaration that can be given and taken away again, but is displayed in the fact that Christ in fact "died for us while we were yet sinners." We can rejoice, therefore, "in God through our Lord Jesus Christ, through whom we have now received our reconciliation" (5:6–11).

Here Paul does not argue for the truth of a Trinitarian way of speaking about reconciliation and the form of Christian life it commends. Instead, as in 1 Corinthians 12 and elsewhere, Paul's hermeneutical moves presuppose a fundamentally Trinitarian pattern. The way to articulate reconciliation theologically, that is, includes a reference to God the Father (with whom we now have peace, whose love is given to us, etc.), the Lord Jesus Christ (through whom we have been given such gifts), and the Holy Spirit (through whom such gifts are spiritually efficacious, "poured into our hearts"). What argumentative logic we can detect in this portion of Romans thus rests more basically upon the linguistic ability to speak of the reconciling act of "God by the death of his Son" in relation to the Holy Spirit's work in forming Christian life. The entirety of Paul's language about reconciliation in Romans 5:1–8 requires a Trinitarian grammar for its intelligibility.

Ephesians 4

The so-called deutero-Pauline epistles are no less indebted to a Trinitarian grammar for their theological language than are the Pauline letters proper. Ephesians 4, for example, in which Paul urges the Ephesians toward Christian unity, couches its plea in an appeal to the unity of God himself. The Ephesians should "maintain the unity of the Spirit in the bond of peace"; for "there is one body and one Spirit, just as you were called to the one hope of your calling: one Lord, one faith, one baptism, one God and Father of us all, who is over all and through all and in all" (4:3–6).

It is remarkable that, in an attempt to ground Christian unity—one faith, one baptism—in the unity of God, Paul's language moves seamlessly between "one Spirit," "one Lord," and "one God." The implication of such language is that the Spirit, Jesus the Lord, and God the Father constitute the unity of God that makes intelligible Paul's exhortation. To embody unity in the life of the church is precisely to display the unity of the Spirit, Jesus the Lord, and God the Father.

But, once again, the argument at this point in Ephesians presupposes rather than argues for a Trinitarian pattern when speaking of the unity of God. Paul does not, that is, argue one way or another about how Jesus's identity as Lord does not threaten the Lord God the Father; it is simply assumed in the course

Part 2: Biblical Studies and Theology in Practice

of the chapter that the theologically proper way to admonish the Ephesians toward unity is to speak of the unity of God—and this with the language of Spirit, Jesus the Lord, and God the Father.

Titus

The short letter to Titus is striking for its focus on salvation (e.g., 1:3, 4; 2:10, 11, 13; 3:4, 5, 6). For the purposes of this chapter the most important aspect of this focus can be seen through the fact that if one were to ask, "Who is the Savior?" the theological grammar of Titus would require us to answer at once both God and Jesus. After first speaking of God in 1:3 as "God our Savior," the letter moves only a sentence later to speak of Jesus as "our Savior": "Grace and peace from God the Father and Christ Jesus our Savior" (1:4).

In 2:10 the reader hears again of "God our Savior" and then immediately learns of the work of "our Savior Jesus Christ" (2:13). And in 3:4 God is "our Savior" just as in 3:6 it is Jesus Christ "our Savior": "When the goodness and loving kindness of God our Savior appeared, he saved us, not because of deeds done by us in righteousness, but in virtue of his own mercy, by the washing of regeneration and renewal in the Holy Spirit, which he poured out upon us richly through Jesus Christ our Savior" (3:4–6).

Attending to the language of salvation in Titus thus discloses a necessity to speak of God the Father and Jesus Christ together in one breath as "the Savior." So doing extends the OT's soteriological language about the God of Israel to Jesus Christ. The "Savior God of Israel" (Isa 45:15) has become God/Jesus Christ our Savior. Moreover, at least in 3:4–6, the connection between God the Savior and Jesus Christ the Savior is the Holy Spirit: the Spirit is the way in which God's loving and merciful good work in Jesus Christ is mediated to the Christian community.

As in the other NT examples above, the letter to Titus does not actually argue for the legitimacy of the new theological grammar. The legitimacy is rather presupposed. It is in fact the foundation upon which Titus explicates the various facets of salvation for its readers.

Taking Hebrews and the Pauline corpus together, we can discern several common themes that together emphasize the hermeneutical importance of Trinitarian reflection. First, as in all the texts of the NT, both the Pauline letters and Hebrews presuppose that the referent of the common noun "God" is the God of the OT. The letters' arguments and exhortations, that is, are not constructed on a general or amorphous theological basis but are instead the quite particular outworking of the God of Israel's salvific self-disclosure.

Second, the explicitly theological language employed in the passages considered above forms a single linguistic skein: to remove either "Jesus Christ" or the "Holy Spirit" or "God" from the argument of the passage would not be simply to truncate the strength of the argument—as if Paul's argument in Romans 5 could proceed with reference to Jesus but not to the Spirit. It would rather be to dismantle the sense of the passage as a whole. The significance of such linguistic unity inheres in the fact that to speak of salvation and of the one who saves requires a theological grammar sufficiently supple to speak of a final unity of identity and act between three distinct "persons."

Third, as a whole Hebrews and the Pauline letters presuppose rather than argue for any specific Trinitarian judgments. Though it explicitly addresses the question of the worship of the Son, even Hebrews does not engage in a debate about exactly how a ubiquitous God could be localized in a particular human being, how Creator and creature could coexist in one life, how the Son of God could actually die, and so forth.

Such presupposition is significant precisely because it manifests a pattern of speaking that Trinitarian reasoning later uncovers. Or, to put it more precisely, the reciprocally interpreting and overlapping ways to speak truly about the one God of Israel constitute the theological ground of the biblical texts' linguistic freedom.

Conclusion

As this brief survey of Hebrews and Pauline texts suggests, attending carefully to the linguistic pattern of the texts' speech about God requires us to look behind the actual arguments of the texts to the theological judgments that make such language possible. To put it simply: the sense that the NT language makes depends upon a larger pattern of theological judgments that makes the sense. This larger theological pattern of sense-making is precisely what we call Trinitarian reasoning. To speak in the manner of Hebrews and the Pauline letters is already to presuppose a Trinitarian range of linguistic possibilities vis-à-vis the identity of God. In just this way Trinitarian reasoning proves to be exegetically illuminating—indeed, the requisite theological language by which to receive Scripture's grammatical moves.

To be clear: such exegetical illumination occurs not because the conceptual apparatus of the author of Hebrews or the Pauline texts was outfitted with ideas that were still two or three centuries in the future. Finitude—in intellectual terms, the intractable historicity of our reflection—conditioned the authors of

Part 2: Biblical Studies and Theology in Practice

Scripture, as it does all human inquiry. It is rather because Trinitarian judgments about the identity of God underlie the intelligibility of the linguistic patterns of the texts. Trinitarian reasoning works on the level of what must be the case to make theological sense of the way Paul and Hebrews speak of the OT God's salvific act in Jesus Christ through the Holy Spirit. Precisely for this reason, to read Scripture within a Trinitarian framework of theological understanding is to move within the deep theological pattern of thinking that Scripture itself requires.

New Testament Iconography?

◆ SITUATING PAUL IN THE ABSENCE OF MATERIAL EVIDENCE

We shall never agree about the nature of art.

—E. R. Goodenough, "Early Christian and Jewish Art"

The Problem

"New Testament iconography" can be read in two ways: (1) an attempt to trace the development of iconography inspired by NT motifs, and so on;[1] (2) a discipline that reads the NT in connection to the wider iconographic culture in the Greco-Roman world in the effort to illuminate particular NT passages.[2] While the latter is the focus of many essays in the volume *Picturing the New Testament*, the former is what occupies us here, but in a kind of fundamental and rather different way: there is no NT iconography before circa AD 200.

---

1. See, e.g., Gertrud Schiller, *Ikonographie der christlichen Kunst*, Bd. 2, *Die Passion Jesu Christ* (Gütersloh: Gütersloher Verlagshaus G. Mohn, 1969).

2. Annette Weissenrieder, "'He is a God!' Acts 28:1-9 in the Light of Iconographical and Textual Sources Related to Medicine," in *Picturing the New Testament: Studies in Ancient Visual Images*, ed. Annette Weissenrieder, Friederike Wendt, and Petra von Gemünden (Tübingen: Mohr Siebeck, 2005), 127-56.

"New Testament Iconography? Situating Paul in the Absence of Material Evidence" was originally published in *Picturing the New Testament: Studies in Ancient Visual Images*, ed. Annette Weissenrieder, Friederike Wendt, and Petra von Gemünden, WUNT 2/193 (Tübingen: Mohr Siebeck, 2005), 289-312. It is reproduced with permission.

In addition to the editors (Annette Weissenrieder and Friederike Wendt) of the volume in which this essay originally appeared, I would like to thank Gerry Warren and Jonathan Robker, both of the Media Center at the Divinity School of Duke University, for their help with the technological matters needed for the essay.

Part 2: Biblical Studies and Theology in Practice

Material evidence of visual interpretation of the NT, insofar as we know, simply does not exist until about the beginning of the third century. Why not?[3]

Broadly speaking, scholars have given one of two answers to this vexing question: (1) Because of their Jewish roots, the earliest Christians were deeply aniconic in their worship and thus in principle eschewed material representations of the divine.[4] Hence Theodor Klauser thematized the entire issue with the question: "Wann hat die christliche Kirche das zweite Gebot endgültig über Bord geworfen?"[5] This answer has in addition frequently entailed a corresponding Harnack-like judgment about the nature of the church once it began to develop an artistic tradition—namely, that it was "backsliding" into paganism: "Der Schmuck der römischen Katakomben und der frühchristlichen Sarkophage . . . [ist] in erster Linie zweifellos das gewesen, was auch Irenaus, Eusebios und Epiphanios in ihnen sehen, nämlich ein Zeichen der groben Paganisierung, des Synkretismus."[6]

(2) In contrast to the first answer, recent efforts have stressed social reality—lack of land and capital, for example—as that which best explains the

---

3. In the introduction to his widely acclaimed book, Paul Zanker, *The Power of Images in the Age of Augustus* (Ann Arbor: University of Michigan Press, 1988), writes: "I am not primarily concerned with the interpretation of individual monuments. . . . My interest is instead in the totality of images that a contemporary would have experienced. This includes not only 'works of art,' buildings, and poetic imagery, but also religious ritual, clothing, state ceremony. . . . I am concerned with the contexts of these images and with the effect of this tapestry of images on the viewer" (3). The actual iconographical concern in this essay is rather similar in that I do not analyze the accompanying figures individually or in detail but treat them illustratively—i.e., as representatives of daily iconographic reality in the Roman Empire. The purpose is to put a little flesh on the textual skeleton and, hence, to deepen the awareness of the intersection between texts and iconic reality in the ancient world. For criticism of Zanker's view of art as a "reflection" of society (rather than in part constitutive of it), see Jeremy Tanner, "Portraits, Power, and Patronage in the Late Roman Republic," *JRS* 90 (2000): 18–50, esp. 20.

4. So, e.g., Ernst Kitzinger, "The Cult of Images in the Age before Iconoclasm," *DOP* 8 (1954): 85–150; Hugo Koch, *Die altchristliche Bilderfrage nach den literarischen Quellen* (Göttingen: Vandenhoeck & Ruprecht, 1917). See the concise survey by Sister Charles Murray, "Art in the Early Church," *JTS* 28 (1977): 303–45, esp. 303–6. For a discussion of the LXX version of the second commandment, see W. Barnes Tatum, "The LXX Version of the Second Commandment (Ex. 20,3–6 = Deut. 5,7–10): A Polemic Against Idols, Not Images," *JSJ* 17, no. 2 (1986): 177–95, who also treats succinctly the evidence from Josephus and Philo.

5. Theodor Klauser, "Erwägungen zur Entstehung der altchristlichen Kunst," *Zeitschrift für Kirchengeschichte* 76 (1965): 2.

6. Hans F. von Campenhausen, "Die Bilderfrage als Theologisches Problem der alten Kirche," *Zeitschrift für Theologie und Kirche* 49 (1952): 36. For an insightful critique of the handling of the literary evidence (Epiphanius, etc.) in this first line of research, see Murray, "Art in the Early Church."

New Testament Iconography?

absence of a distinctive, or at least perceivable, Christian material culture in the earliest period.[7] On this reading of the evidence, the earliest Christians need not have been aniconically oriented[8]; rather, they simply did not have the means at their disposal for the creation of artistic work: "With the community control of real property came the creation of pictorial art."[9] The explanation of the "tardy arrival" of Christian material culture is not to be found in the alleged opposition to iconography but instead in the "unintended consequence of political, social, and economic factors."[10]

What is interesting in this discussion is the apparent lack of attention to the NT itself.[11] This situation is readily understandable, on two counts in particular. First, the NT texts never address the subject of Christian art directly. Second, the Apologists and church fathers actually do. Moreover, the Apologists are more or less contemporaneous with the emergence of Christian art. It is therefore not surprising that their views on such matters receive the bulk of attention.

Yet it is worth asking to what degree the retrojection of the issues of later deliberations—however cautiously done—can actually illuminate the mid to

---

7. See the comprehensive work of Paul Corby Finney, *The Invisible God: The Earliest Christians on Art* (Oxford: Oxford University Press, 1994). In her recent book, Robin Margaret Jensen, *Understanding Early Christian Art* (London: Routledge, 2000), 14f., seems to endorse Finney's position with only minor qualifications.

8. This view obviously garners support from the "discovery" of a considerable Jewish artistic tradition, e.g., in Dura-Europos, Beth Alpha, Hammath Tiberias, etc. (see the material in Erwin R. Goodenough, *Jewish Symbols in the Greco-Roman World*, 13 vols. [New York: Pantheon Books, 1953–1968], though it should be noted that there are no direct depictions of the God of Israel himself in the early period. In this respect, David Freedberg's well-known reflections bury in a by-the-way remark what is perhaps the definitive theological exception to his thesis: "There is a deep and persistent historiographic myth that provides us with insight into one of the most profound aspects of people's attitudes to all figured imagery. This is the myth that certain cultures, usually monotheistic or primitively pure cultures, have no images at all, or no figurative imagery, or no images of the deity. *Abstinence from figuring the deity does occasionally occur*, but for the rest the notion of aniconism is wholly untenable. It is clouded in vagueness and has its roots in confusion" (*The Power of Images: Studies in the History and Theory of Response* [Chicago: University of Chicago Press, 1989], 54; emphasis added). Aniconism with respect to God himself is hardly peripheral to Judaism, however else the second commandment gets interpreted in Jewish thought and practice (cf. the depiction of humans, etc. in the Dura frescoes).

9. Finney, *Invisible God*, 110.

10. Finney, *Invisible God*, 291.

11. The two exceptions that occasionally get a cursory hearing both have to do with Caesar's image (Mark 12:13–17 // Matt 22:15–22 // Luke 20:20–26 and the latter parts of Revelation), but the results have been meager at best.

Part 2: Biblical Studies and Theology in Practice

late first century without corroborating data from that time period and, further, whether or not our firsthand sources for this period might have more to say about our problem than has been heretofore acknowledged. Perhaps in the case of the NT at least, early evidence is, as R. L. Gordon quipped, a "function not so much of matter as of questions."[12] In such light, this chapter will attempt to situate Paul in the debate to position his piece within the larger puzzle that is the absence of early Christian iconography.[13] The most direct way to do this is to examine the Pauline use of εἰκών specifically in relation to our topic. Εἰκών not only bears a linguistic and cognitive connection to matters of iconography but also propels us immediately into the heart of the problem, as its use encompasses both pagan idols and the substance of Pauline theological convictions.[14] After considerable exegetical analysis—let us hear Paul well on this matter—the paper will conclude with the implications of the exegesis for our topic.

Paul and the Εἰκών

The *religionsgeschichtliche* investigation of εἰκών in Hellenistic Judaism, the Greco-Roman world, magical papyri, and so on has been done extensively.[15] So, too, in addition to lexical study,[16] there has been considerable discussion of Paul's use of εἰκών in relation to its Jewish and Greco-Roman cultural antecedents,[17] to

---

12. R. L. Gordon, "The Real and the Imaginary: Production and Religion in the Graeco-Roman World," *Art History* 2 (1979): 5.

13. The article is thus to be understood as a kind of Pauline test case. Whether or not a more extensive combing of the NT writings (esp. John) would yield productive insights for this question is worth further consideration.

14. Obviously in an essay of this length, many critical-exegetical issues will be passed over in silence. Yet to those trained in NT matters, the positions taken within the relevant debates should be clear, as should my indebtedness to the relevant secondary literature.

15. See, e.g., Friedrich-Wilhelm Eltester, *Eikon im Neuen Testament* (Berlin: Töpelmann, 1958); Jacob Jervell, *Imago Dei: Gen 1,26f. im Spätjudentum, in der Gnosis und in den Paulinischen Briefen* (Göttingen: Vandenhoeck & Ruprecht, 1960); G. von Rad, G. Kittel, and H. Kleinknecht, "Art. εἰκών," *ThWNT* 2:378–96.

16. E.g., Dave Steenburg, "The Case against the Synonymity of Morphē and Eikōn," *JSNT* 34 (1988): 77–86.

17. E.g., Jarl Fossum, "Colossians 1.15–18a in the Light of Jewish Mysticism and Gnosticism," *NTS* 35 (1989): 183–201; Joseph A. Fitzmyer, "Glory Reflected on the Face of Christ (2 Cor 3:7–4:6) and a Palestinian Jewish Motif," *Theological Studies* 42 (1981): 630–44.

New Testament Iconography?

Adam-Christ typology,[18] and to its meaning within its epistolary contexts.[19] Yet, insofar as I know, no one has probed Paul's use of εἰκών in relation to the question of early Christian iconography.[20]

In his commentary on 2 Corinthians, C. K. Barrett writes that "it is impossible to draw together into a unity the various occurrences in the Pauline writings of the word *image*."[21] If by "unity" Barrett means to suggest uniformity, then he is obviously correct. But if we understand "unity" as something more akin to coherence, then a different picture emerges, for it is in fact possible to group the Pauline uses of εἰκών under three distinct headings. These distinctions, it will be argued, turn out to fit coherently together.[22]

Romans 1:23: Εἰκών as Εἴδωλον

Romans 1:18-23 is the first section of a larger argument in which Paul attempts to demolish the righteousness of human beings before God. In this particular section of the argument Paul focuses upon pagan worship and practice.

Paul's critique of pagan religiosity hinges on what E. P. Sanders once suggested was "Judaism's most important single contribution to civiliza-

---

18. E.g., James D. G. Dunn, *Christology in the Making: A New Testament Inquiry into the Origins of the Doctrine of the Incarnation*, 2nd ed. (Grand Rapids: Eerdmans, 1989), esp. 107-13. See now Stephen Hultgren, "The Origin of Paul's Doctrine of the Two Adams in 1 Corinthians 15.45-49," *JSNT* 25 (2003): 343-70.

19. So, e.g., Edvin Larsson, *Christus als Vorbild: Eine Untersuchung zu den paulinischen Tauf- und Eikontexten* (Uppsala: Almqvist & Wiksells, 1962); S. Vernon McCasland, "The Image of God according to Paul," *JBL* 69 (1950): 85-100.

20. There are some who discuss Paul's use of εἰκών in relation to later theological developments (e.g., Peter Schwanz, *Imago Dei als christolgisch-anthropologisches Problem in der Geschichte der Alten Kirche von Paulus bis Clemens von Alexandrien* [Halle: Niemeyer, 1970]), but the question of a distinctively Christian material culture is not in view. Conversely, there are also studies that mention Paul's εἰκών texts in relation to, e.g., later iconographic controversies (e.g., Christoph von Schönborn, *L'Icône du Christ: Fondements théologiques élaborés entre le Ier et le IIe Concile de Nicée* [325-787], [Fribourg: Éditions universitaires, 1976]), but actual exegesis of the texts is absent, as is the specific question of the lack of early Christian iconography. Due to the plethora of studies on the subjects mentioned in nn. 16-21, these matters will be taken up in the exegesis only where they have direct bearing upon the interpretation of a passage in light of our particular question.

21. C. K. Barrett, *The Second Epistle to the Corinthians* (Peabody, MA: Hendrickson, 1973), 132.

22. To be clear: Though it will not be treated, 1 Cor 11:7, if from Paul, fits within his general use of εἰκών for humans as bearers of the divine image. The reason for its omission is that this text adds nothing of a substantive nature to our discussion.

253

Part 2: Biblical Studies and Theology in Practice

tion"[23]—namely, the conviction that the εἷς ὁ Θεός (Rom 3:30) is the Creator of the world (ἀπὸ κτίσεως κόσμου, 1:20; ὁ κτίσας, 1:25). That is to say, the Jewish God is not, as with Aristotle's Prime Mover, the "top story" of the cosmos, but rather is other than the cosmos. To put this conviction into modern, if thetic, terms: God is ontologically other than the world and as its Creator stands in the order of being over against the world.[24]

This differentiation between God and the world inherent in the Jewish view of creation constitutes, for Paul as for other Jews, the ground of right worship. To worship anything other than God collapses the distinction between God and the world and moves immediately into idolatry, the exaltation of creation to the place of God. Such is the logic of Paul's language of "exchange":

1:23: καὶ ἤλλαξαν τὴν δόξαν τοῦ ἀφθάρτου Θεοῦ ἐν ὁμοιώματι εἰκόνος φθαρτοῦ ἀνθρώπου καὶ πετεινῶν καὶ τετραπόδων καὶ ἑρπετῶν

1:25: οἵτινες μετήλλαξαν τὴν ἀλήθειαν τοῦ Θεοῦ ἐν τῷ ψεύδει καὶ ἐσεβάσθησαν καὶ ἐλάτρευσαν τῇ κτίσει παρὰ τὸν κτίσαντα

Moving backward, then, to exchange the truth of God for a lie and to reverence and worship the creation rather than the Creator is precisely to exchange the glory of the imperishable God for the likeness of an εἰκών of perishable creation: ἄνθρωποι, πετεινά, τετράποδα, ἑρπετά.

In a still-important article, M. D. Hooker once suggested that we yoke εἰκών specifically to ἄνθρωπος, rather than take εἰκών together with the various animals, and translate ἐν ὁμοιώματι κτλ. "for a likeness of (a) an image of corruptible man, (b) various types of animals."[25] Yet the plurals πετεινά and so on do not require such a restriction of εἰκών or the concomitant broadening of ὁμοίωμα (also singular[26]). Nor is the reach of εἰκών limited by the singular ἄνθρωπος because, being anarthrous, it could easily be rendered "humanity": to use outmoded language for clarification, "for the likeness of an image of mortal man, and of birds, etc." Moreover, this generic sense retains the emphasis on the universality of "creation"—humanity, animals—as that which has been exchanged for the glory of the "Creator" and, to borrow somewhat freely

---

23. E. P. Sanders, *Judaism: Practice and Belief 63 BCE–66 CE* (London: SCM, 1992), 247.
24. The terms "ontological" and "being" are not meant here to convey the entire Greek metaphysical tradition but rather are used in as plain a sense as possible to express in philosophical or theological language the significance of this fundamental Jewish confession.
25. M. D. Hooker, "Adam in Romans 1," *NTS* 6 (1959/1960): 304.
26. From Ps 105:20 LXX.

a *terminus technicus* from elsewhere, allows the *sensus literalis* to remain in the foreground: on the face of it, instead of a subtle reflection on Genesis 1, Paul here comprehensively condemns the pagan iconic veneration of creation.[27]

Käsemann saw in the list of 1:23 a direct reference to "konkret ägyptische Religiosität, welche schon Sap. Sal 11,15; 12,24 empörte."[28] It is certainly true that Paul, if not dependent upon Wisdom of Solomon,[29] obviously shares the same general Jewish tradition (cf. Deut 4:16f.; Let. Aris. 134f.; Jubilees 12:1f., etc.), and that Egyptian religion with its animal-like gods was a common "whipping boy" not only for Jews but also for pagans and early Christians.[30] But specificity such as Käsemann's is again unnecessary and blunts the impact of Paul's main point, the creature-Creator exchange. On the contrary, it seems better to allow the breadth of Paul's description to remain.

It is impossible to know, in any kind of particular sense, exactly which εἰκόνες would have come to mind for Christians in Rome (and elsewhere in the empire as the *corpus Paulinum* began to come together), and this fact maximizes rather than minimizes the effectiveness of the epistolary *Wirkung*. By virtue of its universality Paul's target is as large as it can be, and thus could the Roman Christians have connected the Pauline polemic to any number of εἰκόνες that permeated public space: major deities with impressive temples such as Mars Ultor;[31] statues or busts

---

27. This is not to exclude the influence of the creation narratives on Paul's thought or in this passage, but rather to say that they are not specifically in the foreground.

28. Ernst Käsemann, *An die Römer*, 3rd ed., Handbuch zum Neuen Testament 8a (Tübingen: Mohr, 1974), 41.

29. E.g., Wisdom of Solomon speaks of a woodcutter's (13:11) carving as εἰκόνι ἀνθρώπου (13:13).

30. See, e.g., Cicero, *Nat. d.* 1.36 §101; Justin Martyr, *1 Apol.* 24. Cf. the interesting figures in Erwin R. Goodenough, *Jewish Symbols in the Greco-Roman World*, vol. 7, *Pagan Symbols in Judaism* (New York: Pantheon Books, 1958) (e.g., figs. 145–47, Khensu, etc.).

31. A colossal marble copy of Mars Ultor (the Avenger) stood in a temple built by Augustus (*Res gestae* 4.21) at the center of the Forum. The cult statue stood in the apse of the temple on a podium. Another cuirassed (though naked to the waist) representation of Mars Ultor can be seen on a relief from a large Carthaginian altar (see fig 7.2 in Mary Beard, John North, and Simon Price, *Religions of Rome*, 2 vols. [Cambridge: Cambridge University Press, 1998], 1:332), and a draped figure is visible on the temple pediment on the so-called *Ara Pietatis* (see the detail of this relief of fig. 150 in Zanker, *Power of Images*, 96). For a concise discussion of Mars Ultor and the plan of the Roman temple, see Beard, North, and Price, *Religions of Rome*, 1:199f. and 2:80f.; and for a copy of the cult statue, see Zanker, *Power of Images*, 200, or the brief treatment in Diana E. E. Kleiner, *Roman Sculpture* (New Haven: Yale University Press, 1992), 181–82. For the Forum of Augustus, see Paul Zanker, *Forum Augustum: das Bildprogramm* (Tübingen: Wasmuth, 1968).

Part 2: Biblical Studies and Theology in Practice

of the imperial family;[32] personified virtues or abstractions;[33] gods associated with Rome's mythic origin and reconstitution under Augustus;[34] divine figures upon vessels of travel, jewelry, decorative items, and so on;[35] and of course the near ubiquitous *Dea Roma*, who was herself often joined with the emperor both in temples and on coins.[36] Private religious devotion involving various εἰκόνες

---

32. Zanker discusses a classicizing statue of the emperor Tiberius (Ny Carlsberg Glyptotek, inv. 538), which he says fits within the type first created for a cult statue of the *Divus Iulius* (see Zanker, *Power of Images*, 249 [fig. 194]). On this statue in particular, see V. Poulsen, *Les Portraits Romains*, vol. 1, *République et Dynastie Julienne* (Copenhagen: Glyptothèque Ny Carlsberg, 1962), 84 and fig. 47 (plates 51, 52). For a perspicuous treatment of imperial statues, see Simon R. F. Price, *Rituals and Power: The Roman Imperial Cult in Asia Minor* (Cambridge: Cambridge University Press, 1984). See also a related statue of Livia (Ny Carlsberg Glyptotek, inv. 531).

33. See Cicero, *Nat. d.* 11.23 §61: "In other cases some exceptionally potent force is designated by a title of divinity, for example, Faith and Mind. . . . You see the temple of Virtue, restored as the temple of Honor . . . the temples of Wealth, Safety, Concord, Liberty, and Victory. The names of Desire, Pleasure and Venus Lubentina have been deified" (trans. Rackham, LCL; cf. *Res gestae* 2.11). The personified deities Honor and Virtue, e.g., were portrayed together frequently on coins from at least 67 BC (see, e.g., C. Lochin, "Honos," *LIMC* V.1, 498–502; and V.2, 341, fig. 10 [Honos 10]). So, too, the personifications often took statue form. For example, the Livia referenced in the preceding note is a personified abstraction styled as Livia. Poulsen's identification of this particular statue is more specific on the basis of the cornucopia: "la statue représente la déesse de la Fortune" (Poulsen, *Portraits Romains*, 1:73 [fig. 38]). See Paul Zanker, *Pompeii: Public and Private Life*, trans. Deborah Lucas Schneider (Cambridge, MA: Harvard University Press, 1998), 98 (fig. 48).

34. Cf. the upper right panel on the west side (entrance) of the *Ara Pacis Augustae*, which depicts the sacrifice of Aeneas, the legendary ancestor of the Roman people, in front of the shrine of the Penates.

35. Cf., e.g., the multiplicity of Triton images in *LIMC* VIII.2, or the mention of the Gemini in Acts 28:11.

36. Cf. Josephus's description of the Roma-Augustus temple built by Herod in Caesarea Maritima: "On an eminence facing the mouth of the harbor stood Caesar's temple, remarkable for its beauty and grand proportions; and in it was a colossal statue of Caesar [καῖσαρ], not inferior to the Olympian Zeus [διός], for which it had been modeled, and another of Roma, equal to that of Hera at Argos" (*B. J.* 1.21.7 §414). A Nero/Roma coin from the mint in Rome illustrates well the intersection of the economic plane with the cultic and the potential religious significance of everyday materials. The head of Nero, with a hairstyle that evokes Alexander and his Diadochi (see Hans Peter L'Orange, *Apotheosis in Ancient Portraiture* [Oslo: Aschehoug, 1947], 58f.), is on the obverse. The goddess Roma is displayed on the reverse, along with the *Senatus Consulto* (SC). Note, too, the personification of Victory, held in the outstretched right hand of Roma. A picture of this coin is found in Harold Mattingly, *Coins of the Roman Empire in the British Museum*, vol. 1, *Augustus to Vitellius* (London: British Museum, 1923), plate 43, coin 1. For similar coins but from different principates, see the relevant plates in Mattingly, *Coins*. From the second century, one might also compare

would also come into play, and perhaps especially so in light of the meetings of early Christians in "house churches."[37] We obviously have no idea of the exact religious furniture of the particular houses of the early Gentile Christians in Rome (prior to their "conversion"), but it would be surprising if they did not contain some physical representation of the *lares*, often rendered "household gods."[38] Statuettes of these deities were "a common feature of Roman houses" and, if the monetary resources were available, were evidently placed in a household shrine, a *lararium*.[39]

So, too, recent research has shown that Ovid's remarks from his life of exile were not mere bootlicking;[40] rather, iconic expressions of devotion or fidelity

---

the excellent relief of the apotheosis of Antoninus Pius (d. 161) on a column erected in his honor, where Dea Roma is similarly depicted (Beard, North, and Price, *Religions of Rome*, 2:52, fig. 2.8b).

37. The house church is now a well-established feature of early Christianity in Rome and of Pauline communities in general (cf., e.g., καὶ τῇ κατ' οἶκόν σου ἐκκλησίᾳ, Phlm 2). See, e.g., David L. Balch, "Paul, Families, and Households," in *Paul in the Greco-Roman World*, ed. J. Paul Sampley (Harrisburg: Trinity International Press, 2003), 258–92; the rev. ed. of Peter Lampe's dissertation, *From Paul to Valentinus: Christians at Rome in the First Two Centuries* (Minneapolis: Fortress, 2003); and L. Michael White, *The Social Origins of Christian Architecture* (Valley Forge, PA: Trinity Press, 1990). For a recent treatment of Romans that makes use of such research, see Philip F. Esler, *Conflict and Identity in Romans: The Social Setting of Paul's Letter* (Minneapolis: Fortress, 2003), esp. 120f. On the difference between ancient and modern conceptions of "private space," Zanker, *Pompeii*, 9f., is lucid.

38. Beard, North, and Price, *Religions of Rome*, 1:185, caution against this as an "automatic" translation. They prefer "protecting spirits of place," presumably in light of the fact that the Lares "were worshipped in various contexts: in the house, at the crossroads, in the city (as guardians of the state)" (2:30). To what degree normal (i.e., not religiously explicit) furnishings—sphinx tables, etc.—would have been seen as εἰκόνες is impossible to know for certain.

39. The *lararia* differed in decoration and elaborateness, and they are found in kitchens, gardens, atria, etc. More wealthy persons could afford what amounted to mini-temples (there were provisions for sacrifice) with richly done frescoes, while other *lararia* were plainer. A rather elaborate *lararium*—an *aedicula* from Pompeii, Casa delle Pareti Rosse (Deutsches Archäologisches Institut Rom 71.114)—was found with the statuettes inside. A *lar* was placed on the far right and left. The additional figures in between are Aesculapius, Apollo, Mercury, and Hercules. In Pompeii there were twenty-seven *lararia* with statuettes in them (George K. Boyce, *Corpus of the Lararia of Pompeii*, Memoirs of the Academy in Rome 14 [Rome: American Academy in Rome, 1937], 107). See the pictures and report of Boyce, *Corpus of the Lararia of Pompeii*. The elaborate *lararium* described above is found on plate 31. For excellent and copious pictures of statuettes of the *lares*, which apparently exhibited a standard form, see *LIMC* VI.2, 97–102.

40. Ovid, *Epistulae ex Ponto* 4.9: "The foreign country sees that there is a shrine of Caesar in my house. Beside him stand his pious son and priestly wife [Tiberius and Livia],

Part 2: Biblical Studies and Theology in Practice

to the emperor were often part of life in the home,[41] as is probably also true of the "gods of the interior," the *penates* (if not merged together with the *lares*).[42] Moreover, "foreign" deities, as evidenced for example by the recovery of many Isis statuettes,[43] were also incorporated and serve to indicate the panoply of possibilities for worship in the home.

Drawing a direct line from these general realities of religious life in Rome and the wider Roman world to particular Roman house churches is impossible, but the picture given above is nonetheless quite useful in that it sets into sharp relief the difference between "normal" life in Rome—wherein both public and private space were filled, and indeed constructed, with religious materials—and Paul's radical critique. For those who would take Paul seriously, the perception of both public and private space at the point of images is configured around the break between God and the world. In Paul's view as expressed in Romans 1, this break necessitates the theological eradication of an εἰκών as a legitimate form of religious devotion. In this sense Paul's theology of creation and its corresponding critique of pagan εἰκόνες are indeed deeply and resolutely aniconic: εἰκών here is synonymous with εἴδωλον.

Christ as the Εἰκὼν Τοῦ Θεοῦ

(a) 2 Corinthians 4:4: The use of εἰκών in Romans 1 sets the problem in stark terms. If Paul's critique is pressed, the question becomes, Can God be imaged

---

deities no less important than himself now that he has become a god. To make the household group complete, both of the grandsons are there, one by the side of his grandmother, the other by that of his father. To these I offer incense and words of prayer as often as the day rises from the east" (trans. Wheeler, LCL, altered).

41. Cf., from Italy, Horace, *Carm.* 4.5.29f. Devotion to the emperor within the private household has only recently received sufficient attention. See Ittai Gradel, *Emperor Worship and Roman Religion* (Oxford: Oxford University Press, 2002), 198–212.

42. Cicero, *Nat. d.* 11.27 §68. See Annie Dubourdieu, *Les Origines et le développement du culte des Pénates à Rome* (Rome: Ecole française de Rome, 1989), 94f., esp. 101–10. Dubourdieu concludes: "Les Pénates ont donc été rapprochés d'un certain nombre de pluralités divines, *di patrii, di parentum*, et Lares, ou identifies avec elles" (110). See also Pedar W. Foss, "Watchful Lares: Roman Household Organization and the Rituals of Cooking and Eating," in *Domestic Space in the Roman World: Pompeii and Beyond*, ed. Ray Laurence and Andrew Wallace-Hadrill (Portsmouth, RI: JRA, 1997), 197–218; D. G. Orr, "Roman Domestic Religion," *ANRW* 2.16.2 (1978): 1557–91, esp. 1562f. The *penates* were also part of public life (e.g., Augustus built separate temples to the *lares* and the *di penates* [*Res gestae* 4.19; cf. Tacitus, *Ann.* 15.41]).

43. Cf. the pair of Isiac frescoes found in Herculaneum, probably in a private house (Beard, North, and Price, *Religions of Rome*, 2:303).

if God is other than the world? That is, does not the attempt to figure God in an εἰκών lie at the heart of idolatry exactly on Paul's own construal?

In 2 Corinthians 4:4 Paul writes that Christ is the εἰκὼν τοῦ θεοῦ. The background of this statement has frequently been sought,[44] and it is as likely as not that Jewish Wisdom traditions are close at hand. Wisdom, for example, is spoken of as the εἰκὼν τῆς ἀγαθότητος [τοῦ θεοῦ] (Wis 7:26; cf. 1 Cor 1:24). Yet the turn to such traditions — or, for example, Philo's λόγος as the εἰκὼν θεοῦ for that matter — does not lessen the intensity of Paul's claim, for in fact Paul has focused these traditions entirely onto one human being and, at that, one who was executed.

The shape, then, of God's image is in a very definite sense anthropological. That is to say, for Paul, Christ is always an ἄνθρωπος (cf. esp. Rom 5:15-21; Phil 2:7), and thus God's εἰκών is an image of a human.[45] In this way, πρόσωπον in 2 Corinthians 4:6 is probably best rendered "person," rather than "face," so that the stress lies not so much on the appearance — though this may certainly be implied — as on the totality of the Lord Jesus Christ as the one who is the light of the knowledge of the δόξα of God.[46] The εἰκών is the person himself.

It is worth noting the striking difference here from the remarkable vision in Ezekiel 1:26-28, where ὁμοίωμα ὡς εἶδος ἀνθρώπου occurs as a description of God (moreover, 1:27 tells of an ὄψιν ἠλέκτρου, a face of gold). In Ezekiel, the mode is rather apophatic. To avoid identification between the anthropological comparison and God himself, the comparison takes place within the visionary's stress on the distance of what is seen from the reality: he does not see a throne, but a likeness of a throne; not God as a human, but a likeness of a (visible) form of a human; not the glory of the Lord, but a likeness of the glory, and so on. In point of fact, ὁμοίωμα is used four and ὡς five times in

---

44. See, e.g., Frank J. Matera, *II Corinthians: A Commentary* (Louisville: Westminster John Knox, 2003).

45. In the context of this section of 2 Corinthians, this point is seen clearly through the frequent use of the proper name Ἰησοῦς in 4:5 and 4:7-15 — "für Paulus eine ganz singuläre Häufung." See further the discussion in Ulrich Mauser, *Gottesbild und Menschwerdung: Eine Untersuchung zur Einheit des Alten und Neuen Testaments* (Tübingen: Mohr, 1971), 136f.

46. Contra Jervell, *Imago Dei*, 214f.: e.g., "Hier ist darauf zu achten, daß nur der erhöhte, auferstandene, himmlische Christus die Eikon Gottes ist." Paul does not separate the earthly from the heavenly Christ but instead conceives of Jesus Christ in the entirety of his existence as "ein einziges Subjekt" (Mauser, *Gottesbild*, 140). In Jervell's interpretation, Paul's thought in this passage is strained far too vigorously through the filter of an alleged gnostic background.

this brief span of three verses. By contrast, Paul's explicit statement involves a direct identification of a particular, concrete human as the εἰκὼν θεοῦ.

That the person of Christ as God's εἰκών is the knowledge of God's δόξα —"Gottes Wesens- und Wirkungsart, das heißt, Gott selbst"[47]—has led some scholars to emphasize the divinity of Christ: "Wie wir aus 2Kor 4,1–6 sehen, zielt nun die Gottebenbildlichkeit Christi darauf, daß die Menschen dadurch zur Erkenntnis der Göttlichkeit Christi kommen sollen, bes. V.6."[48] Yet, as Barrett rightly notes, "it would be nearer to Paul's thought to say that through Christ as the image of God men come to apprehend the Göttlichkeit of God— that is . . . what it means . . . to be God."[49] It is precisely in this sense that Paul is deeply iconic—God does have an image, and this image is first of all a human being.

(b) Colossians 1:15: The so-called hymn of Colossians 1:15–20 has been the "intensivster Gegenstand der Forschung"[50] in the study of this epistle. Despite Wright's sobering remarks on the dangers of constructing earlier versions,[51] scholars continue to debate what should be counted "in" or "out" prior to the verses as we have them.[52] For this chapter, we shall take the crucial phrase—ὅς ἐστιν εἰκὼν τοῦ θεοῦ τοῦ ἀοράτου—as it is, especially because it evidences an important connection to a later portion of the letter and thus speaks at least for its strategic incorporation (3:10, see below).

The conjunction of εἰκών and ἀόρατος has consistently baffled interpreters: "Wie soll von Unsichtbarem ein Bild möglich sein?"[53] The answer often given is similar to that of Lightfoot a century ago: "representation" and "manifesta-

---

47. Jervell, *Imago Dei*, 216. Cf. Carey C. Newman, "Resurrection as Glory: Divine Presence and Christian Origins," in *The Resurrection: An Interdisciplinary Symposium on the Resurrection of Jesus*, ed. Stephen T. Davis, Daniel Kendall, and Gerald O'Collins (Oxford: Oxford University Press, 1997), 59–89: "the visible, movable divine presence" (62).

48. Jervell, *Imago Dei*, 218.

49. Barrett, *2 Corinthians*, 132.

50. Joachim Gnilka, *Der Kolosserbrief*, HThKNT X/1 (Freiburg im Breisgau: Herder, 1980), 51.

51. N. T. Wright, "Poetry and Theology in Colossians 1.15–20," *NTS* 36 (1990): esp. 444–51.

52. E.g., A. T. Lincoln, "The Letter to the Colossians," in *The New Interpreter's Bible*, vol. 11, *2 Corinthians, Galatians, Ephesians, Philippians, Colossians, 1 & 2 Thessalonians, 1 & 2 Timothy, Titus, Philemon* (Nashville: Abingdon, 2000), 602f.

53. Ernst Lohmeyer, *Der Brief an die Kolosser und an Philemon* (Göttingen: Vandenhoeck & Ruprecht, 1929), 54. Cf. Eduard Schweizer, *Der Brief an die Kolosser* (Neukirchen-Vluyn: Neukirchener Verlag, 1976): "Wie kann man aber von einem 'unsichtbaren Bild' reden?" (57).

tion."⁵⁴ There is, on this reading, only a "semantische," rather than a "logische Aporie," for "das Bild [wird] vor allem als Abbild charakterisiert."⁵⁵ Yet, even where gnostic-like interpretations such as Jervell's are not endorsed,⁵⁶ such *Abbild* language continues nonetheless to allow a type of Gnostic or Platonic influence with the consequence that through semantic imprecision something resembling Plotinus's later emanationism sneaks in: Christ is removed from the reality of God to become a mere reflection, representation, or mirror image of the God who in fact remains invisible.

But the emphasis in Colossians is hardly upon Christ as an archetype of reality in this way. Instead, Christ, as the author would have it, is the mystery of God (2:2). God, that is, is really known in him visibly—there is neither cleft nor distance between the εἰκών of God and God *in se*. The anthropological force of σωματικῶς in 2:9 ruptures any connection to Platonism or Gnosticism, as "bodily" fullness of deity is their very antithesis (cf. 1:19–20: εὐδόκησεν πᾶν τὸ πλήρωμα κατοικῆσαι . . . εἰρηνοποιήσας διὰ τοῦ αἵματος τοῦ σταυροῦ αὐτοῦ).

Rather than a representation of the invisible God, Christ is the movement of the invisible God into visibility in the life of a human being, ἐν τῷ σώματι τῆς σαρκός (1:22). The Pauline view of revelation is not cheapened gnostically or platonically in Colossians. Gnilka comes close to the point:

> Als Bild Gottes bleibt Christus nicht hinter dem Abgebildeten zurück wie die platonische Eikon, wird er nicht zum minderen Ersatz Gottes, mit dem wir uns begnügen müssten . . . sondern steht er ganz auf seiten Gottes. Zöge man die an sich richtige Konsequenz und sagte, man kann jetzt nicht mehr von Gott reden, ohne von Christus reden zu müssen, wäre es doch zutreffender, es umgekehrt und positiv zu formulieren: Wer von Christus spricht, spricht von Gott.⁵⁷

Hence the logic of the Pauline εἰκών: to speak of the life of a human being is to speak of God. Contra Jervell, in no way can "der Eikonzustand Christi" be understood as "ganz 'gnostisch,'" and his conclusion—"Deshalb kommt in

---

54. J. B. Lightfoot, *St. Paul's Epistles to the Colossians and to Philemon* (London: Macmillan, 1904), 143.
55. Petr Pokorný, *Der Brief des Paulus an die Kolosser* (Berlin: Evangelischer Verlagsanstalt, 1987), 63.
56. Jervell, *Imago Dei*, 225.
57. Gnilka, *Kolosserbrief*, 61.

Part 2: Biblical Studies and Theology in Practice

Eikon die Gottheit Christi und nicht seine Menschheit zum Ausdruck"[58]—we may restate thus: Wenn in Eikon die Gottheit Christi zum Ausdruck kommt, kommt damit auch seine Menschheit zum Ausdruck. That is to say, as the εἰκὼν τοῦ θεοῦ τοῦ ἀοράτου, Christ stands on the side of God in his humanity. Paul's earliest interpreters have gotten him right: the invisible God turns out to be visible precisely in his human image.

Human Transformation and the Εἰκὼν Χριστοῦ

(a) 1 Corinthians 15: Paul's extended argument about the resurrection of the dead "anchors the whole discussion" of the letter.[59] Near the end of the argument, Paul employs the term εἰκών within his Adam-Christ typology (15:21–22, 45–49) in order to make the point that the resurrection of believers will in fact be a bodily one:

15:49a: καὶ καθὼς ἐφορέσαμεν τὴν εἰκόνα τοῦ χοϊκοῦ

15:49b: φορέσομεν[60] καὶ τὴν εἰκόνα τοῦ ἐπουρανίου

In the context of his argument and debate with the Corinthians, εἰκών has to do not with some primordial godlike image within but with the character, stamp, or shape of bodily life. It is on the one hand "of dust" or "weakness" and on the other "of heaven" or "power." Yet the two are not mutually exclusive: human beings bear the εἰκών of both Adam and Christ. But the relation of the images is not simply one of temporal succession, as it might seem on a first reading.[61] In fact, there is a profound tension created by the tense of Paul's verbs: aorist (ἐφορέσαμεν) and future (φορέσομεν). "We have borne" (or "wore"[62]) and "we will bear" combine to leave the present strangely undetermined. What is the εἰκών of the present? The clue to the Pauline answer to this question lies in the logic of participation and the eschatological determination

---

58. Jervell, *Imago Dei*, 225: "So ist also der Eikonzustand Christi ganz 'gnostisch' verstanden."

59. Richard B. Hays, *First Corinthians* (Louisville: Westminster John Knox, 1997), 252.

60. Despite the weak textual attestation, φορέσομεν (rather than φορέσωμεν) is probably the better reading in light of the context (emphasis on resurrection, etc.). See, e.g., Anthony C. Thiselton, *The First Epistle to the Corinthians* (Grand Rapids: Eerdmans, 2000), 1288–89.

61. Cf. 1 Cor 15:22: "For as all die in Adam, so all will be made alive in Christ."

62. See "φορέω" in BDAG, 1064.

of time, but to see the connection to image-bearing in particular we must turn to Romans 8 and 2 Corinthians 3.

(b) Romans 8:29: In Romans 8:18-38 Paul unpacks the συν- compounds of 8:17 (συμπάσχομεν, συνδοξασθῶμεν) as he reflects on the suffering and hope of Christians in the present—the focal point, with respect to time, of the passage. In a move that attempts to relate God's sovereignty and care to present experience, God is said to have predetermined those whom he foreknew συμμόρφους τῆς εἰκόνος τοῦ υἱοῦ αὐτοῦ (8:29). The awkwardness in the phrase finally resists felicitous translation, but an approximation that keeps the relation of σύμμορφος to εἰκών nevertheless seems possible: "to share the form of the image of his Son."

The central question regarding the breadth—and, hence, interpretation—of εἰκών is frequently skewed by the construction of an antithesis that the text does not support. Dunn, for example, against the backdrop of an "Adam Christology," develops an exegesis that situates the εἰκών entirely on the side of resurrection: "Paul has in view the *risen* Christ, the exalted Christ of the last age, not Jesus as he was on earth."[63] Yet, for Paul there is no such antithesis, Christ versus Jesus or resurrection/exaltation versus present suffering. Instead, Jesus Christ is one subject who in his unity embraces the totality of his life, death, and resurrection; moreover, resurrection is not something that is divorced from present suffering. Indeed, present suffering is constitutive of what it means to live the life that ends in resurrection. In this sense, to suffer and die in the present with the hope of resurrection is in a precise sense to be in the εἰκών τοῦ υἱοῦ or to share the form (σύμμορφος) of his image: the pattern that is the life, death, and resurrection of Jesus Christ.[64]

The use of εἰκών in Romans 8:29 is thus startlingly different from the earlier use of the word in Romans 1:23 and helps to fill in the space of the "present" left between the past (aorist) and future in 1 Corinthians 15:49. Here in 8:29 εἰκών is determined eschatologically—that is to say, as both/and or now/not

---

63. James D. G. Dunn, *Romans 1-8* (Dallas: Word, 1988), 483. Dunn does not deny that Christians suffer but insists that the image to which the Christians are to be conformed is the resurrected Christ of glory; e.g., "the image to which they are to be conformed is that of the resurrected one" (484). Cf., e.g., Jervell, *Imago Dei*, 189-90, who mentions Rom 8:29 in the context of 2 Cor 3:18.

64. After writing this article, I noticed that C. F. D. Moule, *The Epistles of Paul the Apostle to the Colossians and to Philemon* (Cambridge: Cambridge University Press, 1957), also speaks in the context of his brief remarks on Col 3:10 of "the pattern of Christ" as a way to talk about the image of God (100). Moule, however, does not develop this thought in any way and leaves the pattern unspecified.

Part 2: Biblical Studies and Theology in Practice

yet[65]—and refers not to static pagan images (εἴδωλα) but to human existence in light of participation in Christ, this pattern of life that flows from being "in Christ" and comes to expression in the present as suffering and hope.[66]

(c) 2 Corinthians 3:18: The use of εἰκών in 2 Corinthians 3:18 comes at the end of Paul's notoriously difficult ruminations on Moses and the "old covenant" (3:14). Thankfully, we do not need to enter the heart of this bramble thicket and may instead come to an understanding of εἰκών in 3:18 through its correlation with Paul's opening remarks in 3:2-3:

> You are our letter, inscribed on our hearts, known and read by all people. You reveal that you are a letter of Christ [ἐπιστολὴ Χριστοῦ], delivered [lit. ministered] by us, inscribed not with ink but by the Spirit of the living God, not on stone tablets but on the tablets of fleshy hearts.

In his elegant exegesis of the entire unit (3:1-4:6), Richard Hays demonstrated that Paul employs his discussion of Moses's veil and so on to develop and buttress his claim that the Corinthians themselves are in fact a letter of Christ.[67] The immediate conclusion of this discussion in 3:18, then, is to be read in counterpoint with the opening claim in 3:2-3 cited just above. Second Corinthians 3:18 is thus a description of what it means for the Corinthians to be a letter of Christ. Beholding the δόξαν κυρίου they are in fact being transformed (μεταμορφόω) into τὴν αὐτὴν εἰκόνα from glory into glory (ἀπὸ δόξης εἰς δόξαν).

The close association of a μορφή compound with εἰκών bears a linguistic similarity to Romans 8:29, and here the present participle focuses the claim ex-

---

65. Esler, *Conflict and Identity*, 261f., contends that to express Pauline eschatology in a "now/not yet" schema is to impose anachronistically modern notions of "future." For Paul, as for other Mediterraneans, the future is a natural outcome of the present (citing the metaphor of Rom 8:22). Esler's discussion, however, (1) overlooks the significance of "inbreaking" that attends the notion of ἀποκάλυψις in the Pauline conception of time (cf., if authentic, esp. Rom 16:25-26), (2) simplifies ancient constructions of time (cf., e.g., the dialogue in Cicero's *De natura deorum*, or the interesting article of Peter J. Holliday, "Time, History, and Ritual on the Ara Pacis Augustae," *Art Bulletin* 72 [1990]: 542-57), and (3) except in what it denies, sounds in its alternative proposal remarkably like what is usually meant by the tensive language of now/not yet (e.g., "Now the glory is forthcoming, rather than future and has a direct, organic connection with present experience. It [glory] exists on the horizon of the present, even if it is not already here" [265]).

66. Cf. Rom 5:1-5; 6:5, etc.

67. Which of course serves to further the argument for Paul's own authority. See Richard B. Hays, *Echoes of Scripture in the Letters of Paul* (New Haven: Yale University Press, 1989), 122-53.

plicitly on ecclesial life in the present: the Corinthians "are being transformed" into the same εἰκών. But as Hays notes, "the same image" leaves the question of the referent of εἰκών open. The auditor/reader has to wait until 2 Corinthians 4:6, when at last the referent of the εἰκών is specified more precisely:

> The imagery of 3:18 paints a picture of the community ... being transformed as they contemplate a vision of glory, but does not yet show the reader what they are gazing at. The source and character of the radiance remain, as it were, offstage. The progression reaches its consummation in 4:6, as Paul ... declares that it is "the face [sic] of Jesus Christ," that manifests the glory. Christ is the glory-bearing *eikōn* into which the community is being transformed, the paradigm for the prosopography of the new covenant.[68]

Hence, to be changed into the form of the εἰκών is to bear the image of Christ in a pattern of communal life, to "manifest the life of Jesus in [the] mortal flesh (cf. 2 Cor 4:11)."[69] The similarity to Romans 8:29 occurs at the level of the "deeper nature of things."[70] The life of those who by their belief participate in the εἰκών θεοῦ is indeed transformed into this same εἰκών, and the contour of this image in the present is traced along the curve that constitutes the pattern that is the life, death, and resurrection of Jesus Christ.

(d) Colossians 3:10: This second use of εἰκών in Colossians occurs in the middle of an extended section in which the emphasis falls on what it means in practice to have died and risen with Christ—that is, to participate in him (3:1–3; cf. 2:11–12). The author exhorts his audience not to lie, for Christians have discarded τὸν παλαιὸν ἄνθρωπον σὺν ταῖς πράξεσιν αὐτοῦ and put on τὸν νέον τὸν ἀνακαινούμενον εἰς ἐπίγνωσιν κατ' εἰκόνα τοῦ κτίσαντος αὐτόν (3:9–10).

In light of Colossians 1:15 the phrase εἰκόνα τοῦ κτίσαντος reads as circumlocution for εἰκὼν τοῦ θεοῦ.[71] Yet here the participle—in a way that the

---

68. Hays, *Echoes*, 153.
69. Hays, *Echoes*, 144.
70. Note, too, the contrast between the δόξα usage in Rom 1:23 and 2 Cor 3:18.
71. This is not, however, to dismantle the connection between creation and Christology found in Col 1:16. Chrysostom et al. read τοῦ κτίσαντος of Christ. Lightfoot, *Colossians*, 214, argues that the allusion to Gen 1:26 requires God rather than Christ. Three points are in order: (1) In light of Col 1:16 it is not the case that the well-known allusion to Gen 1:26–27 precludes the possibility of reading the participle of Christ. (2) As noted above, in light of Col 1:15 where Christ is explicitly called the εἰκὼν τοῦ θεοῦ, epistolary context pushes the reading here in 3:10 toward θεός as the grammatically preferable immediate referent

Part 2: Biblical Studies and Theology in Practice

simple noun does not—places an emphasis on an action that continues into the present[72] and, moreover, emphasizes the present as the process of re-creation, of ἀνακαίνωσις (cf. τὸν ἀνακαινούμενον). But the focus of such renewal and transformation is not, in the context of Colossians, on the individual but rather on the community, for the author continues immediately: ὅπου οὐκ ἔνι Ἕλλην καὶ Ἰουδαῖος, περιτομὴ καὶ ἀκροβυστία, βάρβαρος, Σκύθης, δοῦλος, ἐλεύθερος, ἀλλὰ τὰ πάντα καὶ ἐν πᾶσιν Χριστός (3:11).

To see the unity of the ἐκκλησία is, therefore, to see the image of God. Indeed, not only is Christ said to be ἡ ζωή of the Colossians (3:4), their community is actually his very body (1:24; cf. 2:19). For the author of Colossians, the transformation of the Christian community turns out to be revelation, as the invisible God is seen in the world through the life of a community that is re-created in his image. The image of God is thus anthropological in a double—and very Pauline—sense: Jesus Christ, and the community of human beings that participate in him.

The Pauline Theology of Εἰκών

In light of the foregoing exegesis, we may conclude that the various Pauline uses of εἰκών constitute a basic unity. This unity derives not from semantic uniformity—words cannot be torn free of their context—but from the theological coherence that attends the εἰκών language of Paul and his earliest interpreters as it relates to God. In the person of Jesus Christ and his christologically shaped community, the God of Israel does in fact have an image.

Yet to affirm that God has an image is also to acknowledge the possibility of error or illegitimacy, wherein the true εἰκὼν θεοῦ is exchanged for a false image. Εἰκών in this sense is construed as εἴδωλον; hence, Paul's critique in Romans 1. The shift in the meaning of εἰκών from image to idol or true to false reflects the word's connection to its divine object.

The Pauline theology of εἰκών thus finds its coherence in the notion of revelation—that is, how God is known. On the one hand, God makes himself known in his εἰκών, Jesus Christ, and in the community that is transformed according to this image. And on the other, through human folly the knowledge of God is obfuscated, and such obfuscation manifests itself in εἰκόνες.

(Gnilka, *Kolosserbrief*, 188, sees this second point, but he ignores the first). (3) When pressed, in this context there is actually no difference in ultimate meaning: the Colossians are being re-created in Christ, who is the image of God, and they thus bear Christ's image.

72. Cf., e.g., David M. Hay, *Colossians*, ANTC (Nashville: Abingdon, 2000), 126, who treats the participle more like a simple aorist verb.

The Impact of Pauline Theology

To assess the impact of the exegesis on our larger question, we would do well to remember that religious or theological matters are never solely ideational; rather, as anthropologists have long insisted, "religious 'experience' relates to something in the social world believers live in."[73] Not even abstract thinking, that is, takes place in final abstraction from the world. Texts, moreover, are neither created nor received in a vacuum; instead they make their way into an already existing spatial reality.

In view of these reminders, the force of Paul's aniconic critique in Romans 1 can best be seen in terms of the theological construal of social space. Despite Halbertal's fascinating essay on the Mishnah,[74] it seems clear that social space is "never neutral."[75] It is always bound up with ideological, and in this case theological, articulation.[76] With respect to pagan images, Paul's aim in Romans 1 is not to carve out a place of neutral coexistence but rather to attack "an entire set of symbolic meanings,"[77] or, in more directly theological terms, to challenge the heart of the pagan knowledge of God:

> People knew their gods *through* the statues which depicted them, with a statue's particular attributes in a specific site often marking a local myth or ritual variation of a more general sacred cult. Ancient polytheism was not a religion of written scriptures and doctrines.... Images and myths provided

---

73. Talal Asad, "Anthropological Conceptions of Religion: Reflections on Geertz," *Man* 18 (1983): 249. Here "experience" is not to be understood narrowly (e.g., in rigorously Schleiermacherian terms) but rather in a sense broad enough to encompass even sophisticated secondary reflection (this type of thinking is, after all, also part of experience).

74. Moshe Halbertal, "Coexisting with the Enemy: Jews and Pagans in the Mishnah," in *Tolerance and Intolerance in Early Judaism and Christianity*, ed. Graham N. Stanton and Guy G. Stroumsa (Cambridge: Cambridge University Press, 1998), 159-72.

75. Hilda Kuper, "The Language of Sites in the Politics of Space," *American Anthropologist* 74 (1972): 421. With respect to the essay mentioned in the previous note, Halbertal himself acknowledges, with reference to the work of Charles Taylor, that the attempt to create "neutral space" as an approach to "tolerance" would probably not "survive serious philosophical scrutiny" (163).

76. Price, *Rituals and Power*, grasps this point clearly (see esp. ch. 6 on architecture). Cf. Ray Laurence, "Space and Text," in *Domestic Space in the Roman World: Pompeii and Beyond*, ed. Ray Laurence and Andrew Wallace-Hadrill (Portsmouth, RI: JRA, 1997), 14: "Spatial practice does not simply take place within an ideological environment but is involved in its maintenance as well."

77. Gordon, "The Real," 17.

Part 2: Biblical Studies and Theology in Practice

the main forms of "theology" in the ancient world—giving worshippers the means to recognize and think about their gods.[78]

Images, in other words, were, as Elsner rightly discerned, "not merely passive representations or adornments. They [were] active."[79] Social space—the areas in which life was lived—for pagans was thus in a sense alive with images, mythologized. The statues in the temples and around the cities, the reliefs on the altars, the busts and statuettes of the home, and so on all, with varying degrees of intensity to be sure, figured the divine or, better for ancient polytheism, the divinities. The notion of a separate, secular realm devoid of religious penetration is of course a modern invention (if not itself a fiction). For ancient pagans, space was religious.

Paul's reading of εἰκόνες as εἴδωλα thus demythologizes social space in the far-reaching sense that it removes—or, perhaps, exorcises—the divine from its image and leaves in its place a lump of stone or piece of wood.[80] For Gentile converts, Paul's critique alters radically their "experience of space, the values attached through facts of social and personal existence."[81] Old ways of knowing and living get deconstructed, with the result that the traditional civic tem-

---

78. Jaś Elsner, *Imperial Rome and Christian Triumph: The Art of the Roman Empire AD 100–450* (Oxford: Oxford University Press, 1998), 12. Cf. Elsner, *Art and the Roman Viewer: The Transformation of Art from the Pagan World to Christianity* (Cambridge: Cambridge University Press, 1995), 214; Robin Lane Fox, *Pagans and Christians* (New York: Knopf, 1987), esp. 133f.; and R. L. Gordon, "The Real," esp. 7f.

79. Elsner, *Imperial Rome*, 30. Cf. Elsner, "Image and Ritual: Reflections on the Religious Appreciation of Classical Art," *CQ* 46 (1996): 515–31, esp. 518, 529. This was no less true for a sophisticated or "symbolic" view of images (cf. in a slightly different context Lane Fox, *Pagans*, 135: "Statues were not only the symbols of a god's presence. From the first century A. D. onwards, we know of secret rites which were thought to 'animate' them and draw a divine 'presence' into their material"). On this long philosophic or symbolic tradition, see, e.g., ch. 3 in Finney, *Invisible God*, 162f. For the later, rabbinic interaction with this view, see E. E. Urbach, "The Rabbinical Laws of Idolatry in the Second and Third Centuries in the Light of Archaeological and Historical Facts," *Israel Exploration Journal* 9 (1959): 162–63. Gordon, "The Real," 10, is insightful on the relation of philosophical criticism to the "majority" view of the ancient world.

80. Note Paul's careful delineation in 1 Cor 10:19-20: the actual material image, the εἴδωλον, is nothing, while the numinous realities to which the sacrifice is, as it were, really made are named δαιμόνια. Cf. 1 Cor 8:4 where Paul, whether agreeing with the Corinthian assertion or making the statement himself, also remarks that an idol is nothing. So, too, the statement from 1 Thess 1:9 cited below contrasts dead images (idols) with the "living" God. For the rabbinic view of this matter, see Urbach, "Rabbinical Laws," 154–55, esp. n. 19.

81. Kuper, "Language," 411.

ples and deities are problematized under the rubric of idolatry; the statues of the imperial family, rather than images to be venerated, have become idols to be avoided; the lararium, rather than the shrine of the house, has become—at best—decoration. Statuettes and portable images, such as those of Apuleius,[82] turn into raw matter, no longer capable of being invoked. In short, rather than figuring the divine, the pagan religious furniture becomes just that, simple furniture. Paul's critique thus undoes the pagan conceptualization of social space, as much of its material culture is stripped of theological significance.

The question then arises as to how, on Paul's counter-construal, that space now emptied, as it were, of its former meaning is to be filled. Space, we remember, is never neutral. And, in fact, inherent in Paul's critique is the battle over the proper understanding of the world in which one lives and moves.

There are stories—and evidence—of imperial "head-swapping," wherein, upon the transition of emperors, ancient sculptors made a new head and simply replaced the old with the new, leaving the rest of the statue intact.[83] The statues received a facelift, a little cosmetic surgery that nonetheless left the basic structure unbroken. By analogy, Paul's work is fundamentally dissimilar. It is not one of replacement but one of reconstruction, reconstitution, a reordering of social space not around εἰκόνες but around community.

Instead of statues, altars, and so on,[84] Paul posits not different statues or statues remade but a human community, the ἐκκλησία.[85] The conceptualization

---

82. In his defense against the charge of sorcery, Apuleius remarks: "I usually carry with me, wherever I go, a statuette of some god.... On feasts I offer up incense and wine to it, and sometimes an animal victim. So just now... I ordered someone to run and get my small Mercury" (*Apologia* 63). Apuleius's speech is obviously much later than and geographically removed from Paul (ca. 158–159, North Africa), but in light of the numerous remaining statuettes from a variety of periods and locations, there is no reason to think his remarks are inapplicable to the first century. For the Latin text of Apuleius's *Apologia*, see Vincent Hunink, ed., *Apuleius: Pro Se De Magia* (Amsterdam: Gieben, 1997). Hunink also has an excellent English translation, which I use here: Stephen Harrison, ed., *Apuleius: Rhetorical Works*, trans. Stephen Harrison, John Hilton, and Vincent Hunink (Oxford: Oxford University Press, 2001).

83. See Price, *Rituals and Power*, 193f. Price notes that "in principle the image was permanent," but in cases of official disgrace "the standard constraints were lifted" (193; see also 177–78). So, e.g., statues of Caligula, Nero, and Domitian were reworked. Price's concern is primarily with matters at the official level, and from the Ephesian inscription he cites (193, 189 n. 99), one might actually infer that, on an unofficial level at least, refashioning imperial images was a well-established practice.

84. On painted images, cf. Price, *Rituals and Power*, 188: "We do know that painted images of Augustus, Livia and Tiberius were set up in the theatre for the imperial festival at Gytheum with a table and incense burner in front, where sacrifices were offered."

85. For the Byzantine period, cf. Milton V. Anastos, "The Ethical Theory of Images

Part 2: Biblical Studies and Theology in Practice

and hence filling of social space is thus, for Pauline thought, not iconic in the traditional sense but anthropological, and precisely for that reason theological. That is to say that the justification for the Pauline reconstruction is that this community itself, by virtue of its participation in the εἰκὼν θεοῦ, is an image. Revelation—or, to switch for the moment to the language of phenomenology, "religious experience"—comes no longer through and is no longer bound up with material images. Rather, to know God is to see his image in the pattern of human community that is the life of Jesus Christ.

The shift from a pagan to a Pauline theology of image is tectonic and results in a basic break between them that cannot be bridged. Yet the Pauline view itself appears to result in something of a paradox. On the one hand, Paul and his interpreters are resolutely aniconic in every normal sense of the word. But on the other, Pauline theology affirms without hesitation that God has and is known in an εἰκών.

Concluding Reflections: NT Iconography

In his important book, P. C. Finney frequently adjures his readers to observe the crucial difference, known to "every undergraduate history major," between "the absence of evidence" and "negative evidence."[86] While knowledge of the latter sort would constitute firm ground for hypotheses regarding distinctively Christian material evidence before AD 200, we do not have it. But the former, which describes the present situation, only allows archaeological arguments that are, so Finney, *e silentio*—hence the current scholarly pickle.

Yet, despite the fact that "life and literature are not the same thing,"[87] the possibility nevertheless exists that the relation between literature that was authoritative for a particular community and the archaeological record of that community might amount to more than simple coincidence. The Pauline texts—not to mention the apostle himself (see, e.g., from Rome, 1 Clement)—were, after all, taken as authoritative by early Christians (to wit, long before the

---

Formulated by the Iconoclasts in 754 and 815," *DOP* 8 (1954): 153–60, who notes that even the later iconoclasts had a "conception of an image, which described the virtues of the saints as living images" (153).

86. E.g., Finney, *Invisible God*, 100: "The major pitfall [in the history of interpretation] is the tendency to confuse absence of evidence with negative evidence: as any undergraduate history major can tell you, they are not the same. Not knowing if a thing exists is different from knowing it does not."

87. Finney, *Invisible God*, 103.

beginning of the third century) and would have shaped the sensibilities and imaginations of the readers/auditors. Indeed, as every undergraduate religion major ought to know, one of the greatest differences between paganism and earliest Christianity was that the latter was fundamentally a religion of the text rather than the image.[88] It seems, in other words, ipso facto probable that the material production of a textually shaped community would be related—even if only indirectly—to the texts that shaped it. So, to put our question again: Does the Pauline εἰκών theology give us any bearing on the problem of the absence of distinctively Christian material evidence before AD 200?

In my judgment, a blanket and definitive answer to this question would be illegitimate. Yet Pauline εἰκών theology does allow for concrete suggestions, though obviously illative in nature, that might provide some insight into the earlier period. On the one hand, the archaeologically empty space, or absence of evidence, actually corresponds well to Paul's demythologizing critique and reconstrual of social space at the point of εἰκόνες. For those Christians who took Paul seriously, sculptured εἰκόνες such as those of the Cleveland marbles, if Christian,[89] or the statues in Caesarea Philippi of which Eusebius tells[90]

---

88. Elsner, *Imperial Rome*, 12, saw this point with clarity: "With the coming of Christianity, the role of art in religion changed radically, though it did not lose its central importance. The Christian God, unlike His pagan predecessors, was known not through graven images but through a sacred scripture."

89. See, e.g., the discussion in Ernst Kitzinger, "The Cleveland Marbles," in *Art, Archaeology, and Architecture of Early Christianity*, ed. Paul Corby Finney (New York: Garland, 1993), 117–39. Cf. Eusebius, *Vita Constantini* 3.49, where Constantine is said to have commissioned σύμβολα of the Good Shepherd, Daniel, and the "salvific Passion" to be put up around public fountains in Constantinople. Immediately prior, Eusebius praises Constantine for eliminating εἰδωλολατρία and removing the ἀγάλματα of the pagan gods, so it is doubtful that the σύμβολα were statues (cf. n. 91 below). Kitzinger elsewhere wrote that "no literary statement from the period prior to the year 300 would make one suspect the existence of any Christian images other than the most laconic and hieroglyphic of symbols" ("Cult of Images," 86). Much depends of course on what exactly one means by "laconic" and "hieroglyphic," which are in this case rather unspecified. His opinion is endorsed by, among others, Joseph Gutmann in his prolegomenon to the important collection of essays in *No Graven Images: Studies in Art and the Hebrew Bible* (New York: Ktav, 1971), xviii.

90. *Hist. eccl.* 7.18. Eusebius speaks of the Jesus statue as an εἰκών (the other is of the woman with an issue of blood). Eusebius also mentions having seen εἰκόνας . . . διὰ χρωμάτων ἐν γραφαῖς of Paul, Peter, and "Christ himself." Both statues and colored pictures are attributed to pagan habit (cf. the polemic of Irenaeus, *Haer.* 1.25.6, against Carpocratian Gnostics who venerate *imagines* of Jesus and other famous philosophers; and, e.g., Epiphanius, *Pan.* 27.6.10: στήσαντες . . . τὰς εἰκόνας τὰ τῶν ἐθνῶν ἔθη λοιπὸν ποιοῦσι, "After images are put up, the customs of the pagans do the rest"). Of interest in this connection,

Part 2: Biblical Studies and Theology in Practice

would almost certainly be rejected. The similarity to lararium statuettes or cultic figures would have brought considerable and unwanted accompanying baggage to groups struggling to break from paganism, to turn, that is, "from idols to serve the living God" (1 Thess 1:9). The conversion of pagans to Christianity would, on Paul's terms, require aniconic ground clearing.[91] The archaeological reality and the Pauline critique are coincident with one another.

On the other hand, however, the filling of this newly empty space is deeply iconic in that it involves the life of ἄνθρωποι as the εἰκὼν θεοῦ. God's image is a human image, and thus a living image.[92] Paul's iconism is not about a static image but a life story, first of a particular human and then of the community that embodies the pattern which is the story of that human life: in Jesus Christ and the community of the ἐκκλησία God stands on the side of humanity and is known humanly. In this way the image of God is in fact God's humanity.

It is in this sense that room exists within Pauline iconic theology for artistic depictions. Paul of course never addressed this matter directly, but his conviction that the stories of human life can be or become the εἰκὼν of God moves to reconstruct space in terms that tell the story that is God's εἰκὼν. If the story that is the life of the ἐκκλησία is told in pictures that themselves are expressions of and make reference to that same story—ecclesial "narrative art," to borrow from Jensen[93]—objections that could be raised would not come from Pauline

---

of course, is the absence of honorific statues at Dura. On Greek terminology for images in general, Price, *Rituals and Power*, 176–79, is concise.

91. This is emphatically not to say violent iconoclastic action. Not until much later did Christian aniconism turn sourly to violent destruction.

92. Cf. Gal 6:17: ἐγὼ τὰ στίγματα τοῦ Ἰησοῦ ἐν τῷ σώματι μου βαστάζω.

93. Jensen, *Understanding Early Christian Art*. In her second chapter, Jensen also treats "non-narrative" images (the *orans* figure, Orpheus, good shepherd, fish and loaves, etc.), which have their pagan counterparts and which, she avers, have no "direct textual references" (32f.). It is certainly true that, e.g., Orpheus does not have the same direct relation to the biblical material as does the depiction of the raising of Lazarus (though a fish and a basket with fives loaves, e.g., in the Callistus catacomb comes considerably closer than Orpheus). Yet the distinction between narrative and non-narrative images becomes problematic exactly at the point where Jensen (persuasively) treats the "non-narrative" symbols in relation to a Christian context. Apart from the Christian context, we would have no reason to read these symbols Christianly: to read them Christianly is to presuppose, consciously or not, the story that itself creates the context. There is no such thing, in other words, as Christian art that is non-narrative: to grant the possibility that an image could evoke a Christian interpretation at all is to presuppose knowledge of the Christian story in the reading of the image. In an otherwise illuminating discussion, e.g., Jensen writes of one of the first portraits of Christ (from the ceiling in cubiculum Leonis of the Commodilla catacomb): "No elements of scriptural narrative appear in this image—it is a simple

theology. Indeed, is it not significant that the first Christian art is funeral art, that expression of suffering and hope for resurrection which is the Pauline christological pattern of the εἰκὼν θεοῦ in the present?

Yet for most of the Gentile converts, the initial break with paganism and the counter-narration, as it were, into another story required such enormous effort—to think only of the Corinthians[94]—that the production of legitimate art would have likely been secondary to the concern with illegitimate εἰκόνες. The oft-noted "tentative" nature of the earliest catacomb art (OT typology, mundane symbols, etc.) betrays, it would seem, the rather recent appearance of active thought about distinctively Christian art. And the fact that portraits of Jesus come only much later (fourth century),[95] almost simultaneously with the working out of the doctrine of the incarnation, sketches further the outline of the concern to tread carefully within the development of Christian artistic sensibilities.

Perhaps, then, the deconstruction and reconstruction of images is the harrowing and cultivating movement in a single historical process, which is to say that the Pauline aniconism and iconism fit the mold of history with the shape of time. The critical reconceptualization of space and concomitant reconstitution of the iconic imagination could not be an overnight affair. The time it took for the dialectic that is both rejection and acceptance of εἰκόνες to receive adequate reflection may well be the absence and subsequent advent of distinctively Christian material evidence.

---

portrait. On either side of Christ's head are the letters Alpha and Omega" (103). Yet Christ as the alpha and omega comes directly from the book of Revelation and, moreover, makes reference to the entire story, as it were, from beginning to end. For the catacomb material, see (with excellent color photographs) Vincenzo Fiocchi Nicolai, Fabrizio Bisconti, and Danilo Mazzoleni, eds., *The Christian Catacombs of Rome: History, Decoration, Inscriptions* (Regensburg: Schnell & Steiner, 1999) (see plate 1 for the Christ portrait).

94. See Richard B. Hays, "The Conversion of the Imagination: Scripture and Eschatology in 1 Corinthians," *NTS* 45 (1999): 391–412.

95. See Jensen, *Understanding*, 94f. In taking seriously the "dogmatic" question involved in the doctrine of the incarnation as it relates to images (cf., too, esp. 29f.), Jensen's work is at this point a substantive advance in historical perception over works that would dismiss dogmatic matters as mere rhetoric (as, e.g., Finney, *Invisible God*, comes close to doing when he speaks of the Apologists' "iconophobia") or subordinate them entirely to social processes.

Romans 10:13

♦ WHAT IS THE NAME OF THE LORD?

The Problem: The Identity of God and the Relation of the Testaments

The unity of the Old and New Testaments as a single book is a necessary and fundamental presupposition of Christian biblical theology. This chapter hopes to contribute to the task of biblical theology by raising, through exegesis and theological reflection, significant questions pertaining to this unity of the Old Testament with the New.[1] My approach will be to look at only one statement of Paul's, which, if understood correctly, presses the question of the unity of the testaments at its fault line; that is, at that exact place where the enterprise of Christian biblical theology rises or falls—the doctrine of God. It may be stated bluntly and categorically: if the God of the OT is a different God than the God of the NT, the unity of the testaments is destroyed. It is my thesis that in Romans 10:13 Paul makes a startling claim regarding the relation between Jesus and God that has profound implications for the understanding of the identity of the God of the OT in relation to the God of whom Paul writes.

Various scholars have correctly characterized Paul's letter to the Romans as theocentric. Indeed, θεός (God) occurs more than any other word in the

---

1. As regards my interpretative posture, I am working within the confessional community of the Christian church that confesses one Christian Bible, composed of the Old and New Testaments. I understand Christian biblical theology as a discipline that reads the two testaments together as one book.

"Romans 10:13: What Is the Name of the Lord?" was originally published in *Horizons in Biblical Theology* 22, no. 2 (2000): 135–73. Republished with permission of Brill; permission conveyed through Copyright Clearance Center, Inc.

letter (except for such words as the article, καί, ἐν, αὐτός, etc.).[2] What has not received enough exegetical and theological scrutiny, however, is just exactly who this God is. The reasons for this lack of attention are many, but it will suffice to mention two of the most significant. First, despite Dahl's insightful essay twenty-five years ago,[3] the question about the identity of God is simply not asked with force and consistency, if it is asked at all.[4] Second, and perhaps contributing to the general neglect of the question, is that, on the face of it, the answer is readily at hand: God is the God of Israel, the one who raised Jesus Christ. This is certainly true, but the bare statement alone lacks the theological penetration needed to express the complex and deeply dynamic relation between the two component parts of the statement—the God of Israel, that is, YHWH, and the human person Jesus Christ. In a chapter of this length, one obviously cannot tackle all the pertinent texts in Romans. My task will be rather modest. I will attempt to show that Paul's use of Joel 3:5 (LXX and MT; EV 2:32) in Romans 10:13, if taken at all as instructive for the way in which Paul conceives of God's relation to Christ, eliminates the possibility of thinking of the God of Israel, YHWH, as apart from the human being Jesus.[5] This unitive relationship is dialectical and hinges in fact on unreserved identification of one with the other as well as on clear differentiation. Romans 10:13 sounds the note of the first side of this theological dialectic with unmistakable clarity and, in so doing, brings forth an astonishing image of God.

The interpretation of Romans 10:13 can be conducted neither apart from a thorough exegesis of this verse within its proper context nor apart from his-

---

2. Joseph Fitzmyer, *Romans*, AB 33 (New York: Doubleday, 1993), 104.

3. Nils Dahl, "The Neglected Factor in New Testament Theology," in *Jesus the Christ: The Historical Origins of Christological Doctrine*, ed. Donald H. Juel (Minneapolis: Fortress, 1991), 153–64; originally published in *Reflections* 75 (1975): 5–8.

4. Some of N. T. Wright's work (e.g., *The New Testament and the People of God*, vol. 1 of *Christian Origins and the Question of God* [Minneapolis: Fortress, 1992]) is an exception.

5. There are a few especially instructive studies with regard to the relation between Jesus and God and the language used to express this relation: David B. Capes, *Old Testament Yahweh Texts in Paul's Christology*, WUNT 2/47 (Tübingen: Mohr Siebeck, 1992); Nils Dahl, "Sources of Christological Language," in Juel, *Jesus the Christ*, 113–36; Carl Judson Davis, *The Name and Way of the Lord: Old Testament Themes, New Testament Christology*, JSNTSup 129 (Sheffield: Sheffield Academic, 1996); James D. G. Dunn, "Christology as an Aspect of Theology," in *The Future of Christology: Essays in Honor of Leander E. Keck*, ed. Abraham J. Malherbe and Wayne A. Meeks (Minneapolis: Fortress, 1993), 202–12; Leander E. Keck, "Toward the Renewal of New Testament Christology," *NTS* 32 (1986): 362–77; L. Joseph Kreitzer, *Jesus and God in Paul's Eschatology*, JSNTSup 19 (Sheffield: JSOT Press, 1987); and Neil Richardson, *Paul's Language about God*, JSNTSup 99 (Sheffield: Sheffield Academic, 1994).

Part 2: Biblical Studies and Theology in Practice

torical concerns relevant to Paul in his first-century situatedness, in particular Jewish "monotheistic" theology and monolatrous worship. Thus, this chapter will consist of four main sections as follows: the larger context of Romans 10:13; an exegetical interpretation of Romans 10:13 within the immediate context of 10:11–13; historical/theological reflections upon Jewish monotheism and the implications of Romans 10:13 therein; and theological reflections upon the unity of the Christian Bible and the doctrine of God.

THE LARGER CONTEXT OF ROMANS 10:13

Happily correcting an interpretive deficiency in older critical exegesis that tended to see Romans 9–11 as unrelated to 1–8 and as unimportant as a whole,[6] more recent scholars have labored to assign Romans 9–11 its proper weight in the letter. It is now seen that Paul's discussion of the salvation of Israel is in fact indispensably integral to the thought pattern of the letter and indeed strikes at the heart of its principal theological themes.[7] The logic and thought flow of Romans 9–11 have been analyzed in many different ways. Nevertheless, allowing for variation and nuance, there seems to be a general consensus that chapters 9–11 best make sense in the following form: 9:1–5 (opening oath and doxological declaration regarding the Christ [and God/as God]); 9:6–29 (the unfailing power of God's word and election); 9:30–10:21 (Israel's disobedience to the gospel); 11:1–32 (the electing God's eschatological faithfulness); 11:33–36 (closing doxological hymn of praise to God).[8] This general outline is sound

---

6. Three outstanding examples are Rudolph Bultmann, *Theology of the New Testament* (New York: Charles Scribner's Sons, 1951–1955), who ignores Rom 9–11; C. H. Dodd, *The Epistle of Paul to the Romans* (New York: Harper & Brothers, 1932); and William Sanday and Arthur C. Headlam, *A Critical and Exegetical Commentary on the Epistle to the Romans*, ICC (New York: Charles Scribner's Sons, 1898).

7. See C. E. B. Cranfield, *A Critical and Exegetical Commentary on the Epistle to the Romans*, ICC (Edinburgh: T&T Clark, 1979), 2:445–50; Nils Dahl, "The Future of Israel," in *Studies in Paul: Theology for the Early Christian Mission* (Minneapolis: Augsburg, 1977), 137–58, esp. 138–42; James D. G. Dunn, *Romans 9–16*, WBC (Dallas: Word, 1988), 519–21; Richard B. Hays, *Echoes of Scripture in the Letters of Paul* (New Haven: Yale University Press, 1989), 63–64; E. Elizabeth Johnson, *The Function of Apocalyptic and Wisdom Traditions in Romans 9–11*, SBLDS 109 (Atlanta: Scholars Press, 1989), 110–23; and Ernst Käsemann, *Commentary on Romans* (Grand Rapids: Eerdmans, 1980), 253–57.

8. For concise treatment of the thought flow of Rom 9–11, see James Aageson, "Scripture and Structure in the Development of the Argument in Romans 9–11," *CBQ* 48 (1986): 265–89, esp. 286–87; Hays, *Echoes*, 74–75; Johnson, *Function of Apocalyptic*, 116ff.; E. Eliza-

and captures well the movement of 9–11. However, within the central section of the argument, 9:30–10:21, an important emphasis needs to be made that proves significant for our later exegesis, and for the interpretation of 9–11 as a whole. Though chapters 9–11 are, in a sense, rightly said to be "theocentric," the character and content of Israel's disobedience to the gospel are in fact *christological* (9:32, 33; 10:4, 6, 7, 9, 11, 12, 13, 14, 16, 17).[9] Israel's rejection of/disobedience to God and subsequent acceptance and salvation by God revolve around and find their center in the figure of Jesus Christ.[10] That is to say, in Romans 9–11 one cannot think either of rejection (Israel as object and subject; God as subject and object) or of salvation (Israel as object; God as subject) apart from Jesus Christ.

The central section of 9:30–10:21 is itself knitted tightly together with threads linguistic (e.g., πίστις, δικαιοσύνη, Χριστός, κύριος, πᾶς), logical

---

beth Johnson, "Romans 9–11: The Faithfulness and Impartiality of God," in *Pauline Theology*, vol. 3, *Romans*, ed. David M. Hay and E. Elizabeth Johnson (Minneapolis: Fortress, 1995), 211–39, esp. 211–22; Käsemann, *Romans*, 253ff.; Douglas Moo, "The Theology of Romans 9–11: A Response to E. Elizabeth Johnson," in Hay and Johnson, *Pauline Theology*, vol. 3, *Romans*, esp. 242–43.

9. Markus Barth, "One God, One Christ, One People," *ExAud* 4 (1988): 8–26, recognizes the importance of Christ in ch. 10 in his otherwise unconvincing outline and structural analysis (11ff.). "Theocentrism" is an appropriate term to describe Rom 9–11 only insofar as it includes the christological emphasis of ch. 10. (Ἰησοῦς Χριστός is used directly at least five times, as is θεός. However, indirect references can vary widely depending on whom or what one takes to be the stone/rock, whom one takes to be the κύριος ["Lord"], and to whom one takes the surrounding pronouns to refer. For example, if one takes the stone/rock to refer to Christ, the κύριος to be Christ, and the surrounding pronouns to refer to Christ, then reference is made to him no less than seventeen times in 9:30–10:21. In slight contrast, thirteen is the highest number of possible references to θεός.) But to set the "theocentrism" of Rom 9–11 over against "christocentrism" (as does Johnson, *Function of Apocalyptic*, 204) is to misunderstand altogether the relationship between God and Jesus Christ, and, resultantly, the salvation of the Jews.

10. Perhaps a word should be mentioned here regarding God, Jesus Christ, and the gospel. I take it on the basis of Paul's mutually interchangeable expressions "gospel of God" (1:1; 15:16) and "gospel of Christ/God's Son" (1:9; 15:19), as well as Paul's larger theology, that God, Jesus Christ, and the gospel are so bound up with each other that to speak of one is to speak of the others. And though the relation between God and Jesus Christ cannot always be drawn with razor-sharp precision (but that is part of Paul's theological point, as we will see), it is nonetheless clear that to reject and disobey the gospel is to reject and disobey God and Jesus Christ, God in Jesus Christ, what God has done through Jesus Christ, etc. Thus, Israel's disobedience to the gospel (10:16, etc.) is inherently disobedience to God precisely and just so as it is to Jesus Christ. (Paul can also speak of "my gospel" [2:16], but it is overwhelmingly clear that he means his gospel about Jesus Christ/God, and not his gospel about himself, except insofar as his apostleship is derivative of the gospel.)

Part 2: Biblical Studies and Theology in Practice

(e.g., how can they call upon one of whom they have not heard?), and theological (e.g., use of OT for christological theology and defense of Gentile inclusion in connection with Israel's disobedience), with a clear turning point signaled by the Πῶς οὖν ("How then") in 10:14. Thus within 9:30–10:21 it is possible to see two distinct but clearly connected sections: 9:30–10:13 and 10:14–21. In addition, four further internal structural observations pertaining to 9:30–10:13 can be made. First, 9:30–33 is clearly connected to what follows[11] and can be taken as a sort of preface to 10:1ff. In this way, 10:1ff. functions, at least in part, to give christological content to the righteousness that is ἐκ πίστεως ("from, based on faith," 9:30, 32), and christological identity to the stone/rock (τῷ λίθῳ τοῦ προσκόμματος ["the stone of stumbling," 9:32], λίθον προσκόμματος [9:33], πέτραν σκανδάλου ["rock of offense," 9:33], and ἐπ᾽ αὐτῷ ["in him/it," 9:33]). Second, this would ease the tension of the otherwise slightly startling return to direct address (Ἀδελφοί, "brothers") in 10:1. Third, 10:1 and 10:13 form an (albeit slightly imperfect) *inclusio* linguistically and thematically constituted in "salvation." In 10:1 Paul writes that the desire of his heart and the entreaty to God on behalf of Israel is for salvation (σωτηρίαν).[12] In 10:13 Paul writes that all (πᾶς) who call upon the name of the Lord will be saved (σωθήσεται). Further, in 10:9 the result of confessing and believing "the word of faith" (10:8) that Paul preaches is salvation (σωθήσῃ; cf. 10:10). This suggests that we read 10:1–13 as a rhetorical unit giving christological content not only to the righteousness that is ἐκ πίστεως but also to the concept of salvation as it relates to Paul's desire for Israel (10:1) and to Israel's disobedience (9:30–33 and 10:14–21). Fourth, when one attends closely to the rhetoric of 10:1–13, it becomes apparent that 10:13 is the rhetorical (and theological) climax of 10:1–13 (and, indeed, of 9:30–10:13).[13] Because

---

11. The connection is made clear through the continuation of faith and righteousness language, the repetition of Isa 28:16 in 10:11, and the language and concepts that compel a christological answer to the unavoidable question raised by the use of Isa 28:16 in 9:33 of who or what the stone (9:32, 33), the scandalous rock/rock of offense (9:33), actually is.

12. The meaning of salvation is, of course, not immediately clear from this one verse. It is, rather, drawn out over the next several verses (esp. 10:13) and culminates at the end of ch. 11, where it seems clear that Paul is referring to eschatological salvation.

13. Contra Käsemann, *Romans*, 290, who thinks the accent of the "whole passage" falls on 10:8. Even the emphasis on 10:8 as the climax of Paul's interpretation of Deut 30:12–14 is misplaced. Two considerations bring me to this judgment. First, the threefold repetition of τοῦτ᾽ ἔστιν ("that is," 10:6, 7, 8) points the reader forward, creating a sense of expectation that τὸ ῥῆμα τῆς πίστεως ὃ κηρύσσομεν ("the word of faith that we proclaim"), if seen as the climactic conclusion, cannot satisfy—the question instantly arises, what word? For the

of the enigmatic nature of the expression "for Christ is the τέλος ["end" or "goal"] of the law" (10:4), an enormous amount of scholarly attention has been given to 10:4, and the rhetorical movement of the passage toward 10:13 overlooked.[14] Many commentators correctly note that the γάρ ("for") in 10:5 links 10:5ff. to the preceding material.[15] What is generally missed, however, is the cumulative rhetorical effect of the return to the use of the connective γάρ in 10:10, 11, 12 [2×], 13, in conjunction with both the thematic coherence of the opening sentence in 10:1 with 10:13 and the shifting logical question of 10:14.[16] The use of γάρ five times within 10:10-13 not only connects the phrases to each other but also gives the reader a sense of being pulled or drawn toward some expected end:

> *for* in the heart it is believed . . .
> *for* the Scripture says . . .
> *for* there is no distinction . . .
> *for* the same Lord is Lord of all . . .
> *for* all who call on the name of the Lord shall be saved.

This progression (i) recalls Paul's initial entreaty in 10:1, (ii) picks up the four uses of γάρ (10:2, 3, 4, 5) preceding Paul's rereading of Deuteronomy, and (iii) deepens the "you will be saved" (σωθήσῃ) of 10:9 (cf. σωτηρίαν in 10:10) even as it (iv) presses forward with rhetorical force toward the climactic quotation of Joel 3:5 in 10:13.

---

answer to this question, and Paul anticipates our question, we must read on to 10:9. Second, the ὅτι ("for, because") in 10:9 should be stressed as a connective, for it is explanatory not only in the sense of giving immediate content to the word of faith that Paul preaches, but also in that it explains the way in which one/all is/are saved (Paul's entreaty in 10:1 on behalf of the Jews). Thus, 10:9 should not be separated from Paul's scriptural interpretation of Deut 32:12-14 and should receive the accent.

14. An exception is Steven Richard Bechtler, "Christ, the Τέλος of the Law: The Goal of Romans 10:4," *CBQ* 56 (1994): 288-308, who sees 10:11-13 as the climax of this section of the argument.

15. E.g., Cranfield, *Romans*, 2:520; Dunn, *Romans 9-16*, 599-600; and Käsemann, *Romans*, 284.

16. The question in 10:14 follows logically from Paul's statement in 10:13 and marks only a minor shift (9:30-10:21 is a tightly knit whole as we have observed above). Nonetheless, this shift signals to the reader that 10:13 closes a particular thought unit, and thereby, attention is in yet another way directed to 10:13. Dunn (*Romans 9-16*, 599) wrongly asserts that in 10:11-13 Paul begins a new line of thought—it begins in 10:14ff.

Part 2: Biblical Studies and Theology in Practice

Exegesis of Romans 10:13 within Its Immediate Context

Having given our attention to pertinent matters within the larger structural setting and context of 10:13, we may now turn to the most immediate context within which 10:13 is to be interpreted: 10:11-13. Verses 11-13 follow closely on the heels of Paul's radical christological interpretation of Deuteronomy 30:12-14, draw language and theological themes from earlier in the letter, and use the OT to present an astonishing theological claim about the Lord who saves.

(1) Romans 10:11. Though for our purposes it is not necessary to explore in great detail Paul's use of Isaiah 28:16 in 10:11,[17] several important points that have direct bearing on the significance and interpretation of 10:13 must nevertheless be mentioned.

(*a*) The addition of πᾶς to Isaiah 28:16. The fact that Paul has so recently quoted Isaiah 28:16 (9:33) without the πᾶς (which is also, of course, not in any LXX MS) strongly suggests that the addition is quite intentional.[18] Its linguistic effect is to create a rhetorical link with 10:12-13 (πάντων [12], πάντας [12], πᾶς [13])[19] and to bring Isaiah 28:16 into conformity with Paul's programmatic statement in 1:16, repeated and echoed powerfully throughout Romans (3:22; 4:11; 10:4). This rhetorical skill undergirds 10:9-10 with scriptural evidence[20] and champions yet again one of the fundamental theological themes of Romans: the gospel to be believed is for *all*. To give a rather free paraphrase, with the addition of πᾶς Paul essentially says: "For where the Scripture says 'the one believing in/upon him will not be put to shame,' it means *everyone* who believes in him."

---

17. For Paul's use of Isa 28:16 here in Rom 10:11, see Dietrich-Alex Koch, *Die Schrift als Zeuge des Evangeliums: Untersuchungen zur Verwendung und zum Verständnis der Schrift bei Paulus*, Beiträge zur historischen Theologie 69 (Tübingen: Mohr Siebeck, 1986), 133-34; Christopher Stanley, *Paul and the Language of Scripture: Citation Technique in the Pauline Epistles and Contemporary Literature*, SNTSMS 74 (Cambridge: Cambridge University Press, 1992), 119-25, 133-34; and Florian Wilk, *Die Bedeutung des Jesajabuches für Paulus*, FRLANT 179 (Göttingen: Vandenhoeck & Ruprecht, 1998), 47, 60-62.

18. So Stanley, *Paul and the Language of Scripture*, 133-34, and many others.

19. So, among others, Aageson, "Scripture and Structure," 276; Cranfield, *Romans*, 2:532; Dunn, *Romans 9-16*, 609; Stanley, *Paul and the Language of Scripture*, 134; Wilk, *Bedeutung des Jesajabuches*, 47.

20. Wilk (*Bedeutung des Jesajabuches*, 61) argues that Paul's use of Isa 28:16 is not to support 10:10 (against Koch, *Schrift als Zeuge*, 133), but only 10:9. I find this unconvincing. Rom 10:10 is simply an expansion and explanation of, and therefore not to be separated from, 10:9. Paul cites Isa 28:16 to support vv. 9 and 10, taken together as a unit.

(b) Jesus as the referent of the ἐπ' αὐτῷ ("in him/it").[21] Admittedly, it is not immediately obvious that Jesus is the one of whom the Isaiah quotation speaks. Two objections might weigh against this interpretative option. First, it could be asserted that in its original Isaianic context the ἐπ' αὐτῷ refers to the stone that the Lord will set in Zion. However, this objection does little more than caution against a simple and immediate symbolic leap from the stone to Jesus Christ.[22] Does it really make any sense to say that Paul wants his readers to believe in the stone that has been set in Zion, and leave it at that? No. Surely it is *someone* in whom we are to believe. In this respect the other, and more reasonable, objection may be that the ἐπ' αὐτῷ refers to God. This objection finds its strongest point in the assertion that with the use of πιστεύσῃς ("you believe") in 10:9, faith is directed toward God (believe/trust in your heart that *God* raised him) or at least toward something *God* has done.[23] The verbal link with ὁ πιστεύων in 10:11 would then be seen as establishing continuity of divine object. Nevertheless, neither of these objections is strong enough to outweigh the interpretation that here the ἐπ' αὐτῷ refers to Jesus Christ.[24] Four considerations point strongly in this direction (but in the case of the fourth we must await the exegesis of vv. 12–13 to see its full strength). First, in 10:9 Paul says that "Jesus is Lord" and that God raised "him" (αὐτόν).[25] This αὐτόν

---

21. For some reason Kreitzer (*Jesus and God*, 124) asserts that ἐπ' αὐτῷ is absent from "all copies of the LXX of Isaiah." Stanley (*Paul and the Language of Scripture*, 124), however, notes that while ἐπ' αὐτῷ is absent from the most important MSS, the "Pauline wording is well-grounded in the testimony of the uncials A Q S, the Lucianic and Catena texts, and a variety of other witnesses." Further, the more complete and explicit citation of Isa 28:16 in 1 Pet 2:6 includes ἐπ' αὐτῷ and thus suggests that Paul does not add these words here in Rom 10:11 (or 9:33) himself (unless, of course, 1 Peter is dependent upon Paul). See C. H. Dodd, *According to the Scriptures: The Sub-structure of New Testament Theology* (London: Nisbet, 1952), 42ff., for the possible "stone testimonies" of the early church.

22. It is far from clear just what the "stone" is in Isa 28:16. Is it a metaphorical symbol for God's message? For God himself? (What would be the theological difference?) Neither? In Isa 8:14 it seems as if God himself is the "stone." Perhaps on the basis of Paul's conflation of these two passages in 9:33 (cf. 9:32), one could argue that Paul thought of the "stone" in Isa 28:16 as the same stone (i.e., God himself) of Isa 8:14, but the argument would be highly conjectural and require substantial evidence beyond the observation itself.

23. Though he, too, takes ἐπ' αὐτῷ to refer to Christ, Cranfield, *Romans*, 2:531, is the only one of the major commentators to even notice that the use of ὁ θεός in 10:9 might have bearing on the way in which one reads the rest of the section.

24. So the vast majority of scholars, e.g., Dunn, *Romans 9–16*, 610; Fitzmyer, *Romans*, 592; Sanday and Headlam, *Romans*, 211. Ulrich Wilckens, *Der Brief an die Römer*, EKKNT (Zürich: Benziger; Neukirchen-Vluyn: Neukirchener Verlag, 1980), 2:228.

25. There is general agreement that this was an early Christian baptismal confession (or

indisputably refers back to Jesus and is the clearest antecedent of the αὐτῷ in 10:11. Thus, it is most natural grammatically to take αὐτῷ as continuing the use of the pronoun αὐτόν from 10:9 to refer to Jesus.[26] Second, the statements in 10:9 do not require us to emphasize *either* Jesus or God, because they are, in fact, inseparable: *Jesus is Lord* because *God raised him* from the dead. The confession is thus christo-theological—it concerns both Jesus and God, not one without the other.[27] This mutual interweaving of subjects (Jesus and God) in conjunction with a clear object (Jesus) gives more force to the grammatical point made above, simply because one cannot make clear judgments about the referent of the αὐτῷ from the antecedent "names" alone. Third, Paul uses Isaiah 28:16 in 9:33 to refer to Christ,[28] and so it makes sense, given the proximity of the citations, to see the same referent here. Fourth, the identification of the κύριος ("Lord") in 10:12–13 as Jesus (see below) makes it almost beyond doubt that the αὐτῷ in 10:11 refers to Jesus.

(c) The use of καταισχυνθήσεται ("will be put to shame"). Here, as noted above, Paul's use of "shaming" vocabulary draws upon earlier uses in the letter (1:16; 5:5). Bultmann[29] and E. Elizabeth Johnson[30] have shown that αἰσχύνω compounds can and often do refer to eschatological shame in the face of God's judgment. Given that Paul's concern as stated in 10:1 immediately follows the use of the same Isaiah citation, that the concern is explicitly for "salvation,"[31] and that the use of Joel 3:5 in 10:13 clearly brings eschatological judgment into view (see below), we may conclude that here in 10:11 Paul uses καταισχυνθήσεται eschatologically.

---

creedal formula) and most likely part of Christian worship as well. See Bultmann, *Theology of the New Testament*, 1:81, 312; Dodd, *Romans*, 166; Dunn, *Romans 9–16*, 607; Käsemann, *Romans*, 291; Werner Kramer, *Christ, Lord, Son of God* (London: SCM, 1966), 65ff.

26. Cf. Rom 15:12 where the Gentiles are said to hope ἐπ' αὐτῷ. Here, Paul is clearly using Isa 11:10 to refer to Jesus (the root of Jesse). Cf. also Gal 2:16 where Christ Jesus is clearly the object of faith: καὶ ἡμεῖς εἰς Χριστὸν Ἰησοῦν ἐπιστεύσαμεν ("even we believed in Christ Jesus").

27. Cf. Keck, "Renewal," 363, who notes that "every statement about Christ implicates God." Here, the focus is a soteriological unity in which God and Christ coincide. On the unity of the act of God and of Christ, see Max Meinertz, *Theologie des Neuen Testamentes 2* (Bonn: Hanstein, 1950), 71–72.

28. This, too, is not an uncontested point. See Cranfield, *Romans*, 2:511–12; Dunn, *Romans 9–16*, 584, 594.

29. Rudolph Bultmann, "αἰσχύνω," *TDNT* 1:189–91.

30. Johnson, *Function of Apocalyptic*, 127–28.

31. Johnson also lists σώζω, κτλ. as part of Paul's apocalyptic vocabulary (*Function of Apocalyptic*, 127–28).

Following on vv. 9–10, the effect of (a), (b), and (c) together is to present *Jesus* as the one in whom *all* must believe to avoid eschatological shame and to receive *salvation*. Paul thus not only takes the words of Isaiah to refer to Jesus but also uses the Scripture to formulate his christological statements. This same hermeneutical move can be seen in 10:13, only with a more radical claim. A more complete paraphrase is now in order: "That Jesus is Lord and that God raised him from the dead mean that at God's eschatological judgment 'the one believing in Jesus [him] will not be put to shame.' When the Scripture says this, it means *everyone* who *believes* in *Jesus*. For as I said earlier . . ."

(2) Romans 10:12. Given Paul's addition of πᾶς in v. 11, v. 12 follows both rhetorically and logically. As with 10:11, it is not necessary to explore every nook and cranny of 10:12. We can best understand 10:12 as befits our purposes by making a few observations in regard to each of its component parts.

(a) Verse 12a: "no distinction." The statement that there is no distinction between Jew and Greek is a bit startling to find within the chapters that deal so explicitly with Israel.[32] Nonetheless, the statement must be understood within its context—that is, with respect to Paul's concern for the salvation of the Jews (chs. 9–11 as a whole and, within the present context, 10:1, 9, 10, 13). Its initial function in the present context is to continue the universal emphasis as an immediate explanation of the addition of πᾶς in 10:11. This emphasis upon universality is analogous to that of the οὐ γάρ ἐστιν διαστολή . . . πάντες ("for there is no distinction . . . all")[33] in 3:22. There, however, the universality was one of human sinfulness; here, the universality is one of eschatological salvation through faith—10:12a is the positive point of 3:22.[34] The correlation of the positive and negative sides of the same statement presents us with the picture of anthropological universality we find Paul painting fully in Romans 5:12–21: all sin, and precisely so there is no distinction; all find salvation in Christ, and

---

32. Dunn, *Romans 9–16*, 617, quite rightly notes that this statement would be shocking to Jews. I would add: to Romans as well. The Jews were well known in the Mediterranean world for their "peculiar" practices and views that set them apart as a distinct people (see, e.g., Juvenal, *Sat.* 14.96ff.; Tacitus, *Historiae* 5.5). In addition, in this context (as in Rom 1:14, 16), I take Ἕλληνος ("Greek") to refer more broadly to Gentiles in general, and so will use the terms interchangeably.

33. By setting up the citation in this way, my intention is to include the πάντες rather than to make punctuation suggestions regarding 3:22-23. I am inclined, however, to think that one should put a full stop after διαστολή and begin the next sentence πάντες γάρ. Regardless, the point made here is the same. Cf. also Gal 3:28: οὐκ ἔνι Ἰουδαῖος οὐδὲ Ἕλλην . . . πάντες γὰρ ὑμεῖς εἷς ἐστε ἐν Χριστῷ Ἰησοῦ ("there is no Jew nor Gentile . . . for you are all one in Christ Jesus").

34. So Cranfield, *Romans*, 2:531, and following him, Dunn, *Romans 9–16*, 610.

Part 2: Biblical Studies and Theology in Practice

precisely so there is no distinction. This anthropological assertion finds its ground in the theological universality that it assumes.

(*b*) Verse 12b: "the same Lord is Lord of all." This phrase, pregnant with theological meaning, raises a crucial question that must be answered prior to its interpretation: Who is the κύριος? Though Paul uses κύριος for both God and Jesus Christ,[35] it is hard to see how in 10:12b the κύριος could be anyone other than Jesus.[36] The resounding confession "Jesus is Lord" in 10:9 is reason enough to conclude that this very next use of κύριος is meant to refer to Jesus. Yet we may add that if our interpretation of ἐπ' αὐτῷ in 10:11 is correct, then this also lends support to the claim that the ὁ αὐτὸς κύριος ("the same Lord") is Jesus.

As with οὐ γάρ ἐστιν διαστολὴ Ἰουδαίου τε καὶ Ἕλληνος ("for there is no distinction between Jew and Greek") so, too, ὁ αὐτὸς κύριος has a theological counterpart in the culminating section of chapter 3. There εἷς ὁ θεός ("God [is] one," 3:30) was the ground of the justification of the circumcised and the uncircumcised by faith.[37] So also here in 10:12b ὁ αὐτὸς κύριος is the ground of v. 12a (and of 10:11, 13[38]). Grammatically, the γάρ of v. 12b shows clearly the relation

---

35. Of Christ, e.g., 1:4, 7; 5:21; 6:23; 14:4, 6, 8, 14, etc. Of God, e.g., 9:28, 29; 11:3. Jews around the time of the NT could also speak of God as κύριος: e.g., Josephus, *A. J.* 20.90 (Izates addresses YHWH as ὦ δέσποτα κύριε); Philo, *Conf.* 1 (κύριος [2]); 156 (κύριος); 173 (Moses addresses YHWH as κύριε, κύριε).

36. So Cranfield, *Romans*, 2:531; Dodd, *Romans*, 169; Dunn, *Romans 9–16*, 610; Fitzmyer, *Romans*, 592; and Käsemann, *Romans*, 292. Johnson wants to read this phrase as "the same God is Lord of all" in support of her driving affirmation of God's impartiality (*Function of Apocalyptic*, 154, 171). What has happened, however, is that she has ignored the immediate context for the sake of her larger concern. She does the same thing in "Romans 9–11," 219. Cf. Acts 10:36: . . . Ἰησοῦ Χριστοῦ, οὗτός ἐστιν πάντων κύριος (". . . Jesus Christ, this one is Lord of all"). So also, Luke Timothy Johnson reads κύριος here as God, and mistranslates, "the same God is of all people" (*Reading Romans* [New York: Crossroad, 1997], 161).

37. It is important to note the centrality of εἷς ὁ θεός in 3:29–30: (A) Jews and Gentiles have the same God, (B) God is one, (A') circumcised and uncircumcised justified by the same God, on the same ground. Jouette M. Bassler incorrectly sees "no distinction" and "one God" as two different grounds, both used to support God's "radical impartiality" in justifying Jews and Gentiles by faith (*Divine Impartiality: Paul and a Theological Axiom*, SBLDS 59 [Chico, CA: Scholars Press, 1982], 156–58). It is, rather, as argued above, the identity of the one God that is primary and the shape of the one community without distinction that follows.

38. Though, as I will argue, the more directly startling claim comes in 10:13, ὁ αὐτὸς κύριος is the theological centerpiece of 10:11–13 in that the reality of the same Lord is the ground for both the claims made in 10:11 and 10:13: there is one Lord of all, therefore "all

of the dependence of v. 12a: "for there is no distinction . . . *for* the same Lord is Lord of all." Theologically, it is because the Jews and Greeks have the same Lord that there is no distinction between them. That is, because there is *one* Lord (cf. 1 Cor 8:6), there is one human community (πᾶς).³⁹ The theological universality (v. 12b) is the ground of the anthropological universality (v. 12a).⁴⁰ This dialectical correlation of the One to the one (both in sin and in salvation) is a theme that runs strongly throughout Romans and opens before us the profound depth and panoramic expansiveness of Paul's theological vision.⁴¹

Further, I do not think it too fanciful to suggest that in ὁ αὐτὸς κύριος we can hear a foundational theological resonance, as we almost certainly would in εἷς ὁ θεός in 3:30,⁴² with the Shema:⁴³

---

who believe," "no distinction," "all who call upon him," etc. This theological point can be seen structurally as well:
All who believe in him will not be put to shame
No distinction between Jew and Greek
Same Lord is Lord of all
Generous to all who call upon him
All who call upon the name of the Lord will be saved
Bechtler does not go far enough and wrongly grounds the anthropological universality of 10:11 in the "no distinction" itself ("Christ, the Τέλος of the Law," 306).

39. Ulrich Mauser, "Εἷς θεός und Μόνος θεός in Biblischer Theologie," *Jahrbuch für Biblische Theologie* 1 (1986): 71-87, correctly observes that this anthropological conclusion could be seen by Jews around the time of Paul as quite polemical. There is evidence of a conviction that the oneness of God was thought to be mirrored in the uniqueness of the Jewish people. See, e.g., Let. Aris. 132ff. (God's oneness leads to Jewish separation in worship, practice, etc.); Philo, *De specialibus legibus* 1.67 (ἐπειδὴ εἷς ὁ θεός καὶ ἱερὸν ἓν εἶναι μόνον ["Since God is one, there should be also only one Temple"]); Josephus, *A. J.* 4.200ff. (ἱερὰ πόλις ἔστω μία . . . νεὼς εἷς . . . βωμὸς εἷς . . . ἐν ἑτέρᾳ δὲ πόλει μήτε βωμὸς μήτε νεὼς ἔστω, θεὸς γὰρ εἷς καὶ τὸ Ἑβραίων γένος ἕν ["Let there be one sacred city . . . one temple . . . one altar . . . and in another city let there be neither altar nor temple, for God is one and the Hebrew race is one"]); Josephus, *C. Ap.* 2.193 (Εἷς ναὸς ἑνὸς θεοῦ ["The one temple of the one God"]). Cf. also Josephus, *A. J.* 5.112; *B. J.* 2.117-118.

40. Mauser, "Εἷς θεός," 71-87, has several particularly helpful insights on this point.

41. Rom 3:9-20, 21-31; 4:11, 13; 5:12-21; 8:22, 32; 11:15, 26, 32, 36; 12:4, 5; 14:10, 11, 12; 15:6, 10, 11; 16:26, 27. The theme merits further study in the Pauline corpus as a central driving theological vision.

42. See Nils Dahl, "The One God of Jews and Gentiles," in *Studies in Paul*, 178-91, for a brief and lucid discussion of Rom 3:29-30 in connection with Greek "monotheism" and the later rabbinic sources.

43. If m. Berakhot 1.1ff. is taken as at all instructive for Jewish practice in the time of Paul, then it is hard to imagine that his Jewish readers, at least, would not have heard the overtones with the Shema. Cf. in the NT: Mark 10:18; 12:29; Matt 23:9; John 5:44; 17:3; 1 Cor 8:4-6; Gal 3:20; Eph 4:6; 1 Tim 1:17; 2:5; Jas 2:19; Jude 25. An older but still very interesting study is

Part 2: Biblical Studies and Theology in Practice

> The Lord our God, the Lord is one [κύριος ὁ θεὸς ἡμῶν, κύριος εἷς ἐστι]. (Deut 6:4 LXX)

This fundamental confession of the OT[44] is picked up in Zechariah 14:9–10a, 16–17 (LXX), where it is given an eschatological and universal interpretation:[45]

> And the Lord [κύριος] will be king over all the earth [πᾶσαν τὴν γῆν];
> On that day, the Lord will be one [κύριος εἷς] and his name one [τὸ ὄνομα αὐτοῦ ἕν], surrounding all the earth [κυκλῶν πᾶσαν τὴν γῆν]. . . .
> And it will be that whosoever is left of all the Gentiles [ἐκ πάντων τῶν ἐθνῶν] that come against Jerusalem, they also will go up every year to worship the king, the Lord Almighty [τῷ βασιλεῖ κυρίῳ παντοκράτορι].
> . . . And it will be that whoever does not come up of all the families of the earth [πασῶν τῶν φυλῶν τῆς γῆς] to Jerusalem to worship the king, the Lord Almighty [τῷ βασιλεῖ κυρίῳ παντοκράτορι], even these will be added to the others.[46]

Paul's theological thinking and confession draw upon this universalizing vision of the worship of the one Lord by Jew and Gentile alike and radicalize it by proclaiming that Jesus is in fact Lord (10:9, 12) and that in him the distinction between Jew and Gentile is *at present* abolished.[47] The possibility of the worship of the one true God is now open to the one human community—that

---

that of Vernon Neufeld, *The Earliest Christian Confessions* (Grand Rapids: Eerdmans, 1963), 34–41, who concludes that in the period of 200 BC to AD 100 "the confession εἷς ὁ θεός was the basic *homologia* of Judaism, epitomizing the longer *Shema*"" (41). See, e.g., 2 Macc 7:37 (μόνος αὐτὸς θεός ἐστιν ["he alone is God"]); Let. Aris. 132 (μόνος ὁ θεός ["the only/one God"]), 139 (τὸν μόνον θεόν); Josephus, *A. J.* 5.112 (θεόν τε ἕνα ["the one God"]); 8.335 (ὃς μόνος ἐστὶ θεός ["who is the only God"]), 337 (θεὸν ἀληθῆ καὶ μόνον ["the true and only God"]), 343 (ἕνα θεὸν καὶ μέγιστον καὶ ἀληθῆ μόνον ["the one and only great and true God"]); 20.90 (μόνον . . . κύριον ["the only Lord"]); Philo, *Conf.* 171 (εἷς ὢν ὁ θεός ["God is one"]); *Legat.* 115 (ἕνα νομίζειν τὸν πατέρα καὶ ποιητὴν τοῦ κόσμου θεόν ["to acknowledge the one God, the Father and Maker of the world"]). Cf. also Sibylline Oracles 3.11, 629, 760; 4.30; [8.377; late]; Apocalypse of Abraham 7.10; 17.

44. E.g., Deut 32:39; 1 Sam 2:2; Isa 43–46; Hos 13:4; Joel 2:27.

45. Mauser, "Εἷς θεός," 74. Cf. also esp. Mal 2:10: οὐχὶ πατὴρ εἷς πάντων ὑμῶν; οὐχὶ θεὸς εἷς ἔκτισεν ὑμᾶς; ("Do you not all have one Father? Did not the one God create you?").

46. Instead of "even these will be added to the others" (LXX), Zech 14:17b MT reads "there will be no rain upon them" (ולא עליהם יהיה הגשם).

47. Paul's statements that the gospel is to the "Jew first" do not stand in contradiction to his strong emphasis upon no distinction. In fact they can stand quite naturally together. See Dahl, "Future of Israel," 157.

is, all (πᾶς)—in Christ. Zechariah's vision of the Gentiles streaming to Jerusalem is being fulfilled in Paul's mission to the Gentiles as Jews and Gentiles join together in Christ and with one voice glorify God (cf. 15:6). And yet, as we have noted, Paul's vision in our immediate context is also about future eschatological salvation (10:11, 12c, 13), and his concerns are about the salvation of the disobedient of *Israel*. Thus there is a profound reversal from the eschatological unity of Zechariah—it is now the *Jews* that must join with the Gentiles in acknowledging the one Lord. And so they shall (11:26). Through this theological correlation of the one and same Lord of all with the "all" of no distinction, we begin to feel the undercurrent pulling us along to 11:26 and, ultimately, 11:32.

But, and upon this we must later press, this clear christological transmutation raises crucially important questions. In 10:12 *Jesus* is the Lord of all, the one to whom the unbelieving Jews are disobedient (9:32-33; 10:14ff.) and the one by whom they are saved (10:9-13). However, quite obviously, in the OT the Lord who is over all is *YHWH*, the one and only God of Israel.[48] The crucial theological questions that arise are: In what way can what is constitutive of the very identity of YHWH in the OT be said to be constitutive of the identity of a human being, an ἄνθρωπος, even one who is risen from the dead? Who really is Paul's God? What is his name? For now, we must postpone these profoundly central questions until later in the chapter, because the use of Joel 3:5 in 10:13 sets them in sharpest relief. Suffice it to say at this point that Paul in no way thought his Jewish monotheistic roots to have been severed[49] and that, as his interchangeable use of κύριος shows (see n. 35), he did not set the lordship of Christ over against that of God, but rather held them together.

(c) Verse 12c: "giving richly to all who call upon him." The conclusion of 10:12 continues the emphasis of the universal breadth (πάντας) of eschatological salvation in relation to the Lord Jesus[50] and, in so doing, draws us toward

---

48. So, too, Jews near the time of Paul could use "Lord of all" of YHWH (e.g., Josephus, *A. J.* 20.90 [τῶν πάντων δὲ δικαίως μόνον καὶ πρῶτον ἥγημαι κύριος, "(you are) the first and only rightful Lord of all"]; 1QapGen 20.13: "for You [God] are Lord and Master of everything" [in F. Garcia Martínez and E. G. C. Tigchelaar, eds., *The Dead Sea Scrolls Study Edition* (Leiden: Brill, 1997-1998), 1:26-48]).

49. There is quite a scholarly consensus on this matter. See, e.g., Matthew Black, "The Christological Use of the Old Testament in the New Testament," *NTS* 18, no. 1 (1971): 1-14; Dahl, "The One God of Jews and Gentiles"; N. T. Wright, *The Climax of the Covenant* (Minneapolis: Fortress, 1991), 120-36. However, to state whether Paul's assumptions in this regard are theologically correct is quite another matter (Jews to this day think they are not).

50. If I am right that the κύριος in 10:12b is Jesus, then the αὐτόν at the end of 10:12c necessarily refers to him as well. In regard to the Lord giving richly, Käsemann, *Romans*,

Part 2: Biblical Studies and Theology in Practice

the beginning of the Joel 3:5 (EV 2:32) citation in 10:13 (πᾶς). Paul's soteriology is here decidedly christological (continuing 10:9ff.), and for that reason the significant use of ἐπικαλουμένους ("calling upon") deserves brief mention. In addition to recalling the oracular dimension of vv. 9–10 (ὁμολογήσῃς, ὁμολογεῖται, "you confess," "it is confessed"), ἐπικαλουμένους sounds a resonating note with the OT that could be lost only on the most tone-deaf of readers.[51] The use of "call upon" to describe one's action toward YHWH was exceedingly prevalent, spanning both genre and historical period.[52] The act of "calling upon" varies from worship (e.g., Gen 13:4; 21:33), to prayer for deliverance (e.g., 2 Sam 22 [Ps 18]), to apocalyptic or eschatological vision (Zech 13:9; Joel 3:5), but in each case, the one upon whom the people call is *YHWH*, the one God of Israel. This is particularly emphasized in those passages that speak of calling upon "the name" of the Lord.[53] It is sufficient at this point to note that Paul uses this same terminology of *Jesus* in 10:12c and thereby prepares us for the eschatological citation of Joel 3:5 in 10:13.

Thus far, to add to our earlier paraphrases, Paul essentially says: "That Jesus is Lord and that God raised him from the dead mean that at God's eschatological judgment 'the one believing in Jesus [him] will not be put to shame.' When the Scripture says this, it means everyone who believes in Jesus. For, as I said earlier, there is no distinction between Jew and Gentile in respect to sin or to salvation. This is because there is only one Lord, Jesus. And he will give richly to all, Jew and Gentile alike, when they call upon him. For the Scripture says . . ."

(3) Romans 10:13. Although there is no explicit citation formula signaling an OT citation,[54] it is beyond dispute that Paul here cites Joel 3:5a word for word with only a very minor change.[55] It would be hard to overestimate the

---

292, correctly notes that Paul "often speaks of riches as the fullness of eschatological grace." Friedrich Hauck and Wilhelm Kasch, "πλοῦτος," *TDNT* 6:328–29, collect all the pertinent references in the Pauline corpus and show, interestingly, that πλοῦτος, κτλ. is used interchangeably in relation to God, Christ, and the Christian community.

51. For the use of ἐπικαλέω in pagan Greek (to call upon a god), see the references in BAGD, 294.

52. See the non-exhaustive list of over twenty texts in Dunn, *Romans 9–16*, 610.

53. See Davis, *Name and Way of the Lord*, 118–22, for a very helpful chart comparing the NT texts that have "call upon the name of the Lord" (Acts 2:21; 9:14, 21; 22:16; Rom 10:13; 1 Cor 1:2), where applicable, with their LXX, MT, and Qumran antecedents/parallels.

54. Stanley, *Paul and the Language of Scripture*, 134 n. 159, excludes 10:13 from his study precisely because of the absence of an "explicit indication."

55. Paul does not cite καὶ ἔσται, which occurs at the beginning of Joel 3:5 (EV 2:32). This, however, is not very significant and can probably be explained on rhetorical or stylistic

theological potency of this use of Joel 3:5a. It is my contention that we are to hear the echoes of this sentence in its original context, but now with a christological transformation that has the profoundest implications for Paul's "doctrine" of God and, as such, for the salvation of Israel. But before we consider these matters, it would serve us well to make a few brief structural and rhetorical observations to situate 10:13 within its immediate context.

(*a*) Romans 10:13 within 10:11–13. First, the opening πᾶς of Paul's citation is the last in the string of four (10:11, 12 [2×]), and with it we are shown where Paul has been leading us. Further, that πᾶς occurs as part of Joel 3:5a but not of Isaiah 28:16 is evidence that Paul's addition of πᾶς in 10:11 was to bring Isaiah 28:16 into conformity with Joel 3:5a. Joel 3:5a is thus in this immediate context the scriptural lens through which Paul reinterprets universally Isaiah 28:16.[56] Second, ἐπικαλέσηται carries forth the motif of v. 12c (ἐπικαλουμένους)[57] and grounds it in Scripture in explicit connection with salvation. Third, in addition to its link with 10:9–10 (σωθήσῃ, σωτηρίαν), σωθήσεται reaches back to 10:1 (σωτηρίαν) and implicitly provides an answer of "how" it is that Israel can/will be saved.[58] It is by calling on the name of the Lord.

(*b*) The echoes of Joel 3:5a. Although the book of Joel is certainly connected with historical realities (e.g., 1:6; 2:20), its tone is much more that of an apocalyptic drama. The day of the Lord is near (1:15; 2:1; 3:4, etc.), and it will be one of apocalyptic portents (2:2; 3:4, etc.), prophesying (3:1–2), judgment and destruction (2:2–11, etc.), and eventual restoration for Israel (2:26–27; 4:1, etc.). Joel 3:5a occurs at the tail end of an apocalyptic vision containing God's declaration that he will restore his people (2:18–3:5). We need only to listen to the promise in two of its component parts to hear the linguistic and theological echoes present within Paul's argument:

---

grounds. Contra Capes, who thinks Paul omits these words to emphasize that Joel's "day of the Lord" had already dawned (*Old Testament Yahweh Texts*, 121). Such an interpretation does not really fit either the immediate context of God's promise in Joel or the context of Paul's argument in Rom 10 and his larger concern for the salvation of Israel in Rom 9–11. In fact, where Paul has taken over the idea of the "day of Lord," it refers to a time of judgment/restoration that has not yet occurred. (Capes's idea also fails to make sense of why Paul would then leave ἐπικαλέσηται and σωθήσεται in the future tense.) Also, of course, the postpositive γάρ must come after the πᾶς.

56. Contra Koch, *Schrift als Zeuge*, 134 n. 10.

57. It also sets up the first question in 10:14 (ἐπικαλέσηται).

58. It also, as we will see, looks forward to 11:26: πᾶς Ἰσραὴλ σωθήσεται ("all Israel will be saved").

Part 2: Biblical Studies and Theology in Practice

> You will eat abundantly and be satisfied, and praise the name of the Lord your God [τὸ ὄνομα κυρίου τοῦ θεοῦ ὑμῶν], who has dealt wondrously with you.
> And my people will never ever be put to shame [οὐ μὴ καταισχύνθῃ].
> You will know that I am in the midst of Israel,
> and that I am the Lord your God [ἐγὼ κύριος ὁ θεὸς ὑμῶν] and there is no one except me.
> And all of my people will never ever ever be put to shame[59] [οὐ μὴ καταισχυνθῶσιν οὐκέτι πᾶς ὁ λαός μου εἰς τὸν αἰῶνα]. (Joel 2:26-27 LXX)

> And I will show portents in heaven and upon the earth, blood and fire and vapors of smoke. The sun will be turned into darkness and the moon into blood, before the great and glorious/terrible day of the Lord [κυρίου] comes. And it will be that all who call upon the name of the Lord will be saved [πᾶς ὃς ἂν ἐπικαλέσηται τὸ ὄνομα κυρίου σωθήσεται]. For in Mount Zion and in Jerusalem the saved one [ἀνασῳζόμενος] will be just as the Lord [κύριος] has said, and those whom the Lord [κύριος] has called [προσκέκληται] will have the good news proclaimed [εὐαγγελιζόμενοι] to them. (Joel 3:3-5 LXX)

This Joel text[60] paints a picture of YHWH's apocalyptic salvation and vindication of all of his people Israel and, within the context of Joel, leads one through the judgment of all the Gentiles (πάντα τὰ ἔθνη [4:2, 11, 12 (2×); cf. 4:9 LXX]) to the finale of the book wherein "Judea will be inhabited forever, and Jerusalem to all generations . . . and the Lord [κύριος] will dwell in Zion" (4:20-21). There is a clear eschatological emphasis on the finality and irrevocability of Israel's salvation. Further, this salvation of *all* Israel is grounded in the theological singularity of *YHWH*, the only God of Israel. It is his name, the name of this Lord, upon which Israel must call, for it is they who have been called by him. And it is to them that the good news of their salvation will be proclaimed.

It is not terribly difficult to see the relevance of these themes to Paul's argument in Romans 9-11, nor in our more immediate context of chapter 10. It

---

59. I realize, of course, that this translation is a little awkward, but I am purposely trying to capture the quite emphatic note of the οὐ μὴ + οὐκέτι + εἰς τὸν αἰῶνα.

60. Joel 3:1-5 is also quoted virtually in full in Acts 2:17-21. It was on this basis (passages cited by two or more NT authors in prima facie independence of one another; cf. 1 Cor 1:2) that C. H. Dodd advanced his testimonia argument regarding Joel 3:1-5 (*According to the Scriptures*, 28-29). Because he took Isa 28:16 and Joel 3:5 both as testimonia, Dodd proposed the thesis that Paul was here constructing his argument from these testimonia (48).

is a bit more difficult, however, to see how they play out, both on the level of straightforward discourse and on the level of the rumbling echoes underneath. In order to attempt this task, we may begin at the discursive level.

The emphasis in Joel's prophecy is undeniably upon the salvation of all Israel and the judgment of all the Gentiles. The πᾶς of Joel 3:5a is quite clearly all *Israel*.[61] The Gentiles, concurrently with Israel's eschatological salvation, are, simply, judged and destroyed. The πᾶς of Joel 3:5a does not apply to them. It is this narrow meaning of πᾶς that Paul, the apostle to the Gentiles, subverts. He does so by leading up to Romans 10:13 in such a fashion that we have no confusion about the full meaning of πᾶς. First, in 10:11 he universalizes Isaiah 28:16 with the addition of πᾶς (recalling 9:33; 10:4). Second, in 10:12a he repeats himself (3:22) and bluntly and categorically declares that there is no distinction between Jew and Greek. Third, in 10:12b with the assertion "the same Lord is Lord of all," he grounds these prior moves in the same theological confession of singularity that served in Joel as the foundation for the uniqueness of God's people Israel and their salvation: "I am the Lord your God, and there is no one except me" (Joel 2:27).[62] Fourth, in 10:12c he uses "call upon" just following his correlation of no distinction and one Lord to pick up on its use in Joel 3:5a, but here he expands its range unmistakably to a universal "all" (πάντας). By the time he cites Joel 3:5a in Romans 10:13, it is clear that Paul is rereading this prophecy to refer not only to the Jews but also to the Gentiles. Paul has interpreted the once restrictive πᾶς universally.

Running simultaneously underneath this explicit level of discourse is a strong undercurrent that appropriates Joel's prophecy to foreshadow and proleptically announce the salvation of all of Israel that receives explicit expression in Romans 11:26. This undercurrent moves on the level of echoes, exemplifying the literary and rhetorical trope of metalepsis.[63] Through Paul's use of Joel 3:5a the attentive reader, prepared also by the citation of Isaiah 28:16 in 9:33 and 10:11, would most certainly hear the echoes from the preceding verses in Joel's prophecy:

---

61. This is clear not only from the linguistic connection with Joel 2:27 (πᾶς ὁ λαός μου, "all my people") but also from the following context in Joel, which describes the judgment of all Gentiles and the salvation of all Israel.

62. This connection comes primarily in the realm of allusion but nevertheless functions on the level of Paul's discursive argument.

63. I use the term as Hays defines it: "allusive echo functions to suggest to the reader that text B [Romans] should be understood in light of a broad interplay with text A [Joel], encompassing aspects of A beyond those explicitly cited" (*Echoes*, 20).

Part 2: Biblical Studies and Theology in Practice

> You will . . . praise the name of the Lord your God. . . .
> My people will never ever be put to shame. . . .
> I am the Lord your God. . . .
> All of my people will never ever ever be put to shame. . . .
> *All who call upon the name of the Lord will be saved;*
> . . . those whom the Lord has called. (Joel 2:26–27; 3:5 LXX)

Paul's subtle evocation proclaims the promise of YHWH's faithfulness to all his people Israel. Paul's universal reinterpretation of πᾶς is therefore by no means construed so as to now exclude the Jews: to Israel belong the promises (Rom 9:4); God's word has not "fallen out" (9:6). Rather, Paul plays in the space created by this now double meaning of πᾶς. Through the echoes of Joel's prophetic promise the question is raised in the mind of the reader that simultaneously adumbrates the coming answer: Will all Israel be saved? This question stays with the reader through the rest of Paul's discussion until he makes known the truth of God's promise in Joel: *all Israel will be saved* (11:26: πᾶς Ἰσραὴλ σωθήσεται); the *calling of God* (ἡ κλῆσις τοῦ θεοῦ) is irrevocable (11:29). Thus the undercurrent carries one along in the profound dissonance between God's promise in Joel and its fulfillment. The resolution of this dissonance comes only in the fusion of the echoes of the promise with Paul's outright statement of its fulfillment in 11:26.

We may say, then, that the discursive argument and the undercurrent of the echoes blend in harmonious counterpoint. Each one plays off the other, and in combination they foreshadow their dramatic and doxological unity wherein Paul's universal reinterpretation and expansion of πᾶς to include the Gentiles and his affirmation of God's faithfulness to his promise to all Israel receive eschatological fulfillment:

> For God has imprisoned all [τοὺς πάντας] to disobedience, in order that he might have mercy on all [τοὺς πάντας]. . . .
> For from him and through him and to him are all things [τὰ πάντα].
> (Rom 11:32, 36)

(c) The christological transformation. In the discussion of 10:13 thus far, we have purposefully avoided speaking of the κύριος of 10:13 as either YHWH, God, or Jesus Christ, for the simple reason that to make this identification raises theological questions that are better tackled following the discussion above, and that will lead directly into the last two sections of the chapter. So then, the κύριος of Romans 10:13 is Jesus.[64] This identification depends on (i) the confession "Jesus is Lord" in 10:9; (ii) our arguments above regarding the identification of ἐπ' αὐτῷ (10:11), ὁ αὐτὸς κύριος (10:12), and the αὐτόν (10:12) all as Jesus; and (iii) the clear evidence of 10:14.[65] Thus there is a startling christological transformation in that whereas the κύριος in the original setting was YHWH, now, in Romans 10:13, it is Jesus Christ.[66] In light of this transformation, two questions will shape the remainder of our exegesis: How does this transformation affect our interpretation of Romans 10:13 within its context? What implications does this have for Paul's "doctrine" of God?

We will begin by addressing the former question. That the κύριος in Romans 10:13 is Jesus has in fact been shaping our entire interpretation to this point, and it now remains for us to elucidate two further strands of thought through which the picture of the whole will be brought together and by which

---

64. So also Cranfield, *Romans*, 532; Dunn, *Romans 9–16*, 617; Sanday and Headlam, *Romans*, 291–92. Thus, the correct identification is common. The larger historical and theological significance, however, is almost nowhere to be found (though the books of Capes, *Old Testament Yahweh Texts*; Davis, *Name and Way of the Lord*; and Richardson, *Paul's Language*, have moments of illuminating theological insight).

65. Rom 10:14 says, "How then are they to call upon [one] in whom [referring back to the κύριος of 10:13] they have not believed? And how are they to believe [in one] of whom they have not heard? And how can they hear [of him] apart from preaching?" Since Paul's concern in these chapters is for Israel, it is crystal clear that these questions could not possibly be speaking of the God of Israel.

66. The debate concerning whether or not κύριος was written in the LXX for יהוה is complicated and without consensus. See Dunn, *Romans 9–16*, 608; Fitzmyer, *Romans*, 112–13; Fitzmyer, "The Semitic Background of the New Testament *Kyrios*-Title," in *A Wandering Aramean: Collected Aramaic Essays* (Chico, CA: Scholars Press, 1979), 115–42; George Howard, "The Tetragram and the New Testament," *JBL* 96 (1977): 63–83; and Albert Pietersma, "Kyrios or Tetragram: A Renewed Quest for the Original Septuagint," in *De Septuaginta: Studies in Honour of John William Wevers on His Sixty-Fifth Birthday*, ed. Albert Pietersma and Claude Cox (Mississauga: Benben, 1984), 85–101. I tend to think for our purposes the debate is a bit misdirected. If our NT MSS of Romans are at all trustworthy, then whether Paul read κύριος or יהוה (or an abbreviation thereof) is not as significant as it might seem. Regardless of what he saw in the LXX MSS, he wrote κύριος where the OT LXX citations clearly mean YHWH and correspond to the MT (Koch, *Schrift als Zeuge*, 86, counts eleven such instances). Thus it would seem that Paul himself read κύριος for the God of Israel. (The recurring question of Fitzmyer, "Semitic Background," 121, "Where did the NT writers get the kyrios-title for God [Yahweh]?" gets at this; cf. esp. Rom 11:3 where Paul adds the vocative κύριε, which is not in the LXX, to refer to YHWH.) Howard's arguments regarding the alteration of NT MSS from יהוה (or an abbreviation) to κύριος in the second and third centuries are unpersuasive in light of the lack of NT MSS evidence.

Part 2: Biblical Studies and Theology in Practice

we will come to the theological implications of this christological transformation. First, Jesus is the focal point of Paul's pressing questions about Israel's salvation (9:1–4; 10:1). It is in him that they have not believed (9:32–33; 10:14, 17), and it is through his name that they will be saved. God's promise to Israel through the prophet Joel will indeed find its fulfillment, but the christological shift makes it clear that this fulfillment will be through the name of Jesus Christ. Consequently, one cannot legitimately speak about the disobedience or salvation of Israel apart from Jesus Christ.[67] Second, Jesus is clearly at the center and is the focal point of the salvation of non-Jews. In this respect there is no distinction between Jew and non-Jew. All, and not all Israel alone, who call upon the name of Jesus Christ will be saved. The πᾶς of Joel 3:5 is universally expanded in light of Jesus Christ. Paul's discursive argument and the echoes he invokes with the citation of Joel 3:5 both are centered on and depend upon the figure of Jesus. It is this Lord to whom the Scripture bears witness (cf. Rom 1:2–3; 3:21), and, in turn, it is through this Lord that the promises contained in the Scriptures will find their eschatological fulfillment in the mercy of the inscrutable God.

The question of what this transformation might actually mean for Paul's "doctrine" of God is at once both refreshingly simple and exceedingly complex. Simple, because one might simply observe that 10:13 is an essential part of the theological picture to be completed in Romans 11:32, 35. Hence, Paul's soteriology is both strongly christological and theological, and can be neither one without the other. Complex, because this christological shift is not merely one of emphasis or even of function;[68] it is also one of identity.

The importance and theological significance in the OT of the name of the God of Israel, YHWH, hardly needs comment.[69] It may suffice to note a few aspects of its cardinal significance. First, YHWH is God's self-revelation. This name is who God declares himself to be. It is, as Childs notes, the summary of "God's own testimony to himself."[70] Second, as self-revealed, YHWH is the

---

67. It is thus inappropriate to speak of ch. 10 as a digression or detour in the argument of chs. 9–11.

68. Especially interesting in terms of an overlap of function (while maintaining a clear differentiation between persons) is 8:34 where the answer to the question "Who is to condemn?" is "Christ Jesus . . . who is at the right hand of God."

69. Gerhard von Rad notes that the name YHWH appears in the OT some 6,700 times (*Old Testament Theology*, 2 vols. [New York: Harper & Row, 1962, 1965], 1:186). See Brevard S. Childs, *The Book of Exodus: A Critical, Theological Commentary* (Philadelphia: Westminster, 1974), 411–12, for a summary list of the manifold uses of the divine name in the OT.

70. Childs, *Exodus*, 409.

one and only name of Israel's God. Israel "never had any idea of piling up many names upon Jahweh. Jahweh was in fact one, as Deuteronomy says."[71] There is a profoundly unitive theological correlation between the one Lord (Deut 6:4) and his name as YHWH. Hence, the foundation of the entire Decalogue, "I am YHWH," is inextricably bound with the fundamental prohibitions of the first two commandments: "God's right as Yahweh is somehow at stake."[72] Third, there is no disjunction between the divine name and the divine being.[73] The divine subject was present in his name.[74] Thus YHWH is not some *thing* that is called the name of God, but is rather the one Lord himself. Fourth, the misuse of the divine name is strictly prohibited and, when misused, results in the severest consequences, as it is an affront to God himself.[75]

It is quite astonishing, then, that Paul explicitly uses the τὸ ὄνομα κυρίου ("the name of the Lord") of Joel 3:5 to refer to Jesus. In this way he makes an unreserved identification of Jesus with YHWH, the unique Lord and only God of Israel.[76] However, since Paul is not foremost a propositional theologian,[77] he

---

71. Von Rad, *Old Testament Theology*, 1:185.

72. Childs, *Exodus*, 407.

73. There are a few passages that can give rise to the question of whether God's name is distinct from God himself (the clearest is Isa 30:27-28), but what is emphasized is actually YHWH's immanence or self-manifestation, and not at all the name YHWH as a distinct entity apart from God (this is particularly clear in the LXX where τὸ ὄνομα κυρίου is most naturally understood as a circumlocution for YHWH). In addition, these slightly ambiguous texts should be read in light of the overwhelming witness of the rest of the OT. See Davis, *Name and Way of the Lord*, 110-14, for a brief discussion of the matter of the name of the Lord as distinct from God. He also includes Philo (who does identify the name of the Lord as the Logos) and a reference from Josephus (*A. J.* 6.186) that causes him to doubt that Josephus understood the name as distinct from God.

74. On this, see von Rad, *Old Testament Theology*, 1:181ff. Cf. Christopher Seitz, "The Call of Moses and the 'Revelation' of the Divine Name," in *Theological Exegesis: Essays in Honor of Brevard S. Childs*, ed. Christopher Seitz and Kathryn Greene-McCreight (Grand Rapids: Eerdmans, 1999), 145-61, who writes that "God's 'name' involves his freedom to act and be who he most fully is" (159). Cf. also Childs, *Exodus*, 411.

75. Cf., e.g., Deut 5:11 [LXX], which has the future emphatic negation construction and could be translated: "For the Lord your God will never cleanse [acquit] the one who takes his name in vain." See E. P. Sanders, *Paul and Palestinian Judaism* (Philadelphia: Fortress, 1977), 159ff., who shows that in rabbinic Judaism "the only transgression about which there was any doubt as to whether or not there was an appropriate means of atonement" was the third commandment.

76. Cf., of course, Phil 2:9-11 and 1 Cor 8:6.

77. I am reminded of Barth's humorously wise comments: Romans "is not a system of dogmatics: for this reason the launching against it of anti-dogmatic tirades fails to confute it.... The man who busily engages himself in launching attacks against Paulinism as a

Part 2: Biblical Studies and Theology in Practice

does not simply say, "Jesus is YHWH." His theological medium is instead that of overlap and resonance,[78] such that he creates the overlapping conceptual space wherein this resonating identification occurs.[79] The identification within this unquestionable resonance and "conceptual overlap"[80] is one of dialectical *identity*. The name that is the God of Israel alone is now the name that is Jesus. The saving name in its original context was YHWH; now "the saving name is Christ's."[81] In Joel the Israelites would have called out "YHWH" to be saved, and now in Romans, all would call out "Jesus." "The name of the Lord" = YHWH has become, through Paul's OT citation, "the name of the Lord" = Jesus.[82] There is an overlap and an identity of *subject*. Our final paraphrase may thus run as follows:

> That Jesus is Lord and that God raised him from the dead mean that at God's eschatological judgment "the one believing in Jesus [him] will not be put to shame." When the Scripture says this, it means everyone who believes in Jesus. For, as I said earlier, there is no distinction between Jew and Gentile in respect to sin or to salvation. This is because there is only one Lord, Jesus. And he will give richly to all, Jew and Gentile alike, when they call upon him. For YHWH's promise about himself still stands: all Israel and all Gentiles who call upon his name—that is, Jesus—will be saved.

'system' is simply tilting at windmills; he betrays himself as one who has learnt nothing and forgotten nothing" (Karl Barth, *The Epistle to the Romans* [New York: Oxford University Press, 1968], 527).

78. Hays's *Echoes* is the clear example of a discernment of this mode of thinking.

79. Interestingly, Robert W. Jenson, in discussing Jesus Christ as "of one being with the Father," writes about the created resonance between God and Christ through the use of the title κύριος for both: "This resonance is itself the doctrine" (*Systematic Theology*, 2 vols. [New York: Oxford University Press, 1997–1999], 1:92). His question, "To whom is one speaking when one says 'Lord' to the heavens?" is a good one to bring the point into focus.

80. The term "conceptual overlap" is from Kreitzer, *Jesus and God in Paul's Eschatology*, 25, 29, 62, and is, I think, a particularly good one.

81. Adolf Schlatter, *Romans: The Righteousness of God* (Peabody, MA: Hendrickson, 1995), 216. Capes also recognizes the strong identification of YHWH and Jesus (*Old Testament Yahweh Texts*, 123ff.).

82. Luther captures the essence of the identification through resonance and overlap (cited in Anders Nygren, *Der Römerbrief* [Göttingen: Vandenhoeck & Ruprecht, 1951], 275):
> "Fragst du, wer der ist?
> Er heißt Jesus Christ,
> Der Herr Zebaoth,
> Und ist kein anderer Gott."

The force of potential contradiction in this very notion of the identification of identity between YHWH and Jesus must be pressed. To state the matter succinctly: the identification of identity that Paul sees is between the human being (ἄνθρωπος) Jesus[83] and YHWH the one Lord of Israel who cannot be imaged in the form of a human being. The first two commandments of the Decalogue guard against such imaging, and, for Paul the Jew, they remained unshakably in place. In Romans 1:18–32 Paul grounds his critique of pagan religion and morality in the theological insistence of the OT that as Creator of the world YHWH stands transcendently over against it. Idolatry is fundamentally an exchange of worship of the Creator for that of the creation (1:25). God is, as God, unable to be imaged or fashioned in visible form analogous to any part of creation: he is, "as θεός, absolutely and completely beyond the ken and grasp of human disposition, by nature beyond and above all created life."[84] Thus, of the pagan idolaters it may be said that they "exchanged the glory of the immortal God [ἀφθάρτου θεοῦ] for the likeness of an image of a mortal *human being* [φθαρτοῦ ἀνθρώπου]" (1:23). It would thus seem that the identification of identity between Jesus and the God of Israel is indeed fundamentally contradictory on *Paul's own terms*, which are grounded in those of the OT *itself*.[85] Is

---

83. That Rom 10 is clearly speaking about the risen Jesus does not lessen the force of the point. He is, as elsewhere in Paul, ἄνθρωπος. The commonly asserted idea that Paul does not refer often to the life of the earthly Jesus (which needs to be modified) does not matter here at all. It is beyond a shadow of a doubt that whether or not Paul often refers to the earthly Jesus, Paul believed that Jesus lived on this earth as a human being. C. K. Barrett suggests that Jesus is confessed and believed as one who stands both within and outside history (*A Commentary on the Epistle to the Romans* [London: Black, 1962], 201). I find this a helpful way of holding together the earthly life and death of the ἄνθρωπος Jesus within history, and his subsequent resurrection and exaltation as one who now stands outside of history (though, of course, theologically we would say of the resurrected Jesus, both within and without). See also Ulrich Mauser, *Gottesbild und Menschwerdung: Eine Untersuchung zur Einheit des Alten und Neuen Testaments* (Tübingen: Mohr Siebeck, 1971), 137–38, on the paradoxical unity of identity between the *crucified*, earthly Jesus and the resurrected Lord.

84. Ulrich Mauser, "One God and Trinitarian Language in the Letters of Paul," *HBT* 20, no. 2 (1998): 99–108, esp. 104.

85. The anthropomorphic representations of God in the OT are entirely in "concept and language" and not in a cultic image or mediator of revelation (see von Rad, *Old Testament Theology*, 1–219). Nonetheless, these anthropomorphic representations provide valuable clues for biblical theology. Gen 1:26 could be seen as anticipatory in that human beings can bear the image of God; however, there is no sense of an overlap of identity such that the Creator/creature or God/human being distinction is ever blurred. See Iain Provan, "To Highlight All Our Idols: Worshipping God in Nietzsche's World," *ExAud* 15 (1999): 19–38, esp. 25–26.

not the idea of an overlap between Jesus and YHWH to confuse the Creator with a creature, one who is ἄνθρωπος? Does not Paul spurn his Jewish "monotheistic" roots and the oneness of YHWH?[86] That is, does not Paul speak of *another god* other than the transcendent creator YHWH? Must not the unity of the OT and NT come apart as there exists a contradiction so deep between the very nature of YHWH and the prohibitions that guard that nature, and Paul's radical anthropological theology? For if the God of the OT is not the same God of whom Paul speaks in the NT, then the unity of the testaments is destroyed. The question could not be any greater: Who, then, really is Paul's God? We are thus at the door of our two final considerations, the "monotheism" of Second Temple Judaism and the theological doctrine of God.

The Significance of Romans 10:13 for Second Temple Jewish Monotheism

Second Temple Jewish "monotheism" is an enormous field in itself and countless books, monographs, and articles have been published on the relations between the Christology of the early church and the theology of the Jews of the Second Temple period.[87] It is, of course, always perilous to generalize, but

---

86. See Hans Joachim Schoeps, *Paul: The Theology of the Apostle in the Light of Jewish Religious History* (Philadelphia: Westminster, 1959), esp. 160–67.

87. The relevant literature is extraordinary in scope. Among others, see esp. Richard Bauckham, *God Crucified: Monotheism and Christology in the New Testament* (Grand Rapids: Eerdmans, 1998); Bauckham, "Jesus, Worship Of," *ABD* 3:812–19; Wilhelm Bousset, *Kyrios Christos: A History of the Belief in Christ from the Beginnings of Christianity to Irenaeus* (Nashville: Abingdon, 1970); P. M. Casey, *From Jewish Prophet to Gentile God: The Origins and Development of New Testament Christology* (Louisville: Westminster John Knox, 1991); James D. G. Dunn, *Christology in the Making: A New Testament Inquiry into the Origins of the Doctrine of the Incarnation*, 2nd ed. (London: SCM, 1989), 129ff.; Robert M. Grant, *Gods and the One God* (Philadelphia: Westminster, 1986); Larry Hurtado, *One God, One Lord: Early Christian Devotion and Ancient Jewish Monotheism*, 2nd ed. (Edinburgh: T&T Clark, 1998); H. Kleinknecht, et al., "θεός," *TDNT* 3:65–123; Kramer, *Christ, Lord, Son of God*; G. Quell and W. Foerster, "κύριος," *TDNT* 3:1039–98; Alan F. Segal, *Two Powers in Heaven: Early Rabbinic Reports About Christianity and Gnosticism*, Studies in Judaism in Late Antiquity 25 (Leiden: Brill, 1977); Wright, *Climax of the Covenant*, 120–36; Wright, "Jesus and the Identity of God," *ExAud* 14 (1998): 42–56; Wright, "One God, One Lord, One People: Incarnational Christology for a Church in a Pagan Environment," *ExAud* 7 (1991): 45–58; and Wright, *New Testament*. I should mention at the outset that I find the arguments of Hurtado, Bauckham, Wright, et al. persuasive that Jewish thought is the primary context in which we are to situate our discussion of Christology (at least Pauline Christology), rather than

when working within a chapter generalizations are inevitable. What I will attempt to do, then, is give a brief and broad sketch of the way I see the situation of the question, highlight two of the more promising recent endeavors, and offer a brief and pointed critique.

It is clear that the issue addressed, more or less explicitly, has been the question of what it meant in the Jewish theology of the Second Temple period to say that God is one, and how this might or might not be compatible with early christological formulations. How "open" or "closed" is God's oneness? Put crudely, where does the incredibly close (if not full) identification of Jesus Christ with this one God fit in? How can it? Various scholars have come at these questions in different ways; nevertheless, following Richard Bauckham,[88] it does seem reasonable to suggest three general approaches. First, some scholars argue that the oneness of YHWH was such that it was impossible within Jewish monotheistic theology to attribute divine status to Jesus (or any figure other than YHWH) or to worship him without jeopardizing the oneness of God. To do these things would therefore constitute a radical break from Jewish monotheism.[89] As a result, this view tends either to downplay potentially high Christology or to advocate a break from a Jewish understanding of YHWH's oneness. Second, there are those who argue that the veritable explosion of "semi-divine" figures in the Second Temple period—angels, exalted humans, personifications of the attributes of God, and so on—create a working space in the oneness of God wherein Jesus could be placed without a full identification with YHWH, but also without compromising the oneness of YHWH. There is thus the possibility of high Christology without a break with Jewish monotheism, as the concept of God's oneness in the Second Temple period was open to such a development.[90]

---

in the context of Hellenistic influence (Bousset, Kramer, et al.). The two primary reasons are that I agree that the highest Christology is very early (and therefore less susceptible to direct pagan influence), and that "there is simply no comparable tradition of exclusivist monotheism in pagan religions [or philosophies] of the Greco-Roman period" (Hurtado, *One God, One Lord*, 6; cf. Dahl, "One God of Jews and Gentiles," 179–80, and Grant, *Gods and the One God*, 29ff.).

88. Bauckham, *God Crucified*, 1–3. He suggests two usual approaches, and his is the third.

89. See, e.g., Casey, *From Jewish Prophet to Gentile God*. Cf. Dunn's extended critique of Casey, "The Making of Christology—Evolution or Unfolding?," in *Jesus of Nazareth: Lord and Christ*, ed. Joel B. Green and Max Turner (Grand Rapids: Eerdmans, 1994), 437–52.

90. Hurtado's *One God, One Lord*, is the strongest book in this vein. He argues that the "principal agent" motif is the primary conceptual category of the early Christians, but acknowledges that it is not adequate to account for the larger and more significant features of early Christian devotion. Rather, the religious experience of the early Christians caused

Third, there are the recent endeavors of Bauckham and N. T. Wright.[91] Though there are considerable differences between their respective approaches, unlike the first two, they both see Christ as completely identified with the God of Israel. Bauckham seeks to show this through a reformulation of the two approaches above wherein he holds both to a "strict" interpretation of YHWH's oneness and to the assertion that the early Christology was very high (and vice versa), though the intermediary figures are not "of any decisive importance for the study of early Christology."[92] Second Temple monotheism was self-consciously rigorous in its theological exclusiveness of the meaning of God's oneness—his unique identity—and drew the demarcating line clearly between the creator God and everything else, the creation. The intermediary figures do not represent a blurring between God and all other reality. They are either aspects of God's unique reality (i.e., God himself) or his creatures. The first Christians set Jesus "within the unique identity of the God of Israel. They did so by including Jesus in the unique, defining characteristics by which Jewish monotheism identified God as unique."[93] This radical inclusion was not the end of a process but rather de novo.[94] However, this was not to break with Jewish monotheism, for Jewish monotheism was "structurally open to the development of the christological monotheism that we find in the New Testament texts."[95] Thus, the early Christians did not find Jewish monotheism antithetical to their theology, but instead used its resources for their formulations.

N. T. Wright has advanced the view, stated in many different ways, that first-century Jewish monotheism was "never a numerical analysis of the being of the one God." Rather, it was primarily polemical, a way of saying "our God is the true God, and your gods are worthless idols." This monotheism took shape around three central aspects of Jewish theology: creation, providence, and covenant. Creational monotheism affirms that the one Lord, YHWH, is the Creator of the world and is other than his creation. Providential monotheism maintains that while God is other than the world, he remains in close relation with it through active involvement (angels, etc.). Covenantal monotheism confesses that this one Creator has called the Jews to be his unique people. The

---

a "mutation" or "innovation" within this motif to link the principal agent with God as one who could receive cultic veneration.

91. See n. 87.
92. Bauckham, *God Crucified*, 4.
93. Bauckham, *God Crucified*, vii–viii.
94. Bauckham, *God Crucified*, 28.
95. Bauckham, *God Crucified*, viii.

Jewish theologians expressed these convictions about God in five ways, which present a "swirling sense of a rhythm of mutual relations within the very being of the one God": Spirit, Word, Torah, Presence/Glory, Wisdom. The important christological texts in relation to Jewish monotheistic theology are "all highly dependent on this way of thinking [and] offer a very high, completely Jewish, and extremely early christology."[96] The final way to speak about God for the early Christians was Messiah/Son. With this addition (which is itself Jewish, of course) the early Christians "could say what they felt obliged to say about Jesus (and the Spirit) . . . in the Jewish language of Spirit, Word, Torah, Presence/Glory, Wisdom, and now Messiah/Son. It is as though they discovered Jesus within the Jewish monotheistic categories they already had. The categories seemed to have been made for him. They fitted him like a glove. And . . . it was the *human* Jesus, the *earthly* Jesus, that they fitted."[97]

This did give shape to a christological monotheism (as exemplified in the redefinition of the Shema in 1 Cor 8:6), but this new content did not "cancel out the content it used to have within the Hebrew Bible and subsequent Jewish writing, but rather actually emphasizes it."[98] YHWH had now "made himself known in and through, and even *as*, Jesus and the divine spirit."[99] The NT authors "can be shown to be expressing a fully . . . trinitarian theology, and to be doing so as a fresh and creative variation from within, not an abandonment of, their Second Temple Jewish god-view."[100] Thus, for Wright as for Bauckham, Jesus Christ can be seen in *complete identification* with the God of Israel *within* Jewish monotheism.

Briefly, there are five major strengths of these two recent approaches, the first three shared, the last two distinctive to Bauckham. First, they both make extraordinarily compelling cases (as does Hurtado for that matter) that one does not need to look outside of the Jewish sources to pagan influences to explain high, early Christology. Second, they both speak of *christological* monotheism. That is, while asserting continuity, they acknowledge that there is, even if from within its own categories, a fundamental redefinition of Jewish

---

96. Wright, "Jesus and the Identity of God," 45–46; *New Testament*, 250ff., 259; *Climax of the Covenant*, 125.

97. Wright, "Jesus and the Identity of God," 49.

98. Wright, *Climax of the Covenant*, 136, 130.

99. Wright, *New Testament*, 474. Cf. Wright, "Jesus and the Identity of God," 51: "Did he [Jesus] think he was in any sense the embodiment of Israel's God? I cannot myself see that an orthodox christology or atonement theology can give a negative answer . . . without running into serious difficulties."

100. Wright, "Jesus and the Identity of God," 46–47.

Part 2: Biblical Studies and Theology in Practice

monotheism in the light of Jesus Christ. Third, they both eschew philosophical monadism as a way of understanding the oneness of YHWH either in the OT or in the Second Temple period. There is dynamism within the one God. Fourth, Bauckham in particular focuses on the crucial question of the difference between Creator and creation, and he keeps this persistently in view. Finally, Bauckham flatly denies that an evolutionary model of the development of Christology helps to explain the early Christians' *initial* identification of Jesus with YHWH. This radical first step was taken de novo and makes no more sense at the end of a long process of development.

My critique centers on the implications of the full identification of YHWH, the Creator, with Jesus, an ἄνθρωπος, *born of a woman* (Gal 4:4)—that is, a *creature*. My contention, straightforwardly put, is that nowhere in Second Temple literature is there a warrant for making the identification that YHWH is an ἄνθρωπος born of a woman. No Jewish theologians thought that, because, as yet, they could not *in principle* think it—imaging and, of course, identifying YHWH as a human being is categorically ruled out by the foundational first two commandments of the Decalogue. Thus, I cannot agree with Bauckham that Second Temple Jewish monotheism was "structurally open" to conceiving of the identity of YHWH as an ἄνθρωπος in the way we see it in the highest Pauline christological texts (e.g., Rom 10:13; 1 Cor 8:6; Phil 2:5-6; Col 1:15-16; 2:9; Eph 1:20).

One example is sufficient to point out the difficulty in his approach. It is generally recognized that there are two categories of potential candidates for divine or semi-divine beings: (i) intermediary figures, principal angels and exalted patriarchs (angelic or human figures who play an important part in God's rule over the world), and (ii) personifications or hypostatizations of aspects of the one God (Spirit, Word, Wisdom). Bauckham argues that the figures in the first category are, in the relevant Jewish literature, excluded from God's unique identity; that is, they are creatures. The second category of personifications and so on is included in God's unique identity; that is, the personifications are God.[101] The problem that instantly arises, of course, is that Jesus identified as Divine Wisdom (e.g., in the texts mentioned above) belongs in category two, but identified as a human being born of a woman (implicit wherever Jesus Christ is mentioned) belongs in category one. Thus the figure of Jesus Christ himself breaks through these neatly opposed categorizations as in him they find their unity.[102]

---

101. Bauckham, *God Crucified*, 17ff.
102. Bauckham also holds that the Son of Man in the Similitudes of Enoch is the single

There are a few problems with Wright's expansive account,[103] but suffice it to mention two. First, he does not distinguish clearly enough between Creator and creature. Wright speaks of angels, Wisdom, the *Shekinah*, and so on all equally as expressions of the one God. Yet angels (and certainly the exalted patriarchs), which he sees as a theological way of speaking of the transcendent God's action within the world (an attempt to hold together creational and providential monotheism),[104] are in fact not manifestations or expressions of the one God himself but are his *creatures*, his servants, as Bauckham stresses. Wright gives us a theological interpretation of angelic beings[105] but in so doing confuses God himself with what are clearly his creatures. However, as he does recognize, God's Wisdom, Spirit, Word, Presence are by and large actual expressions of God himself. It would seem then that Wright has blurred a line that was in place for Jewish theology. Second, he seems to underestimate the difference between metaphorical speech and an actual human being. He is unquestionably correct to note that the Jews spoke of God in ways that allowed for his immanence (in particular the *Shekinah*), but this was metaphorical or representational speech. What Second Temple Jewish theology did not say (and could not yet say, on their own grounds) was that YHWH was present as an ἄνθρωπος born of a woman; that is, YHWH was imaged as a human

---

exception wherein an angelic figure/exalted patriarch is included in the divine identity. Thus, this figure, too, breaks his categories. Cf. Bauckham's article "Jesus, Worship Of," *ABD* 3:816, where he states, "It is not too much to say that Jewish monotheism was defined by its adherence to the first and second commandments."

103. For example, his constant insistence upon the fact that first-century Jewish theology was not concerned with a numerical analysis of the being of God is correct, helpful, and crucial. However, what he does not see (or else speak of) is that the Christ event forced this question out into the open, and very quickly. Segal concludes that "all such doctrines ["two powers"], whether in apocalypticism, Christianity or philosophical speculations, were probably condemned by the rabbis as early as the end of the first century and the beginning of the second" (*Two Powers*, 264).

104. Wright, e.g., *New Testament*, 258ff.

105. Wright, *New Testament*, 258. Wright seems to assume that to polemicize theologically against and avoid lapsing into dualism or paganism, one must have angels or else God becomes an "absentee landlord" (258); otherwise, his transcendence is compromised and the move toward paganism (or pantheism) is made (angels are how one deals with the "theological problem" of how to hold together providence and belief in a transcendent God). If I understand him correctly, then this idea is theologically quite false. There is nothing in principle that rules out the Creator's direct action within his creation—unless, contrary to Jewish and Christian theology, one is completely wedded to the Greek philosophical concept of an absolute transcendent deity. Robert Jenson's *Systematic Theology* is a single, sustained demolition of this way of thinking.

Part 2: Biblical Studies and Theology in Practice

being, a man. It is one thing to speak metaphorically of the presence of the one God who cannot be imaged; it is quite another to speak of the identification of identity of this same God with an actual fleshly ἄνθρωπος who was tortured and died a criminal's death by crucifixion. This way of speaking, I submit, was not part of Second Temple Jewish theology, even of the category of Messiah/Son.[106] Thus, Wright's easy and complete continuity between Jewish monotheism and early Christian affirmations about YHWH obscures the radical claim of the *humanity of God*.

In this light, both Bauckham and Wright (and Hurtado et al.), though correctly recognizing that it is Jesus as a human being with whom we must deal, by and large get at the central question the wrong way around. That is to say, their studies move in the direction of how it is that Jesus can be identified with YHWH (the *divinity* of *Jesus*), the one God of Jewish monotheism. It is the implicit underside of this question, however, that needs the attention and creates problems for their theses—how can the *creator YHWH*, the one who cannot be imaged as a *human creature*, be totally identified in his identity with the *human creature* Jesus?

The Theological Implications of Romans 10:13 for Biblical Theology

We have, then, to set forward our judgment of Paul's seemingly contradictory anthropological theology expressed in Romans 10:13,[107] to account for it, and to probe its implications for the doctrine of God. We can attend to these three tasks in order, but there will be mutual interweaving and overlap, as a judgment about one of them will have bearing on the others.

It may be said that Paul did *not* sever the Jewish monotheistic roots of the OT. However, and this is the crux, this can *only be said in the light of the advent of Jesus Christ*, the confession that in Jesus Christ God has become human (the inner necessity and essential justification of which is the resurrection). That is, without the Christian theological confession that YHWH, the one God of Israel unable to be imaged, was indeed in Christ (2 Cor 5:19), the unity of

---

106. This is something Wright would know as well as anyone else today. Jesus's messiahship was, in the end, seemingly different from that expected during the Second Temple period. After all, he was *killed*.

107. By this term I do not mean that Paul based his theology off of humanity. That would obviously be projection and a nice lunch for Feuerbachian critics. Rather, I mean simply to emphasize the humanity of God.

Paul's writing with the OT falls apart, for Paul has introduced *another god*, an image of YHWH. The overlapping identity of subjects, the human Jesus and YHWH, the coordination of creature and Creator, when properly understood, is tantamount to a theological paradigm shift in the doctrine of God, in light of which one rereads the entire OT. It is within this confession of the identity and humanity of God that one can see the theological trajectory in the OT of the anthropomorphism of God and the theomorphism of human beings as pointing toward their unity in Christ. The OT's vivid portrayal of YHWH as a self-humbling God who by nature loves to condescend to and to participate in human history and the corresponding representation of God and God's condition in the prophet of Israel as he participates in God's life (e.g., Hosea) find their fulfillment in the total identification of YHWH with humanity and humanity with YHWH in one human life, that of Jesus of Nazareth.[108] It is also within this confession that the dynamism within the being of YHWH depicted in the OT allows for Trinitarian developments. The OT's personifications and hypostatizations of God are expressions of the inner vitality of the living God made known to his creation. Through the correlation of the unity of the one κύριος (the identification of identity between YHWH and Jesus) and through the retained distinction between Jesus and God, the dynamism of the one God's life necessitates binitarian formulation. The identity and role of the Spirit in relation to the life of the God of the OT and in relation to the life, death, and resurrection of Jesus further necessitate triadic formulation and lead logically to Trinitarian thinking and confession.[109] However, these affirmations can only be made within this incarnational confession of the unity of the transcendence and immanence of God. Apart from this confession, one cannot read through the OT and the Second Temple literature and come up with the idea that YHWH is to be identified in his identity with a human being born of a woman, a creature. Thus, Paul's statement in Romans 10:13 is a particularly forceful example of the fact that it must be the *same God* through which the OT and NT are held together. And Paul's God and the God of Israel

---

108. See Mauser, *Gottesbild*, and Mauser, "Image of God and Incarnation," *Int* 24 (1970): 336–56. Cf. also von Rad, *Old Testament Theology*, 1:219, and Abraham J. Heschel, *The Prophets* (Harper & Row, 1962), esp. ch. 12.

109. I have not dealt with the role of the Spirit here simply because the text with which I have been working does not mention the Spirit. For key Pauline texts, see 2 Cor 3:1–4:6 (esp. 3:17–18); 13:13 (EV 13:14); 1 Cor 12:4–6; Eph 4:4–6. Cf. also Rom 5:5; 8:3–4, 9–11, 15–18, 26–27; 1 Cor 2:4–5, 10–12; 6:11; 2 Cor 1:21–22; Gal 3:1–5; 4:4–6; Phil 1:19; Eph 1:3–14; 2:17–22; 3:14–19; 5:18–20; 2 Thess 2:13. See also Gordon D. Fee, *God's Empowering Presence: The Holy Spirit in the Letters of Paul* (Peabody, MA: Hendrickson, 1994).

are the same God only if YHWH is so identified with Jesus and Jesus with YHWH that the first two commandments are not violated.

Paul was a devout and learned Jew, one who knew the Scripture inside and out. Would he not be aware of such a potential theological disaster in his own thinking about YHWH (he certainly was in regard to pagans; see Rom 1)? Admittedly, Paul was not a rigid systematician, but I find it impossible to believe that one who was "to the law as a Pharisee" could simply think himself into this seemingly idolatrous theological blunder. Put crudely, Saul's reading of the OT and his immersion in the theology of the Second Temple period do not add up to Paul. The only feasible explanation is the one that is always so unsettling and quite frustrating to historians of Christian origins—the appearance of the risen Christ to Paul (Gal 1; Acts 9). This encounter cannot be overestimated and was of such a magnitude that it shook the foundations of Paul's life.

Thus, Paul could reread the first two commandments, and indeed all of Scripture, in dialectical harmony with his proclamation of the gospel of the risen Jesus Christ. The entire Torah (Scripture as narrative) pointed toward and bore witness to this One who had appeared to him. And so, Paul formed his statements about Jesus from Scripture itself. But we must notice the logic of rereading. Jesus Christ was revealed, and *then* the Scripture was read as a witness to him—not the other way around. Paul's anthropological theology and the identification of identity between YHWH and Jesus came out of his confrontation with the risen Jesus Christ.

The implications of the overlap of subjects, the identification of the human Jesus with YHWH the one God of Israel, have been discussed throughout the history of the church. Obviously not all of these implications can be traced here. I will note only a few points. First, a reading of Paul's "doctrine" of God must yield the conclusion that in Pauline theology we see either a complete contradiction with the OT (as many Jews today would still hold) or a fundamental theological seed of Nicaea. Athanasius had it right. If Jesus cannot be identified with YHWH and, we may add, if God's being does not somehow include his humanity, then Christian thinkers and worshipers have been idolaters (on the theological grounds of the OT) since day one, and we have no claim to the Jewish Scriptures as an OT prefiguring, pointing toward, and belonging inseparably with an NT. Second, God is to be understood christologically. This would entail the affirmation of the humanity of God: "God in his deity is human."[110] To follow Barth's lines, this is also an affirmation that

110. Karl Barth, "The Humanity of God," in *The Humanity of God* (Richmond, VA: John

it is not *alien* to God to be human (a rather polemical notion against Greek philosophical conceptions of deity). This must be held to with force if YHWH as the God who cannot be imaged is to be taken seriously at all in conjunction with Jesus Christ. Third, Jesus Christ is to be understood theologically. This affirmation entails not only Jesus's deity (as it must for an identification with YHWH) but also the affirmation of the hiddenness of God. God makes himself known as a tortured and crucified human being, the Lord of glory. Hence, christological theology and theological Christology bring us to affirm that in the narrative of the life of Jesus we see the identity of God.[111] In the life, death, and resurrection of Jesus, God fully adopts the depths of human depravity and misery and assumes even the ultimate contradiction of death into his own life as the life-giving and ever-living God. Finally, because of the identification of identity between YHWH and Jesus Christ, the OT is to be read as a witness to Jesus Christ, the two testaments together as one Bible bearing witness to the same Lord of all. How this would be done is the history of the exegesis of the church, a subject for another chapter, indeed for a lifetime.

Knox, 1963), 37–65, esp. 55. Cf. the fully developed treatment in Barth, *Church Dogmatics* IV/1 (Edinburgh: T&T Clark, 1956), §59.

111. Bauckham's last chapter of *God Crucified* is an admirable step in such reflection. For how this notion is worked out in recent systematic theology, see Jenson's *Systematic Theology*.

Bibliography

Aageson, James. "Scripture and Structure in the Development of the Argument in Romans 9–11." *CBQ* 48 (1986): 265–89.

Adolphe, Jane, Robert L. Fastiggi, and Michael Vacca, eds. *St. Paul, the Natural Law, and Contemporary Legal Theory*. Lanham, MD: Lexington Books, 2012.

Alexander, Loveday. "Ancient Book Production and the Circulation of the Gospels." In Bauckham, *Gospels for All Christians*, 71–112.

———. "Formal Elements and Genre: Which Greco-Roman Prologues Most Closely Parallel the Lukan Prologues?" In *Jesus and the Heritage of Israel: Luke's Narrative Claim upon Israel's Legacy*, edited by David P. Moessner, 9–26. Harrisburg, PA: Trinity Press International, 1999.

———. *The Preface to Luke's Gospel: Literary Convention and Social Context in Luke 1.1–4 and Acts 1.1*. SNTSMS 78. Cambridge: Cambridge University Press, 1993.

Alföldy, Géza. "Subject and Ruler, Subjects and Methods: An Attempt at a Conclusion." In Small, *Subject and Ruler*, 254–61.

Aly, Zaki, and Ludwig Koenen. *Three Rolls of the Early Septuagint: Genesis and Deuteronomy*. Bonn: Rudolf Habelt, 1980.

Anastos, Milton V. "The Ethical Theory of Images Formulated by the Iconoclasts in 754 and 815." *DOP* 8 (1954): 153–60.

Ando, Clifford. *Imperial Ideology and Provincial Loyalty in the Roman Empire*. Berkeley: University of California Press, 2000.

Arendt, Hannah. *On Violence*. New York: Harcourt, Brace & World, 1969.

Aristotle. *Metaphysics*. Vol. 2, *Books 10–14*. Translated by Hugh Tredennick and G. Cyril Armstrong. 2 vols. LCL. Cambridge: Harvard University Press, 1935.

Asad, Talal. "Anthropological Conceptions of Religion: Reflections on Geertz." *Man* 18 (1983): 237–59.

Athanassiadi, Polymnia, and Michael Frede, eds. *Pagan Monotheism in Late Antiquity*. Oxford: Clarendon, 1999.

Bibliography

Attridge, Harold W. "The Philosophical Critique of Religion under the Early Empire." *ANRW* 2.16.1 (1978): 45-78.

Babut, Daniel. *La religion des philosophes grecs: de Thalès aux Stoïciens*. Paris: Presses Universitaires de France, 1974.

Balch, David L. "Paul, Families, and Households." In *Paul in the Greco-Roman World*, edited by J. Paul Sampley, 258-92. Harrisburg: Trinity International Press, 2003.

Balia, Peter. "Does Acts 2.36 Represent an Adoptionist Christology?" *European Journal of Theology* 5, no. 2 (1996): 137-42.

Barclay, John. "Pushing Back: Some Questions for Discussion." *JSNT* 33, no. 3 (2011): 321-26.

Barnes, Timothy D. "An Apostle on Trial." *JTS* 20 (1969): 407-19.

———. "Legislation against the Christians." *JRS* 58 (1968): 32-50.

Barr, James. *Biblical Faith and Natural Theology*. Oxford: Oxford University Press, 1994.

———. *The Semantics of Biblical Language*. London: Oxford University Press, 1961.

Barrett, C. K. "Acts and Christian Consensus." In *Context: Essays in Honour of Peder Johan Borgen*, edited by P. W. Bøckman and R. E. Kristiansen, 19-33. Trondheim: Tapir, 1987.

———. *A Commentary on the Epistle to the Romans*. London: Black, 1962.

———. *A Critical and Exegetical Commentary on the Acts of the Apostles*. 2 vols. ICC. Edinburgh: T&T Clark, 1994-1998.

———. *The Holy Spirit and the Gospel Tradition*. New York: Macmillan, 1947.

———. *Luke the Historian in Recent Study*. Philadelphia: Fortress, 1970.

———. *The Second Epistle to the Corinthians*. Peabody, MA: Hendrickson, 1973.

———. "Submerged Christology in Acts." In *Anfänge der Christologie*, edited by Cilliers Breytenbach and Henning Paulsen, 237-44. Göttingen: Vandenhoeck & Ruprecht, 1991.

———. "The Third Gospel as a Preface to Acts? Some Reflections." In *The Four Gospels, 1992*, edited by F. Van Segbroeck et al., 2:1451-66. Leuven: Leuven University Press, 1992.

Barth, Karl. *Church Dogmatics*. Edinburgh: T&T Clark, 1936-1970.

———. *Dogmatics in Outline*. Translated by G. T. Thomson. New York: Harper & Row, 1959.

———. *The Epistle to the Romans*. New York: Oxford University Press, 1968.

———. "The Humanity of God." In *The Humanity of God*, 37-65. Richmond, VA: John Knox, 1963.

———. *Die Kirchliche Dogmatik* I/1. Zollikon-Zürich: Evangelischer Verlag, 1932.

Barth, Markus. "One God, One Christ, One People." *ExAud* 4 (1988): 8-26.

Barton, S. C. "Can We Identify the Gospel Audiences?" In Bauckham, *Gospels for All Christians*, 173-94.

Bassler, Jouette M. *Divine Impartiality: Paul and a Theological Axiom*. SBLDS 59. Chico, CA: Scholars Press, 1982.

Bauckham, Richard. *God Crucified: Monotheism and Christology in the New Testament*. Grand Rapids: Eerdmans, 1998.

———, ed. *The Gospels for All Christians: Rethinking the Gospel Audiences*. Grand Rapids: Eerdmans, 1998.

Baudissin, W. W. Graf. *KYRIOS als Gottesname im Judentum und seine Stelle in der Religionsgeschichte: Erster Teil: Der Gebrauch des Gottesname Kyrios in Septuaginta*. Giessen: Töpelmann, 1929.

Beard, Mary, John North, and Simon Price. *Religions of Rome*. 2 vols. Cambridge: Cambridge University Press, 1998.

Bechtler, Steven Richard. "Christ, the Τέλος of the Law: The Goal of Romans 10:4." *CBQ* 56 (1994): 288-308.

Bellinzoni, Arthur J. "The Gospel of Luke in the Apostolic Fathers." In *Trajectories through the New Testament and the Apostolic Fathers*, edited by Andrew F. Gregory and Christopher M. Tuckett, 45-68. Oxford: Oxford University Press, 2005.

———. "The Gospel of Luke in the Second Century CE." In Thompson and Phillips, *Literary Studies in Luke-Acts*, 59-76.

Beurlier, Émile. "Saint Paul et L'Aréopage." *Revue d'histoire et de littérature religieuses* 1 (1896): 344-66.

Beyschlag, Willibald. *New Testament Theology, Or, Historical Account of the Teaching of Jesus and of Primitive Christianity according to the New Testament Sources*. 2 vols. Edinburgh: T&T Clark, 1899.

Bickerman, Elias. "Consecratio." In den Boer, *Le culte des souverains dans l'empire romain*, 3-25.

Bird, Michael F. "The Unity of Luke-Acts in Recent Discussion." *JSNT* 29, no. 4 (2007): 425-48.

Black, Matthew. "The Christological Use of the Old Testament in the New Testament." *NTS* 18, no. 1 (1971): 1-14.

Bleek, Friedrich. *Synoptische Erklärung der drei ersten Evangelien*. Leipzig: Wilhelm Engelmann, 1862.

Bockmuehl, Markus. *Jewish Law in Gentile Churches: Halakhah and the Beginning of Christian Public Ethics*. Edinburgh: T&T Clark, 2000.

———. *Seeing the Word: Refocusing New Testament Study*. Studies in Theological Interpretation. Grand Rapids: Baker Academic, 2006.

Bibliography

———. "Why Not Let Acts Be Acts? In Conversation with C. Kavin Rowe." *JSNT* 28, no. 2 (2005): 163–66.

Boer, Willem den. *Le culte des souverains dans l'empire romain*. Geneva: Fondation Hardt, 1973.

Boring, Eugene. "The Christology of Mark: Hermeneutical Issues for Systematic Theology." *Semeia* 30 (1985): 125–53.

Botha, P. J. J. "Community and Conviction in Luke-Acts." *Neotestamentica* 29, no. 2 (1995): 145–65.

Bousset, Wilhelm. *The Faith of a Modern Protestant*. New York: Charles Scribner's Sons, 1909.

———. *Kyrios Christos: A History of the Belief in Christ from the Beginnings of Christianity to Irenaeus*. Nashville: Abingdon, 1970.

Bovon, François. "The Apostolic Memories in Ancient Christianity." In *Studies in Early Christianity*, 1–16. WUNT 161. Tübingen: Mohr Siebeck, 2003.

———. *Das Evangelium nach Lukas*. Vol. 1. EKKNT 3. Zürich: Benziger; Neukirchen-Vluyn: Neukirchener Verlag, 1989.

———. *Luke*. Vol. 1, *A Commentary on the Gospel of Luke 1:1–9:50*. Hermeneia. Minneapolis: Fortress, 2002.

———. "The Reception and Use of the Gospel of Luke in the Second Century." In *Reading Luke: Interpretation, Reflection, Formation*, edited by Craig Bartholomew et al., 379–400. Grand Rapids: Zondervan, 2005.

Braaten, Carl E. "Response to Russell Hittinger." In Cromartie, *A Preserving Grace*, 31–40.

Brent, Allen. *The Imperial Cult and the Development of Church Order: Concepts and Images of Authority in Paganism and Early Christianity before the Age of Cyprian*. Leiden: Brill, 1999.

Breytenbach, Cilliers. "Zeus und der lebendige Gott: Anmerkungen zu Apostelgeschichte 14.11–17." *NTS* 39 (1993): 396–413.

Broughton, T. R. S. "The Roman Army." In Foakes Jackson and Lake, *Beginnings of Christianity*, 5:427–45.

Brock, Ann Graham. *Mary Magdalene, the First Apostle: The Struggle for Authority*. Harvard Theological Studies 51. Cambridge, MA: Harvard University Press, 2003.

Brown, Raymond E. *The Birth of the Messiah*. Garden City, NY: Doubleday, 1977.

———. *An Introduction to New Testament Christology*. New York: Paulist, 1994.

———. *An Introduction to the Gospel of John*. Edited by Francis J. Moloney. New York: Doubleday, 2003.

———. *An Introduction to the New Testament*. New York: Paulist, 1994.

———. "Luke's Method in the Annunciation Narratives of Chapter One." In *Per-*

spectives on Luke-Acts, edited by Charles Talbert, 126–38. Edinburgh: T&T Clark, 1978.

Bruce, F. F. *The Book of the Acts*. Grand Rapids: Eerdmans, 1954.

Brunner, Emil. *Dogmatics*. Vol. 1, *The Christian Doctrine of God*. Philadelphia: Westminster, 1950.

Buckley, James J., and David S. Yeago, eds. *Knowing the Triune God: The Work of the Spirit in the Practices of the Church*. Grand Rapids: Eerdmans, 2001.

Buckwalter, H. Douglas. *The Character and Purpose of Luke's Christology*. SNTSMS 89. Cambridge: Cambridge University Press, 1996.

Bultmann, Rudolf. "Anknüpfung und Widerspruch: Zur Frage nach der Anknüpfung der neutestamentlichen Verkündigung an die natürliche Theologie der Stoa, die hellenistischen Mysterienreligionen und die Gnosis." *Theologische Zeitschrift* 2 (1946): 401–18.

———. "The Christological Confession of the World Council of Churches." In *Essays: Philosophical and Theological*, 273–90. New York: Macmillan, 1955.

———. "The Christology of the New Testament." In *Faith and Understanding*, 262–85. Philadelphia: Fortress, 1969.

———. *Theology of the New Testament*. 2 vols. New York: Charles Scribner's Sons, 1951, 1955.

Burkert, Walter. *Greek Religion*. Cambridge, MA: Harvard University Press, 1985.

Cadbury, Henry J. *The Book of Acts in History*. Eugene, OR: Wipf & Stock, 2004. First published 1995 by Harper & Brothers.

———. *The Making of Luke-Acts*. London: Macmillan, 1927.

———. "The Speeches in Acts." In Foakes Jackson and Lake, *Beginnings of Christianity*, 5:402–27.

———. "The Titles of Jesus in Acts." In Foakes Jackson and Lake, *Beginnings of Christianity*, 5:354–75.

Campenhausen, Hans von. "Die Bilderfrage als Theologisches Problem der alten Kirche." *Zeitschrift für Theologie und Kirche* 49 (1952): 33–60.

———. *Ecclesiastical Authority and Spiritual Power in the Church of the First Three Centuries*. Translated by J. A. Baker. Peabody, MA: Hendrickson, 1997.

———. *The Formation of the Christian Bible*. Translated by J. A. Baker. Philadelphia: Fortress, 1972.

Capes, David B. *Old Testament Yahweh Texts in Paul's Christology*. WUNT 2/47. Tübingen: Mohr Siebeck, 1992.

Carroll, John T. "The God of Israel and the Salvation of the Nations." In *The Forgotten God: Perspectives in Biblical Theology: Essays in Honor of Paul J. Achtemeier on the Occasion of His Seventy-Fifth Birthday*, edited by A. Andrew Das and Frank J. Matera, 91–106. Louisville: Westminster John Knox, 2002.

Bibliography

Casey, P. M. *From Jewish Prophet to Gentile God: The Origins and Development of New Testament Christology.* Louisville: Westminster John Knox, 1991.

Cassidy, Richard. "St. Paul: Between the Law of Caesar and the Justice of Christ in Second Timothy." In Adolphe, Fastiggi, and Vacca, *St. Paul, the Natural Law, and Contemporary Legal Theory*, 1–20.

Cassidy, Richard J., and Philip J. Scharper, eds. *Political Issues in Luke-Acts.* Maryknoll, NY: Orbis Books, 1983.

Chadwick, Henry. "Florilegium." In *Reallexikon für Antike und Christentum*, edited by Theodor Klauser et al., 7:1131–60. Stuttgart: Hiersemann, 1950–.

Chapman, Stephen B. *The Law and the Prophets: A Study in Old Testament Canon Formation.* Forschungen zum Alten Testament 27. Tübingen: Mohr Siebeck, 2000.

Charlesworth, M. P. "The Refusal of Divine Honours: An Augustan Formula." *PBSR* 15 (1939): 1–10.

Childs, Brevard S. *Biblical Theology of the Old and New Testaments.* Minneapolis: Fortress, 1992.

———. *The Book of Exodus: A Critical, Theological Commentary.* Philadelphia: Westminster, 1974.

———. *The New Testament as Canon: An Introduction.* Philadelphia: Fortress, 1984.

Cicero. *On Divination.* Translated by W. A. Falconer. LCL. Cambridge: Harvard University Press, 1923.

———. *On the Laws.* Translated by Clinton W. Keyes. LCL. Cambridge: Harvard University Press, 1928.

———. *On the Nature of the Gods.* Translated by H. Rackham. LCL. Cambridge: Harvard University Press, 1933.

Clauss, Manfred. *Kaiser und Gott: Herrscherkult im römischen Reich.* Stuttgart: Teubner, 1999.

Coleman, K. M. "The Emperor Domitian and Literature." *ANRW* 2.32.5 (1986): 3087–115.

Conybeare, F. C. "Ein Zeugnis Ephräms über das Fehlen von c. 1 und 2 im Texte des Lucas." *ZNW* 3 (1902): 192–97.

Conzelmann, Hans. *Acts of the Apostles.* Hermeneia. Philadelphia: Fortress, 1987.

———. *Die Mitte der Zeit.* Tübingen: Mohr Siebeck, 1954. Published in English translation as *The Theology of St. Luke.* London: Faber & Faber, 1960.

Cook, Arthur Bernard. *Zeus: A Study in Ancient Religion.* 3 vols. Cambridge: Cambridge University Press, 1914–1940.

Cranfield, C. E. B. *A Critical and Exegetical Commentary on the Epistle to the Romans.* ICC. Edinburgh: T&T Clark, 1979.

Cromartie, Michael, ed. *A Preserving Grace: Protestants, Catholics, and Natural Law*. Grand Rapids: Eerdmans, 1997.
Crossan, John Dominic. *The Historical Jesus: The Life of a Mediterranean Jewish Peasant*. San Francisco: HarperSanFrancisco, 1991.
———. *Jesus: A Revolutionary Biography*. San Francisco: HarperSanFrancisco, 1994.
Crowe, Michael Bertram. *The Changing Profile of the Natural Law*. The Hague: Martinus Nijhoff, 1977.
Cullmann, Oscar. *The Christology of the New Testament*. Rev. ed. Translated by Shirley C. Guthrie and Charles A. M. Hall. Philadelphia: Westminster, 1963. German edition 1957.
Cuss, Dominique. *Imperial Cult and Honorary Terms in the New Testament*. Fribourg: University Press, 1974.
Dahl, Nils, A. "The Future of Israel." In *Studies in Paul: Theology for the Early Christian Mission*, 137-58. Minneapolis: Augsburg, 1977.
———. "The Neglected Factor in New Testament Theology." In Juel, *Jesus the Christ*, 153-64. Originally published in *Reflections* 75 (1975): 5-8.
———. "The One God of Jews and Gentiles." In *Studies in Paul: Theology for the Early Christian Mission*, 178-91. Minneapolis: Augsburg, 1977.
———. "A People for His Name (Acts xv. 14)." *NTS* 4 (1957-1958): 319-27.
———. "Sources of Christological Language." In Juel, *Jesus the Christ*, 113-36.
———. "The Story of Abraham in Luke-Acts." In Keck and Martyn, *Studies in Luke-Acts*, 139-58.
———. "Trinitarian Baptismal Creeds and New Testament Christology." In Juel, *Jesus the Christ*, 163-86.
Dahl, Nils A., and Alan F. Segal. "Philo and the Rabbis on the Names of God." *JSJ* 9, no. 1 (1978): 1-28.
Davis, Carl Judson. *The Name and Way of the Lord: Old Testament Themes, New Testament Christology*. JSNTSup 129. Sheffield: Sheffield Academic, 1996.
Davis, Ellen F., and Richard B. Hays, eds. *The Art of Reading Scripture*. Grand Rapids: Eerdmans, 2003.
Deissmann, Adolf. *Light from the Ancient East*. New York: Doran, 1927.
Dibelius, Martin. "Jungfrauensohn und Krippenkind. Untersuchungen zur Geburtsgeschichte Jesu im Lukas-Evangelium." In *Botschaft und Geschichte: Gesammelte Aufsätze von Martin Dibelius*, 2 vols., edited by Gunther Bornkamm, 1:1-78. Tübingen: Mohr Siebeck, 1953-1955.
———. "Paul in Athens." In *Studies in the Acts of the Apostles*, 78-83. London: SCM, 1956.
Dittenberger, Wilhelm, ed. *Sylloge Inscriptionum Graecarum*. 3rd ed. Leipzig: Herzelium, 1917.

Bibliography

Dodd, C. H. *According to the Scriptures: The Sub-structure of New Testament Theology.* London: Nisbet, 1952.

———. *The Epistle of Paul to the Romans.* New York: Harper & Brothers, 1932.

Dodds, E. R. *The Greeks and the Irrational.* Berkeley: University of California Press, 1951.

Donahue, John R. "The Literary Turn and New Testament Theology: Detour or New Direction?" *JR* (1996): 250–75.

Donaldson, Terence L., ed. *Religious Rivalries and the Struggle for Success in Caesarea Maritima.* Studies in Christianity and Judaism 8. Waterloo, ON: Wilfrid Laurier University Press, 2000.

Downing, F. Gerald. "Common Ground with Paganism in Luke and Josephus." *NTS* 28 (1982): 546–59.

———. *Doing Things with Words in the First Christian Century.* JSNTSup 200. Sheffield: Sheffield Academic, 2000.

Dubourdieu, Annie. *Les Origines et le développement du culte des Pénates à Rome.* Rome: Ecole française de Rome, 1989.

Dunn, James D. G. *The Acts of the Apostles.* Epworth Commentaries. Peterborough: Epworth, 1996.

———. "Christology as an Aspect of Theology." In Malherbe and Meeks, *Future of Christology,* 202–12.

———. *Christology in the Making: A New Testament Inquiry into the Origins of the Doctrine of the Incarnation.* 2nd ed. Grand Rapids: Eerdmans, 1989.

———. "ΚΥΡΙΟΣ in Acts." In *The Christ and the Spirit.* Vol. 1, *Christology,* 241–53. Grand Rapids: Eerdmans, 1998.

———. "The Making of Christology—Evolution or Unfolding?" In *Jesus of Nazareth: Lord and Christ,* edited by Joel B. Green and Max Turner, 437–52. Grand Rapids: Eerdmans, 1994.

———. *Romans 1–8.* WBC. Dallas: Word, 1988.

———. *Romans 9–16.* WBC. Dallas: Word, 1988.

Dupont, Jacques. "Les discours missionaires des Actes des Apôtres d'après un ouvrage recent." *Revue biblique* 69, no. 1 (1962): 37–60.

Edwards, Mark, Martin Goodman, Simon Price, and Christopher Rowland, eds. *Apologetics in the Roman Empire: Pagans, Jews, and Christians.* Oxford: Oxford University Press, 1999.

Elliott, John H. "The Jesus Movement Was Not Egalitarian but Family-Oriented." *Biblical Interpretation* 11 (2003): 173–210.

———. "Jesus Was Not an Egalitarian: A Critique of an Anachronistic and Idealist Theory." *Biblical Theology Bulletin* 32, no. 2 (2002): 75–91.

Ellis, E. Earle. *The Gospel of Luke*. New Century Bible. 2nd ed. Grand Rapids: Eerdmans, 1981.

Elsner, Jaś. *Art and the Roman Viewer: The Transformation of Art from the Pagan World to Christianity*. Cambridge: Cambridge University Press, 1995.

———. "Image and Ritual: Reflections on the Religious Appreciation of Classical Art." *CQ* 46 (1996): 515-31.

———. *Imperial Rome and Christian Triumph: The Art of the Roman Empire AD 100-450*. Oxford: Oxford University Press, 1998.

Eltester, Friedrich-Wilhelm. *Eikon im Neuen Testament*. Berlin: Töpelmann, 1958.

Engelhardt, H. Tristram, Jr. *The Foundations of Bioethics*. 2nd ed. Oxford: Oxford University Press, 1996.

Esler, Philip F. "Community and Gospel in Early Christianity: A Response to Richard Bauckham's *Gospels for All Christians*." *SJT* 51 (1998): 235-48.

———. *Community and Gospel in Luke-Acts: The Social and Political Motivations of Lucan Theology*. SNTSMS 57. Cambridge: Cambridge University Press, 1987.

———. *Conflict and Identity in Romans: The Social Setting of Paul's Letter*. Minneapolis: Fortress, 2003.

Evans, C. F. *Saint Luke*. London: SCM, 1990.

Farrer, Austin M. "The Ministry in the New Testament." In *The Apostolic Ministry: Essays on the History and the Doctrine of the Episcopacy*, edited by Kenneth E. Kirk, 113-82. New York: Morehouse-Gorham, 1946.

Fee, Gordon D. *God's Empowering Presence: The Holy Spirit in the Letters of Paul*. Peabody, MA: Hendrickson, 1994.

Finney, Paul Corby. *The Invisible God: The Earliest Christians on Art*. Oxford: Oxford University Press, 1994.

Fishwick, Duncan. *The Imperial Cult in the Latin West: Studies in the Ruler Cult in the Western Provinces of the Roman Empire*. 2 vols. Leiden: Brill, 1989-1992.

Fitzmyer, Joseph A. *The Acts of the Apostles: A New Translation with Introduction and Commentary*. AB 31. New York: Doubleday, 1998.

———. "Glory Reflected on the Face of Christ (2 Cor 3:7-4:6) and a Palestinian Jewish Motif." *Theological Studies* 42 (1981): 630-44.

———. *The Gospel according to Luke*. 2 vols. AB 28/28A. Garden City, NY: Doubleday, 1981-1985.

———. "The Languages of Palestine in the First Century A. D." In *A Wandering Aramean: Collected Aramaic Essays*, 29-56. Chico, CA: Scholars Press, 1979.

———. *Luke the Theologian: Aspects of His Teaching*. New York: Paulist, 1989.

———. "New Testament *Kyrios* and *Maranatha* and Their Aramaic Background." In *To Advance the Gospel: New Testament Studies*, 2nd ed., 218-35. Grand Rapids: Eerdmans, 1998.

Bibliography

———. *Romans.* AB 33. New York: Doubleday, 1993.

———. "The Semitic Background of the New Testament *Kyrios*-Title." In *A Wandering Aramean: Collected Aramaic Essays*, 115–42. Chico, CA: Scholars Press, 1979.

Foakes Jackson, F. J., and Kirsopp Lake, eds. *The Beginnings of Christianity, Part I: The Acts of the Apostles.* 5 vols. London: Macmillan, 1920–1933.

Foakes Jackson, F. J., and Kirsopp Lake. "Christology." In Foakes Jackson and Lake, *Beginnings of Christianity*, 1:345–418.

Foss, Pedar W. "Watchful Lares: Roman Household Organization and the Rituals of Cooking and Eating." In Laurence and Wallace-Hadrill, *Domestic Space in the Roman World*, 197–218.

Fossum, Jarl. "Colossians 1.15–18a in the Light of Jewish Mysticism and Gnosticism." *NTS* 35 (1989): 183–201.

Foucault, Michel. *Discipline and Punish: The Birth of the Prison.* New York: Vintage Books, 1977.

Franklin, Eric. *Christ the Lord: A Study in the Purpose and Theology of Luke-Acts.* Philadelphia: Westminster, 1975.

Freedberg, David. *The Power of Images: Studies in the History and Theory of Response.* Chicago: University of Chicago Press, 1989.

Frei, Hans W. *The Eclipse of Biblical Narrative: A Study in Eighteenth and Nineteenth Century Hermeneutics.* New Haven: Yale University Press, 1974.

———. "Theological Reflections on the Accounts of Jesus' Death and Resurrection." In *Theology and Narrative: Selected Essays*, edited by George Hunsinger and William C. Placher, 45–93. New York: Oxford University Press, 1993.

Friesen, Steven J. *Imperial Cults and the Apocalypse of John: Reading Revelation in the Ruins.* Oxford: Oxford University Press, 2001.

———. *Twice Neokoros: Ephesus, Asia and the Cult of the Flavian Imperial Family.* Leiden: Brill, 1993.

Fuller, Reginald H. *The Foundations of New Testament Christology.* New York: Scribner, 1965.

Gabler, Johann Philipp. *De justo discrimine theologiae biblicae et dogmaticae regundisque recte utriusque finibus* (1787). Translated by J. Sandys-Wunsch and L. Eldredge as "On the Proper Distinction between Biblical and Dogmatic Theology and the Specific Objectives of Each." *SJT* 33 (1980): 133–58.

Gamble, Harry Y. *Books and Readers in the Early Church: A History of Early Christian Texts.* New Haven: Yale University Press, 1995.

Garnsey, Peter. "Religious Toleration in Classical Antiquity." In *Persecution and Toleration*, edited by W. J. Shells, 1–27. London: Blackwell, 1984.

Garrett, Susan R. "Beloved Physician of the Soul? Luke as Advocate for Ascetic

Practice." In *Asceticism and the New Testament*, edited by Leif E. Vaage and Vincent L. Wimbush, 71–95. New York: Routledge, 1999.

Gasque, W. Ward. *A History of the Criticism of the Acts of the Apostles*. Beiträge zur Geschichte der biblischen Exegese 17. Tübingen: Mohr Siebeck, 1975.

Gathercole, Simon J. "A Law unto Themselves: The Gentiles in Romans 2.14–15 Revisited." *JSNT* 24, no. 3 (2002): 27–49.

Gaventa, Beverly Roberts. *The Acts of the Apostles*. ANTC. Nashville: Abingdon, 2003.

———. "Toward a Theology of Acts: Reading and Rereading." *Int* 42 (1988): 146–57.

Gebhardt, H. "Die an die Heiden gerichtete Missionsrede der Apostel und das Johannesevangelium." *ZNW* 6 (1905): 236–49.

Gilbert, Gary. "Roman Propaganda and Christian Identity in the Worldview of Luke-Acts." In *Contextualizing Acts: Lukan Narrative and Greco-Roman Discourse*, edited by Todd Penner and Caroline Vander Stichele, 233–56. Society of Biblical Literature Symposium Series 20. Atlanta: Society of Biblical Literature, 2003.

Gilmour, Samuel MacLean. "The Gospel according to St Luke." In *The Interpreter's Bible*, edited by George A. Buttrick et al., 8:15–16. New York: Abingdon, 1952.

Gnilka, Joachim. *Der Kolosserbrief*. HThKNT X/l. Freiburg im Breisgau: Herder, 1980.

Goldingay, John. "Biblical Narrative and Systematic Theology." In *Between Two Horizons: Spanning New Testament Studies and Systematic Theology*, edited by Joel B. Green and Max Turner, 123–42. Grand Rapids: Eerdmans, 2000.

Goodenough, Erwin R. *Jewish Symbols in the Greco-Roman World*. 13 vols. New York: Pantheon Books, 1953–1968.

Gordon, R. L. "The Real and the Imaginary: Production and Religion in the Graeco-Roman World." *Art History* 2 (1979): 5–34.

Gradel, Ittai. *Emperor Worship and Roman Religion*. Oxford: Oxford University Press, 2002.

Grant, Robert M. *Gods and the One God*. Philadelphia: Westminster, 1986.

Green, Joel B. *The Gospel of Luke*. NICNT. Grand Rapids: Eerdmans, 1997.

———. "The Problem of a Beginning: Israel's Scriptures in Luke 1–2." *BBR* 4, no. 1 (1994): 61–85.

———. *The Theology of the Gospel of Luke*. Cambridge: Cambridge University Press, 1995.

Gregory, Andrew. "The Reception of Luke and Acts and the Unity of Luke-Acts." *JSNT* 29, no. 4 (2007): 459–72.

———. *The Reception of Luke and Acts in the Period before Irenaeus: Looking for Luke in the Second Century*. WUNT 2/169. Tübingen: Mohr Siebeck, 2003.

Bibliography

Griffiths, Paul. "'Allah Is My Lord and Yours': Talking with Ahmadinejad." *Christian Century*, October 17, 2006.

Gutmann, Joseph, ed. *No Graven Images: Studies in Art and the Hebrew Bible*. New York: Ktav, 1971.

Hadot, Pierre. *Philosophy as a Way of Life: Spiritual Exercises from Socrates to Foucault*. Oxford: Blackwell, 1995.

———. *The Present Alone Is Our Happiness: Conversations with Jeannie Carlier and Arnold I. Davidson*. Stanford, CA: Stanford University Press, 2009.

———. *What Is Ancient Philosophy?* Cambridge, MA: Harvard University Press, 2002.

Haenchen, Ernst. *The Acts of the Apostles: A Commentary*. Translated by Bernard Noble and Gerald Shinn. Revised by R. McL. Wilson (EV from 14th German edition of 1965). Philadelphia: Westminster, 1971.

Hahn, Ferdinand. *The Titles of Jesus in Christology: Their History in Early Christianity*. New York: Word, 1969. German edition 1963.

Halbertal, Moshe. "Coexisting with the Enemy: Jews and Pagans in the Mishnah." In *Tolerance and Intolerance in Early Judaism and Christianity*, edited by Graham N. Stanton and Guy G. Stroumsa, 159–72. Cambridge: Cambridge University Press, 1998.

Halbertal, Moshe, and Avishai Margalit. *Idolatry*. Translated by Naomi Goldblum. Cambridge, MA: Harvard University Press, 1992.

Harnack, Adolf von. *Lehrbuch der Dogmengeschichte*. 3 vols. Tübingen: Mohr Siebeck, 1909.

———. *Marcion: Das Evangelium vom fremden Gott: Eine Monographie zur Geschichte der Grundlegung der katholischen Kirche*. 2nd ed. Darmstadt: Wissenschaftliche Buchgesellschaft, 1996.

———. *The Origin of the New Testament and the Most Important Consequences of the New Creation*. London: Williams & Northgate, 1925.

———. *What Is Christianity?* Philadelphia: Fortress, 1986.

Harris, Murray J. *Jesus as God: The New Testament Use of Theos in Reference to Jesus*. Grand Rapids: Baker, 1992.

Harrison, Stephen, ed. *Apuleius: Rhetorical Works*. Translated by Stephen Harrison, John Hilton, and Vincent Hunink. Oxford: Oxford University Press, 2001.

Hart, David Bentley. *Atheist Delusions: The Christian Revolution and Its Fashionable Enemies*. New Haven: Yale University Press, 2009.

Hauerwas, Stanley. "Authority and the Profession of Medicine." In *Suffering Presence: Theological Reflections on Medicine, the Mentally Handicapped, and the Church*, 39–62. Notre Dame: University of Notre Dame Press, 1986.

Havel, Vaclav. "The Power of the Powerless." In *Living in the Truth*, 36–122. London: Faber & Faber, 1986.
Hay, David M. *Colossians*. ANTC. Nashville: Abingdon, 2000.
Hays, Richard B. "The Conversion of the Imagination: Scripture and Eschatology in 1 Corinthians." *NTS* 45 (1999): 391–412.
———. *Echoes of Scripture in the Letters of Paul*. New Haven: Yale University Press, 1989.
Healy, Mary. "St. Paul, Ephesians 5, and Same-Sex Marriage." In Adolphe, Fastiggi, and Vacca, *St. Paul, the Natural Law, and Contemporary Legal Theory*, 147–59.
Hengel, Martin. "Christological Titles in Early Christianity." In *The Messiah: Developments in Earliest Judaism and Christianity*, edited by James H. Charlesworth, 425–60. Minneapolis: Fortress, 1992.
Hermann, Wilhelm. *The Communion of the Christian with God*. Philadelphia: Fortress, 1971.
Heschel, Abraham J. *The Prophets*. Harper & Row, 1962.
Hill, Charles E. *The Johannine Corpus in the Early Church*. Oxford: Oxford University Press, 2004.
Hittinger, Russell. "Natural Law and Catholic Moral Theology." In Cromartie, *A Preserving Grace*, 1–30.
Hoff, Michael C. "The Politics and Architecture of the Athenian Imperial Cult." In Small, *Subject and Ruler*, 185–200.
Holladay, Carl R. *Fragments from Hellenistic Jewish Authors*. Vol. 1, *Historians*. Chico, CA: Scholars Press, 1983.
———. *Fragments from Hellenistic Jewish Authors*. Vol. 3, *Aristobulus*. Atlanta: Scholars Press, 1995.
Holliday, Peter J. "Time, History, and Ritual on the Ara Pacis Augustae." *Art Bulletin* 72 (1990): 542–57.
Holtzmann, H. J. *Hand-Commentar zum Neuen Testament. Erster Band: Die Synoptiker—Die Apostelgeschichte*. Freiburg im Breisgau: Mohr Siebeck, 1889.
Homer. *Odyssey*. Vol. 2, *Books 13–24*. Translated by A. T. Murray. Revised by George E. Dimock. LCL. Cambridge: Harvard University Press, 1919.
Hooker, M. D. "Adam in Romans 1." *NTS* 6 (1959/1960): 304.
Horrell, David G. "The Label Χριστιανός: 1 Peter 4:16 and the Formation of Christian Identity." *JBL* 126 (2007): 361–81.
Horsley, Richard A. *The Liberation of Christmas: The Infancy Narratives in Social Context*. New York: Crossroad, 1989.
Horst, P. W. van der. "The Unknown God." In *Knowledge of God in the Graeco-*

Roman World, edited by R. van den Broek, T. Baarda, and J. Mansfeld, 19–42. Leiden: Brill, 1988.

Howard, George. "The Tetragram and the New Testament." *JBL* 96 (1977): 63–83.

Hultgren, Stephen. "The Origin of Paul's Doctrine of the Two Adams in 1 Corinthians 15.45–49." *JSNT* 25 (2003): 343–70.

Humphrey, Edith M. Review of *Mary Magdalene, the First Apostle: The Struggle for Authority*, by Ann Graham Brock. *Review of Biblical Literature* 6 (2004): 366–70.

Hunink, Vincent, ed., *Apuleius: Pro Se De Magia*. Amsterdam: Gieben, 1997.

Hurtado, Larry. *One God, One Lord: Early Christian Devotion and Ancient Jewish Monotheism*. 2nd ed. Edinburgh: T&T Clark, 1998.

Jeanrond, Werner G. "After Hermeneutics: The Relationship between Theology and Biblical Studies." In *The Open Text: New Directions for Biblical Studies*, edited by Francis Watson, 85–102. London: SCM, 1993.

———. "Criteria for New Biblical Theologies." *JR* 76, no. 2 (1996): 233–49.

Jensen, Robin Margaret. *Understanding Early Christian Art*. London: Routledge, 2000.

Jenson, Robert. *Systematic Theology*. 2 vols. Oxford: Oxford University Press, 1997–1999.

Jeremias, Joachim. *Die Sprache des Lukasevangeliums: Redaktion und Tradition im Nicht-Markusstoff des dritten Evangeliums*. Göttingen: Vandenhoeck & Ruprecht, 1980.

Jervell, Jacob. *Die Apostelgeschichte: Übersetzt und erklärt*. KEK 3. Göttingen: Vandenhoeck & Ruprecht, 1998.

———. *Imago Dei: Gen 1,26f. im Spätjudentum, in der Gnosis und in den Paulinischen Briefen*. Göttingen: Vandenhoeck & Ruprecht, 1960.

———. *Luke and the People of God: A New Look at Luke-Acts*. Minneapolis: Augsburg, 1972.

———. *The Theology of the Acts of the Apostles*. Cambridge: Cambridge University Press, 1996.

Johnson, E. Elizabeth. *The Function of Apocalyptic and Wisdom Traditions in Romans 9–11*. SBLDS 109. Atlanta: Scholars Press, 1989.

———. "Romans 9–11: The Faithfulness and Impartiality of God." In *Pauline Theology*. Vol. 3, *Romans*, edited by David M. Hay and E. Elizabeth Johnson, 211–39. Minneapolis: Fortress, 1995.

Johnson, Luke Timothy. *The Acts of the Apostles*. SP 5. Collegeville, MN: Liturgical Press, 1992.

———. "The Christology of Luke-Acts." In *Who Do You Say That I Am? Essays on Christology*, edited by Mark Allan Powell and David R. Bauer, 49-65. Louisville: Westminster John Knox, 1999.

———. *The Gospel of Luke.* SP 3. Collegeville, MN: Liturgical Press, 1991.

———. "Literary Criticism of Luke-Acts: Is Reception History Pertinent?" *JSNT* 28, no. 2 (2005): 159-62.

———. *Reading Romans.* New York: Crossroad, 1997.

Jones, Donald L. "The Title Kyrios in Luke-Acts." *SBLSP* 74, no. 2 (1974): 85-101.

Josephus. *Against Apion.* Translated by H. St. J. Thackeray. LCL. Cambridge: Harvard University Press, 1926.

Juel, Donald H., ed. *Jesus the Christ: The Historical Origins of Christological Doctrine.* Minneapolis: Fortress, 1991.

Käsemann, Ernst. *An die Römer.* 3rd ed. Handbuch zum Neuen Testament 8a. Tübingen: Mohr, 1974.

———. *Commentary on Romans.* Grand Rapids: Eerdmans, 1980.

Keck, Leander. "Toward the Renewal of New Testament Christology." *NTS* 32, no. 3 (1986): 362-77.

———. *Who Is Jesus? History in Perfect Tense.* Columbia: University of South Carolina Press, 2000.

Keck, Leander E., and J. Louis Martyn. *Studies in Luke-Acts.* Philadelphia: Fortress, 1966.

Kelhoffer, James A. "'How Soon a Book' Revisited: ΕΥΑΓΓΕΛΙΟΝ as a Reference to 'Gospel' Materials in the First Half of the Second Century." *ZNW* 95 (2004): 1-34.

Kingsbury, Jack Dean. *Conflict in Luke: Jesus, Authorities, Disciples.* Minneapolis: Fortress, 1991.

———. "Jesus as the 'Prophetic Messiah' in Luke's Gospel." In Malherbe and Meeks, *Future of Christology*, 29-42.

———. *Matthew as Story.* Minneapolis: Fortress, 1988.

Kitzinger, Ernst. "The Cleveland Marbles." In *Art, Archaeology, and Architecture of Early Christianity*, edited by Paul Corby Finney, 117-39. New York: Garland, 1993.

———. "The Cult of Images in the Age before Iconoclasm." *DOP* 8 (1954): 85-150.

Klauck, Hans-Josef. *Allegorie und Allegorese in synoptischen Gleichnistexten.* Neutestamentliche Abhandlungen 13. Münster: Aschendorff, 1978.

———. "Des Kaisers schöne Stimme. Herrscherkritik in Apg 12,20-23." In *Religion und Gesellschaft im frühen Christentum: Neutestamentliche Studien*, 251-67. WUNT 152. Tübingen: Mohr Siebeck, 2003.

———. *Magic and Paganism in Early Christianity: The World of the Acts of the Apostles.* Edinburgh: T&T Clark, 1999.

Bibliography

———. *The Religious Context of Early Christianity*. Edinburgh: T&T Clark, 2000.
Klauser, Theodor. "Erwägungen zur Entstehung der altchristlichen Kunst." *Zeitschrift für Kirchengeschichte* 76 (1965): 1–11.
Klein, Günther. *Die Zwölf Apostel: Ursprung und Gehalt einer Idee*. FRLANT 59. Göttingen: Vandenhoeck & Ruprecht, 1961.
Kleiner, Diana E. E. *Roman Sculpture*. New Haven: Yale University Press, 1992.
Klostermann, Erich. *Das Lukasevangelium*. Handbuch zum Neuen Testament. Tübingen: Mohr Siebeck, 1919.
Knight, G. A. F. *A Biblical Approach to the Doctrine of the Trinity*. SJT Occasional Papers 1. Edinburgh: Oliver and Boyd, 1953.
Knox, John. *Marcion and the New Testament: An Essay in the Early History of the Canon*. Chicago: University of Chicago Press, 1942.
Koch, Dietrich-Alex. *Die Schrift als Zeuge des Evangeliums: Untersuchungen zur Verwendung und zum Verständnis der Schrift bei Paulus*. Beiträge zur historischen Theologie 69. Tübingen: Mohr Siebeck, 1986.
Koch, Hugo. *Die altchristliche Bilderfrage nach den literarischen Quellen*. Göttingen: Vandenhoeck & Ruprecht, 1917.
Koester, Helmut. *Ancient Christian Gospels: Their History and Development*. Harrisburg, PA: Trinity Press International, 1990.
———. "Writings and the Spirit: Authority and Politics in Ancient Christianity." *Harvard Theological Review* 84 (1991): 353–72.
Koets, P. J. Δεισιδαιμονία: *A Contribution to the Knowledge of the Religious Terminology in Greek*. Purmerend: Muusses, 1929.
Köhler, W.-D. *Die Rezeption des Matthäusevangeliums in der Zeit vor Irenäus*. WUNT 2/24. Tübingen: Mohr Siebeck, 1987.
Kramer, Werner. *Christ, Lord, Son of God*. London: SCM, 1966.
Kreitzer, L. Joseph. *Jesus and God in Paul's Eschatology*. JSNTSup 19. Sheffield: JSOT Press, 1987.
Kuper, Hilda. "The Language of Sites in the Politics of Space." *American Anthropologist* 74 (1972): 411–25.
Kurz, William S. *Reading Luke-Acts: Dynamics of Biblical Narrative*. Louisville: Westminster John Knox, 1993.
Lampe, G. W. H., ed. *A Patristic Greek Lexicon*. Oxford: Clarendon Press, 1961.
Lampe, Peter. "Acta 19 im Spiegel der ephesischen Inschritten." *Biblische Zeitschrift* 36 (1992): 59–76.
———. *From Paul to Valentinus: Christians at Rome in the First Two Centuries*. Minneapolis: Fortress, 2003.
Lane Fox, Robin. *Pagans and Christians*. New York: Knopf, 1986.

Larsson, Edvin. *Christus als Vorbild: Eine Untersuchung zu den paulinischen Tauf- und Eikontexten.* Uppsala: Almqvist & Wiksells, 1962.

Lash, Nicholas. *Voices of Authority.* Shepherdstown: Patmos, 1976.

Laurence, Ray. "Space and Text." In Laurence and Wallace-Hadrill, *Domestic Space in the Roman World,* 7–14.

Laurence, Ray, and Andrew Wallace-Hadrill, eds. *Domestic Space in the Roman World: Pompeii and Beyond.* Portsmouth, RI: JRA, 1997.

Laurentin, René. *Structure et théologie de Luc I–II.* Paris: Gabalda, 1957.

Lawson, J. *The Biblical Theology of Saint Irenaeus.* London: Epworth, 1948.

Leaney, A. R. C. *A Commentary on the Gospel according to St. Luke.* Black's New Testament Commentaries. London: Black, 1958.

Le Bohec, Yann. *The Imperial Roman Army.* London: Batsford, 1994.

Lightfoot, J. B. *St. Paul's Epistles to the Colossians and to Philemon.* London: Macmillan, 1904.

Lincoln, A. T. "The Letter to the Colossians." In *The New Interpreter's Bible.* Vol. 11, *2 Corinthians, Galatians, Ephesians, Philippians, Colossians, 1 & 2 Thessalonians, 1 & 2 Timothy, Titus, Philemon.* Nashville: Abingdon, 2000.

Lindbeck, George A. *The Nature of Doctrine: Religion and Theology in a Postliberal Age.* Philadelphia: Westminster, 1984.

Lohmeyer, Ernst. *Christuskult und Kaiserkult.* Tübingen: Mohr Siebeck, 1919.

———. *Der Brief an die Kolosser und an Philemon.* Göttingen: Vandenhoeck & Ruprecht, 1929.

Longenecker, Bruce W. "Lukan Aversion to Humps and Hollows: The Case of Acts 11.27–12.25." *NTS* 50 (2004): 185–204.

L'Orange, Hans Peter. *Apotheosis in Ancient Portraiture.* Oslo: Aschehoug, 1947.

Lucian. *Alexander the False Prophet.* Translated by A. M. Harmon. LCL. Cambridge: Harvard University Press, 1925.

Lust, Johan. "Mic 5,1–3 in Qumran and in the New Testament and Messianism in the Septuagint." In *The Scriptures and the Gospels,* edited by C. M. Tuckett, 65–88. Leuven: Leuven University Press, 1997.

Luther, Martin. *Luther's Works.* Vol. 25, *Lectures on Romans [Scholia].* St. Louis: Concordia, 1972.

MacIntyre, Alasdair. "Patients as Agents." In *Philosophical Medical Ethics: Its Nature and Significance,* edited by Stuart F. Spicker and H. Tristram Engelhardt Jr., 197–212. Boston: Reidel, 1977.

MacMullen, Ramsay. *Christianizing the Roman Empire: A. D. 100–400.* New Haven: Yale University Press, 1984.

———. *Enemies of the Roman Order: Treason, Unrest, and Alienation in the Empire.* Cambridge, MA: Harvard University Press, 1966.

Bibliography

———. *Paganism in the Roman Empire*. New Haven: Yale University Press, 1981.
Malherbe, Abraham J. *Social Aspects of Early Christianity*. Philadelphia: Fortress, 1983.
Malherbe, Abraham J., and Wayne A. Meeks, eds. *The Future of Christology: Essays in Honor of Leander E. Keck*. Minneapolis: Fortress, 1993.
Manson, William. *The Gospel of Luke*. Moffatt New Testament Commentary. London: Hodder & Stoughton, 1930.
Marcovich, Miroslav. *Iustini Martyris Apologiae Pro Christianis*. Berlin: de Gruyter, 1994.
Marcus, Joel. *Mark 1–8: A New Translation with Introduction and Commentary*. AB 27. New York: Doubleday, 2000.
Marguerat, Daniel. "Luc-Actes entre Jérusalem et Rome: Un procédé lucanien de double signification." *NTS* 45 (1999): 70–87.
———. "Paul après Paul: une histoire de réception." *NTS* 54 (2008): 317–37.
Marshall, Bruce D. *Trinity and Truth*. Cambridge: Cambridge University Press, 2000.
Marshall, I. Howard. "Acts and the 'Former Treatise.'" In *The Book of Acts in Its Ancient Literary Setting*, edited by Bruce W. Winter and Andrew D. Clarke, 163–82. Grand Rapids: Eerdmans, 1993.
———. *The Gospel of Luke: A Commentary on the Greek Text*. Exeter: Paternoster, 1978.
Martin, Dale B. *Inventing Superstition: From the Hippocratics to the Christians*. Cambridge, MA: Harvard University Press, 2004.
Martinez, F. Garcia, and E. G. C. Tigchelaar, eds. *The Dead Sea Scrolls Study Edition*. 2 vols. Leiden: Brill, 1997–1998.
Matera, Frank J. *II Corinthians: A Commentary*. Louisville: Westminster John Knox, 2003.
———. *New Testament Christology*. Louisville: Westminster John Knox, 1999.
Mattingly, Harold. *Coins of the Roman Empire in the British Museum*. Vol. 1, *Augustus to Vitellius*. London: British Museum, 1923.
Mauser, Ulrich. "Εἷς θεός und Μόνος θεός in Biblischer Theologie." *Jahrbuch für Biblische Theologie* 1 (1986): 71–87.
———. *The Gospel of Peace*. Louisville: Westminster John Knox, 1992.
———. *Gottesbild und Menschwerdung: Eine Untersuchung zur Einheit des Alten und Neuen Testaments*. Tübingen: Mohr, 1971.
———. "Image of God and Incarnation." *Int* 24 (1970): 336–56.
———. "One God and Trinitarian Language in the Letters of Paul." *HBT* 20, no. 2 (1998): 99–108.
May, Gerhard, and Katharina Greschat, eds., together with Martin Meiser. *Mar-

cion und seine Kirchengeschichtliche Wirkung / Marcion and His Impact on Church History. TU 150. Berlin: de Gruyter, 2002.

McCabe, Herbert. "Obedience." In *God Matters*, 226-34. London: Chapman, 1987.

McCasland, S. Vernon. "The Image of God according to Paul." *JBL* 69 (1950): 85-100.

Meeks, Wayne. *The First Urban Christians*. New Haven: Yale University Press, 1983.

Meinertz, Max. *Theologie des Neuen Testamentes 2*. Bonn: Hanstein, 1950.

Metzger, Bruce M. *The Canon of the New Testament: Its Origin, Development, and Significance*. Oxford: Clarendon, 1997.

Meyer, P. M., ed. *Griechische Texte aus Ägypten*. Berlin: Weidmannsche Buchhandlung, 1916.

Millar, F. "The Emperor, the Senate and the Provinces." In *Rome, the Greek World, and the East*, edited by Hannah M. Cotton and Guy M. Rogers. Vol. 1, *The Roman Republic and the Augustan Revolution*, 271-91. Chapel Hill: University of North Carolina Press, 2002.

———. "The Imperial Cult and the Persecutions." In den Boer, *Le culte des souverains dans l'empire romain*, 145-65.

Minear, Paul S. "Luke's Use of the Birth Stories." In Keck and Martyn, *Studies in Luke-Acts*, 111-30.

Mitchell, Stephen. *Anatolia: Land, Men, and Gods in Asia Minor*. 2 vols. Oxford: Clarendon, 1993.

———. "The Cult of Theos Hypsistos between Pagans, Jews, and Christians." In Athanassiadi and Frede, *Pagan Monotheism in Late Antiquity*, 81-148.

Moessner, David P. "Two Lords 'at the Right Hand'? The Psalms and an Intertextual Reading of Peter's Pentecost Speech (Acts 2.14-36)." In Thompson and Phillips, *Literary Studies in Luke-Acts*, 215-32.

Moltmann, Jürgen. *The Trinity and the Kingdom*. Minneapolis: Fortress, 1993.

Momigliano, Arnaldo. "Pagan and Christian Historiography in the Fourth Century AD." In *The Conflict between Paganism and Christianity in the Fourth Century*, edited by A. Momigliano, 79-99. Oxford: Clarendon, 1963.

Moo, Douglas. "The Theology of Romans 9-11: A Response to E. Elizabeth Johnson." In *Pauline Theology*. Vol. 3, *Romans*, edited by David M. Hay and E. Elizabeth Johnson, 240-58. Minneapolis: Fortress, 1995.

Moule, C. F. D. *The Epistles of Paul the Apostle to the Colossians and to Philemon*. Cambridge: Cambridge University Press, 1957.

———. *The Origin of Christology*. Cambridge: Cambridge University Press, 1977.

Murray, Sister Charles. "Art in the Early Church." *JTS* 28 (1977): 303-45.

Nagel, Titus. *Die Rezeption des Johannesevangeliums im 2. Jahrhundert: Studien zur vorirenäischen Aneignung und Auslegung des vierten Evangeliums in*

Bibliography

christlicher und christlich-gnostischer Literatur. Leipzig: Evangelische Verlagsanstalt, 2000.

Neagoe, Alexandru. *The Trial of the Gospel: An Apologetic Reading of Luke's Trial Narratives*. SNTSMS 116. Cambridge: Cambridge University Press, 2002.

Neufeld, Vernon. *The Earliest Christian Confessions*. Grand Rapids: Eerdmans, 1963.

Newman, Carey C. "Resurrection as Glory: Divine Presence and Christian Origins." In *The Resurrection: An Interdisciplinary Symposium on the Resurrection of Jesus*, edited by Stephen T. Davis, Daniel Kendall, and Gerald O'Collins, 59–89. Oxford: Oxford University Press, 1997.

Neyrey, Jerome H. "The Symbolic Universe of Luke-Acts: 'They Turn the World Upside Down.'" In *The Social World of Luke-Acts: Models for Interpretation*, 271–304. Peabody: Hendrickson, 1991.

Nicolai, Vincenzo Fiocchi, Fabrizio Bisconti, and Danilo Mazzoleni, eds. *The Christian Catacombs of Rome: History, Decoration, Inscriptions*. Regensburg: Schnell & Steiner, 1999.

Nietzsche, Friedrich. *The Portable Nietzsche*. Translated by Walter Kaufmann. New York: Viking, 1954.

Nock, Arthur Darby. *Conversion*. Oxford: Clarendon, 1933.

———. *Early Gentile Christianity and Its Hellenistic Background*. New York: Harper & Row, 1964.

———. "The Guild of Zeus Hypsistos." In *Essays on Religion in the Ancient World*, edited by Zeph Stewart, 1:414–43. Oxford: Clarendon, 1972.

———. "Religious Attitudes of the Ancient Greeks." In *Essays on Religion and the Ancient World*, edited by Zeph Stewart, 2:534–50. Oxford: Clarendon, 1972.

———. "Religious Developments from the Close of the Republic to the Reign of Nero." In *The Cambridge Ancient History*, 10:465–511. Cambridge: University Press, 1934.

Nussbaum, Martha. "Narrative Emotions: Beckett's Genealogy of Love." *Ethics* 98 (1988): 225–54.

Nygren, Anders. *Der Römerbrief*. Göttingen: Vandenhoeck & Ruprecht, 1951.

O'Day, Gail R. *Revelation in the Fourth Gospel: Narrative Mode and Theological Claim*. Philadelphia: Fortress, 1986.

O'Donovan, Oliver. *The Desire of the Nations: Rediscovering the Roots of Political Theology*. Cambridge: Cambridge University Press, 1996.

O'Neill, J. C. "The Use of Kyrios in the Book of Acts." *SJT* 8, no. 2 (1955): 155–74.

Origen. *Contra Celsum*. Edited and translated by Henry Chadwick. Cambridge: Cambridge University Press, 1980.

Orr, D. G. "Roman Domestic Religion." *ANRW* 2.16.2 (1978): 1557–91.

Oster, Richard. "The Ephesian Artemis as an Opponent of Early Christianity." *Jahrbuch für Antike und Christentum* 19 (1976): 24-44.
Ovid. *Ex Ponto*. Translated by A. L. Wheeler. Revised by G. P. Goold. LCL. Cambridge: Harvard University Press, 1924.
———. *Metamorphoses*. Vol. 1, *Books 1-8*. Translated by Frank Justus Miller. Revised by G. P. Goold. LCL. Cambridge: Harvard University Press, 1916.
Page, T. E. *The Acts of the Apostles*. London: Macmillan, 1911.
Pannenberg, Wolfhart. *Systematic Theology*. 3 vols. Grand Rapids: Eerdmans, 1991-1998.
Parker, Robert. *Athenian Religion: A History*. Oxford: Clarendon, 1996.
Parsons, Mikeal C., and Richard I. Pervo. *Rethinking the Unity of Luke and Acts*. Minneapolis: Fortress, 1993.
Pausanias. *Description of Greece*. Translated by W. H. S. Jones. 5 vols. LCL. Cambridge: Harvard University Press, 1918.
Pelikan, Jaroslav. *Christianity and Classical Culture: The Metamorphosis of Natural Theology in the Christian Encounter with Hellenism*. New Haven: Yale University Press, 1993.
Penner, Todd. "Madness in the Method? The Acts of the Apostles in Current Study." *Currents in Biblical Research* 2, no. 2 (2004): 223-93.
Pesch, Rudolf. *Die Apostelgeschichte*. 2 vols. EKKNT 5. Neukirchener-Vluyn: Neukirchener Verlag, 1986.
Philipose, John. "Kurios in Luke: A Diagnosis." *Bible Translator* 43, no. 3 (1992): 325-33.
Pietersma, Albert. "Kyrios or Tetragram: A Renewed Quest for the Original Septuagint." In *De Septuaginta: Studies in Honour of John William Wevers on His Sixty-Fifth Birthday*, edited by Albert Pietersma and Claude Cox, 85-101. Mississauga: Benben, 1984.
Plümacher, Eckhard. *Lukas als hellenistischer Schriftsteller: Studien zur Apostelgeschichte*. Studien zur Umwelt des Neuen Testaments 9. Göttingen: Vandenhoeck & Ruprecht, 1972.
Plummer, Alfred. *A Critical and Exegetical Commentary on the Gospel according to St. Luke*. ICC. New York: Charles Scribner's Sons, 1898.
Plutarch. *Moralia*. Vol. 13, part 2, *Stoic Essays*. Translated by Harold Cherniss. LCL. Cambridge: Harvard University Press, 1976.
———. *Moralia*. Vol. 5, *The Oracles at Delphi No Longer Given in Verse*. Translated by Frank Cole Babbitt. LCL. Cambridge: Harvard University Press, 1936.
Pokorný, Petr. *Der Brief des Paulus an die Kolosser*. Berlin: Evangelischer Verlagsanstalt, 1987.

Bibliography

———. *Theologie der lukanischen Schriften*. Göttingen: Vandenhoeck & Ruprecht, 1998.
Poulsen, V. *Les Portraits Romains*. Vol. 1, *République et Dynastie Julienne*. Copenhagen: Glyptothèque Ny Carlsberg, 1962.
Price, Simon R. F. *Religions of the Ancient Greeks*. Cambridge: Cambridge University Press, 1999.
———. *Rituals and Power: The Roman Imperial Cult in Asia Minor*. Cambridge: Cambridge University Press, 1984.
Provan, Iain. "To Highlight All Our Idols: Worshipping God in Nietzsche's World." *ExAud* 15 (1999): 19–38.
Pseudo-Callisthenes. *The Life of Alexander of Macedon*. Translated and edited by Elizabeth Hazelton Haight. New York: Longmans, 1955.
Raban, Avner, and Kenneth G. Holum, eds. *Caesarea Maritima: A Retrospective after Two Millennia*. Leiden: Brill, 1996.
Rad, Gerhard von. *Old Testament Theology*. 2 vols. New York: Harper & Row, 1962–1965.
Räisänen, Heikki. *Beyond New Testament Theology*. London: SCM, 1990.
Rese, Martin. *Alttestamentliche Motive in der Christologie des Lukas*. Studien zum Neuen Testament 1. Gütersloh: Gütersloher Verlagshaus Gerd Mohn, 1969.
———. "Die Aussagen über Jesu Tod und Auferstehung in der Apostelgeschichte—ältestes Kerygma oder lukanische Theologumena?" *NTS* 30, no. 3 (1984): 335–53.
———. "Formeln und Lieder im Neuen Testament. Einige notwendige Anmerkungen." *Verkündigung und Forschung* 15, no. 2 (1970): 75–95.
———. "Das Lukas-Evangelium. Ein Forschungsbericht." *ANRW* 2.25.3 (1985): 2258–328.
Rhoads, David, and Donald Michie. *Mark as Story: An Introduction to the Narrative of a Gospel*. Philadelphia: Fortress, 1982.
Rice, George Edward. "The Alterations of Luke's Tradition by the Textual Variants in Codex Bezae." PhD diss., Case Western Reserve University, 1974.
Richardson, Neil. *Paul's Language about God*. JSNTSup 99. Sheffield: Sheffield Academic, 1994.
Ricoeur, Paul. *Oneself as Another*. Translated by Kathleen Blarney. Chicago: University of Chicago Press, 1992.
Riesenfeld, Harald. "The Text of Acts x.36." In *Text and Interpretation: Studies in the New Testament*, edited by Ernest Best and R. McL. Wilson, 191–94. Cambridge: Cambridge University Press, 1979.
Rives, James B. *Religion and Authority in Roman Carthage*. New York: Oxford University Press, 1995.

———. *Religion in the Roman Empire*. London: Blackwell, 2007.
Robinson, J. A., ed. *The Passion of S. Perpetua*. Cambridge: Cambridge University Press, 1891.
Robinson, J. A. T. *Redating the New Testament*. Philadelphia: Westminster, 1976.
Roloff, Jürgen. *Die Apostelgeschichte*. NTD 5. Göttingen: Vandenhoeck & Ruprecht, 1981.
Roscher, W. H. *Ausführliches Lexikon der griechischen und römischen Mythologie*. Leipzig: Teubner, 1884–1937.
Rösel, Martin. *Adonaq—warum Gott "Herr" genannt wird*. Tübingen: Mohr Siebeck, 2000.
Rowe, C. Kavin. "Biblical Pressure and Trinitarian Hermeneutics." *ProEccl* 11 (2002): 295–312.
———. *Early Narrative Christology: The Lord in the Gospel of Luke*. 2006. Reprint, Grand Rapids: Baker Academic, 2009.
———. *One True Life: The Stoics and Early Christians as Rival Traditions*. New Haven: Yale University Press, 2016.
———. *World Upside Down: Reading Acts in the Graeco-Roman Age*. Oxford: Oxford University Press, 2009.
Rusam, Dietrich. *Das Alte Testament bei Lukas*. BZNW 112. Berlin: de Gruyter, 2003.
Sagnard, F. *Irénée de Lyon: Contre les hérésies, Livre III*. SC 34. Paris: Cerf, 1952.
Sanday, William, and Arthur C. Headlam. *A Critical and Exegetical Commentary on the Epistle to the Romans*. ICC. New York: Charles Scribner's Sons, 1898.
Sanday, William, and C. H. Turner. *Novum Testamentum Sancti Irenaei Episcopi Lugdunensis*. Oxford: Clarendon, 1923.
Sanders, E. P. "Jesus' Galilee." In *Fair Play: Diversity and Conflicts in Early Christianity; Essays in Honour of Heikki Räisänen*, edited by Ismo Dunderberg, Christopher Tuckett, and Kari Syreeni, 3–41. Leiden: Brill, 2002.
———. *Judaism: Practice and Belief 63 BCE–66 CE*. London: SCM, 1992.
———. *Paul and Palestinian Judaism*. Philadelphia: Fortress, 1977.
Sandmel, Samuel. "Parallelomania." *JBL* 81 (1962): 1–13.
Schiller, Gertrud. *Ikonographie der christlichen Kunst*. Bd. 2, *Die Passion Jesu Christ*. Gütersloh: Gütersloher Verlagshaus G. Mohn, 1969.
Schlatter, Adolf. *Romans: The Righteousness of God*. Peabody, MA: Hendrickson, 1995.
Schmidt, K. L. "Le problème du Christianisme primitif." *Revue d'histoire et de philosophie religieuses* 18 (1938): 126–73.
Schmithals, Walter. *The Office of Apostle in the Early Church*. Translated by John E. Steely. Nashville: Abingdon, 1969.

Bibliography

Schneider, Gerhard. "Anknüpfung, Kontinuität und Widerspruch in der Areopagrede Apg 17,22–31." In *Kontinuität und Einheit*, edited by Paul-Gerhard Müller and Werner Stenger, 173–78. Freiburg: Herder, 1981.

———. *Das Evangelium nach Lukas: kapitel 1–10*. Ökumenischer Taschenbuchkommentar zum Neuen Testament. Gütersloh: Gütersloher Verlagshaus Mohn; Würzburg: Echter-Verlag, 1977.

———. *Die Apostelgeschichte*. 2 vols. HThKNT. Freiburg: Herder, 1980–1982.

———. "Gott und Christus als Kyrios nach der Apostelgeschichte." In *Begegnung mit dem Wort*, edited by J. Zmijewski and E. Nellessen, 161–74. BBB 53. Bonn: Peter Hanstein Verlag, 1980.

Schoeps, Hans Joachim. *Paul: The Theology of the Apostle in the Light of Jewish Religious History*. Philadelphia: Westminster, 1959.

Schönborn, Christoph von. *L'Icône du Christ: Fondements théologiques élaborés entre le Ier et le IIe Concile de Nicée [325–787]*. Fribourg: Éditions universitaires, 1976.

Schreiner, Susan E. "Calvin's Use of Natural Law." In Cromartie, *A Preserving Grace*, 51–76.

Schubert, Paul. "The Place of the Areopagus Speech in the Composition of Acts." In *Transitions in Biblical Scholarship*, edited by J. Coert Rylaarsdam, 235–61. Chicago: University of Chicago Press, 1968.

Schürmann, Heinz. *Das Lukasevangelium*. 2 vols. Herders theologischer Kommentar zum Neuen Testament Bd. 3. Freiburg: Herder, 1969–1982.

Schüssler Fiorenza, Elisabeth. *Discipleship of Equals: Critical Feminist Ekklesia-logy of Liberation*. New York: Crossroad, 1993.

———. *Jesus: Miriam's Child, Sophia's Prophet*. New York: Continuum, 1994.

Schütz, John Howard. *Paul and the Anatomy of Apostolic Authority*. Cambridge: Cambridge University Press, 1975.

Schwanz, Peter. *Imago Dei als christolgisch-anthropologisches Problem in der Geschichte der Alten Kirche von Paulus bis Clemens von Alexandrien*. Halle: Niemeyer, 1970.

Schweizer, Eduard. *Der Brief an die Kolosser*. Neukirchen-Vluyn: Neukirchener Verlag, 1976.

———. *The Good News according to Luke*. Atlanta: John Knox, 1984.

———. "Jesus Christus I." In *Theologische Realenzyklopädie*, ed. Gerhard Müller. Berlin: de Gruyter, 1987.

Segal, Alan F. *Two Powers in Heaven: Early Rabbinic Reports About Christianity and Gnosticism*. Studies in Judaism in Late Antiquity 25. Leiden: Brill, 1977.

Seitz, Christopher. "The Call of Moses and the 'Revelation' of the Divine Name." In *Theological Exegesis: Essays in Honor of Brevard S. Childs*, edited by

Christopher Seitz and Kathryn Greene-McCreight, 145–61. Grand Rapids: Eerdmans, 1999.

———. "Handing Over the Name: Christian Reflection on the Divine Name YHWH." In *Trinity, Time, and Church: A Response to the Theology of Robert W. Jenson*, edited by Colin E. Gunton, 23–41. Grand Rapids: Eerdmans, 2000.

Seneca. *Epistles*. Translated by Richard M. Gummere. 3 vols. LCL. Cambridge: Harvard University Press, 1920.

Sherwin-White, A. N. *Roman Law and Roman Society in the New Testament*. Grand Rapids: Baker, 1992.

Sim, David. "The Gospels for All Christians? A Response to Richard Bauckham." *JSNT* 84 (2001): 3–27.

Simon, Yves R. *A General Theory of Authority*. Notre Dame: University of Notre Dame Press, 1962.

Skehan, Patrick W. "The Divine Name at Qumran, in the Masada Scroll, and in the Septuagint." *Bulletin of the International Organization for Septuagint and Cognate Studies* 13 (1980): 14–44.

Sleeman, Matthew. *Geography and the Ascension Narrative in Acts*. SNTSMS 146. Cambridge: Cambridge University Press, 2009.

———. "The Vision of Acts: World Right Way Up." *JSNT* 33, no. 3 (2011): 327–33.

Small, Alastair, ed. *Subject and Ruler: The Cult of the Ruling Power in Classical Antiquity*. Dexter, MI: Thompson-Shore, 1996.

Smith, D. Moody. "When Did the Gospels Become Scripture?" *JBL* 119 (2000): 3–20.

Soards, Marion L. *The Speeches in Acts: Their Content, Context, and Concerns*. Louisville: Westminster John Knox, 1994.

Söder, Rosa. *Die apokryphen Apostelgeschichten und die romanhafte Literatur der Antike*. 1932; Stuttgart: Kohlhammer, 1969.

Souter, Alexander. *The Text and Canon of the New Testament*. New York: Charles Scribner's Sons, 1920.

Speidel, Michael P. "The Cult of the Genii in the Roman Army and a New Military Deity." *ANRW* 2.16.2 (1978): 1542–55.

———. "The Roman Army in Judaea under the Procurators." *Ancient Society* 13/14 (1982/1983): 233–40.

Spencer, F. Scott. *Acts*. Sheffield: Sheffield Academic, 1997.

St John, Henry. Preface to *Authority in a Changing Church*. Edited by John Dalrymple et al. London: Sheed and Ward, 1968.

Stählin, Gustav. *Die Apostelgeschichte*. NTD 5. Göttingen: Vandenhoeck & Ruprecht, 1962.

Bibliography

Stählin, Otto. *Clemens Alexandrinus* II. Updated by Ludwig Früchtel. Die griechischen christlichen Schriftsteller 15. Berlin: Academie, 1960.

Stanley, Christopher. *Paul and the Language of Scripture: Citation Technique in the Pauline Epistles and Contemporary Literature.* SNTSMS 74. Cambridge: Cambridge University Press, 1992.

Stanton, Graham N. "The Fourfold Gospel." *NTS* 43 (1997): 317–46.

Starr, Raymond J. "The Circulation of Literary Texts in the Roman World." *CQ* 37, no. 1 (1987): 213–23.

Statius. *Thebaid.* Translated by J. H. Mozley. 2 vols. LCL. New York: G. P. Putnam's Sons, 1928.

Steenburg, Dave. "The Case against the Synonymity of Morphē and Eikōn." *JSNT* 34 (1988): 77–86.

Stenschke, Christoph W. *Luke's Portrait of Gentiles Prior to Their Coming to Faith.* WUNT 2/108. Tübingen: Mohr Siebeck, 1999.

Stern, Menahem. *Greek and Latin Authors on Jews and Judaism.* 3 vols. Jerusalem: Israel Academy of Sciences and Humanities, 1974–1984.

Strange, W. A. *The Problem of the Text of Acts.* SNTSMS 71. Cambridge: Cambridge University Press, 1992.

Talbert, Charles H. "On Reading Luke and Acts." In *Reading Luke-Acts in Its Mediterranean Milieu,* 1–18. Leiden: Brill, 2003.

———. "Paul, Judaism, and the Revisionists." *CBQ* 63 (2001): 1–22.

———. "The Place of the Resurrection in the Theology of Luke." *Int* 46 (1992): 19–30.

———. "Prophecies of Future Greatness: The Contributions of Greco-Roman Biographies to an Understanding of Luke 1.5–4.1." In *Reading Luke-Acts in Its Mediterranean Milieu,* 65–77. Leiden: Brill, 2003. First published in *The Divine Helmsman: Studies on God's Control of Human Events Presented to Lou H. Silberman,* edited by James L. Crenshaw and Samuel Sandmel, 129–41. New York: Ktav, 1980.

———. *Reading Acts: A Literary and Theological Commentary on the Acts of the Apostles.* Reading the New Testament. Macon, GA: Smyth & Helwys, 2005. First published 1997 by Crossroad.

———. *Reading Luke: A Literary and Theological Commentary on the Third Gospel.* New York: Crossroad, 1982.

Talbert, Charles H., with Perry Stepp. "Succession in Luke-Acts and in the Lukan Milieu." In *Reading Luke-Acts in Its Mediterranean Milieu,* 19–55. Leiden: Brill, 2003.

Tannehill, Robert C. *Luke.* ANTC. Nashville: Abingdon, 1996.

———. *The Narrative Unity of Luke-Acts: A Literary Interpretation*. 2 vols. Minneapolis: Fortress, 1986–1990.

Tanner, Jeremy. "Portraits, Power, and Patronage in the Late Roman Republic." *JRS* 90 (2000): 18–50

Tatum, W. Barnes. "The LXX Version of the Second Commandment (Ex. 20,3–6 = Deut. 5,7–10): A Polemic Against Idols, Not Images." *JSJ* 17, no. 2 (1986): 177–95.

Taylor, Charles. *Philosophical Arguments*. Cambridge, MA: Harvard University Press, 1995.

———. *A Secular Age*. Cambridge, MA: Harvard University Press, 2007.

Taylor, Lily Ross. *The Divinity of the Roman Emperor*. Middletown, CT: American Philological Association, 1931.

Taylor, Vincent. *The Names of Jesus*. London: Macmillan, 1962.

———. *The Person of Christ in New Testament Teaching*. London: Macmillan, 1958.

Tertullian. *Adversus Marcionem*. Edited and translated by Ernest Evans. Oxford: Clarendon 1972.

Thiselton, Anthony C. *The First Epistle to the Corinthians*. Grand Rapids: Eerdmans, 2000.

Thompson, Leonard L. *The Book of Revelation: Apocalypse and Empire*. Oxford: Oxford University Press, 1990.

Thompson, M. B. "The Holy Internet: Communication between Churches in the First Christian Generation." In Bauckham, *Gospels for All Christians*, 49–70.

Thompson, Richard P., and Thomas E. Phillips, eds. *Literary Studies in Luke-Acts: Essays in Honor of Joseph B. Tyson*. Macon, GA: Mercer University Press, 1998.

Torrance, T. F. "Phusikos kai Theologikos Logos, St Paul and Athenagoras at Athens." *SJT* 41 (1988): 11–26.

Tracy, David. *The Analogical Imagination: Christian Theology and the Culture of Pluralism*. New York: Crossroad, 1981.

Trebilco, Paul R. *Jewish Communities in Asia Minor*. SNTSMS 69. Cambridge: Cambridge University Press, 1991.

Troeltsch, Ernst. "Faith and History." In *Religion in History*. Minneapolis: Fortress, 1991.

Tuckett, Christopher M. "The Christology of Luke-Acts." In Verheyden, *Unity of Luke-Acts*, 133–64.

Ulrich, E. "The Biblical Scrolls from Qumran Cave 4: An Overview and a Progress Report on Their Publication." *Revue de Qumran* 14 (1989): 207–28.

Urbach, E. E. "The Rabbinical Laws of Idolatry in the Second and Third Centu-

Bibliography

ries in the Light of Archaeological and Historical Facts." *Israel Exploration Journal* 9 (1959): 149–65, 229–45.

Vaggione, Richard Paul. *Eunomius of Cyzicus and the Nicene Revolution*. Oxford Early Christian Studies. Oxford: Oxford University Press, 2000.

———. *Eunomius: The Extant Works*. Oxford Early Christian Texts. Oxford: Clarendon, 1987.

Verheyden, J., ed. *The Unity of Luke-Acts*. Leuven: Leuven University Press, 1999.

———. "The Unity of Luke-Acts: What Are We Up To?" In Verheyden, *Unity of Luke-Acts*, 3–56.

Vielhauer, Philipp. "On the 'Paulinism' of Acts." In Keck and Martyn, *Studies in Luke-Acts*, 33–50.

Waddell, W. G. "The Tetragrammaton in the LXX." *JTS* 45 (1944): 158–61.

Wainwright, Arthur W. *The Trinity in the New Testament*. London: SPCK, 1962.

Wainwright, Geoffrey. "The Holy Spirit." In *The Cambridge Companion to Christian Doctrine*, edited by Colin E. Gunton, 273–96. Cambridge: Cambridge University Press, 1997.

Walaskay, Paul. *Acts*. Louisville: Westminster John Knox, 1998.

Watson, Francis. *Text and Truth: Redefining Biblical Theology*. Grand Rapids: Eerdmans, 1997.

Weiser, Alfons. *Die Apostelgeschichte*. 2 vols. Gütersloh: Gerd Mohn, 1981–1985.

Weiss, Bernhard. *Die Evangelien des Markus und Lukas*. Meyer Kritisch exegesticher Kommentar über das Neue Testament. 9th ed. Göttingen: Vandenhoeck & Ruprecht, 1901.

Weiss, Bernhard, and Johannes Weiss. *Die Evangelien des Markus und Lukas*. Meyer Kritisch exegesticher Kommentar über das Neue Testament. 8th ed. Göttingen: Vandenhoeck & Ruprecht, 1892. (The eighth edition of the Meyer series commentary was done by Johannes.)

Weiss, Johannes. *Die Schriften des Neuen Testament. Erster Band: Die drei älteren Evangelien. Die Apostelgeschichte*. Göttingen: Vandenhoeck & Ruprecht, 1906.

———. *Über die Absicht und den literarischen Charakter der Apostelgeschichte*. Göttingen: Vandenhoeck & Ruprecht, 1897.

Weissenrieder, Annette. "'He Is a God!' Acts 28:1–9 in the Light of Iconographical and Textual Sources Related to Medicine." In *Picturing the New Testament: Studies in Ancient Visual Images*, edited by Annette Weissenrieder, Friedericke Wendt, and Petra von Gemünden, 127–56. Tübingen: Mohr Siebeck, 2005.

Wellhausen, Julius. *Das Evangelium Lucae*. Berlin: Reimer, 1904.

Westberg, Daniel. "The Reformed Tradition and Natural Law." In Cromartie, *A Preserving Grace*, 103-17.

White, L. Michael. *The Social Origins of Christian Architecture*. Valley Forge, PA: Trinity Press, 1990.

Wilckens, Ulrich. *Der Brief an die Römer*. Vol. 2. EKKNT 6. Zürich: Benziger; Neukirchen-Vluyn: Neukirchener Verlag, 1980.

———. *Die Missionsreden der Apostelgeschichte: Form- und traditionsgeschichtliche Untersuchungen*. Neukirchen-Vluyn: Neukirchener Verlag, 1961.

Wilk, Florian. *Die Bedeutung des Jesajabuches für Paulus*. FRLANT 179. Göttingen: Vandenhoeck & Ruprecht, 1998.

Wilken, Robert Louis. *The Christians as the Romans Saw Them*. 2nd ed. New Haven: Yale University Press, 2003.

Williams, David Salter. "Reconsidering Marcion's Gospel." *JBL* 108 (1989): 477-96.

Williams, Frank. *The Panarion of Epiphanius of Salamis*. 2 vols. Nag Hammadi Studies 35. Leiden: Brill, 1987-1994.

Wilson, Stephen G. *The Gentiles and the Gentile Mission in Luke-Acts*. SNTSMS 23. Cambridge: Cambridge University Press, 1973.

Winter, Paul. "Lukanische Miszellen." *ZNW* 49 (1958): 65-75.

Witherington, Ben, III. *The Acts of the Apostles: A Socio-rhetorical Commentary*. Grand Rapids: Eerdmans, 1998.

Wolter, Michael. "'Wann wurde Maria schwanger?' Eine vernachlässigte Frage und ihre Bedeutung für das Verständnis der lukanischen Vorgeschichte (Lk 1-2)." In *Von Jesus zum Christus: Christologische Studien*, edited by Rudolf Hoppe and Ulrich Busse, 405-22. BZNW 93. Berlin: de Gruyter, 1998.

Wrede, William. *The Messianic Secret*. Translated by J. C. G. Grieg. Cambridge: Clarke, 1971.

———. "Über Aufgabe und Methode der sogenannten neutestamentlichen Theologie" (1897). Translated by Robert Morgan as "The Task and Methods of 'New Testament Theology.'" In *The Nature of New Testament Theology*, edited by Robert Morgan. Naperville, IL: Allenson, 1973.

Wright, N. T. *The Climax of the Covenant*. Minneapolis: Fortress, 1991.

———. "Jesus and the Identity of God." *Ex Aud* 14 (1998): 42-56.

———. *The New Testament and the People of God*. Vol. 1 of *Christian Origins and the Question of God*. Minneapolis: Fortress, 1992.

———. "One God, One Lord, One People: Incarnational Christology for a Church in a Pagan Environment." *Ex Aud* 7 (1991): 45-58.

———. "Poetry and Theology in Colossians 1.15-20." *NTS* 36 (1990): esp. 444-68.

Yeago, David S. "The New Testament and Nicene Dogma: A Contribution to the Recovery of Theological Exegesis." *ProEccl* 3, no. 2 (1994): 152-64.

Bibliography

Young, Frances M. *Biblical Exegesis and the Formation of Christian Culture*. Cambridge: Cambridge University Press, 1997.

———. "The 'Mind' of Scripture: Theological Readings of the Bible in the Fathers." *International Journal of Systematic Theology* 7, no. 2 (2005): 126–41.

Young, Francis M., and David F. Ford. *Meaning and Truth in Second Corinthians*. Grand Rapids: Eerdmans, 1988.

Zanker, Paul. *Forum Augustum: das Bildprogramm*. Tübingen: Wasmuth, 1968.

———. *Pompeii: Public and Private Life*. Translated by Deborah Lucas Schneider. Cambridge, MA: Harvard University Press, 1998.

———. *The Power of Images in the Age of Augustus*. Ann Arbor: University of Michigan Press, 1988.

Zehnle, Richard F. *Peter's Pentecost Discourse: Tradition and Lukan Reinterpretation in Peter's Speeches of Acts 2 and 3*. Society of Biblical Literature Monograph Series 15. Nashville: Abingdon, 1971.

Index of Authors

Aageson, James, 276n8, 280n19
Adolphe, Jane, 217n1, 219n4
Alexander, Loveday, 153n27, 155, 156n34, 158n46, 169n69, 173n6
Alföldy, Géza, 6n14
Aly, Zaki, 53n20
Anastos, Milton V., 269n85
Ando, Clifford, 100n12
Aquinas, Saint Thomas, 74–75
Arendt, Hannah, 204n8
Asad, Talal, 267n73
Athanassiadi, Polymnia, 86n45, 125n69
Attridge, Harold W., 115n22, 119n41

Babut, Daniel, 115n22
Balch, David L., 257n37
Balia, Peter, 197n58
Barclay, John, 95–106, 108n34
Barnes, Timothy D., 11, 80, 129n88
Barr, James, 77n16, 193, 198n65
Barrett, C. K., 12, 14n41, 60n39, 75n9, 82n35, 87n49, 89n52, 117n31, 120n50, 121, 124n67, 125n68, 126n76, 157n42, 163n58, 170n70, 186, 188, 191, 197n56, 198n60, 226, 253, 260, 297n83
Barth, Karl, 34n30, 49n9, 50n14, 52n18, 63n44, 68n58, 110, 295n77, 306
Barth, Markus, 277n9
Barton, S. C., 158n46
Bassler, Jouette M., 207n16, 209n20, 284n37
Bauckham, Richard, 4, 60n39, 158n46, 298n87, 299–304, 307n11
Baudissin, W. W. Graf, 53n20
Beard, Mary, 100, 255n31, 256n36, 257n38, 258n43

Bechtler, Steven Richard, 279n14, 285n38
Bellinzoni, Arthur J., 147n5, 172n3
Beurlier, Émile, 73n1
Beyschlag, Willibald, 47n5
Bickerman, Elias, 4n6, 22n68
Bird, Michael F., 174n9
Bisconti, Fabrizio, 272n93
Black, Matthew, 287n49
Bleek, Friedrich, 36n36, 39n42
Bockmuehl, Markus, 174–75, 217n2, 218n4, 223n10
Boer, Willem den, 4n6, 22nn67–68
Boring, Eugene, 58n34
Botha, P. J. J., 163n57
Bousset, Wilhelm, 47n5, 54n24, 298n87
Bovon, François, 36, 37n37, 39, 155n33, 172n3, 210
Braaten, Carl E., 219n5
Brent, Allen, 9n24, 51n16
Breytenbach, Cilliers, 117n32, 121n54, 122, 198n60
Brock, Ann Graham, 210n24
Broughton, T. R. S., 13n37
Brown, Raymond, 28, 30, 36n35, 49n11, 58n37, 59n38, 164
Bruce, F. F., 76n12
Brunner, Emil, 47
Buckwalter, H. Douglas, 199n68
Bultmann, Rudolf, 24, 47n6, 77n17, 185, 276n6, 282
Burkert, Walter, 114n19

Cadbury, Henry J., 36n35, 43n56, 63n44, 114n16, 154nn28–29, 155n33, 156n38, 157n40, 157n42, 159n48, 173, 187n30
Calvin, John, 75

Index of Authors

Campenhausen, Hans von, 150–51, 210n22, 210n25, 212n28, 250n6
Capes, David B., 275n5, 288n55, 293n64, 296n81
Carroll, John T., 163
Casey, P. M., 298n87, 299n89
Cassidy, Richard J., 11, 218n4
Chadwick, Henry, 115n21
Chapman, Stephen B., 52n19
Charlesworth, M. P., 16n49, 119n39
Childs, Brevard, 52, 66n53, 69n59, 155n33, 166n62, 294, 295n72, 295n74
Clauss, Manfred, 4n5, 51n16
Coleman, K. M., 7n16
Conybeare, F. C., 27n11
Conzelmann, Hans, 29, 41, 58, 76, 185n22, 199n67
Cook, Arthur Bernard, 122n57, 124n67
Cranfield, C. E. B., 276n7, 279n15, 280n19, 281n23, 282n28, 283n34, 284n36, 293n64
Cromartie, Michael, 217n1, 219n5, 229n16
Crossan, John Dominic, 205n10
Crowe, Michael Bertram, 218n3
Cullmann, Oscar, 49n11, 184n17, 185
Cuss, Dominique, 51n16

Dahl, Nils, 30, 50n14, 53n22, 112n7, 160n50, 275, 276n7, 285n42, 286n46, 287n49, 298n87
Davis, Carl Judson, 275n5, 288n53, 293n64, 295n73
Deissmann, Adolf, 17n55, 21n62, 23, 51n16
Dibelius, Martin, 28, 36, 75n10, 86n45
Dittenberger, Wilhelm, 16n50, 16n52
Dodd, C. H., 276n6, 281n21, 281n25, 284n36, 290n60
Dodds, E. R., 126n75, 127n82
Donahue, John R., 58n34
Donaldson, Terence L., 14n39
Downing, F. Gerald, 129, 163n57
Dubourdieu, Annie, 258n42
Dunn, James D. G., 20n61, 186n27, 191, 253n18, 263, 275n5, 276n7, 279nn15–16, 280n19, 281nn24–25, 282n28, 283n32, 283n34, 284n36, 288n52, 293n64, 293n66, 298n87, 299n89
Dupont, Jacques, 185n22

Eco, Umberto, 113n11
Edwards, Mark, 51n16
Elliot, John H., 205n11, 206n12
Ellis, E. Earle, 35n32
Elsner, Jaś, 268, 271n88
Eltester, Friedrich-Wilhelm, 252n15
Engelhardt, H. Tristram, Jr., 213n30, 231n18
Esler, Philip F., 158n46, 163n58, 257n37, 264n65
Evans, C. F., 36n36, 39n44

Farrer, Austin M., 211
Fastiggi, Robert L., 217n1, 218n4
Fee, Gordon D., 305n109
Finney, Paul Corby, 251nn9–10, 251n27, 268n79, 270, 271n89, 273
Fishwick, Duncan, 4n4
Fitzmyer, Joseph A., 4n2, 8n22, 18n57, 27n11, 29n16, 35–36, 37n37, 43n57, 53nn20–21, 54nn26–27, 59n38, 63, 66–67, 76, 158n46, 188n33, 252n17, 275n2, 281n24, 284n36, 293n66
Foakes Jackson, F. J., 13n37, 186n26
Foerster, Werner, 32n26, 51n16, 126n74, 298n87
Fohrer, G., 51n16
Forcellini, A., 23n72
Foss, Pedar W., 258n42
Fossum, Jarl, 252
Foucault, Michael, 212n28
Franklin, Eric, 199n67
Frede, Michael, 86n45, 125n69
Freedberg, David, 251n8
Frei, Hans W., 44, 57
Friesen, Steven J., 4n5, 5nn9–10, 10n26
Fuller, Reginald H., 66n52

Gabler, Johann Philipp, 46n3
Gadamer, Hans-Georg, 85n43, 105, 229
Gamble, Harry Y., 33n27, 154n29, 177n17
Garnsey, Peter, 81n29
Garrett, Susan R., 26n8
Gärtner, Bertil, 75n10
Gasque, W. Ward, 168n67
Gathercole, Simon J., 221n8
Gaventa, Beverly Roberts, 14n41, 15n45, 126n77, 188, 198n62, 206n14

Index of Authors

Gebhardt, H., 75n8
Gilbert, Gary, 162
Gilmour, Samuel MacLean, 159n49
Gnilka, Joachim, 260n50, 261, 265n71
Goldingay, John, 48
Goodenough, Erwin R., 251n8, 255n30
Goodman, Martin, 51n16
Gordon, R. L., 252, 267n77, 268nn78–79
Gradel, Ittai, 258n41
Grant, Robert M., 298n87
Green, Joel B., 30n17, 31n25, 39, 48n7, 58, 63n44, 65, 78n21
Gregory, Andrew, 74n4, 147–50, 151n15, 152–53, 154nn29–30, 155n33, 156n35, 156n37, 158n45, 159–60, 171–72, 174, 177n17
Griffiths, Paul, 143n10
Gutmann, Joseph, 271n89

Hadot, Pierre, 90, 91nn60–61, 91n63
Haenchen, Ernst, 13n34, 82nn33–34, 118, 123n62, 186n27, 191
Hahn, Ferdinand, 49n11, 186n27, 192n42, 197n58
Halbertal, Moshe, 124n64, 267
Harnack, Adolf von, 26, 27n10, 47, 157nn43–44, 185n21
Harris, Murray J., 49n11
Harrison, Stephen, 269n82
Hart, David Bentley, 145n14
Hauck, Friedrich, 287n50
Hauerwas, Stanley, 204
Havel, Václav, 108–9
Hay, David M., 266n72, 276n8
Hays, Richard B., 262n59, 264–65, 273n94, 276nn7–8, 291n63, 296n78
Headlam, Arthur C., 276n6, 281n24, 293n64
Healy, Mary, 218n4
Hengel, Martin, 54n27
Hermann, Wilhelm, 47n5
Heschel, Abraham, 305n108
Hill, Charles E., 147n4
Hittinger, Russell, 217n1, 230
Hoff, Michael C., 5n12
Holladay, Carl R., 86n48, 117n33, 122n58
Holliday, Peter J., 264n65
Holtzmann, H. J., 36n36

Holum, Kenneth G., 14n39
Hooker, Morna D., 254
Horrell, David G., 111n6
Horsley, Richard A., 11n28
Horst, P. W. van der, 83n38, 122n59
Howard, George, 53n20, 54n25, 293n66
Hultgren, Stephen, 253n18
Humphrey, Edith M., 210n24
Hunink, Vincent, 269n82
Hurtado, Larry, 60n39, 298n87, 299n90

Jeanrond, Werner G., 48n7
Jensen, Robin Margaret, 251n7, 272, 273n95
Jenson, Robert, 50n14, 57, 296n79, 303n105, 307n111
Jeremias, Joachim, 37n37
Jervell, Jacob, 7n18, 13n35, 73n2, 123n61, 123n63, 252n15, 259n46, 260nn47–48, 261, 262n58, 263n63
Johnson, E. Elizabeth, 276nn7–8, 282, 284n36
Johnson, Luke Timothy, 30, 52n17, 62n41, 63n44, 117n31, 118n38, 119n39, 121, 123n62, 146n1, 160–62, 164n59, 167, 173n6, 174, 178, 188n34, 189nn35–36, 284n36
Jones, Donald L., 63n44, 199n67
Juel, Donald H., 50n14, 275n3, 275n5

Kasch, Wilhelm, 287n50
Käsemann, Ernst, 255, 276nn7–8, 278n13, 279n15, 281n25, 284n36, 287n50
Keck, Leander E., 30n20, 31n24, 52n17, 58n37, 73n2, 160n50, 202n4, 275n5, 282n27
Kelhoffer, James A., 155n31
Kingsbury, Jack Dean, 52n17, 58n34
Kittel, G., 193, 252n15
Kitzinger, Ernst, 250n4, 271n89
Klauck, Hans-Josef, 6n15, 9n25, 18n58, 82, 83n36, 112n7, 117n31, 118n37, 123n61, 126
Klauser, Theodor, 115n21, 250
Klein, Günther, 210n23
Kleiner, Diana E. E., 255n31
Kleinknecht, H., 252n15, 298n87
Klostermann, Erich, 36n36, 36n39
Knight, G. A. F., 60n39
Knox, John, 27n11

341

Index of Authors

Koch, Dietrich-Alex, 280n17, 280n20, 289n56, 293n66
Koch, Hugo, 250n4
Koenen, Ludwig, 53n20
Koester, Helmut, 155n33, 159n47, 203n5
Koets, P. J., 82n34, 119n40
Köhler, W.-D., 147n4
Kramer, Werner, 281n25, 298n87
Kreitzer, L. Joseph, 275n5, 281n21, 296n80
Kuper, Hilda, 267n75, 268n81
Kurz, William S., 189n35

Lake, Kirsopp, 13n37, 43n56, 63n44, 186n26, 187n30
Lampe, G. W. H., 34n31
Lampe, Peter, 113n12, 158n46, 257n37
Lane Fox, Robin, 100n12, 111n3, 111n5, 113n13, 114n19, 115n20, 115n21, 115n25, 116n28, 118, 124n65, 128n84, 131n95, 268nn78–79
Larsson, Edvin, 253n19
Lash, Nicholas, 207n17
Laurence, Ray, 258n42, 267n76
Laurentin, René, 67n55
Lawson, J., 149n11
Leaney, A. R. C., 37n37
Le Bohec, Yann, 13n37
Lightfoot, J. B., 260, 261n54, 265n71
Lincoln, A. T., 260n52
Lindbeck, George A., 57
Lochin, C., 256n33
Lohmeyer, Ernst, 51n16, 260n53
Lohse, Eduard, 209n20
Longenecker, Bruce W., 149n12, 153n26, 196n54
L'Orange, Hans Peter, 256n36
Lust, Johan, 53n20, 54n26
Luther, Martin, 184n16, 229, 296n82
Luz, Ulrich, 147n4

MacIntyre, Alasdair, 213
MacMullen, Ramsay, 111n4, 114n18, 115n25, 128, 131n93
Malherbe, Abraham J., 52n17, 158n46, 275n5
Manson, William, 37n37
Marcovich, Miroslav, 74n4

Marcus, Joel, 184n18
Margalit, Avishai, 124n64
Marguerat, Daniel, 76n14, 83n36, 87n50
Marshall, Bruce D., 68n56
Marshall, I. Howard, 39n41, 146n3
Martin, Dale B., 82n34
Martínez, F. Garcia, 287n48
Matera, Frank J., 163n57, 199, 259n44
Mattingly, Harold, 256n36
Mauser, Ulrich, 21n63, 49n12, 259nn45–46, 285nn39–40, 286n45, 297nn83–84, 305n108
May, Gerhard, 25n3
Mazzoleni, Danilo, 272n93
McCabe, Herbert, 202n3
McCasland, S. Vernon, 253n19
Meeks, Wayne, 52n17, 158n46, 275n5
Meinertz, Max, 282n27
Metzger, Bruce M., 152n19, 152n22, 156n35, 157n41, 177n15
Meyer, P. M., 16n51
Michie, Donald, 58n34
Millar, Fergus, 3, 22n67
Milton, John, 77n16
Minear, Paul S., 31, 58n37, 62n42
Mitchell, Stephen, 6n13, 125
Moessner, David P., 169n69, 189n36
Moltmann, Jürgen, 50n14
Momigliano, Arnaldo, 187n30
Mommsen, Theodor, 226
Moo, Douglas, 276n8
Morgan, Robert, 46n1
Moule, C. F. D., 195n49, 263n64
Murray, Sister Charles, 250n4

Nagel, Titus, 147n4
Neagoe, Alexandru, 11n27, 165–66
Neufeld, Vernon, 285n43
Newman, Carey C., 260n47
Neyrey, Jerome H., 207nn16–17
Nicolai, Vincenzo Fiocchi, 272n93
Nietzsche, Friedrich, 130n91
Nock, A. D., 4n7, 6n15, 17n54, 21n64, 90n56, 114n19, 117n34, 118n38, 124n67, 126n72, 131
North, John, 255n31, 256n36

Index of Authors

Nussbaum, Martha, 130
Nygren, Anders, 296n82

O'Day, Gail R., 58n34
O'Donovan, Oliver, 97n2, 98
O'Neill, J. C., 63n44
Orr, D. G., 258n42
Oster, Richard, 135n4

Page, T. E., 15n42
Pannenberg, Wolfhart, 50n14, 68n57
Parker, Robert, 115n26, 132
Parsons, Mikeal C., 146n3, 148n6, 155n33, 173–74, 177n16
Pelikan, Jaroslav, 74n6
Penner, Todd, 113n10, 162n56
Pervo, Richard I., 146n3, 148n6, 155n33, 173–74, 177n16
Pesch, Rudolf, 76n12, 120n47, 123n62, 184n17, 206n14
Philipose, John, 63n44
Phillips, Thomas E., 147n5, 189n36
Pietersma, Albert, 53n20, 293n66
Plümacher, Eckhard, 187n32
Plummer, Alfred, 36, 39n44, 62
Pokorný, Petr, 198n61, 261n55
Poulsen, V., 256n32
Price, Simon R. F., 5n10, 6n14, 9n25, 10n26, 12, 21n64, 51n16, 111n5, 114n19, 115n22, 119n39, 119nn41–42, 132n97, 255n31, 256n32, 256n36, 257n38, 258n43, 267n76, 269nn83–84, 271n90
Provan, Iain, 297n85

Quell, G., 32n26, 51n16, 298n87

Raban, Avner, 14n39
Rad, Gerhard von, 66n53, 252n15, 294n69, 295n74, 297n85, 305n108
Räisänen, Heikki, 46n4
Rese, Martin, 31n22, 169n68, 186–87, 193n45
Rhoads, David, 58n34
Rice, George Edward, 40n46
Richardson, Neil, 275n5, 293n64
Ricoeur, Paul, 42n52, 43n53
Riesenfeld, Harald, 14n40

Rives, James B., 100
Robinson, J. A., 23n72
Robinson, J. A. T., 8
Roloff, Jürgen, 191n41
Roscher, W. H., 15n44
Rösel, Martin, 54n26
Rowe, C. Kavin, 67n54, 78n20, 83n37, 89n54, 97n5, 101n15, 102n17, 104n23, 121n51, 131n92, 135n3, 137n7, 139n9, 144n12, 171n2, 175n12, 194n47, 195n51, 196n54, 208n18, 218n3, 224n11, 226n13
Rowland, Christopher, 51n16
Rusam, Dietrich, 30n18

Sagnard, F., 149n10
Sanday, William, 149n11, 276n6, 281n24, 293n64
Sanders, E. P., 24, 193n46, 253, 254n23, 295n75
Sandmel, Samuel, 9n23
Scharper, Philip J., 11n28
Schiller, Gertrud, 249n1
Schlatter, Adolf, 296n81
Schmidt, K. L., 50n14, 61n40
Schmithals, Walter, 210
Schneider, Gerhard, 36n36, 39, 63n44, 73n1, 77n17, 93n68, 123n61, 184n17, 199n67
Schoeps, Hans Joachim, 298n86
Schönborn, Christoph von, 253n20
Schreiner, Susan E., 229n16
Schubert, Paul, 73
Schürmann, Heinz, 39
Schüssler Fiorenza, Elisabeth, 205n10, 206n12
Schütz, John Howard, 201
Schwanz, Peter, 253n20
Schweizer, Eduard, 61n40, 186n25, 260n53
Segal, Alan F., 53n22, 298n87, 303n103
Seitz, Christopher, 66n53, 295n74
Sherwin-White, A. N., 13n36
Sim, David, 158n46
Simon, Yves R., 203n6
Skehan, Patrick W., 53n20
Sleeman, Matthew, 95–98
Small, Alastair, 5n12, 6n14
Smith, D. Moody, 160n50

343

Index of Authors

Soards, Marion L., 187n32
Söder, Rosa, 115n20
Souter, Alexander, 157n41, 177n15
Speidel, Michael P., 13nn36–37
Spencer, F. Scott, 189n35, 198n63
Spinoza, Baruch, 88
Stählin, Gustav, 122n60
Stählin, Otto, 77n18
Stanley, Christopher, 280nn17–19, 281n21, 288n54
Stanton, Graham N., 151n17, 152n19, 153nn23–24, 153n26, 155n33, 156n35, 157, 158n46, 168n66, 267n74
Starr, Raymond J., 177n17
Steenburg, Dave, 252n16
Stenschke, Christoph W., 112n7
Stepp, Perry, 146n2
Stern, Menahem, 125n70, 129n86
St. John, Henry, 203n5
Strange, W. A., 155n33, 157n44

Talbert, Charles H., 24n1, 30n21, 42n50, 58n34, 59n38, 146n2, 167n64, 189n35, 196, 228n14
Tannehill, Robert C., 14n41, 58n34, 58n37, 189
Tanner, Jeremy, 250n3
Tatum, W. Barnes, 250n4
Taylor, Charles, 130n90, 132n96, 144n13, 267n75
Taylor, Lily Ross, 51n16
Taylor, Vincent, 49n11
Thiselton, Anthony C., 262n60
Thompson, Leonard L., 16n49
Thompson, M. B., 158n46
Thompson, Richard P., 147n5, 189n36
Tigchelaar, E. G. C., 287n48
Torrance, T. F., 75n7
Tracy, David, 57n32
Trebilco, Paul R., 125n69
Troeltsch, Ernst, 47n5
Tuckett, Christopher M., 53n20, 172n3, 187–88, 193n46

Turner, C. H., 149n11
Turner, Max, 48n7, 299n89

Ulrich, E., 54n26
Urbach, E. E., 268nn79–80

Vacca, Michael, 217n1, 218n4
Vaggione, Richard Paul, 181nn4–5
Verheyden, J., 146n3, 147n5, 187n32
Vielhauer, Philipp, 73, 76n11

Waddell, W. G., 53n20
Wainwright, Arthur W., 50n14
Wainwright, Geoffrey, 61n40
Walaskay, Paul, 76n13
Wall, Robert, 166n62
Watson, Francis, 48n7
Weiser, Alfons, 89n53
Weiss, Bernhard, 37nn38–39
Weiss, Johannes, 7n20, 37
Weissenrieder, Annette, 249n2
Wellhausen, Julius, 29n14
Westberg, Daniel, 229n16
White, L. Michael, 257n37
Wilckens, Ulrich, 14n41, 120n50, 185–86, 199, 281n24
Wilk, Florian, 280n17, 280nn19–20
Wilken, Robert Louis, 111n5
Williams, David Salter, 27n9
Williams, Frank, 182n10
Wilson, Stephen G., 76n13
Winter, Paul, 35n33
Witherington, Ben, III, 86n45
Wittgenstein, Ludwig, 230, 231n19
Wolter, Michael, 179n1
Wrede, William, 46–47, 184, 192
Wright, N. T., 60n39, 260, 275n4, 287n49, 298n87, 300–301, 303–4

Yeago, David S., 49n10
Young, Frances M., 111n4, 131n95, 190n37

Zanker, Paul, 250n3, 255n31 256nn32–33, 257n37
Zehnle, Richard F., 187n28

Index of Subjects

Adam, 87–88, 225, 262
adoptionism, in the Christology of Acts, 184–85
allegiance, political, 17, 33, 100, 102, 140, 143
ambiguity, 20, 36–41, 62–65, 83, 124–26, 224–25. *See also* hermeneutics; tension, in Luke's political vision
angels, Jesus's supremacy to, 239–40. *See also* God; Trinity
aniconicism, in Paul, 258, 267. *See also* iconography
Anknüpfungspunkt, 76–77
anthropology: and epistemological incapacity, 222; and image of God, in Paul, 259, 266, 269–70; modern individualist and autonomous, 202; Paul's theological, 221, 305; relation of authority and community within modern, 202–3; and theomorphism of humans in OT, 305. *See also* community; image(s)
anthropomorphism, in ancient paganism, 115, 119. *See also* philosophy
Antitheses (Marcion), 25–26
appearance, of Jesus to Paul, 306
Areopagus speech, 73–94, 223–26; the narrative's hermeneutical significance for, 78–82, 223–24; patristic and modern exegesis of, 74–77; as a presentation of an alternative pattern of life, 77, 88–92; the Socratic resonances with, 81, 224. *See also* natural law; philosophy
Arian controversy, 180
ascension, 98
Ausgangspunkt: for canonical separation of Luke and Acts, 154, 175–77. *See also* hermeneutics; history

authorial intention, ignorance of Luke's, 10
authority: and anthropology, 202–3; as constitutive of community, 213; of God/Jesus in Acts, 207–9; positive nature of in Acts, 214; in postmodernity, 201. *See also* community; equality

baptism, 221, 243
birth-infancy narratives, 28–30

canon: and Hebrews' circulation with the *corpus Paulinum*, 233; and varied placement of Acts in canonical lists, 176–77. *See also* hermeneutics; history; Luke-Acts: reception of
captatio benevolentiae, 82, 224
chain-link style, 196
Christology, in Acts: and disputed subordinationist reading of Acts 2:36 in antiquity, 181–84; and dogmatic interpretive context of patristic disputes about Acts 2:36, 189–90; and importance of Luke's narrative framework for interpretation, 188, 192–94; and "making" of the Son's divinity, 181–82; and "making" of the Son's humanity, 182–83; and proto-adoptionist reading of Acts 2:36 in modernity, 184–86; and reconstructing context of Acts 2:36, 190–92; and source derivation of Acts 2:36, 186–88. *See also* adoptionism, in the Christology of Acts; *Kyrios*
Christuskult, 21
community: in Acts, 97–99; as alternative to religious images in Paul's theology, 269; and anthropology, 203, 266; the image of God in the Christian, 266;

345

Index of Subjects

of Jew and gentile in Acts, 206–7; and Lukan narrative, 204. *See also* authority; ecclesiology; equality

continuity, of Luke's Christology, 179–200

creation: the damage and healing of in Paul's christological cosmology, 222; and monotheism, 300; and question of the Son's generation, 180–84, 239; worship of, 254–55

critique: deconstructive and constructive, 121, 268–70, 273; of pagan cult in Acts, 120, 131

cult: in ancient paganism, 116; to Artemis in ancient Ephesus, 135–36; of emperors, 3–23. *See also* paganism; politics; polytheism; theology; worship

culture: and Christianity's theological clash with paganism, 111–12, 120–22, 127–28, 130, 136; and cultural encyclopedia, 113

dicta probantia/classica, 234–35

dogma: biblical theology's antithesis to, in Wrede, 46; and creedal transformation of Jesus faith in Harnack, 47; and absence of Trinitarian conviction in the NT in Brunner and Goldingay, 47–48. *See also* theology; Trinity

ecclesiology: and Acts' vision of being Christian, 134; and the church as image of God, 266, 269; and multiplicity of Christian communities in Acts, 133; and obedience to the Lord, 145; and refusal to relegate church to a private sphere, 145. *See also* authority; community; equality; image(s)

economics: antiquity's political and religious interconnection to, 99, 138; Christianity's theological collision with pagan, 126–28, 136, 138. *See also* politics; theology

eikon. *See* image(s)

epistles, occasional character of Paul's, 242

equality: and ethics, 205–6; as function of Jesus's universal Lordship, 208, 213; as function of theology, 207, 213; between Jew and gentile in Acts, 206–7; between Jew and gentile in Romans, 283; relation of hierarchy to, 212. *See also* authority; community; ecclesiology

eschatology: in Acts, 87–88, 92–93, 204; in the OT, 286, 289–90; in Paul, 221, 263–64, 278, 282–83, 287

ethics, in Acts, 202

evidence, the difference between absence of and negative, 270–71

finitude, human, 247–48

freedom, and Christianity's ad hoc relation to law/laws, 231–32. *See also* natural law

God: as ground of human equality, 207; and Hebrews' confession of the triune, 238–41; and human being Jesus, 275, 306; humanity of, in OT, 305; importance of, for Christianity's way of life, 110–11; importance of question of identity of, 275, 306; as measure of all things, 110, 131–32; Paul's Trinitarian grammar for, 242–46; and qualitative distinction from the cosmos, 254, 300, 303; as reason for Christianity's clash with paganism, 111–13, 120–22, 131, 136; and unity of Old and New Testament, 274. *See also* Christology, in Acts; *Kyrios*; theology; worship

gods: appearance of, in ancient paganism, 114–15; Christianity's collision with, 129, 131; importance of, in ancient paganism, 100, 268; in pagan households, 257–58; philosophical acceptance of cult to the, 119; in public space, 268. *See also* cult; imperial cult; paganism; polytheism; worship

grammar: the NT's Trinitarian, 50, 59, 236–37, 241–46; and patterns of life, 86, 88, 93, 231. *See also* hermeneutics; Trinity

Hebrews, authorship of, 233

hermeneutics: and dependence of meaning on textual context, 192–92, 218, 235; and early Christian reading of Acts with the four Gospels, 151–53, 172; and historical problem of reading Luke and Acts as two-volume work, 148–50, 159–70, 172;

Index of Subjects

and identity of God, 110–11, 236; and integral role of Luke's narrative sequence, 29, 78–79, 113, 188–200; and Lukan ambiguity, 20, 36–41, 62–65, 83, 124–26, 224–25; and Luke's use of OT, 30–31, 36–39, 41–42, 57–58, 64; and necessity of interpretive schemata for interpretation, 234–35; and Paul's reading of OT, 280–83, 288–92, 306; and Trinitarian interpretation of biblical texts, 234–37; as way of life, 88–93. *See also* Areopagus speech; history; Luke-Acts: reception of; Luke-Acts, literary unity of; Trinity

Herrscherkult, 6

hierarchy: in Christian community in Acts, 210–12; relation of human equality to, 212. *See also* authority; community; equality

history: and developmental approach to Trinitarian doctrine, 236; and hermeneutical choice of reading Luke and Acts as Luke-Acts, 158–70; and reception of Hebrews vis-à-vis Paul, 233–34; and reception of Luke-Acts, 146–59, 172. *See also* hermeneutics; Luke-Acts: reception of; Luke-Acts, literary unity of

Holy Spirit, in relation to God and Jesus, 240–43, 305. *See also* Trinity

house churches, religious art in, 257. *See also* iconography

humanity: of God, 304, 306; of Jesus, 238–39

iconography: absence of, in early Christian, 249, 252, 271–73; and economic deficit of early Christians as possible reason for their aniconism, 251; and Jewish character of aniconism, 250–51; and lack of NT commentary on, 251–52; relation of Paul's theology to early Christian, 253, 271–73

identity, potential contradiction of, in relation of Jesus's and God's, 297–98. *See also Kyrios*

idolatry, 254, 268–69, 297, 306. *See also* cult; gods; paganism; polytheism; theology

image(s): Christ/the human being as God's, in Paul, 258–62; Christian community as God's, 262–66, 269–70; and Gnostic and Platonic influence in Paul, 261; of God/gods in pagan antiquity, 84–85, 136, 267–68; and Paul's expansive critique of idolatry, 254–58, 266–69, 297; and tension between aniconicism and iconicism in Paul, 270–73; ubiquitous presence of, in ancient social space, 268–69. *See also* anthropology; community; cult; iconography; worship

imperial cult: and acclamation of Roman emperor as *kyrios*, 16–17, 43, 139; apparent ignorance of, in Luke-Acts, 4–8; critical relevance of Luke's *kyrios* Christology in Acts 10 to, 15, 43, 139–40; and images of imperial family, 256, 269. *See also* Christology; cult; *Kyrios*; worship

incarnation, in Luke's Gospel, 59

Kaiserkult, 6–7, 21

knowledge, of God, 74, 76, 219–20, 222, 226, 267. *See also* Areopagus speech

Kyrios: absence of, in Jesus's trial and death in Luke, 196; emperor as, 16–17, 43, 139; in Luke-Acts, 18–20, 41–44, 139–40, 194–97; in Luke's birth-infancy narrative, 32–40, 59–60; in OT, 53–55, 240, 294–95; in Paul, 284, 287, 292–98; relation of Luke's use of *Christos* to, 18, 35; and rival claim to universal lordship, 21, 43, 102–3, 139; and role of Holy Spirit, 34, 60–61, 68; and Trinitarian formulation, 51, 59–61, 240; and unity and distinction of identity between Jesus and God, 34–41, 43–44, 63, 67–68, 240. *See also* Christology; God; Holy Spirit; imperial cult; Trinity; worship

language: practical character of, 102; theological judgments presupposed in NT, 247

language game, 230

lararia/lararium. *See* gods

law, application of, 105, 229

Lokalkolorit, 113

347

Index of Subjects

Lordship, as service in Luke-Acts, 22
Luke-Acts: dating of, 8–9; reception of, 146–78 (*see also* hermeneutics; history)
Luke-Acts, literary unity of: and canonical placement of Luke and Acts in antiquity, 156–57; and common authorship, 151–52; and different forms of text of Acts, 176; external evidence for, 171–72; internal evidence for, 173; Irenaeus's view of, 148–51; Muratorian Fragment's view of, 152–53; as an open question, 168–70; and placement of Acts in canonical lists, 176–77; and preface in Acts, 153–56, 173; and question of a Lukan community, 158, 163, 167; reception history as a distinct question from, 173–74; and scholarly methods of reading Luke-Acts, 159–70; and separate publication/circulation of Luke and Acts, 177. *See also* hermeneutics; history; Luke-Acts: reception of

metalepsis, 291
mission, in Acts, 99–101, 105, 129
monotheism, Jewish: absence of God's identification with a human in, 301, 304; and christological monotheism, 301; and Christ's identification with God, 300–302; and distinction between Creator and creature, 300, 303; high, early Christology within, 301; in N. T. Wright, 300–303; Paul's continuity with, 304; and question of God's oneness, 299; and representational speech about God, 303; in Richard Bauckham, 300–302; and semidivine figures in Judaism, 299–300, 302; and theories of early Christology, 298–99. *See also* Christology, in Acts; God; *Kyrios*; theology; Trinity
moral law. *See* natural law

narrative: and Lukan theology, 58, 188; as theology, 57–58, 67
natural law: in Areopagus speech, 223–26; and Christian freedom, 231–32; and Christian wisdom, 232; different uses of, 230; Paul's contribution to question of, 228–31; and Paul's use of his Roman citizenship, 227; and Paul's use of Roman law in Acts, 226; relation of Torah to, in Paul, 217; in Romans, 219–23; and the Stoics, 218. *See also* Areopagus speech
natural theology, 75–77, 83–84, 228–31

oikoumenē, 239
Old Testament: unity of NT with, 274, 298, 304–5; as witness to Jesus Christ, 307. *See also* hermeneutics; unity

paganism: Christian critique of, 255, 267; Christian encounters with, 129, 131, 223; common horizon of, 101; conflict and competition within, 100; myth of tolerance in, 131; and politics, 102; and popular piety, 115–18, 127. *See also* critique; cult; idolatry; imperial cult; politics; polytheism; theology
pax Romana, 8, 137
parallelomania, 9
participation, in Christ: and dying and rising with Christ, 265–66; and transformation into Christ's image, 262–65, 270. *See also* transformation, into Christ's image
Paul, and parallels with Peter, in Acts, 211
penates. *See* gods
Peter, and parallels with Paul, in Acts, 211
philosophy: acceptability of pagan cultic practice in ancient, 119, 131; critique of anthropomorphism and superstition in ancient, 115, 119, 131; as pattern of life, 90–92, 131; and refusal of divine honors, 118–19; relation of NT to pagan, 223. *See also* anthropomorphism, philosophical critique of, in ancient paganism; Areopagus speech; natural law
polemic, danger of: in portraying opponents, 24; in understanding Marcion, 25
politics: and accusation of Christian rebellion, 104, 138, 140, 144; Acts' vision of, 96, 104, 144; antiquity's economic and religious interconnection with, 99, 138; and Christian rejection of the gods and allegiance to the emperor, 104, 136;

Index of Subjects

complexity and tension of Lukan, 11–12, 21, 106–9, 137–43; and resurrection, 98, 140, 143. *See also* economics; paganism; polytheism; Roman Empire; *stasis*; theology

polytheism: ability to absorb many gods in, 125, 131–32, 224, 258; antiquity's economic and political integration within, 99; and Christianity's prohibition of devotion to the gods, 99, 131, 223, 255; cultural limits of, 132; as lived pattern, 99; perdurance of, 115. *See also* critique; cult; economics; gods; imperial cult; paganism; politics; theology

predication, 49, 235. *See also theos*

prooftexting, 234, 236. *See also* hermeneutics

prophecy-fulfillment scheme, 31

reason, and gentile idolatry, 220–21

resurrection, 42–43, 98, 140, 143

revelation, and the knowledge of God, 266. *See also* knowledge, of God

Roman Empire: Luke's complex attitude toward, 11, 21; and nature of the imperial cult, 4, 9–10; provincial character of, 3. *See also* allegiance, political; imperial cult; politics

Roman law, 105, 226; Christian tactical use of, 228

salvation: of Israel, 276–78, 283, 289, 294; in Romans 10, 282. *See also sōtēr*

Seinsweise, 34

shame, eschatological, 282

slavery, to sin in Paul, 221, 229–30

sōtēr: in Lukan birth narrative, 61–62; in OT, 55–57; in Titus, 246

speech composition, in antiquity, 187

stasis, 103–4, 128, 137–39, 143, 226. *See also* economics; politics; theology

subordinationism, 180–84. *See also* Arian controversy

supersessionism, 237–38. *See also Antitheses* (Marcion); unity

tension, in Luke's political vision, 106–9, 141–43. *See also* ambiguity; politics

Tetraevangelium, 172

Tetragrammaton, 34, 53–55. *See also Kyrios*

text-criticism, in Acts, 176

theocentrism: and Christology, 277; in Romans, 274–75

theology: and biblical critique of idolatry, 120–24, 220–21, 254–58; and identity of Jesus, 307; interconnections of ancient politics and economics with, 99, 138, 144; as reason for equality between Jew and gentile, 284–85; as way of life, 110, 129–30, 132, 144. *See also* Christology, in Acts; economics; God; *Kyrios*; politics

theos, 238–40. *See also* God; *Kyrios*; predication

transformation, into Christ's image, 264–65. *See also* participation, in Christ

translation, of traditions, 86, 88, 90, 92. *See also* Areopagus speech; hermeneutics

Trinity: as antecedent theological logic of biblical texts, 234, 236, 241–43; the exegetical necessity of creedal formulation of the, 48–50, 68–69, 237, 247; as ground of biblical patterns of speech, 242–46; in Hebrews, 237–42; John and Paul as primary sources for doctrine of, 50; in Lukan birth narrative, 59–61; and NT presuppositions about God's identity, 236, 241, 244–47; ontological priority of the immanent to the economic, 236; in Paul, 242–47, 305; pressure toward the, in narrative of Luke-Acts, 51–52, 60–68, 70–72; relation of biblical message to, 47–48, 68–69, 241; and *theos* predication in the NT, 49, 235. *See also* Christology, in Acts; God; hermeneutics; *Kyrios*

two-kingdoms theology, 142–43

typology, Adam-Christ, 262

unity: the canon's theological, 25–26, 44–45; of God in Luke's infancy narratives, 27, 31–32; of God in Paul, 243, 245–47, 298; of God in relation to Marcion's the-

349

Index of Subjects

ology of separation, 26, 43, 45; of identity between Jesus and God in Luke-Acts, 34, 43–45, 63; of identity between Jesus and God in Paul, 296–98; of Luke-Acts and reception history, 146–70; of Old and New Testaments and the doctrine of God, 274, 298, 304–5

universal gospel/eschatology, in Romans, 283, 291–92

Verbindlichkeit, 28, 44. *See also* unity

will, bondage of the, 229

Wirkungsgeschichte, in Codex Bezae's rendition of Luke, 40–41

wisdom, 232

worship: of God by the nations in the end time, 286; Jesus's reception of, alongside God, 239; as prerogative of Israel's Creator God, 13–14, 254; as sacrifice in antiquity, 116. *See also* cult; God; gods; idolatry; imperial cult; paganism; polytheism

Index of Scripture

OLD TESTAMENT

Genesis
1	88, 225, 255
1:2	60n39
1:26	265n71, 297n85
1:26–27	265n71
2	225
11–21	30n19, 57n33
13:4	288
21:33	288

Exodus
20:5	70

Leviticus
17:7	120n46

Deuteronomy
4:16f.	255
4:29	225
5:9	70
5:11	295n75
6:4	43n56, 55, 61, 68, 286, 295
6:13	70
6:16	70
7:18	54n23
30:12–14	278n13
32:12–14	278–79n13
32:39	286n44

Judges
3:9	55n28
3:15	55n28
12:3	55n28
13:2–25	30n19, 57n33

1 Samuel
1:1–2:10	30n19, 57n33
2:2	286n44

2 Samuel
7:12–16	30n19, 57n33
22	288

Nehemiah
9:6	43, 55

Esther
5:2	55

Psalms
15:8 LXX	196
16:8–11	72
18	288
26:1	56
33:6	60n39
33:51	60n39
44:7	238, 240, 241
61:3	56
64:6	56
78:9	56
101:26 LXX	240
104:30	60n39
105:20 LXX	254n26
109:1 LXX	42, 196
110:1	41, 42
110:4	54n23, 240
118:26	67, 71
139:7	60n39

Proverbs
8:22	181, 238

Isaiah
2:9–12	30n19, 57n33
2:11	43n56
2:17	43n56
7:14	30n19, 57n33
9:6–7	30n19, 57n33
11:2	60n39
11:10	282n26
12:2–6	56
19:19	53n21
28:16	278n11, 280, 281n21, 281n22, 282, 289, 290n60, 291
30:27–28	66–67n53, 295n73
32:6	120n46
32:15	60n39
40:3	38–39, 40n46, 64–65
40:3–5	38, 40n46, 64, 65n48
40:5	38, 64
42:1	60n39
42:6	30n19, 57n33, 112
42:8	43n56, 55
43–46	286n44
44:3–5	60n39

Index of Scripture

45:15	246
49:6	30n19, 57n33
49:9	112
52:6	72
52:10	30n19, 57n33
55:6	225
61	114n14
61:1f.	70
62:11	56
63:10–14	60n39

Jeremiah

10:3	120n46
10:15	120n46
31	240
31:31–34 (38:31–34 LXX)	220
31:33–34	241

Ezekiel

1:26–28	259
1:27	259
8:10	120n46
36:27	60n39
37:1–14	60n39
39:7	43n56

Daniel

2:47	54n26
5:23	54n26
7–10	30n19, 57n33

Hosea

13:4	286n44

Joel

1:6	289
1:15	289
2:1	289
2:2	289
2:2–11	289
2:18–3:5	289
2:20	289
2:26–27	289, 290, 292
2:27	286n44, 291
2:32 (EV)	275, 288–89
3:1–2	289
3:1–5	60n39, 72, 290n60
3:3–5	290
3:4	289
3:5	275, 279, 282, 287–89, 290n60, 292, 294, 295–96
3:5a	288–89, 291
4:1	289
4:2	290
4:9	290
4:11	290
4:12	290
4:20–21	290

Amos

2:4	120n46
9:11–12	72

Micah

4:7–5:5	30n19, 57n33
7:7	56

Zephaniah

3:14–17	30n19, 57n33

Haggai

2:5	60n39

Zechariah

2:14–17	112n7
2:15 LXX	112n7
4:6	60n39
13:9	288
14:9	55
14:9–10a	286
14:16–17	286
14:17b MT	286n44

Malachi

2:10	286n44
3:1	30n19, 57n33
3:1ff.	67n55
4:5–6	30n19, 57n33

Deuterocanonical Books

Judith

6:4	16n50

Wisdom of Solomon

7:26	259
13:11	255n29

Sirach

51:1	57

2 Maccabees

7:37	285–86n43

2 Esdras

19:6 LXX	43, 55

New Testament

Matthew

17:4	19n59
22:15–22	251n11
23:9	285n43
24:43–44	18
24:45–51	18
26:29–40	156n35
26:65	120n47
28:19	50n13
28:19–20	172n4

Mark

1:3	39, 54, 65n48
3:14	198–99n65
5:19	71
6:5	195
9:5	19n59
10:18	285n43
10:46–52	195
12:13–17	251n11
12:29	285n43
14:63	120n47

Index of Scripture

Luke							
1–2	29, 30–32, 36, 43, 51, 52, 57–63	2:11	19, 20, 35–36, 41, 61, 179, 194n47, 195	8:39	71
		2:15	35, 36	8:48	71
1:1	38, 64, 162	2:23	30, 57	9:1	210n22
1:1–4	108	2:24	30, 57	9:12	210n22
1:1–4:30	28	2:25	196	9:33	19n59
1:4	198	2:26	35, 36, 41	9:43	71
1:5–24	30n19, 57n33	2:30–31	30n19, 57n33	10:1	195
1:5–38	59, 61	2:30–32	112	10:3	80n25
1:5–2:52	30n19, 57n33	2:32	30n19, 57n33, 173	10:17	195
1:6	32, 33, 59	2:34	196	10:21	20, 43, 71, 212
1:9	32, 33, 41n47, 59	2:46	80n25	10:38–42	195
1:11	33, 59	3:1	8, 27, 29n14, 38, 64	10:39	195n48
1:15	33	3:1–6	51, 59	10:41	195n48
1:16	33, 59	3:4	38–39, 64–65	11:3	35
1:16–17	37n39, 62–63n43, 64n45	3:4–6	36–41, 63, 64	11:13	71
		3:6	38, 64, 65	11:20	71
1:17	30n19, 33, 57n33, 59	3:16	70	11:39	195n48
1:25	33	3:21–22	70	12:30	11n31
1:26–33	30n19, 57n33	3:38	87	12:37	22
1:26–38	30n19, 57n33	4:1	70	12:39–40	18
1:27	30n19, 57n33, 60	4:2	70	12:41–42	18, 71, 195
1:28	33	4:5	11n31	12:42	195n48
1:32	33, 59	4:8	70	12:42b–48	18
1:32–33	30n19, 57n33	4:12	70	13:12–13	71
1:35	60, 62	4:14	70	13:15	41, 195n48
1:38	32, 33, 59	4:18	70	13:35	67, 71
1:39	32, 59	4:18–19	114n14	14:21–23	195
1:42	32	5:1–11	19	17:5	195n48
1:43	19, 32–35, 41, 42, 59, 62–63n43, 67, 71, 194	5:8	70, 72, 195, 196n52	17:6	195n48
		5:12	195	17:15–19	71, 72
		5:17–26	70, 114n14	17:19	71
1:45	33	5:50	71	18:6	195n48
1:46	33	6:46	19	18:32–33	11n31
1:46–55	30n19, 57n33	7:1–10	11n30, 173	18:35–43	195
1:47	61	7:6	195	18:41	19, 195
1:51	198–99n65	7:13	18, 41, 195	19:8	18, 195, 195n48
1:68	32, 70	7:16	70	19:38	11n31, 67, 71
1:76	30n19, 36–40, 57n33, 62–63n43, 64, 65	7:19	19, 195n48	19:44	70
		7:22	114n14	20:20–26	251n11
		7:31	195n48	20:41–44	41–42
1:78–79	70	7:48f.	70	20:44	41
1:79	30n19, 57n33	7:50	71	21:12–13	11n31
2:1	8	8:1	29n16, 210n22	22:3	210n22
2:1–14	30n19, 57n33	8:7	80n25	22:24	11n31
2:9	35, 36	8:28	124n66	22:25–27	22
				22:27	80n25

353

Index of Scripture

22:47	210n22	2:21	67, 288n53	9:36–41	211n27
22:52	42n51, 131n92	2:22	80n25, 183	9:42	72
22:61	19, 41, 195n48	2:25	54, 67	10	13
22:61–62	196	2:25–28	72	10:1–11:18	13n34
23:14–15	131n92	2:32	211	10:14	207
23:18	131n92	2:33	71, 183n13	10:25	72
23:20	131n92	2:34–35	20	10:25–26	117
23:22	131n92	2:36	15n43, 20, 42–44,	10:26	121, 211n27
23:25	131n92		179–200, 208n18	10:28	206–7
23:26	80n24	2:36b	42	10:33	14
23:47	11n30, 42n51,	2:42	213	10:34	207
	107n31, 131n92	3:1–10	114n14, 211n27	10:36	14n40, 17, 20, 22–23,
24:3	41n47, 195n48, 196	3:13	11n30		35, 42–44, 72, 197,
24:34	19, 71, 196	3:15	72, 194n47, 211		208, 284n36
24:36	80n25	3:16	72	10:36–37	14, 208n18
24:48	211	3:24	29n16	10:36–38	140
24:49	60, 71, 148–49	4:2	125n71	10:37	14n40
24:52	70, 72	4:10–11	72	10:39	211
24:52–53	71	4:11	11n31	10:41	209, 211
		4:12	72, 126, 208	10:42	208
John		4:24	102	10:43	208
1:1	235	4:25–26	11n31	11:1	72
1:1–18	49–50n12	4:29	71	11:17	72
1:18	235	4:31	72	11:18	12–13, 206n13
5:44	285n43	4:32–35	211	11:20	72, 209n21
14:26	149n11	4:33	20, 211	11:25–26	13, 206n13
16:13	149n11	5:3–9	72	11:26	111–12n6
17:3	285n43	5:16	211n27	11:30	13, 206n13
20:28	49–50n12	5:31	194n47	12:6–11	211n27
		5:32	211	12:20–23	6n15
Acts		5:40	72	12:25	13, 206n13
1:1	29, 153–54, 198–99n65	6:2	210n22	13:5	72
1:1–2	153–55	6:7	72	13:7–8	11n30
1:2	71, 211	7	136	13:38	125n71
1:4	71	7:54–8:1	71	13:44	72
1:7	204n7	7:59	196	13:47	112
1:8	148–49, 211	8:12	72	13:48	123
1:8a	148–49	8:14–17	211n27	13:48–49	72
1:8b	148–49	8:16	20, 196	13:50–14:6	123n62
1:15	80n25	8:25	72	14	7, 113–24, 136
1:21	20, 71, 196	9	306	14:1	209n21
1:21–22	211	9:10–11	18, 195	14:2	123
1:24	71	9:14	288n53	14:4	114n15, 210
2:14	179	9:15	12, 206n13	14:5	209n21
2:17–21	72, 290n60	9:21	288n53	14:7	114, 123n62
2:20–21	72	9:27	72	14:8–10	211n27
		9:33–10:1	156n35	14:8–18	117

14:8–19	113	16:36	128	19:29	136
14:8–20	72	16:37–38	129n86	19:31	11n30
14:9	123n62	16:39	129	19:37	11n30
14:9a	114	17	73–94, 134, 136, 141–44,	20:9–12	211n27
14:9bc	114		223–26	20:17–38	228n14
14:11	114	17:1–9	141	20:21	72
14:11–13	114	17:3	125n71, 208n18	21:30	80n24
14:13	114n17, 116	17:6	80n24, 104	21:33	80n24
14:14	114n15, 114n17, 210	17:6–7	141	22:10	195
14:14–18	114	17:7	103, 104	22:15	211
14:15	13n38, 121, 211n27	17:16	79, 82, 223	22:16	288n53
14:15–18	122n60	17:16–20	79	22:17	211
14:16	123	17:16–21	83	22:22	209n21
14:17	121	17:18	81, 125n71, 224	22:25	227
14:18	114n17, 116	17:19	80	23:10	131n92
14:18–19	123	17:19–20	81	23:11	211
14:19	114, 114n17, 123n61	17:21	81	24:1–26:32	138
14:19–15:5	124	17:22	80, 82, 119n40, 224	24:2–3	82
14:22	123n62	17:22–28	74n6	24:5	111n6, 131n92
15:3	120	17:23	74n4, 125n71, 224	24:16–17	226
15:6	210	17:24	20, 43n57, 88,	24:24	72
15:8–9	208		208n18, 212, 224	25–26	134, 138–41
15:14	112, 131	17:24–25	84, 85, 129	25:7–8	104
15:16–17	72	17:24–27	88	25:8	139
15:23	210	17:26	87, 88	25:11	80, 227
15:36	72	17:26–30	87	25:13–27	17
16	124–29, 136	17:27	85, 87n51, 224	25:19	119n40, 212
16:7	72	17:27–28	74	25:26	17, 23, 34, 51n16, 139
16:10	124	17:28	85, 225	26:15	195
16:13	125n69	17:28–29	88	26:16	211
16:14–15	124	17:28a	85	26:20	120
16:16	125n69, 127	17:28b	85	26:22	211
16:16–24	113	17:29	85, 129	26:23	125n71, 140
16:17	124–25	17:30	89, 92	26:24	140, 212
16:18	124, 126–27, 211n27	17:30–31	87, 88	26:28	111–12n6
16:19	80n24, 128	17:31	87, 89–90	26:32	227
16:19–24	126	17:33	80	27:21	80n25
16:19–40	21	18:14	103	28:1–10	117
16:20	111n6, 128	18:14–15	226	28:9	211n27
16:21	11n31, 104, 125n71,	18:17	80n24	28:11	256n35
	128	18:23	29n16	28:23	72
16:22–23	124, 129	19	134–38	28:31	72, 142
16:22–24	129	19:1–7	211n27		
16:24–34	211n27	19:1–11	134	**Romans**	
16:31	72	19:8	72	1	75, 306
16:32	72	19:25–27	135	1–4	244
16:34	72	19:28	136		

Index of Scripture

1–8	276	6:23	222, 284n35	10:9	277, 278, 279, 280n20, 281–82, 283, 284, 286, 293
1:1	277n10	7:14–25	222n9		
1:1–3:31	219–21	8:3–4	305n109		
1:2–3	294	8:9–11	305n109	10:9–10	280, 283, 288, 289
1:3–4	184n16	8:15–18	305n109		
1:4	185, 284n35	8:17	263	10:9–13	287
1:7	284n35	8:18–38	263	10:9ff.	288
1:9	277n10	8:21	222	10:10	278, 279, 280n20, 283
1:14	283n32	8:22	264n65, 285n41		
1:16	280, 282	8:22–30	222	10:10–13	279
1:18–23	253	8:26–27	305n109	10:11	277, 278n11, 279, 280–83, 284, 291, 293
1:18–32	221, 297	8:29	239, 263, 264–65		
1:19–20	219	8:33	285n41		
1:20	254	8:34	294n68	10:11–13	276, 279n14, 279n16, 280, 284–85n38, 289
1:22	219	9–11	244, 276–77, 283, 288–89n55		
1:23	253–58, 263, 265n70, 297				
		9:1–4	294	10:12	277, 279, 280, 283–88, 289, 293
1:25	220, 254, 297	9:1–5	276		
2:11	209n20	9:4	292	10:12–13	280, 281, 282
2:14–16	220	9:5	235	10:12a	283, 284–85, 291
2:16	277n10	9:6	292	10:12b	284–87, 287n50, 291
2:17–29	220	9:6–29	276	10:12c	287–88, 289, 291
3	244	9:28	284n35	10:13	54, 67, 274–307
3:9–20	285n41	9:29	284n35	10:14	277, 278, 279, 289n57, 293, 294
3:21	294	9:30	278		
3:21–31	285n41	9:30–33	278	10:14–21	278
3:22	280, 283, 291	9:30–10:13	278	10:16	277, 277n10
3:22–23	283n33	9:30–10:21	276, 277–78, 279n16	10:17	277, 294
3:29–30	284n37, 285n42			11:1–32	276
3:30	254, 284, 285	9:32	277, 278, 281n22	11:3	284n35, 293n66
4:11	280, 285n41	9:32–33	287, 294	11:15	285n41
4:13	285n41	9:33	277, 278, 280, 281n21, 281n22, 282, 291	11:26	285n41, 287, 289n58, 291, 292
5	244–45				
5:1	244			11:29	292
5:1–5	264n66	10:1	278, 279, 283, 289, 294	11:32	285n41, 287, 292, 294
5:1–8	245				
5:1–11	244–45	10:1–13	278	11:33–36	276
5:2–3	244	10:1ff.	278	11:35	294
5:5	244, 282, 305n109	10:2	279	11:36	285n41, 292
5:6–11	245	10:3	279	12:4	285n41
5:12–21	87, 283, 285n41	10:4	277, 279, 280, 291	12:5	285n41
5:15–21	259	10:5	279	13:1–7	218n4
5:21	284n35	10:5ff.	279	14:4	284n35
6–8	221–23	10:6	277, 278n13	14:6	284n35
6:5	264n66	10:7	277, 278n13	14:8	284n35
6:15–23	221	10:8	278, 278n13	14:10	285n41

356

14:11	285n41	3:17–18	305n109	1:15–16	302
14:12	285n41	3:18	68n57, 263n63, 264–65	1:15–20	49–50n12, 260
14:14	284n35	4:4	258–60	1:16	265n71
14:14ff.	287	4:6	259, 265	1:18	239
15:6	285n41, 287	4:11	265	1:19–20	261
15:10	285n41	5:19	304	1:22	261
15:11	285n41	12:4–6	305n109	1:24	266
15:12	282n26	13:13	49–50n12, 244, 305n109	2:2	261
15:16	277n10			2:9	302
15:19	277n10	13:14 (EV)	305n109	2:11–12	265
16:25–26	264n65			2:19	266
16:26	285n41	**Galatians**		3:1–3	265
16:27	285n41	1	306	3:4	266
		2:16	282n26	3:9–10	265
1 Corinthians		3:1–5	244, 305n109	3:10	260, 265–66
1:2	288n53, 290n60	3:20	285n43	3:25	209n20
1:24	259	3:28	283n33		
2:2–5	244	4:4	302	**1 Thessalonians**	
2:4–5	305n109	4:4–6	305n109	1:9	111, 120n50, 268n80, 272
2:10–12	305n109	6:17	272n92		
6:1–11	218n4			**2 Thessalonians**	
6:11	305n109	**Ephesians**		2:13	305n109
8:4	268n80	1:3–14	305n109		
8:4–6	285n43	1:20	302	**1 Timothy**	
8:6	285, 295n76, 301, 302	2:17–22	305n109	1:17	285n43
10:19–20	268n80	3:14–19	305n109	2:5	285n43
11:7	253n22	4	245–46	6:13	23n69
12	242–44, 245	4:3–6	245	6:15	23n69
12:3	243	4:4–6	49–50n12, 305n109		
12:4–6	49–50n12, 243	4:6	285n43	**Titus**	
12:12–13	243	5:18–20	305n109	1:3	246
15	262–63	6:9	209n20	1:4	246
15:21–22	262			2:10	246
15:22	262n61	**Philippians**		2:11	246
15:45–49	262	1:19	305n109	2:13	246
15:49	263	2:5–6	302	3:4	246
15:49a	262	2:5–11	33n28, 49–50n12, 59, 185	3:4–6	246
15:49b	262			3:5	246
16:22	54n24	2:6–11	66n51	3:6	246
		2:7	259		
2 Corinthians		2:9–11	67, 295n76	**Hebrews**	
1:21–22	305n109	3:3	244	1	237, 238
3:1–4:6	264, 305n109			1–2	241
3:2–3	264	**Colossians**		1:2	238
3:14	264	1:15	181, 239, 260–62, 265–66	1:3	238, 240
3:17	68n57				

357

Index of Scripture

1:4	239	9:8	240	3:15	102n20
1:5–6	239, 240	9:13–14	241	4:16	102n20, 111–12n6
1:8	238, 240, 241	9:14	240		
1:8–9	49–50n12, 240	10:12	240	**2 Peter**	
1:10–12	240	10:15	240	2:1	49–50n12
1:13–14	240	10:15–17	241		
2:3–4	241	10:29	240–41	**1 John**	
2:4	240	12:2	239, 240	5:7	49–50n12
2:9	238	13:20	240	5:20	49–50n12
2:14	239				
2:17	240	**James**		**Jude**	
2:18	239	2:1	209n20	25	285n43
3:7	240, 241	2:9	209n20		
4:15	239	2:19	285n43	**Revelation**	
6:4	240–41			1:5	239
7:14	240	**1 Peter**		17:14	23
7:21	240	2:6	281n21	19:16	23
8:8	240	2:17	102	22:20b	54n24

Index of Other Ancient Sources

Pseudepigrapha

Apocalypse of Abraham
7.10	285–86n43
17	285–86n43

Jubilees
12:1f.	255

Letter of Aristeas
132	285–86n43
132ff.	285n39
134f.	255
139	285–86n43
155	54n23

Sibylline Oracles
3.11	285–86n43
3.629	285–86n43
3.760	285–86n43
4.30	285–86n43
8.377	285–86n43

Dead Sea Scrolls

1QapGen	54n26
20.13	287n48
22.16	43n57
4Q126	54n26

Ancient Jewish Writers

Josephus

Antiquitates judaicae
4.200ff.	285n39
5.112	285n39, 285–86n43
6.186	295n73
8.335	285–86n43
8.337	285–86n43
8.343	285–86n43
13.68	53n21
20.90	53n21, 284n35, 285–86n43, 287n48

Bellum judaicum
1.21.7 §414	5n11, 256n36
2.10.4 §197	7n19
2.13.7	13n36
2.17.2 §409	7n19
2.117–118	285n39
6.2.5 §134	16n53
7.10.1 §§418–419	23n70

Contra Apionem
2.193	285n39
2.239–242 §§33–34	115n24
2.251 §35	121n52
2.262–264	81n30
2.267–268	81n31

Philo

De confusione linguarum
1	284n35
156	284n35
171	285–86n43
173	284n35

De specialibus legibus
1.67	285n39

Legatio ad Gaium
115	285–86n43
157	7n19
286	16n53
317	7n19
356	16n53
357	102–3n20

Rabbinic Works

Mishnah

m. Berakhot
1.1ff.	285n43

m. Sanhedrin
7.5	120n47

Early Christian Writings

Acts of the Scillitan Martyrs
1	23n71

359

Index of Other Ancient Sources

5	23n71	65	180n3	**Irenaeus**	
6	23n72	69.42.1–6	181n8	*Adversus haereses*	
		69.42.2	182n10	1.25.6	271n90
Ambrose		*Epistle to Diognetus*		1.27.2	26n5
Epistola		7.7	23	3.1	172
43	74n6			3.1.1	148–50
De fide		**Eunomius**		3.11.8	151n17
1.15.95	181n8, 182n10	*Liber apologeticus*		3.11.9	150, 151n16
		28	181n6	3.12.2	180n2
Apostolic Constitutions				3.14.3–4	151n16
Can. 85	176	**Eusebius**			
		Historia ecclesiastica		**Jerome**	
Athanasius		3.25.1	176	Ep. 25	54n27
Orationes contra Arianos		5.28	185n21		
2.15.11	181n8	7.18	271n90	**John Chrysostom**	
2.15.12	182n10, 183n15	7.30	180n3	*Homiliae in Acta apostolorum*	
2.15.13	180n3	*Praeparatio evangelica*		38	76n14
		9.27.6	117n33		
Augustine		13.12	86n48, 122n58	*Homiliae in epistulam ad Hebraeos*	
De civitate Dei		*Vita Constantini*		3.1	181n5, 182n10
6.10	85n41	3.49	271n89		
Basil of Caesarea		**Eustathius of Antioch**		**Justin Martyr**	
De Spiritu Sancto		*Fragmenta*		*Apologia i*	
46	34n31	72.6–10	182n10	5.4	81n30
				24	255n30
Clement of Alexandria		**Gregory of Nyssa**		50.12	172
Stromateis		*Contra Eunomium*		*Apologia ii*	
1.19	74n5, 77n17	1	34n31	10.6	74n4
Codex Claromontanus		5.2	181n7, 182n9		
	172–73n5, 176	5.3	183n12, 183n13	**Martyrdom of Polycarp**	
		5.5	183n11	8.2	23n70
Didache					
10:6	54n24	**Hippolytus**		**Origen**	
		Against the Heresy of Noetus		*Contra Celsum*	
Epiphanius				1.1	104
Panarion		10	60n39	5.41	125n70
27.6.10	271n90				

360

Index of Other Ancient Sources

Philodemus

On Piety   119n41

Pseudo-Clement

Homilies
9.16.3   126n77

Tertullian

Adversus Marcionem
4.1   25–26

Adversus Praxean
5   60n39
28.3–4   180n2

Apologeticus
2.7   22n68
10.1–2   105
34.1   23n73, 102n18

GRECO-ROMAN LITERATURE

Amphilochius of Iconium

Fragmenta
1.4–5   182n10

Apuleius

Apologia
63   269n82

Metamorphoses
10.7   82n33
10.33   81n32

Aratus

Phaenomena   74–75, 77, 85, 86, 88, 122n58, 225

Aristotle

Metaphysica
12.8.18   115n23

Augustus

Res gestae
2.11   256n33
4.19   258n42
4.21   255n31

Cassius Dio

Historiae Romanae
62.29.4   7n16
67.13.2–4   7n16

Cicero

De divinatione
1.4ff.   127
2.132–133   128n83

De legibus
2.19.47   119n42

De natura deorum
1.2.4   119
1.6.14   119
1.21.60   201
1.30.85   120n45
1.30.123   120n45
1.36 §101   255n30
1.37.77   120n49
1.115   91n62
2.3.9   127
2.30.76   120n44
3.1.3   120n45
11.23 §61   256n33
11.27 §68   258n42

Tusculanae disputationes
5.1   91n58
5.5   91n58

Damascius

Isidorus
141   125n70

Demosthenes

De corona
18.127 [269]   79n22

Dio Chrysostom

Discourses
1.56   126n77
12.28   85n42
32.9   79n22
45.4   17n54

Diogenes Laertius

Lives
2.40   81n30

Epictetus

Discourses
4.1.12   16n47, 43n54

Euripides

Bacchae
lines 255–259   81n31

Homer

Odyssey
7.266   122n56
17.485–486   115n20

Horace

Carmina
1.2, lines 40–45   117n34
4.5.29f.   258n41

Index of Other Ancient Sources

Juvenal

Satirae
2.29–33	7n17
4.38	7n17
14.96ff.	283n32

Lucian

Alexander (Pseudomantis)
9	126n77
13	116n26
14	116n27
25	92n66
36	92n66
38	119n41, 120n44

Athletics
19	82n33

Vera historia
55	149n12
58	187n31

Macrobius

Mart. Apoll.
3	23n72

Saturnalia
3.9.10	122n59

Martial

Epigrams
5.8.1	16n49
8.2.5–6	16n49
10.72.3	16n49

Ovid

Epistulae ex Ponto
4.9	257–58n40

Metamorphoses
1.200–220	116n29
8.628–629	117n30
8.707–708	117

Pausanias

Graeciae descriptio
1.32.2	122n56
5.11.10–11	84n40
8.9.2	121n55

Plato

Apologia
24BC	81n30
28E–30E	81n30

Phaedo 92n65

Respublica
2.364B–C	128n83
7.517Cff.	120n49

Pliny

Epistulae
3.5	7n16
10.96	111

Plutarch

An seni respublica gerenda sit (Whether an Old Man Should Engage in Public Affairs)
26	91n59

De defectu oraculorum
417	127n79
418D	127n80
421A–E	126n77
438C–D	127n80

De Iside et Osiride
355	51n16

De Pythiae oraculis
402B–C	127n80

De Stoicorum repugnatis (On Stoic Self-Contradictions) 91n59

De superstitione
167	85n41

Moralia
1034B	120n43
1034C	120n45

Numa
8.7–8	85n41

Pseudo-Aristotle

De mundo
401A	122n58

Pseudo-Callisthenes

Alexander Romance (The Life of Alexander of Macedon)
2.14	119n39
2.22	119n39

Seneca

De clementia
1.2	22n65

De superstitione 85n41

Epistulae morales
41.1	85n42, 224–25
90	131n95

Statius

Silvae
1.6.80	16n49

Thebaid
1.696–720	122n58

Suetonius

Divus Augustus
53.1–2	16n49

362

Index of Other Ancient Sources

Domitianus
13.2   16n48

Tacitus

Annales
1.1   7n16
14.52   7n16
15.41   258n42

Historiae
5.5   283n32

Thucydides

Historia belli Peloponnesiaci
1.22   187n31

Xenophon

Memorabilia
1.1.1   81n30
1.1.3   81n30

OTHER ANCIENT WORKS

Papyri
Papyrus 4   156n37
Papyrus 45   176
Papyrus 46   233
Papyrus 53   156n35, 176
Papyrus 74   176
Papyrus Fouad 266 [848]
                    53n20
Payrus Oxyrynchus 899
    (line 31)   80